lonely planet

P9-DGH-629

Cambodia

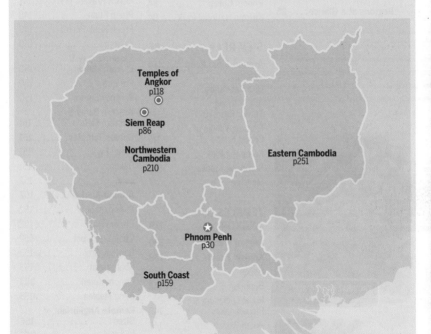

Temples of
Angkor
p118

Siem Reap
p86

Northwestern
Cambodia
p210

Eastern Cambodia
p251

Phnom Penh
p30

South Coast
p159

THIS EDITION WRITTEN AND RESEARCHED BY
Nick Ray, Greg Bloom

PLAN YOUR TRIP

ITAL VITA/GETTY IMAGES ©

TROPICAL FRUIT (P317)

TIM BARKER/GETTY IMAGES ©

KOH KONG (P161)

ON THE ROAD

Contents

Welcome to Cambodia

Ascend to the realm of the gods, Angkor Wat. Descend into hell at Tuol Sleng prison. With a history both inspiring and depressing, Cambodia delivers an intoxicating present.

An Empire of Temples

Contemporary Cambodia is the successor state to the mighty Khmer empire, which, during the Angkorian period, ruled much of what is now Laos, Thailand and Vietnam. The remains of this empire can be seen at the fabled temples of Angkor, monuments unrivalled in scale and grandeur in Southeast Asia. The traveller's first glimpse of Angkor Wat, the ultimate expression of Khmer genius, is sublime and is matched by only a few select spots on earth, such as Machu Picchu and Petra.

Upcountry Adventures

Siem Reap and Phnom Penh may be the heavyweights, but to some extent they are a bubble, a world away from the Cambodia of the countryside. This is the place to experience the rhythm of rural life and timeless landscapes of dazzling rice paddies and swaying sugar palms. The South Coast is fringed by tropical islands, with just a handful of beach huts in sight. Inland from the coast lie the Cardamom Mountains, part of a vast tropical wilderness that provides a home to elusive wildlife and is the gateway to emerging ecotourism adventures. The mighty Mekong River cuts through the country and is home to some of the region's last remaining freshwater dolphins. The northeast is a world unto itself, its wild and mountainous landscapes a home for Cambodia's ethnic minorities and an abundance of natural attractions.

The Comeback Capital

Just as Angkor is more than its wat, so too is Cambodia more than its temples. The chaotic yet charismatic capital of Phnom Penh is a hub of political intrigue, economic vitality and intellectual debate. All too often overlooked by hit-and-run tourists ticking off Angkor on a regional tour, the revitalised city is finally earning plaudits in its own right thanks to a gorgeous riverside location, a cultural renaissance and a wining and dining scene to rival anywhere in the region.

The Cambodian Spirit

Despite having the eighth wonder of the world in its backyard, Cambodia's real treasure is its people. The Khmers have been to hell and back, struggling through years of bloodshed, poverty and political instability. Thanks to an unbreakable spirit and infectious optimism, they have prevailed with their smiles intact. No visitor comes away without a measure of admiration and affection for the inhabitants of this enigmatic kingdom.

Why I Love Cambodia

By Nick Ray, Author

Where to start? I first came through Cambodia as a young backpacker in 1995 and the intoxicating history captured my attention. However, the people were the most memorable part of that first trip, their smiles infectious. Angkor is spectacular and special and continues to reward, no matter how many times you visit. The coastline is beautiful and blissfully undeveloped compared with some of the region. And it remains a frontier for motorbike rides from the Cardamoms in the southwest to Mondulkiri and Ratanakiri in the northeast. Even as it evolves, Cambodia remains a real adventure.

For more about our authors, see page 368

Above: Produce seller, near Siem Reap

Cambodia

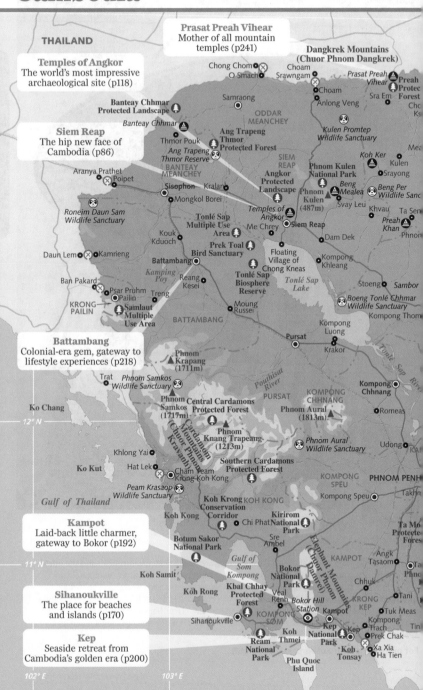

THAILAND

Temples of Angkor
The world's most impressive archaeological site (p118)

Prasat Preah Vihear
Mother of all mountain temples (p241)

Dangkrek Mountains
(Chuor Phnom Dangkrek)

Chong Chom ⊗ Choam
O Smach ○ Choam Srawngam ○ *Prasat Preah* ▲ Preah
Vihear ▲ Protec
⊗ Choam ○ Sra Em Forest
Anlong Veng ○ Cho
Ks

Banteay Chhmar
Protected Landscape ▲

Banteay Chhmar ▲

Samraong ○

ODDAR
MEANCHEY

Kulen Promtep
Wildlife Sanctuary ⊗

Siem Reap
The hip new face of Cambodia (p86)

Thmor Pouk ○ **Ang Trapeng**
Thmor
Protected Forest ▲

Ang Trapeng
Thmor Reserve ▲

Koh Ker ○
Kulen

Aranya Prathet
⊗ Poipet

BANTEAY
MEANCHEY

SIEM
REAP
Angkor
Protected
Landscape ▲

○ Srayong
Beng ▲ *Beng Per*
Mealea *Wildlife Sanc*

Phnom ▲
Kulen

Svay Leu ○
Khvau
Ta Sen

○ Sisophon ○ Kralan
○ Mongkol Borei

Phnom
Kulen
National Park ▲

Phnom
Kulen (487m) ▲
Temples of
Angkor ▲

Roneim Daun Sam
Wildlife Sanctuary ⊗

Kouk
Kduoch

Tonlé Sap
Multiple Use
Area ▲

Me Chrey ○ ●Siem Reap

Preah ▲
Khan
Phnom

Daun Lem ⊗ ○Kamrieng

Prek Toal ▲
Bird Sanctuary

Dam Dek ○

Ban Pakard ○

○ Battambang

Floating
Village of
Chong Kneas

Kompong
Khleang ○

Psar Pruhm ⊗
○ Pailin
Treng

Kamping
Poy

Reang ○
Kesei

Tonlé Sap
Biosphere
Reserve

Tonlé Sap
Lake

Stoeng ○ *Sambor*

KRONG
PAILIN

Samlaut
Multiple
Use Area ▲

BATTAMBANG

Moung ○
Russei

Boeng Tonlé Chhmar ⊗
Wildlife Sanctuary
Kompong Thom

Battambang
Colonial-era gem, gateway to lifestyle experiences (p218)

Trat ○

Kompong
Luong ○

Pursat ●
○ Krakor

Tonlé Sap Rive

Phnom ▲
Krapang
(1711m)

Pouthisat
River

Phnom Samkos
Wildlife Sanctuary ⊗

PURSAT

KOMPONG
CHHNANG

Kompong ○
Chhnang

Ko Chang

— 12° N —

▲
Phnom **Central Cardamons**
Samkos **Protected Forest** ▲
(1717m)

Phnom Aural
(1813m) ▲

○ Romeas

▲
Phnom
Knang Trapeang
(1213m)

Khlong Yai ○

Udong ○

Cardamon
Mountains
(Chuor Phnom
Kravanh)

Southern Cardamons
Protected Forest ▲

Phnom Aural
Wildlife Sanctuary ⊗

Ko Kut

Hat Lek ○
⊗ Cham Yeam
Krong-Koh Kong

KOMPONG
SPEU

PHNOM PENH

Ta Mo
Protecte
Fores

Peam Krasaop ⊗
Wildlife Sanctuary

Kompong Speu ○
Takh

Gulf of Thailand

Koh Krong
Conservation
Corridor

Koh Kong ○

KOH KONG

Kirirom
Chi Phat ○ **National** ▲
Sre **Park**
Ambel

Angk
Tasaom ○

KAMPOT

Ta
Phno

Kampot
Laid-back little charmer, gateway to Bokor (p192)

Botum Sakor
National Park ▲

Gulf of
Som
Kompong

Bokor ▲
National
Park

Chhuk ○

KRONG
KEP

— 11° N —

Koh Samit ○

Elephant Mountains
(Chuor Phnom Damrei)

Tani ○

Tuk Meas ○

Sihanoukville
The place for beaches and islands (p170)

Kôh Rong ○

Veal ○
Renh

Kbal Chhay
Protected
Forest ▲

Bokor Hill
Station ◉

KOMPONG
SÔM

Kampot ◉

Kep ◉ Kep

Kompong
Trach ○
○ Prek Chak

Sihanoukville ●

Kep
Seaside retreat from Cambodia's golden era (p200)

Koh
Thmei

Ream
National
Park ▲

Kep
National
Park ▲

Koh
Tonsay

⊗ Xa Xia
○ Ha Tien

Phu Quoc
Island

102° E

103° E

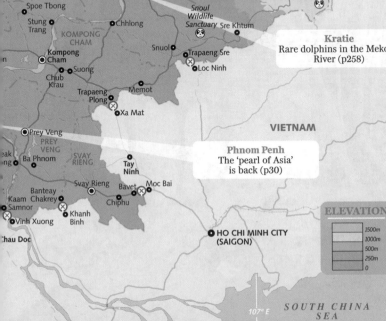

Ratanakiri
Jungle romps and adrenalin-fuelled excursions (p266)

Mondulkiri
The wild east (p275)

Kratie
Rare dolphins in the Mekong River (p258)

Phnom Penh
The 'pearl of Asia' is back (p30)

LAOS

Preah Vihear Protected Forest

Muang Khong

Siem Pang

Virachey National Park

Voen Sai

RATANAKIRI

Nong Nok Khiene

Ko Chheuteal Thom

Trapaeng Kriel

Anlong Seima

STUNG TRENG

Ban Lung

O'Yadaw

Le Tanh

Stung Treng Ramsar Site

Tonlé Kong

Tonlé San

Boeng Yeak Lom

Bokheo

Thala Boravit

Rovieng

Stung Treng

Lumphat

Lomphat Wildlife Sanctuary

Koh Nhek

Mekong River

Phnom Prich Wildlife Sanctuary

MONDULKIRI

Mondulkiri Protected Forest

MPONG THOM

Sambor

Sandan

KRATIE

Nam Lear Wildlife Sanctuary

Kratie

Sen Monorom

ay

Spoe Tbong

Stung Trang

Chhlong

Snoul Wildlife Sanctuary

Sre Khtum

KOMPONG CHAM

Snuol

Trapaeng Sre

Kompong Cham

Suong

Loc Ninh

Chub Krau

Trapaeng Plong

Memot

Xa Mat

VIETNAM

Prey Veng

PREY VENG

SVAY RIENG

eak

Ba Phnom

ng

Tay Ninh

Svay Rieng

Bavet

Moc Bai

Banteay Chakrey

Chiphu

Kaam Samnor

Khanh Binh

Vinh Xuong

hau Doc

HO CHI MINH CITY (SAIGON)

SOUTH CHINA SEA

107° E

108° E

ELEVATION

1500m
1000m
500m
250m
0

0 — 50 km
0 — 25 miles

Cambodia's
Top 10

Siem Reap & the Temples of Angkor

1 One of the world's most magnificent sights, the temples of Angkor (p118) are so much better than the superlatives. Choose from Angkor Wat, the world's largest religious building; Bayon, one of the world's weirdest, with its immense stone faces; or Ta Prohm, where nature runs amok. Buzzing Siem Reap (p86), with a superb selection of restaurants and bars, is the base for temple exploration. Beyond lie floating villages on the Tonlé Sap lake (p216), adrenalin-fuelled activities like quad biking and ziplining, and such cultured pursuits as cooking classes and birdwatching. Monks at Ta Prohm (p146)

Phnom Penh

2 The Cambodian capital (p30) is a chaotic yet charming city that has thrown off the shadows of the past to embrace a brighter future. Boasting one of the most beautiful riverfronts in the region, Phnom Penh is in the midst of a boom, with hip hotels, designer restaurants and funky bars ready to welcome urban explorers. Experience emotional extremes at the inspiring National Museum (p35) and the depressing Tuol Sleng prison (p35), showcasing the best and worst of Cambodian history. Once the 'Pearl of Asia', Phnom Penh is fast regaining its shine. Dancer, Phnom Penh's Royal Palace (p31)

3

4

Sihanoukville

3 Despite a reputation for backpacker hedonism, Sihanoukville's real appeal lies in its beaches (p171). On nearby islands like Koh Rong and Koh Rong Samloem (p188), resorts are creating a laid-back beach-bungalow vibe. On the mainland, it's only 5km from Sihanoukville's grittier central beach, Occheuteal, to Otres Beach, mellow and sublime despite the long-looming threat of development. More central Victory Beach, Independence Beach, Sokha Beach, and even Occheuteal and backpacker favourite Serendipity Beach all have their charms.

Battambang

4 The real Cambodia, far from the jet-set destinations of Phnom Penh and Siem Reap. Unfurling along the banks of the Sangker River, Battambang (p218) is one of the country's best-preserved colonial-era towns Shophouses host everything from fair-trade cafes to bike excursions. Beyond the town lie the Cambodian countryside and a cluster of ancient temples – while they're not exactly Angkor Wat, they do, mercifully, lack the crowds. Further afield is Prek Toal Bird Sanctuary (p114), a world-class bird sanctuary. Battambang in a word? Charming.

Kampot & Kep

5 These South Coast retreats form the perfect combination for those looking to get beyond the beaches of Sihanoukville. In laid-back Kampot (p192), take in the wonderful colonial architecture, explore the pretty river by paddleboard or kayak, and day-trip to wild Bokor National Park. Sleepier Kep (p200) offers its famous Crab Market, hiking in Kep National Park and hidden resorts to escape from it all. Crumbling half-century-old villas in both towns offer glimpses of a time when these were prime destinations for Phnom Penh's privileged few. Colonial buildings, Kampot

Mondulkiri

6 Eventually the endless rice fields and sugar palms that characterise the Cambodian landscape give way to rolling hills. Mondulkiri (p275) is the wild east, home to the hardy Bunong people, who still practise animism and ancestor worship. Elephants are used here, but better than riding them is visiting them at the Elephant Valley Project (p280), where you can experience 'walking with the herd'. Add thunderous waterfalls, jungle treks and spotting black-shanked douc to the mix and you have the right recipe for adventure.

COREY BARNES/GETTY IMAGES ©

Ratanakiri

7 The setting for Colonel Kurtz's jungle camp in *Apocalypse Now,* Ratanakiri (p266) is one of Cambodia's most remote and pretty provinces. Home to Virachey National Park, one of the largest protected areas in the country, this is serious trekking country. Possible animal encounters here include elephants and gibbons. Swimming is popular too, with jungle waterfalls and a beautiful crater lake within striking distance of provincial capital Ban Lung. Home to a diverse mosaic of ethnic-minority people, Ratanakiri is a world away from lowland Cambodia. Kinchaan waterfall (p267)

Kratie

8 Gateway to the rare freshwater Irrawaddy dolphins of the Mekong River (p258), Kratie is emerging as a crossroads on the overland route between Phnom Penh and northeastern Cambodia or southern Laos. The town (p258) has a decaying colonial grandeur and some of the country's best Mekong sunsets. Nearby Koh Trong island (p260) is a relaxing place to experience a homestay or explore on two wheels. North of Kratie the Mekong Discovery Trail (p262) has adventures themed around the mother river, including community-based homestays, bicycle rides and boat trips.

Prasat Preah Vihear

9 The mother of all mountain temples, Prasat Preah Vihear (p242 stands majestically atop the Dangkrek Mountains, forming a controversial border post between Cambodia and Thailand. The foundation stones of the temple stretch to the edge of the cliff as it falls away to the plains below, and the views across northern Cambodia are incredible. The 300-year chronology its construction offers an in sight into the metamorpho sis of carving and sculptur in the Angkorian period. It's all about location, and i doesn't get better than this

Khmer Cuisine

10 Everyone has tried Thai and Vietnamese specialities before they hit the region, but Khmer cuisine remains under the culinary radar. *Amok* (baked fish with lemongrass, chilli and coconut) is the national dish, but sumptuous seafood and fresh-fish dishes are plentiful, including Kep crab infused with Kampot pepper. It wouldn't be Asia without street snacks and Cambodia delivers everything from noodles *(mee)* and congee *(bobor;* rice porridge) to deep-fried tarantulas and roasted crickets. With subtle spices and delicate herbs, Cambodian food is an unexpected epicurean experience.

OTTO STADLER/GETTY IMAGES ©

Need to Know

For more information, see Survival Guide (p327)

Currency
Riel (r); US dollars (US$) are universally accepted

Language
Khmer; English and Chinese widely spoken

Visas
A tourist visa valid for one month costs US$20 on arrival and requires one passport-sized photo. Easily extendable business visas are available for US$25.

Money
ATMs are widely available, including in all major tourist centres and provincial capitals. Credit cards are accepted by many hotels and restaurants in larger cities.

Mobile Phones
Roaming is possible but is generally very expensive. Local SIM cards and unlocked mobile phones are readily available.

Time
Indochina Time Zone (GMT/UTC plus seven hours)

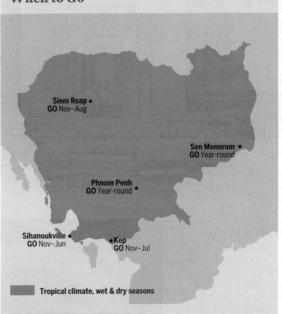

When to Go

Siem Reap •
GO Nov–Aug

Sen Monorom •
GO Year-round

Phnom Penh
GO Year-round •

Sihanoukville •
GO Nov–Jun

• Kep
GO Nov–Jul

Tropical climate, wet & dry seasons

High Season
(Nov–Mar)

➡ Cool and windy, with almost Mediterranean temperatures; the best all-round time to be here.

➡ Book accommodation in advance during the peak Christmas and New Year period.

Shoulder
(Jul–Aug)

➡ Wet in most parts of Cambodia, with high humidity, but the landscapes are emerald green.

➡ South Coast can be busy as Western visitors escape for summer holidays while school is out.

Low Season
(Apr–Jun & Sep–Oct)

➡ April and May spells the hot season, when the mercury hits 40°C and visitors melt.

➡ September and October can be wet, but awesome storms and cloud formations accompany the deluge.

Useful Websites

Lonely Planet (www.lonely planet.com) Online authority on travel in the Mekong region.

Phnom Penh Post (www. phnompenhpost.com) Cambodia's newspaper of record.

Travelfish (www.travelfish. org) Opinionated articles and reviews.

Andy Brouwer's Cambodia Tales (blog.andybrouwer.co.uk) Gateway to all things Cambodian; includes a popular blog.

Khmer Rouge Tribunal (www. cambodiatribunal.org) Detailed coverage of the Khmer Rouge trials.

Important Numbers

Drop the 0 from a regional (city) code when calling Cambodia from another country.

Cambodia code	☏855
International access code	☏001
Ambulance	☏119
Fire	☏118
Police	☏117

Exchange Rates

Australia	A$1	3711r
Canada	C$1	3777r
Euro zone	€1	5353r
Japan	¥100	3952r
New Zealand	NZ$1	3296r
Thailand	1B	124r
UK	UK£1	6377r
USA	US$1	3954r

For current exchange rates see www.xe.com.

Daily Costs

Budget: US$20–50

➡ Cheap guesthouse room: US$5–10

➡ Local meals and street eats: US$1–3

➡ Local buses: US$2–3 per 100km

Midrange: US$50–200

➡ Air-con hotel room: US$15–50

➡ Decent local restaurant meal: US$5–10

➡ Local tour guide per day: US$25

Top End: More than US$200

➡ Boutique hotel or resort: US$50–500

➡ Gastronomic meal with drinks: US$25–50

➡ 4WD rental per day: US$60–120

Opening Hours

Opening hours vary throughout the year. We've provided the high-season opening hours; hours will generally decrease in the shoulder and low seasons.

Banks 8am-3.30pm Monday to Friday

Bars 5pm to late

Government offices 7.30am-11.30am and 2-5pm Monday to Friday

Restaurants 7am-9pm or meal times

Shops 8am-6pm daily

Arriving in Cambodia

Phnom Penh Airport (p148) The airport is 7km west of central Phnom Penh. Official taxis/*remarks* to anywhere in the city cost a flat US$9/7 (30 minutes).

Siem Reap Airport (p339) The airport is 7km from the town centre. Taxis cost US$7 (15 minutes). A trip on the back of a *moto* is US$2. Many city hotels and guesthouses offer a free airport pick-up service with advance bookings.

Land borders (p340) Shared with Laos, Thailand and Vietnam; Cambodian visas available on arrival. Most borders are open during the core hours of 7am to 5pm. Overcharging for the Cambodian visa is very common at the borders with Thailand. Poipet and Cham Yeam (Koh Kong) are particularly notorious, so some travellers like the convenience of arranging an e-visa in advance.

Getting Around

Bus The most popular form of transport for most travellers, connecting all major towns and cities.

Car Private car or 4WD is an affordable option for those who value time above money.

Motorbike An amazing way to travel around Cambodia for experienced riders.

Air Relatively expensive domestic flights link Phnom Penh and Siem Reap.

Boat Less common than in the old days of bad roads, but Siem Reap to either Battambang or Phnom Penh remain popular routes.

For much more on **getting around**, see p342

If You Like...

Temples

Angkor Wat The one and only; the temple that puts all others in the shade. (p130)

Ta Prohm Iconic tree roots locked in a muscular embrace with ancient stones. (p146)

Prasat Preah Vihear The most mountainous of all the Khmer mountain temples, it is perched imperiously on the cliff-face of the Dangkrek Mountains. (p242)

Sambor Prei Kuk The pre-Angkorian capital of Isanapura was the first temple city in the Mekong region and is a chronological staging post on the road to Angkor. (p248)

Islands & Beaches

Sihanoukville King of the Cambodian beach resorts, with a headland ringed by squeaky white sands. (p170)

Koh Rong & Koh Rong Samloem More and more resorts are cropping up on the long, lonely white-sand beaches of these neighbouring islands located two hours off Sihanoukville. (p188)

Koh Kong There's no shortage of dreamy beaches on practically uninhabited Koh Kong Island and the cluster of islands just off Botum Sakor National Park. (p165)

Kep Cambodia's original beach resort, Kep was devastated by war but has resurrected itself in recent years with boutique resorts and delicious seafood. (p200)

Epicurean Experiences

Phnom Penh Dine to make a difference at one of Phnom Penh's many training restaurants to help the disadvantaged. (p57)

Siem Reap Browse the lively restaurants of the Old Market area and choose from exotic barbecues, mod Khmer cuisine or stop-and-dip market stalls. (p102)

Sihanoukville Sample succulent seafood at Cambodia's leading beach resort, including fresh crab, prawn and squid, cooked up with Kampot pepper. (p180)

Battambang Discover the delights of Cambodian cooking with a cheap and cheerful cooking class in this relaxed riverside town. (p221)

Water Features

Mekong Discovery Trail See rare freshwater dolphins, cycle around remote Mekong islands or experience a local family homestay. (p262)

Tonlé Sap lake Discover floating villages, bamboo skyscrapers, flooded forest and rare birdlife by taking a boat trip on Cambodia's Great Lake. (p15)

Boeng Yeak Lom Small but perfectly formed, this jungle-clad crater lake is Cambodia's most inviting natural swimming pool. (p267)

Bou Sraa Waterfall One of Cambodia's biggest set of falls, this roars out of the jungle in remote Mondulkiri Province. (p280)

IF YOU LIKE... ALTERNATIVE AEROBICS

Phnom Penh (p40) is the place to join in some aerobics en masse with early morning/early evening sessions along the bustling riverfront or overlooking the landmark Olympic Stadium.

Off-the-Beaten-Track Adventures

Elephant Valley Project Learn about elephants in their element by experiencing a walk with the herd in remote Mondulkiri Province. (p280)

Virachey National Park Disappear for a week into the wildlife-rich forests of this remote northeastern Cambodian natural treasure. (p273)

Kampot Cave Pagodas Go under ground at Kampot Province's cave pagodas, perfectly preserved since the 6th century in their own microclimate. (p198)

Cardamom Mountains Penetrate the vast rainforests of the remote Cardamoms like an explorer of old. (p166)

'Route 66' to Preah Khan Motorcycle along the ancient Angkorian highway from Beng Mealea to Preah Khan temple in Preah Vihear Province. (p245)

Nightlife

Phnom Penh This is where Cambodia rocks. Warm up with a riverfront happy hour, crawl around the Wat Langka area and end up in a nightclub. (p66)

Siem Reap There are so many bars around the Old Market that one strip has earned itself the accolade of Pub St. Stay late for the alternative Angkor sunrise. (p106)

Sihanoukville Home to a hedonistic crowd, the beachfront strips of Serendipity and Occheuteal have long been party central on the coast. (p183)

PLAN YOUR TRIP IF YOU LIKE...

(above) A hotel chef leads a market tour, Siem Reap (p93)
(below) Outdoor aerobics class, Phnom Penh (p40)

Month by Month

TOP EVENTS

Khmer New Year, April

Chinese New Year, January/February

P'chum Ben, September/October

Bon Om Tuk, October/November

Angkor Wat International Half Marathon, December

January

This is peak tourist season in Cambodia with Phnom Penh, Siem Reap and the South Coast heaving as Europeans and Americans escape the winter chill. Chinese and Vietnamese New Years sometimes fall in this month too.

✨ Chaul Chnam Chen (Chinese New Year)

The Chinese inhabitants of Cambodia celebrate their New Year somewhere between late January and mid-February – for the Vietnamese, this is Tet. As many of Phnom Penh's businesses are run by Chinese, commerce grinds to a halt around this time and there are dragon dances all over town. Many Vietnamese living in Cambodia return to their homeland for a week or more.

February

Still one of the busiest times of year for tourist arrivals, February is also often the month for Chinese and Vietnamese New Years. Young Cambodians swoon as Valentine's Day comes around.

✨ Giant Puppet Parade

This colourful annual fundraising event takes place in Siem Reap. Local organisations, orphanages and businesses come together to create giant puppets in the shape of animals, deities and contemporary characters, and the whole ensemble winds its way along the Siem Reap River like a scene from the Mardi Gras.

April

This is the most important month in the calendar for Khmers, as the New Year comes in the middle of April. For tourists it's a possible month to avoid, as the mercury regularly hits 40°C.

✨ Chaul Chnam Khmer (Khmer New Year)

This is a three-day celebration of the Khmer New Year, and it's like Christmas, New Year and a birthday all rolled into one. Cambodians make offerings at wats, clean out their homes and exchange gifts. It is a lively time to visit the country as the Khmers go wild with water in the countryside. Throngs of Khmers flock to Angkor, and it's absolute madness at most temples, so avoid the celebration if you want a quiet, reflective Angkor experience. That said, it is nowhere near as excessive as in Thailand or Laos, so it might seem tame by comparison.

May

This is the beginning of the low season for visitors as the monsoon arrives (and lasts till October), but there may be a last blast of hot weather to welcome mango season and some delicious ripe fruits.

⚜ Chat Preah Nengkal (Royal Ploughing Ceremony)

Led by the royal family, the Royal Ploughing Ceremony is a ritual agricultural festival held to mark the traditional beginning of the rice-growing season. It takes place in early May in front of the National Museum, near the Royal Palace in Phnom Penh, and the royal oxen are said to have a nose for whether it will be a good harvest or a bad one.

⚜ Visakha Puja (Buddha Day)

A celebration of Buddha's birth, enlightenment and *parinibbana* (passing). Activities are centred on wats. It falls on the eighth day of the fourth moon (May or June) and is best observed at Angkor Wat, where you can see candle-lit processions of monks.

September

Traditionally the wettest month in Cambodia, September is usually a time of sporadic flooding along the Mekong. The second most important festival, P'chum Ben, usually falls in this month.

⚜ P'chum Ben (Festival of the Dead)

This is a kind of All Souls' Day, when respects are paid to the dead through offerings made at wats. Offerings include paper money, candles, flowers and incense, as well as food and drink, all passed through the medium of the monks. P'chum Ben lasts for several days and devout Buddhists are expected to visit seven wats during the festival. Head to the village of Vihear Sour in Kandal Province, about 35km northeast of Phnom Penh, to witness authentic bareback buffalo racing and traditional Khmer wrestling.

October

The rains often linger long into October and this has led to some major flooding in Siem Reap in recent years. The countryside is extraordinarily green at this time.

⚜ Bon Om Tuk (Water Festival)

Celebrating the epic victory of Jayavarman VII over the Chams, who occupied Angkor in 1177, this also marks the extraordinary natural phenomenon of the reversal of the current of Tonlé Sap River. It's one of the most important festivals in the Khmer calendar and is a wonderful, chaotic time to be in Phnom Penh or Siem Reap. Boat races are held on the Tonlé Sap and Siem Reap Rivers, with each boat colourfully decorated and holding 40 rowers. As many as two million people flood the capital for the fun and frolics, so be sure to book ahead for accommodation. Sadly, this event was marred by tragedy in 2010 when a stampede developed on a bridge connecting the city with nearby Koh Pich (Diamond Island). More than 350 people died in the resulting crush. The event has subsequently been cancelled three years in a row: 2011, 2012 and 2013.

November

November brings the dry, windy season and signals the start of the best period to be in the country (which extends through until January or February). Bon Om Tuk often comes around in November.

⚜ Angkor Photo Festival

This photo festival has become a regular on the Siem Reap calendar. Resident and regional photographers descend on the temples and team up with local youths to teach them the tricks of the trade. Photography exhibitions are staged all over town.

December

Christmas and New Year are the peak of the peak season at Angkor and leading beach resorts; book a long way ahead. Sign up for a marathon or cycle ride if you fancy doing something for charity.

🏃 Angkor Wat International Half Marathon

This event has been a fixture in the Angkor calendar for more than 15 years now. Choose from a 21km half marathon, a 10km fun run or various bicycle races and rides. It may not be as famous as the London or New York marathons, but it's hard to imagine a better backdrop to a road race than the incredible temples of Angkor.

Plan Your Trip
Itineraries

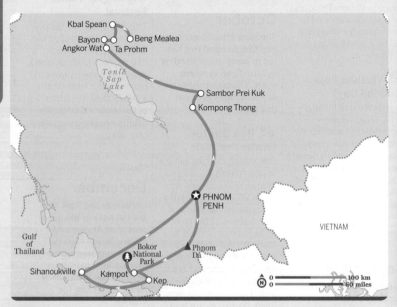

2 WEEKS Cambodia Snapshot

This is the ultimate journey, via temples, beaches and the capital. It can be run in any direction, but it is best followed to the letter, starting in the capital, exploring the coastline and winding up at the world's most impressive collection of temples, Angkor.

Hit **Phnom Penh** for its impressive National Museum and stunning Silver Pagoda. There's superb shopping at the Psar Tuol Tom Pong, and a night shift that never sleeps.

Take a fast boat to the hilltop temple of **Phnom Da**, which dates from the pre-Angkorian time, and then continue south to the colonial-era town of **Kampot**, which makes a good base for exploring this area. From here, visit the seaside town of **Kep** (and nearby Rabbit Island off the coast) and nearby cave pagodas. It is also possible to make a side trip to **Bokor National Park** or visit a pepper plantation.

Go west to **Sihanoukville**, Cambodia's beach capital, to sample the seafood, dive or snorkel the nearby waters or just enjoy soaking up the sun. Choose from

Bayon complex (p139), Angkor Thom

the party-central Serendipity Beach, chilled-out Otres Beach or the up-and-coming islands of Koh Rong or Koh Rong Samloem.

Backtrack via Phnom Penh to **Kompong Thom** and visit the pre-Angkorian brick temples of **Sambor Prei Kuk**.

Finish the trip at Angkor; it's a mind-blowing experience with which few sights can compare. See **Angkor Wat**, perfection in stone; **Bayon**, weirdness in stone; and **Ta Prohm**, nature triumphing over stone – before venturing further afield to **Kbal Spean** or jungle-clad **Beng Mealea**.

This trip can take two weeks at a steady pace or three weeks at a slow pace. Public transport serves most of this route, although some of the side trips will require chartered transport or a motorbike trip.

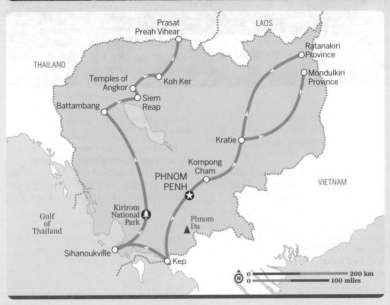

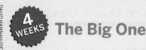

4 WEEKS The Big One

Cambodia is a small country and even though the roads are sometimes bad and travel can be slow, most of the big hitters can be visited in a month.

Setting out from the hip capital that is **Phnom Penh**, pass through the bustling Mekong town of **Kompong Cham** before heading on to **Kratie**, for an encounter with the elusive Irrawaddy river dolphins. Then it is time to make a tricky choice to experience the beauty of the northeast. Choose between **Ratanakiri Province** and the volcanic crater lake of Boeng Yeak Lom, or **Mondulkiri Province** and the original Elephant Valley Project to ensure maximum time elsewhere. Both offer new primate experiences for those that fancy a bit of monkey business along the way. Tough choice...can't decide? Flip a coin, if you can find one in this coinless country.

Head to the south coast. Take your time and consider a few nights in **Kep** or on one of the nearby islands, and a boat trip from **Sihanoukville** to explore the up-and-coming islands off the coast. Turning back inland, check out **Kirirom National Park**, home to pine trees, black bears and some spectacular views of the Cardamom Mountains.

Then it's time to go northwest to charming **Battambang**, one of Cambodia's best-preserved colonial-era towns and a base from which to discover rural life. Take the proverbial slow boat to **Siem Reap**, passing through stunning scenery along the snaking Sangker River, and turn your attention to the **temples of Angkor**.

Visit all the greatest hits in and around Angkor, but set aside some extra time to venture further to the rival capital of **Koh Ker**, which is cloaked in thick jungle, or **Prasat Preah Vihear**, a mountain temple perched precariously atop a cliff on the Thai border.

Overlanders can run this route in reverse, setting out from Siem Reap and exiting Cambodia by river into Vietnam or Laos. Entering from Laos, divert east to Ratanakiri before heading south. Getting around is generally easy, as there are buses on the big roads, taxis on the small roads and buzzing boats on the many rivers.

loating vegetable sales, Battambang Province (p218)
m: French colonial architecture, Battambang (p218)

Off the Beaten Track: Cambodia

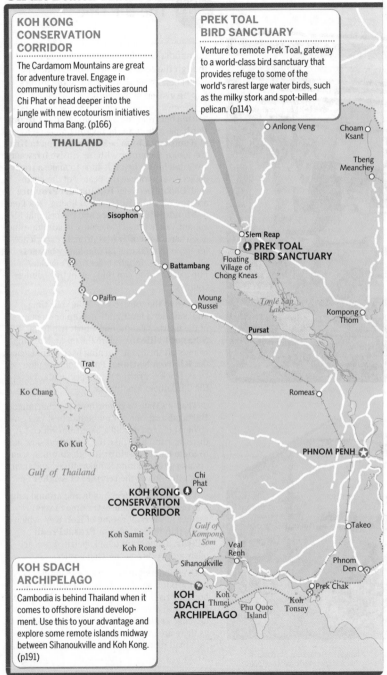

KOH KONG CONSERVATION CORRIDOR

The Cardamom Mountains are great for adventure travel. Engage in community tourism activities around Chi Phat or head deeper into the jungle with new ecotourism initiatives around Thma Bang. (p166)

PREK TOAL BIRD SANCTUARY

Venture to remote Prek Toal, gateway to a world-class bird sanctuary that provides refuge to some of the world's rarest large water birds, such as the milky stork and spot-billed pelican. (p114)

KOH SDACH ARCHIPELAGO

Cambodia is behind Thailand when it comes to offshore island development. Use this to your advantage and explore some remote islands midway between Sihanoukville and Koh Kong. (p191)

THAILAND

Anlong Veng
Choam Ksant
Tbeng Meanchey
Sisophon
Siem Reap
PREK TOAL BIRD SANCTUARY
Floating Village of Chong Kneas
Battambang
Moung Russei
Tonlé Sap Lake
Kompong Thom
Pailin
Pursat
Trat
Ko Chang
Romeas
Ko Kut
Gulf of Thailand
PHNOM PENH
Chi Phat
KOH KONG CONSERVATION CORRIDOR
Gulf of Kompong Som
Takeo
Koh Samit
Koh Rong
Veal Renh
Sihanoukville
Phnom Den
KOH SDACH ARCHIPELAGO
Koh Thmei
Phu Quoc Island
Koh Tonsay
Prek Chak

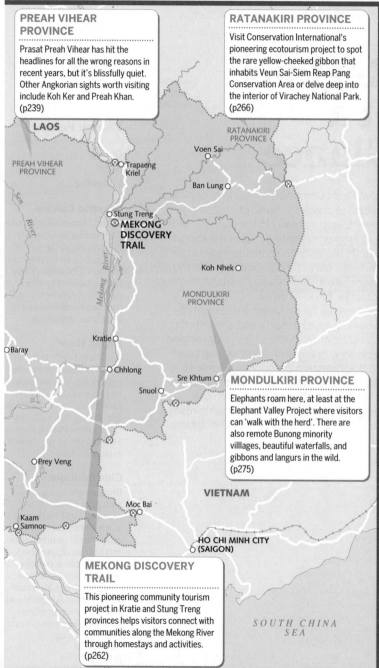

N   0 _____ 50 km
    0 _____ 30 miles

PREAH VIHEAR PROVINCE

Prasat Preah Vihear has hit the headlines for all the wrong reasons in recent years, but it's blissfully quiet. Other Angkorian sights worth visiting include Koh Ker and Preah Khan. (p239)

RATANAKIRI PROVINCE

Visit Conservation International's pioneering ecotourism project to spot the rare yellow-cheeked gibbon that inhabits Veun Sai-Siem Reap Pang Conservation Area or delve deep into the interior of Virachey National Park. (p266)

MONDULKIRI PROVINCE

Elephants roam here, at least at the Elephant Valley Project where visitors can 'walk with the herd'. There are also remote Bunong minority villlages, beautiful waterfalls, and gibbons and langurs in the wild. (p275)

MEKONG DISCOVERY TRAIL

This pioneering community tourism project in Kratie and Stung Treng provinces helps visitors connect with communities along the Mekong River through homestays and activities. (p262)

LAOS

PREAH VIHEAR PROVINCE

Sen River

Trapaeng Kriel

RATANAKIRI PROVINCE

Voen Sai

Ban Lung

Stung Treng
MEKONG DISCOVERY TRAIL

Mekong River

Koh Nhek

MONDULKIRI PROVINCE

Kratie

Baray

Chhlong

Sre Khtum

Snuol

Prey Veng

VIETNAM

Moc Bai

Kaam Samnor

HO CHI MINH CITY (SAIGON)

SOUTH CHINA SEA

Regions at a Glance

Phnom Penh, Cambodia's resurgent capital, is the place to check the pulse of contemporary life. Siem Reap, gateway to the majestic temples of Angkor, is starting to give the capital a run for its money with sophisticated restaurants, funky bars and chic boutiques. World Heritage Site Angkor houses some of the most spectacular temples on earth.

Down on the South Coast are several up-and-coming beach resorts and a smattering of tropical islands that are very undeveloped compared with those of neighbouring countries. Northwestern Cambodia is home to Battambang, a slice of more traditional life, and several remote jungle temples. The country's wild east is where elephants roam, waterfalls thunder and freshwater dolphins can be found.

Phnom Penh

Dining
Bars
Shopping

Creative Cuisine

French bistros abound, and outstanding fusion restaurants blend the best of Cambodian and European flavours. Ubiquitous Cambodian barbecues offer a more local experience or try gourmet Khmer cuisine in a designer restaurant.

Happy Hour

Get started early in a breezy establishment overlooking the Mekong, move on to one of the many live-music bars, and top it off by dancing till dawn in a legendary club. Phnom Penh is 24/7 and one of the liveliest capitals in Asia.

Chic Boutiques

Bring an extra bag to fill with gifts. Choose from colourful local markets where bargains abound on name-brand clothing, silks and handicrafts, or check out the impressive collections of several local and expat designers. There are also plenty of fair trade and good cause shops where your spending assists development projects.

p30

Siem Reap

Temples
Dining
Activities

Divine Inspiration

Many visitors arrive at Angkor under the misconception that it's all about Angkor Wat. True, it's one of the world's most iconic buildings, but just down the road are the enigmatic faces of the Bayon, the jungle temple of Ta Prohm and the carvings of Banteay Srei.

Eclectic Epicurean Experiences

Contemporary Khmer cuisine, spiced-up street food, fine French dining and a whole host more; Siem Reap is a dining destination in itself. Continue the night along Pub St or the more gentrified alleys beyond.

Beyond Angkor

Take to the skies by hot-air balloon or helicopter to see Angkor from a different angle. Learn the secrets of Cambodian cuisine with a cooking class. Play a round of golf on a world-class course or try Angkor-themed mini-golf. Too much hard work? Indulge in a massage in one of the many spas around town.

p86

South Coast

Beaches
Activities
Dining

Tropical Bliss

Thailand's beaches create more buzz, but on Cambodia's islands you can have a strip of powdery sand all to yourself, or relax in a beachfront bar that's still under the radar. Choose life in the fast lane in Sihanoukville, the slow lane in Kep or no lanes on the islands.

Land or Sea

National parks and other protected areas dot the region, offering trekking, mountain biking, kayaking, rock climbing and kitesurfing. Watersports abound, including windsurfing, wakeboarding and boating. Venture underwater to experience scuba diving or snorkelling around the islands.

Seafood Specialities

Each coastal town has its speciality. In Kep, it's delectable crab. In Takeo, it's lobster. In Kampot, it's anything cooked with the region's famous pepper. Sihanoukville has bargain beachside barbecues and seafood prepared in every style from sashimi to spicy.

p159

Northwestern Cambodia

Temples
Towns
Boat Trips

Beyond the Crowds

Heard enough about Angkor Wat? Don't forget the pre-Angkorian capital of Sambor Prei Kuk, the region's first temple city, or the remote jungle temples of Preah Vihear Province. Other noteworthy temples include Banteay Chhmar in the far northwest and hilltop Wat Banan near Battambang.

The Real Cambodia

Battambang has some of the best preserved French architecture in the country, a lively dining scene and a beautiful riverside setting. Kompongs Chhnang and Thom are well off the tourist trail and offer a slice of the real Cambodia.

Floating Villages

One of the most memorable boat rides in Cambodia links Battambang to Siem Reap following the Sangker River and the Tonlé Sap lake through timeless local communities. Explore the largest floating village on the Tonlé Sap lake, Kompong Luong.

p210

Eastern Cambodia

Wildlife
Culture
River Life

Jungle is Massive

View rare freshwater river dolphins around Kratie, walk with a herd of elephants in Mondulkiri or spot primates in newly launched community-based forest treks around Mondulkiri or Ratanakiri. The northeast is one of the best regions in Cambodia for guaranteed wildlife spotting.

Minority Report

Northeast Cambodia is home to a mosaic of ethnic minorities. Encounter the friendly Bunong people of Mondulkiri or venture up jungle rivers to visit remote tribal cemeteries in Ratanakiri. The culture in this region is a world away from lowland Cambodia.

The Mighty Mekong

The Mekong cuts through the region's heart; along it is the Mekong Discovery Trail, a community-based tourism initiative to develop homestays, lifestyle adventures and activities. Beyond the Mekong are some important tributaries in Ratanakiri and Mondulkiri, including the Tonle Srepok, as depicted in *Apocalypse Now*.

p251

On the Road

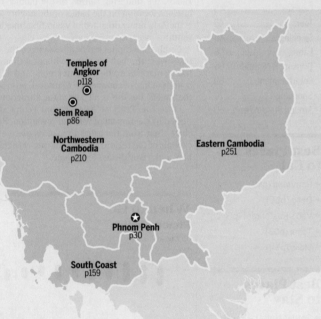

Phnom Penh

023 / POP 2 MILLION / AREA 290 SQ KM

Best Places to Eat

➡ Romdeng (p59)
➡ Deco (p65)
➡ Van's Restaurant (p63)
➡ Tepui (p58)
➡ Malis (p64)

Best Places to Stay

➡ Raffles Hotel Le Royal (p51)
➡ Eighty8 Backpackers (p47)
➡ Foreign Correspondents' Club (p47)
➡ Pavilion (p53)
➡ Villa Langka (p54)

Why Go?

Phnom Penh (ភ្នំ ពេញ): the name can't help but conjure up an image of the exotic. The glimmering spires of the Royal Palace, the fluttering saffron of the monks' robes and the luscious location on the banks of the mighty Mekong – this is the Asia many dreamed of when first imagining their adventures overseas.

Cambodia's capital can be an assault on the senses. Motorbikes whiz through laneways without a thought for pedestrians; markets exude pungent scents; and all the while the sounds of life, of commerce, of survival, reverberate through the streets. But this is all part of the attraction.

Once the 'Pearl of Asia', Phnom Penh's shine was tarnished by the impact of war and revolution. But the city has since risen from the ashes to take its place among the hip capitals of the region, with an alluring cafe culture, bustling bars and a world-class food scene.

When to Go
Phnom Penh

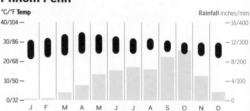

Jan–Feb The holiday crush is over and pleasant northeasterly breezes massage the riverfront.

Sep–Oct Heavy rains provide relief from searing sun; many hotels offer steep low-season discounts.

Oct–Nov Bon Om Tuk, or Water Festival, is one giant street party (when it's not suspended!).

History

Legend has it that the city of Phnom Penh was founded when an old woman named Penh found four Buddha images that had come to rest on the banks of the Mekong River. She housed them on a nearby hill, and the town that grew up here came to be known as Phnom Penh (Hill of Penh).

In the 1430s, Angkor was abandoned and Phnom Penh chosen as the site of the new Cambodian capital. Angkor was poorly situated for trade and subject to attacks from the Siamese (Thai) kingdom of Ayuthaya. Phnom Penh commanded a more central position in the Khmer territories and was perfectly located for riverine trade with Laos and China, via the Mekong Delta.

By the mid-16th century, trade had turned Phnom Penh into a regional power. Indonesian and Chinese traders were drawn to the city in large numbers. A century later, however, the landlocked and increasingly isolated kingdom had become a little more than a buffer between ascendant Thais and Vietnamese, until the French took over in 1863.

The French protectorate in Cambodia gave Phnom Penh the layout we know today. They divided the city into districts or *quartiers* – the French and European traders inhabited the area north of Wat Phnom between Monivong Blvd and Tonlé Sap River. By the time the French departed in 1953, they had left many important landmarks, including the Royal Palace, National Museum, Psar Thmei (Central Market) and many impressive government ministries.

Phnom Penh grew quickly in the post-independence peacetime years of Norodom Sihanouk's rule. By the time he was overthrown in 1970, the population of the city was approximately 500,000. As the Vietnam War spread into Cambodian territory, the city's population swelled with refugees and reached nearly three million in early 1975. The Khmer Rouge took the city on 17 April 1975 and, as part of its radical revolution, immediately forced the entire population into the countryside. Whole families were split up on those first fateful days of 'liberation'.

During the time of Democratic Kampuchea, many tens of thousands of former Phnom Penhois – including the vast majority of the capital's educated residents – were killed. The population of Phnom Penh during the Khmer Rouge regime was never more than about 50,000, a figure made up of senior party members, factory workers and trusted military leaders.

Repopulation of the city began when the Vietnamese arrived in 1979, although at first it was strictly controlled by the new government. During much of the 1980s, cows were more common than cars on the streets of the capital. The 1990s were boom years for some: along with the arrival of the UN Transitional Authority in Cambodia (Untac) came US$2 billion (much of it in salaries for expats).

Phnom Penh has really begun to change in the last 15 years, with roads being repaired, sewage pipes laid, parks inaugurated and riverbanks reclaimed. Business is booming in many parts of the city, with skyscrapers under development, investors rubbing their hands with the sort of glee once reserved for Bangkok or Hanoi, and swanky new restaurants opening. Phnom Penh is back, and bigger changes are set to come.

◎ Sights

Phnom Penh is a relatively small city and easy to navigate as it is laid out in a numbered grid. The most important cultural sights can be visited on foot and are located near the riverfront in the most beautiful part of the city. Most other sights are also fairly central – just a short *remork-moto* ride from the riverfront.

★ Royal Palace PALACE
(ព្រះបរមរាជវាំង; Map p36; Sothearos Blvd; admission incl camera/video 25,000r, guide per hr US$10; ⊙ 8-11am & 2-5pm) With its classic Khmer roofs and ornate gilding, the Royal Palace dominates the diminutive skyline of Phnom Penh. It is a striking structure near the riverfront, bearing a remarkable likeness to its counterpart in Bangkok.

Being the official residence of King Sihamoni, parts of the massive palace compound are closed to the public. Visitors are only allowed to visit the throne hall and a clutch of buildings surrounding it. Adjacent to the palace, the Silver Pagoda complex is also open to the public.

Visitors need to wear shorts that reach to the knee, and T-shirts or blouses that reach to the elbow; otherwise they will have to rent an appropriate covering. The palace gets very busy on Sundays when countryside Khmers come to pay their respects, but this can be a fun way to experience the place, thronging with locals.

Phnom Penh Highlights

1 Discover the world's finest collection of Khmer sculpture at the stunning **National Museum** (p35)

2 Delve into the dark side of Cambodian history with visits to the **Tuol Sleng Museum** (p35) and the **Killing Fields** (p37)

3 Be dazzled by the 5000 silver floor tiles of the **Silver Pagoda** (p31), part of the Royal Palace

4 Dive into Phnom Penh's frenzied **nightlife** (p66) with a happy-hour cocktail, a bar crawl and a late-night cameo in a legendary disco

5 Shop till you drop (of heat exhaustion) at bounteous **Russian Market** (p70)

6 Put your hands in the air like you just don't care during public **aerobics sessions** (p40) at landmark Olympic Stadium

7 Cruise the mighty Mekong, cocktail in hand, on a **sunset boat cruise** (p40)

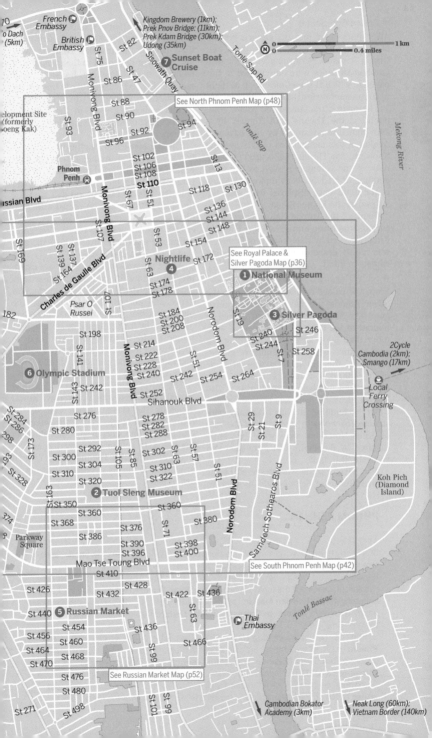

➤ Palace Compound

All visitors enter into the eastern portion of the palace compound near the Chan Chaya Pavilion. Performances of classical Cambodian dance were once staged in this pavilion, which is sometimes lit up at night to commemorate festivals or anniversaries.

The main attraction in the palace compound is the Throne Hall. Topped by a 59m-high tower inspired by the Bayon at Angkor, it was inaugurated in 1919 by King Sisowath. The Throne Hall is used for coronations and ceremonies such as the presentation of credentials by diplomats. Many of the items once displayed here were destroyed by the Khmer Rouge.

South of the Throne Hall, check out the curious iron Napoleon II Pavilion. Given to King Norodom by Napoleon III of France, it was hardly designed with the Cambodian climate in mind.

➤ Silver Pagoda Complex

From the palace compound you enter the Silver Pagoda complex through its north gate. The Silver Pagoda was so named in honour of the floor, which is covered with more than 5000 silver tiles weighing 1kg each, adding up to five tonnes of gleaming silver. You can sneak a peek at some of the 5000 tiles near the entrance – most are covered for their protection. It is also known as Wat Preah Keo (Pagoda of the Emerald Buddha). It was originally constructed of wood in 1892 during the rule of King Norodom, who was apparently inspired by Bangkok's Wat Phra Keo, and was rebuilt in 1962.

The Silver Pagoda was preserved by the Khmer Rouge to demonstrate its concern for the conservation of Cambodia's cultural riches to the outside world. Although more than half of the pagoda's contents were lost, stolen or destroyed in the turmoil that followed the Vietnamese invasion, what remains is spectacular. This is one of the few places in Cambodia where bejewelled objects embodying some of the brilliance and richness of Khmer civilisation can still be seen.

The staircase leading to the Silver Pagoda is made of Italian marble. Inside, the Emerald Buddha, believed to be made of Baccarat crystal, sits on a gilded pedestal high atop the dais. In front of the dais stands a life-sized gold Buddha decorated with 2086 diamonds, the largest of which, set in the crown, is a whopping 25 carats. Created in the palace workshops around 1907, the gold Buddha weighs in at 90kg.

Along the walls of the pagoda are examples of extraordinary Khmer artisanship, including intricate masks used in classical dance and dozens of gold Buddhas. The many precious gifts given to Cambodia's monarchs by foreign heads of state appear rather spiritless when displayed next to such diverse and exuberant Khmer art. Photography is not permitted inside the Silver Pagoda.

The Silver Pagoda complex is enclosed by walls plastered with an extensive mural depicting the classic Indian epic of the *Ramayana* (known as the *Reamker* in Cambodia). The story begins just south of the east gate and includes vivid images of the battle of Lanka. The mural was created around 1900 and is definitely showing its age in parts.

PHNOM PENH IN...

Two Days

Start early to observe the aerobics sessions on the riverfront, then grab breakfast before venturing into the **Royal Palace** (p31). Next is the **National Museum** (p35) and the world's most wondrous collection of Khmer sculpture. After lunch at **Friends** (p57) restaurant, check out the funky architecture of **Psar Thmei** (p70), but save the heavy shopping for the **Russian Market** (p70). Celebrate your shopping coups with a riverside happy-hour drink at **Foreign Correspondents' Club** (p67), and then a night out on the town.

Start day two with a **walking tour** (p45) of the centre, or just wander around **Wat Phnom** (p37), where Khmers pray for luck. Have lunch on the riverside, then visit the sobering **Tuol Sleng Museum** (p35) before continuing on to the **Killing Fields of Choeung Ek** (p37). It is a grim afternoon, but essential for understanding just how far Cambodia has come in the intervening years. Wind up your weekend with a **sunset cruise** (p40) on the Mekong River, offering a beautiful view over the Royal Palace.

Other structures to be found in the complex (listed clockwise from the north gate) include the mondap (library), which once housed richly decorated sacred texts written on palm leaves (now moved to the safety of air-conditioned storage); the shrine of King Norodom (r 1860–1904); an equestrian statue of King Norodom; the shrine of King Ang Duong (r 1845–59); a pavilion housing a huge footprint of the Buddha; Phnom Mondap, an artificial hill with a structure containing a bronze footprint of the Buddha from Sri Lanka; a shrine dedicated to one of Prince Sihanouk's daughters; a pavilion for celebrations held by the royal family; the shrine of Prince Sihanouk's father, King Norodom Suramarit (r 1955–60); and a bell tower, where the bell is rung to order the gates to be opened or closed.

★ National Museum of Cambodia MUSEUM
(សារមន្ទីរជាតិ; Map p48; www.cambodia museum.info; cnr St 13 & St 178; admission US$5; ☉8am-5pm) Located just north of the Royal Palace, the National Museum of Cambodia is housed in a graceful terracotta structure of traditional design (built 1917-20), with an inviting courtyard garden. The museum is home to the world's finest collection of Khmer sculpture – more than a millennium's worth of masterful Khmer design.

The museum comprises four pavilions, facing the pretty garden. Most visitors start left and continue in a clockwise, chronological direction. The first significant sculpture to greet visitors is a large fragment – including the relatively intact head, shoulders and two arms – of an immense bronze reclining Vishnu statue recovered from the Western Mebon temple near Angkor Wat in 1936.

Continue into the left pavilion, where the pre-Angkorian collection begins. It illustrates the journey from the human form of Indian sculpture to the more divine form of Khmer sculpture from the 5th to 8th centuries. Highlights include an imposing eight-armed Vishnu statue from the 6th century found at Phnom Da, and a staring Harihara, combining the attributes of Shiva and Vishnu, from Prasat Andet in Kompong Thom province. The Angkor collection includes several striking statues of Shiva from the 9th, 10th and 11th centuries; a giant pair of wrestling monkeys (Ko Ker, 10th century); a beautiful 12th-century stele (stone) from Oddar Meanchey inscribed with scenes from

the life of Shiva; and the sublime statue of a seated Jayavarman VII (r 1181–1219), his head bowed slightly in a meditative pose (Angkor Thom, late 12th century).

The museum also contains displays of pottery and bronzes dating from the pre-Angkorian periods of Funan and Chenla (4th to 9th centuries), the Indravarman period (9th and 10th centuries) and the classical Angkorian period (10th to 14th centuries), as well as more recent works such as a beautiful wooden royal barge.

Unfortunately, it is not possible to photograph the collection - only the courtyard. English-, French- and Japanese-speaking guides (US$6) are available. A comprehensive booklet, *The New Guide to the National Museum*, is available at the front desk (US$10), while the smaller *Khmer Art in Stone* covers some of the signature pieces (US$2).

★ Tuol Sleng Museum MUSEUM
(សារមន្ទីរទួលស្លែង; Map p42; cnr St 113 & 350; admission/guide US$2/6; ☉7am-5.30pm) In 1975, Tuol Svay Prey High School was taken over by Pol Pot's security forces and turned into a prison known as Security Prison 21 (S-21). This soon became the largest centre of detention and torture in the country. Between 1975 and 1978 more than 17,000 people held at S-21 were taken to the killing fields of Choeung Ek.

S-21 has been turned into the Tuol Sleng Museum, which serves as a testament to the crimes of the Khmer Rouge.

Like the Nazis, the Khmer Rouge leaders were meticulous in keeping records of their barbarism. Each prisoner who passed through S-21 was photographed, sometimes before and after torture. The museum displays include room after room of harrowing black-and-white photographs; virtually all of the men, women and children pictured were later killed. You can tell which year a picture was taken by the style of number-board that appears on the prisoner's chest. Several foreigners from Australia, New Zealand and the USA were also held at S-21 before being murdered. It is worth hiring a guide, as they can tell you the stories behind some of the people in the photographs.

As the Khmer Rouge 'revolution' reached ever greater heights of insanity, it began devouring its own. Generations of torturers and executioners who worked here were in turn killed by those who took their places. During early 1977, when the party purges of

Royal Palace & Silver Pagoda

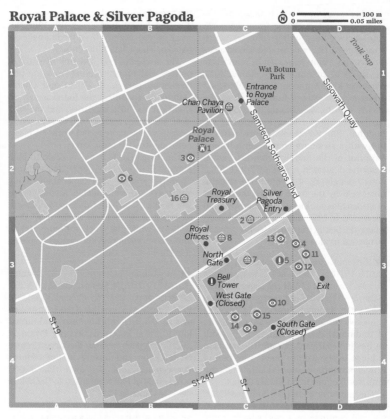

Royal Palace & Silver Pagoda

Eastern Zone cadres were getting underway, S-21 claimed an average of 100 victims a day.

When the Vietnamese army liberated Phnom Penh in early 1979, there were only seven prisoners alive at S-21, all of whom had used their skills, such as painting or photography, to stay alive. Fourteen others had been tortured to death as Vietnamese forces were closing in on the city. Photographs of their gruesome deaths are on display in the rooms where their decomposing corpses were found. Their graves are nearby in the courtyard.

Altogether, a visit to Tuol Sleng is a profoundly depressing experience. The sheer ordinariness of the place makes it even more horrific: the suburban setting, the plain school buildings, the grassy playing area where children kick around balls juxtaposed with rusted beds, instruments of torture and wall after wall of disturbing portraits. It demonstrates the darkest side of the human spirit that lurks within us all. Tuol Sleng is not for the squeamish.

Behind many of the displays at Tuol Sleng is the **Documentation Center of Cambodia** (DC-Cam; www.dccam.org). DC-Cam was established in 1995 through Yale University's **Cambodian Genocide Program** (www.yale.edu/cgp) to research and document the crimes of the Khmer Rouge. It became an independent organisation in 1997 and researchers have spent years translating confessions and paperwork from Tuol Sleng, mapping mass graves, and preserving evidence of Khmer Rouge crimes.

French-Cambodian director Rithy Panh's 1996 film *Bophana* tells the true story of Hout Bophana, a beautiful young woman, and Ly Sitha, a regional Khmer Rouge leader, who fall in love but are made to pay for this 'crime' with imprisonment and execution at S-21 prison. It is well worth investing an hour to watch this powerful documentary, which is screened here at 10am and 3pm daily. A DC-Cam slide presentation takes place Monday and Friday at 2pm and Wednesday at 9am.

Killing Fields of Choeung Ek   MUSEUM

(វាលពិឃាតជើងឯក; admission incl audio tour US$5; ⊙7.30am-5.30pm) Between 1975 and 1978 about 17,000 men, women, children and infants who had been detained and tortured at S-21 were transported to the extermination camp of Choeung Ek. They were often bludgeoned to death to avoid wasting precious bullets.

The remains of 8985 people, many of whom were bound and blindfolded, were exhumed in 1980 from mass graves in this one-time longan orchard; 43 of the 129 communal graves here have been left untouched. Fragments of human bone and bits of cloth are scattered around the disinterred pits. More than 8000 skulls, arranged by sex and age, are visible behind the clear glass panels of the Memorial Stupa, which was erected in 1988. It is a peaceful place today, masking the horrors that unfolded here less than three decades ago.

Admission to the Killing Fields includes an excellent audio tour, available in several languages, which includes stories by those who survived the Khmer Rouge, as well as a chilling account by Choeung Ek guard and executioner Him Huy about some of the techniques they used to kill innocent prisoners and defenceless women and children.

The museum here has some interesting information on the Khmer Rouge leadership and the ongoing trial. A memorial ceremony is held annually at Choeung Ek on 9 May.

To get to the Killing Fields of Choeung Ek, take Monireth Blvd southwest out of the city. The site is well signposted in English about 7.5km from the bridge near St 271. Figure on about US$10 for a *remork* (drivers will ask US$15 to US$20).

Wat Phnom   BUDDHIST TEMPLE

(វត្តភ្នំ; Map p48; temple/museum admission US$1/2; ⊙7am-6.30pm, museum 7am-6pm) Set on top of a 27m-high tree-covered knoll, Wat Phnom is on the only 'hill' in town. According to legend, the first pagoda on this site was erected in 1373 to house four statues of Buddha deposited here by the waters of the Mekong River and discovered by Madame Penh. The main entrance to Wat Phnom is via the grand eastern staircase, which is guarded by lions and *naga* (mythical serpent) balustrades.

Today, many people come here to pray for good luck and success in school exams or business affairs. When a wish is granted, the faithful return to deliver on the offering promised, such as a garland of jasmine flowers or a bunch of bananas, of which the spirits are said to be especially fond.

The *vihara* (temple sanctuary) was rebuilt in 1434, 1806, 1894 and 1926. West of the *vihara* is a huge stupa containing the ashes of King Ponhea Yat (r 1405–67). In a pavilion on the southern side of the passage between the *vihara* and the stupa is a statue of a smiling and rather plump Madame Penh.

A bit to the north of and below the *vihara* is an eclectic shrine dedicated to the genie Preah Chau, who is especially revered by the Vietnamese. On either side of the entrance to the central altar containing a statue of Preah Chau are guardian spirits bearing iron bats. In the chamber to the right of the statue (if you are looking at it) are drawings of Confucius, as well as two Chinese-style figures of the sages Thang Cheng (on the right) and Thang Thay (on the left).

Down the hill from the *vihara* in the northwest corner of the complex is a museum with some old statues and historical artefacts, which can probably be skipped if you've been to the National Museum.

Wat Phnom can be a bit of a circus, with beggars, street urchins, women selling drinks and children selling birds in cages (you pay to set the bird free, but the birds are trained to return to their cage afterwards).

Wat Ounalom BUDDHIST TEMPLE

(វត្តឧណ្ណាលោម; Map p48; Sothearos Blvd; ⊙6am-6pm) This wat is the headquarters of Cambodian Buddhism. It was founded in 1443 and comprises 44 structures. It received a battering during the Pol Pot era, but today the wat has come back to life. The head of the country's Buddhist brotherhood lives here, along with a large number of monks.

On the 2nd floor of the main building, to the left of the dais, is a statue of Huot Tat, fourth patriarch of Cambodian Buddhism, who was killed by Pol Pot. The statue, made in 1971 when the patriarch was 80 years old, was thrown in the Mekong by the Khmer Rouge to show that Buddhism was no longer the driving force in Cambodia. It was retrieved after 1979. To the right of the dais is a statue of a former patriarch of the Thummayuth sect, to which the royal family belongs.

Seek out the stairway to the left behind the dais. It leads up to the 3rd floor, where a glass case houses a small marble Buddha of Burmese origin that was broken into pieces by the Khmer Rouge and later reassembled. There are nice views of the Mekong up here.

Behind the main building is a stupa containing an eyebrow hair of Buddha with an inscription in Pali (an ancient Indian language) over the entrance.

Olympic Stadium LANDMARK

(ពហុកីឡដ្ឋានអូឡាំពិក; Map p42; near cnr Sihanouk & Monireth Blvds) Known collectively as the National Sports Complex, the Olympic Stadium is a striking example of 1960s Khmer architecture and includes a sports arena and facilities for boxing, gymnastics, volleyball and other sports. Turn up after 5pm to see countless football matches, *pétanque* duels or badminton games.

Wat Moha Montrei BUDDHIST TEMPLE

(វត្តមហាមន្ត្រី; Map p42; Sihanouk Blvd) Situated close to the Olympic Stadium, Wat Moha Montrei was named in honour of one of King Monivong's ministers, Chakrue Ponn, who initiated the founding of the pagoda (*moha montrei* means 'the great minister'). The cement *vihara*, topped with a 35m-high tower, was completed in 1970. Between 1975 and 1979, it was used by the Khmer Rouge to store rice and corn.

Check out the assorted Cambodian touches incorporated into the wall murals of the *vihara*, which tell the story of Buddha. The angels accompanying Buddha to heaven are dressed as classical Khmer dancers and the assembled officials wear the white military uniforms of the Sihanouk period.

Independence Monument MONUMENT

(វិមានឯករាជ្យ; Map p42; cnr Norodom & Sihanouk Blvds) Modelled on the central tower of Angkor Wat, Independence Monument was built in 1958 to commemorate the country's independence from France in 1953. It also serves as a memorial to Cambodia's war dead. Wreaths are laid here on national holidays. In the park just east of here is a new statue (Map p42; Sihanouk Blvd) of the legendary former king/prime minister/statesman Norodom Sihanouk (p293), who died a national hero in 2012.

Nearby, in Wat Botum Park opposite photogenic Wat Botum (Map p42; btwn Sts 7 & 19), is the optimistically named Cambodia-Vietnam Friendship Monument (Map p42; Wat Botum Park), built to a Vietnamese (and rather communist) design in 1979. Concerts are often held in the park, which springs to life with aerobics, football and *takraw* (foot juggling with a rattan ball) enthusiasts after 5pm.

Vann Nath Gallery ART GALLERY

(Map p42; 33B St 169, Kith Eng Restaurant) FREE The late Cambodian artist Vann Nath is famous the world over for his depictions of Khmer Rouge torture scenes at Phnom Penh's notorious S-21 Security Prison, where he was one of only seven survivors. He continued to paint vivid canvases of S-21 right up until he died in 2011.

Many of Vann Nath's later works can be viewed here at his family's Kith Eng Restaurant. There are no set hours, just drop by and usually his wife or his son-in-law (who speaks English) will let you in.

Some of Vann Nath's most famous images are on display at the Tuol Sleng Museum. The Vietnamese brought him back to S-21 from 1980 to 1982 specifically to paint these. 'We must think of the souls of those who died there,' Vann Nath told us in an interview not long before he passed away. 'These souls died without hope, without light, without a future. They had no life. So I paint my scenes to tell the world the stories of those who did not survive.'

In the wake of Vann Nath's death, fellow prisoners Chum Mey and Bou Meng are the last remaining survivors of S-21.

French Embassy LANDMARK
(☎023-430020; 1 Monivong Blvd) At the northern end of Monivong Blvd, the French embassy played a significant role in the dramas that unfolded after the fall of Phnom Penh on 17 April 1975. About 800 foreigners and 600 Cambodians took refuge in the embassy. Within 48 hours, the Khmer Rouge informed the French vice-consul that the new government did not recognise diplomatic privileges and that if all the Cambodians in the compound were not handed over, the lives of the foreigners inside would also be forfeited.

Cambodian women married to foreigners could stay; Cambodian men married to foreign women could not. Foreigners wept as servants, colleagues, friends, lovers and husbands were escorted out of the embassy gates. At the end of the month the foreigners were expelled from Cambodia by truck. Many of the Cambodians were never seen again. Today a high whitewashed wall surrounds the massive complex and the French have returned to Cambodia in a big way, promoting French language and culture in their former colony.

Prayuvong Buddha Factories BUDDHIST
(កន្លែងកសាងព្រះពុទ្ធបព្រះយួរវង្ស; Map p42; btwn St 308 & St 310) In order to replace the countless Buddhas and ritual objects smashed by the Khmer Rouge, a whole neighbourhood of private workshops making cement Buddhas, *naga* and small stupas has grown up on the grounds of Wat Prayuvong. While the graceless cement figures painted in gaudy colours are hardly works of art, they are an effort by the Cambodian people to restore Buddhism to a place of honour in their culture. The Prayuvong Buddha factories are about 300m south of Independence Monument.

National Library LANDMARK
(បណ្ណាល័យជាតិ | Bibliothèque Nationale; Map p48; St 92; ⊗8-11am & 2-5pm Mon-Fri) The National Library is in a graceful old building

PHNOM PENH FOR CHILDREN

With chaotic traffic, a lack of green spaces and sights that are predominantly morbid, Phnom Penh would not seem like the most child-friendly city. Think again. There are plenty of little gems to help you pass the time with your children in the capital. Plus, what kid doesn't love a *remork* ride?

One rule of thumb is that kids also love Buddhist temples – especially colourful temples like Wat Langka (p44) or Wat Ounalom (p38), and hill temples like Wat Phnom (p37) or, outside of town, Udong (p81). Shimmering gold Buddhas, shiny stupas, animal statues and the occasional monkey give children plenty of visual stimulation (just keep their eyes averted from potentially scary demons). The Royal Palace (p31) is similarly rich in Buddhist iconography.

If your kids ride two-wheelers, consider renting bicycles and crossing the Mekong by ferry from the dock behind Imperial Garden Hotel. On the other side, smooth roads and trails lead 15km or so north to Smango (☎016994555; www.smangohouse.com; pool admission US$5), a guesthouse with decent food and a refreshing swimming pool. Check its website for exact directions.

Phnom Penh has decent public play spaces, including a playground (Map p42; Sothearos Blvd) northwest of the Cambodia-Vietnam Friendship Memorial in Wat Botum Park, and another playground (Map p48) just south of Wat Phnom.

To escape the heat (or the rain), Kids City (Map p42; www.kidscityasia.com; Sihanouk Blvd; 1hr from US$5; ⊗8am-9.30pm) is a vast indoor play palace, with a first-rate climbing gym, an elaborate jungle gym, a science gallery and an ice rink. Other indoor playgrounds (bring socks) with elaborate slides, bouncy castles and the like can be found at amusement park Dream Land (Map p42; www.dreamland.com.kh; 8 Sisowath Quay; admission US$6, playground 2000r; ⊗9am-9pm), which also has a ferris wheel and other rides; and, for younger children, Monkey Business (Map p42; St 370 cnr St 57; child US$2-4, adult free; ⊗9am-7pm), which has wi-fi and a cafe for adults.

Many of the restaurants and cafes are child-friendly, but there are a few specifically aimed at families, including Le Jardin (p64).

The most interesting attraction is beyond the city limits and makes a good day trip: Phnom Tamao Wildlife Sanctuary (p83), a rescue centre for Cambodia's incredible wildlife.

ⓘ WARNING: BAG SNATCHING

Bag snatching has become a real problem in Phnom Penh and foreigners are often targeted. Hot spots include the riverfront and busy areas around popular markets, but there is no real pattern – the speeding motorbike thieves, usually operating in pairs, can strike any time, any place. Countless expats and tourists have been injured falling off their bikes in the process of being robbed, and in 2007 a young French woman was killed after being dragged from a speeding *moto* (moto-taxi) into the path of a vehicle. Try to wear close-fitting bags such as backpacks that don't dangle from the body temptingly. Don't hang expensive cameras around the neck and keep things close to the body and out of sight, particularly when walking along the road, crossing the road or travelling by *remork-moto (tuk tuk)* or especially by *moto*. These guys are real pros and only need one chance.

constructed in 1924, near Wat Phnom. During its rule, the Khmer Rouge turned the building into a stable and destroyed most of the books. Many were thrown out into the streets and picked up by people, some of whom donated them back to the library after 1979; others used them as food wrappings. Today it houses, among other things, a time-worn collection of English and French titles, including some ancient Lonely Planet books.

🏃 Activities

Aerobics

Every morning at the crack of dawn, and again at dusk, Cambodians gather in several pockets throughout the city to participate in quirky and colourful aerobics sessions. This quintessential Cambodian phenomenon sees a ring-leader, equipped with boom box and microphone, whip protégés into shape with a mix of 1980s-Soviet-style calisthenics and *Thriller*-inspired line-dancing moves. It's favoured by middle-aged Khmer women, but you'll see both sexes and all ages participating, and tourists are more than welcome.

There are many places to join in the fun or just observe. Olympic Stadium is probably the best spot because of the sheer volume of participants. Here several instructors compete for clients and the upper level of the grandstand becomes a cacophony of competing boom boxes.

The riverfront usually sees some action; the patch opposite Blue Pumpkin at the terminus of St 144 is a good bet. Another popular place that usually sees several groups getting their collective freaks on is Wat Botum Park along Sothedros Blvd.

Boat Cruises

Boat trips on the Tonlé Sap and Mekong Rivers are very popular with visitors. Sunset cruises are ideal, the burning sun sinking slowly behind the glistening spires of the Royal Palace. A slew of cruising boats is available for hire on the riverfront about 500m north of the tourist boat dock. Just rock up and arrange one on the spot for US$15 to US$20 an hour, depending on negotiations and numbers. You can bring your own drinks or buy beer and soft drinks on the boat.

Public river cruises are another option. They leave every 30 minutes from 5pm to 7.30pm from the tourist boat dock (p76) and last about 45 minutes (US$5 per head).

Cycling

You can hire a bike and go it alone – Koh Dach is a doable DIY trip, or venture across the Mekong River on a local ferry (1000r including bike) behind Imperial Garden Hotel and pick up bucolic back roads on the other side. Or opt for something more organised with or without a guide through one of the companies below. Vicious Cycle and Offroad Cambodia both run daily group tours to Udong or Koh Dach, departing before 8am.

2Cycle Cambodia CYCLING
(📱 015696376; www.2cyclecambodia.com) 2Cycle specialises in trips across the Mekong, including an overnight tour with a village homestay. Local-ish mountain bikes cost US$2 per hour to US$6 for the day, and smaller bikes are available for children. Book the day before you plan to ride.

Bike Shop CYCLING
(Map p42; 📱089834704; www.bicyclecambodia rental.com; 31 St 302) Has premium mountain and road bikes for rent (US$10 to US$30) and specialises in multiday cycling tours that criss-cross the country (from US$80 per day per person for a couple).

Offroad Cambodia CYCLING
(Map p42; 📱 0888555123; http://offroad-cambodia .com; 2 St 215) Rents quality Trek mountain

bikes for US$7 per day and runs a variety of day and multiday tours, including mountain biking in Kirirom National Park. As the name suggests, tours tend to steer well clear of sealed highways.

Vicious Cycle CYCLING
(Map p48; ☑012430622; www.grasshopper adventures.com; 23 St 144; road/mountain bike per day US$4/8) Plenty of excellent mountain and other bikes are available here. Kiddie seats can be attached to your mountain bike for US$3. Vicious represents well-respected Grasshopper Adventures in Phnom Penh.

Fitness Centres & Swimming

The fanciest hotels listed in this chapter will let you use their gyms and pools for a stiff fee, while Sofitel (p55) and Imperial Garden (p54) add tennis courts. A few of the midrange pool-equipped boutique hotels will let you swim if you buy a few bucks' worth of food or cocktails – try Teahouse (p53), Hotel Nine (p55) and the 252 (p53). But keep in mind that the pools at these places are pretty small – more for dipping and cooling off than for doing laps. Most other midrange boutiques charge US$5 for pool rights.

Himawari Hotel SWIMMING
(Map p42; ☑023-214555; 313 Sisowath Quay; admission weekday/weekend US$7/8) Has a larger pool fit for laps.

Long Beach Plaza Hotel SWIMMING
(Map p32; ☑023-998007; 3 St 289; US$1) A bargain for a lap-sized pool but far away from the centre.

Muscle Fitness GYM
(Map p52; cnr Sts 95 & 386; per session US$3.50; ☺6am-8pm) A pretty good deal considering the range of equipment, albeit with dysfunctional air-con.

The Place GYM
(Map p42; ☑023-999799; 11 St 51; walk-in US$15; ☺6am-10pm) This is absolutely state of the art, with myriad machines, a big pool and a range of cardio classes.

Go-Carting

Kambol Kart Raceway GO CARTS
(☑012232332; per 10min US$12) Kambol Kart Raceway is a professional circuit in a rural setting just outside of Phnom Penh. Prices include helmets and racing suits. It's about 2km off the road to Sihanoukville. Look for a hard-to-spot sign on the right, 8km beyond

the airport; if you hit the toll booth, you've gone too far.

Golf

If you can't survive without a swing, Phnom Penh has three 18-hole courses, all with club rental for about US$10: Royal Cambodia Phnom Penh Golf Club (☑011253703; off NH4; weekend/weekday US$70/50, shoe/club hire US$7/10), located down an access road off NH4 about 3km west of the airport; Cambodia Golf & Country Club (☑012811778; NH4; weekend/weekday US$45/38), close to the highway about 30km beyond the airport; and the new Garden City Golf Club (☑0889966852; www.gardencityclub.com; weekend/weekday US$103/83), 30km north of the city over the Prek Pnov Bridge. Closer to the centre is the nine-hole pitch-and-putt City Golf Club (☑0889966852; www.gardencityclub. com; weekend/weekday US$103/83).

Massage & Spas

There are plenty of massage parlours in Phnom Penh, but some are purveying 'naughty' massages. However, there are also scores of legitimate massage centres and some superb spas for that pampering palace experience.

Spa Bliss SPA
(Map p42; ☑023-215754; http://blissspacambodia .com; 29 St 240; massages from US$22) One of the most established spas in town, set in a lovely old French house on popular St 240.

Bodia Spa SPA
(Map p48; ☑023-226199; www.bodia-spa.com; cnr Sothearos Blvd & St 178; massages from US$26; ☺10am-11pm) About the best rub-downs in town, in a Zen-like setting (albeit with some street noise).

O Spa SPA
(☑023-992405; www.ospacambodia.com; 4B St 75; body massages from US$20; ☺11am-10pm) An oasis of calm with rejuvenating hot-stone massage, plus Balinese and Thai treatments, and virtually no street noise.

Daughters FOOT SPA
(Map p48; ☑077657678; www.daughtersof cambodia.org; 65 St 178; 1hr foot spa US$10; ☺9am-5.30pm Mon-Sat) Hand and food massages administered by participants in this NGO's vocational training program for at-risk women. Shorter (15- to 30-minute) treatments available.

South Phnom Penh

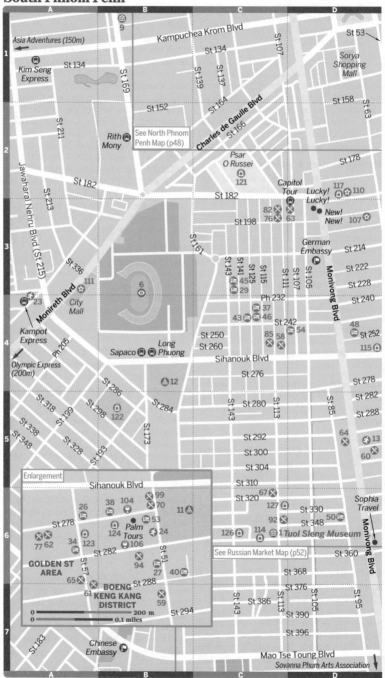

Asia Adventures (150m)

Kim Seng Express

St 134

St 211

Jawaharal Nehru Blvd (St 215)

St 213

St 182

St 336

Monireth Blvd

23

Kampot Express

Olympic Express (200m)

Ph 205

St 286

St 318

St 199

St 298

St 338

St 328

St 348

St 193

St 173

St 284

122

Kampuchea Krom Blvd

St 134

St 139

St 137

St 169

St 152

St 164

Charles de Gaulle Blvd

St 166

Rith Mony

See North Phnom Penh Map (p48)

9

St 107

St 53

Sorya Shopping Mall

St 158

St 63

Psar O Russei

121

St 178

Capitol Tour

Lucky! Lucky!

117

110

St 182

82 76 63

New! New!

107

St 198

German Embassy

St 214

St 161

St 143

St 141

St 125

St 115

St 141

St 111

St 107

St 105

Monivong Blvd

St 222

St 228

45

29

St 240

111

City Mall

6

Ph 232

37

43 46

St 242

54

48

St 252

115

St 250

St 260

85 58

Long Phuong

Sapaco

Sihanouk Blvd

St 276

St 278

St 282

St 288

12

St 280

St 143

St 113

St 85

64

13

60

St 292

St 300

St 304

St 310

St 320

67

127

Sophia Travel

St 330

92

St 348

50

126

114

1 Tuol Sleng Museum

See Russian Market Map (p52)

St 360

Monivong Blvd

Enlargement

Sihanouk Blvd

26

38

104

99

70

11

St 278

124

Palm Tours

53

24

106

34

123

St 282

77 62

GOLDEN ST AREA

St 57

94

St 51

27

40

65

61

BOENG KENG KANG DISTRICT

59

St 288

St 294

0   200 m
0   0.1 miles

St 183

St 368

St 376

St 143

St 386

St 113

St 390

St 105

St 95

Chinese Embassy

St 396

Mao Tse Toung Blvd

Sovanna Phum Arts Association

See Royal Palace &
Silver Pagoda Map (p36)

South Phnom Penh

Nail Bar   MASSAGE, SALON
(Map p48; www.mithsamlanh.org; Friends n' Stuff store, 215 St 13; massages per 30/60min US$4/7; ⊙11am-9pm) Cheap manicures, pedicures, foot massages, hand massages and nail painting, all to help Mith Samlanh train street children in a new vocation.

Seeing Hands Massage   MASSAGE
(⊙7.30am-10pm) Helps you ease those aches and pains; helps blind masseurs stay self-sufficient. Massages average US$7 per hour, making it one of the best-value massages in the capital. There are several other cooperatives around town including **Riverside** (Map p48; 12 St 13) and **St 108** (Map p48; 34 St 108; ⊙8am-9pm).

Meditation & Yoga

Free one-hour Vipassana meditation sessions take place in the central *vihara* of **Wat Langka** (Map p42; cnr St 51 & Sihanouk Blvd) at 6pm on Mondays, Thursdays and Saturdays, and on Sunday morning at 8am. Warning: if you've never done it before, an hour will seem like an eternity. It's OK to just do 20 or 30 minutes.

The following studios hold regular yoga classes – check their websites for schedules. Both offer discounts for multiple classes.

NaṭaRāj Yoga   YOGA
(Map p42; ☎ 090311341; www.yogacambodia.com; 52 St 302) Popular yoga studio with a range of classes from US$9.

Yoga Phnom Penh YOGA
(Map p42; ☑012739419; www.yogaphnompenh. com; 172 Norodom Blvd) Yoga Phnom Penh has a wide variety of yoga classes starting from US$8.

Running

Hash House Harriers RUNNING, DRINKING
(www.p2h3.com) A good opportunity to meet local expatriates is via the Hash House Harriers, usually referred to simply as 'the Hash'. A run/walk takes place every Sunday. Participants meet in front of Phnom Penh train station at 2pm. The fee of US$5 includes refreshments (mainly a lot of beer) at the end.

🍜 Courses

Cambodia Cooking Class COOKING COURSE
(Map p42; ☑012524801; www.cambodia-cooking-class.com; booking office 67 St 240, classes near Russian embassy; half/full day US$15/23) Learn the art of Khmer cuisine through Frizz Restaurant. Reserve ahead.

👉 Tours

If you want an organised city tour, most of the leading guesthouses and travel agencies can arrange one for about US$6 per person, not including entrance fees. Tour operator **Asia Adventures** (☑023-882955; www.asia-adventures.com; 578 Kampuchea Krom Blvd) can tailor a good one that takes in sights outside of Phnom Penh as well. What follows are some interesting niche tours in and around Phnom Penh.

Khmer Architecture Tours
ARCHITECTURE

(www.ka-tours.org; tours US$8-15) Those interested in the new-wave Khmer architecture from the Sangkum era (1953–70) should look no further. These two- to three-hour introductory tours take in some of the most prominent buildings in the city and take place on foot or by *cyclo*, starting at 8.30am two or three Sundays per month. The website also includes a DIY map of the most popular walking tour. For more on this landmark architecture, pick up a copy of *Cultures of Independence* (2001) or *Building Cambodia: New Khmer Architecture 1953–70* (2006).

Cambodian Living Arts
CULTURAL TOURS

(CLA; Map p42; ☑ 017998570; www.cambodianlivingarts.org; 128 Sothearos Blvd) Cambodian Living Arts supports elder Cambodian musicians to train young and mostly at-risk Cambodians in traditional music, dance and other forms. You can visit many of these classes through CLA's 'Living Arts Tours'. Among the most interesting is the Pinpeat ensemble class (Map p42; ☺ 10.45am-12.15pm Mon-Fri) in the decrepit modernist 'White Building', where students learn to play melodies that were used in the royal courts of Angkor to accompany ceremonies, dances and masked plays.

There are many more tours, both in Phnom Penh and in Siem Reap, Takeo and other provinces – see the website for details.

Cyclo Centre
CYCLING

(Map p48; ☑ 0977009762; www.cyclo.org.kh; 95 St 158; per hour/day from US$3/12) Dedicated to supporting cyclo drivers in Phnom Penh, these tours are a great way to see the sights. Themed trips such as pub crawls or cultural tours are also available.

Kingdom Brewery
BREWERY TOUR

(☑ 023-430180; 1748 NH5; tours US$6; ☺ 1-5pm Mon-Fri) It costs just US$6 to tour the facilities of Kingdom Brewery. Tours include two beers and you don't even have to book ahead – just show up. It's exactly 1km north of the Japanese Bridge on NH5.

Nature Cambodia
QUAD BIKING

(☑ 012676381; www.nature-cambodia.com) Offers quad biking in the countryside around Phnom Penh. The quads are automatic, and so are easy to handle for beginners, and tour prices are US$25 per bike (maximum two passengers) for 90 minutes, US$55 for a half day and US$110 for a full-day taking in Tonlé Bati and Phnom Tamao. Despite its proximity to the capital, this is rural Cambodia and very beautiful. Longer trips and jeep tours are also available. Follow signs to the Killing Fields of Choeung Ek and it is about 300m before the entrance. Call ahead as numbers are limited.

🛏 Sleeping

Accommodation in Phnom Penh, as in the rest of the country, is terrific value no matter your budget and there are hundreds of guesthouses and hotels to choose from.

CAMBODIAN FIGHT CLUB

The whole world knows about *muay Thai* (Thai boxing) and the sport of kickboxing, but what is not so well known is that this contact sport probably originated in Cambodia. *Pradal serey* (literally 'free fighting') is Cambodia's very own version of kickboxing and it is possible to see some fights in Phnom Penh. Popular Cambodian TV channel CTN hosts live bouts at 2pm on Friday, Saturday and Sunday out at its main studio on National Hwy 5. It is about 4km north of the Japanese Bridge. Entry is free and there is usually a rowdy local crowd surreptitiously betting on the fights. Most bouts are ended by a violent elbow move and there is a lot more ducking and diving than with other kickboxing genres.

An even older martial art is *bokator*, or *labokatao*, which some say dates back to the time of Angkor. It translates as 'pounding a lion' and was originally conceived for battlefield confrontations. Weapons include bamboo staffs and short sticks, as well as the *krama* (scarf) in certain situations. The Pras Khan Chey Bokator School (Map p48; ☑ 095455555, 0766690096; www.bokatorcambodia.com; 10 St 109 ; ☺ 8-10am & 6-8pm) in Phnom Penh offers lessons (US$5 per hour) or full brown-belt courses (US$1500). Call ahead to ensure you get an English-speaking instructor.

Centre North (Riverfront)

While the idea of roosting riverfront has obvious appeal, you'll find much better value elsewhere. Also keep in mind that hotels along the river tend to be noisy, and most budget rooms are windowless or face away from the river. A few superb options exist at the top end, but worthwhile pickings are much slimmer in the budget and midrange categories.

Osaka Ya GUESTHOUSE $
(Map p48; ☎023-6509423; www.osakayaguesthouse.com; 171 Sisowath Quay; r US$15-25; ✳️🛜) This Japanese-run high-rise raises the bar for budget riverside lodging, with none of the stink and mould that plague other hotels of this ilk. Swathe yourself in imported linens in snug rooms (the cheapest are windowless) offset by high ceilings; the entire joint is tasteful and spotless. There's a common balcony on the top floor and a Japanese restaurant on the bottom.

Camory Hostel HOSTEL $
(Map p48; ☎012664567; www.camoryhostelandrestaurant.com; 167 Sisowath Quay; dm incl breakfast US$12; ✳️🛜) Yes, the dorm beds are pricey, but when you consider that you're smack dab in the middle of the riverfront strip and that breakfast is included, they start looking like a better deal. Plus they are much smarter than your average dorm room. The common balcony over the river is a nice bonus. No private rooms.

★Foreign Correspondents' Club BOUTIQUE HOTEL $$
(FCC; Map p48; ☎023-210142; www.fcccambodia.com; 363 Sisowath Quay; standard/deluxe r incl breakfast US$84/97; ✳️🛜) This landmark location is a fine place to recapture the heady days of the war correspondents. The eight rooms are exquisitely finished in polished wood and include fine art, top-of-the-line furniture and vintage *Phnom Penh Post* covers on the wall. The deluxe rooms have pleasing balconies with prime river views.

The Quay BOUTIQUE HOTEL $$
(Map p48; ☎023-224894; www.thequayhotel.com; 277 Sisowath Quay; r/ste incl breakfast from US$60/110; ✳️@🛜) The Quay is a temple of contemporary style right on the riverfront. The river-view panoramic suites, with balconies done right, are the beds of choice, as they are far more spacious than the still-stylish but dark rooms at the rear. Ascend to the roof-top Chow bar to catch breezes off the Tonlé Sap.

Bougainvillier Hotel HOTEL $$
(Map p48; ☎023-220528; www.bougainvillierhotel.com; 277G Sisowath Quay; r off/on river incl breakfast from US$51/98; ✳️🛜) You could swing a giant Mekong catfish in the huge river-facing suites, but they are far from modern. Riverfront rooms get a balcony and you can walk up to the rooftop bar for serious views.

Amanjaya Pancam Hotel BOUTIQUE HOTEL $$$
(Map p48; ☎023-214747; www.amanjaya-pancam-hotel.com; 1 St 154; r incl breakfast US$135-185; ✳️@🛜) One of Phnom's original Asian Zen–style boutiques, it boasts a superb riverfront location and capacious rooms with dark-wood floors, elegant Khmer drapes and tropical furnishings. Luscious Le Moon bar is on the roof, trendy K West cafe at ground-level.

River 108 BOUTIQUE HOTEL $$$
(Map p48; ☎023-218785; www.river108.com; 2 St 108; ste incl breakfast US$85-105; ✳️@🛜) Hip boutique hotel near the riverfront with a chic chintz look to it. Rooms include flat-screen TVs and ample bathrooms; some have partial river-view terraces.

Centre North (Off-river)

If you want to be near the riverfront but not pay riverfront prices, this area is your ticket. Be aware, though, that the blocks running west off the river from St 104 to about St 144 are gritty and contain pockets of sleaze. A handful of delectable new boutique hotels point to eventual gentrification of this prime real estate. Meanwhile, St 172 between St 19 and St 13 has become Phnom Penh's most popular backpacker area.

★Eighty8 Backpackers HOSTEL $
(Map p48; ☎023-5002440; www.88backpackers.com; 98 St 88; dm US$5-7, d US$20-24; ✳️@🛜🏊) A hostel with a swimming pool has to be a good thing, right? Duh. The pool and the premises – a magnificent, rambling villa – set this place apart from the rest of Phnom Penh's hostels. The courtyard is anchored by a big, sturdy bar, with billiards and plenty of places to lounge within range of the pool.

Dorms come in air-con and fan varieties, plus a female dorm. The private rooms can't compare to the public spaces, but what can?

Me Mate's Place GUESTHOUSE $
(Map p48; ☎023-5002497; www.mematesplace.com; 5 St 90; dm US$7, s/d from US$15/20; ✳️@🛜🏊) This is a smart little guesthouse-bar on a quiet strip north of Wat Phnom.

North Phnom Penh

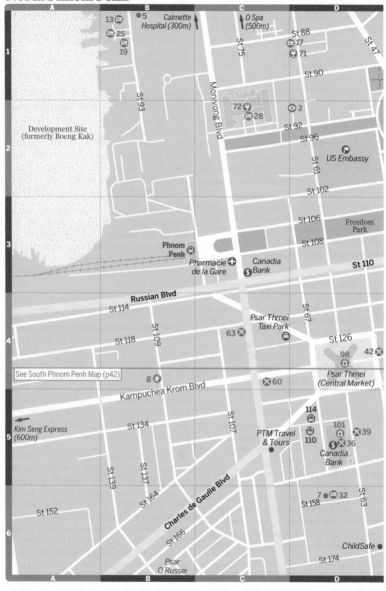

The high price tag on the six-bed dorms is redeemed by sturdy double-wide bunk beds and crisp air-con. The spartan private rooms, some windowless, are a bit of a let-down by comparison. Guests here get free reign at Eighty8 Backpackers' swimming pool.

Pra-Tna Guesthouse HOTEL **$**
(Map p48; ☏ 023-6661818; pratna_guesthouse@ live.com; 54 St 13; r with fan/air-con US$10/15; ❋ 🛜) Passable budget hotels this close to the river (it's just one block away) are rare in Phnom Penh. Well-managed Pra-Tna

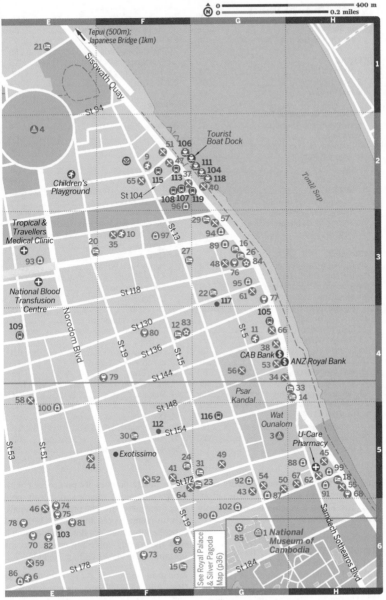

has clean rooms with small flat-screen TVs, mint-green walls, windows and a Bon Cafe branch downstairs. Bathrooms fall flat but otherwise it's terrific value.

11 Happy Backpacker   HOSTEL **$**
(Map p48; ☎0887777421; happy11gt@hotmail. com; 87-89 St 136; dm US$5, r US$8-30; ❋@☜) The sprawling rooftop bar/restaurant/chill-out area here has cosy chairs, a pool table and a flat-screen. Mellow by day, fun by

North Phnom Penh

night. The white-tiled rooms hardly compare but are clean and have no major problems. The Flicks 2 cinema is conveniently located downstairs.

Royal Guesthouse　　　　　　　HOTEL **$**
(Map p48; ☑ 023-218026; hou_leng@yahoo.com; 91 St 154; s US$6-13, d US$8-15, tr from US$15; ❈@🛜) This old-time high-rise is getting a bit tired, but it's priced right and the family in charge are super friendly and dole out travel info aplenty. The rooms are spacious but some are dark, so check a few.

★ **Blue Lime**　　　　　　BOUTIQUE HOTEL **$$**
(Map p48; ☑ 023-222260; www.bluelime.asia; 42 St 19z; r incl breakfast US$45-80; ❈@🛜🏊) The follow-up act of the team behind the Pavilion nearly outdoes its predecessor with smart, minimalist rooms and a leafy pool area done just right. The pricier rooms have private plunge pools, four-poster beds and concrete love seats. You don't lose too much with the equally appealing cheaper rooms upstairs in the main building. No kids.

Monsoon Hotel　　　　BOUTIQUE HOTEL **$$**
(Map p48; ☑ 023-989856; www.monsoonhotel. com; 53-55 Street 130; r incl breakfast US$39-45; ❈@🛜) Blink and you'll miss this little oasis on chaotic St 130. Hidden inside are attractive rooms with polished-concrete walls and floors, blonde-wood bathroom counters and pleasing murals. A super price considering the sophistication of the design and a location so close to the river.

The Billabong BOUTIQUE HOTEL $$
(Map p48; ☎023-223703; www.thebillabong hotel.com; 5 St 158; s/d/tr incl breakfast from US$34/55/80; ☀@☎☜) Near Psar Thmei but an oasis of calm by comparison, Billabong has 41 stylish rooms surrounding an open courtyard with a large swimming pool in the middle. Shoot for the ground-level pool-view rooms, which have private verandas and more space compared with rooms at the back.

Natural House Boutique Hotel HOTEL $$
(Map p48; ☎0972634160; www.naturalhouse.asia; 52-54 St 172; r incl breakfast US$20-35; ☀☎) The best-looking $20 rooms in the St 172 area are here. Plush bedding and kitchenettes in all rooms are the highlights. Breakfast is opposite at the Bistro Corner, owned by the same Japanese expat. Also opposite is newly opened **Natural Inn Backpacker Hostel** (Map p48; ☎0972634160; www.naturalhouse.asi; Off St 172; dm US$3-8; ☀☎).

Sundance Inn & Saloon GUESTHOUSE $$
(Map p48; ☎016802090; www.sundancecam bodia.com; 61 St 172; r US$25-30; ☀@☎☜) Sundance separates itself from the pack on St 172 with positively giant beds, designer bathrooms, kitchenettes and computers that hook up to flat-screens in every room. With open-mic Mondays, frequent live music, all-day US$1 cocktails and a pool out back, it can become quite the party pad.

★**Raffles Hotel Le Royal** HISTORIC HOTEL $$$
(Map p48; ☎023-981888; www.raffles.com/ phnompenh; cnr Monivong Blvd & St 92; r from

Russian Market

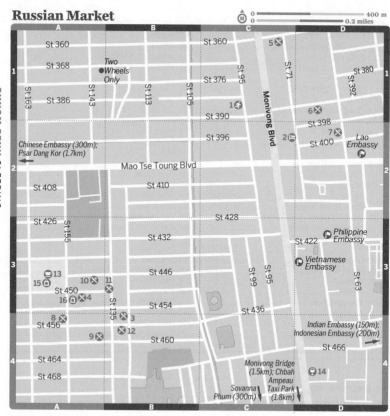

US$299; ✳@🛜🏊) From the golden age of travel, this is one of Asia's grand old palaces, belonging in the illustrious company of the Oriental in Bangkok and Raffles in Singapore. This classic colonial-era property is Phnom Penh's leading address, with a heritage to match its service and style. Indulgent diversions include two swimming pools, a gym, spa and lavish bars and restaurants.

Between 1970 and 1975 many famous journalists working in Phnom Penh stayed here.

★**La Maison D'Ambre**   BOUTIQUE HOTEL **$$$**
(Map p48; ☎023-222780; www.lamaisondambre.com; 123 St 110; ste incl breakfast US$120-210; ✳@🛜) Associated with respected clothing boutique Ambre, this place is fit for a fashion shoot. The ample themed suites feature stunning contemporary art, space-age lamps, extra-long sofas and designer kitchens. The *coup de grâce* is the psych-edelic rooftop bar. With prime views of Wat Phnom and funky furniture, it's a great place for breakfast or happy hour.

🛏 St 240 & Around

The hotels in this zone are ideally positioned on or within walking distance of the river, close to the Royal Palace and well south of the chaos and girlie bars of the north-central area. Cosy boutique hotels set around a pool are in abundance here. Walk-in backpackers can target St 258, which has a clutch of guesthouses with rooms in the US$5 to US$10 range.

Same Same Backpackers   HOSTEL **$**
(Map p42; ☎077717174; theatoch@yahoo.com; 5 St 258; dm US$4, d with fan/air-con from US$7/10; ✳@🛜) Nothing fancy, just simple rooms priced right on the well-located mini backpacker strip known as St 258. The air-con dorm room has no bunks, just 10 beds in

Russian Market

close proximity to each other and a single bathroom.

Lazy Gecko Guesthouse GUESTHOUSE $
(Map p42; ☏078786025; lazygeckocafe@gmail.com; St 258; r with fan US$6-10, with air-con US$14-18; ❇🛜) Best known as a cafe, Lazy Gecko's rooms are a mixed bag. The air-con doubles are nondescript but do have flat-screen TVs and plenty of space, while the fan rooms are mostly dark and grotty. But hey, you're paying for the location amid the backpacker haunts of St 258.

★Pavilion BOUTIQUE HOTEL $$
(Map p42; ☏023-222280; www.thepavilion.asia; 227 St 19; r incl breakfast US$50-100, apt US$110-120; ❇@🛜☒) Housed in an elegant French villa, this immensely popular and atmospheric place helped popularise the Phnom Penh poolside boutique hotel. All rooms have inviting four-poster beds, stunning furniture, personal computers and iPod docks. Recently expanded to 27 rooms, some of the newer rooms include a private plunge pool. Guests can use bamboo bikes for free. No children allowed.

Circa 51 BOUTIQUE HOTEL $$
(Map p42; ☏012585714; www.circa51.com; 155 St 222; s/d incl breakfast from US$46/56; ❇🛜☒)

In a classic '60s villa, Circa 51 has just 10 rooms and they are lovely. The ground level is layered in original chequerboard tiles, and the spacious rooms have ambient lighting, cool furniture, minimalist art, flat-screen TVs and silk robes. A banyan tree shades the luscious pool area within arm's length of the bar.

The 252 BOUTIQUE HOTEL $$
(Map p42; ☏023-998252; www.the-252.com; 19 St 152; d incl breakfast US$50-60, tr US$65; ⊖❇@🛜☒) This terrific-value place has attractive lime-striped rooms that are a tad small for hangin', but prime lounging spots lurk around the pool. The charismatic French owner makes guests feel welcome.

Teahouse BOUTIQUE HOTEL $$
(Map p42; ☏023-212789; www.theteahouse.asia; 32 St 242; r incl breakfast US$38-50; ❇@🛜☒) This new property is a smaller, cheaper version of sister hotel Plantation. While the rooms and pool are smaller than Plantation's, they are similarly comfortable and chic. The open-air reception area under a Chinese-style pavilion has comfy seating and internet-enabled PCs. Exceptional value.

Manor House GUESTHOUSE $$
(Map p42; ☏023-992566; www.manorhousecambodia.com; 21 St 262; s/d incl breakfast from US$42/49; ❇@🛜☒) Set in a small villa, this gay-friendly guesthouse offers artfully decorated rooms and a compact hangout area around a small swimming pool. The nifty 'basic' rooms are great value, or upgrade to the much bigger standard rooms, with huge flat-screen TVs and love seats. Kids aren't allowed.

Kabiki BOUTIQUE HOTEL $$
(Map p42; ☏023-222290; www.thekabiki.com; 22 St 264; r incl breakfast US$50-80; ❇@🛜☒) The most family-friendly place in town offers an extensive garden and an inviting swimming pool with a kiddie pool. Family rooms include bunks and most rooms have a private garden terrace.

The Plantation BOUTIQUE HOTEL $$$
(Map p42; ☏023-215151; www.theplantation.asia; 28 St 184; r incl breakfast US$85-100; ❇@🛜☒) This is the unmatched Pavilion group's largest and most ambitious property. It's more impersonal than its kin, but it still has the goods: high ceilings, top-grade furniture and fixtures, open-plan bathrooms and balconies

(pay more to have one overlooking the glorious pool area).

Imperial Garden   SERVICED APARTMENTS $$$
(Map p42; ☎023-219991; www.imperialgarden
-hotel.com; 315 Sisowath Quay; d/apt incl breakfast
from US$120/250; ❄@🛜☀) Rooms here are
a bit pricey but big discounts are usually
available if you ask. Rooms have outstanding river views, while apartments are off-
river, closer to the road.

🛏 Boeng Keng Kang & Tonlé Bassac

Popular among NGO workers and other expats, the Boeng Keng Kang (BKK) and Tonlé
Bassac districts south of Independence Monument comprise the flashpacker zone, with
an expanding selection of fine midrange hotels to go with a wealth of trendy bars and
restaurants, plus a few good hostels. Many
of the hotels are centred on St 278, dubbed
'Golden St' because of the preponderance of
hotels that feature 'Golden' in their name.
Golden St is less than a 10-minute *remork*
ride from the riverfront.

★**Mad Monkey**   HOSTEL $
(Map p42; ☎023-987091; www.phnompenh
hostels.com; 26 St 302; dm US$7, r without/with
bathroom US$15/20; ❄@🛜) This colourful
and arty hostel is justifiably popular. The
spacious dorms have air-con and sleep six to
twenty; the smaller ones have double-wide
bunk beds that can sleep two (US$9 per couple). The private rooms are snazzy for the
price but lack TVs and, usually, windows.
They vary, so check out a few.

The rooftop bar serves free beer for an
hour on Monday and Saturday.

Top Banana Guesthouse   HOSTEL $
(Map p42; ☎012885572; www.topbanana.biz; 9 St
278; dm US$6, r US$7-20; ❄@🛜) 'Great bar,
so-so hostel' has long been the mantra here.
Now a facelift has seen the rooms improved
and three dorm rooms added, including a
four-bed female dorm. They are clean and
have wide beds. The brilliant location high
above Golden St and comfy open-air chill-
out area remain the top selling point, however. Book way ahead.

The White Rabbit   HOSTEL $
(Map p42; www.whiterabbitguesthouse.com; 40A
St 294; dm with fan/air-con US$4/5, d US$12-
15; ❄🛜) This convivial hostel is a hidden
gem, with an attractive ground-level bar

and hang-out area where you can play Play-
station on a big screen. The two private
rooms are pretty good value, but most opt
for the comfortable dorms with clean bath-
rooms and wide bunk beds. Good food too.

Blue Dog Guesthouse   HOSTEL $
(Map p42; ☎012658075; bluedogguesthouse@
gmail.com; 13 St 51; dm US$5-6, s/d US$6/10;
@🛜) Location and price are right, plus
there's a cosy common area and a popular
bar downstairs, so you don't have to spend
too much time in the clean but basic rooms.

New Golden Bridge Guesthouse   HOTEL $
(Map p42; ☎023-721396; www.goldenbridgehtl.
com; 7 St 278; s/d/tr US$15/18/20; ❄🛜) It's
close, but this is our favourite among the
'Golden' hotels on St 278. Rooms are huge if a
bit dark, with clean linen, low bamboo beds,
desks, fine bathrooms and no funky smells
like in some of its neighbours. Like most of
the Golden hotels, it offers free laundry.

★**Villa Langka**   BOUTIQUE HOTEL $$
(Map p42; ☎023-726771; www.villalangka.com;
14 St 282; r incl breakfast US$48-120; ❄@🛜☀)
One of the first players in the poolside-
boutique game, it's now firmly cemented
as a Phnom Penh favourite. Rooms ooze
post-modern panache. People complain that
it has become too big and impersonal – 48
rooms at last count – but the flip side is
more variety. The leafy pool area is perfect.

★**Rambutan**   BOUTIQUE HOTEL $$
(Map p52; ☎017992240; www.rambutanresort.
com; 29 St 71; r incl breakfast US$55-120; ❄🛜☀)
Sixties-groovy, gay friendly and extremely
well-run, this striking villa once belonged to
the American Embassy. The soaring original
structure and a newer wing shade a boot-
shaped swimming pool – you could practi-
cally swan-dive into it from the balconies
of the pricier rooms. Concrete floors set an
industrial tone in the 19 smart rooms, which
are outfitted with top-quality everything.

Khmer Surin Boutique Guesthouse   BOUTIQUE HOTEL $$
(Map p42; ☎012731909; www.khmersurin.com.kh;
11A St 57; r incl breakfast US$50-60; ❄🛜) This
guesthouse is attached to the long-running
restaurant of the same name in a sumptuous
villa near Golden St (St 278). The 19 rooms
come with flat-screen TVs, leafy and lavish
balconies, and loads of antique furniture,
not to mention bathrooms that would put
most four-star properties to shame. With all

the museum-quality furniture lying around, rooms might seem busy to some.

The Willow
BOUTIQUE HOTEL **$$**

(Map p42; ☎023-996256; www.thewillowpp.com; 1 St 21; r incl breakfast US$53-80; ❄️📶) Another fashionable boutique hotel, the Willow has twelve spacious rooms in a splendid 1960s villa. Four-poster beds, modern art, wood furniture, furnished balconies (in some rooms), rain showers and flat screens set an enticing mood. Also known for its sandwiches and its Wednesday night pub quizzes.

Anise
HOTEL **$$**

(Map p42; ☎023-222522; www.anisehotel.com.kh; 2C St 278; s incl breakfast US$42-72, d US$47-77; ❄️@📶) If the leafy boutique hotel around pool isn't the thing for you, Anise is the best midrange high-rise in town. Indigenous textiles and handsome wood trim add character to rooms that already boast extras like DVD players. Pricier rooms are gargantuan. Free laundry.

One Up Banana
HOTEL **$$**

(Map p42; ☎023-211344; www.1uphotelcambodia.com; 132 St 51; r US$32-60; ❄️@📶) The backpacker-oriented Banana franchise ventures into flashpacker territory here. The slick highrise features arty, ambient-lit rooms with nice desks and even kitchenettes. All rooms have somewhat hard king beds – no twins.

Hotel Nine
BOUTIQUE HOTEL **$$**

(Map p42; ☎023-215964; www.hotel-nine.com; 48 St 9; r/ste incl breakfast US$45/65; ❄️@📶🏊) A study in white-washed minimalism, with an agreeable little pool, cosy beds and 16 attractive rooms. A safe and central choice in the boutique-by-the-pool genre. Knock US$10 off room prices June to September.

Patio
HOTEL **$$$**

(Map p42; ☎023-997900; www.patio-hotel.com; 134 St 51; s/d incl breakfast from US$90/110; ❄️@📶🏊) The main selling point here is the infinity pool, 10 storeys up on the rooftop. It's a must for a sundowner (and/or a moonriser if you time it right). It's a bit hot and unprotected during the day, however. Rooms have top-quality furnishings and the pricier ones have small balconies.

Governor's House
BOUTIQUE HOTEL **$$$**

(Map p42; ☎023-987025; www.governorshouse.net; 3 Mao Tse Tung Blvd; s/d incl breakfast from US$75/125; ❄️📶🏊) There's a high 'wow' factor at Governor's House, predictable when you furnish sumptuous rooms and common

areas with centuries-old European furniture (property of the antique-dealing Belgian owner). The building itself, a restored colonial number, also impresses and the suites are fit for Belgian royalty. The slightly out-of-the-way location on a busy thoroughfare isn't perfect but you can't have everything.

Sofitel Phnom Penh Phokeethra
LUXURY HOTEL **$$$**

(Map p42; ☎023-999200; www.sofitel.com; 26 Sothearos Blvd; r from US$210; ❄️@📶🏊) Phnom Penh's latest five-star property boasts spacious rooms and a gazillion facilities, including numerous tennis courts and several restaurants. Absolutely first class, but feels somewhat large and impersonal and the location isn't perfect.

🛏 Psar O Russei & Tuol Sleng

With the downfall of the Boeng Kak area, the zone south of Psar O Russei has emerged as a popular alternative for budget travellers. It's a mix of high-rise hotels and backpacker-oriented guesthouses. The hotels are particularly appealing – you won't come close to finding better US$15 air-con rooms elsewhere in the centre.

★ Narin Guesthouse
GUESTHOUSE **$**

(Map p42; ☎099881133; www.naringuesthouse.com; 50 St 125; r with fan/air-con US$12/17; ❄️@📶) One of the stalwarts of the Phnom Penh guesthouse scene (we first stayed here back in 1995). Rooms are smart, bathrooms smarter still and the price is nice. There is a super-relaxed open-air restaurant-terrace for taking some time out.

Smiley's Hotel
HOTEL **$**

(Map p42; ☎012365959; smileyhotel.pp@gmail.com; 37 St 125; s with fan US$6, d US$15-20; ❄️@📶) A migrant from Siem Reap, Smiley's is a huge seven-storey hotel with a choice of 40 spacious rooms that border on chic. The US$20 rooms have big flat-screen TVs. Includes a lift.

Town View Hotel
HOTEL **$**

(Map p42; ☎023-992949; www.townviewhotel.com; 30 St 111; d US$15; ❄️@📶) Yet another fantastic-value spot in the Psar O Russei area. All rooms include a fully-stocked minibar, sparkling bathrooms, soft beds and a table, plus there's a lift.

Fairyland Guesthouse
HOTEL **$**

(Map p42; ☎023-214510; 99 St 141; r US$14-16; ❄️@📶) This towering maroon guesthouse has large, bright rooms, decent linen, smart bathrooms and a lift. You can squeeze three into the more expensive rooms, which include queen and single beds – albeit hard beds. Still, exceptional value.

Sunday Guesthouse
GUESTHOUSE $

(Map p42; ☐ 023-211623; gech_sundayguesthouse@hotmail.com; 97 St 141; d/tr from US$7/11; ❄@🛜) A *real* guesthouse, this is a three-storey walk-up affair run by an amiable family who can cook meals and help with travel arrangements.

Tat Guesthouse
GUESTHOUSE $

(Map p42; ☐ 012921211; tatcambodia@yahoo.com; 52 St 125; s without bathroom US$4, d with bathroom US$7-12; ❄@🛜) A super-friendly spot with breezy rooftop hangout that's perfect for chilling. The rooms aren't going to wow you but they are functional. US$12 gets you air-con – not bad.

The Terrace on 95
BOUTIQUE HOTEL $$

(Map p42; ☐023-996143; www.theterraceon95.com; 43 St 95; r US$50; ❄) This hotel is a revelation in the sleepy Tuol Sleng district. The six attractively furnished rooms share an impeccably restored traditional house with the vegan-friendly K'nyay restaurant upstairs.

Boeng Kak Area

This was backpacker central – a lakeside version of Bangkok's Khao San Rd – until Boeng Kak (ie the lake) was completely filled in with sand in 2011 as part of a massive development project. A couple of holdouts remain, offering up basic rooms, cheap cocktails, free laundry and happy snacks. A semblance of the crusty old backpacker spirit survives, but it's very quiet and the location isn't great – a good place to hide.

Grand View Guesthouse
GUESTHOUSE $

(Map p48; ☐023-430766; www.grandview.netfirms.com; 4 St 93; r US$5-8; ❄@🛜) Tall, skinny structure with basic rooms and unrivalled views of the sandlot formerly known as Boeng Kak.

Number 10 Lakeside Guesthouse
GUESTHOUSE $

(Map p48; ☐012970989; phil.chea@yahoo.com; 10 St 93; s/d with fan US$4/6, with air-con US$8/12; ❄@🛜) Long-time stalwart with some bargain rooms with shared bathroom, or bigger rooms with hot water and cable TV.

11 Happy Guesthouse
BACKPACKER $

(Map p48; ☐ 0887777421; 11 St 93; s US$3, d US$5-10; ❄@🛜) Also known as Simon's, this old-timer was closed for renovations at the time of research but should be back.

Eating

For foodies, Phnom Penh is a real delight, boasting a superb selection of restaurants that showcase the best in Khmer cooking, as well as the greatest hits from world cuisine such as Chinese, Vietnamese, Thai, Indian, French, Italian, Spanish, Mexican and more. Visitors to Phnom Penh are quite literally spoilt for choice these days.

Centre North (Riverfront)

Blue Pumpkin
CAFE $

(Map p48; 245 Sisowath Quay; mains US$3-7; ⊗6am-11pm; ❄🛜) The beloved Siem Reap cafe with the alluring white upholstery has opened its doors in Phnom Penh and proved a smashing success. Healthy breakfasts, pasta, sandwiches and the capital's best ice cream lead the menu, and you can watch the nightly aerobics spectacle on the riverfront as you eat. Other branches in **BKK** (Map p42; 12A St 57; ⊗6am-10pm; ❄🛜) and at Kids City (p39) and Monument Books (p73).

Cantina
MEXICAN $

(Map p48; 347 Sisowath Quay; mains US$4-6; ⊗2.30-11pm, closed Sat; 🛜) This is the spot for tostadas, fajitas and other Mexican favourites, all freshly prepared. It's also a journo hangout and a lively bar with expertly made margaritas and tequilas.

Beirut
LEBANESE $

(Map p48; ☐ 023-720011; 117 Sisowath Quay; dishes US$3-7; ⊗11am-10.30pm; ❄🛜♪) Lilliputian eatery with super deals on wraps, kebabs and saucy appetisers like hummus with pita bread, plus shisha pipes (hookahs) for US$6 to US$8. Keep in mind that river views are obstructed up here.

Anjali/Karma Cafe
CAFE $

(Map p48; 273 Sisowath Quay; mains US$3-6; ⊗7am-late) Twin-sister restaurants practically under one roof, with prices that are more than reasonable for this part of town. Anjali has some Indian offerings; otherwise, they share an identical menu – pub grub and some Asian highlights.

¡Viva! MEXICAN $

(Map p48; 111 Sisowath Quay; dishes US$4-6; ☻10am-11pm; ❋🐾) It doesn't look like much, but this Siem Reap import has raised the bar for Mexican food in Phnom Penh. A bucket of margaritas costs US$5. It's on the same strip as Indian, Lebanese and noodle restaurants if you'd rather window shop.

Pop Café ITALIAN $$

(Map p48; ☎012562892; 371 Sisowath Quay; pasta dishes US$6-9; ☻11am-2pm & 6-10pm; ❋) Owner Giorgio welcomes diners as if you are coming to his own home for dinner, making this a popular spot for authentic Italian cooking. Thin-crust pizza, homemade pasta and tasty gnocchi – it could be Roma.

GOOD-CAUSE DINING

There are several restaurants around town that are run by aid organisations to help fund their social programs in Cambodia. These are worth seeking out, as the proceeds of a hearty meal go towards helping Cambodia's recovery and allow restaurant staff to gain valuable work experience.

Centre North

Friends (Map p48; ☎012802072; www.friends-international.org; 215 St 13; tapas US$4-7, mains from US$6; ☻11am-9pm; ❋🐾) One of Phnom Penh's best-loved restaurants, this place is a must, with tasty tapas bites, heavenly smoothies and creative cocktails. It offers former street children a head start in the hospitality industry.

Sugar 'n Spice Cafe (Map p48; www.daughtersofcambodia.org; 65 St 178; sandwiches US$3.50-7; ☻9am-6pm Mon-Sat; ❋🐾) This fantastic cafe on the top floor of the Daughters visitors centre features soups, smoothies, original coffee drinks, cupcakes and fusion-y mains served by former sex workers being trained by Daughters to reintegrate into society.

Veiyo Tonlé (Map p48; 237 Sisowath Quay; mains US$3.50-6.50; ☻7am-11pm; 🐾) A little restaurant on the riverfront, the menu here features mainly Khmer and Italian cuisine, including yummy pizza. Some proceeds go towards helping a local orphanage.

Centre South

Café Yejj (Map p52; www.cafeyejj.com; 170 St 450; mains US$3.50-6; ☻8am-9pm; ❋🐾) An air-con escape from Russian Market (walk upstairs), this bistro-style cafe uses many organic ingredients to prepare pasta, salads, wraps and more ambitious dishes like Moroccan lamb stew and chilli con carne. Promotes fair trade and responsible employment.

Hagar (Map p42; 44 St 310; lunch/dinner buffet US$6.50/11; ☻7am-2pm & 6-9pm Thu-Sat, 7am-2pm Sun-Wed) Proceeds from the all-you-can-eat buffets go towards assisting destitute or abused women. The spread is usually Asian fusion or barbecue, except for Wednesday lunch and Thursday dinner, when Hagar lays out its legendary Italian buffet.

Jars of Clay (Map p52; 39B St 155; cakes US$1.50, mains US$3-5.25; ☻7.30am-9pm Mon-Sat; ❋🐾) Much more than just a bakery, with rich Khmer mains like their patented *lok lak*, plus thirst-quenching drinks and welcome air-conditioning on a hot day. Ten per cent of profits go to those in need, including women rescued from trafficking.

Le Lotus Blanc (Map p42; 152 St 51; mains US$4-8.50; ☻7am-10pm Mon-Sat; ❋🐾) This upmarket diner acts as a training centre for youths who previously scoured the city dump. Run by French NGO Pour un Sourire d'Enfant (For the Smile of a Child), it serves classy French and Khmer cuisine.

Craft Peace Cafe (Map p52; 14 St 392; ❋🐾) This Jesuit-run cafe produces smoothies, fresh juices, fair-trade coffee, salads and delicious pocket sandwiches, plus textiles crafted by their disabled staff. Cosy, attractive and well air-conditioned – a good place for some laptop time.

Ebony Tree (Map p42; St 29, cnr St 294; mains US$3.50-7.50; ☻11am-11pm; 🐾) A stylish little cafe serving health shakes, vegetarian treats and Khmer food. Twenty per cent of the profits go to the Apsara Arts Association and an HIV orphanage/hospital.

La Croisette INTERNATIONAL $$
(Map p48; ☑023-220554; 241 Sisowath Quay; mains US$5-18; ⊘7am-1am; ✳🛜) The stylish La Croisette is a popular riverfront spot with homemade pasta and gnocchi plus hearty steaks, lamb chops and even some Cambodian offerings.

Limoncello ITALIAN $$
(Map p48; 81 Sisowath Quay; pizza US$5.50-8; ⊘11.30am-2pm & 5.30-10pm; ✳🛜) They don't get everything perfect but their pizza is simply outstanding – arguably the best in town, and in a plum riverfront setting to boot. Great desserts too.

Fish SEAFOOD $$
(Map p48; ☑023-222685; cnr Sts 108 & Sisowath Quay; mains US$6-17; ⊘7am-11pm; ✳🛜) No prizes for guessing the speciality of the house. Sophisticated tapas and mains, including a superb bouillabaisse, dot the menu. The Pacific dory fish and chips are among the best in town. Stylish and fun.

Khmer Borane CAMBODIAN $$
(Map p48; 95 Sisowath Quay; mains US$5-7; ⊘11am-11pm) A great choice for traditional Khmer recipes; choose from *trey kor* (steamed fish with sugar palm) or *lok lak* (fried diced beef with a salt, pepper and lemon dip).

Happy Herb Pizza PIZZA $$
(Map p48; ☑012921915; 345 Sisowath Quay; medium pizza US$6-8.50; ⊘8am-11pm; 🛜) No, happy doesn't mean it comes with free toppings; it means pizza à la ganja. The non-marijuana pizzas are also pretty good, but don't involve the free buzz. Good place to sip a cheap beer as well. Delivery available.

Bopha Phnom Penh Restaurant CAMBODIAN $$
(Map p48; Sisowath Quay; mains US$5-10; ⊘6am-11pm; 🛜) Also known as Titanic, it's right on the river and designed to impress, with Angkorian-style carvings and elegant wicker furniture. The menu is thick with the exotic, especially water buffalo, and there's a Western menu for the less adventurous.

★**Tepui** LATIN AMERICAN $$$
(☑023-991514; 45 Sisowath Quay, cnr St 84; mains US$12-20; ⊘5-10.30pm Mon-Sat) Housed in the Chinese House, one of the city's true colonial-era masterpieces, Tepui is worth a visit for the ambience alone. The Venezuelan chef fabricates South American-inspired concoctions like red snapper ceviche, Brazilian beef tenderloin and calamari black-ink paella. Creative specials and cocktails too.

Metro FUSION $$$
(Map p48; ☑023-222275; 271 Sisowath Quay; plates US$4-8, large plates US$8-24; ⊘9.30am-1am; ✳🛜) Metro is the trendiest spot on the riverfront strip thanks to a striking design and an adventurous menu. Small plates are for sampling and include beef with red ants and tequila black-pepper prawns, while large plates include steaks and honey-soy-roasted chicken. Also does a mean eggs Benedict.

Sister restaurant **Rahu** (Map p48; 159 Sisowath Quay; mains US$4-18; ⊘5pm-2am; ✳🛜) up the way has the same menu but adds sushi.

✘ Centre North (Off-river)

★**Sam Doo Restaurant** CHINESE $
(Map p48; 56-58 Kampuchea Krom Blvd; mains US$2.80-5; ⊘7am-2am; ✳) Many Chinese Khmers swear this upstairs eatery near Central Market has the best food in town. Choose from signature Sam Doo fried rice, *trey chamhoy* (steamed fish with soy sauce and ginger), fresh seafood, hot pots and dim sum.

Warung Bali INDONESIAN $
(Map p48; 25 St 178; dishes US$1.50-3; ⊘8.30am-9pm) Here you'll encounter spicy Indonesian favourites like fish in sweet soy bean sauce and beef rendang (beef cooked in coconut milk and spices). It's busy and fragrant.

Special Pho VIETNAMESE $
(Map p48; 11 St 178; mains from US$2.50-4.50; ⊘8am-9pm) Great location near the riverfront for good *pho,* the noodle soup that keeps Vietnam moving forward, plus dirt-cheap fried rice and fried noodles.

Laughing Fatman CAMBODIAN $
(Map p48; St 172; mains US$2.50-6.50; ⊘7am-midnight) A welcoming backpacker cafe with cheap food and big breakfasts, formerly called Oh My Buddha – 'New name, same body', the corpulent owner joked.

Kebab Felafel KEBAB $
(Map p48; 156 St 51; wraps US$2.50-3; ⊘9pm-6am; ☑) One of several establishments that exist solely to provide late-night edibles to St 51 bar crawlers, this is the pick of the bunch, best known for its veggie felafel wraps.

Restaurant Soksan CAMBODIAN $
(Map p48; 30 St 136; mains 4000-10,000r; ⊘5.30am-9pm) This local curbside eatery, a

stumble away from Psar Thmei, is popular for *lok lak,* spicy fried chicken and noodle soups.

Bonbon   ICE CREAM $
(Map p48; 38 St 63; scoop US$1.25; ⊙noon-10pm; ✳🖫) Bonbon indeed. The French-crafted ice-cream creations (combine them with crepes or waffles) are a pleasure, especially after sweating it out in nearby Psar Thmei.

Sorya Food Court   FAST FOOD $
(Map p48; St 63; ⊙9am-9pm) The top-floor food court is a more sanitised way to experience a variety of local fare. Also up here is McDonald's imitator **BB World** (Map p48; burgers from US$1.75; ✳🖫).

Thai Huot   SUPERMARKET $
(Map p48; 103 Monivong Blvd; ⊙7.30am-8.30pm) This is the place for French travellers who are missing home, as it stocks many French products, including Bonne Maman jam and Hénaff pâté. Additional location in **BKK** (Map p42; cnr St 63 & St 352; ⊙7.30am-8.30pm).

★The Chat n' Chew   CAMBODIAN $$
(Map p48; 54 St 172; mains US$3-10; ⊙7.30am-11pm; 🖫) This is kind of like an upmarket backpacker cafe, popular with expats and serving a range of Cambodian and international dishes. With enjoyable music, a wine list and some care given to presentation, it's a step above most dining options on the busy St 172 strip.

★Romdeng   CAMBODIAN $$
(Map p48; ☏092219565; 74 St 174; mains US$5-8; ⊙11am-9pm; 🖫) Set in a gorgeous colonial villa with a small pool, Romdeng specialises in Cambodian country fare, including a famous fish *amok,* two-toned pomelo salad and tiger-prawn curry. Sample deep-fried tarantulas or stir-fried tree ants with beef and holy basil if you dare – this is *the* place to do it.

Part of the Friends' extended family, it is staffed by fomer street youths and their teachers.

Sher-e-Punjab   INDIAN $$
(Map p48; ☏023-216360; 16 St 130; mains US$3-7; ⊙11am-11pm; 🖉) The top spot for a curry fix according to many members of Phnom Penh's Indian community; the tandoori dishes are particularly good. Even the prawn dishes cost under US$6.

Opera Cafe   ITALIAN $$
(Map p48; ☏016969275; 188 St 13; mains US$3.50-8; ⊙10am-midnight; 🖫) More than a restaurant, this diminutive Italian eatery hosts movie and opera screenings, dance classes and even speed dating sessions. The real reason to come is for the food – mostly Italian, along with burgers and some Khmer selections. The perfectly al dente pasta is an opus in its own right.

Le Wok   FUSION $$
(Map p48; ☏092821857; 33 St 178; mains US$7.50-12; ⊙8am-11pm; 🖫) The name says it all – French flair with an Asian flavour. Choose from a tempting menu of regular meals, or an assortment of Khmer tapas, or daring specials like snail cassoulet.

Lone Star   TEX-MEX $$
(Map p48; 30 St 23; US$4.50-7; ⊙7am-11pm; 🖫) Missing America? You won't after a morning in here watching American football via satellite and digging into the calorific mains like meat loaf and Baha fish tacos. The smoked pork ribs and the wings each have a claim to being the best in town.

Le Bistrot de Paris   FRENCH $$
(Map p48; 52 St 51; mains US$3.50-7; ⊙8am-11pm) With a few tables tossed haphazardly on the pavement of bar-packed St 51, Le Bistrot doesn't look like much, but don't be fooled. The excellent food is French bistro fare all the way, served with a choice of four excellent sauces.

La Patate   BELGIAN $$
(Map p48; 14 St 5; mains US$4-14; ⊙7am-2am; 🖫) Come here for hearty Belgian fare and gourmet coffee ground by moustachioed chef/host Didier. Meat dishes arrive swimming in one of several rich sauces. If you're really hungry, try the foot-long 'bazooka burger' on a king-sized bed of Phnom Penh's best fries.

Lemongrass   THAI $$
(Map p48; ☏012996707; 14 St 130; mains US$4.50-9; ⊙9am-11pm; ✳🖫) A higher-class Thai restaurant with a selection of Khmer classics. Prices are pretty reasonable given the look of the place. Splurge for the *choo chee goong* (ocean tiger prawns in red curry).

Buffalo Sister   DELI $$
(Map p48; ☏017879403; 128 St 19; sandwiches from US$4.25; ⊙11am-7.30pm; 🖫) The extensive sandwich list is written on a chalkboard above the counter at this self-described carvery. Dig into a roast pork with apple sauce sandwich or a bowl of creamy mashed potatoes with gravy, or go healthy with a roast veggie or felafel wrap.

Phnom Penh

Cambodia's capital casts its spell over all who enter. It might be the gleaming spires of the Royal Palace, or the graceful French architecture, a waft of lemongrass from a street stall, or the infectious buzz of the cafe-lined riverfront. Somehow, some way, Phnom Penh will grab you. It always does.

1. Royal Palace (p31)
Buddhist monks walk the grounds of the king's official residence.

2. Phnom Penh streets (p30)
A family rides the capital's busy streets.

3. Food market (p62)
Phnom Penh is packed with busy markets selling fresh food.

4. Throne Hall (p34)
Used for coronations and important ceremonies, it features classic Khmer roofs and ornate gilding.

Genova   ITALIAN $$
(Map p48; 19 St 154; mains US$2.50-7; ☺10.30am-10.30pm) An authentic Italian streetside *trattoria* in the heart of Phnom Penh? You betcha. Friendly proprietor Roberto puts plenty of TLC into his pint-sized eatery, and the delicious food is fine value. Linguini in the 'best pesto in Cambodia' is the house speciality.

GOING LOCAL

Khmer Barbecues & Soup Restaurants

After dark, Khmer eateries scattered across town illuminate their Cambodia Beer signs, hailing locals in for fine fare and generous jugs of draught beer. Don't be shy, and heed the call – the food is great and the atmosphere lively.

The speciality at most of these places is grilled strips of meat or seafood, but they also serve fried noodles and rice, curries and other pan-fried faves along with some veggie options.

Many of these places also offer *phnom pleung* (hill of fire), which amounts to cook-your-own meat over a personal barbecue. Another speciality is *soup chhnang dei* (cook-your-own soup in a clay pot), which are great fun if you go in a group. Other diners will often help with protocol, as it is important to cook things in the right order so as not to overcook half the ingredients and eat the rest raw.

Khmer barbecues are literally all over town, so it won't be hard to find one. Koh Pich (Diamond Island), beyond (east of) hulking Naga World casino, has a cluster of well-reputed barbecues. Other recommended local eateries:

City Corner (Map p52; City Villa, cnr St 71 & 360; mains US$1.50-2.50; ☺10.30am-1.30pm & 4pm-midnight) Here you can cook your own meat *phnom pleung* and wash it down with US$5 towers of draught beer.

Red Cow (Map p42; 126 Norodom Blvd; mains US$2.50-7; ☺4-11pm) Grills up everything imaginable – eel, eggplant, frog, pig intestine, quail – along with curries and other tradi-tional Khmer dishes.

Sovanna (Map p42; 2C St 21; mains US$2-3; ☺6-11am & 3-11pm) Always jumping with locals and even a smattering of expats who have made this their barbecue of choice. It's as good a place as any to sample the national breakfast, *bei sach chrouk* (pork and rice).

Sonivid (Map p42; 39 St 242; meals US$5-10; ☺3pm-midnight) Steamed or fried crab, squid, fish and shellfish are the specialities at this wildly popular corner eatery. It's not a barbecue, it just looks like one.

Master Suki (Map p48; 7th fl, Sorya Shopping Centre; soup from US$5; ☺9am-10pm) It may be a Japanese concept, but it has a very Khmer touch and is a great way to try soup *chhnang dei*, with photos to help choose the ingredients. Great views as well. Additional outlets all over the city.

Street Fare & Markets

Street fare is not quite as familiar or user-friendly as in, say, Bangkok. But if you're a little adventurous and want to save boatloads of money, look no further. Breakfast is when the street-side eateries really get hopping, as most Cambodian men eat out for breakfast. Look for bums on seats and you can't go wrong.

Phnom Penh's many markets all have large central eating areas where stalls serve up local faves like noodle soup and fried noodles. Most dishes cost a reasonable 4000r to 6000r. The best market for eating is Russian Market (p70) with an interior food zone that's easy to find and with a nice variety of Cambodian specialities. Psar Thmei (p70) and Psar O Russei (p70) are other great choices. Psar Kandal (Map p48; Btwn Sts 144 & 154), just off the riverfont between Sts 144 & 154, gets going a little later and is an early-evening option.

If markets are too hot or claustrophobic for your taste, look out for mobile street sellers carrying their wares on their shoulders or wheeling around small carts. Another popular all-day option is a row of curry noodle stalls (Map p42) opposite Wat Botum Park.

Dim Sum Emporers
CHINESE $$

(Map p48; 48 St 130; dim sum US$2-2.50; ☻7am-9pm; ✳☎) Wildly popular for both its dim sum and its blasting air-con, which comes as welcome relief after a shopping session at nearby Psar Thmei.

★Van's Restaurant
FRENCH $$$

(Map p48; ☎023-722067; 5 St 13; mains US$16-43; ☻11.30am-2.30pm & 5-10.30pm; ✳) In one of the city's grandest buildings, the former Banque Indochine, you can still see the old vault doors en route to the refined dining room upstairs. Dishes are presented with decorative flourishes and menu highlights include langoustine ravioli, tender veal and boneless quail. Business lunches available for US$15, including a glass of wine.

Armand's
FRENCH $$$

(Map p48; ☎015548966; 33 St 108; meals US$12-25; ☻from 6pm, closed Mon; ✳) The best steaks in town are served flambé style by the eponymous owner of this French bistro. The steaks are nonpareil, and every item on the chalkboard menu shines. Space is tight so book ahead.

✗ St 240 Area

The Vegetarian
CAMBODIAN $

(Map p42; 158 St 19; mains US$1.75-2.50; ☻10.30am-8.30pm Mon-Sat; ☑) This is one of the best-value spots in Phnom Penh. All dishes are US$2.50 or under and it doesn't skimp on portions either. Noodles and fried rice are the specialities. The leafy setting in a quiet nook off central Sihanouk Blvd is yet another plus.

Mercy House
Coffee Restaurant
VEGETARIAN $

(Map p42; 157 St 51; mains 7500-15,000r; ☻7am-6pm; ☑) This outdoor vegetarian eatery serves Japanese dishes with a Cambodian twist. Go for the teppanyaki hot plates – sizzling fake meat topped with an egg and served over rice – or the sweet and sour 'pork ribs'. The 'snow shakes' and frothy 'sand ice shakes' are as delicious as they are quirkily named.

★The Shop
CAFE $$

(Map p42; ☎023-986964; 39 St 240; mains US$3.50-6; ☻7am-7pm, to 3pm Sun; ☎☑) If you are craving the deli back home, make for this haven, with a changing selection of sandwiches and salads with healthy and creative ingredients like wild lentils, wild 'shrooms

and lamb. The pastries, cakes and chocolates are delectable and worth the indulgence.

ARTillery
CAFE $$

(Map p42; St 240½; mains US$4-6; ☻7.30am-9pm Tue-Sun, to 5pm Mon; ☎☑) Healthy salads, sandwiches, shakes and snacks like hummus and felafel are served in this creative space on an artsy alley off St 240. The menu leans vegetarian, and pizza is among the offerings on its small raw-food menu. The daily specials are worth asking about. Another branch (Map p42; 13 St 278; ☻7.30am-5pm) is on St 278.

Sonoma Oyster Bar
SEAFOOD $$

(Map p42; ☎077723911; sonomaoyster@gmail.com; 159 St 222; 6-oyster platters US$7.50-9; ☻5-11pm; ✳) The owner here sells premium imported oysters wholesale to top-end hotels – or sells them here to you at bargain prices. A must for raw-oyster lovers. Scallops and steaks are among other tempting options.

Public House
FUSION $$

(Map p42; ☎017770754; St 240½; mains US$5-8; ☻11.30am-11pm Tue-Sun; ✳) The trendiest restaurant on trendy St 240½, Kiwi-owned Public House attracts hip expats with its long bar, linear design and overpriced beer. The food is the real highlight, however, a mix of fusion fare (roast duck breast on couscous) and spruced-up pub grub (fish 'n' chips). High tea is from 3pm to 5.30pm (reserve ahead).

Dolce Italia
ITALIAN $$

(Map p42; ☎012562892; 96 Sothearos Blvd; pizza US$6-11, pasta US$7-11; ✳☎) This is the sister pizzeria of Italian eatery Pop Cafe on the Riverside. Neopolitan-style pies have soft, thick crust and a loyal fan base among Phnom Penh expats. Sit upstairs on the appealing balcony overlooking Wat Botum Park.

Naturae
ORGANIC $$

(Map p42; 83 St 240; wraps US$5.50; ☻7am-9pm; ☎☑) A delightful spot with delicious all-organic salads and wraps and grass growing in the tables, plus a health-food store.

Yi Sang
CHINESE $$

(Map p42; Sisowath Quay; US$6-20; ☻6am-11pm) Yi Sang is all about contemporary Chinese cuisine. The menu includes live seafood, or at least recently alive, plus just about the best dim sum in town (available before 5pm only). The riverfront location, with an abbreviated menu, is one of the best places in the city for a relaxing sunset cocktail. Also located at the Almond Hotel (Map p42; 128 Sothearos Blvd; ☎).

⭐**La Residence**   FRENCH **$$$**

(Map p42; ☎023-224582; 22 St 214; mains US$15-100, set lunches US$15-30; ☺11.30am-2pm & 6.30-10pm Mon-Fri, 6.30-10pm Sat & Sun; ✺🛜) Princess Marie's daughter Ratana has converted part of the family home into this elegant French restaurant. Pass through the immense wooden doors and enjoy fine French food, including braised lamb shanks with raisin couscous, superb seafood, and steaks in Café de Paris sauce.

Origami   JAPANESE **$$$**

(Map p42; ☎012968095; 88 Sothearos Blvd; sushi sets from US$25; ☺11.30am-2pm & 6-10pm; ✺🛜) This outstanding Japanese eatery takes the art of Japanese food to another level. Yes, it's very expensive, but real sushi connoisseurs wouldn't settle for anything less. Set menus include beautifully presented sushi, sashimi and tempura boxes.

🍴 Boeng Keng Kang & Tonlé Bassac

⭐**Dosa Corner**   INDIAN **$**

(Map p42; 5E St 51; mains US$1.50-3; ☺8.30am-2pm & 5-10pm) Fans of Indian dosas will be pleased to discover this place does just what it says on the label, namely a generous variety of savoury pancakes from the south. Great value.

⭐**Ayotaya**   THAI **$**

(Map p42; 58 St 302; dishes US$3.50-4.50; ☺10.30am-2pm & 5-9pm Mon-Sat; ✺) No punches are pulled for tourists here: the dishes are pure Thai fire. Besides the trademark pad thai, you'll find plenty delicious papaya salads, zippy red curry and scrumptious lime-steamed fish. The interior isn't much but the air-con is nice.

Café Soleil   VEGETARIAN **$**

(Map p42; 22D St 278; mains US$2-4; 🛜💼) Cheap-as-chips veggie dishes like fried noodles, pumpkin curry, hummus and salads.

Friendly House   CAMBODIAN **$**

(Map p42; 203 St 310; mains 4000-8000r; ☺7am-8pm) Draws a mostly local crowd who appreciate affordable Cambodian and Vietnamese dishes like lemongrass chicken and fried noodles with seafood.

⭐**Malis**   CAMBODIAN **$$**

(Map p42; 136 Norodom Blvd; mains US$6-12; 🛜) The leading Khmer restaurant in the Cambodian capital, Malis is a chic place to dine

al fresco. The original menu includes beef bites in bamboo, goby with Kampot peppercorns, and traditional soups and salads. Popular for a boutique breakfast; sets are a good deal at US$3 to US$4.

Java Café   CAFE **$$**

(Map p42; www.javaarts.org; 56 Sihanouk Blvd; mains US$4-8; ✺🛜💼) Consistently popular thanks to a breezy balcony and a creative menu that includes crisp salads, delicious homemade sandwiches, burgers (do try the vegetarian one) and excellent coffee from several continents. The upstairs doubles as an art gallery, the downstairs as a bakery.

Taste Budz   INDIAN **$$**

(Map p42; ☎092961554; 13E St 282; mains US$3-6; ☺10am-2.30pm & 5-10pm; ✺) This pint-sized outfit with the funny name (rasta inspired?) is the most toothsome of Phnom Penh's many Indian restaurants. The speciality is Kerala (South Indian) cuisine. The spicy *kedai* dishes are divine. Order *porotta* (flatbread) on the side and dig in (with your hands, naturally).

Piccola Italia Da Luigi   PIZZERIA **$$**

(Map p42; ☎017323273; 36 St 308; pizza US$4.50-9; ☺11am-2pm & 6-10pm) A bustling curbside eatery, just like in Italy, 'Luigi's' certainly has a claim to making some of the best pizza in Phnom Penh. Also has a small deli attached if you're in the mood for some zingy antipasti. Reservations not a bad idea.

Le Jardin   CAFE **$$**

(Map p42; ☎011723399; 16 St 360; mains US$3.50-6; ☺9am-10pm; 🛜) Taking full advantage of a garden laden with jackfruit trees, this family-oriented cafe has a sandpit and a play house. The light menu includes tapas (pick three for US$7), *galettes*, sandwiches and salads. Live music most Friday nights and Sunday afternoon jazz in the garden.

Vego Salad Bar   CAFE **$$**

(Map p42; 21B St 294; salads US$4-5.50; ☺7.30am-9pm; 💼) Vego attracts health nuts with its build-it-yourself salads and wraps. The space is the real draw, however, awash in blonde wood and strewn with cosy seating. A great place to spend a wi-fi-enabled afternoon sipping a latte. There's also a **mini-branch** (Map p42; St 51, cnr St 278; ☺7.30am-9pm) opposite Wat Langka in the BKK area.

La Plaza   SPANISH **$$**

(Map p42; 22B St 278; tapas US$2.50-10; ☺11am-2pm & 5-10pm; ✺🛜) An authentic Spanish tapas bar in a snug shophouse on Golden St, La Plaza's wide-ranging menu covers the basics (garlic shrimp, Spanish meatballs) and adds Cambodia-inspired creations like *boquerones del Mekong* (small Mekong fish in vinegar). Happy hour (5pm to 6.30pm) sees US$1.50 *patatas bravas* and US$2 sangria.

Comme à la Maison FRENCH $$

(Map p42; 13 St 57; mains US$5-9; ⊘ 6am-10.30pm; 🖀) This attractive open-air restaurant under a thatched Balinese-style roof has a compact menu of provincial French fare, plus pizza and pasta and enticing weekly specials. An on-site bakery makes this a good spot for an early *petit déjeuner*.

Aussie XL INTERNATIONAL $$

(Map p42; 205A St 51; mains US$7-14; ⊘ 9am-11pm) The name is telling – this is a place for serious fill-ups. Super-sized fish, lamb, chicken, steak and about every other type of burger imaginable is available. Weekends sometimes see pigs roasted on spits. The place for Aussie sports on the telly.

Doo.re KOREAN $$

(Map p52; 245 St 63; mains US$5-6; ⊘ 9am-10pm; 🖀) Korean expats flock to this diminutive eatery to eat bowls of home-cooked *bibimbap* (rice mixed with lots of stuff) and *sundubu jjigae* (spicy Korean stew).

Sushi Bar JAPANESE $$

(Map p42; 2D St 302; sushi sets from US$6; ⊘ 11am-10pm; 🍲🖀) Purists will scoff at the low prices, but it's always packed for a reason. Definitely the best place in town for quick-and-easy raw fish. Sit downstairs at the bar, outside on the patio or in private rooms upstairs.

★ Deco EUROPEAN $$$

(Map p42; ☑ 017577327; cnr Sts 352 & 57; mains US$9-13; ⊘ noon-2pm & 5-10pm; 🍲) With an enviable setting in an impeccably restored '60s modernist house, and a rotating menu of progressive European cuisine, Deco is one of Phnom Penh's most sophisticated restaurants. The menu might include duck breast or Kampot crab cakes at any given time, and the creative cocktails are legendary.

Duck INTERNATIONAL $$$

(Map p42; ☑ 089823704; 49 Sothearos Blvd; mains US$9-15, steaks US$21-39; ⊘ 9am-3pm & 6-11pm; 🍲🖀) Owned by a Kiwi, Duck is a Soho-style bistro in the heart of Phnom Penh, with sherry-red wood tables, suave chill-out music and some of the most exciting cuisine in the capital. You won't regret splurging on the wagyu scotch fillet (US$39). They do great things with mushrooms here and have brunch on weekends.

The Common Tiger FUSION $$$

(Map p42; ☑ 077505234; 20 St 294; mains US$10-13, degustation menu US$40; ⊘ noon-3pm & 7-9.30pm; 🍲🖀) Everything about this delectable eatery is minimalist, including the portions, so do go ahead and order an appetiser. The South African chef personally presents his creations to diners on super-sized plates. The constantly rotating menu usually includes just two main courses. Delicious homemade bread and desserts top things off.

🍴 Psar O'Russei & Tuol Sleng

★ Asian Spice SINGAPOREAN $

(Map p42; 79 St 111; mains US$2.30-2.80; ⊘ 6am-9pm; 🖀) The house speciality is the zesty Singapore laksa (yellow curry noodles), but you'll also find a host of appropriately spicy Indonesian and Malaysian specialities on the menu, along with some Western fare. One of Phnom Penh's best bargains.

Noodle Café CAMBODIAN $

(Map p42; 67 St 113; US$3-4; ⊘ 6am-9pm; 🍲🖀) Surprisingly contemporary for these parts. Relax in body-swallowing couches under industrial lamps and sup on Peking duck wonton soup. Also serves coffee, bread and ice cream. The air-con is blissful.

Cyclo CAFE $

(Map p42; 29A St 113; mains US$2-3; ⊘ 8am-5pm; 🍲🖀) The perfect air-conditioned escape after sweating it out at Tuol Sleng. It's mainly a coffee-and-wi-fi kind of place, but a picture menu displays a few Khmer mains and pasta at very affordable prices.

Mama Restaurant CAMBODIAN $

(Map p42; 10C St 111; mains US$1.50-4; ⊘ 7.30am-8.30pm) This long-running backpacker cafe in the heart of the Psar O Russei area serves tasty French-influenced Khmer food, plus shepherd's pie. Try the beef stew.

King Kong Bamboo CAMBODIAN $

(Map p42; St 111; US$1.50-3; ⊘ 6am-8.30pm) Bold name for such a tiny space – just two tables plopped on the pavement out front. Khmer specialities like grilled eggplant are fresh and pack a fiery punch. It's a real bargain.

Spider Restaurant
CAMBODIAN $

(Map p42; 50 St 113; mains US$2.50-6; ⊙8am-5pm; 🖥) A relaxing little fan-cooled cafe opposite Tuol Sleng with good curries, coffee, jazz tunes playing and a charming chequerboard floor.

Chinese Noodle/China Restaurant
CHINESE $

(Map p42; 553 Monivong Blvd; mains US$1.50-2.50) Twin bargain eateries popular among locals and expats alike. Chinese Noodle is all about – what else – noodles, with anything from duck to pig stomach. China Restaurant is famous for its dumpling-like pork buns.

Capitol Restaurant
CAMBODIAN $

(Map p42; 14 St 182; mains US$1.50-2.50; ⊙6am-9pm) Long-running Capitol, under the cheap guesthouse of the same name, is popular for a reason – namely really cheap food and a good selection of both Western and Khmer favourites. Breakfasts are an especially good deal.

★K'nyay
VEGAN $$

(Map p42; 📞011454282; 43 St 95; mains US$4-7; ⊙noon-10pm Tue-Fri, 8am-10pm Sat-Sun, closed Mon; 🖥💻) A handsome restaurant upstairs at The Terraces boutique hotel, K'nyay complements its meat-infused traditional Cambodian fare with a vegan menu, and also prepares vegan lunch boxes for daytrippers. Try the tasty banana or pumpkin curry (ask them to spice it up). Or drop by for an original health shake after visiting sweltering the Tuol Sleng Museum nearby.

Russian Market Area

There is nothing better than an iced coffee or fresh fruit shake after surviving the scrum that is the Russian Market. In the market's central food stall area, look out for the charismatic **Mr Bounnareth** (Map p52; Russian Market, Shop 547), whose patented 'best iced coffee in Phnom Penh' has been living up to its name for some 35 years. Other stalls sell fried noodles and *banh chav* (meat or seafood and veggies wrapped inside a thin egg pancake and lettuce leaf) for US$1.

The streets emanating east and south from Russian Market are home to several stand-out lunch spots, some so successful that they are now open for dinner.

★Sesame Noodle Bar
NOODLES $

(Map p52; www.sesamenoodlebar.com; 9 St 460; mains US$3.75-4.50; ⊙11.30am-2.30pm & 5-9.30pm) A Japanese-American duo is behind Russian Market's trendiest lunch spot. Didn't know you liked cold noodles? We didn't either. They arrive in vegetarian or egg varieties and come heaped with an egg and carmelised pork or grilled tofu. Delicious.

Alma Cucina Mexicana
MEXICAN $

(Map p52; 43A St 454; meals US$3-5; ⊙7am-2pm; 🖥) How real home-cooked Mexican cuisine made its way here we'll never guess, but we're glad it did. The scrumptious rotating menu might include chorizo quesadillas one day, *bistec encebollado* (steak and onions) the next. The *huevos rancheros* breakfasts are legendary.

Sumatra
INDONESIAN $

(Map p52; 35 St 456; mains US$1.50-3.50; ⊙11am-8pm; 🖥💻) The vegetarian dishes, which average about US$2, are fantastic value, although big eaters may have to order two. The spicy *balado* (tomato and chilli sauce) dishes are good. Seating is on a leafy garden patio under a tin roof.

Spring Vale
JAPANESE $

(Map p52; 27 St 450; mains US$3.50-5.50; ⊙11am-3pm Mon-Fri; ✽🖥) A relaxing corner lunch stop where the friendly Japanese host whips up classic lunch fare from his homeland, including steaming rice bowls, curry noodles and affordable sushi.

Sisters
BAKERY $

(Map p52; 26B St 446; sandwiches US$2.50-3.50; ⊙7am-6pm; 🖥) A tiny little place that punches above its weight with light bites, all-day breakfasts, a few Cambodian mains and excellent homemade cakes, including 25-cent cupcakes (yum).

Drinking & Nightlife

Phnom Penh has some great bars and clubs and it's definitely worth planning at least one big night on the town. Many venues are clustered around the intersection of St 51 and St 172, where seemingly everybody ends up late at night. 'Golden St' (St 278) is popular and the riverfront also has its share of bars.

Happy hours are a big thing in Phnom Penh so it pays to get started early, when even such luminaries as the FCC and the Raffles offer two-for-one specials. There are some great hostel bars in Phnom Penh – besides those listed below, check out Blue Dog's streetside bar or the rooftop bar at Mad Monkey. Drop by trendy little St 240½ to see what's happening as well. Most bars are open until at least midnight, which is about the time that Phnom Penh's rollicking nightclubs swing into action.

Bars

⭐ **Elephant Bar**   BAR
(Map p48; St 92; ☺ happy hour 4-9pm) Few places are more atmospheric than this sophisticated bar at the Raffles. It has been drawing journalists, politicos, and the rich and famous for more than 80 years. Singapore slings and everything else are half-price during happy hour.

⭐ **FCC**   BAR
(Foreign Correspondents' Club; Map p48; 363 Sisowath Quay; ☺ 6am-midnight; 🕾) A Phnom Penh institution, the 'F' is housed in a colonial gem with great views and cool breezes. One of those must-see places in Cambodia, almost everyone swings by for a drink – happy hours are 5pm to 7pm and 10pm to midnight. If the main bar is too crowded, head up to the rooftop, which often sees live music at weekends. Has decent if expensive food as well.

Chow   BAR
(Map p48; 277 Sisowath Quay; ☺ 7am-11pm) The Quay hotel's swanky rooftop has river views, cooling breezes, a plunge pool and happy hours (half price off US$6 drinks) from 4pm to 8.30pm. The creative cocktail list includes zesty infusions like ginger and lemongrass, plus a passionfruit caipirinha.

Top Banana   BAR
(Map p42; 9 St 278) There's no question where the top backpacker party spot in Phnom Penh is. The rooftop bar of this guesthouse goes off practically every night of the week – sometimes with spontaneous dancing into the wee hours.

Howie Bar   BAR
(Map p48; 32 St 51; ☺ 7pm-6am) Friendly, fun and unpredictable, 'way-cool' Howie is the perfect spillover when the famous Heart of Darkness is packed.

Zeppelin Café   BAR
(Map p48; 109 St 51; ☺ 6.30pm-late) Who says vinyl is dead? It lives on in the Cambodian capital, thanks to the owner of this old-school rock bar manning the turntables every night.

Eighty8 Backpackers   BAR
(Map p48; 98 St 88) A well-stocked, perfectly oval bar commands the courtyard of this villa-like hostel. Great tunes, great ambience and regular first-Friday parties see the expat and backpacker worlds collide.

Rainbow Bar   BAR
(Map p48; 134 St 136) Phnom Penh's friendliest, most laid-back gay bar, with a 10pm drag show every night.

Dusk Till Dawn   BAR
(Map p48; 46 St 172) Also known as Reggae Bar because of the clientele and the music, the rooftop setting makes it a great spot for a sundowner, but the party lasts well into the evening. Ride the lift to the top floor in the tall building opposite Pontoon.

Paddy Rice   IRISH PUB
(Map p48; 213 Sisowath Quay; ☺ 24hr) A real jack of all trades – good pub grub, big screens for sports viewing, and occasional live music. Thursday is open-mic night. All this in a perfect riverside location.

Bouchon   WINE BAR
(Map p42; 3/4 St 246; ☺ 4pm-midnight) Bouchon has a great selection of French wines, plus pâtés and other French nibbles, in a contemporary space on a quiet side street opposite the Himawari Hotel. A glass of house red costs US$3.50.

Le Moon   BAR
(Map p48; 1 St 154; ☺ 5pm-1am) Another hotel bar, the Amanjaya's rooftop offering scores points for atmosphere and views, but service is spotty. Bring patience.

Blue Chili   BAR
(Map p48; 36 St 178; ☺ 6pm-late) The owner of this gay-friendly bar stages his own drag show every Friday and Saturday at 10.30pm.

Score   SPORTS BAR
(Map p42; 📞 023-221357; 5 St 282; ☺ 8am-late) With its ginormous screen, this spacious bar is the best place to watch the big game. Several pool tables tempt those who would rather play than watch.

Dodo Rhum House   BAR
(Map p48; 42C St 178; ☺ 5pm-late) Specialising in homemade flavoured rums, this French

favourite also offers an excellent fish fillet and other tasty treats.

Gym Bar
SPORTS BAR

(Map p48; 42 St 178; ☺11am-late) The only workout here is raising glasses. This is a top sports bar with ample big and small screens.

Live Music

Phnom Penh boasts a surprisingly active music scene, with several talented expat and mixed Khmer-expat bands.

Equinox
BAR

(Map p42; 3A St 278; ☺8am-late; 🖻) At the heart of the action, this is a popular place with a lively outdoor bar downstairs as well as bands upstairs from Thursday to Saturday. It works well as just a bar on other nights.

Memphis Pub
LIVE MUSIC

(Map p48; 🖉023-871263; 3 St 118; ☺4pm-late, closed Sun) It's not closed, it just has sound-proof doors. Memphis has a decent house cover band and frequently attracts more diverse acts. There's an open-mic jam session on Monday night.

Slur
BAR

(Map p48; 28 St 172; ☺11am-2am) Slur consistently draws some of Phnom Penh's best musical talent. Worth stopping by to see who's on stage and throw back a Jägerbomb.

The Doors
LIVE MUSIC

(18 St 84; ☺7am-midnight; 🖻) Self-described as a 'music and tapas' bar, the Doors is a sophisticated place with a long bar, mouth-watering Spanish bites, expensive drinks and classy live jazz, piano and more.

Sharky
LIVE MUSIC

(Map p48; www.sharkybarblog.com; 126 St 130; ☺5pm-late) An old-school Phnom Penh hangout long famous for billiards and babes, Sharky's has done a good job of redirecting some of its focus towards quality live music.

Nightclubs

For the lowdown on club nights, check out **Phnom Penh Underground** (www.phnom-penh-underground.com), a roving party of sorts that promotes gigs for various electro troupes in Phnom Penh and beyond.

★Heart of Darkness
NIGHTCLUB

(Map p48; 26 St 51; ☺8pm-late) This Phnom Penh institution with the alluring Angkor theme has evolved into a nightclub more than a bar over the years. It goes off every night of the week, attracting all – and we mean all – sorts. Everybody should stop in at least once just to bask in the aura and history of the place.

Pontoon
NIGHTCLUB

(Map p48; www.pontoonclub.com; 80 St 172; admission weekends US$3-5, weekdays free; ☺9.30pm-late) After floating from pier to pier for a few years (hence the name), the city's premier nightclub has finally found a permanent home on *terra firma*. It draws top local DJs and occasional big foreign acts. Thursday is gay-friendly night, with a 1am lady-boy show.

Meta House
NIGHTCLUB

(Map p42; 37 Sothearos Blvd) The venerable movie house hosts Tech Penh and other public parties from 9pm every Friday and some Thursdays and Saturdays.

Backstage Cocktail Bar
CLUB, LOUNGE

(Map p48; 377 Sisowath Quay; ☺till late) A little bolt hole of a place, it can be sneaky fun and is worth popping by late-night if you're looking for some riverfront dance action.

Rock
NIGHTCLUB

(Map p52; 468 Monivong Blvd; admission varies; ☺until late) If you want a more authentic local experience, Rock is your best bet. Looks like a gigantic Home Depot, but Khmers go crazy for it, complete with karaoke rooms.

FLOWER POWER

Anyone who spends a night or two on the town in Phnom Penh will soon be familiar with young girls and boys hovering around popular bars and restaurants to sell decorative flowers. The kids are incredibly sweet and most people succumb to their charms and buy a flower or two. All these late nights for young children might not be so bad if they were benefiting from their hard-earned cash, but usually they are not. Look down the road and there will be a *moto* driver with an ice bucket full of these flowers waiting to ferry the children to another popular spot. Yet again, the charms of children are exploited for the benefit of adults who should know better but are too poor to worry about it. Think twice before buying from them, as the child probably won't reap the reward.

☆ Entertainment

For news on what's happening in town, grab a copy of free listings newspaper *The Advisor* or check out *7 Days* in the Friday issue of the *Phnom Penh Post*. *AsiaLife* is a free monthly with entertainment features and some listings. Online, try www.ladypenh. com or Khmer440.com.

Cinemas

★ Meta House CINEMA
(Map p42; www.meta-house.com; 37 Sothearos Blvd; ⊙4pm-midnight Tue-Sun; 🛜) This German-run open-air theatre screens art-house films, documentaries and shorts from Cambodia and around the world most evenings at 4pm (admission free) and 7pm (admission US$2). Films are sometimes followed by Q&As with those involved. Order German sausages, pizza-like 'flamecakes' and beer to supplement your viewing experience.

Flicks CINEMA
(Map p42; www.theflicks-cambodia.com; 39B St 95; tickets US$3.50; 🛜) Flicks shows at least two movies a day in an uber-comfortable air-conditioned screening room. You can watch both on one ticket. A second **Flicks** (Map p48; 90 St 136) is downstairs at 11 Happy Backpacker.

Legend Cinema CINEMA
(Map p42; ☑095300400; www.legend.com.kh; 3rd fl, City Mall, Monirith Blvd; tickets US$3-5) Large Western-style theatre.

Platinum Cineplex CINEMA
(Map p48; ☑086666210; www.platinumcineplex. com.kh; Sorya Shopping Centre; tickets US$4-6) Screens Western blockbusters on the top floor of Phnom's premier shopping mall.

Bophana Centre FILM CENTRE
(Map p42; ☑023-992174; www.bophana.org; 64 St 200; admission free; ⊙8am-noon & 2-6pm Mon-Fri, 2-6pm Sat) Established by Cambodian-French filmmaker Rithy Panh, this is an audiovisual resource for filmmakers and researchers, and visitors can explore its archive of old photographs and films and attend free film screenings on Saturdays at 4pm.

French Institute CINEMA
(Institut Français; Map p42; ☑023-213124; www. institutfrancais-cambodge.com; 218 St 184) Has frequent movie screenings in French during the week, usually kicking off at 6.30pm, as well as a French library, bookstore and gallery space.

The cinema and the garden cafe out the back were being rebuilt at the time of research.

Mekong River Restaurant CINEMA
(Map p48; cnr St 118 & Sisowath Quay) Screens two original films in English or French, one covering the Khmer Rouge and the other on the subject of landmines. Showings are hourly from 11am to 9pm and cost US$3.

Classical Dance & Arts

Plae Pakaa PERFORMING ARTS
(Fruitful; Map p48; ☑023-986032; www.cambodianlivingarts.org; National Museum, St 178; adult/child US$15/6; ⊙7pm Mon-Sat Oct-Mar, Fri & Sat May-Sep, closed Apr) Plae Pakaa is a series of must-see performances put on by Cambodian Living Arts (p46). There are three rotating shows, each lasting about an hour. *Children of Bassac* showcases traditional dance styles. *Passage of Life* depicts the celebrations and rituals that Khmers go through in their lifetimes – weddings, funerals etc. *Mak Therng* is a traditional *yike* opera.

Apsara Arts Association DANCE
(☑012979335; www.apsara-art.org; 71 St 598; tickets US$6-7) 🏵 Alternate performances of classical dance and folk dance are held most Saturdays at 7pm (call to confirm). Visitors are also welcome from 7.30am to 10.30am and from 2pm to 5pm Monday to Saturday to watch the students in training (suggested donation: US$3). However, it is important to remember that this is a training school – noise and flash photography should be kept to a minimum. It's in Tuol Kork district, in the far north of the city.

Sovanna Phum Arts Association SHADOW PUPPETS
(☑023-987564; www.shadow-puppets.org; 166 St 99, btwn Sts 484 & 498; adult/child US$5/3) 🏵 Regular traditional shadow-puppet performances and occasional classical dance and traditional drum shows are held here at 7.30pm every Friday and Saturday night. Audience members are invited to try their hand at the shadow puppets after the 50-minute performance. Classes are available here in the art of shadow puppetry, puppet making, classical and folk dance, and traditional Khmer musical instruments.

Chatomuk Theatre THEATRE
(Map p42; Sisowath Quay) Check the flyer out front for information on performances at the Chatomuk Theatre, located just north of the Hotel Cambodiana. Officially, it has

been turned into a government conference centre, but it regularly plays host to cultural performances.

Shopping

There is some great shopping to be had in Phnom Penh, but don't forget to bargain in the markets or you'll have your 'head shaved' – local-speak for being ripped off.

Markets & Malls

As well as the markets, there are now some shopping malls in Phnom Penh. While these may not be quite as glamorous as the likes of the Siam Paragon in Bangkok, they are good places to browse thanks to the air-conditioning.

Russian Market   MARKET
(Psar Tuol Tom Pong; Map p52; ⊙6am-5pm) This sweltering bazaar is the one market all visitors should come to at least once during a trip to Phnom Penh. It is *the* place to shop for souvenirs and discounted Western name-brand clothing. We can't vouch for the authenticity of everything, but along with plenty of knock-offs you will find genuine articles stitched in local factories. You'll pay as little as 10% of the price you'll pay back home for brands like Banana Republic, Billabong, Calvin Klein, Colombia, Gap and Next.

Russian Market – so-called by foreigners because the predominantly Russian expat population shopped here in the 1980s – also has a large range of handicrafts and antiquities (many fake), including miniature Buddhas, woodcarvings, betel-nut boxes, silks, silver jewellery, musical instruments and so on. Bargain hard, as hundreds of tourists pass through here every day.

Psar Thmei   MARKET
(ផ្សារធ្មី, Central Market; Map p48; ⊙6.30am-5.30pm) A landmark building in the capital, the art deco Psar Thmei is often called the Central Market, a reference to its location and size. The huge domed hall resembles a Babylonian ziggurat and some claim it ranks as one of the 10 largest domes in the world. The design allows for maximum ventilation, and even on a sweltering day the central hall is cool and airy. The market was recently renovated with French government assistance and is looking in fine fettle these days.

The market has four wings filled with stalls selling gold and silver jewellery, antique coins, dodgy watches, clothing and other such items. For photographers, the fresh food section affords many opportunities. For a local lunch, there are a host of food stalls located on the western side, which faces Monivong Blvd.

Psar Thmei is undoubtedly the best market for browsing. However, it has a reputation among Cambodians for overcharging on most products.

Psar O Russei   MARKET
(Map p42; ⊙6.30am-5.30pm) Much bigger than either Psar Thmei or Russian Market, Psar O Russei sells foodstuffs, costume jewellery, imported toiletries, secondhand clothes and everything else you can imagine from hundreds of stalls. The market is housed in a huge labyrinth of a building that looks like a shopping mall from the outside.

Sorya Shopping Centre   MALL
(Map p48; cnr Sts 63 & 154; ⊙9am-9pm) The pick of the malls in Phnom Penh, with a good range of shops, a central location, a Western-style cinema and superb views over the more traditional Psar Thmei.

Night Market   MARKET
(Psar Reatrey; Map p48; St 108 & Sisowath Quay; ⊙5-11pm Fri-Sun) A cooler al fresco version of Russian Market, this night market takes place every Friday, Saturday and Sunday evening, if rain doesn't stop play. Bargain vigorously, as prices can be on the high side. Interestingly, it's probably more popular with Khmers than foreigners.

Psar Chaa   MARKET
(Map p48; St 108; ⊙6am-5.30pm) This is a scruffy place that deals in household goods, clothes and jewellery. There are small restaurants, food vendors and jewellery stalls, as well as some good fresh-fruit stalls outside.

Clothing, Silks & Accessories

While the markets are best-known for knock-off clothing, a few shops surrounding Russian Market sell authentic brand-name gear, mostly made in Vietnam. There are also several boutiques around town specialising in silk furnishings and stylish original clothing, as well as glam accessories. Many are conveniently located on St 240, Cambodia's answer to London's King's Rd.

DAH Export   CLOTHING
(Map p42; 87 Sihanouk Blvd; ⊙9am-9pm) This is the biggest and best of the factory overrun outlets, with an impressive winter collection (North Face Gortex ski jackets for US$99, anyone?), plenty of kiddie clothing and a

LOCAL KNOWLEDGE

ARN CHORN-POND, MUSICIAN

Arn Chorn-Pond is the founder of Cambodian Living Arts (CLA; p46), an organisation dedicated to reviving traditional music, dance and other Cambodian art forms that were nearly lost during the Khmer Rouge years. Arn himself almost didn't survive that dark time. His parents ran a respected traditional opera company in Battambang. This made them immediate targets of the Khmer Rouge, which slaughtered more than 90% of performing artists, according to Arn. Twenty-five members of Arn's immediate family, including five of his eight siblings, were killed.

But the Khmer Rouge needed to keep some musicians around to play their revolutionary hymns. Arn was among several children in Battambang recruited to dance and play the flute and the *khim* (a traditional Cambodian string instrument) at a local killing temple.

'They killed three kids who were slow to learn,' Arn says. 'I was a fast learner because I had music in my blood. If there was no music at that time, I probably would have been killed. Music saved my life.'

At the killing temple, Arn witnessed all sorts of atrocities. The Khmer Rouge made him play music to drown out the sounds of the screams. In the late 1970s, at the age of 12, Arn was forced to trade in his *khim* for a gun as he was recruited into the beleaguered Khmer Rouge army. He eventually managed to escape over the border to a refugee camp in Thailand, where he was ultimately adopted along with several other refugees by an American family from New Hampshire.

When Arn returned to Cambodia several years later, people in Battambang still recognised him as 'that little boy who played the *khim*'. He founded CLA in 1998.

Arn shared with us his top five places for cultural connections in Phnom Penh.

Amrita Performing Arts (www.amritaperformingarts.org) 'They work with traditional Apsara dancers to create new stories, and worked closely with CLA to organise the "Season of Cambodia" in New York in 2013.'

Apsara Arts Association (p69) 'A great family-run organisation that's working with a new generation of kids to preserve forms like Apsara and traditional folk dance.'

Plae Pakaa (p69) 'CLA puts on these performances almost every evening in front of the National Museum.'

CLA's Yike Class (Map p42; 65 Sothearos Blvd) 'These daily traditional-opera classes for at-risk youth are run by master theatre performer Ieng Sithul and are open to tourists. Many of the kids here would be prostitutes if not for this class.'

Sovanna Phum (p69) 'They do a great job creating new stories and new dances out of old Cambodian traditional forms.'

prominent location. A lifetime 20% discount kicks in if you spend US$250.

Ambre   SILK
(Map p48; 📞 023-217935; 37 St 178; ⊘10am-6pm) Leading Cambodian fashion designer Romyda Keth has turned this striking French-era mansion into an ideal showcase for her stunning silk collection.

Couleurs d'Asie   ACCESSORIES
(Map p42; www.couleursdasie.net; 33 St 240; ⊘8am-7pm) A great place for gift shopping, with lots of kids' clothes, silks, chunky jewellery, beautiful bags, knick-knacks and fragrant soaps, lotions, incense and oils.

Paperdolls   CLOTHING
(Map p42; 82 St 240½; ⊘10am-6pm Tue-Sun) Great stuff for girls – sundresses, shoes, movie-star shades, handbags, jewellery, you name it.

Waterlily   ACCESSORIES
(Map p42; 37 St 240; ⊘10am-7pm Mon-Fri, 9am-5pm Sat) Strikingly original bags, jewellery, art and dolls. Everything is made from recycled materials.

Bliss Boutique   CLOTHING
(Map p42; 29 St 240; ⊘9am-9pm) Casual dresses, blouses and men's shirts made of wonderfully airy materials, plus pillows and scented creams and oils.

SHOPPING TO HELP CAMBODIA

There are a host of tasteful shops selling handicrafts and textiles to raise money for projects to assist disadvantaged Cambodians. These are a good place to spend some dollars, as it helps to put a little bit back into the country.

A.N.D. (Map p42; www.artisandesigners.com; 52B/C St 240; ⊙8am-7pm) Specialises in ikat sundresses and *kramas*, plus reliable T-shirts and original bags and jewellery made from quirky recycled materials. A fair-trade brand, A.N.D. supports disabled and indigenous artisans, including Watthan Artisans Cambodia.

Cambodian Handicraft Association (CHA; Map p42; 1 St 350; ⊙8am-7pm) This well-stocked showroom and workshop sells fine handmade silk clothing, scarves, toys and bags produced by people disabled by landmines and polio.

Daughters (Map p48; www.daughtersofcambodia.org; 65 St 178; ⊙9am-6pm Mon-Sat) Daughters is an NGO that runs a range of programs to train and assist former prostitutes and victims of sex trafficking. The fashionable clothes, bags and accessories here are made with eco-friendly cotton and natural dyes by program participants.

Friends n' Stuff (Map p48; 215 St 13; ⊙11am-9pm) Part of the charitable Friends/Mith Samlanh empire, it carries a good range of new and secondhand products sold to generate money to help street children. Also trains tailors.

KeoK'jay (Map p48; www.keokjay.com; cnr St 110 & Sisowath Quay; ⊙11am-10pm) Original women's clothing and accessories stiched by HIV-positive women.

Mekong Blue (Map p48; www.bluesilk.org; 9 St 130; ⊙8am-6pm) Phnom Penh boutique for Stung Treng's best-known silk cooperative to empower women. Produces beautiful scarves and shawls, as well as jewellery.

Mekong Quilts (Map p42; www.mekong-quilts.org; 49 St 240; ⊙9am-7pm) Incredible queen- and king-sized quilts cost US$375 to US$450 for silk, US$250 to US$350 for cotton. Bamboo bikes and baskets too. Helps women in remote villages.

Peace Handicrafts (Map p52; www.peacehandicraft.com; 39C St 155; ⊙7.30am-6pm) Carries an impressive range of higher-end souvenirs, including affordable Buddha heads and other

---

Spicy Green Mango   CLOTHING
(Map p42; www.spicygreenmango.com; 4A St 278; ⊙9am-9pm) *The* place to shop for original and creative kids' clothes, plus quality T-shirts and a hippyesque adult female line.

Kambuja   CLOTHING
(Map p48; 165 St 110; ⊙8am-6pm) Blending the best of East and West, the Cambodian and American designers focus on female fashion but also produce some quality embroidered men's shirts.

Subtyl   CLOTHING
(Map p42; www.subtyl.com; 43 St 240; ⊙9am-7pm) French-run boutique offering stylish accessories and clothes for women, plus the Chilli Kids line for hip youngsters.

Smateria   BAGS
(Map p48; 7 St 178; ⊙9am-9.30pm) They do some clothing but the specialty is bags, including a line of quirky kids' backpacks, made from fishing net and other recycled

materials. There's another branch in BKK (Map p42; 8 St 57; ⊙8am-9pm).

Tuol Sleng Shoes   SHOES
(Map p42; 136 St 143; ⊙7.30am-5pm) Scary name, but there's nothing scary about the price of these custom-fit, handmade shoes. Nearby Beautiful Shoes is another good option.

Art & Books

Plenty of shops sell locally produced paintings along St 178, opposite the Royal University of Fine Arts between streets 13 and 19. With a new generation of artists coming up, the selection is much stronger than it once was. Do bargain. Lots of reproduction busts of famous Angkorian sculptures are available along this stretch – great for the mantelpiece back home.

Artisans d'Angkor   HANDICRAFTS
(Map p48; 12 St 13; ⊙9am-6pm) Phnom Penh branch of the venerable Siem Reap sculpture and silk specialist.

statues, stationary and silks. Employs landmine victims and other disabled people in the workshop upstairs.

Rajana (Map p52; www.rajanacrafts.org; 170 St 450; ☉7am-6pm Mon-Sat, 10.30am-5pm Sun) One of the best all-around handicraft stores, Rajana aims to promote fair wages and training. It has a beautiful selection of cards, some quirky metalware products, quality jewellery, bamboo crafts, lovely shirts, gorgeous wall hangings, pepper, candles – you name it. Has a second market store (p72).

Rehab Craft (Map p42; 1 St 278; ☉9am-9pm) Carvings, weavings, wallets, jewellery and bags, all produced in the workshop by disabled artisans, often using recycled materials.

Sobbhana (Map p48; www.sobbhana.org; 23 St 144; ☉8am-noon & 1-6pm) Established by Princess Marie, the Sobbhana Foundation is a not-for-profit organisation training women in traditional weaving. Beautiful silks in a stylish boutique.

Ta Prohm Souvenir (Map p48; 49 St 178; ☉8am-7pm) Bags of all shapes and sizes, pillows, throws and shirts. Started by a disabled person to employ poor and/or disabled people. Also a **branch** (Map p52; 168A St 155; ☉7am-6pm) near the Russian Market.

Tabitha (Map p42; 239 St 360; ☉7am-6pm Mon-Sat) A leading NGO shop with a good collection of silk bags, tableware, bedroom decorations and children's toys. Proceeds go towards rural community development, such as well drilling.

Villageworks (Map p42; www.villageworks.biz; 118 St 113; ☉8am-5pm Mon-Sat) Opposite Tuol Sleng Museum, this shop has the inevitable silk and bags, as well as coconut-shell utensils made by poor and disadvantaged artisans in Kompong Thom province.

Watthan Artisans (Map p42; www.wac.khmerproducts.com; 180 Norodom Blvd; ☉8am-6.30pm) Located at the entrance to Wat Than, it sells silk and other products, including wonderful contemporary handbags, made by a project-supported cooperative of landmine and polio victims. You can visit the on-site woodworking and weaving workshops.

Women for Women (WFW; Map p48; www.womanforwoman.net; 9 St 178; ☉7am-10pm) Pillows, throws, bags, scarves, jewellery, silver and more, made by women with disabilities.

Asasax Art Gallery GALLERY
(Map p48; 192 St 178; ☉8am-7.30pm) High-end gallery featuring the striking work of artist Asasax.

French Institute GALLERY
(Map p42; www.institutfrancais-cambodge.com; 218 St 184; ☉11am-7pm Mon-Sat) Regularly hosts top-notch art and architecture exhibitions in its large galleries.

Citadel Knives KNIVES
(Map p48; ☎023-217617; www.knives-citadel.com; 10 St 110; ☉9am-10pm) Premium knives and swords, locally produced.

Monument Books BOOKS
(Map p42; 111 Norodom Blvd; ☉7am-8.30pm) This is the best-stocked bookshop in town, with almost every Cambodia-related book available, a superb maps and travel section, plus a wi-fi-enabled branch of Blue Pumpkin cafe.

International Book Center ALL-PURPOSE
(IBC; Map p42; 59 Sihanouk Blvd; ☉8am-8pm) High-quality headphones, flashlights, swimming goggles, notebooks, pens, sneakers – you name it.

Open Book BOOKS
(Map p42; 41 St 240; ☉10am-5pm) Run by an NGO, this is essentially a library where you can drop in to read a variety of books in French or English. Also has a fair selection of Cambodia-themed children's books for sale.

D's Books BOOKS
(Map p48; 7 St 178; 9am-9pm) The largest chain of secondhand bookshops in the capital, with a good range of titles. There's a second **branch** (Map p42; 79 St 240; ☉9am-9pm) just east of Norodom Blvd.

Bohr's Books BOOKS
(Map p48; 5 Sothearos Blvd; ☉8am-8pm) Secondhand bookshop near the riverfront with a great selection of novels and nonfiction.

ⓘ Information

DANGERS & ANNOYANCES

Phnom Penh is not as dangerous as people imagine, but it is important to take care. Armed robberies do sometimes occur, but statistically you would be very unlucky to be a victim. However, bag (and smartphone) snatching is a huge problem, and victims are often hurt when they are dragged off their bicycles or motorbikes.

Should you become the victim of a robbery, do not panic and do not, under any circumstances, struggle. Calmly raise your hands and let your attacker take what they want. *Do not* reach for your pockets, as the assailant may think you are reaching for a gun. Do not carry a bag at night, because it is more likely to make you a target.

If you ride your own motorbike during the day, some police may try to fine you for the most trivial of offences, such as turning left in violation of a no-left-turn sign. At their most audacious, they may try to get you for riding with your headlights on during the day although, worryingly, it does not seem to be illegal for Cambodians to travel without their headlights on at night. The police will most likely demand US$5 from you and threaten to take you to the police station for an official US$20 fine if you do not pay. If you are patient with them and smile, you can usually get away with handing over US$1. The trick is to not stop in the first place by not catching their eye.

The riverfront area of Phnom Penh, particularly places with outdoor seating, attracts many beggars, as do Psar Thmei and Russian Market. Generally, however, there is little in the way of push and shove.

Flooding is a major problem in the wet season (June to October), and heavy downpours see some streets turn into canals for a few hours.

EMERGENCY

In the event of a medical emergency it may be necessary to be evacuated to Bangkok.

Ambulance (☑119, in English 724891)
Fire (☑in Khmer 118)
Police (☑117)

CHILD PROSTITUTION

The sexual abuse of children by foreign paedophiles is a serious problem in Cambodia. Paedophilia is a crime in Cambodia and several foreigners have served or are serving jail sentences. There is no such thing as an isolation unit for sex offenders in Cambodia. Countries such as Australia, France, Germany, the UK and the USA have also introduced much-needed legislation that sees nationals prosecuted in their home country for having under-age sex abroad.

This child abuse is slowly but surely being combated, although in a country as poor as Cambodia, money can tempt people into selling babies for adoption and children for sex. The trafficking of innocent children has many shapes and forms, and the sex trade is just the thin end of the wedge. Poor parents have been known to rent out their children as beggars, labourers or sellers; many child prostitutes in Cambodia are Vietnamese and have been sold into the business by family back in Vietnam. Once in the trade, it is difficult to escape a life of violence and abuse. Drugs are also being used to keep children dependent on their pimps, with bosses giving out *yama* (a dirty metaamphetamine) or heroin to dull their senses.

Paedophilia is not unique to Western societies and it is a big problem with Asian tourists as well. The problem is that some of the home governments don't treat it as seriously as some of their Western counterparts. Even more problematic is the domestic industry of virgin-buying in Cambodia, founded on the superstition that taking a virgin will enhance one's power. Even if NGOs succeed in putting off Western paedophiles, confronting local traditions may be a greater challenge.

Visitors can do their bit by keeping an eye out for any suspicious behaviour. Don't ignore it – pass on any relevant information such as the name and nationality of the individual to the embassy concerned. To report abuse there is a Cambodian **hotline** (☑023-997919) and ChildSafe (p76) maintains confidential hotlines in **Phnom Penh** (☑012311112), **Siem Reap** (☑017358758) and **Sihanoukville** (☑012478100). When booking into a hotel or jumping on transport, look out for the ChildSafe logo, as each establishment or driver who earns this logo is trained to identify and respond to child abuse. **End Child Prostitution and Trafficking** (ECPAT; www.ecpat.net) is a global network aimed at stopping child prostitution, child pornography and the trafficking of children for sexual purposes, and has affiliates in most Western countries.

INTERNET ACCESS

Phnom Penh is now well and truly wired, with prices dropping to less than US$0.50 per hour. Internet cafes are all over the city and you'll find plenty of computer terminals on the main backpacker strips – St 258, St 278, St 172 and Boeng Kak. Most internet cafes are set up for Skype or similar services, and offer cheap VOIP calls as well.

Pretty much all hotels and most cafes and restaurants offer wi-fi connections, usually free.

MEDIA

Phnom Penh has two excellent English-language newspapers – the *Cambodia Daily* and the *Phnom Penh Post,* both widely circulated. They mix original local-news content with international stories pulled from wire services. *AsiaLife* is a monthly listings mag full of features targeted at Phnom Penh's expat community. The *Phnom Penh Visitors Guide* is brimming with useful information on the capital and beyond, plus detailed maps of the entire city.

MEDICAL SERVICES

It is important to be aware of the difference between a clinic and a hospital in Phnom Penh. Clinics are good for most situations, but in a genuine emergency it is best to make for one of the hospitals.

Calmette Hospital (☑023-426948; 3 Monivong Blvd; ⊙24hr) The best of the local hospitals, with the most comprehensive services and an intensive care unit.

European Dental Clinic (Map p42; ☑023-211363; 160A Norodom Blvd; ⊙8am-noon & 2-7pm Mon-Fri, 8am-noon Sat, closed Sun) With international dental services and a good reputation.

International SOS Medical Centre (Map p42; ☑012816911, 023-216911; www.international sos.com; 161 St 51; ⊙8am-5.30pm Mon-Fri, 8am-noon Sat, emergency 24hr) Top clinic with a host of Western doctors, and prices to match.

Naga Clinic (Map p42; ☑023-211300; www.nagaclinic.com; 11 St 254; ⊙24hr) A French-run clinic for reliable consultations.

Pharmacie de la Gare (Map p48; 81 Monivong Blvd; ⊙7am-9pm) A pharmacy with English-and French-speaking consultants.

Royal Rattanak Hospital (☑023-991000; www.royalrattanakhospital.com; 11 St 592; ⊙24hr) International hospital affiliated with Bangkok Hospital and boasting top facilities. Expensive.

Tropical & Travellers Medical Clinic (Map p48; ☑023-306802; www.travellersmedical clinic.com; 88 St 108; ⊙9.30-11.30am & 2.30-5pm Mon-Fri, 9.30-11.30am Sat) Well-regarded clinic run for more than a decade by a British general practioner.

U-Care Pharmacy (Map p48; 26 Sothearos Blvd; ⊙8am-10pm) International-style pharmacy with a convenient location near the river.

MONEY

There's little need to turn US dollars into riel, as greenbacks are universally accepted in the capital. You can change a wide variety of other currencies into dollars or riel in the jewellery stalls around Psar Thmei and Russian Market. Many upmarket hotels offer 24-hour money-changing services, although this is usually reserved for their guests. Banks with ATMs and money-changing facilities are ubiquitous – malls and supermarkets are good bets, and there are dozens of ATMs along the riverfront.

ANZ Royal Bank (Map p48; 265 Sisowath Quay; ⊙8.30am-4pm Mon-Fri, 8.30am-noon Sat) ANZ has ATMs galore all over town, including at supermarkets and petrol stations, but there is a US$4 charge per transaction.

CAB Bank (Map p48; 263 Sisowath Quay; ⊙8am-9pm) Convenient hours and location; cashes travellers cheques in a range of currencies (3% commission). There's also a Western Union office here (one of several in the city).

Canadia Bank (Map p48; cnr St 110 & Monivong Blvd; ⊙8am-3.30pm Mon-Fri, 8-11.30am Sat) Canadia Bank ATMs around town incur no transaction charges. Here at their flagship branch you can also change travellers cheques of several currencies for a 2% commission, plus get free cash advances on MasterCard and Visa. Canadia Bank also represents MoneyGram. Additional branches at Sorya Shopping Centre (Map p48; Sorya Shopping Centre, cnr Sts 63 & 154) and on Norodom Blvd (Map p42; Norodom Blvd).

POST

Central Post Office (Map p48; St 13; ⊙8am-6pm) A landmark, it's in a charming building just east of Wat Phnom.

TOURIST INFORMATION

ChildSafe (Map p48; ☑hotline 012311112, office 023-986601; www.childsafe-cambodia.org; 71 St 174; ⊙8am-5pm Mon-Fri) There's a centre here for tourists to learn about best behaviour relating to child begging, the dangers of orphanage tours, exploitation and other risks to children (see www.thinkchildsafe.org for a tips checklist). You can also look out for the ChildSafe logo on *remorks* and hotels. This network of people are trained to protect children.

Visitor Information Centre (Map p42; Sisowath Quay; ⊗8am-5pm Mon-Sat) Located on the riverfront near the Chatomuk Theatre; while it doesn't carry a whole lot of information, it does offer free internet access, free wi-fi, aircon and clean public toilets.

TRAVEL AGENCIES

There are plenty of travel agents around town. The following are good bets for air tickets and all manner of domestic excursions, and can also arrange local transport and tour guides in multiple languages.

Exotissimo (Map p48; ☑023-218948; www.exotissimo.com; 66 Norodom Blvd) Runs tours all over Cambodia and the Mekong region.

Hanuman Travel (Map p42; ☑023-218396; www.hanumantravel.com; 12 St 310) Guides in several languages, tours and more, all over the country.

Palm Tours (Map p42; ☑023-726291; www.palmtours.biz; 1B St 278; ⊗8am-9pm) Efficient Volak and her team are a great option for bus tickets (no commission) and the like. In the heart of all the action on St 278.

PTM Travel & Tours (Map p48; ☑023-219268; www.ptmcambodia.com; 200 Monivong Blvd; ⊗8am-5.30pm Mon-Sat) Good bet for outgoing air tickets.

Sophia Travel (Map p42; ☑023-222455; www.sophiyatours.com; 216B St 63) Professional service, good for tickets and tours.

🛈 Getting There & Away

AIR

Many international air services (p339) run to/from Phnom. Domestically, **Cambodia Angkor Air** (Map p42; ☑023-666 6786; www.cambodia angkorair.com; 206A Norodom Blvd) flies four to six times daily to Siem Reap (about US$100, 30 minutes).

BOAT

Fast boats up the Tonlé Sap to Siem Reap and down the Mekong to Chau Doc, Vietnam, operate from the **tourist boat dock** (Map p48; 93 Sisowath Quay) at the eastern end of St 104. Services also run to Chau Doc and the Mekong Delta (p80). Public boats up the Mekong to Kompong Cham and Kratie stopped running years ago.

The fast boats to Siem Reap (US$35, five to six hours) aren't as popular as they used to be. When it costs just US$6 for an air-conditioned bus or US$35 to be bundled on the roof of a boat, it is not hard to see why. It is better to save your boat experience for elsewhere in Cambodia. Several companies have daily services departing at 7am and usually take it in turns to make the run. The first stretch of the journey along the river is scenic, but once the boat hits the lake, the fun is over as it resembles a vast inland sea with not a village in sight. The boats to Siem Reap run from roughly late July to late March (water levels are too low at other times).

LAND
Bus

All major towns in Cambodia are accessible by air-conditioned bus from Phnom Penh. Most buses leave from company offices, which are generally clustered around Psar Thmei or located near the corner of St 106 and Sisowath Quay. Buying tickets in advance is a good idea for peace of mind, although it's not always necessary.

Not all buses are created equal, or priced the same for that matter. Buses run by Capitol Tour and Phnom Penh Sorya are usually among the cheapest; Mekong Express and Giant Ibis buses are somewhat upmarket and pricier.

Most of the long-distance buses drop off and pick up in major towns along the way, such as Kompong Thom en route to Siem Reap, Pursat

---

GETTING TO VIETNAM: PHNOM PENH TO HO CHI MINH CITY

Getting to the border The original Bavet/Moc Bai land crossing between Vietnam and Cambodia has seen steady traffic for two decades. The easiest way to get to Ho Chi Minh City (Saigon) is to catch an international bus (US$8 to US$13, seven hours) from Phnom Penh. We recommend taking a Vietnamese company, such as Sapaco, as it will speed entry into Vietnam in the event of long lines at the border. There are several companies making this trip (p78).

At the border Long lines entering either country are not uncommon, but otherwise it's straightforward provided you purchase a Vietnamese visa in advance.

Moving on If you are not on the international bus, it's not hard to find onward transport to Ho Chi Minh City or elsewhere.

on the way to Battambang, or Kompong Cham en route to Kratie. However, full fare is usually charged anyway.

Another popular bus route is to Ho Chi Minh City (p76).

Capitol Tour (☑023-724104; 14 St 182)

Giant Ibis (Map p48; ☑023-999333; www.giantibis.com; 3 St 106; 🛜) 'VIP' bus and express van specialist. Big bus to Siem Reap has plenty of legroom and dysfunctional wi-fi. A portion of profits go toward giant ibis conservation.

Gold VIP (Map p48; ☑070988888; 3 St 106)

GST (US Liang Express Bus; Map p48; ☑023-218114; 13 St 142)

Long Phuong (Map p42; ☑0973110999; 274 Sihanouk Blvd)

Mekong Express (☑023-427518; www.catmekongexpress.com; 2020 NH5) Has a riverside booking office (Map p48; Sisowath Quay).

Olympic Express (☑092868782; 70 Monireth Blvd)

Phnom Penh Sorya (Map p48; ☑023-210359; Psar Thmei area)

Rith Mony (Map p42; ☑0978889447; St 169) Also has a riverfront terminal (Map p48; ☑017525388; 24 St 102).

Sapaco (Map p42; ☑023-210300; www.sapacotourist.com; Sihanouk Blvd)

Virak Buntham (Kampuchea Angkor Express; Map p48; ☑016786270; St 106) Night bus specialist.

Express Van

Speedy express vans (minibuses) with 12 to 14 seats serve popular destinations like Siem Reap and Sihanoukville. These cut travel times significantly, but they tend to be cramped and often travel at very high speeds – not for the faint of heart. Several of the big bus companies also run vans, most famously Mekong Express. It's a good idea to book express vans in advance.

Express-van companies include the following:

CTT Net (Map p48; ☑023-217217; 223 Sisowath Quay)

Golden Bayon Express (Map p48; ☑023-966968; 3 St 126)

Kampot Express (Map p42; ☑077555123; kampotexress@gmail.com; 2 St 215)

Kim Seng Express (Map p42; ☑012786000; 506 Kampuchea Krom Blvd)

Mex Hong Transport (☑023-6372722) Call for pick-up.

Neak Krorhorm (Map p48; ☑092966669; 4 St 108)

Seila Angkor (Map p48; ☑077888080; 43 St 154)

Share Taxi, Minibus & Pick-up

Share taxis, pick-ups and local minibuses leave Phnom Penh for destinations all over the country. Taxis to Kampot, Kep and Takeo leave from **Psar Dang Kor** (Mao Tse Toung Blvd), while packed local minibuses and taxis for most other places leave from the northwest corner of **Psar Thmei** (Map p48).

Vehicles for the Vietnam border leave from Chbah Ampeau taxi park on the eastern side of Monivong Bridge in the south of town. You may have to wait awhile (possibly until the next day if you arrive in the afternoon) before your vehicle fills up, or else pay for the vacant seats yourself.

DESTINATION	PRICE	DURATION
Battambang	US$55	4½hr
Kampot	US$35	3hr
Kep	US$40	3hr
Koh Kong	US$65	4½hr
Kompong Cham	US$35	2½hr
Kompong Thom	US$45	3hr
Kratie	US$50	5hr
Pursat	US$45	3hr
Siem Reap	US$70	5hr
Sihanoukville	US$50	4hr
Takeo	US$25	1¾hr
Vietnam Border	US$50	3hr

Local minibuses and pick-ups aren't much fun and are best avoided when there are larger air-con buses or faster share taxis available, which is pretty much everywhere. However, they will save you a buck or two if you're pinching pennies.

Train

There are currently no passenger services operating on the Cambodian rail network, but this should be seen as a blessing in disguise, given that the trains are extremely slow, travelling at about 20km/h. Yes, for a few minutes at least, you can outrun the train!

Just for reference, Phnom Penh's train station is located at the western end of St 106 and St 108, in a grand old colonial-era building that is a shambles inside. The railway is being overhauled and has been reopened to cargo services, so there may be the option of passenger services at some point in the future.

🛈 Getting Around

Being such a small city, Phnom Penh is quite easy to get around, although the traffic is getting worse by the year and traffic jams are common around the morning and evening rush hour, particularly around the two main north–south boulevards, Monivong and Norodom.

TRANSPORT FROM PHNOM PENH

Bus

DESTINATION	DURATION	PRICE	COMPANIES	FREQUENCY
Ban Lung	11hr	US$13	PP Sorya, Rith Mony, Thong Ly	morning only
Bangkok	12hr	US$18-23	Mekong Exp, PP Sorya, Virak Buntham	daily per company
Battambang (day)	6hr	US$5-6	GST, PP Sorya, Rith Mony	several per company
Battambang (night)	6hr	US$8-10	Virak Buntham	4 per night
Ho Chi Minh City	7hr	US$8-13	Capitol Tour, Long Phuong, Mekong Exp, PP Sorya, Sapaco, Virak Buntham (night)	several per company until about 3pm
Kampot (direct)	3hr	US$5.50-6	Capitol Tour, Rith Mony	2 daily per company
Kampot (via Kep)	4hr	US$5.50	PP Sorya	7.30am, 9.30am, 2.45pm
Kep	3hr	US$5.25	PP Sorya	7.30am, 9.30am, 2.45pm
Koh Kong	5½hr	US$5	Olympic Exp, PP Sorya, Virak Buntham	2-3 per company to noon
Kompong Cham	3hr	US$5	PP Sorya	hourly to 4pm
Kratie	6-8hr	US$8	PP Sorya	6.45am, 7.15am, 7.30am, 9.30am, 10.30am
Pakse via Don Det	12-14hr	US$28	PP Sorya	6.45am
Poipet (day)	8hr	US$9-11	Capitol Tour, Gold VIP, PP Sorya, Rith Mony	frequent until noon
Poipet (night)	7hr	US$10-11	Gold VIP, Virak Buntham, Rith Mony	1 per company
Preah Vihear City	7hr	US$10	GST, Rith Mony	morning only
Sen Monorom	8hr	US$8	PP Sorya	7.30am
Siem Reap (day)	6hr	US$5-8	most companies	frequent
Siem Reap (VIP)	6hr	US$13	Giant Ibis	7.45am, 8.45am, 12.30pm
Siem Reap (night)	6hr	US$10	Gold VIP, Virak Buntham	6pm, 8pm, 11pm, 12.30am
Sihanoukville	5½hr	US$5-6	Capitol Tour, GST, Mekong Exp, PP Sorya, Rith Mony, Virak Buntham	frequent
Stung Treng	9hr	US$12.50	PP Sorya	6.45am, 7.30am

Express Van

DESTINATION	DURATION	PRICE	COMPANIES	FREQUENCY
Battambang	4½hr	US$10-12	Mekong Exp, Golden Bayon	several per company
Kampot	2hr	US$7-8	Giant Ibis, Kampot Exp, Olympic Exp	3 per company
Kep	2½hr	US$7	Olympic Exp	7.15am, 1.30pm
Sen Monorom	5½hr	US$10	Kim Seng	7am, 7.30am, 11am, 1.30pm
Siem Reap	5hr	US$10-12	Golden Bayon, Mekong Exp, Mex Hong, Neak Krohorm, Olympic Exp, Seila Angkor	3-5 per company
Sihanoukville	4hr	US$10-12	CTT Net, Giant Ibis, Golden Bayon, Mekong Exp, Mex Hong	2-4 per company

TO/FROM THE AIRPORT

Phnom Penh International Airport is 7km west of central Phnom Penh, via Russian Blvd.

An official booth outside the airport arrivals area arranges taxis to the centre for US$9 to US$12; a *remork* costs a flat US$9/7. You can get a *remork* for $US4 and a *moto* for half that if you walk one minute out to the street. Heading to the airport from central Phnom Penh, a taxi/ *remork*/*moto* will cost about US$9/4/2. The journey usually takes about 30 minutes.

BICYCLE

It is possible to hire bicycles at some of the guesthouses around town for about US$1 to US$2 a day, but take a look at the chaotic traffic conditions before venturing forth. Once you get used to the anarchy, it can be a fun way to get around.

CAR & MOTORCYCLE

Exploring Phnom Penh and the surrounding areas on a motorbike is a very liberating experience if you are used to chaotic traffic conditions.

There are numerous motorbike hire places around town. A 100cc Honda costs US$4 to US$7 per day and 250cc dirt bikes run from US$12 to US$30 per day. You'll have to leave your passport – a driver's licence or other form of ID won't do. Remember you usually get what you pay for when choosing a steel steed.

A Cambodia licence isn't a bad idea if you'll be doing extensive riding. Motorbike rental shops can arrange to get you one for about US$40. Otherwise you technically need an international licence to drive in Cambodia (although a small bribe gets you out of most infractions if you don't have one). If you want to purchase insurance (available at motorbike rental shops for about US$22 per month), you'll need an international or Cambodian licence. Remember to lock your bike, as motorbike theft is common.

Car hire is available through travel agencies, guesthouses and hotels in Phnom Penh. Everything from cars (from US$25) to 4WDs (from US$60) are available for travelling around the city, but prices rise if you venture beyond.

In addition to the following popular motorcycle rental shops, Palm Tours (p76) rents motorbikes for US$5 to US$7. The Bike Shop (p40) has excellent 250cc to 600cc bikes for US$30 to US$55 per day, and smaller motorbikes for US$6 per day.

Angkor Motorcycles (Map p48; ☎012722098; 92 St 51) Huge selection of trail bikes (day/ week rentals US$15/100), plus motorbikes at US$5 to US$7 per day.

Harley Tours Cambodia (Map p42; ☎012948529; www.harleycambodia.com) For those looking for a little more muscle on the road, Harley Tours organise Harley rides around Phnom Penh, including overnighters to places like Kompong Cham or Kep. Day rental is available, but prices are similar to luxury-car rental back home.

Little Bikes (Map p48; ☎017329338; 97 St 154) High-quality trail bikes from US$18, and 125cc bikes for US$7/30 per day/week.

Lucky! Lucky! (Map p42; ☎023-212788; 413 Monivong Blvd) Motorbikes are US$4 to US$7 per day, less for multiple days. Trail bikes from US$12.

New! New! (Map p42; ☎012855488; 417 Monivong Blvd) Motorbikes start at US$4 per day, and trail bikes from US$12.

Two Wheels Only (Map p52; ☎012200513; www.twocambodia.com; 34L St 368) Has well-maintained bikes available to rent (motorbike/ trail bike per day US$25/5).

Vannak Bikes Rental (Map p48; 46 St 130) Has high-performance trail bikes up to 600cc for US$15 to US$30 per day, and smaller motorbikes for US$5 to US$7.

CYCLO

Travelling by *cyclo* (pedicab) is a more relaxing way to see the sights in the centre of town, although they don't work well for long distances. For a day of sightseeing, expect to pay around US$10 – find one on your own or negotiate a tour through the Cyclo Centre (p46). For short one-way jaunts costs are similar to *moto* fares. You won't see many cyclos on the road late at night.

MOTO

In areas frequented by foreigners, *moto* drivers generally speak English and sometimes a little French. Elsewhere around town it can be difficult to find anyone who understands where you want to go. Most short trips are about 2000r, although if you want to get from one end of the city to the other, you have to pay up to US$1.

WHAT'S IN A NAME?

For obscure reasons, two Phnom Penh bus companies are known by different names in the provinces: Virak Buntham (known as Kampuchea Angkor Express elsewhere) and GST (known as Liang US Express elsewhere). In this book we use the Phnom Penh name in Phnom Penh, and the local name as appropriate elsewhere. In addition, Rith Mony is still sometimes referred to as Paramount Angkor, its former sister company (now off the road after a series of accidents).

Cambodians never negotiate when taking rides (they just pay what they think is fair) but foreigners should always work out the price in advance, especially with *motodups* who hang out in touristy areas like the riverside or outside luxury hotels. Likewise, night owls taking a *moto* home from popular drinking holes should definitely negotiate to avoid an expensive surprise.

Many of the *moto* drivers who wait outside the popular guesthouses and hotels have good English and are able to act as guides for a daily rate of about US$8 to US$10, depending on the destinations.

REMORK-MOTO

Better known as *tuk-tuks*, *remorks* are motorbikes with carriages and are the main way of getting around Phnom Penh for tourists. Average fares are about double those of *moto* – US$1.50 for short rides around the cente, US$2 to US$2.50 for slightly longer trips. *Remork* drivers will try to charge more for multiple passengers but don't let them – pay per ride not per person (although groups of five or more might pay an extra US$1 or so).

TAXI

Taxis are cheap at 3000r per kilometre but don't expect to flag one down on the street. Call **Global Meter Taxi** (☑ 011311888), **Choice Taxi** (☑ 010888010, 023-888023) or **Taxi Vantha** (☑ 012855000) for a pick-up.

AROUND PHNOM PENH

There are several attractions around Phnom Penh that make good day trips. Koh Dach is the easiest trip and is best done by mountain bike, *moto* or *remork*. The other sights listed here are at least an hour by car and longer still by *moto* or *remork*.

The Angkorian temple of Tonlé Bati, Phnom Tamao Wildlife Rescue Centre and the hilltop pagoda of Phnom Chisor are near each other off NH2. You can easily combine two of these into one trip (all three might be a stretch). These can also be built into a journey south to either Takeo or Kep/Kampot.

Udong, once the capital of Cambodia, is a separate half-day trip and can be combined with a visit to Kompong Chhnang, known for being a 'genuine' Cambodian town. Kirirom National Park lies further afield, about halfway to Sihanoukville off NH4.

Koh Dach   កោះដាច់

Known as 'Silk Island' by foreigners, this is actually a pair of islands lying in the Mekong River about 5km northeast of the Japanese Friendship Bridge. They make for an easy half-day DIY excursion for those who want to experience the 'real Cambodia'. The

---

GETTING TO VIETNAM: PHNOM PENH TO CHAU DOC

The most scenic way to end your travels in Cambodia is to sail the Mekong to Kaam Samnor, about 100km south-southeast of Phnom Penh, cross the border to Vinh Xuong in Vietnam, and proceed to Chau Doc on the Tonlé Bassac River via a small channel or overland. Chau Doc has onward land and river connections to points in the Mekong Delta and elsewhere in Vietnam.

Various companies do trips all the way through to Chau Doc using a single boat or some combination of bus and boat; prices vary according to speed and level of service. **Delta Adventure Co** (Map p48; ☑ 012733191; www.deltaadventure.info; US$23) departs Phnom Penh at 8am, **Capitol Tour** (Map p42; ☑ 023-217627; 14 St 182; US$23) departs at 8am and **Hang Chau** (Map p48; ☑ 0888787871; US$24) departs at noon, while the more upmarket and slightly faster **Blue Cruiser** (Map p48; ☑ 023-6333666; www.bluecruiser. com; US$35) pulls out at 1.30pm. **Victoria Hotels** (Map p48; www.victoriahotelsasia.com; US$97) also has a boat making several runs a week between Phnom Penh and its Victoria Chau Doc Hotel. These companies take about four hours, including a slow border check, and use a single boat to Chau Doc. Backpacker guesthouses and tour companies offer cheaper bus/boat combo trips. All boats depart from Phnom Penh's **tourist boat dock** (93 Sisowath Quay).

You can go it alone, but it won't save you much money (if any). Make your own way overland to Neak Luong, on the Mekong east of Phnom Penh, and look for the pier about 300m south of the ferry landing on the west bank of the Mekong. From the pier a slow morning passenger boat departs around 9am for Kaam Samnor. Or hire a speedboat (US$50, one hour). In Vinh Xuong, local Vietnamese transport waits to transfer you to Chau Doc, an hour away.

hustle and bustle of Phnom Penh feels light years away here.

The name derives from the preponderance of silk weavers who inhabit the islands. When you arrive by ferry, you'll undoubtedly be approached by one or more smiling women who speak a bit of English and will invite you to their house to observe weavers in action and – they hope – buy some *kramas,* sarongs or other silk items. If you are in the market for silk, you might follow them and have a look. Otherwise, feel free to smile back and politely decline their offer – you'll see plenty of weavers as you journey around the islands.

Other attractions include a few colourful modern temple complexes and the rural scenery.

❶ Getting There & Around

Remork drivers offer half-day tours to Koh Dach; US$20 should do it (less if you just want to be dropped off at the ferry), but they have been known to charge as much as US$40. The daily **boat tours** (per person US$10) from the tourist boat dock, departing at 8.30am, 9.30am and 1pm, are another option (minimum four people).

Otherwise, hire a mountain bike or motorbike and go it alone. Ferries cross the Mekong in three places and cost 500r per person, plus 500r per bike. The southernmost ferry crossing is the most convenient; it takes you to the larger, closer island. Cross the Japanese Bridge and follow NH6 for 4km, then turn right just before the Medical Supply Pharmaceutical Enterprise. You immediately hit a small dirt road that parallels the Mekong. Turn left and follow it north for about 500m until you see the ferry crossing.

Over on the larger island, you are just a short cycle ride to a bridge that links the two islands. The smaller island (technically named Koh Okhna Tey, or Mekong Island) has better infrastructure, including a paved main road; the larger island is more rustic and remote feeling, especially as you venture north.

Udong · ឧត្តុង្គ

Udong (the Victorious) served as the capital of Cambodia under several sovereigns between 1618 and 1866, during which time 'victorious' was an optimistic epithet, as Cambodia was in terminal decline. A number of kings, including King Norodom, were crowned here. The main attractions today are the twin humps of **Phnom Udong**, which have several stupas on them. Both ends of the ridge have good views of the Cambodian countryside dotted with innumerable sugar palm trees.

The larger main ridge – the one you'll hit first if approaching from NH5 – is known as **Phnom Preah Reach Throap** (Hill of the Royal Fortune). It is so named because a 16th-century Khmer king is said to have hidden the national treasury here during a war with the Thais.

Ascending the main, monkey-lined north stairway from the parking area, the first structure you come to at the top of the ridge is a modern temple that comtained a relic of the Buddha, believed to be an eyebrow hair and fragments of teeth and bones. The relics were brazenly stolen in late 2013. Follow the path behind this stupa along the ridge and you'll come to a line of three large stupas. The first (northwesternmost) is **Damrei Sam Poan**, built by King Chey Chetha II (r 1618–26) for the ashes of his predecessor, King Soriyopor. The second stupa, **Ang Doung**, is decorated with coloured tiles; it was built in 1891 by King Norodom to house the ashes of his father, King Ang Duong (r 1845–59), but some say King Ang Duong was in fact buried next to the Silver Pagoda in Phnom Penh. The last stupa is **Mak Proum**, the final resting place of King Monivong (r 1927–41). Decorated with *garudas* (mythical half-man, half-bird creatures), floral designs and elephants, it has four faces on top.

Continuing along the path beyond Mak Proum, you'll pass a stone *vihara* with a cement roof and a seated Buddha inside (looking resplendent in a sailor's cap when we dropped in), then arrive at a clearing dotted by a gaggle of structures, including three small *vihara* and a stupa. The first *vihara* you come to is **Vihear Prak Neak**, its cracked walls topped with a tin roof. Inside this *vihara* is a seated Buddha who is guarded by a *naga* (*prak neak* means 'protected by a *naga*'). The second structure also has a seated Buddha inside. The third structure is **Vihear Preah Keo**, a cement-roofed structure that contains a statue of Preah Ko, the sacred bull; the original statue was carried away by the Thais long ago. Beyond this, near the stupa, red and black mountain lions guard the entrance to a modern brick-walled *vihara*.

Continue southeast along a lotus-flower-lined concrete path to the most impressive structure on Phnom Preah Reach Throap, **Vihear Preah Ath Roes**. The *vihara* and an enormous seated Buddha, dedicated in

1911 by King Sisowath, were blown up by the Khmer Rouge in 1977. The *vihara,* supported by eight enormous columns and topped by a soaring tin roof, was recently rebuilt, as was the 20m high Buddha.

At the base of the main (northern) staircase leading up to Phnom Preah Reach Throap, near the restaurants, is a **memorial** to the victims of Pol Pot. It contains the bones of some of the people who were buried in approximately 100 mass graves, each containing about a dozen bodies. Instruments of torture were unearthed along with the bones when a number of the pits were disinterred in 1981 and 1982. Just north of the memorial is a pavilion decorated with graphic murals depicting Khmer Rouge atrocities.

Southeast of Phnom Preah Reach Throap, the smaller ridge has two structures and several stupas on top. **Ta San Mosque** faces westward towards Mecca. Across the plains to the south of the mosque you can see **Phnom Vihear Leu**, a small hill on which a vihara (temple sanctuary) stands between two white poles. To the right of the *vihara* is a building used as a prison under Pol Pot's rule. To the left of the *vihara* and below it is a pagoda known as **Arey Ka Sap**.

Phnom Udong really fills up with locals at weekends but is quiet during the week. Admission is free but myriad beggars and vendors will do their best to get money out of you.

🛏 Sleeping & Eating

The sprawling and impressive **Cambodia Vipassana Dhura Buddhist Meditation Centre** (✆contact Mr Um Sovann 016883090; www.cambodiavipassanacenter.com) is near the base of the western staircase up Phnom

Preah Reach Throap. Foreigners are welcome to practise meditation here with experienced monks or nuns for one or several days. Meditation sessions are daily from 7am to 9pm and from 2pm to 5pm. In between you can hang out in the library, which contains scores of books on Buddhism, not to mention an impressive collection of pirated Lonely Planet books. The en-suite guest rooms are fairly comfortable by monastic standards, albeit sans mattresses (wicker mats are as good as it gets). You'll be fed breakfast and lunch, but no dinner. There is no fixed price for a meditative retreat here, so donate according to your means; US$25 per day would be considered about average. Meditation sessions are free.

There are scores of food stalls around the bustling main parking area at the base of the northern staircase.

ℹ Getting There & Away

Udong is 37km from the capital. To get there take a Phnom Penh Sorya bus bound for Kompong Chhnang (10,000r, one hour to Udong). It will drop you off at the access road to Phnom Udong, and from there it's 3km (4000r by *moto*). Other bus companies also make the trip to Udong. To return to Phnom Penh flag down a bus on NH5 or take a *moto* (US$6 to US$10, depending on your haggling skills).

If going it alone, head north out of Phnom Penh on NH5 and turn left (south) at a prominent archway between the 36km and 37km markers.

A taxi for the day trip from Phnom Penh will cost around US$40. *Moto* drivers also run people to Udong for about US$15 or so for the day, but compared with the bus this isn't the most pleasant way to go, as the road is pretty busy and very dusty.

THE SHOOTING RANGES

Shooting ranges have long been a popular activity for gung-ho travellers visiting Cambodia. Cambodia's lack of law enforcement and culture of impunity allowed visitors to do pretty much anything they wanted in the bad old days. A number of military bases near Phnom Penh were transformed into shooting ranges and rapidly became popular with tourists wanting to try their luck with an AK-47, M-60 or B-40 grenade launcher. The government periodically launched crackdowns, but the business continued largely unabated.

And so the show goes on. The most popular one is located just beyond the go-cart track in Kambol district off NH4. Visitors can try out a range of weapons, but most of the machine guns work out at about US$1 a bullet. Handguns are available at the lower end, while at the other extreme it is possible to try shooting a B-40 rocket-propelled grenade launcher (US$350).

Tonlé Bati ទន្លេបាទី

Tonlé Bati (admission US$3) is the collective name for a pair of old Angkorian-era temples and a popular lakeside picnic area. It's worth a detour if you are on the way to Phnom Tamao and Phnom Chisor. You can eat at one of several restaurants here and hire an innertube to float around the lake for 2000r. Just avoid Tonlé Bati at weekends, when it's mobbed by locals.

◎ Sights

Ta Prohm HINDU TEMPLE

(តាព្រហ្ម) The laterite temple of Ta Prohm was built by King Jayavarman VII (r 1181–1219) on the site of an ancient 6th-century Khmer shrine. The main sanctuary consists of five chambers, each containing a modern buddha. The facades of the chambers contain intricate and well-preserved bas-reliefs. In the central chamber is a linga (phallic symbol) that shows signs of the destruction wrought by the Khmer Rouge.

Yeay Peau HINDU TEMPLE

(យាយពៅ) Yeay Peau temple, named after King Prohm's mother, is 150m north of Ta Prohm in the grounds of a modern pagoda. Legend has it that Peau gave birth to a son, Prohm. When Prohm discovered his father was King Preah Ket Mealea, he set off to live with the king. After a few years, he returned to his mother but did not recognise her and, taken by her beauty, asked her to become his wife. He refused to believe Peau's protests that she was his mother. To put off his advances, she suggested a contest to avoid the impending marriage. For the outcome of the contest, see p256.

❶ Getting There & Away

The access road heading to Tonlé Bati is signposted on the right on NH2, 33km south of Independence Monument in Phnom Penh. The entrance to the complex is 1.8km from the highway.

Most people hire private transport to get here. Figure on US$12/25 return for a *moto/remork* from Phnom Penh. Add US$5 to combine with Phnom Tamao, and more still to throw Phnom Chisor into the mix.

Another option is to take a Takeo-bound Phnom Penh Sorya bus (four daily – shoot for the 7am or the 10.30am) and jump off at the access road. Returning to Phnom Penh can be problematic, however. The best advice is to buy a ticket in advance on Sorya's Takeo–Phnom Penh bus. Otherwise, hire a *moto*.

Phnom Tamao Wildlife Rescue Centre
ភ្នំតាម៉ៅ (សួនសត្វ)

This wonderful wildlife sanctuary (adult/child US$5/2; ⊙ 8am-5pm) for rescued animals is home to gibbons, sun bears, elephants, tigers, lions, deer, ginormous pythons and a massive bird enclosure. They were all taken from poachers or abusive owners and receive care and shelter here as part of a sustainable breeding program. Wherever possible animals are released back into the wild once they have recovered. The centre operates breeding programs for a number of globally threatened species.

The sanctuary occupies a vast site south of the capital and its animals are kept in excellent conditions by Southeast Asian standards, with plenty of room to roam in enclosures that have been improved and expanded over the years with help from international wildlife NGOs. Spread out as it is, it feels like a zoo crossed with a safari park.

The centre is home to the world's largest captive collections of pileated gibbons and Malayan sun bears, as well as other rarities such as Siamese crocodiles and greater adjutant storks. Other popular enclosures include huge areas for the large tiger population, and there are elephants that sometimes take part in activities such as painting. You'll also find a walk-through area with macaques and deer, and a huge aviary.

Cambodia's wildlife is usually very difficult to spot, as larger mammals inhabit remote areas of the country. Phnom Tamao is the perfect place to discover more about the incredible variety of animals in Cambodia. If you don't like zoos, you might not like this wildlife sanctuary, but remember that these animals have been rescued from traffickers and poachers and need a home. Visitors that come here will be doing their own small bit to help in the protection and survival of Cambodia's varied and wonderful wildlife.

☞ Tours

Free the Bears TOUR

(Map p42; www.freethebears.org) Free the Bears operates a Bear Keeper for a Day program to allow students and adults with a genuine interest in wildlife a better understanding of the Asian black bear and Malayan sun bear. Participants have no contact with the bears, but spend the day behind the scenes of the sanctuary learning the ins and outs of caring for the 130-plus bears being looked after here. One- to 12-week volunteer positions are also available.

Wildlife Tours TOUR
(☏095970175; wildlifetourspt@wildlifealliance.org; minimum donation US$150) Wildlife Alliance has created an exciting full-day interactive tour to raise funds for Phnom Tamao. Donors get to interact with a variety of rescued animals, including elephants, macaques and gibbons, and get up close with tigers, crocodiles and what is possibly the world's only captive hairy-nosed otter. Tours include walks with elephants in the forest and you get to feed various baby animals in the sanctuary's nursery, which is normally off-limits to the public. All proceeds go toward the rescue and care of wildlife at Phnom Tamao.

Betelnut Jeep Tours TOUR
(Map p48; ☏012619924; www.betelnuttours.com; per person US$40) Betelnut Jeep Tours offers guided open-top jeep trips to Phnom Tamao from Tuesday to Saturday, departing at 9.45am from the Lazy Gecko Guesthouse (p53) in Phnom Penh. The price includes admission, lunch and a *krama* (scarf) to protect against the elements.

❶ Getting There & Away

The access road to Phnom Tamao is clearly signposted on the right 6.5km south of the turnoff to Tonlé Bati on NH2. The sanctuary is 5km from the highway on an incredibly dusty road lined with elderly beggars. If coming by bus ask to be let off at the turnoff, where *motos* await to whisk you to the sanctuary.

Phnom Chisor ភ្នំជីស្

A temple from the Angkorian era, **Phnom Chisor** (admission US$2, levied at the summit) is set upon a solitary hill in Takeo Province, offering superb views of the countryside. Try to get to Phnom Chisor early in the morning or late in the afternoon, as it is an uncomfortable climb in the heat of the midday sun.

The main temple stands on the eastern side of the hilltop. Constructed of laterite and brick with carved sandstone lintels, the complex is surrounded by the partially ruined walls of a 2.5m-wide gallery with windows. Inscriptions found here date from the 11th century, when this site was known as Suryagiri.

On the plain to the west of Phnom Chisor are the sanctuaries of **Sen Thmol**, just below Phnom Chisor, and **Sen Ravang**, plus the former sacred pond of **Tonlé Om**. All three features form a straight line from Phnom Chisor in the direction of Angkor. During rituals held here 900 years ago, the king, his Brahmans and their entourage would climb a monumental 400 steps to Suryagiri from this direction.

If you haven't got the stamina for an overland adventure to Preah Vihear or Phnom Bayong (near Takeo), this is the next best thing for a temple with a view. Near the main temple is a modern Buddhist *vihara* that is used by resident monks.

❶ Getting There & Away

The eastward-bound access road to Phnom Chisor is signposted (in Khmer) on the left 12km south of the Phnom Tamao turnoff on NH2. The temple is 4.5km from the highway – *motos* wait at the turnoff. To get here follow the directions for Tonlé Bati and Phnom Tamao, adding yet another few dollars if you are hiring private transport.

Kirirom National Park ឧទ្យានជាតិគិរីរម្យ

You can really get away from it all at this lush elevated **park** (admission US$5) a two-hour drive southwest of Phnom Penh. Winding trails lead through pine forests to cascading wet-season waterfalls and cliffs with amazing views of the Cardamom Mountains, and there's some great mountain-biking to be done if you're feeling adventurous.

From the NH4 highway it's 10km on a sealed road to a small village near the park entrance. From the village you have two choices: the left fork takes you 50m to the park entrance and then 17km up a fairly steep sealed road to the unmanned **Kirirom Information Centre** inside the park proper; the right fork takes you 10km along the perimeter of the park on a dirt road to **Chambok commune**, site of an excellent **community based ecotourism** (CBET; ☏012698529, 012938920; mlup@online.com.kh; adult/child US$3/1) program. These are two vastly different experiences, and they are nowhere near each other, so it's recommended to devote a day to each.

Park Proper

Up in the park proper, you'll find myriad walking trails and dirt roads that lead to small wet-season waterfalls, lakes, wats and abandoned buildings, but you'll need a map or a guide to navigate them. There's a great map of the park trails and roads made by a Phnom Penh-based mountain-bike enthusiast – we bought one for US$3 at the Kirirom Guesthouse & Restaurant.

Mr Mik (☑015810271) is a park ranger and guide who can usually be found at the barbecue shacks near the busy main parking area, about 500m northeast of the information centre. For US$10 he can take you on a two-hour hike up to Phnom Dat Chivit (End of Life Mountain), where an abrupt cliff face offers an unbroken view of the Elephant Mountains and Cardamom Mountains to the west.

Chambok Commune

The main attraction at the Chambok CBET site is a 4km hike to a series of three waterfalls (no guide required). The second waterfall has a swimming hole. The third one is an impressive 40m-high waterfall. Bikes are available for US$1.50 but won't get you very far as the trail deteriorates fairly quickly. Other attractions include traditional ox-cart rides, a bat cave and guided nature walks (guides cost US$15 per day).

🛏 Sleeping & Eating

Chambok Homestays   HOMESTAY **$**
(☑012938920; per person US$3, plus US$3 per home-cooked meal) Multiple homestays are available in Chambok commune proper as part of the CBET program.

Romantic Waterfall & Cafe   GUESTHOUSE **$**
(☑012733694; www.romantic-cafe.org; r US$8) About 1km south of Chambok commune, Romantic has a few basic rooms and a Khmer restaurant – be sure to pre-order.

Kirirom Guesthouse &
Restaurant   GUESTHOUSE **$$**
(☑012957 700; r US$20) This bare-bones guesthouse, nestled amid pine trees, is the only place to stay up in the park proper. It's cold at night so bring something warm to wear. Look for the sign to the guesthouse on the left about 3km south of the information centre.

Kirirom Hillside Resort   RESORT **$$**
(☑016303888, in Phnom Penh 023-216471; www.kiriromresort.com; room/bungalow from US$50/65; ✳🛜🏊) Much more upscale, the Kirirom Hillside Resort is located down the hill near the park entrance and the junction to Chambok commune. Attractive if dysfunctional Scandinavian-style bungalows, some with glorious balconies overlooking a small lake, dot the sprawling grounds. There's a nice pool, a hit-or-miss restaurant, a zoo and even a plastic-dinosaur park. Beware: advertised services like horseback riding, wi-fi and mountain-bike rental are rarely available.

ℹ Getting There & Away

Kirirom National Park is accessed from the village of Treng Trayern, which straddles the NH4 87km southwest of Phnom Penh and 139km northeast of Sihanoukville. A taxi from either city is about US$60, or have a bus drop you off at the turnoff in Treng Trayern, where *motos* demand a stiff $5 per person to get you to the entrance (a bit more to Chambok commune, and still more to ascend into the park proper). Bringing your own transport is highly recommended.

Siem Reap

☑ 063 / POP (TOWN) 135,000 / AREA (PROVINCE) 10,299 SQ KM

Best Places to Eat

➡ Chanrey Tree (p105)

➡ Cuisine Wat Damnak (p106)

➡ Green Star (p105)

➡ Haven (p103)

➡ Marum (p103)

Best Places to Stay

➡ HanumanAlaya (p99)

➡ Ivy Guesthouse 2 (p95)

➡ La Résidence d'Angkor (p97)

➡ Soria Moria Hotel (p98)

➡ Steung Siem Reap Hotel (p96)

Why Go?

The life-support system for the temples of Angkor, Siem Reap (*see*-em ree-*ep;* សៀមរាប) was always destined for great things. It has reinvented itself as the epicentre of chic Cambodia, with everything from backpacker party pads to hip hotels, world-class wining and dining, and sumptuous spas.

This is good news for the long-suffering Khmers riding the wave, but it can make the town a little bling in places. Authentic it is not, although just a short distance away lies Siem Reap Province and the real Cambodia of rural beauty. Explore floating villages and rare-bird sanctuaries or just cycle (or quad bike or pony trek) through the paddies as an antidote to the bustle of town.

Angkor is a place to be savoured, not rushed, and this is the base to plan your adventures. Still think three days at the temples is enough? Think again, with Siem Reap on the doorstep.

When to Go
Siem Reap

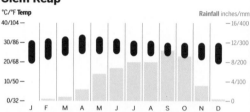

Nov–Mar Peak season; avoid if you want to dodge crowds. Giant Puppet Parade in Feb.

Apr–May Can be shockingly hot, which makes exploring hard work and the countryside barren.

Jun–Oct Wet season; town centre may be under water for long periods in October.

History

Siem Reap was little more than a village when French explorers discovered Angkor in the 19th century. With the return of Angkor to Cambodian – or should that be French – control in 1907, Siem Reap began to grow, absorbing the first wave of tourists. The Grand Hotel d'Angkor opened its doors in 1929 and the temples of Angkor remained one of Asia's leading draws until the late 1960s, luring luminaries such as Char-

lie Chaplin and Jackie Kennedy. With the advent of war and the Khmer Rouge, Siem Reap entered a long slumber from which it only began to awaken in the mid-1990s.

Tourism is the lifeblood of Siem Reap and, without careful management, it could become Siem Reapolinos, the not-so-Costa-del-Culture of Southeast Asia. However, there are promising signs that developers are learning from the mistakes that have blighted other regional hot spots, with

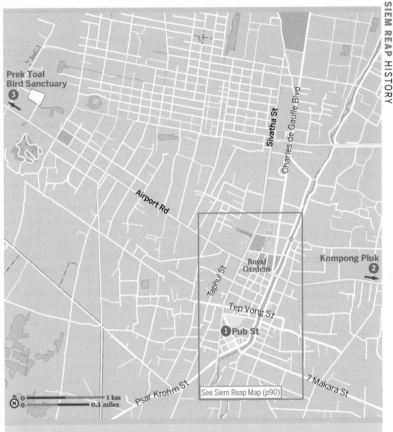

Siem Reap Highlights

1 Dive into **Pub St** (p102), the drinking capital of Siem Reap, and discover nearby restaurants and bars

2 Explore the flooded forest of **Kompong Pluk** (p115), an incredible village of bamboo skyscrapers

3 Encounter some of the world's rarest large water birds at **Prek Toal Bird Sanctuary** (p114)

4 Learn the secrets of Khmer cuisine with a **cooking course** (p93),

the perfect way to impress friends back home

5 Experience some of the **activities** (p92) on offer from horse riding to quad biking or Angkor-themed mini-golf to links golf

restrictions on hotel height and bus size. Either way, Angkor is centre stage on the world travel map right now, and there's no going back for its supply line, Siem Reap.

◉ Sights

Visitors come to Siem Reap to see the temples of Angkor. The sights in and around the town pale in comparison, but they are a good diversion for those who find themselves templed out after a few days. That said, some of the best sights are...yet more temples. The modern pagodas around Siem Reap offer an interesting contrast to the ancient sandstone structures of Angkor.

★ **Angkor National Museum**   MUSEUM
(សារមន្ទីរអង្គរ; Map p90; ☑063-966601; www. angkornationalmuseum.com; 968 Charles de Gaulle Blvd; adult/child under 1.2m US$12/6; ☺8.30am-6pm, to 6.30pm 1 Oct-30 Apr) Looming large on the road to Angkor is the Angkor National Museum, a state-of-the-art showpiece on the Khmer civilisation and the majesty of Angkor. Displays are themed by era, religion and royalty as visitors move through the impressive galleries.

After a short presentation, visitors enter the Zen-like 'Gallery of a Thousand Buddhas', which has a fine collection of images. Other collections include the pre-Angkorian periods of Funan and Chenla, the great Khmer kings, Angkor Wat, Angkor Thom and the inscriptions.

Presentations include touch-screen video, epic commentary and the chance to experience a panoramic sunrise at Angkor Wat, but for all the technology there seems less sculpture on display than in the National Museum (p35) in Phnom Penh. However, it remains a very useful experience for first-time visitors to put the story of Angkor and the Khmer empire in context before exploring the temples. The US$12 admission fee is a little high, given that US$20 buys admission to all the temples at Angkor. Visitors also have to pay a US$2 camera fee, but can't snap everywhere, and an audio tour is available for US$3. Attached to the museum is a 'Cultural Mall', lined with shops, galleries and cafes, but this hasn't really taken off and sees few visitors.

Les Chantiers Écoles   SCHOOL
(កសិដ្ឋានស្ងួយត្រី; Map p90; www.artisansdangkor .com; ☺7.30am-5.30pm, silk farm 7am-5pm) 🕐**FREE** Siem Reap is the epicentre of the drive to revitalise Cambodian traditional culture, which was dealt such a harsh blow by the Khmer Rouge and the years of instability that followed its rule. Les Chantiers Écoles is a school specialising in teaching wood- and stone-carving techniques, traditional silk painting, lacquerware and more to impoverished youngsters.

On the premises the school has a beautiful shop called Artisans d'Angkor (p110), which sells everything from stone and wood reproductions of Angkorian-era statues to household furnishings. Free guided tours are available daily from 7.30am to 5.30pm to learn more about traditional techniques. Tucked down a side road, the school is well signposted from Sivatha St.

There's also a second shop opposite Angkor Wat in the Angkor Cafe building, and

---

THE CAMBODIA LANDMINE MUSEUM

Established by DIY de-miner Aki Ra, the **Cambodia Landmine Museum** (☑012 598951; www.cambodialandminemuseum.org; admission US$2; ☺7.30am-5pm) is very popular with travellers thanks to its informative displays on the curse of landmines in Cambodia. The museum includes an extensive collection of mines, mortars, guns and weaponry used during the civil war. The site includes a mock minefield so that visitors can attempt to spot the deactivated mines. Not only a weapon of war, landmines are a weapon against peace, and proceeds from the museum are ploughed into mine awareness campaigns and support a rehabilitation centre and training facility. The museum is about 25km from Siem Reap in Banteay Srei and is easily combined with a visit to Banteay Srei temple, about 6km beyond.

For those wanting to learn more about the after-effects of an amputation, it is possible to visit the **Physical Rehabilitation Centre** (Map p90; ☺8am-noon & 2-5pm Mon-Fri), run by **Handicap International** (www.handicapinternational.be). There are informative displays including a variety of homemade prosthetics that it has replaced with international-standard artificial limbs, plus it's possible to meet some of the locals receiving assistance here.

outlets at Phnom Penh and Siem Reap international airports. Some profits from sales go back into funding the school and bringing more teenagers into the training program, although the majority shareholder (50%) is now Société Concessionaire d'Aeroport (SCA), a privately owned, French-run airport-management company.

Les Chantiers Écoles also maintains a **silk farm** (⊙ 7.30am-5.30pm), which produces some of the best work in the country, including clothing, interior-design products and accessories. All stages of the production process can be seen here, from the cultivation of mulberry trees through the nurturing of silk worms to the dyeing and weaving of silk. Free tours are available daily between 7am and 5pm and there is a free shuttle bus departing from Les Chantiers Écoles at 9.30am and 1.30pm. The farm is about 16km west of Siem Reap, just off the road to Sisophon in the village of Puok.

Khmer Ceramics Centre ARTS CENTRE
(មជ្ឈមណ្ឌលកុលាលភាជន៍; Map p90; ☑ 017 843014; www.khmerceramics.com; Charles de Gaulle Blvd; ⊙ 8am-7.30pm) 🖉 Located on the road to the temples, this ceramics centre is dedicated to reviving the Khmer tradition of pottery, which was an intricate art during the time of Angkor. It's possible to visit and try your hand at the potter's wheel, and courses in traditional techniques are available from US$15 to US$25.

Shadow Puppets SHADOW PUPPETS
The creation of leather *sbei tuoi* (shadow puppets) is a traditional Khmer art form, and the figures make a memorable souvenir. Characters include gods and demons from the *Reamker,* as well as exquisite elephants with intricate armour. These are a very Cambodian keepsake.

The **House of Peace Association** (Map p116), about 4km down NH6 on the way to the airport, makes these puppets; small pieces start at US$15, while larger ones can be as much as US$150. A second workshop is located at Wat Preah Inkosei. It's possible to watch a shadow-puppet show at La Noria Restaurant (p108).

Miniature Replicas
of Angkor's Temples MINIATURES
(Map p90; admission US$1.50) One of the more quirky places in town is the garden of a local master sculptor, which houses miniature replicas of Angkor Wat, the Bayon, Banteay Srei and other temples. It is a bluffer's way

to get that aerial shot of Angkor without chartering a helicopter, although the astute might question the presence of oversized insects in the shot.

There is also a display of scale miniatures at Preah Ko Temple.

Cambodian Cultural Village CULTURAL VILLAGE
(Map p116; ☑ 063-963836; www.cambodian culturalvillage.com; Airport Rd; adult/child under 1.1m US$9/free; ⊙ 8am-7pm) It may be kitsch, it may be kooky, but it's very popular with Cambodians and provides a diversion for families travelling with children. This is the Cambodian Cultural Village, which tries to represent all of Cambodia in a whirlwind tour of recreated houses and villages.

The visit begins with a wax museum and includes homes of the Cham, Chinese, Kreung and Khmer people, as well as miniature replicas of landmark buildings in Cambodia. There are dance shows and performances throughout the day, but it still doesn't add up to a turn-on for most foreign visitors, unless they have the kids in tow. It's located about midway between Siem Reap and the airport.

Angkor Butterfly Centre WILDLIFE RESERVE
(សួនមេអំបៅបណ្ដាយស្រី; ☑ 097 852 7852; www. angkorbutterfly.com; adult/child US$4/2; ⊙ 9am-5pm) 🖉 The Angkor Butterfly Centre is a worthwhile place to include on a trip to Banteay Srei and the Cambodia Landmine Museum. The largest fully enclosed butterfly centre in southeast Asia, it has more than 30 species of Cambodian butterflies fluttering about. It is a good experience for children, as they can see the whole process from egg to caterpillar to cocoon to butterfly.

The centre is trying to provide a sustainable living for the rural poor and most of the butterflies are farmed around Phnom Kulen. It's located about 7km before Banteay Srei temple on the left-hand side of the road.

Wat Bo BUDDHIST TEMPLE
(វត្តបូ; Map p90; ⊙ 6am-6pm) This is one of the town's oldest temples and has a collection of well-preserved wall paintings from the late 19th century depicting the *Reamker,* Cambodia's interpretation of the *Ramayana.*

Wat Preah Inkosei BUDDHIST TEMPLE
(វត្តព្រះឥន្ទ្រកោសិយ៍; Map p116; ⊙ 6am-6pm) This wat is built on the site of an early Angkorian brick temple north of town, which still stands today at the rear of the compound.

SIEM REAP SIGHTS

Siem Reap

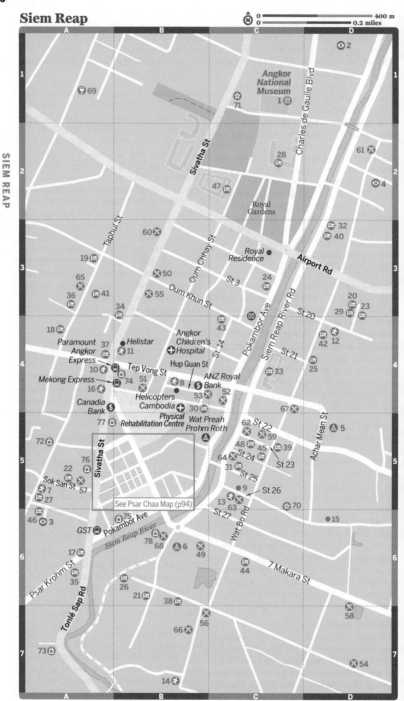

Siem Reap

SIEM REAP SIGHTS

Wat Athvea
BUDDHIST TEMPLE

(វត្តអថ្វា; Map p120; ⊘6am-6pm) South of the city centre, Wat Athvea is an attractive pagoda on the site of an ancient temple. The old temple is still in very good condition and sees far fewer visitors than the main temples in the Angkor area, making it a peaceful spot in the late afternoon.

Wat Thmei
BUDDHIST TEMPLE

(វត្តថ្មី; Map p116; ⊘6am-6pm) On the left fork of the road to Angkor Wat, Wat Thmei has a small memorial stupa containing the skulls and bones of victims of the Khmer Rouge. It also has plenty of young monks eager to practise their English.

Wat Dam Nak BUDDHIST TEMPLE

(វត្តដំណាក់; Map p90; ⊙6am-6pm) Formerly a royal palace during the reign of King Siso-wath, hence the name *dam nak* (palace), to-day the structure is home to the Centre for Khmer Studies (www.khmerstudies.org), an independent institution promoting a great-er understanding of Khmer culture, with a drop-in research library on site.

Activities

There is an incredible array of activities on offer in Siem Reap, ranging from predict-able swimming pools, spa centres and golf courses right through to less predictable horse riding, quad biking and an Angkor-themed mini-golf course. Don't forget to include a visit to the Angkor Centre for Conservation of Biodiversity (p154) out near Kbal Spean, one of the more remote Ang-korian sites.

It's hot work clambering about the tem-ples and there's no better way to wind down than with a dip in a swimming pool. Pay by the day at most hotels for use of the pool and/or gym, ranging from just US$5 at some of the midrange hotels to US$20 at the five-star palaces. More and more of the cheaper hotels and resorts are putting in pools and this can be a worthwhile splash for weary travellers. Locals like to swim in the waters of the Western Baray at the weekend.

Foot massage is a big hit in Siem Reap – not surprising given all those steep stair-ways at the temples. There are half a dozen or more places on the strip running north-west of Psar Chaa offering a massage for about US$6 to US$8 an hour. Some are more authentic than others, so dip your toe in first before selling your sole.

For an alternative foot massage, brave the waters of Dr Fish: dip your feet into a pad-dling pool full of cleaner fish, which nibble away at your dead skin. It's heaven for some, tickly as hell for others. The original was in the Angkor Night Market, but copycats have sprung up all over town, including a dozen or so tanks around Pub St and Psar Chaa.

Angkor Golf Resort GOLF

(Map p116; ☑063-761139; www.angkor-golf.com; green fees US$115) This world-class course was designed by celebrated British golfer Nick Faldo. Fees rise to US$175 with clubs, caddies, carts and all.

Angkor Putt MINI GOLF

(☑012 302330; www.angkorwatputt.com; adult US$5, child US$4; ⊙7.30am-11pm) Crazy golf to the Brits among us, this is a homegrown con-trast with the big golf courses out of town. Navigate mini temples and creative obstacles for 14 holes. Win a beer for a hole in one.

Bodia Spa SPA

(Map p94; ☑063-761593; www.bodia-spa.com; Pithnou St; ⊙10am-midnight) A sophisticated spa near Psar Chaa offering a full range of scrubs, rubs and natural remedies, including its own line of herbal products.

Bodytune SPA

(Map p94; ☑063-764141; www.bodytune.co.th; 293 Pokambor Ave; ⊙10am-10pm) A lavish outpost of a popular Thai spa, this is a fine place to relax and unwind on the riverfront.

Frangipani Spa SPA

(Map p90; ☑063-964391; www.frangipanisiem reap.com; 615 Hup Guan St; ⊙10am-10pm) This delightful hideaway offers massage and a whole range of spa treatments.

FLIGHT OF THE GIBBON ANGKOR

New in 2013, Angkor is the ultimate backdrop for a zipline experience in Asia. Flight of the Gibbon Angkor (☑0969999101; www.treetopasia.com; near Ta Nei Temple, Angkor; per person US$99; ⊙7am-5pm) is located inside the Angkor protected area and the course includes 10 ziplines, 21 treetop platforms, four skybridges and an abseil finish. There is a panoramic refreshment stop at the halfway stage and highlights include a tandem line for couples. Safety is a priority and high-flyers are permanently clipped to lines via cara-biners, with clear English instruction throughout. A conservation element is included in the project with a pair of gibbons released in the surrounding forest and a plan for more introductions in the future. The price includes a transfer to any Siem Reap hotel, plus a lunch before or after the trip near Sra Srang. Located near Ta Nei temple, it's a great new addition to the activities on offer around Siem Reap and Angkor. Watch a Lonely Planet video of the experience at www.youtube.com/watch?v=UJzEtKoITrg.

SIEM REAP FOR CHILDREN

Siem Reap is a great city for children these days thanks to a range of activities beyond the temples. Many of the temples themselves will appeal to older children, particularly the Indiana Jones atmosphere of Ta Prohm and Beng Mealea, the sheer size and scale of Angkor Wat and the weird faces at the Bayon.

Other activities that might be popular include boat trips on the Tonlé Sap to visit other-worldly villages, swimming at a hotel or resort, exploring the countryside on horseback or quad bike, goofing around at the Cambodian Cultural Village, playing mini-golf at the Angkor Putt, exploring the Angkor Butterfly Centre, or just enjoying the cafes and restaurants of Siem Reap at a leisurely pace. Ice-cream shops might be popular, if a little naughty, while the local barbecue restaurants are always enjoyably interactive for older children.

Jungle Junction (7 Makara St; ⊙11.30am-10pm) is specifically aimed at children with indoor and outdoor playgrounds and a small cinema. For big kids, there is a great little restaurant and bar to pass the time.

Happy Ranch
HORSE RIDING

(Map p116; ☑012 920002; www.thehappyranch. com; 1hr/half-day US$25/56) Forget the Wild West and try your hand at riding in the Wild East. Happy Ranch offers the chance to explore Siem Reap on horseback, taking in surrounding villages and secluded temples. This is a calm way to experience the countryside, far from the traffic and crowds elsewhere.

Popular rides take in Wat Athvea, a modern pagoda with an ancient temple on its grounds, and Wat Chedi, a temple set on a flood plain near the Tonlé Sap lake. Riding lessons are also available for children and beginners. Book direct for the best prices.

Krousar Thmey
MASSAGE

(Map p116; massage US$7) ✐ Massage by the blind in the same location as its free Tonlé Sap Exhibition.

Lemongrass Garden Spa
SPA

(Map p90; ☑012 387385; www.lemongrassgarden. com; 105B Sivatha Blvd; ⊙11am-11pm) Smart spa in a central location, offering a range of affordable treatments.

Peace Cafe Yoga
YOGA

(Map p90; ☑063-965210; www.peacecafeangkor. org; per session US$6) A popular community centre-cum-cafe that has daily yoga sessions at 8.30am and 6.30pm, including ashtanga and hatha sessions.

Phokheetra Country Club
GOLF

(☑063-964600; www.sofitel.com; green fees US$100) This club hosts a tournament on the Asian tour annually and includes an ancient Angkor bridge amid its manicured fairways and greens.

Quad Adventure Cambodia
ADVENTURE TOUR

(Map p90; ☑092-787216; www.quad-adventure -cambodia.com; sunset ride US$30, full day US$170) All-terrain biking is alive and well in Siem Reap thanks to this outfit. For those who haven't tried it, all-terrain biking is serious fun and all rides include a short introductory lesson. Rides around Siem Reap involve rice fields at sunset, pretty temples and back roads through traditional villages where children wave and shout.

Seeing Hands Massage 4
MASSAGE

(Map p90; ☑012 836487; 324 Sivatha St; per hr fan/air-con US$5/7) ✐ Seeing Hands trains blind people in the art of massage. Watch out for copycats, as some of these are just exploiting the blind for profit.

☗ Courses

Cooking classes have really taken off in Siem Reap with a number of restaurants and hotels now offering an introduction to the secrets of Cambodian cooking, including many of the top-end places.

Angkor Palm
COOKING COURSE

(Map p94; Pithnou St; per person US$12) Informal cooking classes held from 8am to 5pm.

Cooks in Tuk Tuks
COOKING COURSE

(Map p116; ☑063-963400; www.therivergarden. info; per person US$25) Starts at 10am daily with a visit to Psar Leu market, then returns to the River Garden for a professional class.

Le Tigre de Papier
COOKING COURSE

(Map p94; Pub St; per person US$12) ✐ Starts at 10am daily and includes a visit to the market. Proceeds go to supporting Sala Bai

Psar Chaa

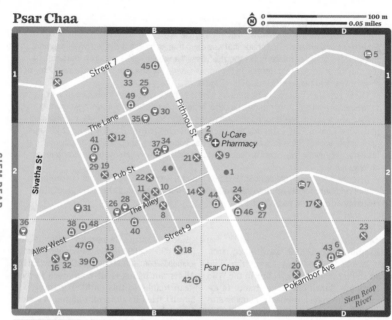

SIEM REAP

Psar Chaa

Hotel & Restaurant School, making it great value and a good cause.

☞ Tours

Most visitors are in Siem Reap to tour the temples of Angkor. See the Temples of Angkor chapter (p127) for recommended tours around the temples.

The beautiful countryside is perfect for two-wheeled adventures. Some of the companies promoting bike tours are listed here.

Grasshopper Adventures   BICYCLE TOUR
(Map p90; ☑012462165; www.grasshopperadventures.com; per person from US$39) Rides around the Siem Reap countryside, plus a dedicated temple tour on two wheels.

Off Track   BICYCLE TOUR
(Map p90; ☑093-903024; http://kko-cambodia.org; tour US$35-40) ✐ Good cause cycling tours around the paths of Angkor or into the countryside beyond the Western Baray. Proceeds go towards Khmer for Khmer Organisation, which supports education and vocational training.

Pure Countryside Cycling Tour BICYCLE TOUR
(www.pureforkids.org; per person US$22) ✐ Long half-day tour that takes in local life around Siem Reap, including lunch with a local family. All proceeds go towards supporting Pure educational and vocational-training projects.

🛏 Sleeping

Siem Reap has the best range of accommodation in Cambodia. A vast number of family-run guesthouses charging US$3 to US$20 a room cater for budget travellers, while those looking for midrange accommodation can choose upmarket guesthouses or small hotels from US$20 per room.

Touts for budget guesthouses wait at the taxi park, Phnom Krom (where the fast boat from Phnom Penh docks) and at the airport. Even if you've not yet decided where to stay in Siem Reap, don't be surprised to see a noticeboard displaying your name, as most guesthouses in Phnom Penh either have partners up here or sell your name on to another guesthouse. This system usually involves a free ride into town. There's no obligation to stay at the guesthouse if you don't like the look of it, but the 'free lift' might suddenly cost US$2 or more.

There are plenty of great midrange deals available thanks to an explosion in quality boutique accommodation. Most rates include a free transfer from the airport or boat dock.

Many top end hotels levy an additional 10% government tax, 2% tourist tax and sometimes an extra 10% for service, but breakfast is included. It's essential to book ahead at most places from November to March, particularly for the glamorous spots.

In the low season (April to September), there are lots of special offers available ranging from 'stay three, pay two' to big discounts in the range of 30% to 50%. Top-end hotels usually publish high- and low-season rates.

There are many more good places around town not listed here, as the total number of guesthouses and hotels is now hovering around the 600 or more mark.

Commission scams abound in Siem Reap, so keep your antennae up.

🛏 Psar Chaa Area

This is the liveliest part of town, brimming with restaurants, bars and boutiques. Staying here can be a lot of fun, but it's not the quietest part of town.

★**Ivy Guesthouse 2**   GUESTHOUSE **$**
(Map p90; ☑012 800860; www.ivy-guesthouse.com; r US$6-15; ❋@🛜) An inviting guesthouse with a chill-out area and bar, the Ivy is a lively place to stay. The restaurant is as good as it gets among the guesthouses in town, with a huge vegetarian selection.

Shadow of Angkor Guesthouse   GUEST HOUSE **$**
(Map p94; ☑063-964774; www.shadowofangkor.com; 353 Pokambor Ave; r US$15-25; ❋@🛜🏊) In a grand old French-era building overlooking the river, this friendly, 15-room place offers affordable air-con in a superb setting. The newer annexe across the river includes a swimming pool.

Downtown Siem Reap Hostel   HOSTEL **$**
(Map p90; ☑012 675881; www.downtownsiemreaphostel.hostel.com; Wat Damnak area; dm US$4-6, r US$13-17; ❋🛜🏊) Also sometimes known as Bamboo Garden, the rates here are particularly attractive when you consider there is a small pool in the garden. Chill out with air-con in the more expensive dorms or rooms. Outside visitors can use the pool with a US$6 spend on food and drink.

A GOLDEN SILK REVIVAL

Golden Silk (☑ 012 596811; www.goldensilk.org; Phum Thmey) is a working silk farm located in Banteay Srei district, about 30km from Siem Reap. Golden silk also happens to be the name of a particularly refined thread of silk produced by the yellow silkworm. Once common in Cambodia, its production has been in decline in recent years due to the fragile constitution of the silkwork and the weaving methods involved in producing silk items. It's an intensive process involving 100kg of cocoons and 1500kg of mulberry leaves just to produce 10kg of silk. Visitors are welcome to visit the weaving centre and learn more about the weaving process. A donation of US$10 is requested to assist the work of the NGO, which employs former orphans and disadvantaged women from the Banteay Srei area.

Prohm Roth Guesthouse GUESTHOUSE **$**
(Map p94; ☑ 012 466495; www.prohmroth-guesthouse.com; near Wat Preah Prohm Roth; r US$12-30; ❄@🖧) Central, yet tucked away down a side street which runs parallel to Wat Preah Prohm Roth, this is a friendly place. Free pick-up from airport, port or bus station.

Mandalay Inn GUESTHOUSE **$**
(Map p90; ☑ 063-761662; www.mandalayinn.com; r US$7-18; ❄@🖧) This smart guesthouse promises Burmese hospitality meets Khmer smiles, offering spotless rooms plus free wi-fi and a rooftop 'gym'. It's a friendly spot.

Angkor Park Guesthouse GUESTHOUSE **$**
(Map p90; ☑ 063-761663; www.angkorparkguesthouse.com; off Sivatha St; r with fan/air-con US$8/13; ❄🖧) A no-frills good value guesthouse that has 22 rooms, including TV and attached bathroom with hot water. It's pretty central for the Psar Chaa and Pub St action.

Steung Siem Reap Hotel HOTEL **$$**
(Map p94; ☑063-965167; www.steungsiemreaphotel.com; near Psar Chaa; r from US$63; ❄@🖧⊠) In keeping with the French-colonial air around Psar Chaa, this hotel has high ceilings, louvre shutters and wrought-iron balconies. Three-star rooms feature smart wooden trim. The location is hard to beat.

Golden Banana BOUTIQUE HOTEL **$$**
(Map p90; ☑063-761259; 063-766655; www.golden-banana.com; B&B r US$22-31, boutique r US$55-136; ❄@🖧⊠) Prepare for some confusion, as this is Siem Reap's Banana Republic. There are now four Golden Bananas occupying this crossroads near Wat Damnak, including the original B&B and a high-rise hotel, plus two boutique hotels under different ownership. We recommend the original B&B or the newer boutique hotels, which offer duplex suites set on two floors. All are gay-friendly.

🛏 Sivatha St Area

The area to the west of Sivatha St includes a good selection of budget guesthouses and midrange boutique hotels.

My Home Tropical Garden Villa GUESTHOUSE **$**
(Map p116; ☑ 063-760035; www.myhomecambodia.com; r US$12-30; ❄@🖧⊠) Offering hotel standards at guesthouse prices, this is a fine place to rest your head. The decor includes some soft silks and the furnishings are tasteful. There's an inviting little swimming pool.

Mad Monkey HOSTEL **$**
(Map p90; www.madmonkeyhostels.com; Sivatha St; dm US$5-6, r US$8-17; ❄@🖧) The Siem Reap outpost of an expanding Monkey business, this is a classic backpacker crashpad with several dorms, good-value rooms for those wanting privacy and the statutory rooftop bar, only this one's a beach bar!

Cashew Nut Guesthouse GUESTHOUSE **$**
(Map p116; ☑063-765015; http://thecashewnut.com; Psar Krom Rd; r incl breakfast US$13-20; ❄@🖧) A lively little place run by a self-proclaimed 'nutter' who previously worked as a tour leader for Intrepid. Artful decoration and slick service propel this into boutique backpacker orbit, plus breakfast is included.

Garden Village GUESTHOUSE **$**
(Map p116; ☑012 217373; www.gardenvillageguesthouse.com; dm US$1, r US$6-13; ❄@🖧) This traditional backpacker hang-out offers some of the cheapest beds in town and is a good place to meet travellers. Options among its 70 rooms include eight-bed dorms at a bargain buck a bed. The rooftop bar is a draw around sunset.

Mommy's Guesthouse GUESTHOUSE **$**
(Map p90; ☑012 941755; mommy_guesthouse@yahoo.com; r US$5-15; ❄@🖧) A warm and welcoming, family-run place, this 13-room

villa has large rooms with air-con, as well as cheap digs with cold showers. The owners really go out of their way to assist travellers.

Golden Temple Villa
HOTEL $$

(Map p90; ☑ 012 943459; www.goldentemplevilla. com; r US$15-40; ❄@⎙) A long-running popular place with funky, colourful decor and fun outlook. There's a bar-restaurant downstairs, plus all sorts of generous freebies ranging from a one-hour massage to a dance show at Temple Club. The newer Golden Temple Hotel offers the four-star high life.

Auberge Mont Royal
HOTEL $$

(Map p90; ☑ 063-964044; www.auberge-mont -royal.com; r US$32-85; ❄@⎙⛱) Set in a classic colonial-style villa, the Auberge has smart rooms at a smart price, with the swimming pool and spa making it a cut above other offerings in this price bracket.

Encore Angkor Guesthouse
HOTEL $$

(Map p90; ☑ 063-969400; www.encoreangkor. com; 456 Sok San St; r US$40-60; ❄@⎙⛱) The stylish lobby sets the tone for a budget boutique experience. Rooms include oversized beds and an in-room safe. Their motto was 'just don't tell anyone', but unfortunately we spilled the beans a few years ago.

Sala Bai Hotel & Restaurant School
HOTEL $$

(Map p90; ☑ 063-963329; www.salabai.com; Taphul St; r US$15-30; ❄@⎙) ⦿ Immerse yourself in the intimate surrounds of this training-school hotel, where the super staff are ever-helpful. The four rooms include silk wall hangings, woven throw pillows and wicker wardrobes, so book ahead.

Tareach Angkor Villa
HOTEL $$

(Map p90; ☑063-963986; www.tareachangkorvilla. com; r US$20-30; ❄⎙) Brand new for 2014, this is a good value flashpacker place to stay, offering smart rooms with flat-screen TV and stylish bathrooms. Triples available for US$25.

Avatar Angkor Hotel
HOTEL $$

(Map p90; ☑ 063-968767; www.avatarangkorhotel. com; Taphul Rd; r US$22-29; ❄⎙) A new budget boutique hotel on Taphul Rd, Avatar has smart contemporary lines and some tasteful local decorative touches. Rooms include flat-screen TVs and crisp white bed linen.

Park Hyatt Siem Reap
LUXURY HOTEL $$$

(Map p90; ☑063-966000; www.parkhyatt.com; Sivatha St; r/ste from US$265/765; ❄@⎙⛱) Formerly the funky Hotel de la Paix, Park Hyatt has risen from the renovations and retained much of the personality of its predecessor, albeit at a more luxurious level. Superb swimming pool and spa areas and contemporary dining ensure it remains one of the most popular luxe hotels in town.

Riverfront & Royal Gardens

The smart end of town, this is where the royal residence is to be found, along with many of the luxury hotels and boutique resorts.

★ La Résidence d'Angkor
BOUTIQUE RESORT $$$

(Map p90; ☑ 063-963390; www.residencedangkor .com; Stung Siem Reap St; r from US$280; ❄@⎙⛱) The 54 wood-appointed rooms, among the most tasteful and inviting in town, come with verandas and huge Jacuzzi-sized tubs. The gorgeous swimming pool is perfect for laps. The newer wing is ultra-contemporary, as is the sumptuous Kong Kea Spa.

Shinta Mani
BOUTIQUE RESORT $$$

(Map p90; ☑063-761998; www.shintamani.com; Oum Khun St; r US$83-230; ❄@⎙⛱) ⦿ Contemporary chic designed by renowned architect Bill Bensley, Shinta Mani Resort offers an inviting central pool, while Shinta Mani Club offers more exclusive rooms. Shinta Mani has won several international awards for responsible tourism practices.

Victoria Angkor Hotel
HOTEL $$$

(Map p90; ☑ 063-760428; www.victoriahotels-asia. com; r from US$150; ❄@⎙⛱) The Victoria is a popular choice for those craving the French touch in Indochine. The classy lobby is the perfect introduction to one of the most impressive courtyard pools in town. The rooms are well finished and many include a striking pool view.

FCC Angkor
BOUTIQUE HOTEL $$$

(Map p90; ☑063-760280; www.fcccambodia.com; Pokambor Ave; r/ste from US$100/160; ❄@⎙⛱) This funky property wouldn't look out of place in any chic European capital. However, there are Khmer touches, and the rooms feature large bath-tubs, Cambodian silks and wi-fi throughout. The black-tiled swimming pool and Visaya Spa complete the picture.

Grand Hotel d'Angkor
HISTORIC HOTEL $$$

(Map p90; ☑ 063-963888; www.raffles.com; r from US$260; ❄@⎙⛱) The hotel with history on its side, this place has been welcoming guests since 1929, including Charlie Chaplin, Charles de Gaulle, Jackie Kennedy and Bill Clinton. Ensconced in such opulent surroundings, you can imagine what it was like to be a tourist in colonial days. Rooms include classic colonial-era touches and a dizzying array of bathroom gifts.

Wat Bo Area

This up-and-coming area features socially responsible guesthouses, as well as some hip boutique hotels. There is a great guesthouse ghetto in a backstreet running parallel to the north end of Wat Bo Rd, which is good for on-the-spot browsing.

Seven Candles Guesthouse　GUESTHOUSE $
(Map p90; ☑963380; www.sevencandlesguesthouse.com; 307 Wat Bo Rd; r US$10-20; ❋@🛜) ∕ A good-cause guesthouse; its profits help a local foundation that seeks to promote education to rural communities. Rooms include hot water, TV and fridge.

Babel Guesthouse　GUESTHOUSE $
(Map p90; ☑063-965474; http://babel-siemreap.com; r incl breakfast US$15-27; ❋@🛜) A Norwegian-run guesthouse set in a relaxing tropical garden, the service and presentation are a cut above the nearby budget places and rates include breakfast. The Babel owners are keen supporters of responsible tourism.

Happy Guesthouse　GUESTHOUSE $
(Map p90; ☑063-963815; www.happyangkorguesthouse.com; r US$3-12; ❋@🛜) This place will really make you happy thanks to welcoming owners who speak very good English *et un peu de Français*. Great-value rooms and free internet.

European Guesthouse　GUESTHOUSE $
(Map p90; ☑012 582237; www.european-guesthouse.com; d US$3-5, r US$15-28; ❋@🛜) ∕ Fun and friendly, the rooms are well presented, the dorms are a bargain and the garden a good place to relax. The European is a member of local NGO networks Childsafe and ConCERT and supports projects like the White Bicycles.

Siem Reap Hostel　HOSTEL $
(Map p90; ☑063-964660; www.thesiemreaphostel.com; 10 Makara St; dm US$6-8, r incl breakfast US$20-39; ❋@🛜🏊) Angkor's original full-on backpacker hostel is pretty slick. The dorms are well tended and the rooms are definitely flashpacker, and include breakfast too. There

is a lively bar-restaurant and a covered pool, plus a well-organised travel desk.

Rosy Guesthouse　GUESTHOUSE $
(Map p90; ☑063-965059; www.rosyguesthouse.com; Stung Siem Reap Rd; r US$8-30; ❋🛜) ∕ A British-owned establishment whose 13 rooms come with TV and DVD. Has a lively pub downstairs with great grub and host regular events to support community causes.

Soria Moria Hotel　BOUTIQUE HOTEL $$
(Map p90; ☑063-964768; www.thesoriamoria.com; Wat Bo Rd; r US$39-63; ❋@🛜🏊) ∕ A hotel with a heart, promoting local causes to help the community, this boutique place has attractive rooms with smart bathroom fittings. Fusion restaurant downstairs, sky hot tub upstairs and a new swimming pool.

Frangipani Villa Hotel　BOUTIQUE HOTEL $$
(Map p90; ☑063-999930; www.frangipanihotel.com; Wat Bo Rd; r incl breakfast US$40-60; ❋@🛜🏊) The Siem Reap outpost of the expanding Frangipani empire, this is chic boutique on the cheap. Rooms include stylish touches like flat-screen TVs, and there's an inviting pool.

Reflections　BOUTIQUE HOTEL $$
(Map p90; ☑063-659 4343; www.reflections-thai.com; Wat Bo Rd; r US$40-80; ❋🛜🏊) An eccentric art hotel with personality, the lobby includes a huge collection of cuddly toys. Rooms are set in art-deco style buildings surrounding a central pool and all are decorated with quirky artworks. Life is Plastic is a shrine to Barbie, just one example of the kitsch originality.

Pippeli Pensione　BOUTIQUE HOTEL $$
(Map p90; ☑063-969011; www.pippelipensione.com; near Wat Damnak; r US$49-59; ❋🛜🏊) Contemporary lodgings nestled in the backstreets on the west bank of the river, Pippeli offers good value and intimacy thanks to just nine rooms. Some lower floor rooms include an outdoor tub and upper floor rooms have a balcony.

La Noria Guesthouse　BOUTIQUE GUESTHOUSE $$
(Map p90; ☑063-964242; www.lanoriaangkor.com; r US$39-59; ❋🛜🏊) Long-running, lovely place set in a lush tropical garden with a pretty swimming pool. Rooms have a traditional trim and veranda but no TV or fridge.

Karavansara　BOUTIQUE HOTEL $$
(Map p90; ☑063-760678; www.karavansara.com; 25 Acha Sva St; r from US$70, ste from US$110;

❋◉⍾⊠) Set in an iconic building from Cambodia's new architecture heyday, this boutique hotel offers tasteful rooms and, across the road, larger apartments for families. The restaurant is set in a delightful relocated traditional house.

Viroth's Hotel BOUTIQUE HOTEL $$$
(Map p90; ☎063-761720; www.viroth-hotel.com; r from US$80; ❋◉⍾⊠) Minimalist and modern, this small gay-friendly boutique property has seven rooms finished in contemporary chic. Facilities include a pool, a hot tub and free wi-fi.

🏠 Further Afield

Don't shy away from venturing further afield, as some of the most memorable boutique hotels lie hidden beyond.

★ HanumanAlaya BOUTIQUE HOTEL $$
(Map p116; ☎063-760582; www.hanumanalaya.com; r US$60-100; ❋◉⍾⊠) The most authentically Cambodian of the boutique hotels in town, HanumanAlaya is set around a lush garden and pretty swimming pool. Rooms are decorated with antiques and handicrafts but include modern touches like flat-screen TV, minibar and safe. It also includes a garden spa and Reahoo Restaurant, popular for authentic Khmer flavours.

★ Pavillon Indochine BOUTIQUE HOTEL $$
(Map p116; ☎012 849681; www.pavillon-indochine.com; r US$55-70, ste US$75-95; ❋◉⍾⊠) The Pavillon offers charming colonial-chic rooms set around a small swimming pool. The trim includes Asian antiques, billowing mosquito nets and a safe. Also included in the rates is a *remork* driver for the day to tour the temples, making it great value.

1961 BOUTIQUE HOTEL $$
(Map p116; ☎063-966961; www.the1961.com; r US$35-55; ❋◉⍾) Part hotel, part art gallery and creative space, this is a memorable little hotel themed around 1961. Galleries (not rooms!) are named after the Norodoms, the Kennedys and famous Khmer architect Vann Molyvann. We like the Norodoms, complete with royal pop art and movie posters.

River Garden BOUTIQUE HOTEL $$
(Map p116; ☎063-963400; www.therivergarden.info; r US$50-105; ❋◉⍾⊠) Invitingly set amid a verdant garden, this wooden resort has a small selection of atmospheric rooms, some with large balconies and deep baths.

SIEM REAP SLEEPING

Renowned for its 'cooks in *tuk-tuks*' culinary class.

Le Rit's GUESTHOUSE $$
(Map p116; ☎063-763390; www.nyemo.com/guesthouse_sr; r US$30-55; ❋◉) 🌿 Run by local NGO Nyemo, this a a guesthouse for a good cause. The rooms are all named after local flowers and plants and include bright silks, a signature product of Nyemo's shops. All proceeds go towards assisting vulnerable women to make a sustainable living.

Lotus Lodge HOTEL $$
(Map p116; ☎063-966140; www.lotus-lodge.com; r US$25-55; ❋◉⍾⊠) A good deal for those wanting a peaceful retreat after a day at the temples. Rooms are clean and comfortable, plus there's a spacious swimming pool. Free bikes and evening shuttles.

Paul Dubrule Hotel & Tourism School HOTEL $$
(Map p116; ☎063-963673; www.ecolepauldubrule.org; Airport Rd; r US$20-35; ❋◉⍾) 🌿 Paul Dubrule co-founded the Accor hotel group, so it's no surprise that his training hotel offers smart rooms and slick service. A great deal.

★ Sala Lodges BOUTIQUE LODGE $$$
(☎063-766699; www.salalodges.com; r US$190-410; ❋⍾⊠) An original concept, Sala Lodges offers 11 traditional Khmer houses that have been retrofitted inside to bring them up the standard of a rustic boutique hotel. Enter the resort and you'll think you have stumbled on an idyllic Cambodian village, but the pool and restaurant will soon confirm you have found a gem.

Siem Reap & Around

Cambodia is the undisputed temple capital of Asia, and we're not just talking about the holiest of holies – the one and only Angkor Wat. Angkor is heaven on earth, but there are also temples dotted all over Siem Reap, the epicentre of the empire, that attest to the glories of Khmer civilisation.

MARTIN PUDDY/GETTY IMAGES ©

1. Ta Prohm (p146)
Jungle trees are entwined with temples at Angkor's most atmospheric ruin.

2. Sra Srang (p147)
Only the stone base remains of the temple that once stood in this peaceful basin.

3. Banteay Srei (p153)
A Hindu temple with stunning stone carvings, known as the art gallery of Angkor.

4. Apsara dancers (p313)
Royal dancers are considered a tangible link to the past glories of Angkor.

B TRENKEL/GETTY IMAGES ©

TRAVELSTOCK44-JUERGEN HELD/GETTY IMAGES ©

Navutu Dreams
BOUTIQUE RESORT $$$

(☎063-688 0607; www.navutudreams.com; US$90-230; ❋❀✿≋) Set in the rural suburbs of Siem Reap, Navutu Dreams offers a selection of open plan villas set around lush gardens and two swimming pools. A new expansion has added a third pool and there are plans to open a yoga and wellness centre here.

Heritage Suites
BOUTIQUE HOTEL $$$

(Map p116; ☎063-969100; www.relaischateaux.com/heritage; Wat Polanka; r from US$200; ❋@✿≋) Designed in the colonial style, the suites here are spectacular and open plan, many including a small garden and freestanding bathtub. Lanterns Restaurant here is highly regarded, plus there's Thursday night jazz.

✗ Eating

The dining scene in Siem Reap is something to savour, offering a superb selection of street food, Asian eateries and sumptuous restaurants. The range encompasses something from every continent, with new temptations constantly on offer. Sample the subtleties of Khmer cuisine in town, or simply indulge in home comforts or gastronomic delights prior to – or after – hitting the remote provinces. Some of the very best restaurants also put something back into community projects or offer vocational training. Check out the boxed text (right) for recommendations.

Tourist numbers mean many top restaurants are heaving during high season. But with so many places to choose from, keep walking and you'll find somewhere more tranquil. Quite a lot of restaurants work with tour groups to some degree. If you prefer to avoid places with tour groups, it's better to stick to the Psar Chaa area and explore on foot. The restaurants reviewed here represent just a fraction of the food on offer.

Some of the budget guesthouses have good menus offering a selection of local dishes and Western meals; while it's easy to order in-house food, it hardly counts as the full Siem Reap experience. Several of the midrange hotels and all the top-end places have restaurants, some excellent. Several hotels and restaurants around town feature dinner and a performance of classical dance.

The Alley is wall-to-wall with good Cambodian restaurants, many of which are family owned. Most have 'Khmer' in the name and offer cheap beers and meal deals. Take a stroll and see what takes your fancy.

Markets are well stocked with fruit and fresh bread. For treats like cheese and chocolate, try the local supermarkets. Eating in the market usually works out cheaper than self-catering, but some folks like to make up a picnic for longer days on the road.

✗ Pub St & Around

Pub St may not seem the most relaxing dining venue, particularly by night, but the alleys and lanes that criss-cross the area reveal some atmospheric places.

Khmer Kitchen Restaurant
CAMBODIAN $

(Map p94; www.khmerkitchens.com; The Alley; mains US$2-5; ⊙11am-10pm) Can't get no (culinary) satisfaction? Follow in the footsteps of Sir Mick Jagger and try this popular place, which offers an affordable selection of Khmer and Thai favourites, including feisty curries.

Red Piano
ASIAN, INTERNATIONAL $

(Map p94; www.redpianocambodia.com; Pub St; mains US$3-6; ✿) Strikingly set in a restored colonial gem, Red Piano has a big balcony for watching the action unfold below. The menu has a reliable selection of Asian and international food, all at decent prices. Former celebrity guest Angelina Jolie has a cocktail named in her honour.

Le Tigre de Papier
INTERNATIONAL $$

(Map p94; www.letigredepapier.com; Pub St; mains US$2-9; ⊙24hr; ✿) One of the best all-rounders in Siem Reap, the popular Tigre serves up authentic Khmer food, great Italian dishes and a selection of favourites from most other corners of the globe. Doubles as a popular bar by night, with frontage on both Pub St and the Alley.

Chamkar
VEGETARIAN $$

(Map p94; www.chamkar-vegetarian.com; The Alley; mains US$4-8; ⊙11am-11pm, closed lunch Sun; ✿) The name translates as 'farm' and the ingredients must be coming from a pretty impressive organic vegetable supplier given the creative dishes on the menu here. Asian flavours predominate, such as stuffed pumpkin or vegetable kebabs in black pepper sauce.

Cambodian BBQ
BARBECUE $$

(Map p94; www.angkorw.com; The Alley; mains US$5-9; ⊙11am-11pm; ✿) Crocodile, snake, ostrich and kangaroo meat add an exotic twist to the traditional *phnom pleung* (hill of fire) grills. It has spawned half a dozen or more copycats in the surrounding streets, many of which offer discount specials.

DINING FOR A CAUSE

These are some good restaurants that support worthy causes or assist in the training of Cambodia's future hospitality staff with a subsidised ticket into the tourism industry. If you dine at the training places, it gives the trainees a good opportunity to hone their skills with real customers.

Blossom Cafe (Map p90; www.blossomcakes.org; St 6; cupcakes US$1.50; ⊙10am-5pm Mon-Sat; 🛜) Cupcakes are elevated to an artform at this elegant cafe, with beautifully presented creations available in a rotating array of 48 flavours. Creative coffees, teas and juices are also available and the profits assist Cambodian women in vocational training.

Common Grounds (Map p90; 719 St 14; light meals US$3-5; ⊙7am-10pm; 🛜) Sophisticated international cafe akin to Starbucks. Great coffee, homemade cakes, light bites, and free wi-fi and internet terminals. Offers free computer classes and English classes for Cambodians, and supports good causes.

Haven (Map p90; ✆078-342404; www.haven-cambodia.com; Sok San St; mains US$3-7; ⊙11am-10pm; 🛜) A culinary haven indeed, dine here for the best of East meets West. The fish fillet with green mango is particularly zesty. Proceeds go towards helping young adult orphans make the step from institution to employment. It regularly occupies top spot on Trip Advisor, so book ahead.

Joe-to-Go (Map p94; near Psar Chaa; mains US$2-5; ⊙7am-9.30pm) If you need coffee coursing through your veins to tackle the temples, then head here. Gourmet coffees, shakes and light bites, with proceeds supporting street children. Upstairs is a small boutique supporting the associated NGO, The Global Child.

Les Jardins des Delices (Map p116; ✆063-963673; Paul Dubrule Hotel & Tourism School, NH6; set lunch US$12; ⊙noon-2pm Mon-Fri) Enjoy Sofitel standards at an affordable price, with a three-course meal of Asian and Western food prepared by students training in the culinary arts.

Marum (Map p90; www.marum-restaurant.org; Wat Polanka area; mains US$3.25-6.75; ⊙11am-10pm Mon-Sat; 🛜) Brings the best of Friends (p57) to Siem Reap. Set in a delightful wooden house with a spacious garden, menu highlights include red tree ant fritters and ginger basil meatballs. There are lots of vegetarian and seafood dishes on the menu, plus some mouthwatering desserts. Part of the Tree Alliance group of training restaurants, the experience is a must.

New Leaf Book Cafe (Map p94; near Psar Chaa; mains US$3-6; ⊙7am-10pm) A new cafe and secondhand bookshop in Siem Reap, all profits go towards supporting NGOs working in Siem Reap province. The menu includes some home favourites, an Italian twist and some local Cambodian specials.

Peace Cafe (Map p90; www.peacecafeangkor.org; St 26; mains US$2.50-4.50; ⊙7am-9pm) Popular garden cafe serving delicious and affordable vegetarian meals. Healthy drinks include a tempting selection of vegetable juices. A focus of community activities, there are vegetarian cooking classes daily at 11am, yoga sessions and Khmer classes every weekend at 4pm.

Sala Bai Hotel and Restaurant School (Map p90; www.salabai.com; set lunch US$8; ⊙7-9am & noon-2pm Mon-Fri) This school trains young Khmers in the art of hospitality and serves an affordable menu of Western and Cambodian cuisine.

Sister Srey Cafe (Map p94; 200 Pokambor Ave; mains US$3-6; ⊙7am-7pm Tue-Sun) A friendly and fun cafe on the riverfront near Psar Chaa, Sister Srey offers an ambitious breakfast menu that is perfect after a sunrise at the temples, including eggs benedelicious. Lunch menu is Western food with a creative twist, including burgers, wraps and salads.

Amok CAMBODIAN **$$**
(Map p94; www.angkorw.com; The Alley; mains US$4-9; ⏱5-11pm; 🛜) The name pays homage to Cambodia's national dish, *amok* (or *amoc*), and this is indeed a fine place to try baked fish curry in banana leaf or, better still, an *amok* tasting platter with four varieties. It is in the heart of the Alley.

Il Forno ITALIAN **$$**
(Map p94; www.ilfornorestaurantsiemreap.com; The Lane; mains US$5-15; ⏱11am-11pm; 🛜) Aficionados of fine Italian cuisine will be delighted to know that there is, as the name suggests, a full-blown brick oven in this cosy little *trattoria*. The menu includes fresh antipasti, authentic pizza and some home-cooked Italian dishes.

AHA FUSION **$$**
(Map p94; tapas US$3-10; 🛜) Trendy little tapas emporium and wine bar with a variety of tasting platters, including cheese, veggie, Khmer and contemporary. Inventive cuisine.

Soup Dragon ASIAN, INTERNATIONAL **$$**
(Map p94; Pub St; Vietnamese mains US$2-10; ⏱6am-11pm; 🛜) Three-level restaurant with a split personality: the ground floor serves up cheap, classic Asian breakfasts, while upstairs serves diverse Asian and international dishes, including Italian and Moroccan.

Little Italy ITALIAN **$$**
(Map p94; Alley West; mains US$4-12; ⏱11am-11pm) An elegant Italian restaurant that is much more affordable than its sophisticated exterior might suggest. Wood-fired pizzas

---

CRAVING ICE CREAM?
....
After a hot day exploring the temples, there's nothing quite like an ice-cream fix and Siem Reap delivers some superb surprises:

Blue Pumpkin (p104) Homemade ice cream in original tropical flavours from ginger to passionfruit.

The Glasshouse (Map p90; Park Hyatt, Sivatha St; cones US$2; ⏱6am-10pm) Velvety ice creams including white chocolate and tangy sorbets.

Swenson's Ice Cream (Map p94; Pokambor Ave; cones US$1.25; ⏱9am-9pm) One of America's favourites has become one of Siem Reap's favourites. Located in the Angkor Trade Centre.

---

are produced upstairs and the menu includes a wide range of homemade pasta and imported Italian cuts.

Sushi Bar Koh Kong JAPANESE **$$**
(Map p94; Pub St; mains US$3-12; ⏱5-11pm) The first sushi bar to open in the heart of old Siem Reap, much of the seafood is locally sourced in Cambodia from – wait for it, Koh Kong – and prices are tempting for Japanese cuisine.

✕ Psar Chaa Area

★ Blue Pumpkin INTERNATIONAL **$**
(Map p94; http://tbpumpkin.com; Pithnou St; mains US$2-6; ⏱6am-10pm; 🛜) Downstairs it could be any old cafe, albeit with a delightful selection of cakes, breads and homemade ice cream. Upstairs is another world of white minimalism, with beds to lounge on and free wi-fi. Light bites, great sandwiches, filling specials and divine shakes, this place is the real deal. Many new branches around town.

Psar Chaa CAMBODIAN **$**
(Map p94; mains US$1.50-4; ⏱7am-9pm) When it comes to cheap Khmer eats, Psar Chaa itself has plenty of food stalls on the northwest side, all with signs and menus in English. These are atmospheric places for a local meal at local-ish prices. Some dishes are on display, others are freshly flash fried to order, but most are wholesome and filling.

Cafe Central INTERNATIONAL **$**
(Map p94; mains US$3-6; ⏱7am-11pm; 🛜) A popular spot looking across to the market, this is as central as it gets. The eclectic menu includes generous all-day breakfasts, good-value pizza, a selection of seven burgers and a diverse choice of mains from lemongrass chicken to steak and Guinness pie.

Angkor Palm CAMBODIAN **$$**
(Map p94; www.angkorpalm.com; Pithnou St; mains US$3-8; ⏱10am-10pm) This popular restaurant offers the authentic taste of Cambodia. Even Khmers rave about the legendary *amok* (baked fish in banana leaf) here, and it offers a great-value sampling platter for just US$7.50. Cooking classes available.

Viva MEXICAN **$$**
(Map p94; www.ivivasiemreap.com; Pithnou St; mains US$2.50-12.50; ⏱7am-late) Spice up your life with Mexican food and margaritas at this long-running place, which has expanded to include a guesthouse. Lively location opposite Psar Chaa.

Sivatha St Area

Curry Walla INDIAN $

(Map p90; Sivatha St; mains US$2-5; ⊙10.30am-11pm) For good-value Indian food, this place is hard to beat. The *thalis* (set meals) are a bargain and the owner knows his share of spicy specials from the subcontinent.

Le Malraux FRENCH-ASIAN $$

(Map p94; www.le-malraux-siem-reap.com; Sivatha St; mains US$5-15; ⊙7am-midnight) A good spot for gastronomes, this classy art-deco cafe-restaurant offers fine French food. Try the combination salmon tartare and carpaccio to start, followed by a quality steak. The Cognac and Armagnac selection is to die for. Asian dishes also available.

Angkor Market SUPERMARKET

(Map p90; Sivatha St) The best all-round supermarket in town, this place has a steady supply of international treats.

Lucky Market SUPERMARKET

(Map p90; Sivatha St) Biggest supermarket in town, part of a shopping mall on Sivatha St.

Wat Bo Area

★**Green Star** CAMBODIAN $

(Map p90; www.greenstarrestaurant.org; mains US$2-5; ⊙11.30am-2pm & 5.30-10.30pm Mon-Sat; 🔊) ✎ Tucked away in a quiet street behind Wat Damnak is this appealing not-for-profit restaurant supporting former street kids in Siem Reap. Authentic Khmer dishes include spicy duck, lemongrass eel and succulent frog. Blackboard specials change regularly.

Le Café CAFE $

(Map p90; snacks US$2-4; ⊙7.30am-9pm; 🔊) ✎ Run in partnership with the Paul Dubrule Hotel & Tourism School, this cafe brings five-star sandwiches, salads and shakes to the French Cultural Centre.

Moloppor Cafe JAPANESE, INTERNATIONAL $

(Map p90; Siem Reap River Rd; mains US$1-4; ⊙10am-11pm; 🔊) One of the cheapest deals in town, it offers Japanese, Asian and Italian dishes at almost giveaway prices for what is a real restaurant. Nice location with river views.

Wat Damnak BBQs BARBECUE $

(Map p90; Wat Damnak St; mains US$2-5; ⊙11am-11pm) Located opposite the venerable Wat Damnak, these local barbecue restaurants are popular for barbecued beef and other local meats and lake fish. They also double as beer emporiums and turn out some of the cheapest draught in town.

Alliance Cafe FRENCH, ASIAN $$

(Map p90; www.allianceangkor.com; mains US$3.50-16; ⊙10am-11pm; 🔊) Set in an attractive French colonial–era villa, this classy French restaurant also pays homage to its Cambodian context with some original Asian recipes. Choose from set menus such as Asian Tradition and Alliance Passion for just US$14. The cafe doubles as an art venue.

Square 24 CAMBODIAN $$

(Map p90; www.thesquare24.com; St 24; mains US$5.50-15; ⊙11.30am-11pm) A stylish venue for contemporary Khmer and Asian cuisine. Billowing silks flutter around the open-plan architecture, making it ideal for a balmy evening. All soups and starters US$5.50 and Asian mains US$8.50.

Viroth's Restaurant CAMBODIAN $$

(Map p90; Wat Bo Rd; mains US$4-8; ⊙lunch & dinner) A sophisticated garden restaurant near Wat Bo, where Khmer cuisine meets Balinese design. It's popular with tour groups but still manages to retain an element of intimacy.

Around Siem Reap

Vitking House VEGETARIAN $

(Map p116; 7 Makara St; mains US$1-3; ⊙7am-9pm; 🔊✎) Popular with students from the nearby university, this is one of the cheapest veggie spots in town, with sizzling platters of shiitake mushrooms and noodles. Worth the detour.

★**Chanrey Tree** CAMBODIAN $$

(Map p90; www.chanreytree.com; Pokambar Ave; mains US$5-12; ⊙11am-10pm) Cool and contemporary, Chantrey Tree is the new face of Khmer cuisine, combining a stylish setting with expressive presentation while retaining the essentials of traditional Cambodia cooking. Try roast chicken in honey, rice brandy, young jackfruit and lemongrass.

Sugar Palm CAMBODIAN $$

(Map p90; www.sugarpalmrestaurant.com; Taphul St; mains US$5-9; ⊙11.30am-3pm & 5.30-10pm Mon-Sat; 🔊) Set in a beautiful wooden house in the west of town, the Sugar Palm is the place to sample traditional flavours infused with herbs and spices, including delicious *char kreung* (curried lemongrass) dishes. Owner Kethana showed celebrity chef Gordon Ramsay how to prepare *amok*.

FCC Angkor
INTERNATIONAL **$$**

(Map p90; ☐ 063-760280; mains US$5-15; ⏱ 7am-midnight; 🛜) This landmark building draws people in from the riverside thanks to a reflective pool, torchlit dining and a garden bar. Inside, the colonial chic continues with lounge chairs and an open kitchen turning out a range of Asian and international food.

Touich
CAMBODIAN **$$**

(Map p116; the-touich-restaurant-bar.blogspot.com; mains US$2.50-8; ⏱ dinner) Hidden away but worth the search, this is a traditional Khmer restaurant set in the backstreet suburbs of Wat Preah Inkosei. The menu includes regional specialities and seafood such as Mekong prawns and Koh Kong red snapper. Check the blog to avoid getting lost.

Mie Cafe
CAMBODIAN, INTERNATIONAL **$$**

(Map p116; miecafe-siemreap.com; near Angkor Conservation; mains US$4-8; ⏱ 11am-10pm) Cambodian eatery offering a fusion take on traditional flavours. Set in a traditional wooden house just off the road to Angkor, it offers romantic set menus for two at US$25. Dishes include everything from fish *amok* to fish and chips.

Tangram Garden
INTERNATIONAL **$$**

(Map p90; www.tangramgarden.com; mains US$4.75-9.50; ⏱ 11am-2pm & 5-10pm; 🛜) An alfresco garden restaurant in a quiet suburb near Wat Damnak, Tangram Garden specialises in barbecue grills, creative vegetarian dishes and Khmer staples. Atmospheric at night, there's also a small children's playground here to keep it family-friendly.

L'Oasi Italiana
ITALIAN **$$**

(Map p116; www.oasiitaliana.com; mains US$5-17, pizza US$5-9; ⏱ 6-10pm Mon, 11am-2pm & 6-10pm Tue-Sun; 🛜) Something of an oasis, hidden away in a forest near Wat Preah Inkosei. Expats swear by the gnocchi and homemade pasta, including ravioli with porcini mushrooms, plus wood-fired pizza.

Madame Butterfly
ASIAN **$$**

(Map p116; www.madamebutterflyrestaurant.com; Airport Rd; mains US$4-10; ⏱ 6-11pm; 🛜) This traditional wooden house has been sumptuously decorated with fine silks and billowing drapes. A lovely atmosphere, but sometimes dampened by the sheer number of tour groups who come to sample the Asian and Khmer cuisine.

Kanell
INTERNATIONAL **$$**

(Map p90; www.kanellrestaurant.com; 7 Makara St; mains US$4-13; ⏱ 10am-10pm; 🛜) Set in a handsome Khmer villa on the edge of town, Kanell offers extensive gardens and a swimming pool (free with US$5 spend) for those seeking to dine and unwind. The menu includes French-accented dishes, plus some Cambodian favourites.

★ Cuisine Wat Damnak
CAMBODIAN **$$$**

(Map p90; www.cuisinewatdamnak.com; Sivatha Blvd; 5-course menu US$22, 6-course menu US$26; ⏱ dinner) Set in a traditional wooden house, this is the highly regarded restaurant from Siem Reap celeb chef Johannes Rivieres. The menu delivers the ultimate contemporary Khmer dining experience. Seasonal set menus focus on market fresh ingredients and change weekly, plus vegetarian options are available with advance notice.

Abacus
FRENCH **$$$**

(Map p116; www.cafeabacus.com; mains US$10-22; ⏱ 11am-late; 🛜) The finest French dining in town, with steaks in black-truffle sauce, succulent lamb and superb seafood, including tuna *maguro*. Dine in the garden or the cool interior. The menu includes some beautifully presented Khmer dishes. Off Airport Rd.

 ## Drinking

The transformation from sleepy overgrown village to an international destination for the jet set has been dramatic and Siem Reap is now firmly on the nightlife map of southeast Asia. By night it feels more like a beach town than a cultural capital. The Psar Chaa area is a good hunting ground, with one street even earning the moniker 'Pub St', where you can dive in and crawl out. Pub St is closed to traffic every evening.

Great spots running parallel to Pub St include the Alley, to the south, where the volume control is just a little lower, plus a series of smaller lanes to the north. There are plenty more places around town, so make sure you plan at least one big night out.

Most of the bars here have happy hours, but so do some of the fancier hotels, which is a good way to sample the high life even if you're not staying at those places, although the atmosphere can be a little austere.

As well as the selection of bars below, a number of restaurants double as lively bars by night, including atmospheric Abacus, classic FCC Angkor, the popular Red Piano and the rooftop Soup Dragon, which donates 7% of the take to the Angkor Children's Hospital, so you're helping someone else's health, if not your own.

Warehouse
BAR

(Map p94; Pithnou St; ⏰10.30am-3am; 📶) This lively bar opposite Psar Chaa has long been popular with resident expats and travellers in Siem Reap. Top tunes, table football, a pool table and devilish drinks keep them coming until the early hours. Charity quiz night on Thursday.

Laundry Bar
BAR, NIGHTCLUB

(Map p94; ⏰4pm-late; 📶) One of the most alluring bars in town thanks to low lighting and discerning decor, this is the place to come for electronica and ambient sounds. It heaves on weekends or when guest DJs crank up the volume. Happy hour until 9pm.

Miss Wong
COCKTAIL BAR

(Map p94; The Lane; ⏰5pm-late; 📶) Miss Wong carries you back to the chic of 1920s Shanghai. The cocktails are a draw here, making it a cool place to while away an evening, with a new menu offering dim sum. Gay-friendly and extremely popular with the well-heeled expat crowd.

Asana
BAR

(Map p94; www.asana-cambodia.com; The Lane; ⏰11am-late; 📶) Also known as the wooden house, this is a traditional Cambodian countryside dwelling dropped into the backstreets of Siem Reap and makes for an atmospheric place to imbibe. Lounge on *capok*-filled rice sacks over a classic cocktail made with infused rice wine. Khmer cocktail classes available at US$15 per person.

The Yellow Sub
BAR

(Map p94; www.theyellow-sub.com; The Lane; ⏰11am-11pm; 📶) No prizes for guessing the theme, but as Beatles tribute bars go, this has to be one of the best. Memorabilia plasters the walls, including signed album covers and artworks. Venture upstairs and there are multi-levels, including a pool table and a 4th-floor whisky bar with single malts. Great food as well, including Beatles-themed burgers.

Silk Garden
BAR

(Map p94; The Lane; ⏰3pm-late; 📶) Hidden away in the maze of lanes, this is a relaxing place to sink some drinks away from the pandemonium of Pub St. Little garden, silk drapes and a chill-out area upstairs.

Mezze Bar
LOUNGE BAR

(Map p94; mezzebarsiemreap.com; St 11; ⏰6pm-late; 📶) One of the hippest bars in Siem Reap, Mezze is located above the madness that surrounds Pub St. Ascend the stairs to

---

THE CAMBODIAN BEER GARDEN EXPERIENCE

There are dozens of beer gardens around Siem Reap that cater to young Cambodians working in the tourism industry. These can be a great experience for cheap beer, local snacks and getting to know some Cambodians beyond your driver or guide. All serve up ice-cold beer, some served in 3L beer towers complete with chiller. They can be a bit laddish by Cambodian standards, so solo female travellers might want to hook up with a traveller crowd before venturing forth.

The best strip is just north of Airport Rd from the first set of traffic lights after Sivatha St. Samut Siem Reap (Map p90; ⏰5pm-late) is one of the best of the bunch, with a huge central bar, regular football on big screens and mighty beer towers. Wander around this area to see where the locals are hanging out.

---

a contemporary lounge bar complete with original art and regular DJs.

Charlie's
BAR

(Map p94; The Alley; ⏰8am-1am; 📶) A popular retro Americana bar with cheap drinks and a convivial crowd. It forms the missing link between the more sophisticated bars around Psar Chaa and the madness unfolding nightly on Pub St.

Linga Bar
COCKTAIL LOUNGE

(Map p94; The Alley; ⏰4pm-late; 📶) This chic gay bar attracts all comers thanks to a relaxed atmosphere, a cracking cocktail list and some big beats, which draw a dancing crowd later into the night.

Angkor What?
BAR

(Map p94; Pub St; ⏰5pm-late; 📶) Siem Reap's original bar claims to have been promoting irresponsible drinking since 1998. The happy hour (to 9pm) lightens the mood for later when everyone's bouncing along to indie anthems, sometimes on the tables, sometimes under them.

Molly Malone's
IRISH PUB

(Map p94; Pub St; ⏰7.30am-midnight; 📶) Siem Reap's original Irish pub brings the sparkle of the Emerald Isle to homesick Irish and a whole host of honorary Dubliners. Serves Powers whiskey, Guinness and excellent pub grub.

Temple Club
BAR

(Map p94; Pub St; ⏱10am-late; ☎) The only worshipping going on at this temple is 'all hail the ale'. This place starts moving early and doesn't stop, but it's not for the hard of hearing as the music is permanently cranked up to 11. Dangerous happy hours from 10am to 10pm.

X Bar
BAR

(Map p94; Sivatha St; ⏱4pm-sunrise; ☎) One of *the* late-night spots in town, X Bar draws revellers for the witching hour when the other places are closing up. Early-evening movies on the big screen, pool tables and even a skateboard pipe...if you're not too hammered.

Picasso
TAPAS BAR

(Map p94; Alley West; ⏱5pm-late; ☎) A tiny tapas bar in the up-and-coming Alley West area, this is a convivial spot for a bit of over-the-counter banter. With only 10 stools, expect spillover into the street, especially once the cheap sangria, worldly wines and cheap Tiger bottles start flowing.

Nest
COCKTAIL LOUNGE

(Map p90; Sivatha St; ⏱11am-late; ☎) A memorable bar thanks to its sweeping sail-like shelters and stylish seating, this place has one of the most creative cocktail lists in town. Curl up in a sleigh bed and relax for the night. Also has an impressive menu of fusion and international cuisine should the munchies strike.

★ Entertainment

Several restaurants and hotels offer cultural performances during the evening, and for many visitors such shows offer the only opportunity to see Cambodian classical dance. While they may be aimed at tourists and are nowhere near as sophisticated as a performance of the Royal Ballet in Phnom Penh, to the untrained eye it is nonetheless graceful and alluring. Prices usually include a buffet meal.

Apsara Theatre
DANCE

(Map p90; ☑063-963561; www.angkorvillage.com/theatre.php; admission US$25) The setting is a striking wooden pavilion finished in the style of a wat, but the set menu is less inspiring. There are two shows per night and it's packed to the rafters with tour groups.

Beatocello
CLASSICAL MUSIC

(Map p116; www.beatocello.com; ⏱7.15pm Sat) 🍴 Better known as Dr Beat Richner, Beatocello performs cello compositions at Jayavarman VII Children's Hospital. Entry is free, but donations are welcome, as they assist the hospital in offering free medical treatment to the children of Cambodia.

La Noria Restaurant
SHADOW PUPPETS

(Map p90; ☑063-964242; show US$6, mains US$4-8) 🍴 For something a bit different, try the Wednesday-evening shadow-puppet show with classical dance at La Noria. Part of the fee is donated to a charity supporting local children.

Rosana Broadway
CABARET SHOW

(☑063-769991; www.rosanabroadway.com; US$25-45; ⏱7.30pm) Bringing a bit of Bangkok-style

ROLL UP, ROLL UP, THE CIRCUS HAS COME TO TOWN

Cambodia's answer to Cirque du Soleil, **Phare** (The Cambodian Circus; Map p90; ☑015 499480; www.pharecambodiancircus.org; behind Angkor National Museum; adult/child US$15/8, premium seats US$35/18; ⏱7.30pm) is so much more than a conventional circus, with an emphasis on performance art and a subtle yet striking social message behind each production. Cambodia's leading circus, theatre and performing arts organisation, Phare Ponleu Selpak opened its big top for nightly shows in 2013 and the results are a unique form of entertainment that should be considered unmissable when staying in Siem Reap. Several generations of performers have graduated through Phare's original Battambang campus and have gone on to perform in international shows around the world. Many of the performers have deeply moving personal stories of abuse and hardship, making their talents a triumph against the odds. An inspiring night out for adults and children alike, all proceeds are reinvested into Phare Ponleu Selpak activities. Animal lovers will be pleased to note there are no animals used in any performance.

Broadway to Siem Reap, this show includes cultural dances from the region and a not-so-cultural ladyboy cabaret, but ticket prices are on the high side.

Smile of Angkor   DINNER SHOW
(☑ 063-655 0168; www.smileofangkor.net; US$45-55; ⊘ 7.15pm) Popular with some Asian tour groups, this is the glitziest dinner-dance show in town, but in reality it doesn't live up to the hefty price tag.

Temple Club   DANCE
(Map p94; Pub St; ⊘ from 7.30pm) Free traditional dance show upstairs from 7.30pm, providing punters order some food and drink from the very reasonably priced menu.

🔒 Shopping

Much of what you see on sale in the markets of Siem Reap can also be purchased from children and vendors throughout the temple area. Some visitors get fed up with the endless sales pitches as they navigate the ancient wonders, while others enjoy the banter and a chance to interact with Cambodian people. It's often children out selling, and some visitors will argue that they should be at school instead. However, most do attend school at least half of the time, joining for morning or afternoon classes, alternating with siblings.

Items touted at the temples include postcards, T-shirts, temple bas-relief rubbings, curious musical instruments, ornamental knives and crossbows – the latter may raise a few eyebrows with customs should you try to take one home! Be sure to bargain, as overcharging is pretty common.

Cheap books on Angkor and Cambodia are hawked by kids around the temples, and by amputees trying to make a new start in Siem Reap. Be aware that many are illegal photocopies and the print quality is poor.

Psar Chaa   MARKET
(Old Market; Map p94) When it comes to shopping in town, Psar Chaa is well stocked with anything you may want to buy, and lots you don't. Silverware, silk, wood carvings, stone carvings, Buddhas, paintings, rubbings, notes and coins, T-shirts, table mats...the list goes on. There are bargains to be had if you haggle patiently and humorously. Avoid buying old stone carvings that vendors claim are from Angkor. Whether or not they are real, buying these artefacts serves only to

encourage their plunder and they will usually be confiscated by customs.

Angkor Night Market   MARKET
(Map p90; www.angkornightmarket.com; ⊘ 4pm-midnight) Near Sivatha St, this is a popular place on the Siem Reap shopping scene. It's packed with stalls selling a variety of handicrafts, souvenirs and silks and is well worth a browse to take advantage of cooler temperatures. It's also possible to chill out in the Island Bar, indulge in a Dr Fish massage or watch a 3D event movie (US$3) about the Khmer Rouge or the scourge of landmines. There are now half a dozen copycats in the near vicinity.

Siem Reap Art Center   NIGHT MARKET
(Map p90; www.siemreapartcenter.com; south bank of Siem Reap River; ⊘ 4-11pm) One of the newer night markets in town, this is pretty similar to the rest, but it is connected to the Psar Chaa area via a traditional wooden bridge across the Siem Reap River.

Bambou Indochine   CLOTHING
(Map p94; Alley West; ⊘ 10am-10pm) Original clothing designs inspired by Indochina. A cut above the average souvenir T-shirts.

Blue Apsara   BOOKS
(Map p94; ⊘ 9am-9pm) Longest-running secondhand bookshop in town, with a good selection of English, French and German titles. Psar Chaa area.

Diwo Gallery   ART GALLERY
(www.tdiwo.com; Wat Svay district; ⊘ 9am-6pm) French photographer and writer Thierry Diwo's collection of art photography from around Angkor and high-quality replica bronze, stone and wood sculptures.

Eric Raisina Workshop   FASHION
(Map p116; ☑ 063-965207; www.ericraisina.com; Wat Thmei area; ⊘ by appointment) Renowned designer Eric Raisina brings a unique cocktail of influences to his couture. Born in Madagascar, raised in France and resident in Cambodia, he offers a striking collection of clothing and accessories.

Jayav Art   SCULPTURE
(Map p116; ☑ 089 588121; A25 Charles de Gaulle Blvd; ⊘ 9am-6pm) Inspired by all the beautiful Angkorian sculpture around the temples, but lacking the excess baggage limit to lug replica statues all the way home? Talk to Jayav Art, which specialises in exquisite papier-mâché replica sculptures in various sizes.

McDermott Gallery
PHOTOGRAPHY

(Map p94; www.mcdermottgallery.com; The Alley; ⊙10am-10pm) These are the famous images you have seen of Angkor. Calendars, cards and striking sepia images of the temples, plus regular exhibitions.

Monument Books
BOOKS

(Map p90; Pokambor Ave; ⊙9am-9pm) Well-stocked new bookstore near Psar Chaa, with an additional branch at the airport.

Mooglee
CLOTHING

(Map p94; www.mooglee.com; The Lane; ⊙10am-10pm) New T-shirt shop with some original designs, including elephants at Angkor, tigers at the temples and old Angkor travel posters.

Rogue
MUSIC

(Map p94; Pithnou St; ⊙10am-10pm) Sells iPods, downloads, accessories and T-shirts.

Spicy Green Mango
FASHION

(Map p94; www.spicygreenmango.com; Alley West; ⊙8am-10pm) Small designer boutique with fun and funky fashion and accessories, in an old house that looks straight out of Provence.

Theam's House
LACQUER GALLERY

(www.theamshouse.com; ⊙8am-7pm) Cambodian artist and designer Theam spent years helping Artisans d'Angkor revitalise Khmer handicrafts and now operates his own studio of lacquer creations and artwork. Highly original – just make sure you find a driver who knows where it is.

Three Seasons
FASHION

(Map p94; The Lane; ⊙10am-10pm) Three shops in one at this new place, including Elsewhere, Zoco and Keo Kjay, a fair-trade fashion enterprise helping HIV-positive women earn a living.

SHOPPING FOR A CAUSE

Several shops support Cambodia's disabled and disenfranchised through their production process or their profits. Consider spending at one of these worthy places:

Artisans d'Angkor (Map p90; www.artisansdangkor.com; ⊙7.30am-6.30pm) High-quality reproduction carvings and exquisite silks are available. Impoverished youngsters are trained in the arts of their ancestors at Les Chantiers Écoles (p88).

IKTT (Map p90; Tonlé Sap Rd; ⊙9am-5pm) A traditional wooden house that is home to the Institute for Khmer Traditional Textiles. Fine *kramas*, scarves, throws and more.

Mekong Quilts (Map p90; www.mekong-quilts.org; 5 Sivatha St; ⊙8am-10pm) Handmade bed covers, quilts, home accessories and more in cotton, linen and silk. Supports women from poor rural areas and helps them earn money within their community.

Nyemo (Map p90; www.nyemo.com; Angkor Night Market; ⊙4pm-midnight) Silk products such as cushions, hangings and throws, plus children's toys. Proceeds are used to help HIV/AIDS sufferers and vulnerable women generally.

Rajana (Map p90; ☑063-964744; www.rajanacrafts.org; Sivatha St; ⊙9am-9pm Mon-Sat) Sells quirky wooden and metalwork objects, well-designed silver jewellery and handmade cards. Rajana promotes fair trade and employment opportunities for Cambodians.

Rehab Craft (Map p94; Pokambar Ave; ⊙8am-5.30pm) Small shop selling traditional scarves, silk items, carvings, paintings and postcards, all to assist the disabled community in Cambodia.

Samatoa (Map p94; ☑012 285930; www.samatoa.com; Pithnou St; ⊙8am-11pm) If you find yourself in need of a party frock, this designer dress shop offers original threads in silk, with the option of a tailored fit in 48 hours. Samatoa promotes fair trade.

Senteurs d'Angkor (Map p94; ☑063-964860; Pithnou St; ⊙8.30am-9.30pm) Opposite Psar Chaa, this shop has an eclectic collection of silk and carvings, as well as a superb range of traditional beauty products and spices, all made locally. It targets rural poor and disadvantaged for jobs and training, and sources local products from farmers. Visit its **Botanic Garden** (⊙7.30am-5.30pm) on Airport Rd, a sort of Willy Wonka's for the senses, where you can sample infused teas and speciality coffees.

Smateria (Map p94; www.smateria.com; Alley West; ⊙10am-10pm) Recycling rocks here, with funky bags made from construction nets, plastic bags, motorbike seat covers and more. Fair-trade enterprise employing some disabled Cambodians.

❶ Orientation

Siem Reap is still a small town at heart and is easy enough to navigate. The centre is around Psar Chaa (Old Market) and accommodation is spread throughout town. National Hwy 6 (NH6) cuts across the northern part of town, passing Psar Leu (Main Market) in the east of town and the Royal Residence and the Grand Hotel d'Angkor in the centre, and then heads to the airport and beyond to the Thai border. The Siem Reap River (Stung Siem Reap) flows north–south through the centre of town, and has enough bridges that you won't have to worry too much about being on the wrong side. As in Phnom Penh, however, street numbering is haphazard to say the least, so take care when hunting down specific addresses.

Angkor Wat and Angkor Thom are only 6km and 8km north of town, respectively.

Buses and share taxis usually drop passengers off at the bus station/taxi park about 3km east of the town centre, from where it's a short *moto* or *remork-moto (tuk-tuk)* ride to nearby guesthouses and hotels. Fast boats from Phnom Penh and Battambang arrive at Phnom Krom, about 11km south of town, and most places to stay include a free transfer by *moto* or minibus. Siem Reap International Airport is 7km west of town and there are plenty of taxis and *motos* available for transfers to the town centre.

❶ Information

Pick up a copy of the *Siem Reap Angkor Visitors Guide* (www.canbypublications.com), which is packed with listings and comes out quarterly. Check out *Drinking and Dining* for the low-down on bars and restaurants, or *Out and About* for shops and services, both produced by **Pocket Guide Cambodia** (www.cambodiapocketguide.com) and widely available.

DANGERS & ANNOYANCES

Siem Reap is a pretty safe city, even at night. However, if you rent a bike, don't keep your bag in the basket, as it will be easy pickings for a drive-by snatch. Likewise, lone females should try to walk home with travelling companions when leaving late-night spots, particularly if heading through poorly lit areas.

There are a lot of commission scams in Siem Reap that involve certain guesthouses and small hotels paying *moto* and taxi drivers to deliver guests. Ways to avoid these scams include booking ahead via the internet and arranging a pick-up, or sticking with a partner guesthouse if you are coming from Phnom Penh. Alternatively, just go with the flow and negotiate with the hotel or guesthouse on arrival.

There are a lot of beggars around town and some visitors quickly develop beggar fatigue.

However, try to remember that with no social-security network and no government support, life is pretty tough for the poorest of the poor in Cambodia. In the case of children, it is often better not to encourage begging, but, if you are compelled to help, then offer food, as money usually ends up being passed on to someone else. These days the problem is less serious, as many have been retrained to sell books or postcards to tourists instead of simply begging.

Watch out for the powder formula scam taking place in Siem Reap. A woman and baby approach asking for help to buy milk for the baby. Visitor agrees and gets asked to buy the most expensive brand in the nearby minimart. Transaction over, woman and baby then take the formula back to the shop and split the profit.

Out at the remote temple sites beyond Angkor, stick to clearly marked trails. There are still landmines at locations such as Phnom Kulen and Koh Ker.

EMERGENCY

Tourist Police (☎ 097 778 0013) Located at the main ticket checkpoint for the Angkor area, this is the place to come and lodge a complaint if you encounter any serious problems while in Siem Reap.

INTERNET ACCESS

Internet shops have spread through town like wildfire and your nearest online fix will never be far away. Prices are US$0.50 to US$1 per hour and most places also offer cheap internet-based telephone calls. The greatest concentration is along Sivatha St and around the Psar Chaa area. Almost all guesthouses and hotels also offer free access for guests, either via a free terminal or free wi-fi. Many of the leading restaurants and bars also offer free wi-fi these days.

MEDICAL SERVICES

Siem Reap now has an international-standard hospital for emergencies. However, any serious complications will still require relocation to Bangkok.

Angkor Children's Hospital (Map p90; ☎ 063-963409; ⏱ 24hr) This international-standard paediatric hospital is the place to take your children if they fall sick. Will also assist adults in an emergency for up to 24 hours. Donations accepted.

Royal Angkor International Hospital (☎ 063-761888; www.royalangkorhospital.com; Airport Rd) A new international facility; affiliated with the Bangkok Hospital, so very expensive.

U-Care Pharmacy (Map p94; ☎ 063-965396; Pithnou St; ⏱ 8am-9pm) Smart pharmacy and shop like Boots in Thailand (and the UK). English spoken.

MONEY

For cash exchanges, markets (usually at jewellery stalls or dedicated money-changing stalls) are faster and less bureaucratic than the banks.

ANZ Royal Bank (Map p90; Achar Mean St) Credit-card advances and can change travellers cheques in most major currencies. Several branches and many ATMs (US$5 per withdrawal) around town.

Canadia Bank (Map p90; Sivatha St) Offers free credit-card cash advances and changes travellers cheques in most major currencies at a 2% commission. International ATM with no transaction fees.

POST

Main Post Office (Map p90; ⊙7am-5.30pm) Services are more reliable these days, but it doesn't hurt to see your stamps franked. Includes a branch of EMS express mail.

TELEPHONE & FAX

Making international calls is straightforward. The cheapest way is to use the major internet cafes, with calls starting at about US$0.10 per minute, but there can be some delay. The cheapest 'unblemished' calls can be arranged with one of the many private booths advertising these telephone services. Hotels impose hefty surcharges on calls, so check the rates before you dial.

TOURIST INFORMATION

It's hard to believe given the sheer number of tourists passing through Siem Reap, but there isn't a dedicated official tourism office in the town. Guesthouses and hotels are often a more reliable source of information, as are fellow travellers who have been in town for a few days.

ⓘ Getting There & Away

AIR

There are direct international flights from Siem Reap to Bangkok in Thailand; Vientiane, Luang Prabang and Pakse in Laos; Ho Chi Minh City (Saigon), Hanoi and Danang in Vietnam; Hong Kong; Kuala Lumpur in Malaysia; Kunming in China; Seoul in South Korea; Singapore; Taipei in Taiwan; and Yangon in Myanmar.

Domestic links are currently limited to Phnom Penh (from US$90 one way) and Sihanoukville (from US$110 one way), and only Cambodia Angkor Airways currently operates these routes. Cheaper specials are sometimes offered, but these are usually restricted to Cambodian nationals. Demand for seats is high during peak season, so book as far in advance as possible.

BOAT

There are daily express boat services between Siem Reap and Phnom Penh (US$35, five to six hours) or Battambang (US$20, four to eight hours or more, depending on the season). The boat to Phnom Penh is rather overpriced these days, given it is just as fast by road and so much cheaper. The Battambang trip is seriously scenic, but breakdowns are *very* common.

Boats from Siem Reap leave from the floating village of Chong Kneas near Phnom Krom, about 11km south of Siem Reap. The boats dock in different places at different times of the year; when the lake recedes in the dry season, both the port and floating village move with it. An all-weather road has improved access around the lake area, but the main road out to the lake takes a pummelling in the annual October floods.

Most of the guesthouses in town sell boat tickets. Buying the ticket from a guesthouse usually includes a *moto* or minibus ride to the port. Otherwise, a *moto* out here costs about US$2, a *remork-moto* about US$5 and a taxi about US$10.

BUS

The road linking Siem Reap to Phnom Penh varies in condition from year to year, but was severely damaged by floods in late-2013, leading to some very bumpy sections between Kompong Thom and Skuon. The road west to Sisophon, Thailand and Battambang has been completely rebuilt and is in great condition.

All buses depart from the bus station/taxi park, which is 3km east of town and nearly 1km south of NH6. Tickets are available at guesthouses, hotels, bus offices, travel agencies

TRANSPORT FROM SIEM REAP

DESTINATION	CAR & MOTORBIKE	BUS	BOAT	AIR
Phnom Penh	6hr	US$5-13, 7hr, frequent	US$35, 5hr, 7am	from US$90, 30min, 4 daily
Kompong Thom	2hr	US$5, 3hr, frequent	N/A	N/A
Battambang	3hr	US$4-5, 4hr, regular	US$20, 6-8hr, 7am	N/A
Poipet	3hr	US$4-5, 4hr, regular	N/A	N/A
Bangkok	8hr	US$12-15, 10hr, frequent	N/A	from US$90, 1hr, 5 daily

and ticket kiosks. Some bus companies send a minibus around to pick up passengers at their place of lodging. Most departures to Phnom Penh are between 7am and 1pm, but there are also some night buses available. Buses to other destinations generally leave early in the morning. Upon arrival in Siem Reap, be prepared for a rugby scrum of eager *moto* drivers when getting off the bus. Express minibus services to Phnom Penh (US$10) are gaining in popularity as they can save considerable time on the poor sections of road. Newcomer Golden Bayon Express is a recommended option.

A number of bus companies serve Siem Reap, and all have booths or offices out at the bus station. Some also have offices in the downtown area where Sivatha St meets the Siem Reap River.

Tickets to Phnom Penh (six hours), via NH6, cost US$5 to US$13, depending on the level of service (air-con, comfy seats, a toilet, a hostess) and whether there's a hotel pick-up. Many companies charge the same price to Kompong Thom as they do to Phnom Penh. Several companies offer direct services to Kompong Cham (US$6, five or six hours), Battambang (US$3.75, three hours), Sisophon (US$3.75, two hours) and Poipet (US$3.75, three hours). GST has a bus to Anlong Veng (US$4, two hours) and on to Sra Em (for Prasat Preah Vihear; US$10, four hours, 7am). There are no through buses to Ho Chi Minh City, but it is possible to change in Phnom Penh.

Advertised direct services to Koh Kong do not actually go direct, but via Sihanoukville, so it is better to take a bus to Phnom Penh and change for Koh Kong there.

Capitol Tour (☑063-963883) Serves Phnom Penh, Poipet, Battambang and Bangkok.

Giant Ibis (www.giantibis.com) Smartest operator with daily service to Phnom Penh (US$13) and free wi-fi on board.

Gold VIP (☑063-632 7600) Express minibuses to Phnom Penh and night bus (US$10) departing at midnight.

GST (Map p90; ☑092 905016) Serves Phnom Penh, Anlong Veng and Sra Em (for Prasat Preah Vihear).

Mekong Express (Map p90; ☑063-963662) Serves Phnom Penh and Ho Chi Minh City.

Neak Kror Horm (☑063-964924) Serves Phnom Penh and Poipet.

Paramount Angkor Express (Map p90; ☑063-966469) Serves Phnom Penh, Sisophon and Battambang.

Phnom Penh Sorya (☑012 235618) Serves Phnom Penh, Poipet and Battambang.

Rith Mony (☑012 344377) Serves Phnom Penh and Kompong Cham.

Virak Buntham (☑017 790440) Night buses to Phnom Penh (US$11) and Sihanoukville (US$17).

SIEM REAP GETTING AROUND

INTERNATIONAL BUS TO BANGKOK

Many guesthouses and travel companies offer 'international' bus tickets to Bangkok (around US$15) with a change of bus at the border. There are even some 'night' buses advertised, but these of pretty pointless given the Poipet border does not open until 7am!

Nattakan (☑078 795333; Sivatha St) offers a 'direct' bus to Bangkok (US$25) daily at 8am departing from its Sivatha St office, including fast-track immigration at the border. It may not be so advantageous departing Cambodia but might prove very useful for travellers entering Cambodia this way. However, visa-overcharging is a risk, so it may be smart to arrange a Cambodian e-visa (US$25) in advance of travel. From Bangkok to Siem Reap, the bus departs Mo Chit Bus Terminal at 9am and tickets cost 750B.

CAR, SHARE TAXI, MINIBUS & PICK-UP

As well as buses, share taxis and other vehicles operate some of the main routes and these can be a little quicker than buses.

Destinations include Phnom Penh (US$10, five hours), Kompong Thom (US$5, two hours), Sisophon (US$5, two hours) and Poipet (US$7, three hours). To get to the temple of Banteay Chhmar, head to Sisophon and arrange onward transport there.

❶ Getting Around

Following are insights into the most common forms of transport used for getting around Siem Reap.

TO/FROM THE AIRPORT

Siem Reap International Airport is 7km from the town centre. Many hotels and guesthouses in Siem Reap offer a free airport pick-up service with advance bookings. Official taxis are available next to the terminal for US$7. A trip to the city centre on the back of a *moto* is US$2. *Remork-motos* are available for about US$5, depending on the hotel or guesthouse location.

BICYCLE

Some of the guesthouses around town hire out bicycles, as do a few shops around Psar Chaa, usually for US$1 to US$2 a day. The **White Bicycles** (www.thewhitebicycles.org) project rents bicycles, with all proceeds going towards supporting local development projects around Siem

Reap. Imported mountain bikes are available from cycling tour operators (p95) for around US$8 to US$10.

CAR & MOTORCYCLE

Most hotels and guesthouses can organise car hire for the day, with a going rate of US$25 and up. Upmarket hotels may charge more. Foreigners are forbidden to rent motorcycles in and around Siem Reap. If you want to get around on your own motorcycle, you need to hire one in Phnom Penh and ride it to Siem Reap.

MOTO

A *moto* with a driver will cost about US$8 to US$10 per day. The average cost for a short trip within town is 2000r or so, more to places strung out along the roads to Angkor or the airport. It is probably best to negotiate in advance these days, as with the tourism boom a lot of drivers have got into the habit of overcharging.

REMORK-MOTO

Remork-motos are sweet little motorcycles with carriages (commonly called *tuk-tuks* around town), and are a nice way for couples to get about Siem Reap, although drivers like to inflate the prices. Try for US$1 on trips around town, although drivers may charge US$2 for a trip to the edges of town at night. Prices rise when you add more people.

AROUND SIEM REAP

Prek Toal Bird Sanctuary ជម្រកបក្សីព្រែកទាល់

Prek Toal is one of three biospheres on Tonlé Sap lake, and this stunning bird sanctuary makes it the most worthwhile and straightforward of the three to visit. It is an ornithologist's fantasy, with a significant number of rare breeds gathered in one small area, including the huge lesser and greater adjutant storks, the milky stork and the spot-billed pelican. Even the uninitiated will be impressed, as these birds have a huge wingspan and build enormous nests.

Visitors during the dry season (December to April) will find the concentration of birds like something out of a Hitchcock film. It is also possible to visit from September, but the concentrations may be lower. As water starts to dry up elsewhere, the birds congregate here. Serious twitchers know that the best time to see birds is early morning or late afternoon and this means an early start or an overnight at Prek Toal's environment office, where there are basic beds for US$15/20 per single/double.

Several ecotourism companies arrange trips out to Prek Toal. Sam Veasna Center (Map p90; ☎063-963710; www.samveasna.org), in the Wat Bo area of Siem Reap, offers trips to Prek Toal that contribute to the conservation of the area. Sam Veasna uses ecotourism to provide an income for local communities in return for a ban on hunting and cutting down the forest. The trips cost about US$100 per person for a group of five or more, with additional charges for smaller groups. Osmose (☎012 832812; www.osmosetonlesap.net) also runs organised day trips to Prek Toal. The day trips cost US$95 per person with a minimum group of four people.

Tours include transport, entrance fees, guides, breakfast, lunch and water. Binoculars are available on request, plus the Sam Veasna Center has spotting scopes. Both outfits can arrange overnight trips for serious enthusiasts. Some proceeds from the tours go towards educating children and villagers about the importance of the birds and the unique flooded-forest environment, and the trip includes a visit to one of the local communities. Day trips include a hotel pick-up around 6am and a return by nightfall.

Getting to the sanctuary under your own steam requires you to take a 20-minute *moto* (US$2 or so) or taxi (US$10 one way) ride to the floating village of Chong Kneas (depending on the time of day additional fees may have to be paid at the new port) and then a boat to the environment office (around US$55 return, one hour each way). From here, a small boat (US$30 including a guide) will take you into the sanctuary, which is about one hour beyond.

Sunscreen and head protection are essential, as it can get very hot in the dry season. The guides are equipped with booklets with the bird names in English, but they speak little English themselves, hence the advantage of travelling with the Sam Veasna Center or Osmose (both of which can provide English-speaking guides).

Ang Trapeng Thmor Reserve អាងត្រពាំងថ្ម(ជម្រកសត្វក្រៀល)

This bird sanctuary (admission US$10) is just across the border in the Phnom Srok region of Banteay Meanchey Province, about 100km from Siem Reap. It's one of only a handful of places in the world where it's possible to see the extremely rare sarus crane, as depicted on bas-reliefs at Bayon. These grey-feathered birds have immensely long legs and striking red heads. The reserve is based around a reservoir created by forced labour during the Khmer Rouge regime, and the facilities are very basic, but it is an incredibly beautiful place. Bring your own binoculars, however, as none are available here.

To reach here, follow the road to Sisophon for about 72km before turning north at Prey Mon. It's 22km to the site, passing through some famous silk-weaving villages. The Sam Veasna Center (see left) arranges birding trips (US$100 per person with a group of four) out here, which is probably the easiest way to undertake the trip.

Floating Village of Chong Kneas ភូមិបណ្ដែតចុងឃ្នាស

This famous floating village is now extremely popular with visitors who want a break from the temples, and it's an easy excursion to arrange yourself. If you want something a bit more peaceful, try venturing to one of the other Tonlé Sap villages further afield. Visitors arriving by boat from Phnom Penh or Battambang get a sneak preview, as the floating village is near Phnom Krom, where the boat docks. It is very scenic in the warm light of early morning or late afternoon and can be combined with a view of the sunset from the hilltop temple of Phnom Krom. The downside is that tour groups tend to take over, and boats end up chugging up and down the channels in convoy. Avoid the crowds by asking your boat driver to take you down some of the back channels.

Visitors should stop in at the Gecko Centre (www.tsbr-ed.org; ⊙8.30am-5.30pm), an informative exhibition that is located in the floating village and helps to unlock the secrets of the Tonlé Sap. It has displays on flora and fauna of the area, as well as information on communities living around the lake.

The village moves depending on the season and you will need to rent a boat to get around it properly. However, Sou Ching, the company that runs the tours here has fixed boat prices at an absurd US$20 per person, plus a US$3 entrance fee. This makes it very

poor value by comparison with the temples of Angkor. In practice it may be possible to pay just US$20 for the boat shared between several people.

One of the best ways to visit for the time being is to hook up with the Tara Boat (☏092 957765; www.taraboat.com), which offers all-inclusive trips with a meal aboard its converted cargo boat. Prices include transfers, entry fees, local boats, a tour guide and a two-course meal, starting from US$27 for a lunch to US$33 for a sunset dinner.

Getting to the floating village from Siem Reap costs US$2 by *moto* each way (more if the driver waits), or US$15 or so by taxi. The trip takes 20 minutes. Or rent a bicycle in town and just pedal out here, as it is a leisurely 11km through pretty villages and rice fields.

Kompong Pluk ព្រែលិចទឹកកំពង់ភ្លុក

More memorable than Chong Kneas, but harder to reach, is the village of Kompong Pluk, an otherworldly place built on soaring stilts. Nearby is a flooded forest, inundated every year when the lake rises to take the Mekong's overflow. As the lake drops, the petrified trees are revealed. Exploring this area by wooden dugout in the wet season is very atmospheric. The village itself is a friendly place, where most of the houses are built on stilts of about 6m high, almost bamboo skyscrapers. It looks like it's straight out of a film set. Rather like Chong Kneas, prices have been fixed at US$20 per person for a boat, plus there is a US$1 entry fee, but again it may be possible to negotiate this as a per boat cost split between a group.

There are two ways to get to Kompong Pluk. One is to come via the floating village of Chong Kneas, where a boat (1¼ hours) can be arranged from US$55 return, and the other is to come via the small town of Roluos by a combination of road (about US$7 by *moto* or US$20 by taxi) and boat (US$8). All said, the road-and-boat route will take up to two hours, but it depends on the season – sometimes it's more by road, sometimes more by boat. The new road brings the dry-season access time to less than one hour. Tara Boat (see above) also offers day trips here for US$60 per person.

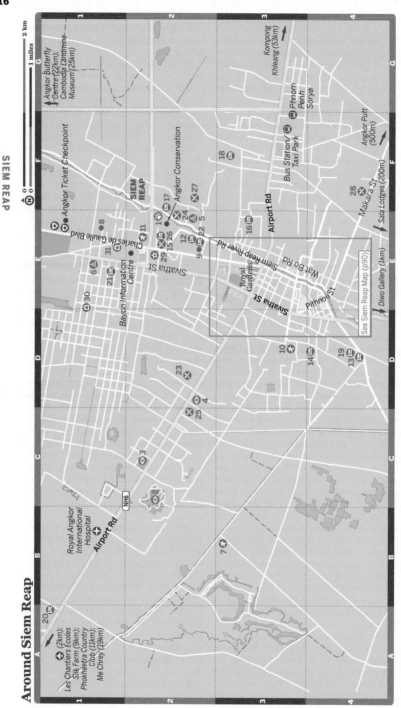

Around Siem Reap

116

SIEM REAP

N 0 — 1 miles
0 — 2 km

Les Chantiers Écoles;
Silk Farm (9km);
Phokheetra Country
Club (11km);
Me Chrey (19km) (2km)

20

NH6

Airport Rd

Royal Angkor
International
Hospital

3

2

7

23

25

4

10

14

19

13

Bayon Information
Centre

Sivatha St

30

6

21

31

29

15 26

9

12

22 5

11

8

Charles de Gaulle Blvd

Angkor Ticket Checkpoint

SIEM
REAP

Angkor Conservation

1

17

24

27

18

16

Airport Rd

Wat Bo Rd

Siem Reap River Rd

Royal
Gardens

Sivatha St

Pithnou St

See Siem Reap Map (p90)

Diwo Gallery (1km)

28

Makara St

Sala Lodges (200m)

Angkor Putt
(500m)

Bus Station/
Taxi Park

Phnom
Penh
Sorya

Kompong
Khleang (53km)

Angkor Butterfly
Centre (22km);
Cambodia Landmine
Museum (25km)

Around Siem Reap

Kompong Khleang កំពង់ឃ្លាំង

One of the largest communities on the Tonlé Sap, Kompong Khleang is more of a town than the other villages, and comes complete with several ornate pagodas. As in Kompong Pluk, most of the houses here are built on towering stilts to allow for a dramatic change in water level. Few tourists visit here compared with the floating villages closer to Siem Reap, but that might be a reason to visit in itself. There is only a small floating community on the lake itself, but the stilted town is an interesting place to browse for an hour or two. A boat trip around the town and out to the lake is about US$20 for a couple of hours, but they may ask for US$30. It is not that difficult to reach from Siem Reap thanks to an all-weather road via the junction town of Dam Dek, but the trip will cost about US$40 return by taxi.

Me Chrey មេជ្រៃ

One of the more recently 'discovered' floating villages, **Me Chrey** (admission US$1) lies midway between Siem Reap and Prek Toal. It is one of the smaller villages in the area but sees far fewer tourists than busy Chong Kneas. Me Chrey moves with the water level and is prettier during the wet season, when houses are anchored around an island pagoda. It is located to the south of Puok district, about 25km from Siem Reap. Arrange transport by road for about US$8 for a *moto* or US$25 for a taxi before switching to a boat (US$15 to US$20 for fewer than 10 people) to explore the area.

SIEM REAP KOMPONG KHLEANG

Temples of Angkor

Best Temples for Sunrise or Sunset

➡ Angkor Wat (p130)

➡ Bayon (p139)

➡ Phnom Bakheng (p144)

➡ Pre Rup (p150)

➡ Sra Srang (p147)

Best Temples for Film Buffs

➡ Angkor Wat (p130)

➡ Bayon (p139)

➡ Beng Mealea (p155)

➡ East Gate of Angkor Thom (p139)

➡ Ta Prohm (p146)

Why Go?

Welcome to heaven on earth. Angkor (ប្រាសាទអង្គរ) is the earthly representation of Mt Meru, the Mt Olympus of the Hindu faith and the abode of ancient gods. The temples are the perfect fusion of creative ambition and spiritual devotion. The Cambodian 'god-kings' of old each strove to better their ancestors in size, scale and symmetry, culminating in the world's largest religious building, Angkor Wat.

The temples of Angkor are a source of inspiration and national pride to all Khmers as they struggle to rebuild their lives after years of terror and trauma. Today, the temples are a point of pilgrimage for all Cambodians, and no traveller to the region will want to miss their extravagant beauty. Angkor is one of the world's foremost ancient sites, with the epic proportions of the Great Wall of China, the detail and intricacy of the Taj Mahal and the symbolism and symmetry of the pyramids, all rolled into one.

Don't Miss

➡ Seeing the sun rise over the holiest of holies, Angkor Wat (p130), the world's largest religious building

➡ Contemplating the serenity and splendour of Bayon (p139), its 216 enigmatic faces staring out into the jungle

➡ Witnessing nature reclaiming the stones at the mysterious ruin of Ta Prohm (p146), the *Tomb Raider* temple

➡ Staring in wonder at the delicate carvings adorning Banteay Srei (p153), the finest seen at Angkor

➡ Trekking deep into the jungle to discover the River of a Thousand Lingas at Kbal Spean (p153)

➡ Exploring the tangled vines, crumbling corridors and jumbled sandstone blocks of Beng Mealea (p155)

History

The Angkorian period spans more than 600 years from AD 802 to 1432. This incredible age saw the construction of the temples of Angkor and the consolidation of the Khmer empire's position as one of the great powers in Southeast Asia. This era encompasses periods of decline and revival, and wars with rival powers in Vietnam, Thailand and Myanmar. This brief history deals only with the periods that produced the temples that can be seen at Angkor.

The hundreds of surviving temples are but the sacred skeleton of the vast political, religious and social centre of Cambodia's ancient Khmer empire; a city that, at its zenith, boasted a population of one million when London was a small town of 50,000. The houses, public buildings and palaces of Angkor were constructed of wood – now long decayed – because the right to dwell in structures of brick or stone was reserved for the gods.

An Empire is Born

The Angkorian period began with the rule of Jayavarman II (r 802–50). He was the first to unify Cambodia's competing kingdoms before the birth of Angkor. His court was situated at various locations, including Phnom Kulen, 40km northeast of Angkor Wat, and Roluos (known then as Hariharalaya), 13km east of Siem Reap.

Jayavarman II proclaimed himself a *devaraja* (god-king), the earthly representative of the Hindu god Shiva, and built a 'temple-mountain' at Phnom Kulen, symbolising Shiva's dwelling place of Mt Meru, the holy mountain at the centre of the universe. This set a precedent that became a dominant feature of the Angkorian period and accounts for the staggering architectural productivity of the Khmers at this time.

Indravarman I (r 877–89) is believed to have been a usurper, and probably inherited the mantle of *devaraja* through conquest. He built a 6.5-sq-km *baray* (reservoir) at Roluos and established Preah Ko. The *baray* was the first stage of an irrigation system that created a hydraulic city, the ancient Khmers mastering the cycle of nature to water their lands. Form and function worked together in harmony, as the *baray* also had religious significance, representing the oceans surrounding Mt Meru. Indravarman's final work was Bakong, a pyramidal representation of Mt Meru.

Indravarman I's son Yasovarman I (r 889–910) looked further afield to celebrate his divinity and glory in a temple-mountain of his own. He first built Lolei on an artificial island in the *baray* established by his father, before beginning work on the Bakheng. Today this hill is known as Phnom Bakheng, a favoured spot for viewing the sunset over Angkor Wat. A raised highway was constructed to connect Phnom Bakheng with Roluos, 16km to the southeast, and a large *baray* was constructed to the east of Phnom Bakheng. Today it is known as the Eastern Baray but has entirely silted up. Yasovarman I also established the temple-mountains of Phnom Krom and Phnom Bok.

After the death of Yasovarman I, power briefly shifted from the Angkor region to Koh Ker, around 80km to the northeast, under another usurper king, Jayavarman IV (r 924–42). In AD 944 power returned again to Angkor under the leadership of Rajendravarman II (r 944–68), who built the Eastern Mebon and Pre Rup. The reign of his son Jayavarman V (r 968–1001) produced the Ta Keo and Banteay Srei temples; the latter was built by a Brahman rather than the king.

The Golden Age of Angkor

The temples that are now the highlight of a visit to Angkor – Angkor Wat and those in and around the walled city of Angkor Thom – were built during the golden age or classical period. While this period is marked by fits of remarkable productivity, it was also a time of turmoil, conquests and setbacks. The great city of Angkor Thom owes its existence to the fact that the old city of Angkor, which stood on the same site, was destroyed during the Cham invasion of 1177.

Suryavarman I (r 1002–49) was a usurper to the throne who won the day through strategic alliances and military conquests. Although he adopted the Hindu cult of the god-king, he is thought to have come from a Mahayana Buddhist tradition and may even have sponsored the growth of Buddhism in Cambodia. Buddhist sculpture certainly became more commonplace in the Angkor region during his time.

Little physical evidence of Suryavarman I's reign remains at Angkor, but his military exploits brought much of central Thailand and southern-central Laos under the control of Angkor. His son Udayadityavarman II (r 1049–65) embarked on further military expeditions, extending the empire once more, and building Baphuon and the Western Mebon. Many major cities in the Mekong region were important Khmer settlements in the 11th and

TEMPLES OF ANGKOR HISTORY

Temples of Angkor

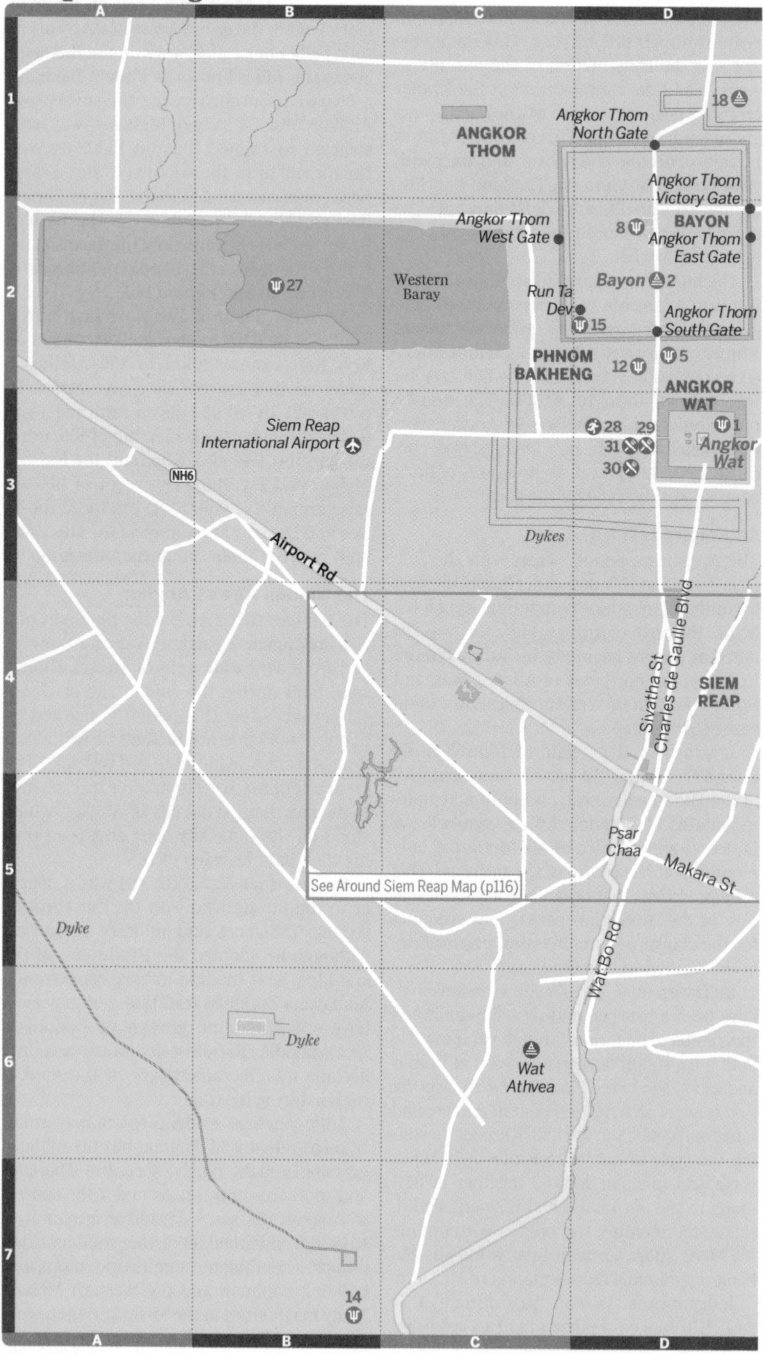

1 18

ANGKOR THOM

Angkor Thom
North Gate

Angkor Thom
Victory Gate

BAYON

8 Angkor Thom
East Gate

Angkor Thom
West Gate

Western
Baray

27

Bayon **2**

Run Ta
Dev

15 Angkor Thom
South Gate

**PHNOM
BAKHENG**

12 **5**

**ANGKOR
WAT**

28 **29** **1**

31 Angkor
Wat

30

Siem Reap
International Airport ✈

Dykes

NH6

Airport Rd

Sivatha St

Charles de Gaulle Blvd

**SIEM
REAP**

Psar
Chaa

Makara St

See Around Siem Reap Map (p116)

Dyke

Wat Bo Rd

Dyke

Wat
Athvea

14

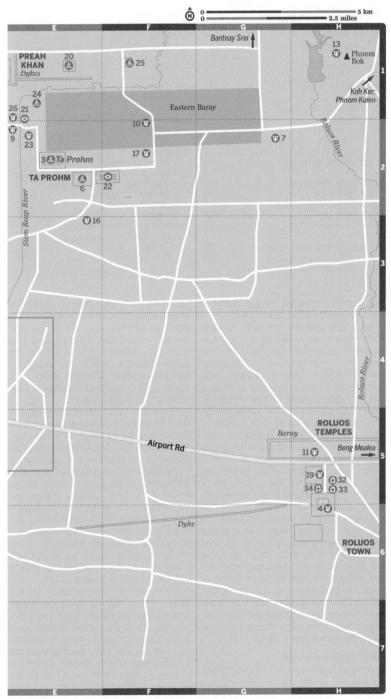

Temples of Angkor

12th centuries, including the Lao capital of Vientiane and the Thai city of Lopburi.

From 1066 until the end of the century, Angkor was again divided as rival factions contested the throne. The first important monarch of this new era was Suryavarman II (r 1112–52), who unified Cambodia and extended Khmer influence to Malaya and Myanmar (Burma). He also set himself apart religiously from earlier kings through his devotion to the Hindu deity Vishnu, to whom he consecrated the largest and arguably most magnificent of all the Angkorian temples, Angkor Wat.

The reign of Suryavarman II and the construction of Angkor Wat signifies one of the high-water marks of Khmer civilisation. However, there were signs that decline was lurking. It is thought that the hydraulic system of reservoirs and canals that supported the agriculture of Angkor had by this time been pushed beyond its limits, and was slowly starting to silt up due to overpopulation and deforestation. The construction of Angkor Wat was a major strain on resources, and, on top of this, Suryavarman II led a disastrous campaign against the Dai Viet (Vietnamese) late in his reign, during the course of which he was killed in battle.

Enter Jayavarman VII

In 1177 the Chams of southern Vietnam, then the Kingdom of Champa and long annexed by the Khmer empire, rose up and sacked Angkor. This attack caught the Khmers completely by surprise, as it came via sea, river and lake rather than the traditional land routes. The Chams burnt the wooden city and plundered its wealth. Four years later Jayavarman VII (r 1181–1219) struck back, emphatically driving the Chams out of Cambodia and reclaiming Angkor.

Jayavarman VII's reign has given scholars much to debate. It represents a radical departure from the reigns of his predecessors. For centuries the fount of royal divinity had reposed in the Hindu deity Shiva (and, occasionally, Vishnu). Jayavarman VII adopted Mahayana Buddhism and looked to Avalokiteshvara, the Bodhisattva of Compassion, for patronage during his reign. In doing so he may well have been converting to a religion that already enjoyed wide popular support among his subjects. It may also be that the destruction of Angkor was such a blow to royal divinity that a new religious foundation was thought to be needed.

During his reign, Jayavarman VII embarked on a dizzying array of temple projects that centred on Baphuon, which was the site of the capital city destroyed by the Chams. Angkor Thom, Jayavarman VII's new city, was surrounded by walls and a moat, which became another component of Angkor's complex irrigation system. The centrepiece of Angkor Thom was Bayon, the temple-mountain studded with faces that, along with Angkor Wat, is the most famous of Cambodia's temples. Other temples built during his reign include Ta Prohm, Banteay Kdei and Preah Khan. Further away, he rebuilt vast temple complexes, such as Banteay Chhmar and Preah Khan in Preah Vihear Province, making him by far the most prolific builder of Angkor's many kings.

Jayavarman VII also embarked on a major public-works program, building roads, schools and hospitals across the empire. Remains of many of these roads and their magnificent bridges can be seen across Cambodia. Spean Praptos at Kompong Kdei, 65km southeast of Siem Reap on National Hwy 6 (NH6), is the most famous, but there are many more lost in the forest on the old Angkorian road to the great Preah Khan, including the now accessible Spean Ta Ong, about 28km east of Beng Mealea near the village of Khvau.

After the death of Jayavarman VII around 1219, the Khmer empire went into decline. The state religion reverted to Hinduism for a century or more and outbreaks of iconoclasm saw Buddhist sculpture adorning the Hindu temples vandalised or altered. The Thais sacked Angkor in 1351, and again with devastating efficiency in 1431. The glorious Siamese capital of Ayuthaya, which enjoyed a golden age from the 14th to the 18th centuries, was in many ways a recreation of the glories of Angkor from which the Thai conquerors drew inspiration. The Khmer court moved to Phnom Penh, only to return fleetingly to Angkor in the 16th century; in the meantime, it was abandoned to pilgrims, holy men and the elements.

Angkor Rediscovered

The French 'discovery' of Angkor in the 1860s made an international splash and created a great deal of outside interest in Cambodia. But 'discovery', with all the romance it implied, was something of a misnomer. When French explorer Henri Mouhot first stumbled across Angkor Wat on his Royal Geographic Society expedition, it included a wealthy, working monastery with monks and slaves. Moreover, Portuguese travellers in the 16th century encountered Angkor, referring to it as the Walled City. Diego do Couto produced an accurate description of Angkor in 1614, but it was not published until 1958. A 17th-century Japanese pilgrim drew a detailed plan of Angkor Wat, though he mistakenly recalled that he had seen it in India.

Still, it was the publication of *Voyage à Siam et dans le Cambodge* by Mouhot, posthumously released in 1868, that first brought Angkor to the public eye. Although the explorer himself made no such claims, by the 1870s he was being celebrated as the discoverer of the lost temple-city of Cambodia. In fact, a French missionary known as Charles-Emile Bouillevaux had visited Angkor 10 years before Mouhot and had published an account of his own findings. However, the Bouillevaux account was roundly ignored and it was Mouhot's account, with its rich descriptions and tantalising pen-and-ink colour sketches of the temples, that turned the ruins into an international obsession.

Soon after Mouhot, other adventurers and explorers began to arrive. Scottish photographer John Thomson took the first photographs of the temples in 1866. He was the first Westerner to posit the idea that they were symbolic representations of the mythical Mt Meru. French architect Lucien Fournereau travelled to Angkor in 1887 and produced plans and meticulously executed cross-sections that were to stand as the best available until the 1960s.

From this time, Angkor became the target of French-financed expeditions and, in 1901, the École Française d'Extrême-Orient (EFEO; www.efeo.fr) began a long association with Angkor by funding an expedition to Bayon. In 1907 Angkor was returned to Cambodia, having been under Thai control for more than a century, and the EFEO took responsibility for clearing and restoring the whole site. In the same year, the first foreign tourists arrived in Angkor – an unprecedented 200 of them in three months. Angkor had been 'rescued' from the jungle and was assuming its place in the modern world.

Archaeology of Angkor

With the exception of Angkor Wat, which was restored for use as a Buddhist shrine in the 16th century by the Khmer royalty, the temples of Angkor were left to the jungle for many centuries. The majority of temples are made of sandstone, which tends to dissolve when in prolonged contact with dampness. Bat droppings took their toll, as did sporadic pilfering of sculptures and cut stones. At some monuments, such as Ta Prohm, the jungle had stealthily waged an all-out invasion, and plant life could only be removed at great risk to the structures it now supported in its web of roots.

Initial attempts to clear Angkor under the aegis of the EFEO were fraught with technical difficulties and theoretical disputes. On a technical front, the jungle tended to grow back as soon as it was cleared; on a theoretical front, scholars debated the extent to which temples should be restored and whether later additions, such as Buddha images in Hindu temples, should be removed.

It was not until the 1920s that a solution was found, known as anastylosis. This was the method the Dutch had used to restore Borobudur in Java. Put simply, it was a way of reconstructing monuments using the original materials and in keeping with the original form of the structure. New materials were permitted only where the originals could not be found, and were to be used discreetly. An example of this method can be seen on the causeway leading to the entrance of Angkor Wat, as the right-hand side was originally restored by the French.

The first major restoration job was carried out on Banteay Srei in 1930. It was deemed such a success that many more extensive restoration projects were undertaken elsewhere around Angkor, culminating in the massive Angkor Wat restoration in the 1960s. Large cranes and earth-moving machines were brought in, and the operation was backed by a veritable army of surveying equipment.

The Khmer Rouge victory and Cambodia's subsequent slide into an intractable civil war resulted in far less damage to Angkor than many had assumed, as EFEO and Ministry of Culture teams had removed many of the statues from the temple sites for protection. Nevertheless, turmoil in Cambodia resulted in a long interruption of restoration work, allowing the jungle to resume its assault on the monuments. The illegal trade of *objets d'art* on the world art market has also been a major threat to Angkor, although it is the more remote sites that have been targeted recently. Angkor has been under the jurisdiction of the UN Educational Scientific and Cultural Organization (Unesco) since 1992 as a World Heritage Site, and international and local efforts continue to preserve and reconstruct the monuments. In a sign of real progress, Angkor was removed from Unesco's endangered list in 2003.

Many of Angkor's secrets remain to be discovered, as most of the work at the temples has concentrated on restoration efforts above ground rather than archaeological digs and surveys below. Underground is where the real story of Angkor and its people lies – the inscriptions on the temples give us only a partial picture of the gods to whom each structure was dedicated, and the kings who built them.

To learn more about Unesco's activities at Angkor, visit http://whc.unesco.org, or take a virtual tour of Angkor in 360 degrees at www.world-heritage-tour.org. For a great online photographic resource on the temples of Angkor, look no further than www.angkor-ruins.com, a Japanese website with an English translation.

TOP 10 KINGS OF ANGKOR

A mind-numbing array of kings ruled the Khmer empire from the 9th to the 14th centuries AD. All of their names include the word '*varman*', which means 'armour' or 'protector'. Forget the small fry and focus on the big fish in our Top 10:

Jayavarman II (r 802–50) Founder of the Khmer empire in AD 802.

Indravarman I (r 877–89) Builder of the first *baray* (reservoir), Preah Ko and Bakong.

Yasovarman I (r 889–910) Moved the capital to Angkor and built Lolei and Phnom Bakheng.

Jayavarman IV (r 924–42) Usurper king who moved the capital to Koh Ker.

Rajendravarman II (r 944–68) Builder of Eastern Mebon, Pre Rup and Phimeanakas.

Jayavarman V (r 968–1001) Oversaw construction of Ta Keo and Banteay Srei.

Suryavarman I (r 1002–49) Expanded the empire into much of Laos and Thailand.

Udayadityavarman II (r 1049–65) Builder of the pyramidal Baphuon and the Western Mebon.

Suryavarman II (r 1112–52) Legendary builder of Angkor Wat and Beng Mealea.

Jayavarman VII (r 1181–1219) The king of the god-kings, building Angkor Thom, Preah Khan and Ta Prohm.

Architectural Styles

From the time of the earliest Angkorian monuments at Roluos, Khmer architecture was continually evolving, often from the rule of one king to the next. Archaeologists therefore divide the monuments of Angkor into nine periods, named after the foremost example of each period's architectural style.

The evolution of Khmer architecture was based on a central theme of the temple-mountain, preferably set on a real hill (but an artificial hill was allowed if there weren't any mountains at hand). The earlier a temple was constructed, the more closely it adheres to this fundamental idea. Essentially, the mountain was represented by a tower mounted on a tiered base. At the summit was the central sanctuary, usually with an open door to the east, and three false doors at the remaining cardinal points of the compass. For Indian Hindus, the Himalayas represent Mt Meru, the home of the gods, while the Khmer kings of old adopted Phnom Kulen as their symbolic Mt Meru.

By the time of the Bakheng period, this layout was being embellished. The summit of the central tower was crowned with five 'peaks' – four at the points of the compass and one in the centre. Angkor Wat features this layout, though on a grandiose scale. Other features that came to be favoured include an entry tower and a causeway lined with *naga* (mythical serpent) balustrades leading up to the temple.

As the temples grew in ambition, the central tower became a less prominent feature, although it remained the focus of the temple. Later temples saw the central tower flanked by courtyards and richly decorated galleries. Smaller towers were placed on gates and on the corners of walls, their overall number often of religious or astrological significance.

These refinements and additions eventually culminated in Angkor Wat, which effectively showcases the evolution of Angkorian architecture. The architecture of the Bayon period breaks with tradition in temples such as Ta Prohm and Preah Khan. In these temples, the horizontal layout of the galleries, corridors and courtyards seems to completely eclipse the central tower.

The curious narrowness of the corridors and doorways in these structures can be explained by the fact that Angkorian architects never mastered the flying buttress to build a full arch. They engineered arches by laying blocks on top of each other, until they met at

TEMPLE ADDICTS

The god-kings of Angkor were dedicated builders. Each king was expected to dedicate a temple to his patron god, most commonly Shiva or Vishnu during the time of Angkor. Then there were the ancestors, including mother, father, and grandparents (both maternal and paternal), which meant another half dozen temples or more. Finally there was the mausoleum or king's temple, intended to deify the monarch and project his power, and each of these had to be bigger and better than one's predecessor. This accounts for the staggering architectural productivity of the Khmers at this time and the epic evolution of temple architecture.

a central point; known as false arches, they can only support very short spans.

Most of the major sandstone blocks around Angkor include small circular holes. These originally held wooden stakes that were used to lift and position the stones during construction before being sawn off.

Climate

Avoid the sweltering temperatures of March to May. November to February is the best time of year to travel, but this is no secret, so it coincides with peak season. And peak season really is mountainous in this day and age, where more than two million visitors a year descend on Angkor. The summer months of July and August can be a surprisingly rewarding time, as the landscape is emerald green, the moats overflowing with water, and the moss and lichen in bright contrast to the grey sandstone.

Itineraries

Back in the early days of tourism, the problem of what to see and in what order came down to two basic temple itineraries: the Small (Petit) Circuit and the Big (Grand) Circuit. It's difficult to imagine that anyone follows these to the letter any more, but in their time they were an essential component of the Angkor experience and were often undertaken on the back of an elephant.

Small Circuit

The 17km Small Circuit begins at Angkor Wat and heads north to Phnom Bakheng, Baksei

Chamkrong and Angkor Thom, including the city wall and gates, the Bayon, the Baphuon, the Royal Enclosure, Phimeanakas, Preah Palilay, the Terrace of the Leper King, the Terrace of Elephants, the Kleangs and Prasat Suor Prat. It exits from Angkor Thom via the Victory Gate in the eastern wall, and continues to Chau Say Tevoda, Thommanon, Spean Thmor and Ta Keo. It then heads northeast of the road to Ta Nei, turns south to Ta Prohm, continues east to Banteay Kdei and Sra Srang, and finally returns to Angkor Wat via Prasat Kravan.

Big Circuit

The 26km Big Circuit is an extension of the Small Circuit: instead of exiting the walled city of Angkor Thom at the east gate, the Grand Circuit exits at the north gate and continues to Preah Khan and Preah Neak Poan, east to Ta Som, then south via the Eastern Mebon to Pre Rup. From there it

MOTIFS, SYMBOLS & CHARACTERS AROUND ANGKOR

The temples of Angkor are intricately carved with myths and legends, symbols and signs, and a cast of characters in the thousands. Deciphering them can be quite a challenge, so here we've highlighted some of the most commonly seen around the majestic temples. For more help understanding the carvings of Angkor, pick up a copy of *Images of the Gods* by Vittorio Roveda.

Apsaras Heavenly nymphs or goddesses, also known as *devadas;* these beautiful female forms decorate the walls of many temples.

Asuras These devils feature extensively in representations of the Churning of the Ocean of Milk, such as at Angkor Wat.

Devas The 'good gods' in the creation myth of the Churning of the Ocean of Milk.

Flame The flame motif is found flanking steps and doorways and is intended to purify pilgrims as they enter the temple.

Garuda Vehicle of Vishnu; this half-man, half-bird creature features in some temples and was combined with his old enemy the *nagas* to promote religious unity under Jayavarman VII.

Kala The temple guardian appointed by Shiva; he had such an appetite that he devoured his own body and appears only as a giant head above doorways. Also known as Rehu.

Linga A phallic symbol of fertility, *lingas* would have originally been located within the towers of most Hindu temples.

Lotus Another symbol of purity, the lotus features extensively in the shape of towers, the shape of steps to entrances and in decoration.

Makara A giant sea serpent with a reticulated jaw; features on the corner of pediments, spewing forth a *naga* or some other creature.

Naga The multiheaded serpent, half-brother and enemy of *garudas*. Controls the rains and, therefore, the prosperity of the kingdom; seen on causeways, doorways and roofs. The seven-headed *naga*, a feature at many temples, represents the rainbow, which acts as a bridge between heaven and earth.

Nandi The mount of Shiva; there are several statues of Nandi dotted about the temples, although many have been damaged or stolen by looters.

Rishi A Hindu wise man or ascetic, also known as *essai;* these bearded characters are often seen sitting cross-legged at the base of pillars or flanking walls.

Vine Yet another symbol of purity, the vine graces doorways and lintels and is meant to help cleanse the visitor on their journey to this heaven on earth, the abode of the gods.

Yama God of death who presides over the underworld and passes judgment on whether people continue to heaven or hell.

Yoni Female fertility symbol that is combined with the *linga* to produce holy water infused with fertility.

HIDDEN RICHES, POLITICAL HITCHES

Angkor Conservation is a Ministry of Culture compound on the banks of the Siem Reap River, about 400m east of the Sofitel Phokheetra Royal Angkor Hotel. The compound houses more than 5000 statues, *lingas* (phallic symbols) and inscribed stelae, stored here to protect them from the wanton looting that has blighted hundreds of sites around Angkor. The finest statuary is hidden away inside Angkor Conservation's warehouses, meticulously numbered and catalogued. Unfortunately, without the right contacts, trying to get a peek at the statues is a lost cause. Some of the statuary is on public display in the Angkor National Museum in Siem Reap, but it is only a fraction of the collection.

Formerly housed at Angkor Conservation, but now going it alone in an impressive headquarters on one of the main roads to Angkor, is **Apsara Authority** (Authority for Protection & Management of Angkor & the Region of Siem Reap; www.autoriteapsara. org). This organisation is responsible for the research, protection and conservation of cultural heritage around Angkor, as well as urban planning in Siem Reap and tourism development in the region. It's quite a mandate and quite a challenge – especially now that the government is taking such a keen interest in its work. Angkor is a money-spinner; it remains to be seen whether Apsara will be empowered to put preservation before profits.

heads west and then southwest on its return to Angkor Wat.

One Day

If you have only one day to visit Angkor, a good itinerary would be Angkor Wat for sunrise and then sticking around to explore the mighty temple while it's quieter. From there continue to the tree roots of Ta Prohm before breaking for lunch. In the afternoon, explore the temples within the walled city of Angkor Thom and the beauty of the Bayon in the late-afternoon light.

Two Days

A two-day itinerary allows time to include some of the other big hitters around Angkor. Spend the first day visiting petite Banteay Srei, with its fabulous carvings; stop at Banteay Samré on the return leg. In the afternoon, visit immense Preah Khan, delicate Preah Neak Poan and the tree roots of Ta Som, before taking in a sunset at Pre Rup. Spend the second day following the one-day itinerary to Angkor Wat, Ta Prohm and Angkor Thom.

Three to Five Days

If you have three to five days to explore Angkor, it's possible to see most of the important sites. One approach is to see as much as possible on the first day or two and then spend the final days combining visits to other sites such as the Roluos temples and Banteay Kdei. Better still is a gradual build-up to the most spectacular monuments. After all, if you see Angkor

Wat on the first day, then a temple like Ta Keo just won't cut it. Another option is a chronological approach, starting with the earliest Angkorian temples and working steadily forwards in time to Angkor Thom, taking stock of the evolution of Khmer architecture and artistry.

It is well worth making the trip to the River of a Thousand Lingas at Kbal Spean for the chance to stretch your legs amid natural and human-made splendour, or the remote, vast and overgrown temple of Beng Mealea. Both can be combined with Banteay Srei in one long day.

One Week

Those with the time to spend a week at Angkor will be richly rewarded. Not only is it possible to fit all the temples of the region into an itinerary, but a longer stay also allows for non-temple activities, such as relaxing by a pool, indulging in a spa treatment or shopping around Siem Reap. Check out the aforementioned itineraries for some ideas on approach, but relax in the knowledge that you'll see it all. You may also want to throw in some of the more remote sites such as Koh Ker, Prasat Preah Vihear or Banteay Chhmar.

Tours

Most budget and midrange travellers not on package tours prefer to take in the temples at their own pace. Plan a dawn-to-dusk itinerary with a long, leisurely lunch to avoid the heat of the midday sun. Alternatively, plan to explore the temples through lunch, when it can be considerably quieter than the peak morning and afternoon visit times. However, it will be hot as hell and the light is not that conducive to photography. The Angkor Wat International Half Marathon takes place annually in December, including the option of bicycle rides for those not into running.

Visitors who have only a day or two at this incredible site may prefer something organised locally.

It is possible to link up with an official tour guide in Siem Reap. The Khmer Angkor Tour Guides Association (☑063-964347; www.khmerangkortourguide.com) represents some of Angkor's authorised guides. English- or French-speaking guides can be booked from US$20 to US$40 a day; guides speaking other languages, such as Italian, German, Spanish, Japanese and Chinese, are available at a higher rate, as there are fewer of them.

For an organised tour around Angkor, check out these recommended Siem Reap–based companies:

Beyond TOUR
(www.beyonduniqueescapes.com) Beng Mealea, Kompong Pluk, cycling trips and cooking classes.

Buffalo Trails TOUR
(☑012297506; www.buffalotrails-cambodia.com) Ecotours and lifestyle adventures around Siem Reap.

Indochine Exploration TOUR
(www.indochineex.com) Me Chrey kayaking, professional birdwatching and remote temples tours.

Sam Veasna Center TOUR
(☑063-963710; www.samveasna.org) Day trips that combine birdwatching with visits to outlying temples.

Terre Cambodge TOUR
(☑077448255; www.terrecambodge.com) Remote sites around Angkor, some by bicycle, plus boat trips on the Tonlé Sap lake.

TEMPLE-PASS WARNING!

Visitors found inside any of the main temples without a ticket will be fined a whopping US$100.

---

❶ Orientation

Heading north from Siem Reap, Angkor Wat is the first major temple, followed by the walled city of Angkor Thom. To the east and west of this city are two vast former reservoirs (the eastern reservoir now completely dried up), which once helped to feed the huge population. Further east are temples including Ta Prohm, Banteay Kdei and Pre Rup. North of Angkor Thom is Preah Khan and, way beyond in the northeast, Banteay Srei, Kbal Spean, Phnom Kulen and Beng Mealea. To the southeast of Siem Reap is the early Angkorian Roluos Group of Temples.

❶ Information

ADMISSION FEES

While the cost of entry to Angkor is relatively expensive by Cambodian standards, the fees represent excellent value. Visitors have a choice of a one-day pass (US$20), a three-day pass (US$40) or a one-week pass (US$60). An improved system was introduced in 2009 that allows three-day passes to run over three non-consecutive days in a one-week period and one-week passes to last for a full month. Purchase the entry pass from the large official entrance booth on the road to Angkor Wat. The **Angkor ticket checkpoint** is due to move in the lifetime of this book and will reopen on a parallel newer road to Angkor. Passes include a digital photo snapped at the entrance booth, so queues can be slow at peak times. Visitors entering after 5pm get a free sunset, as the ticket starts from the following day. The fee includes access to all the monuments in the Siem Reap area but not the sacred mountain of Phnom Kulen (US$20) or the remote complexes of Beng Mealea (US$5) and Koh Ker (US$10).

Entry tickets to the temples of Angkor are controlled by local hotel chain Sokha Hotels, part of a local petroleum conglomerate called Sokimex, which, in return for administrating the site, takes 17% of the revenue. Apsara Authority, the body responsible for protecting and conserving the temples, takes 68% for operating costs, and 15% goes to restoration. A South Korean company is due to take over the concession when the checkpoint moves to the new location.

Most of the major temples now have uniformed guards to check the tickets, which has reduced the opportunity for scams. A pass is not required for excursions to villages around or beyond Angkor, but you still have to stop at the checkpoint to explain your movements to the guards.

DRESS CODE

While the temples of Angkor are not a million miles away from the beaches of Sihanoukville or the Thai islands, it is important to remember that the temples of Angkor represent a sacred

ANGKORIN' FOR LUNCH

Many of the tour groups buzzing around Angkor head back to Siem Reap for lunch. This is as good a reason as any to stick around the temples, taking advantage of the lack of crowds to explore some popular sites and enjoy a local lunch at one of the many stalls. Almost all the major temples have some sort of nourishment available beyond the walls. Anyone travelling with a *moto* or *remork-moto (tuk-tuk)* should ask the driver for tips on cheap eats, as these guys eat around the temples every day. They know the best spots, at the best price, and should be able to sort you out (assuming you are getting along well).

The most extensive selection of restaurants is lined up opposite the entrance to Angkor Wat and includes several restaurants, such as **Khmer Angkor Restaurant** (mains US$3-6) and **Angkor Reach Restaurant** (mains US$3-6). There is also a handy branch of **Blue Pumpkin** (Angkor Cafe; dishes US$2-5) turning out sandwiches, salads and ice creams, as well as the usual divine fruit shakes, all to take away if required. **Chez Sophea** (☑ 012858003; meals US$10-20) offers barbecued meats and fish, accompanied by a cracking homemade salad, but prices are at the high end.

There are dozens of local noodle stalls just north of Angkor Thom's Terrace of the Leper King, which are a good spot for a quick bite to eat. Other central temples with food available include Ta Prohm, Preah Khan and Ta Keo. There is also a cluster of excellent Khmer restaurants located along the northern shore of Sra Srang.

Further afield, Banteay Srei has several small restaurants, complete with ornate wood furnishings cut from Cambodia's forests. Further north at Kbal Spean, food stalls at the bottom of the hill can cook up fried rice or a noodle soup, plus there is the inviting **Borey Sovann Restaurant** (meals US$3-6), which is a great place to wind down before or after an ascent. There are also **stop-and-dip stalls** (dishes US$1-3) near the entrance to Beng Mealea temple.

Water and soft drinks are available throughout the temple area, and many sellers lurk outside the temples, ready to pounce with offers of cold drinks. Sometimes they ask at just the right moment; on other occasions it is the 27th time in an hour that you've been approached and you are ready to scream. Try not to – you'll scare your fellow travellers and lose face with the locals.

religious site to the Khmer people. Inappropriate dress is not appreciated, despite the fact that the friendly Cambodians may say nothing. Vest tops for women, singlets for men, hot pants, short skirts – none of these should be worn when exploring Angkor. Certain temples even stipulate a dress code and it is not possible to visit the highest level of Angkor Wat without upper arms covered and shorts to the knees. It is only likely that authorities will enforce such dress standards at other temples in the future, so remember to dress appropriately.

MAPS

There are several free maps covering Angkor, including the *Siem Reap Angkor 3D Map*, available at certain hotels, guesthouses and restaurants in town. River Books of Thailand publishes a fold-out *Angkor Map*, which is one of the more detailed offerings available.

❶ Getting There & Around

Visitors heading to the temples of Angkor – in other words, pretty much everybody coming to Cambodia – need to consider the most suitable way to travel between the temples. Many of the best-known temples are no more than a few kilometres from the walled city of Angkor Thom, which is just 8km from Siem Reap, and can be visited using anything from a car or motorcycle to a sturdy pair of walking boots. For the independent traveller, there is a daunting range of alternatives to consider.

For the ultimate Angkor experience, try a pick-and-mix approach, with a *moto*, *remork-moto* or car for one day to cover the remote sites, a bicycle to experience the central temples, and an exploration on foot for a spot of peace and serenity.

Transport will be more expensive to remote temples such as Banteay Srei or Beng Mealea, due to extra fuel costs.

BICYCLE

A great way to get around the temples, bicycles are environmentally friendly and are used by most locals. There are few hills and the roads are good, so there's no need for much cycling experience. Moving about at a slower speed, you soon find that you take in more than from out of a car window or on the back of a speeding *moto*.

White Bicycles (www.thewhitebicycles.org; per day US$2) is supported by some guesthouses around town, with proceeds from the hire fee going towards community projects. Many guesthouses and hotels in town rent bikes for around US$1 to US$2 per day.

Some places, like Trek or Giant, offer better mountain bikes for US$7 to US$10 per day. Try Grasshopper Adventures (p95), which offers international mountain bikes and helmets for US$8 per day.

CAR & MOTORCYCLE

Cars are a popular choice for getting about the temples. The obvious advantage is protection from the elements, be it heavy downpours or the punishing sun. Shared between several travellers, they can also be an economical way to explore. The downside is that visitors are a little more isolated from the sights, sounds and smells as they travel between temples. A car for the day around the central temples is US$25 to US$35 and can be arranged with hotels, guesthouses and agencies in town.

Motorcycle rental in Siem Reap is currently prohibited, but some travellers bring a motorcycle from Phnom Penh. If you manage to get a bike up here, leave it at a guarded parking area or with a stallholder outside each temple; otherwise it could get stolen.

ELEPHANT

Travelling by elephant was the traditional way to see the temples way back in the early days of tourism at Angkor, at the start of the 20th century. It is once again possible to take an elephant ride between the south gate of Angkor Thom and the Bayon (US$10) in the morning, or up to the summit of Phnom Bakheng for sunset (US$15). The elephants are owned by the **Angkor Village** (Map p116; www.angkor village.com) resort group. Some visitors have complained about the elephants being poorly treated by handlers.

HELICOPTER & HOT-AIR BALLOON

For those with plenty of spending money, there are tourist flights around Angkor Wat (US$90) and the temples outside Angkor Thom (US$150) with **Helicopters Cambodia** (☑ 012814500; www.helicopterscambodia.com; 658 Hup Quan St, Siem Reap). The company also offers charters to remote temples such as Prasat Preah Vihear and Preah Khan. Newer company **Helistar** (Map p90; ☑ 063-966072; www.helistar cambodia.com; 24 Sivatha St, Siem Reap) is another option for scenic flights and charters.

Angkor Balloon (☑ 012759698; per person US$15) offers a bird's-eye view of Angkor Wat.

The balloon carries up to 30 people, is on a fixed line and rises 200m above the landscape.

MINIBUS

Minibuses are available from various hotels and travel agents around town. A 12-seat minibus costs from US$50 per day, while a 25- or 30-seat coaster bus is around US$80 to US$100 per day.

MOTO

Many independent travellers end up visiting the temples by *moto*. *Moto* drivers accost visitors from the moment they set foot in Siem Reap, but they often end up being knowledgeable and friendly, and good companions for a tour around the temples, starting at around US$10 per day. They can drop you off and pick you up at allotted times and places and even tell you a bit of background about the temples as you zip around. Many of the better drivers go on to become official tour guides.

REMORK-MOTO

Remorks are motorcycles with twee little hooded carriages towed behind, and are also known as *tuk tuks*. They are a popular way to get around Angkor as fellow travellers can still talk to each other as they explore (unlike on the back of a *moto*). They also offer some protection from the rain. As with *moto* drivers, some *remork* drivers are very good companions for a tour of the temples. Prices run from US$15 to US$25 for the day, depending on the destination and number of passengers.

WALKING

Why not forget all these newfangled methods and simply explore on foot? There are obvious limitations to what can be seen, as some temples are just too far from Siem Reap. However, it is easy enough to walk to Angkor Wat and the temples of Angkor Thom, and this is a great way to meet up with villagers in the area. Those who want to get away from the roads should try the peaceful walk along the walls of Angkor Thom. It is about 13km in total, and offers access to several small, remote temples and some bird life. Another rewarding walk is from Ta Nei to Ta Keo through the forest.

ANGKOR WAT

The traveller's first glimpse of Angkor Wat (អង្គរវត្ត; admission to all of Angkor: 1 day/3 days/1 week US$20/40/60), the ultimate expression of Khmer genius, is simply staggering and is matched by only a few select spots on earth such as Machu Picchu and Petra.

Angkor Wat is, quite literally, heaven on earth. Angkor is the earthly representation

DODGING THE CROWDS

Let's be honest: we know some of you are a little cynical when it comes to following our advice on avoiding other tourists. Sure, a lot of other travellers are carrying Lonely Planet's *Cambodia*, but bear in mind that they are a fraction of the overall numbers. Vietnamese, South Korean and Chinese travellers together accounted for around 1.5 million visitors in 2012, or close to half the total number. Very few, if any, are carrying the Lonely Planet guide, but are visiting the temples in groups of 25 to 75 people at a time. So we suggest you pay close attention to the following advice.

Angkor is on the tourist trail and is getting busier by the year but, with a little planning, it is still possible to escape the hordes. One important thing to remember, particularly when it comes to sunrise and sunset, is that places are popular for a reason, and it is worth going with the flow at least once.

It is received wisdom that as Angkor Wat faces west, one should be there for late afternoon, and in the case of the Bayon, which faces east, in the morning. Ta Prohm, most people seem to agree, can be visited in the middle of the day because of its umbrella of foliage. This is all well and good, but if you reverse the order, the temples will still look good – and you can avoid some of the crowds.

The most popular place for sunrise is Angkor Wat. Most tour groups head back to town for breakfast, so stick around and explore the temple while it's cool and quiet between 7am and 9am. Bayon sees far fewer visitors than Angkor Wat in the early hours. Sra Srang is usually pretty quiet, and sunrise here can be spectacular thanks to reflections in the extensive waters. Phnom Bakheng could be an attractive option, because the sun comes up behind Angkor Wat and you are far from the madding crowd that gathers here at sunset, but there are now strict limitations on visitor numbers each day. Ta Prohm is an alternative option, with no sight of sunrise, but a mysterious and magical atmosphere.

The definitive sunset spot is the hilltop temple of Phnom Bakheng. This was getting well out of control, with as many as 1000 tourists clambering around the small structure. However, new restrictions limit visitors to no more than 300 at any one time. It is generally better to check it out for sunrise or early morning and miss the crowds. Staying within the confines of Angkor Wat for sunset is a rewarding option, as it can be pretty peaceful when most tourists head off to Phnom Bakheng around 4.30pm or so. Pre Rup is popular with some for an authentic rural sunset over the countryside, but this is starting to get very busy. Better is the hilltop temple of Phnom Krom, which offers commanding views across Tonlé Sap lake, but involves a long drive back to town in the dark. The Western Baray takes in the sunset from the eastern end, across its vast waters, or from Western Mebon island, and is generally a quiet option.

When it comes to the most popular temples, the middle of the day is generally the quietest time. This is because the majority of the large tour groups head back to Siem Reap for lunch. It is also the hottest part of the day, which makes it tough going around relatively open temples such as Banteay Srei and the Bayon, but fine at well-covered temples such as Ta Prohm, Preah Khan and Beng Mealea, or even the bas-reliefs at Angkor Wat. The busiest times at Angkor Wat are from 6am to 7am and 3pm to 5pm; at the Bayon, from 8am to 10am; and at Banteay Srei, mid-morning and mid-afternoon. However, at other popular temples, such as Ta Prohm and Preah Khan, the crowds are harder to predict, and at most other temples in the Angkor region it's just a case of pot luck. If you pull up outside and see a car park full of tour buses, you may want to move on to somewhere quieter. The wonderful thing about Angkor is that there is always another temple to explore.

of Mt Meru, the Mt Olympus of the Hindu faith and the abode of ancient gods. The 'temple that is a city', Angkor Wat is the perfect fusion of creative ambition and spiritual devotion. The Cambodian god-kings of old each strove to better their ancestors' structures in size, scale and symmetry, culminating in what is believed to be the world's largest religious building, the mother of all temples, Angkor Wat.

Temples of Angkor

THREE-DAY EXPLORATION

The temple complex at Angkor is simply enormous and the superlatives don't do it justice. This is the site of the world's largest religious building, a multitude of temples and a vast, long-abandoned walled city that was arguably Southeast Asia's first metropolis, long before Bangkok and Singapore got in on the action.

Starting at the Roluos group of temples, one of the earliest capitals of Angkor, move on to the big circuit, which includes the Buddhist-Hindu fusion temple of **1 Preah Khan** and the ornate water temple of **2 Preah Neak Poan**.

On the second day downsize to the small circuit, starting with an atmospheric dawn visit to **3 Ta Prohm**, before continuing to the temple pyramid of Ta Keo, the Buddhist monastery of Banteay Kdei and the immense royal bathing pond of **4 Sra Srang**.

Next venture further afield to Banteay Srei temple, the jewel in the crown of Angkorian art, and Beng Mealea, a remote jungle temple.

Saving the biggest and best until last, experience sunrise at **5 Angkor Wat** and stick around for breakfast in the temple to discover its amazing architecture without the crowds. In the afternoon, explore **6 Angkor Thom**, an immense complex that is home to the enigmatic **7 Bayon**.

Three days around Angkor? That's just for starters.

TOP TIPS

» **Dodging the Crowds** Early morning at Ta Prohm, post sunrise at Angkor Wat and lunchtime at Banteay Srei does the trick.

» **Extended Explorations** Three-day passes can now be used on non-consecutive days over the period of a week but be sure to request this.

Bayon
The surreal state temple of legendary king Jayavarman VII, where 216 faces bear down on pilgrims, asserting religious and regal authority.

Terrace of the Leper King
Preah Palilay
Phimeanakas Temple
Tep Pranam
West Gate Angkor Thom
Baphuon Temple
Terrace of the Elephants
7
South Gate Angkor Thom
Phnom Bakheng
Baksei Chamrong
5

Angkor Wat
The world's largest religious building. Experience sunrise at the holiest of holies, then explore the beautiful bas-reliefs – devotion etched in stone.

Angkor Thom

The last great capital of the Khmer empire conceals a wealth of temples and its epic proportions would have inspired and terrified in equal measure.

Preah Khan

A fusion temple dedicated to Buddha, Brahma, Shiva and Vishnu; the immense corridors are like an unending hall of mirrors.

Preah Neak Poan

If Vegas ever adopts the Angkor theme, this will be the swimming pool; a petite tower set in a lake, surrounded by four smaller ponds.

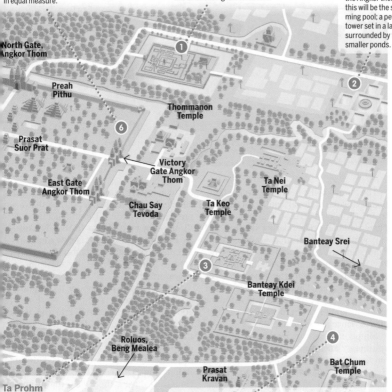

North Gate, Angkor Thom

Preah Pithu

Thommanon Temple

Prasat Suor Prat

Victory Gate Angkor Thom

East Gate Angkor Thom

Chau Say Tevoda

Ta Keo Temple

Ta Nei Temple

Banteay Srei

Banteay Kdei Temple

Roluos, Beng Mealea

Prasat Kravan

Bat Chum Temple

Ta Prohm

Nicknamed the *Tomb Raider* temple; *Indiana Jones* would be equally apt. Nature has run riot, leaving iconic tree roots strangling the surviving stones.

Sra Srang

Once the royal bathing pond, this is the ablutions pool to beat all ablutions pools and makes a good stop for sunset.

Angkor Wat

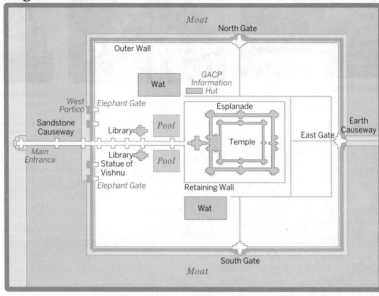

Moat
North Gate

Outer Wall

Wat

GACP Information Hut

West Portico   *Elephant Gate*

Esplanade

Sandstone Causeway

Library

Pool

Temple

East Gate

Earth Causeway

Main Entrance

Library
Statue of Vishnu

Pool

Elephant Gate

Retaining Wall

Wat

South Gate

Moat

The temple is the heart and soul of Cambodia. It is the national symbol, the epicentre of Khmer civilisation and a source of fierce national pride. Soaring skyward and surrounded by a moat that would make its European castle counterparts blush, Angkor Wat is one of the most inspired and spectacular monuments ever conceived by the human mind. Unlike the other Angkor monuments, it was never abandoned to the elements and has been in virtually continuous use since it was built.

Simply unique, it is a stunning blend of spirituality and symmetry, an enduring example of humanity's devotion to its gods. Relish the very first approach, as that spine-tickling moment when you emerge on the inner causeway will rarely be felt again. It is the best-preserved temple at Angkor, and repeat visits are rewarded with previously unnoticed details.

There is much about Angkor Wat that is unique among the temples of Angkor. The most significant fact is that the temple is oriented towards the west. Symbolically, west is the direction of death, which once led a large number of scholars to conclude that Angkor Wat must have existed primarily as a tomb. This idea was supported by the fact that the magnificent bas-reliefs of

the temple were designed to be viewed in an anticlockwise direction, a practice that has precedents in ancient Hindu funerary rites. Vishnu, however, is also frequently associated with the west, and it is now commonly accepted that Angkor Wat most likely served both as a temple and as a mausoleum for Suryavarman II.

Angkor Wat is famous for its beguiling *apsaras* (heavenly nymphs). More than 3000 *apsaras* are carved into the walls of Angkor Wat, each of them unique, and there are 37 different hairstyles for budding stylists to check out. Many of these exquisite *apsaras* were damaged during Indian efforts to clean the temples with chemicals during the 1980s, the ultimate bad acid trip, but they are now being restored by the teams with the German Apsara Conservation Project (GACP; www.gacp-angkor.de). The organisation operates a small information booth in the northwest corner of Angkor Wat, near the modern wat, where beautiful black-and-white postcards and images of Angkor are available for sale.

Allow at least two hours for a visit to Angkor Wat and plan a half day if you want to decipher the bas-reliefs with a tour guide and ascend to Bakan, the upper level.

Symbolism

Visitors to Angkor Wat are struck by its imposing grandeur and, at close quarters, its fascinating decorative flourishes and extensive bas-reliefs. Holy men at the time of Angkor must have revelled in its multilayered levels of meaning in much the same way a contemporary literary scholar might delight in James Joyce's *Ulysses*.

Eleanor Mannikka explains in her book *Angkor Wat: Time, Space and Kingship* that the spatial dimensions of Angkor Wat parallel the lengths of the four ages (Yuga) of classical Hindu thought. Thus the visitor who walks the causeway to the main entrance and through the courtyards to the final main tower, which once contained a statue of Vishnu, is metaphorically travelling back to the first age of the creation of the universe.

Like the other temple-mountains of Angkor, Angkor Wat also replicates the spatial universe in miniature. The central tower is Mt Meru, with its surrounding smaller peaks, bounded in turn by continents (the lower courtyards) and the oceans (the moat). The seven-headed *naga* becomes a symbolic rainbow bridge for man to reach the abode of the gods.

While Suryavarman II may have planned Angkor Wat as his funerary temple or mausoleum, he was never buried there as he died in battle during a failed expedition to subdue the Dai Viet (Vietnamese).

Architectural Layout

Angkor Wat is surrounded by a 190m-wide moat, which forms a giant rectangle measuring 1.5km by 1.3km. From the west, a sandstone causeway crosses the moat. The sandstone blocks from which Angkor Wat was built were quarried more than 50km away (from the holy mountain of Phnom Kulen) and floated down the Siem Reap River on rafts. The logistics of such an operation are mind-blowing, consuming the labour of thousands – an unbelievable feat given the lack of cranes and trucks that we take for granted in contemporary construction projects. According to inscriptions, the construction of Angkor Wat involved 300,000 workers and 6000 elephants, yet it was still not fully completed.

The rectangular outer wall, which measures 1025m by 800m, has a gate on each side, but the main entrance, a 235m-wide porch richly decorated with carvings and sculptures, is on the western side. There is a statue of Vishnu, 3.25m in height and hewn from a single block of sandstone, located in the right-hand tower. Vishnu's eight arms hold a mace, a spear, a disc, a conch and other items. You may also see locks of hair lying about. These are offerings both from young people preparing to get married and from pilgrims giving thanks for their good fortune.

An avenue, 475m long and 9.5m wide and lined with *naga* balustrades, leads from the main entrance to the central temple, passing between two graceful libraries (restored by a Japanese team) and then two pools, the northern one a popular spot from which to watch the sun rise.

The central temple complex consists of three storeys, each made of laterite, which enclose a square surrounded by intricately interlinked galleries. The Gallery of a Thousand Buddhas (Preah Poan) was used to house hundreds of Buddha images before the war, but many of these were removed or stolen, leaving just the handful we see today.

The corners of the second and third storeys are marked by towers, each topped with symbolic lotus-bud towers. Rising 31m above the third level and 55m above the ground is the central tower, which gives the whole grand ensemble its sublime unity.

ON LOCATION WITH TOMB RAIDER

Several sequences for *Tomb Raider*, starring Angelina Jolie as Lara Croft, were shot around the temples of Angkor. The Cambodia shoot opened at Phnom Bakheng, with Lara looking through binoculars for the mysterious temple. The baddies were already trying to break in through the east gate of Angkor Thom by pulling down a giant polystyrene *apsara*. Reunited with her custom Land Rover, Lara made a few laps around Bayon before discovering a back way into the temple from Ta Prohm. After battling a living statue and dodging Daniel Craig (aka 007) by diving off the waterfall at Phnom Kulen, she emerged in a floating market in front of Angkor Wat, as you do. She came ashore here before borrowing a mobile phone from a local monk and venturing into the Gallery of a Thousand Buddhas, where she was healed by the abbot.

Angkor Wat – Central Structure

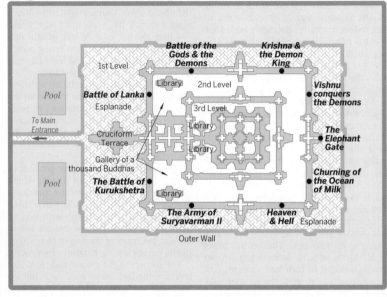

Battle of the Gods & the Demons

Krishna & the Demon King

1st Level

Library

2nd Level

Vishnu conquers the Demons

Battle of Lanka

Esplanade

3rd Level

The Elephant Gate

To Main Entrance

Cruciform Terrace

Library

Pool

Gallery of a thousand Buddhas

Library

Churning of the Ocean of Milk

The Battle of Kurukshetra

Pool

Library

The Army of Suryavarman II

Heaven & Hell Esplanade

Outer Wall

The stairs to the upper level are immensely steep, because reaching the kingdom of the gods was no easy task. Also known as Bakan, the upper level of Angkor Wat was closed to visitors for several years, but it is once again open to a limited number per day with a timed queuing system. This means it is once again possible to complete the pilgrimage with an ascent to the summit: savour the cooling breeze, take in the extensive views and then find yourself a quiet corner in which to contemplate the symmetry and symbolism of this Everest of temples.

⊙ Sights

Stretching around the outside of the central temple complex is an 800m-long series of intricate and astonishing bas-reliefs. The following is a brief description of the epic events depicted on the panels. They are described in the order in which you'll come to them if you begin on the western side and keep the bas-reliefs to your left. The majority of them were completed in the 12th century, but in the 16th century several new reliefs were added to unfinished panels.

The bas-reliefs at Angkor Wat were once sheltered by the cloister's wooden roof, which long ago rotted away except for one

original beam in the western half of the north gallery. The other roofed sections are reconstructions.

The Battle of Kurukshetra   BAS-RELIEF

The southern portion of the west gallery depicts a battle scene from the Hindu *Mahabharata* epic, in which the Kauravas (coming from the north) and the Pandavas (coming from the south) advance upon each other, meeting in furious battle. Infantry are shown on the lowest tier, with officers on elephants, and chiefs on the second and third tiers. Some of the more interesting details (from left to right): a dead chief lying on a pile of arrows, surrounded by his grieving parents and troops; a warrior on an elephant who, by putting down his weapon, has accepted defeat; and a mortally wounded officer, falling from his carriage into the arms of his soldiers. Over the centuries, some sections have been polished (by the millions of hands that fall upon them) to look like black marble. The portico at the southwestern corner is decorated with sculptures representing characters from the *Ramayana*.

The Army of Suryavarman II   BAS-RELIEF

The remarkable western section of the south gallery depicts a triumphal battle march of Suryavarman II's army. In the southwestern corner about 2m from the floor is Suryavarman II on an elephant, wearing the royal tiara and armed with a battleaxe; he is shaded by 15 parasols and fanned by legions of servants. Compare this image of the king and with the image of Rama in the northern gallery and you'll notice an uncanny likeness that helped reinforce the aura of the god-king.

Further on is a procession of well-armed soldiers and officers on horseback; among them are bold and warlike chiefs on elephants. Just before the end of this panel is the rather disorderly Siamese mercenary army, with their long headdresses and ragged marching, at that time allied with the Khmers in their conflict with the Chams. The Khmer troops have square breastplates and are armed with spears; the Thais wear skirts and carry tridents.

The rectangular holes seen in the Army of Suryavarman II relief were created when, so the story goes, Thai soldiers removed pieces of the scene containing inscriptions that reportedly gave clues to the location of the golden treasures of Suryavarman II, later buried during the reign of Jayavarman VII.

Heaven & Hell BAS-RELIEF

The eastern half of the south gallery depicts the punishments and rewards of the 37 heavens and 32 hells. On the left, the upper and middle tiers show fine gentlemen and ladies proceeding towards 18-armed Yama (the judge of the dead) seated on a bull; below him are his assistants, Dharma and Sitragupta. On the lower tier, devils drag the wicked along the road to hell. To Yama's right, the tableau is divided into two parts by a horizontal line of *garudas*: above, the elect dwell in beautiful mansions, served by women and attendants; below, the condemned suffer horrible tortures that might have inspired the Khmer Rouge. The ceiling in this section was restored by the French in the 1930s.

Churning of the Ocean of Milk BAS-RELIEF

The southern section of the east gallery is decorated by the most famous of the bas-relief scenes at Angkor Wat, the Churning of the Ocean of Milk. This brilliantly executed carving depicts 88 *asuras* on the left, and 92 *devas*, with crested helmets, churning up the sea to extract from it the elixir of

GUIDE TO THE GUIDES

Countless books on Angkor have been written over the years, with more and more new titles coming out, reflecting Angkor's rebirth as one of the world's cultural hot spots. Here are just a few of the best:

A Guide to the Angkor Monuments (Maurice Glaize) The definitive guide, downloadable for free at www.theangkorguide.com.

A Passage Through Angkor (Mark Standen) One of the best photographic records of the temples.

A Pilgrimage to Angkor (Pierre Loti) One of the most beautifully written books on Angkor, based on the author's 1910 journey.

Ancient Angkor (Claude Jacques) Written by one of the foremost scholars on Angkor, this is the most readable guide to the temples, with photos by Michael Freeman.

Angkor: An Introduction to the Temples (Dawn Rooney) Probably the most popular contemporary guide.

Angkor – Heart of an Asian Empire (Bruno Dagens) The story of the 'discovery' of Angkor, complete with lavish illustrations.

Angkor: Millennium of Glory (various authors) A fascinating introduction to the history, culture, sculpture and religion of the Angkorian period.

Angkor: Splendours of the Khmer Civilisation (Marilia Albanese) Beautifully photographed guide to the major temples, including some of the more remote places in northern Cambodia.

Khmer Heritage in the Old Siamese Provinces of Cambodia (Etienne Aymonier) Aymonier journeyed through Cambodia in 1901 and visited many of the major temples.

The Customs of Cambodia (Chou Ta-Kuan) The only eyewitness account of Angkor, by a Chinese emissary who spent a year at the Khmer capital in the late 13th century.

Central Area of Angkor Thom

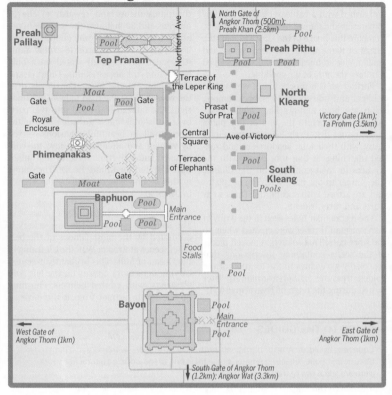

immortality. The demons hold the head of the serpent Vasuki and the gods hold its tail. At the centre of the sea, Vasuki is coiled around Mt Mandala, which turns and churns up the water in the tug of war between the demons and the gods. Vishnu, incarnated as a huge turtle, lends his shell to serve as the base and pivot of Mt Mandala. Brahma, Shiva, Hanuman (the monkey god) and Lakshmi (the goddess of beauty) all make appearances, while overhead a host of heavenly female spirits sing and dance in encouragement. Luckily for us, the gods won through, as the *apsaras* above were too much for the hot-blooded devils to take. Restoration work on this incredible panel by the **World Monuments Fund** (WMF; www.wmf.org) was completed in 2012.

The Elephant Gate   BAS-RELIEF
This gate, which has no stairway, was used by the king and others for mounting and dismounting elephants directly from the gallery. North of the gate is a Khmer inscription recording the erection of a nearby stupa in the 18th century.

Vishnu Conquers the Demons   BAS-RELIEF
The northern section of the east gallery shows a furious and desperate encounter between Vishnu, riding on a *garuda*, and innumerable devils. Needless to say, he slays all comers. This gallery was completed at a later date, most likely in the 16th century, and the later carving is notably inferior to the original work from the 12th century.

Krishna & the Demon King   BAS-RELIEF
The eastern section of the north gallery shows Vishnu incarnated as Krishna riding a *garuda*. He confronts a burning walled city, the residence of Bana, the demon king. The *garuda* puts out the fire and Bana is captured. In the final scene Krishna kneels before Shiva and asks that Bana's life be spared.

Battle of the Gods & the Demons
BAS-RELIEF

The western section of the north gallery depicts the battle between the 21 gods of the Brahmanic pantheon and various demons. The gods are featured with their traditional attributes and mounts. Vishnu has four arms and is seated on a *garuda*, while Shiva rides a sacred goose.

Battle of Lanka
BAS-RELIEF

The northern half of the west gallery shows scenes from the *Ramayana*. In the Battle of Lanka, Rama (on the shoulders of Hanuman), along with his army of monkeys, battles 10-headed, 20-armed Ravana, captor of Rama's beautiful wife Sita. Ravana rides a chariot drawn by monsters and commands an army of giants.

ANGKOR THOM

It is hard to imagine any building bigger or more beautiful than Angkor Wat, but in Angkor Thom the sum of the parts add up to a greater whole. Aptly named, the fortified city of Angkor Thom (អង្គរធំ) is indeed a 'Great City' on an epic scale. The last great capital of the Khmer empire, and set over 10 sq km, Angkor Thom took monumental to a whole new level. It was built in part as a reaction to the surprise sacking of Angkor by the Chams, after Jayavarman VII (r 1181–1219) decided that his empire would never again be vulnerable at home. Beyond the formidable walls is a massive moat that would have stopped all but the hardiest invaders in their tracks. At the city's height, it may have supported a population of one million people in the surrounding region. Centred on Bayon, the mesmerising, if mind-bending, state temple, Angkor Thom is enclosed by a *jayagiri* (square wall) 8m high and 12km in length and encircled by a 100m-wide *jayasindhu* (moat). This architectural layout is yet another expression of Mt Meru surrounded by the oceans.

It is the gates that grab you first, flanked by a vast representation of the Churning of the Ocean of Milk, 54 demons and 54 gods engaged in an epic tug of war on the causeway. Each gate towers above the visitor, the magnanimous faces of the Bodhisattva Avalokiteshvara staring out over the kingdom. Imagine being a peasant in the 13th century approaching the forbidding capital for the first time. It would have been an awe-inspiring yet unsettling experience to enter such a gateway and come face to face with the divine power of the god-kings.

The south gate is most popular with visitors, as it has been fully restored and many of the heads (mostly copies) remain in place. The gate is on the main road into Angkor Thom from Angkor Wat, and it gets very busy. More peaceful are the east and west gates, found at the end of dirt trails. The east gate was used as a location in *Tomb Raider,* where the bad guys broke into the 'tomb' by pulling down a giant (polystyrene!) *apsara*. The causeway at the west gate of Angkor Thom has completely collapsed, leaving a jumble of ancient stones sticking out of the soil, like victims of a terrible historical pile-up.

In the centre of the walled enclosure are the city's most important monuments, including Bayon, Baphuon, the Royal Enclosure, Phimeanakas and the Terrace of Elephants. With all these temples and sites to cover, visitors should set aside a half day to explore Angkor Thom in depth.

Bayon
បាយ័ន

Unique, even among its cherished contemporaries, Bayon is the mesmerising state temple of Cambodia's legendary king, Jayavarman VII. Its architectural audacity epitomises the creative genius and inflated ego of this enigmatic figure. It's a place of stooped corridors, precipitous flights of stairs and, best of all, a collection of 54 towers decorated with 216 coldly smiling, enormous faces of Avalokiteshvara that bear more than a passing resemblance to the great king

---

BAYON INFORMATION CENTER

The **Bayon Information Center** (Map p116; ☏ 092165083; www.angkor-jsa.org/bic; 56 Phum Tropeang Ses, Khum Kokchork, Siem Reap; admission US$2; ◉ 8am-4pm Tue, Wed & Fri-Sun) is a well-presented and informative exhibition on the history of the Khmer empire and the restoration projects around Angkor, including some short documentary films. Set in the beautiful compound of the Japanese government team for Safeguarding Angkor (JSA) on the outskirts of Siem Reap, it's a big saving on the Angkor National Museum.

himself. These huge heads glare down from every angle, exuding power and control with a hint of humanity – this was precisely the blend required to hold sway over such a vast empire, ensuring the disparate and far-flung population yielded to his magnanimous will. As you walk around, a dozen or more of the heads are visible at any one time – full face or in profile, almost level with your eyes or staring down from up high.

Bayon is now known to have been built by Jayavarman VII, though for many years its origins were unknown. Shrouded in dense jungle, it also took researchers some time to realise that it stands in the exact centre of the city of Angkor Thom. There is still much mystery associated with Bayon – such as its exact function and symbolism – and this seems only appropriate for a monument whose signature is an enigmatic smiling face.

The eastward orientation of Bayon leads most people to visit early in the morning, preferably just after sunrise, when the sun inches upwards, lighting face after face. Bayon, however, looks equally good in the late afternoon. A Japanese team is restoring several outer areas of the temple.

Architectural Layout

Unlike Angkor Wat, which looks impressive from all angles, Bayon looks rather like a glorified pile of rubble from a distance. It's only when you enter the temple and make your way up to the third level that its magic becomes apparent.

The basic structure of Bayon a simple three levels, which correspond more or less to three distinct phases of building. This is because Jayavarman VII began construction of this temple at an advanced age, so he was never confident it would be completed. Each time one phase was completed, he moved on to the next. The first two levels are square and adorned with bas-reliefs. They lead up to a third, circular level, with the towers and their faces.

Some say that the Khmer empire was divided into 54 provinces at the time of Bayon's construction, hence the all-seeing eyes of Avalokiteshvara (or Jayavarman VII) keeping watch on the kingdom's outlying subjects.

◎ Sights

Angkor Wat's bas-reliefs may grab the headlines, but Bayon's are even more extensive, decorated with 1.2km of extraordinary carvings depicting more than 11,000 figures. The famous carvings on the outer wall of the first level show vivid scenes of everyday life in 12th-century Cambodia. The bas-reliefs on the second level do not

Bayon

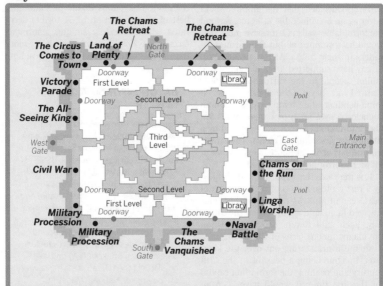

LOCAL KNOWLEDGE

PROFESSOR ANG CHOULEANM, ARCHAEOLOGY EXPERT

What is the most important Khmer temple? Angkor Thom is the most striking and challenging for archaeologists, since it was a living city, humans and gods cohabiting there.

What is the most important archaeological site in Cambodia? Sambor Prei Kuk is among the most important for its homogeneity, given the period and its artistic style.

Who is the most important king in Cambodian history? Suryavarman I, who had a real political vision that can be measured by the monuments he built, such as Preah Vihear and Wat Phu.

What is your position on the debate between romance and restoration at Ta Prohm? It is a matter of balance. The trees are most impressive, but maintaining the monument is our duty.

Which other civilisation interests you greatly? Japanese civilisation, as it is so different from Khmer civilisation, allowing me to better understand mine.

Professor Ang Choulean is one of Cambodia's leading experts on anthropology and archaeology and a renowned scholar on Cambodian history. He was awarded the 2011 Grand Fukuoka Prize for his outstanding contribution to Asian culture.

have the epic proportions of those on the first level and tend to be fragmented. The reliefs described are those on the first level. The sequence assumes that you enter Bayon from the east and view the reliefs in a clockwise direction.

Chams on the Run BAS-RELIEF
Just south of the east gate is a three-level panorama. On the first tier, Khmer soldiers march off to battle – check out the elephants and the oxcarts, which are almost exactly like those still used in Cambodia today. The second tier depicts coffins being carried back from the battlefield. In the centre of the third tier, Jayavarman VII, shaded by parasols, is shown on horseback followed by legions of concubines (to the left).

Linga Worship BAS-RELIEF
The first panel north of the southeastern corner shows Hindus praying to a *linga* (phallic symbol). This image was probably originally a Buddha, later modified by a Hindu king.

Naval Battle BAS-RELIEF
The next panel has some of the best-carved reliefs. The scenes depict a naval battle between the Khmers and the Chams (the latter with head coverings), and everyday life around Tonlé Sap lake, where the battle was fought. Look for images of people picking lice from each other's hair, of hunters and, towards the western end of the panel, a woman giving birth.

The Chams Vanquished BAS-RELIEF
In the next panel, scenes from daily life continue and the battle shifts to the shore, where the Chams are soundly thrashed. Scenes include two people playing chess, a cockfight and women selling fish in the market. The scenes of meals being prepared and served are in celebration of the Khmer victory.

Military Procession BAS-RELIEF
The last section of the south gallery, depicting a military procession, is unfinished, as is the panel showing elephants being led down from the mountains. Brahmans have been chased up two trees by tigers.

Civil War BAS-RELIEF
This panel depicts scenes that some scholars maintain is a civil war. Groups of people, some armed, confront each other, and the violence escalates until elephants and warriors join the melee.

The All-Seeing King BAS-RELIEF
The fighting continues on a smaller scale in the next panel. An antelope is being swallowed by a gargantuan fish; among the smaller fish is a prawn, under which an inscription proclaims that the king will seek out those in hiding.

Victory Parade BAS-RELIEF
This panel depicts a procession that includes the king (carrying a bow). Presumably it is a celebration of his victory.

The Circus Comes to Town
BAS-RELIEF

At the western corner of the northern wall is a Khmer circus. A strongman holds three dwarfs, and a man on his back is spinning a wheel with his feet; above is a group of tightrope walkers. To the right of the circus, the royal court watches from a terrace, below which is a procession of animals. Some of the reliefs in this section remain unfinished.

A Land of Plenty
BAS-RELIEF

The two rivers, one next to the doorpost and the other a few metres to the right, are teeming with fish.

The Chams Retreat
BAS-RELIEF

On the lowest level of this unfinished three-tiered scene, the Cham armies are being defeated and expelled from the Khmer kingdom. The next panel depicts the Cham armies advancing, and the badly deteriorated panel shows the Chams (on the left) chasing the Khmers.

The Sacking of Angkor
BAS-RELIEF

This panel shows the war of 1177, when the Khmers were defeated by the Chams, and Angkor was pillaged. The wounded Khmer king is being lowered from the back of an elephant and a wounded Khmer general is being carried on a hammock suspended from a pole. Directly above, despairing Khmers are getting drunk. The Chams (on the right) are in hot pursuit of their vanquished enemy.

The Chams Enter Angkor
BAS-RELIEF

This panel depicts another meeting of the two armies. Notice the flag bearers among the Cham troops (on the right). The Chams were defeated in the war, which ended in 1181, as depicted on the first panel in the sequence.

Baphuon
បាពួន

Often coined the world's largest jigsaw puzzle, Baphuon was the centre of EFEO restoration efforts when the civil war erupted, and work paused for a quarter of a century. The temple was taken apart piece by piece, in keeping with the anastylosis method of renovation, but all the records were destroyed during the Khmer Rouge years, leaving experts with 300,000 stones to put back into place. The EFEO resumed restoration work in 1995, and continues its efforts today. Baphuon is approached by a 200m elevated walkway made of sandstone, and the central structure is 43m high. Clamber under the elevated causeway leading to Baphuon for an incredible view of the hundreds of pillars supporting it.

In its heyday, Baphuon would have been one of the most spectacular of Angkor's temples. Located 200m northwest of Bayon, it's a pyramidal representation of mythical Mt Meru. Construction probably began under Suryavarman I and was later completed by Udayadityavarman II. It marked the centre of the capital that existed before the construction of Angkor Thom.

Royal Enclosure & Phimeanakas
ភិមានអាកាស

Phimeanakas stands close to the centre of a walled area that once housed the royal palace. There's very little left of the palace today except for two sandstone pools near the northern wall. Once the site of royal ablutions, these are now used as swimming holes by local children. The royal enclosure is fronted to the east by the Terrace of Elephants. Construction of the palace began under Rajendravarman II, although it was used by Jayavarman V and Udayadityavarman I. It was later added to and embellished by Jayavarman VII and his successors.

Phimeanakas means 'Celestial Palace', and some scholars say that it was once topped by a golden spire. Today it only hints at its former splendour and looks a little worse for wear. The temple is another pyramidal representation of Mt Meru, with three levels. Most of the decorative features are broken

---

THE RECLINING BUDDHA OF BAPHUON

On the western side of Baphuon, the retaining wall of the second level was fashioned – apparently in the 15th or 16th century – into a reclining Buddha about 60m in length. The unfinished figure is difficult to make out, but the head is on the northern side of the wall and the gate is where the hips should be; to the left of the gate protrudes an arm. When it comes to the legs and feet – the latter are entirely gone – imagination must suffice. This huge project, undertaken by the Buddhist faithful 500 years ago, reinforces the notion that Angkor was never entirely abandoned.

TREKKING AROUND THE TEMPLES

Spread over a vast area of the steamy tropical lowlands of Cambodia, the temples of Angkor aren't the ideal candidates to tackle on foot. However, the area is blanketed in mature forest, offering plenty of shade, and following back roads into temples is the perfect way to leave behind the crowds.

Angkor Thom is the top trekking spot thanks to its manageable size and plenty of rewarding temples within its walls. Starting out at the spectacular south gate of Angkor Thom, admire the immense representation of the Churning of the Ocean of Milk before bidding farewell to the masses and their motorised transport. Ascend the wall of this ancient city and then head west, enjoying views of the vast moat to the left and the thick jungle to the right. It is often possible to see forest birds along this route, as it is very peaceful. Reaching the southwest corner, admire Prasat Chrung, one of four identical temples marking the corners of the city. Head down below to see the water outlet of Run Ta Dev, as this once powerful city was criss-crossed by canals in its heyday.

Back on the gargantuan wall, continue to the west gate, looking out for a view to the immense Western Baray on your left. Descend at the west gate and admire the artistry of the central tower. Wander east along the path into the heart of Angkor Thom, but don't be diverted by the beauty of Bayon, as this is best saved until last.

Veer north into Baphuon and wander to the back of what some have called the 'world's largest jigsaw puzzle'. Pass through the small temple of Phimeanakas and the former royal palace compound, an area of towering trees, tumbling walls and atmospheric foliage. Continue further north to petite but pretty Preah Palilay.

It's time to make for the mainstream with a walk through the Terrace of the Leper King and along the front of the royal viewing gallery, the Terrace of Elephants. If there is time, you may want to zigzag east to visit the laterite towers of Prasat Suor Prat. Otherwise, continue to the top billing of Bayon: weird yet wonderful, this is one of the most enigmatic of the temples at Angkor. Take your time to decipher the bas-reliefs before venturing up to the legendary faces of the upper level.

or have disappeared. Still, it is worth clambering up to the second and third levels for good views of Baphuon.

The northwestern wall of the Royal Enclosure is very atmospheric, with immense trees and jungle vines cloaking the outer side, easily visible on a forest walk from Preah Palilay to Phimeanakas.

Preah Palilay   ប្រះបាំលីថ្ង្

Preah Palilay is located about 200m north of the Royal Enclosure's northern wall. It was erected during the rule of Jayavarman VII and originally housed a Buddha, which has long since vanished. Sadly, the immense trees that used to loom large over the temple have been cut down, removing some of the romance of the place in the process.

Tep Pranam   ទេពប្រណម្យ

Tep Pranam, an 82m by 34m cruciform Buddhist terrace 150m east of Preah Palilay, was once the base of a pagoda of lightweight construction. Nearby is a Buddha that's 4.5m high, but it's a reconstruction of the original. A group of Buddhist nuns lives in a wooden structure close by.

Preah Pithu   ប្រះពិធ្ធ

Preah Pithu, which is across Northern Ave from Tep Pranam, is a group of 12th-century Hindu and Buddhist temples enclosed by a wall. It includes some beautifully decorated terraces and guardian animals in the form of elephants and lions.

Terrace of the
Leper King   ទិលានប្រះគម្ចង់

The Terrace of the Leper King is just north of the Terrace of Elephants. Dating from the late 12th century, it is a 7m-high platform, on top of which stands a nude, though sexless, statue. It is yet another of Angkor's mysteries. The original of the statue is held at Phnom Penh's National Museum, and various theories have been advanced to explain its meaning. Legend has it that at least two of the Angkor kings had leprosy, and the statue may represent one of them. Another theory – a more likely explanation – is that the statue is of Yama, the god of death, and that the Terrace of the Leper King housed the royal crematorium.

The front retaining walls of the terrace are decorated with at least five tiers of meticulously executed carvings of seated *apsaras;* other figures include kings wearing pointed diadems, armed with short double-edged swords and accompanied by the court and princesses, the latter adorned with beautiful rows of pearls.

On the southern side of the Terrace of the Leper King (facing the Terrace of Elephants), there is access to the front wall of a hidden terrace that was covered up when the outer structure was built – a terrace within a terrace. The four tiers of *apsaras* and other figures, including *nagas,* look as fresh as if they had been carved yesterday, thanks to being covered up for centuries. Some of the figures carry fearsome expressions. As you follow the inner wall of the Terrace of the Leper King, notice the increasingly rough chisel marks on the figures, an indication that this wall was never completed, like many of the temples at Angkor.

Terrace of Elephants ទីលានដល់ដំរី

The 350m-long Terrace of Elephants was used as a giant viewing stand for public ceremonies and served as a base for the king's grand audience hall. As you stand here, try to imagine the pomp and grandeur of the Khmer empire at its height, with infantry, cavalry, horse-drawn chariots and elephants parading across Central Sq in a colourful procession, pennants and standards aloft. Looking on is the god-king, crowned with a gold diadem, shaded by multitiered parasols and attended by mandarins and handmaidens bearing gold and silver utensils.

The Terrace of Elephants has five piers extending towards the Central Sq – three in the centre and one at each end. The middle section of the retaining wall is decorated with life-size *garudas* and lions; towards either end are the two parts of the famous parade of elephants, complete with their Khmer mahouts.

Kleangs & Prasat Suor Prat ឃ្លាំង ប្រាសាទសួរព្រ័ត្រ

Along the east side of Central Sq are two groups of buildings, called Kleangs. The North Kleang and the South Kleang may at one time have been palaces. The North Kleang has been dated from the period of Jayavarman V.

Along Central Sq in front of the two Kleangs are 12 laterite towers – 10 in a row and two more at right angles facing the Ave of Victory – known as the Prasat Suor Prat, meaning 'Temple of the Tightrope Dancers'. Archaeologists believe the towers, which form an honour guard along Central Sq, were constructed by Jayavarman VII. It is likely that each one originally contained either a *linga* or a statue. It is said artists performed for the king on tightropes or rope bridges strung between these towers.

According to Chinese emissary Chou Ta-Kuan, the towers of Prasat Suor Prat were also used for public trials of sorts – during a dispute the two parties would be made to sit inside two towers, one party eventually succumbing to illness and thus proven guilty.

AROUND ANGKOR THOM

Baksei Chamkrong បក្សីចាំក្រុង

Southwest of the south gate of Angkor Thom, this well-proportioned, petite temple is one of the few brick edifices in the immediate vicinity of Angkor and was once decorated with a covering of lime mortar. Like virtually all of the structures of Angkor, it opens to the east. In the early 10th century, Harshavarman I erected five statues in this temple: two of Shiva, one of Vishnu and two of Devi.

Phnom Bakheng ភ្នំបាក់ខែង

Located around 400m south of Angkor Thom, the main attraction at Phnom Bakheng is the sunset view over Angkor Wat. For many years, the whole affair turned into something of a circus, with crowds of tourists ascending the slopes of the hill and jockeying for space once on top. However, numbers have now been restricted to just 300 visitors at any one time. In practice, this means arriving pretty early (4pm) for sunset to guarantee a spot. Some prefer to visit in the early morning, when it's cool (and

Phnom Bakheng

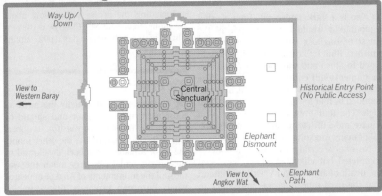

Way Up/Down

View to Western Baray ←

Central Sanctuary

Historical Entry Point (No Public Access)

Elephant Dismount

View to Angkor Wat

Elephant Path

crowds are light), to climb the hill. That said, the sunset over the Western Baray is very impressive from here. Allow about two hours for the sunset experience.

Phnom Bakheng also lays claim to being home to the first of the temple-mountains built in the vicinity of Angkor. Yasovarman I chose Phnom Bakheng over the Roluos area, where the earlier capital (and temple mountains) had been located.

The temple-mountain has five tiers, with seven levels (including the base and the summit). At the base are – or were – 44 towers. Each of the five tiers had 12 towers. The summit of the temple has four towers at the cardinal points of the compass as well as a central sanctuary. All of these numbers are of symbolic significance. The seven levels, for example, represent the seven Hindu heavens, while the total number of towers, excluding the central sanctuary, is 108, a particularly auspicious number and one that correlates to the lunar calendar.

It is possible to arrange an elephant ride up the hill (US$15 one way). Try to book in advance, however, as the rides are very popular with tour groups.

To get a decent picture of Angkor Wat in the warm glow of the late-afternoon sun from the summit of Phnom Bakheng, you will need at least a 300mm lens, as the temple is 1.3km away.

Chau Say Tevoda ចៅសាយទេវតា

Just east of Angkor Thom's east gate is **Chau Say Tevoda**. It was probably built during the second quarter of the 12th century, under the reign of Suryavarman II, and dedicated to Shiva and Vishnu. It has been renovated by the Chinese to bring it up to the condition of its twin temple, Thommanon.

Thommanon ធម្មនន្ទ

Thommanon is just north of Chau Say Tevoda. Although unique, the temple complements its neighbour, as it was built to a similar design around the same time. It was also dedicated to Shiva and Vishnu. Thommanon is in good condition thanks to extensive work by the EFEO in the 1960s.

Spean Thmor ស្ពានថ្ម

Spean Thmor (Stone Bridge), of which an arch and several piers remain, is 200m east of Thommanon. Jayavarman VII constructed many roads with these immense stone bridges spanning watercourses. This is the only large bridge remaining in the immediate vicinity of Angkor. It vividly highlights how the water level has changed course over the centuries and may offer another clue to the collapse of Angkor's extensive irrigation system. Just north of Spean Thmor is a large water wheel.

There are more-spectacular examples of these ancient bridges elsewhere in Siem Reap Province, such as Spean Praptos, with 19 arches, in Kompong Kdei on NH6 from Phnom Penh; and Spean Ta Ong, a 77m bridge with a beautiful *naga*, forgotten in the forest about 28km east of Beng Mealea.

Ta Keo តាកែវ

Ta Keo is a stark, undecorated temple that undoubtedly would have been one of the finest of Angkor's structures, had it been finished. Built by Jayavarman V, it was dedicated to Shiva and was the first Angkorian monument built entirely of sandstone. The summit of the central tower, which is surrounded by four lower towers, is almost 50m high. The four towers at the corners of a square and a fifth tower in the centre is typical of many Angkorian temple-mountains.

No one is certain why work was never completed, but a likely cause may have been the death of Jayavarman V. Others contend that the hard sandstone was impossible to carve and that explains the lack of decoration. According to inscriptions, Ta Keo was struck by lightning during construction, which may have been a bad omen and led to its abandonment.

Allow about 30 minutes to visit Ta Keo.

Ta Nei តានី

Ta Nei, 800m north of Ta Keo, was built by Jayavarman VII. There is something of the spirit of Ta Prohm here, albeit on a lesser scale, with moss and tentacle-like roots covering outer areas of this small temple. The number of visitors is also on a lesser scale, making it very atmospheric. It now houses the training unit of Apsara Authority and can be accessed by walking across the French-built dam. To get to the dam, take the long track on the left, just after the Victory Gate of Angkor Thom when coming from Siem Reap. It is possible to walk from Ta Nei to Ta Keo through the forest, a guaranteed way to leave the crowds behind.

Including the access walk, allow about two hours to visit Ta Nei. Close by is the new Flight of the Gibbon Angkor (p92) zipline experience.

Ta Prohm តាព្រហ្ម

★Ta Prohm is undoubtedly the most atmospheric ruin at Angkor and should be high on the hit list of every visitor. Its appeal lies in the fact that, unlike the other monuments of Angkor, it has been swallowed by the jungle, and looks very much the way most of the monuments of Angkor appeared when European explorers first stumbled upon them. Well, that's the theory, but in fact the jungle is pegged back and only the largest trees are left in place, making it manicured rather than raw like Beng Mealea. Still, a visit to Ta Prohm is a unique, otherworldly experience. The temple is cloaked in dappled shadow, its crumbling towers and walls locked in the slow, muscular embrace of vast root systems. If Angkor Wat, Bayon and other temples are testament to the genius of the ancient Khmers, Ta Prohm reminds us equally of the awesome fecundity and power of the jungle. There is a poetic cycle to this venerable ruin, with humanity first conquering nature to rapidly create, and nature once again conquering humanity to slowly destroy.

Built from 1186 and originally known as Rajavihara (Monastery of the King), Ta Prohm was a Buddhist temple dedicated to the mother of Jayavarman VII. It is one of the few temples in the Angkor region where an inscription provides information about the temple's dependents and inhabitants. Almost 80,000 people were required to maintain or attend at the temple, among them more than 2700 officials and 615 dancers.

Ta Prohm is a temple of towers, closed courtyards and narrow corridors. Many of the corridors are impassable, clogged with jumbled piles of delicately carved stone blocks dislodged by the roots of long-decayed trees. Bas-reliefs on bulging walls are carpeted with lichen, moss and creeping plants, and shrubs sprout from the roofs of monumental porches. Trees, hundreds of years old, tower overhead, their leaves filtering the sunlight and casting a greenish pall over the whole scene.

CUNNING LINGAS

Fertility symbols are prominent around the temples of Angkor. The *linga* is a phallic symbol and would have originally been located within the towers of most Hindu temples. It sits inside a *yoni*, the female fertility symbol, combining to produce holy water, charged with the sexual energy of creation. Brahmans poured the water over the *linga* and it drained through the *yoni* and out of the temples through elaborate gutters to anoint the pilgrims outside.

Ta Prohm

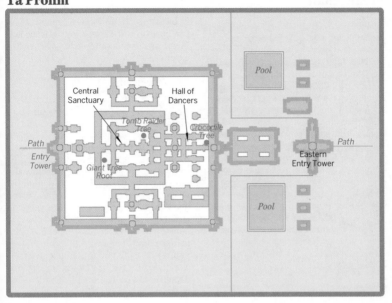

Central Sanctuary

Hall of Dancers

Tomb Raider Tree

Crocodile Tree

Path

Entry Tower

Giant Tree Root

Pool

Pool

Path

Eastern Entry Tower

The most popular of the many strangulating root formations is that on the inside of the easternmost *gopura* (entrance pavilion) of the central enclosure, nicknamed the Crocodile Tree. One of the most famous spots in Ta Prohm is the so-called 'Tomb Raider tree', where Angelina Jolie's Lara Croft picked a jasmine flower before falling through the earth into…Pinewood Studios.

It used to be possible to climb onto the damaged galleries, but this is now prohibited, to protect both temple and visitor. Many of these precariously balanced stones weigh a tonne or more and would do some serious damage if they came down.

Ta Prohm is at its most impressive at dawn before the crowds arrive. Allow as much as two hours to visit, especially if you want to explore the maze-like corridors and iconic tree roots.

Banteay Kdei & Sra Srang   បន្ទាយក្ដីនិងស្រះស្រង់

Banteay Kdei, a massive Buddhist monastery from the latter part of the 12th century, is surrounded by four concentric walls. The outer wall measures 500m by 700m. Each of its four entrances is decorated with *garudas,* which hold aloft one of Jayavarman

VII's favourite themes: the four faces of Avalokiteshvara. The inside of the central tower was never finished and much of the temple is in a ruinous state due to hasty construction. It is considerably less busy than nearby Ta Prohm and this alone can justify a visit.

East of Banteay Kdei is an earlier basin, **Sra Srang** (Pool of Ablutions), measuring 800m by 400m, reserved for the king and his consorts. A tiny island in the middle once bore a wooden temple, of which only the stone base remains. This is a beautiful body of water from which to take in a quiet sunrise.

Allow about one hour to visit Banteay Kdei and take in the view over nearby Sra Srang.

Prasat Kravan   ប្រាសាទក្រវ៉ាន់

Uninspiring from the outside, the interior brick carvings concealed within its towers are the hidden treasure of **Prasat Kravan.** The five brick towers here, which are arranged in a north–south line and oriented to the east, were built for Hindu worship in AD 921. The structure is unusual in that it was not constructed by royalty; this accounts for its slightly distant location, away from the centre of the capital. Prasat Kravan is just south of the road between Angkor Wat and Banteay Kdei.

Preah Khan

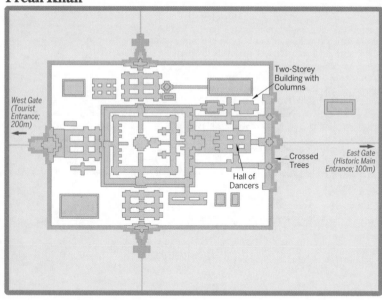

Two-Storey
Building with
Columns

West Gate
(Tourist
Entrance;
200m)

East Gate
(Historic Main
Entrance; 100m)

Crossed
Trees

Hall of
Dancers

Prasat Kravan was partially restored in 1968, returning the brick carvings to their former glory. The images of Vishnu in the largest central tower show the eight-armed deity on the back wall, taking the three gigantic steps with which he reclaimed the world on the left wall; and riding a *garuda* on the right wall. The northernmost tower displays bas-reliefs of Vishnu's consort, Lakshmi.

Preah Khan ព្រះ ខ័ន្ឌ

The temple of **Preah Khan** (Sacred Sword) is one of the largest complexes at Angkor – a maze of vaulted corridors, fine carvings and lichen-clad stonework. It is a good counterpoint to Ta Prohm and generally sees slightly fewer visitors. Preah Khan was built by Jayavarman VII and probably served as his temporary residence while Angkor Thom was being built. Like Ta Prohm it is a place of towered enclosures and shoulder-hugging corridors. Unlike Ta Prohm, however, the temple of Preah Khan is in a reasonable state of preservation thanks to the ongoing restoration efforts of the World Monuments Fund.

The central sanctuary of the temple was dedicated in AD 1191 and a large stone stela tells us much about Preah Khan's role as a centre for worship and learning. Originally located within the first eastern enclosure, this stela is now housed safely at Angkor Conservation. The temple was dedicated to 515 divinities and during the course of a year 18 major festivals took place here, requiring a team of thousands just to maintain the place.

Preah Khan covers a very large area, but the temple itself is within a rectangular enclosing wall of around 700m by 800m. Four processional walkways approach the gates of the temple, and these are bordered by another stunning depiction of the Churning of the Ocean of Milk, as in the approach to Angkor Thom, although most of the heads have disappeared. From the central sanctuary, four long, vaulted galleries extend in the cardinal directions. Many of the interior walls of Preah Khan were once coated with plaster that was held in place by holes in the stone. Today, many delicate reliefs remain, including *rishi* and *apsara* carvings.

The main entrance to Preah Khan is in the east, but most tourists enter at the west gate near the main road, walk the length of the temple to the east gate before doubling back to the central sanctuary, and exit at the north gate. Approaching from the west, there is little clue to nature's genius, but on the outer retaining wall of the east gate is a pair of trees with monstrous roots embracing, one still reaching for the sky. There is also a curious Grecian-style two-storey structure in the temple grounds, the purpose of which is unknown, but it looks like an exile from Athens. Another option is to enter from the north and exit from the east. Given its vast size, it is sensible to set aside at least 90 minutes to explore this temple, even two hours.

Preah Khan is a genuine fusion temple, the eastern entrance dedicated to Mahayana Buddhism with equal-sized doors, and the other cardinal directions dedicated to Shiva, Vishnu and Brahma with successively smaller doors, emphasising the unequal nature of Hinduism.

Preah Neak Poan   ព្រះនាគព័ន្ធ

The Buddhist temple of Preah Neak Poan (Temple of the Intertwined Nagas) is a petite yet perfect temple constructed by – not him again, surely! – Jayavarman VII in the late 12th century. It has a large square pool surrounded by four smaller square pools. In the middle of the central pool is a circular 'island' encircled by the two *nagas* whose intertwined tails give the temple its name. It's a safe bet that if an 'Encore Angkor' casino is

eventually developed in Las Vegas or Macau, Preah Neak Poan will provide the blueprint for the ultimate swimming complex.

In the pool around the central island there were once four statues, but only one remains, reconstructed from the debris by the French archaeologists who cleared the site. The curious figure has the body of a horse supported by a tangle of human legs. It relates to a legend that Avalokiteshvara once saved a group of shipwrecked followers from an island of ghouls by transforming into a flying horse. A beautiful replica of this statue decorates the main roundabout at Siem Reap International Airport.

Water once flowed from the central pool into the four peripheral pools via ornamental spouts, which can still be seen in the pavilions at each axis of the pool. The spouts are in the form of an elephant's head, a horse's head, a lion's head and a human head. The pool was used for ritual purification rites.

Preah Neak Poan was once in the centre of a huge 3km-by-900m *baray* serving Preah Khan, known as Jayatataka, once again partially filled with water due to a new opening in the dyke road. Access is currently restricted to the edge of the complex via a wooden causeway, so a visit takes only 30 minutes.

Preah Neak Poan

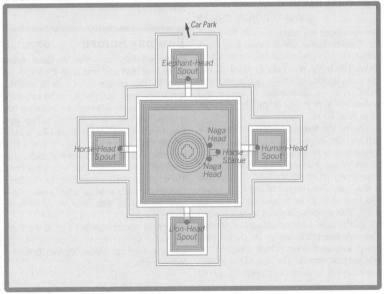

THE LONG STRIDER

One of Vishnu's best-loved incarnations was when he appeared as the dwarf Vamana, and proceeded to reclaim the world from the evil demon king Bali. The dwarf politely asked the demon king for a comfortable patch of ground upon which to meditate, saying that the patch need only be big enough so that he could easily walk across it in three paces. The demon agreed, only to see the dwarf swell into a mighty giant who strode across the universe in three enormous steps. From this legend, depicted at Prasat Kravan, Vishnu is sometimes known as the 'long strider'.

Ta Som   តាសោម

Ta Som, which stands to the east of Preah Neak Poan, is yet another of the late-12th-century Buddhist temples of Jayavarman VII, the Donald Trump of ancient Cambodia. The most impressive feature at Ta Som is the huge tree completely overwhelming the eastern *gopura,* providing one of the most popular photo opportunities in the Angkor area.

Eastern Baray & Eastern Mebon
បារាយណ៍មេបុណ្យខាងកើត

The enormous one-time reservoir known as the Eastern Baray was excavated by Yasovarman I, who marked its four corners with stelae. This basin, now entirely dried up, was the most important of the public works of Yasodharapura, Yasovarman I's capital, and is 7km by 1.8km. It was originally fed by the Siem Reap River.

The Hindu temple known as the **Eastern Mebon**, erected by Rajendravarman II, would have been situated on an islet in the centre of the Eastern Baray reservoir, but is now very much on dry land. This temple is like a smaller version of Pre Rup, which was built 15 to 20 years later and lies to the south. The temple-mountain form is topped off by the now familiar quintet of towers. The elaborate brick shrines are dotted with neatly arranged holes, which attached the original plasterwork. The base of the temple is guarded at its corners by perfectly carved stone figures of elephants, many of which are still in a very good state of preservation.

The Eastern Mebon is flanked by earthen ramps, a clue that this temple was never finished and a good visual guide to how the temples were constructed.

Pre Rup   ប្រែរូប

Pre Rup, built by Rajendravarman II, is about 1km south of the Eastern Mebon. Like its nearby predecessor, the temple consists of a pyramid-shaped temple-mountain with the uppermost of the three tiers carrying five lotus towers. The brick sanctuaries were also once decorated with a plaster coating, fragments of which still remain on the southwestern tower; there are some amazingly detailed lintel carvings here. Several of the outermost eastern towers are perilously close to collapse and are propped up by an army of wooden supports.

Pre Rup means 'Turning the Body' and refers to a traditional method of cremation in which a corpse's outline is traced in the cinders, first in one direction and then in the other; this suggests that the temple may have served as an early royal crematorium.

Pre Rup is one of the most popular sunset spots around Angkor, as the view over the surrounding rice fields of the Eastern Baray was beautiful, although some lofty trees have rather obscured it these days. It also gets pretty crowded.

Banteay Samré   បន្ទាយសំរែ

Banteay Samré dates from the same period as Angkor Wat and was built by Suryavarman II. The temple is in a fairly healthy state of preservation due to some extensive renovation work, although its isolation has resulted in some looting during the past few decades. The area consists of a central temple with four wings, preceded by a hall and also accompanied by two libraries, the southern one remarkably well preserved. The whole ensemble is enclosed by two large concentric walls around what would have been the unique feature of an inner moat, sadly now dry.

Banteay Samré is 400m east of the Eastern Baray. A visit here can be combined with a trip to Banteay Srei or Phnom Bok in a half-day trip.

Western Baray & Western Mebon

បារាយណ៍មេបុណ្យខាងលិច

The Western Baray, measuring an incredible 8km by 2.3km, was excavated by hand to provide water for the intensive cultivation of lands around Angkor. Just for the record, these enormous *barays* weren't dug out, rather huge dykes were built up around the edges. In the centre of the Western Baray is the ruin of the Western Mebon temple, where the giant bronze statue of Vishnu (now in the National Museum) was found. The Western Mebon is accessible by boat (US$10 for the boat) from the dam on the southern shore.

The Western Baray is the main local swimming pool around Siem Reap. There is a small beach of sorts at the western extreme (complete with picnic huts and inner tubes for rent), which attracts plenty of Khmers at weekends.

ROLUOS TEMPLES

The monuments of Roluos (រលួស), which served as Indravarman I's capital, Hariharalaya, are among the earliest large, permanent temples built by the Khmers and mark the dawn of Khmer classical art. Before the construction of Roluos, generally only lighter (and less durable) construction materials such as brick were employed.

The temples can be found 13km east of Siem Reap along NH6 near the modern-day town of Roluos. Plan a half-day visit together with the stilted village of Kompong Pluk (p115) or plan on two to three hours to explore the three temples.

Preah Ko   ព្រះគោ

Preah Ko, erected by Indravarman I in the late 9th century, was dedicated to Shiva. Six *prasats* (stone halls), aligned in two rows and decorated with carved sandstone and plaster reliefs, face east; the central tower of the front row is much larger than the other towers. Preah Ko has some of the best surviving examples of plasterwork seen at Angkor and is currently under restoration by a German team. There are elaborate inscriptions in the ancient Hindu language of Sanskrit on the doorposts of each tower.

The towers of Preah Ko (Sacred Ox) feature three *nandis* (sacred oxen), all of whom look like a few steaks have been sliced off them over the years. Preah Ko was dedicated by Indravarman I to his deified ancestors in AD 880. The front towers relate to male ancestors or gods, the rear towers to female ancestors or goddesses. Lions guard the steps up to the temple.

Bakong   បាគង

Bakong is the largest and most interesting of the Roluos Group of Temples, and has an active Buddhist monastery just to the north of the east entrance. It was built and dedicated to Shiva by Indravarman I. It's a representation of Mt Meru, and it served as the city's central temple. The east-facing complex consists of a five-tier central pyramid of sandstone, 60m square at the base, flanked by eight towers (or their remains) of brick and sandstone and by other minor sanctuaries. A number of the eight towers below the upper central tower are still partly covered by their original plasterwork.

The complex is enclosed by three concentric walls and a moat. There are well-preserved statues of stone elephants on each corner of the first three levels of the central temple. There are 12 stupas – three to each side – on the third tier. The sanctuary on the

GOOD-CAUSE PROJECTS AROUND ROLUOS

Several good-cause initiatives have sprung up around the Roluos area. Look out for **Prolung Khmer** (www.prolungkhmer.blogspot.com) on the road between Preah Ko and Bakong. It's a weaving centre producing stylish cotton *kramas* (scarves), set up as a training collaboration between Cambodia and Japan. Also here is the **Lo-Yuyu** ceramics workshop, producing traditional Angkorian-style pottery.

Right opposite Preah Ko is the **Khmer Group Art of Weaving**, turning out silk and cotton scarves on traditional looms. Also here is **Dy Proeung Master Sculptor** (donations accepted), who has created scale replicas of Preah Ko, Bakong and Lolei, plus Angkor Wat, Preah Vihear and Banteay Srei for good measure.

fifth level of Bakong temple was a later addition during the reign of Suryavarman II, in the style of Angkor Wat's central tower.

On the grounds of the temple, there is also a very old wat, dating back a century or more, which has recently been restored.

Lolei លលៃ

The four brick towers of Lolei, an almost exact replica of the towers of Preah Ko (but in much worse shape), were built on an islet in the centre of a large reservoir – now rice fields – by Yasovarman I, founder of the first city at Angkor. The sandstone carvings in the niches of the temples are worth a look and there are Sanskrit inscriptions on the doorposts. According to one of the inscriptions, the four towers were dedicated by Yasovarman I to his mother, his father and his maternal grandparents on 12 July 893.

AROUND ANGKOR

Phnom Krom ភ្នំក្រោម

The temple of Phnom Krom, 12km south of Siem Reap on a hill overlooking Tonlé Sap lake, dates from the reign of Yasovarman I in the late 9th or early 10th century. The name means 'Lower Hill' and is a reference to its geographic location in relation to its sister temples of Phnom Bakheng and Phnom Bok. The three towers, dedicated (from north to south) to Vishnu, Shiva and Brah-

---

WHEN NATURE CALLS

Angkor is now blessed with some of the finest public toilets in Asia. Designed in wooden chalets and complete with amenities such as electronic flush, they wouldn't be out of place in a fancy hotel. The trouble is that the guardians often choose not to run the generators that power the toilets, meaning it is pretty dark inside the cubicles (but, thankfully, you can flush manually, too!). Entrance is free if you show your Angkor pass; and the toilets are found near most of the major temples.

Remember, in remote areas, don't stray off the path – being seen in a compromising position is infinitely better than stepping on a landmine.

---

ma, are in a ruined state, but Phnom Krom remains one of the more tranquil spots from which to view the sunset, complete with an active wat. The fast boats from Phnom Penh dock near here, but it is not possible to see the temple from beneath the hill. If coming here by *moto* or car, try to get the driver to take you to the summit, as it is a long, hot climb otherwise.

It is now necessary to have an Angkor pass to visit the temple at the summit of Phnom Krom, so don't come all the way out here without one, as the guards won't allow you access to the summit of the hill. Plan on a half-day visit in tandem with exploring the floating village of Chong Kneas (p115).

Phnom Bok ភ្នំបូក

Making up the triumvirate of temple mountains built by Yasovarman I in the late 9th or early 10th century, this peaceful but remote location sees few visitors. The small temple is in reasonable shape and includes two frangipani trees growing out of a pair of ruined towers – they look like some sort of extravagant haircut when in full flower. However, it is the views of Phnom Kulen to the north and the plains of Angkor to the south from this 212m hill that make it worth the trip. The remains of a 5m *linga* are also visible at the opposite end of the hill and it's believed there were similar *linga* at Phnom Bakheng and Phnom Krom. Unfortunately, it is not a sensible place for sunrise or sunset, as it would require a long journey in the dark.

There is a long, winding trail snaking up the hill at Phnom Bok, which takes about 20 minutes to climb, plus a faster cement staircase that is fairly exposed. Avoid the heat of the middle of the day and carry plenty of water, which can be purchased locally.

Phnom Bok is about 25km from Siem Reap and is clearly visible from the road to Banteay Srei. It is accessible by continuing east on the road to Banteay Samré for another 6km. It is possible to loop back to Siem Reap via the temples of Roluos by heading south instead of west on the return journey, and gain some rewarding glimpses of the countryside.

Chau Srei Vibol ចៅស្រីវិបុល

This petite hilltop temple used to see few visitors, as it was difficult to access, but new roads have put it on the temple map at last.

The central sanctuary is in a ruined state but is nicely complemented by the construction of a modern wat nearby. Surrounding the base of the hill are laterite walls, each with a small entrance hall in reasonable condition. To get here, turn east off the Roluos to Anlong Veng highway at a point about 8km north of NH6, or 5km south of Phnom Bok. There is a small sign (easy to miss) that marks the turn. Locals are friendly and helpful should you find yourself lost.

Banteay Srei   បន្ទាយស្រី

The art gallery of Angkor, **Banteay Srei** is considered by many to be the jewel in the crown of Angkorian artisanship. A Hindu temple dedicated to Shiva, it is cut from stone of a pinkish hue and includes some of the finest stone carving seen anywhere on Earth. It is one of the smallest sites at Angkor, but what it lacks in size it makes up for in stature. It is wonderfully well preserved and many of its carvings are three-dimensional. Banteay Srei means 'Citadel of the Women' and it is said that it must have been built by a woman, as the elaborate carvings are supposedly too fine for the hand of a man.

Construction on Banteay Srei began in AD 967 and it is one of the few temples around Angkor to be commissioned not by a king but by a brahman, who may have been a tutor to Jayavarman V. The temple is square and has entrances at the east and west, the east approached by a causeway. Of interest are the lavishly decorated libraries and the three central towers, which are decorated with male and female divinities and beautiful filigree relief work.

Classic carvings at Banteay Srei include delicate women with lotus flowers in hand and traditional skirts clearly visible, as well as breathtaking recreations of scenes from the epic *Ramayana* adorning the library pediments (carved inlays above a lintel). However, the sum of the parts is no greater than the whole – almost every inch of these interior buildings is covered in decoration. Standing watch over such perfect creations are the mythical guardians, all of which are copies of originals stored in the National Museum.

Banteay Srei was the first major temple restoration undertaken by the EFEO in 1930 using the anastylosis method. The project, as evidenced today, was a major success and soon led to other larger projects such as the

> **LANDMINE ALERT!**
>
> At no point during a visit to Kbal Spean or Phnom Kulen should you leave well-trodden paths, as there may be landmines in the area.

restoration of Bayon. Banteay Srei is also the first to have been given a full makeover in terms of facilities, with a large car park, a designated dining and shopping area, clear visitor information and a state-of-the-art exhibition on the history of the temple and its restoration.

When Banteay Srei was first rediscovered, it was assumed to be from the 13th or 14th centuries, as it was thought that the refined carving must have come at the end of the Angkor period. It was later dated to AD 967, from inscriptions found at the site.

In 1923 Frenchman André Malraux was arrested in Phnom Penh for attempting to steal several of Banteay Srei's major statues and pieces of sculpture. Ironically, Malraux was later appointed Minister of Culture under Charles de Gaulle.

Banteay Srei is 21km northeast of Bayon or about 32km from Siem Reap. It is well signposted and the road is surfaced all the way – a trip from Siem Reap should take about 45 minutes. *Moto* and *remork* drivers will want a bit of extra cash to come out here, so agree on a sum first. It is possible to combine a visit to Banteay Srei as part of a long day trip to the River of a Thousand Lingas at Kbal Spean and Beng Mealea. A half-day itinerary might include Banteay Srei, the Cambodia Landmine Museum and Banteay Samre.

Kbal Spean   ក្បាលស្ពាន

A spectacularly carved riverbed, **Kbal Spean** is set deep in the jungle to the northeast of Angkor. More commonly referred to in English as the 'River of a Thousand Lingas', the name actually means 'bridgehead', a reference to the natural rock bridge at the site. Lingas have been elaborately carved into the riverbed, and images of Hindu deities are dotted about the area. Kbal Spean was 'discovered' in 1969, when EFEO ethnologist Jean Boulbet was shown the area by a local hermit; the area was soon off-limits due to the civil war, only becoming safe again in 1998.

It is a 2km uphill walk to the carvings, along a pretty path that winds its way up into the jungle, passing by some interesting boulder formations along the way. Carry plenty of water up the hill, as there is none available beyond the parking area. The path eventually splits to the waterfall or the river carvings. There is an impressive carving of Vishnu on the upper section of the river, followed by a series of carvings at the bridgehead itself, some of which have been tragically hacked off in the past few years. This area is now roped off to protect the carvings from further damage.

Following the river down, there are several more impressive carvings of Vishnu, and Shiva with his consort Uma, and further downstream hundreds of *lingas* appear on the riverbed. At the top of the waterfall are many animal images, including a cow and a frog, and a path winds around the boulders to a wooden staircase leading down to the base of the falls. Visitors between January and May will be disappointed to see very little water here. The best time to visit is between July and December. When exploring Kbal Spean it is best to start with the river carvings and work back down to the waterfall to cool off. From the car park, the visit takes about two hours including the walk, nearer three hours with a natural shower or a picnic. It's the best part of a day trip if you include Angkor Centre for Conservation of Biodiversity, Banteay Srei temple and the Cambodian Landmine Museum.

Kbal Spean is about 50km northeast of Siem Reap or about 18km beyond the temple of Banteay Srei. The road is now excellent, as it forms part of the new road north from NH6 to Anlong Veng and the Thai border, so it takes just one hour or so from town.

Moto drivers will no doubt want a bit of extra money to take you here – a few extra dollars should do, or US$12 to US$15 for the day, including a trip to Banteay Srei. Likewise, *remork* drivers will probably push up the price to US$20 or more. A surcharge is also levied to come out here by car. Admission to Kbal Spean is included in the general Angkor pass; the last entry to the site is at 3.30pm.

Phnom Kulen ភ្នំគូលែន

Considered by Khmers to be the most sacred mountain in Cambodia, Phnom Kulen is a popular place of pilgrimage on weekends and during festivals. It played a significant role in the history of the Khmer empire, as it was from here in AD 802 that Jayavarman II proclaimed himself a *devaraja* (god-king) and announced independence from Java, giving birth to the Cambodian kingdom. There is a small wat (Wat Preah Ang Thom) at the summit of the mountain, which houses a large **reclining Buddha** carved into the sandstone boulder upon which it is built. Nearby is a large **waterfall** and above it are smaller bathing areas and a number of carvings in the riverbed, including numerous *lingas*. A private businessman bulldozed a road up here a decade ago and charges a US$20 toll per foreign visitor, an ambitious fee compared with what you get for your money at Angkor. Very little of the toll goes towards preserving the site.

The road winds its way through some spectacular jungle scenery, emerging on the plateau after a 20km ascent. The road eventually splits: the left fork leads to the picnic spot, waterfalls and ruins of a 9th-century temple; the right fork continues over a bridge and some riverbed carvings to the reclining Buddha. This is the focal point of a pilgrimage here for Khmer people, so it is important to take off your shoes and any head covering before climbing the stairs to the sanctuary. The views from the 487m peak are tremendous, as you can see right across the forested plateau.

ANGKOR CENTRE FOR CONSERVATION OF BIODIVERSITY

Conveniently located near the base of the trail to Kbal Spean is the Angkor Centre for Conservation of Biodiversity (Map p116; www.accb-cambodia.org; US$3 donation; ⊘ tours 1pm), committed to rescuing, rehabilitating and reintroducing threatened wildlife to the Cambodian forests. Tours of the centre are available daily at 1pm, taking about 90 minutes. Species currently under protection here include pangolin, pileated gibbon, silvered langur, slow loris, civet cat and leopard cat. There are also several large water birds, including the impressive sarus crane and the extremely rare giant ibis, the national bird of Cambodia.

The waterfall is an attractive spot but would be much more beautiful if not for all the litter left here by families picnicking at the weekend. Near the top of the waterfall is a jungle-clad temple known as **Prasat Krau Romeas**, dating from the 9th century.

There are plenty of other Angkorian sites on Phnom Kulen, including as many as 20 minor temples around the plateau, the most important of which is **Prasat Rong Chen**, the first pyramid or temple-mountain to be constructed in the Angkor area. Most impressive of all are the giant stone animals or guardians of the mountain, known as **Sra Damrei** (Elephant Pond). These are very difficult to get to, with the trail impassable in the wet season. The few people who make it, however, are rewarded with a life-size replica of a stone elephant – a full 4m long and 3m tall – and smaller statues of lions, a frog and a cow. These were constructed on the southern face of the mountain and from here there are spectacular views across the plains below. Getting to Sra Damrei requires taking a *moto* from Wat Preah Ang Thom for about 12km on very rough trails through thick forest before arriving at a sheer rock face. From here it is a 1km walk to the animals through the forest. Don't try to find it on your own; expect to pay the *moto* driver about US$8 to US$10 (with some hard negotiating) and carry plenty of water.

Phnom Kulen is a huge plateau around 50km from Siem Reap and about 15km from Banteay Srei. To get here on the new toll road, take the well-signposted right fork just before Banteay Srei village and go straight ahead at the crossroads. Just before the road starts to climb the mountain, there is a barrier and it is here that the US$20 charge is levied. It is possible to buy a cheaper entrance ticket to Phnom Kulen for US$12 from the City Angkor Hotel in Siem Reap. It is only possible to go up Phnom Kulen before 11am and only possible to come down after midday, to avoid vehicles meeting on the narrow road. There are plenty of small restaurants and food stalls located near the waterfall or in the small village near Wat Preah Ang Thom.

Moto drivers are likely to want about US$20 or more to bring you out here, and rented cars will hit passengers with a surcharge, more than double the going rate for Angkor; forget coming by *remork* as the hill climb is just too tough. With the long journey here, it is best to plan on spending

THE LOST CITY OF MAHENDRAPRAVARTA

Phnom Kulen hit the headlines in 2013 thanks to the 'discovery' of a lost city known as Mahendrapravarta in Angkorian times. Using ground-piercing LIDAR radar technology, the structures of a more extensive archaeological site have been unveiled beneath the jungle canopy and earth. However, it wasn't quite as dramatic a discovery as initially reported, as Phnom Kulen had long been known as an important archaeological site. The LIDAR research confirmed the size and scale of the ancient city, complete with canals and barays, in the same way NASA satellite imagery had helped identify the size and scale of the greater Angkor hydraulic water system more than a decade ago. Some new temples and features were identified beneath the jungle, but remain remote and inaccessible due to terrain and the possibility of landmines.

the best part of a day exploring, although it can be combined with either Banteay Srei or Beng Mealea.

Beng Mealea   ប៉ឹងមាលា

One of the most mysterious temples at Angkor, **Beng Mealea** (admission US$5) is a spectacular sight to behold as nature has well and truly run riot. Built to the same floor plan as Angkor Wat, this titanic temple is Angkor's ultimate Indiana Jones experience. Built in the 12th century under Suryavarman II, Beng Mealea is enclosed by a massive moat measuring 1.2km by 900m, part of which is now dried up.

The temple used to be utterly consumed by jungle, but some of the dense foliage has been cut back and cleaned up in recent years. Entering from the south, visitors wend their way over piles of finely chiselled sandstone blocks, through long, dark chambers and between hanging vines. The central tower has completely collapsed, but hidden away among the rubble and foliage are several impressive carvings, as well as a well-preserved library in the northeastern quadrant. The temple is a special place and it is worth taking the time to explore it thoroughly –

Beng Mealea

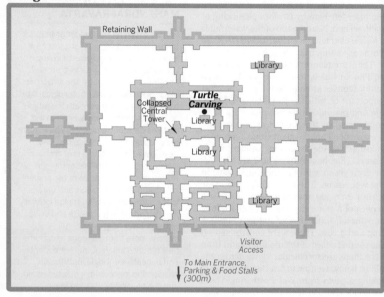

apsara caretakers can show you where rock-hopping and climbing is permitted. The large wooden walkway to and around the centre was originally constructed for the filming of Jean-Jacques Annaud's *Two Brothers* (2004), set in 1930s French Indochina and starring two tiger cubs. The filming included 20 tigers of all ages for continuity throughout the story.

There are very basic, unmarked family homestays a few hundred metres behind the restaurants opposite the temple entrance. The best restaurant is **Romduol Angkor II** (mains US$5), a sister restaurant to the Romduol Angkor near Sra Srang. Wholesome Cambodian food is on offer, plus cold drinks.

It costs US$5 to visit Beng Mealea and there are additional small charges for transport – make sure you work out in advance with the driver or guide who is paying this.

Beng Mealea is about 40km east of Bayon (as the crow flies) and 6.5km southeast of Phnom Kulen. By road it is about 68km (one hour by car, longer by *moto* or *remork*) from Siem Reap. The shortest route is via the junction town of Dam Dek, located on NH6 about 37km from Siem Reap in the direction of Phnom Penh. Turn north immediately after the market and continue on this road for 31km. The entrance to the temple lies just

beyond the left-hand turn to Koh Ker. Allow a half day to visit, including the journey time from Siem Reap or combine it with Koh Ker in a long day trip best undertaken by car or 4WD.

Beng Mealea is at the centre of an ancient Angkorian road connecting Angkor Thom and Preah Khan in Preah Vihear Province, now evocatively numbered NH66. A small Angkorian bridge just west of Chau Srei Vibol temple is the only remaining trace of the old Angkorian road between Beng Mealea and Angkor Thom; between Beng Mealea and Preah Khan there are at least 10 bridges abandoned in the forest. This is a way for extreme adventurers to get to Preah Khan temple; but don't undertake this journey lightly.

REMOTE ANGKORIAN SITES

Koh Ker

Abandoned for centuries to the forests of the north, **Koh Ker** (admission US$10), capital of the Angkorian empire from AD 928 to AD 944, was for a long time one of Cambodia's most remote and inaccessible temple complexes. Now, since the opening of a toll road from Dam Dek (via Beng Mealea), Koh Ker (pronounced ko-*kaye*) is within day-trip distance of Siem Reap. But to really appreciate the temples – the ensemble has 42 major structures in an area that meas-ures 9km by 4km – it's necessary to spend at least one night.

Several of the most impressive sculptures in the National Museum come from Koh Ker, including the huge *garuda* that greets visitors in the entrance hall and a unique

Koh Ker

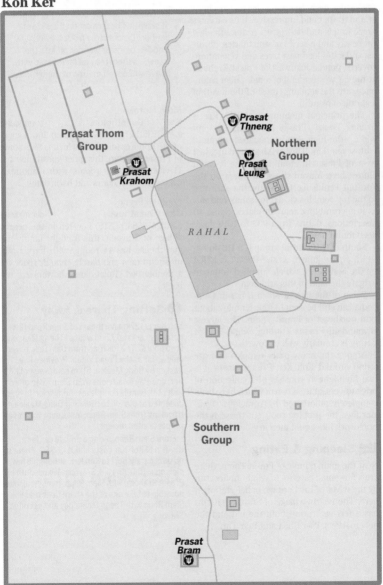

carving depicting a pair of wrestling monkey kings.

Most visitors start at **Prasat Krahom** (Red Temple), the second-largest structure at Koh Ker, named for the red bricks from which it is constructed. Sadly, none of the carved lions for which this temple was once known remain, though there's still plenty to see – stone archways and galleries lean hither and thither and impressive stone carvings grace lintels and doorposts. A *naga*-flanked causeway and a series of sanctuaries, libraries and gates lead past trees and vegetation-covered ponds. Just west of Prasat Krahom, at the far western end of a half-fallen colonnade, are the remains (most of the head) of a statue of Nandin.

The principal monument at Koh Ker is **Prasat Thom** (Prasat Kompeng), a 55m-wide, 40m-high sandstone-faced pyramid with seven tiers. This striking structure, just west of Prasat Krahom, looks like it could almost be a Mayan site somewhere on the Yucatán Peninsula. Currently, the staircase to the top remains closed for safety reasons, as it is crumbling apart in places. Some 40 inscriptions, dating from 932 to 1010, have been found here.

South of this central group is a 1185m-by-548m *baray* known as the **Rahal**. It is fed by the Sen River, which supplied water to irrigate the land in this arid area.

Some of the largest Shiva *linga* in Cambodia can still be seen in four temples about 1km northeast of Prasat Thom. The largest is found in **Prasat Thneng**, while **Prasat Leung** is similarly well endowed.

Among the many other temples that are found around Koh Ker, **Prasat Bram** is a real highlight. It consists of a collection of brick towers, at least two of which have been completely smothered by voracious strangler figs; the probing roots cut through the brickwork like liquid mercury.

Sleeping & Eating

Near the main temple of Prasat Thom, there are a few small eateries (daylight hours) run by the wives of the heritage police stationed here. The nearby village of Srayong (10km) has a few eateries at both the old and the new markets, Psar Chaa and Psar Thmei.

LANDMINE ALERT!

Many of the Koh Ker temples were mined during the war, but by 2008 most had been cleared: de-mining teams reported removing from the area a total of 1382 mines and 1,447,212 pieces of exploded and unexploded ordnance. However, considering what's at stake, it's best to err on the side of caution. Do not stray from previously trodden paths or wander off into the forest, as there may be landmines within a few hundred metres of the temples.

Mom Morokod
Koh Ker Guesthouse GUESTHOUSE $
(☑011935114; r from US$10) About 200m south of the Koh Ker toll plaza, which is 8km south of Prasat Krahom, this quiet guesthouse has 11 clean, spacious rooms with elaborately carved wooden doors and bathrooms.

Ponloeu Preah
Chan Guesthouse GUESTHOUSE $
(☑012489058; r US$5) Located in the nearby village of Srayong, this friendly, family-run guesthouse has 14 rooms with bare walls, mosquito nets and barely enough space for a double bed. Toilets and showers are out back.

Getting There & Away

Koh Ker is 127km northeast of Siem Reap (2½ hours by car) and 72km west of Tbeng Meanchey (two hours). The toll road from Dam Dek, paved only as far as the Preah Vihear Province line, passes by Beng Mealea, 61km southwest of Koh Ker; one-day excursions from Siem Reap often visit both temple complexes. Admission fees are collected at the toll barrier near Beng Mealea if travelling from Siem Reap; make sure you get a proper printed receipt.

From Siem Reap, hiring a private car for a day trip to Koh Ker costs about US$80. There's no public transport to Koh Ker, although a few pick-ups (10,000r) link Srayong, 10km south of Prasat Krahom, with Siem Reap. It might also be possible to take one of the share taxis that link Siem Reap with Tbeng Meanchey and get off at Srayong.

South Coast

POP 2 MILLION / AREA 27,817 SQ KM

Includes ➡

Best Places to Eat

➡ Café Laurent (p163)

➡ Chez Claude (p181)

➡ Rikitikitavi (p197)

➡ Sailing Club (p205)

➡ Sandan (p180)

Best Places to Stay

➡ Four Rivers Floating Ecolodge (p166)

➡ Done Right (p179)

➡ Ropanha Boutique Hotel (p176)

➡ The Columns (p194)

➡ Veranda Natural Resort (p204)

Why Go?

Ever wonder what Southern Thailand was like decades ago, before the crowds arrived? The South Coast (ឆ្នេរខាងត្បូង) of Cambodia might provide some clues. The country's coastline is tiny compared with its illustrious neighbour, but it remains practically deserted save for a clutch of fabulously diverse coastal towns: Koh Kong (the cowboy border town), Sihanoukville (the brash temptress), Kampot (the suave French colonialist) and Kep (the faded monarch).

Around these cities you won't find much besides jungle, a few truly idyllic islands and long stretches of powdery sand marred only by your footprints. Developers have long been drooling over the potential of this richly ecodiverse area, but most large-scale projects have been slow to materialise. Small resort owners have moved in, establishing little colonies of cool on patches of paradise along the coastline. Inland, legitimate ecotourism initiatives tempt adventurous and responsible travellers.

When to Go
Sihanoukville

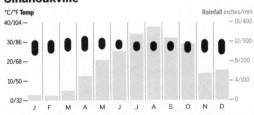

Nov–Feb Coolest months, with balmy weather and blue skies. Peak season; book ahead.

Mar–May It starts heating up in March, and builds to a crescendo in April and May.

Jun–Oct Rains are most severe on the south coast, but the scenery is lush and beautiful.

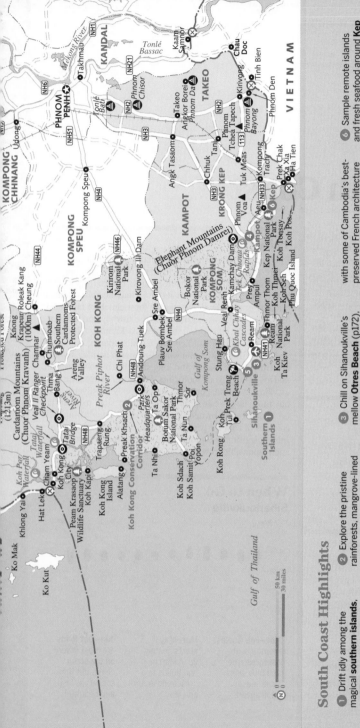

South Coast Highlights

① Drift idly among the magical **southern islands**, (p187) home to low-key resorts and lonely white sand beaches

② Explore the pristine rainforests, mangrove-lined rivers and remote waterfalls of the **Koh Kong Conservation Corridor**(p166), which is now open for ecotourism

③ Chill on Sihanoukville's mellow **Otres Beach** (p172), where exertion consists of yet another cocktail run

④ Kick back in **Kampot** (p192), a charming river town

with some of Cambodia's best-preserved French architecture

⑤ Party on **Occheuteal Beach** (p172), one of southeast Asia's top backpacker spots

⑥ Sample remote islands and fresh seafood around **Kep** (p200), the midcentury mecca of Cambodia's jet set

KOH KONG PROVINCE

Cambodia's vast and sparsely populated far southwestern province of Koh Kong (ខេត្ត កោះកុង) shelters some of the country's most remarkable and important natural sites.

Until relatively recently the entire province was effectively cut off from the rest of the country because of dreadful roads. The capital city of Koh Kong (Krong Koh Kong) was easier to visit from Thailand, the Thai baht was king and the vast majority of foreigners in town were the wrong type of tourists on visa runs from Pattaya. That has all changed as National Hwy 48 (NH48) is now paved and bus connections to Phnom Penh and Sihanoukville are frequent.

The best base for exploring the province's untamed jungle and coastline, spread out along the Koh Kong Conservation Corridor, is the riverine town of Koh Kong, 8km from the Thai border. From here, motorboats can whisk you to rushing waterfalls, secluded islands, sandy coves and Venice-like fishing villages on stilts.

Koh Kong City   ក្រុងកោះកុង

☑ 035 / POP 35,000

Once Cambodia's Wild West, its isolated frontier economy dominated by smuggling, prostitution and gambling, Koh Kong is striding towards respectability as ecotourists shoo away the sleaze. It's a sleepy town on the banks of the Koh Poi River, which spills into the Gulf of Thailand a few kilometres south of the centre.

◉ Sights & Activities

Koh Kong's main draw is adventures in and around the Cardamom Mountains and the Koh Kong Conservation Corridor, but there are a few diversions around town as well. If you want a dip, the pool at the Oasis Bungalow Resort is open to nonguests for US$3 a day.

Sun worshippers will discover additional beaches on the Gulf of Thailand further north near the Thai border.

Koh Yor Beach   BEACH

(ឆ្នេរកោះយ័រនៅប៉ាក់ខ្លង) This long, wind-swept beach is on the far (western) side of the peninsula that forms the west bank of the Koh Poi River opposite Koh Kong. It's not the world's prettiest beach, but it offers good shell collecting and you're pretty much guaranteed to have it to yourself. To

WAT NEANG KOK

A rocky promontory on the right (western) bank of the Koh Poi River is decorated with life-size statues demonstrating the violent punishments that await sinners in the Buddhist hell. This graphic tableau belongs to Wat Neang Kok, a Buddhist temple. To get there, cross the bridge, turn right 600m past the toll booth (*motos* 1200r), and proceed 150m beyond the temple to the statues.

get there, cross the bridge that spans the river north of the town centre, pay the toll on the other side (1200r for a *moto*) and look for a left turn about 1.5km beyond the toll booth. The beach is about 6km from the turn-off.

☞ Tours

Boat tours are an excellent way to view Koh Kong's many coastal attractions. English-speaking **Teur** (☑ 016 278668) hangs around the **boat dock** (cnr Sts 1 & 9) and can help you hire six-passenger (40-horsepower) and three-passenger (15-horsepower) outboards (speedboats). Destinations include Koh Kong Island western beaches (big/small boats US$80/50), around Koh Kong Island (US$120/90) and Peam Krasaop Wildlife Sanctuary (US$40/30).

The most popular tour is to Koh Kong Island (full day per person including lunch and snorkelling equipment US$25, or overnight for US$55). Trips take in some of the mangroves of Peam Krasaop Wildlife Sanctuary, and there's a good chance of spotting Irrawaddy dolphins early in the morning on these trips. Overnight trips involve beach camping or a homestay on the island. Note that tours don't take place in the rainy season (July to October) because of strong onshore (southwesterly) breezes. However, private boat trips to Peam Krasaop are possible year-round.

As tours become more popular, garbage is beginning to pile up on some of the island's western beaches, mainly the fault of irresponsible boatmen and tour operators. The following companies are trustworthy. They all run overland trips in the Cardamom Mountains as well as boat tours.

Blue Moon Guesthouse   JUNGLE TOUR
(☎ 012 946079; bluemoonkohkong@yahoo.com)
Mr Neat offers boat trips and rainforest
overnights in a hammock.

Jungle Cross   MOTORBIKE TOUR
(☎ 015 601633; www.junglecross.com) Specialises
in dirt-bike and jeep safaris deep into the
Cardamoms, with riverside camping in hammocks. Also runs trekking tours to more remote bits of the Cardamoms, with transport
by jeep to the launch point. Based out of Koh
Kong Safari World near the Thai border.

Koh Kong Eco Adventure Tours   TOUR
(☎ 012 707719; www.kohkongecoadventure.com; St
1) Koh Kong's longest running ecotourism

Koh Kong City

operator, Ritthy's excursions include excellent Koh Kong Island boat tours, birdwatching and jungle treks in the Cardamoms.

Neptune Adventure   TOUR
(☎ 088 777 0576; neptuneadventure-cambodia.
com; Tatai River) Well-established ecotourism
operator that is now based at Tatai River
(p166) and offers kayaking trips, as well as
multi-activity adventures with trekking and
cycling thrown in for a sort of triathlon light.

🛏 Sleeping

Koh Kong is becoming a popular holiday
destination for Khmers, so hotels fill up and
raise the rates during Cambodian holidays.
The Tatai River (p166), 18km east of town, has
some appealing eco-accommodation options.

⭐**Koh Kong City Hotel**   HOTEL $
(☎ 035-936777; kkcthotel.netkhmer.com; St 1; r
US$15-20; ❄ @ 🖥) Ludicrous value for what
you get, rooms include a huge bathroom,
two double beds, 50 TV channels, full complement of toiletries, free water and – in the
US$20 rooms – glorious river views.

Apex Koh Kong   HOTEL $
(☎ 016 307919; www.apexkohkong.com; St 6; r with
fan US$10, with air-con US$15-25; ❄ 🖥 🏊) Run
by the ubiquitous Virak Buntham group that
operates transport, hotels and more besides
in Koh Kong, this hotel is absurdly good
value given the central swimming pool and
smart rooms. Includes an inviting garden
restaurant and is usually busy thanks to paying transport commissions to local drivers.

Paddy's Bamboo Guesthouse   GUESTHOUSE $
(☎ 015 533223; ppkohkong@gmail.com; r US$4-8;
🖥) Paddy's targets backpackers with basic
rooms, a balcony for chillin' and a pool table.
Shoot for the wood-floored rooms upstairs
with shared bathrooms. Paddy is also a good

source of travel info and can arrange boat tours and other excursions.

PS Guesthouse GUESTHOUSE $
([icon] 097 729 1600; St 1; r with fan US$7, with air-con US$12; [icons]) A single-storey hotel backing on to the riverfront, the 18 rooms are well-furnished with large beds, flat-screen TVs and tastefully decorared bathrooms. PS: we recommend it.

Blue Moon Guesthouse GUESTHOUSE $
([icon] 012 575741; bluemoonkohkong@yahoo.com; r with fan/air-con US$6/10; [icons]) Nine neat, clean rooms with spiffy furnishings and hot water line a long, narrow courtyard. It's off the street so a peaceful night's sleep is definitely on the cards.

Asian Hotel HOTEL $
([icon] 035-936667; www.asiankohkong.com; St 1; r US$15-20; [icons]) A clean and comfortable hotel near the riverfront, it lacks the river views of its immediate rivals. The popular Baan Peakmai restaurant recently relocated downstairs, but lacks the atmosphere of old.

★**Oasis Bungalow Resort** RESORT $$
([icon] 092 228342; oasisresort.netkhmer.com; d/tr US$25/30; [icons]) In a quiet rural area 2km north of the centre, this oasis of calm has a gorgeous infinity pool with views of the Cardamoms and five cheerful, spacious bungalows with all the amenities. There's a no-sex-tourist policy, which is a refreshing approach for Koh Kong. Blue signs point the way from Acleda Bank.

Koh Kong Bay Hotel BOUTIQUE HOTEL $$
([icon] 035-936367; www.kohkongbay.com; St 1; r US$35-90) Koh Kong's first attempt at a boutique hotel. Rooms come in a variety of shapes and sizes, but it's not worth investing significantly more money in the top-end rooms. The decor is attractive and bathrooms include a rain shower. The pool offers river views and there's a small spa on site.

[icon] Eating & Drinking

The best cheap food stalls are in the southeast corner of Psar Leu (the market); fruit stalls can be found near the southwest corner. Riverfront food carts sell noodles and cans of beer for a few thousand riel, doubling up as sunset drinking spots.

Crab Shack SEAFOOD $
(Koh Yor Beach; mains US$4-8; [icon]11am-9pm) A family-run place over the bridge on Koh Yor, Crab Shack is known for perfect sunsets and heaped portions of fried crab with pepper (on request).

Japanese Food Maruo JAPANESE $
(mains US$2-7; [icon]11am-10pm) Japanese food has come to town and the prices are definitely more Koh Kong than Kyoto. Sushi samples are just US$1 to US$3 and set menus start from just US$5.50. As well as cheap local beers, imported sake is available for an authentic experience.

Bob's Ice CAFE $
(St 1; mains US$2-5; [icon]7am-10pm; [icon]) Popular Bob's Bar has a lively location near the riverfront. Don't be fooled by the name, though: the ice cream is great, but most people here are drinking chilled beers.

★**Café Laurent** INTERNATIONAL $$
(cafelaurent.asia; St 1; mains US$4-15; [icon]11am-10pm; [icon]) This chic, French-style cafe and restaurant offers fine dining in over-water pavilions, including refined Western and Khmer cuisine. French accented dishes include imported steaks and a traditional lamb stew. There is also a huge range of fresh seafood and cheap local classics.

Thmorda Crab House SEAFOOD $$
([icon] 035-690 0324; Neang Kok; US$4-8; [icon]7am-10pm) For dining with a different perspective, head across the bridge to this attractive restaurant set on stilts over the river. Part of the Thmorda Garden Riverside Resort, the restaurant includes some private pavillions for a spot of privacy. Crab is a speciality, plus there's a good range of Thai dishes available.

Blue Moon Shop SELF-CATERING
([icon]7am-9pm) Sells imported meats, cheeses and other goodies.

Fat Sam's BAR
(St 3; [icon]7am-11pm) An informal, Welsh-run bar-restaurant with a decent selection of beers, spirits and wines. The impressive food menu includes fish and chips, pasta, chilli con carne and authentic Khmer and Thai favourites. Useful travel information is dished out for free, plus there's motorbikes available for rent.

[icon] Information

MEDICAL SERVICES

In a medical emergency, evacuation to Thailand via the Cham Yeam/Hat Lek border crossing is possible 24 hours a day. In Thailand there's a hospital in Trat, 92km from the border.

Sen Sok Clinic (☏ 012 555060; kkpao@camintel.com; St 3, cnr St 5; ☺24hr) Has doctors who speak English and French.

MONEY

Thai baht are widely used so there's no urgent need to change baht into dollars or riel. To do so, use one of the many mobile-phone shops around Psar Leu.

Acleda Bank (cnr Sts 3 & 5; ☺8am-3.30pm Mon-Fri, to 11.30am Sat) ATM accepts Visa cards.

Canadia Bank (St 1; ☺8am-3.30pm Mon-Fri, to 11.30am Sat) The ATM here accepts most international plastic and there's no local charge for withdrawals.

TOURIST INFORMATION

Guesthouses, hotels and pubs are the best places to get the local low-down. You can also look for the free *Koh Kong Visitors Guide* (www.koh-kong.com), which is mostly advertisements.

❶ Getting There & Away

Koh Kong is on NH48, 220km northwest of Sihanoukville and 290km west of Phnom Penh. It's linked to the Thai border by a paved toll road that begins on the other side of the 1.9km bridge over the Koh Poi River.

BUS

Most buses drop passengers at Koh Kong's unpaved **bus station** (St 12), on the northeast edge of town, where *motos* and *remorks* await, eager to overcharge tourists. Don't pay more than US$1/2 for the three-minute *moto/remork*

ride into the centre. Pick-ups are at the company offices in town. Bus companies usually offer free transfer by *remork* from your guesthouse to their respective offices.

Rith Mony (☏ 012 640344; St 3), **Olympic Transport** (☏ 011 363678; St 3), **Phnom Penh Sorya** (☏ 077 563447; St 3) and **Virak Buntham** (☏ 089 998760; St 3) each run a couple of buses to Phnom Penh (US$7, six hours) and one or two trips to Sihanoukville (US$7, five hours). Most Sihanoukville trips involve a transfer, but Rith Mony and Virak Buntham have direct buses around 8am. Note that Virak Buntham claims to offer night buses from Siem Reap to Koh Kong, but these arrive in Sihanoukville early morning and require a second five-hour bus to Koh Kong, leaving many a backpacker justifiably annoyed.

Morning trips to Kampot (US$12, five hours) and Kep (US$14, six hours) with Rith Mony and Virak Buntham involve a vehicle change or two. The same two companies offer midday trips to Bangkok with a bus change at the border (US$20, eight hours). There are also trips to Koh Chang (US$14 including ferry) with a change of bus at the border, plus a local ferry to the island.

TAXI

From the taxi lot next to the bus station, shared taxis head to Phnom Penh (US$11, five hours) and occasionally to Sihanoukville (US$10, four hours) and Andoung Tuek (US$5, two hours). As with anywhere, the best chance for a ride is in the morning. Travel agents can easily set you up with shared or private taxi (to Phnom Penh/ Sihanoukville US$55/50).

Hiring a taxi to or from the Thai border costs about US$10 (plus 6000r for the toll), while a *moto/remork* will cost about US$3/8.

GETTING TO THAILAND: KOH KONG CITY TO TRAT

Getting to the border The Cham Yeam/Hat Lek border crossing, between Cambodia's Koh Kong and Trat in Thailand, is popular with travellers linking the beaches of Cambodia and Thailand. It offers connections from Bangkok, Ko Samet and Ko Chang to the Cardamom Mountains, Sihanoukville and Phnom Penh. Leaving Cambodia, take a taxi (US$10 plus toll) or *moto* (US$3 plus toll) from Koh Kong across the toll bridge to the border. Once in Thailand, catch a minibus to Trat, from where there are regular buses to Bangkok.

At the border Departing Cambodia via the Hat Lek border is actually pretty straightforward, as there are no visa scams for immigration to benefit from. Coming in the other direction and arriving in Cambodia via Hat Lek is a bit of a nightmare, as visa overcharging is common – up to 1000B or more than US$30. Avoid this problem by arranging an online e-visa in advance of travel.

Moving on From the Hat Lek border, take a minibus straight to Trat (120B). From here there are regular buses to Bangkok (from 225B, five to six hours) heading to the Thai capital's Eastern or North and Northeastern bus stations. Buses depart regularly from 6am until 11.30pm. Anyone heading to the nearby island of Koh Chang can arrange onward transport in Trat.

ℹ Getting Around

BICYCLE

Paddy's Bamboo Guesthouse and Koh Kong Eco Adventure Tours rent out bicycles for US$1 to US$2 per day.

CAR, MOTO & MOTORBIKE

Short *moto* rides within the centre are 2000r; *remorks* are double that; overcharging is common.

Motorbike hire is available from most guesthouses and from Koh Kong Eco Adventure Tours for US$5. They also have a 250cc Honda Degree available to rent for US$20 per day.

Around Koh Kong City

Koh Kong Island   កោះកុង

Cambodia's largest island towers over seas so crystal clear you can make out individual grains of sand in a couple of metres of water. The island has seven beaches, all of them along the Western coast. Unfortunately, they're becoming increasingly polluted as irresponsible tour operators fail to properly dispose of waste. Hopefully the situation can be reversed, as the island is a real gem.

Several of the beaches, lined with coconut palms and lush vegetation, just as you'd expect in a tropical paradise, are at the mouths of streams. At the sixth beach from the north, a narrow channel leads to a lagoon.

On Koh Kong Island's eastern side, half a dozen forested hills – the highest towering 407m above the sea – drop steeply to the mangrove-lined coast. The Venice-like fishing village of Alatang, with its stilted houses and colourful fishing boats, is on the southeast coast facing the northwest corner of Botum Sakor National Park.

It's forbidden to explore the thickly forested interior, but there is now one bungalow resort, plus overnight camping and homestay options are available with a guide.

🛏 Sleeping

Koh Kong Island Resort   RESORT $$
(☑035-936371; www.kohkongisland.net; Bungalows US$40-90) The first accommodation to open on Koh Kong Island, this could signal a wave of development in the coming years. The bungalows are rustic all-wooden structures, but include some nice decorative flourishes. The superior bungalows are pretty pokey, so it is worth investing in the deluxe options, from US$55.

ℹ Getting There & Away

Koh Kong Island lies about 25km south of Koh Kong City. The most practical way to get there is on a boat tour from Koh Kong City. Koh Kong Island Resort offers daily trips for US$25 per person, departing Koh Kong at 8.30am and returning around 5pm, including lunch.

Peam Krasaop Mangrove Sanctuary ជម្រកសត្វព្រៃបឹងក្រយ៉ក នៅ ក្រាមក្រសោម

Anchored to alluvial islands – some no larger than a house – this 260-sq-km sanctuary's millions of magnificent mangroves protect the coast from erosion, serve as a vital breeding and feeding ground for fish, shrimp and shellfish, and provide a home to myriad birds. The area, which is part of the Koh Kong Conservation Corridor, is all the more valuable from an ecological standpoint because similar forests in Thailand have been trashed by short-sighted development.

To get a feel for the delicate mangrove ecosystem – and to understand how mangrove roots can stop a tsunami dead in its tracks – head to the 600m-long concrete mangrove walk, which wends its way above the briny waters to a 15m observation tower. If you're lucky you'll come upon cavorting monkeys with a fondness for fizzy drinks. The walk (ជម្រកសត្វព្រៃបឹងក្រយ៉ក នៅ ក្រាមក្រសោម; mangrove walk admission 5000r; ⏱mangrove walk 6.30am-6pm) 🚩 begins at the sanctuary entrance, about 5.5km southeast of the city centre. A *moto/remork* costs US$5/10 return from Koh Kong City.

Unfortunately, a new resort has built 30 stilted bungalows amid the mangroves near the sanctuary entrance. The resort is a shrine to wood-crete that falls well short of blending with the beauty of the surroundings and was not fully operational at the time of writing.

You can avoid confronting this eyesore by hiring a motorboat to take you through the sanctuary. Wooden boats (US$10 per hour) are available for hire near the observation tower; a better plan is to head into the park's interior on a boat tour out of Koh Kong. On a boat tour, you'll have a chance to visit fishing hamlets whose residents use spindly traps to catch fish, which they keep alive until market time in partly submerged nets attached to floating wooden frames. Further out, on some of the more remote mangrove islands, you'll pass isolated little beaches where you can land and lounge alongside fearless hermit crabs.

Much of Peam Krasaop Mangrove Sanctuary is on the prestigious **Ramsar List of Wetlands of International Importance** (www.ramsar.org). The area's habitats and fisheries are threatened by the large-scale dredging of sand for Singapore.

Koh Kong Conservation Corridor របៀងអភិរក្សខេត្តកោះកុង

Stretching along both sides of NH48 from Koh Kong to the Gulf of Kompong Som (the bay northwest of Sihanoukville), the Koh Kong Conservation Corridor encompasses many of Cambodia's most outstanding natural sites, including the southern reaches of the fabled Cardamom Mountains, an area of breathtaking beauty and astonishing biodiversity.

The Cardamoms cover 20,000 sq km of southwestern Cambodia. Their remote peaks – up to 1800m high – and 18 major waterways are home to at least 59 globally threatened animal species, including tigers, Asian elephants, bears, Siamese crocodiles, pangolins and eight species of tortoise and turtle.

The second-largest virgin rainforest on mainland southeast Asia, the Cardamoms are one of only two sites in the region where unbroken forests still connect mountain summits with the sea (the other is in Myanmar). Some highland areas receive up to 5m of rain a year. Conservationists hope the Cardamoms will someday be declared a Unesco World Heritage Forest.

While forests and coastlines elsewhere in Southeast Asia were being ravaged by developers and well-connected logging companies, the Cardamom Mountains and the adjacent mangrove forests were protected from the worst ecological outrages by their sheer remoteness and, at least in part, by Cambodia's long civil war. As a result, much of the area is still in pretty good shape, ecologically speaking, so the potential for ecotourism is huge – akin, some say, to that of Kenya's game reserves or Costa Rica's national parks.

The next few years will be critical in determining the future of the Cardamom Mountains. NGOs such as **Conservation International** (CI; www.conservation.org), **Fauna & Flora International** (FFI; www.fauna-flora.org) and **Wildlife Alliance** (www.wildlifealliance.org), and teams of armed enforcement rangers, are working to help protect the area's 16 distinct ecosystems from loggers and poachers. Ecotourism, too, can play a role in providing local people with sustainable alternatives to logging and poaching.

Tatai River & Waterfall ស្ទឹងទឹកធ្លាក់តាតៃ

About 18km east of Koh Kong on the NH48, the Phun Daung (Tatai) Bridge spans the Tatai River (Stung Tatai). Nestled in a lushly forested gorge upstream from the bridge is the Tatai Waterfall, a thundering set of rapids in the wet season, plunging over a 4m rock shelf. Water levels drop in the dry season, but you can swim year-round in refreshing pools around the waterfall. The water is fairly pure, as it comes down from the high Cardamoms, where there are very few human settlements.

🛏 Sleeping

The Tatai River has several excellent eco-accommodation options that are well worth a couple of days or more. All have their own restaurants, some with meals included, and a range of activities on the river and adventures in the surrounding jungle.

Tatai River Bungalows ECOLODGE $$
(☑088 777 0576; neptuneadventure-cambodia.com; bungalows US$25-35) New riverside accommodation from long-running ecotour operator Neptune Adventure, the bunglows here are all wood and thatch affairs with solar power. Meals are available in the restaurant and include a popular communal dinner. Activities on offer include kayaking and tubing, plus original treks into the surrounding jungle.

Rainbow Lodge ECOLODGE $$
(☑097 948 5074; www.rainbowlodgecambodia.com; s/d incl all meals from US$50/75) This supremely tranquil ecolodge has seven bungalows with bathroom, fan and mosquito net. Solar panels provide electricity. Activities include kayaking, a sunset river cruise, a day trek and overnight camping. It's situated 10 minutes upriver from the Tatai Bridge, just a short kayak away from the waterfall. Access is by boat; call ahead for free pick-up at the bridge.

★ **Four Rivers Floating Ecolodge** RESORT $$$
(☑035-690 0650; www.ecolodges.asia; s/d incl breakfast US$203/239; 🖱) Boasting 'top-of-

the-line luxury in harmony with Mother Nature', this ecoresort's 17 South African–made tented villas – each 45 sq metres, with special septic tanks and partial solar power – float on a branch of the Tatai River estuary 6km downriver from NH48. Access is by boat (20 minutes) from the Koh Kong side of the Tatai Bridge.

❶ Getting There & Away

Access to Tatai Waterfall is by car or motorbike. The clearly marked turn-off is on the NH48 about 15km southeast of Koh Kong, or 2.8km northwest of the Tatai Bridge. From the highway it's about 2km to the falls along a rough access road. There's a stream crossing about halfway – you may have to cross it on foot and walk the last kilometre at the height of the wet season.

From Koh Kong, a half-day *moto/remork* excursion to Tatai Waterfall costs US$10/15 return, or less to go one way to the bridge. If travelling by public transport from Phnom Penh to one of the resorts, ask the driver to let you off at the bridge.

Central Cardamoms Protected Forest   ឧទ្យានជាតិជួរភ្នំក្រវាញ

The Central Cardamoms Protected Forest (CCPF; 4013 sq km) encompasses three of Southeast Asia's most threatened ecosystems: lowland evergreen forests, riparian forests and wetlands.

The rangers and military police who protect this vast area from illegal hunting and logging, with the help of Conservation International, are based at six strategically sited ranger stations, including one in Thma Bang, where they run a basic **guesthouse** (per person US$5) with two double rooms and a dorm, with electricity from 6pm to 9pm. The rangers' cook can prepare meals for US$2. Bring warm clothes, as the temperature can drop as low as 10°C.

Mostly covered with dense rainforest, Thma Bang is perfect for birdwatching or hiking to a waterfall with a local guide (rangers can help you find one). The nearby **Areng Valley**, some of whose inhabitants belong to the Khmer Daeum minority community, is home to Asian elephants and the dragonfish (Asian arowana), which is almost extinct in the wild. It also has the world's second-largest population of critically endangered wild Siamese crocodiles, toothy critters up to 3.5m long that don't eat people, preferring fish, snakes, frogs and small mammals. The valley and its fauna are under threat from a huge Chinese-built hydro-electric dam, which, if constructed, will displace 1500 people, flood 90 to 120 sq km of land and inundate an important elephant migration route. Government proponents of the dam counter that this and several additional Chinese-funded dams being built in Cambodia will provide much-needed electricity to a power-starved country.

From December to May, the truly intrepid can take an eight-day trek from Thma Bang north to Kravanh, or from Chamnar (linked to Thma Bang by road) over the mountains to Kravanh, a five- or six-day affair.

An easier, year-round option is the three- or four-day hike from Chumnoab, east of Thma Bang, eastwards to Roleak Kang Cheung, linked to Kompong Speu by road. Between the two is Knong Krapeur (1000m), set amid high-elevation grassland and pines. Inhabited five centuries ago, the area is known for its giant ceramic funeral jars, still filled with human bones.

There's no reservation system in Thma Bang; just show up and arrange trekking and accommodation on the spot.

❶ Getting There & Away

The southern reaches of the CCPF are easiest to reach from the south. The road to Thma Bang from NH48 has been widened and it now takes only about an hour to drive from Koh Kong. Turn off NH48 about 10km east of the Tatai River bridge at the Veal II (Veal Pii) ranger checkpoint.

Thma Bang is linked to Chi Phat by a difficult trail that can be handled by motorbike, but just barely and only in the dry season. From our nightmare experience we don't recommend it. Only attempt it in a large group of experienced bikers to help navigate bikes over the more difficult river crossings and dried out waterfall beds.

An improving road, passable by Toyota Camry or motorbike in the dry season, goes north from Koh Kong through the Cardamoms to Pursat, Pailin and Battambang, passing by remote mountain towns such as Veal Veng, O Som (where there's a ranger station) and Promouy (the main town in the Phnom Samkos Wildlife Sanctuary). Near Koh Kong, the turn-off is on the old road to Phnom Penh past the airport, a few hundred metres beyond the army base. Going south, share taxis link Pursat with Promouy, O Som and Koh Kong in the dry season. In the wet season, it may still be possible to hire a *moto* for the long trip from Pramouy to Koh Kong, depending on local road conditions and seasonal rainfall.

The CCPF's northern sections are accessible from Pursat.

END OF THE LINE FOR THE PANGOLIN?

In China and Vietnam, the meat of the Malayan (Sunda) pangolin – a kind of nocturnal anteater whose only food is ants and termites – is considered a delicacy, and the creature's blood and scales are believed to have healing powers. As a result, villagers in the Cardamom Mountains, who often hunt with dogs, are paid a whopping US$100 per kilo for live pangolins (the price rises to US$175 in Vietnam and as much as US$7000 in China) and pangolin populations have been in freefall. Enforcement personnel are doing their best to crack down on poaching before it's too late.

Botum Sakor National Park
រមណីយដ្ឋានកីរសាតរនិងបទុមសាររ

Occupying almost the entirety of the 35km-wide peninsula west across the Gulf of Kompong Som from Sihanoukville, this 1834-sq-km national park, encircled by mangroves and beaches, is home to a profusion of wildlife, including elephants, deer, leopards and sun bears.

Alas, Botum Sakor appears to be a national park in name only. A US$5 billion Chinese-run tourism project will see the western third of the park developed into seven resort-like 'cities'. Launched in 2010, the project will take 30 years to complete, but construction crews have already laid a four-lane highway through the heart of the park. The new highway, which begins 6km west of Andoung Tuek, provides improved access to the Koh Sdach Archipelago.

Meanwhile, Cambodian businessman Ly Yong Phat has been granted a concession to develop a large central swath of the park.

That leaves the eastern third of the peninsula as the only viable area to visit. Boats can be hired in Andoung Tuek to take you up into four mangrove-lined streams that are – for the time being at least – rich with wildlife, including the pileated gibbon, long-tailed macaque and black-shanked douc langur. The streams are Ta Op, the largest, on the east coast; Ta Nun in the middle of the south coast; and Ta Nhi and Preak Khsach on the east coast.

At the park headquarters (☎ 081 414988, 099 374797), on NH48, 3.5km west of Andoung Tuek, you can arrange a hike with a ranger (US$5 a day) or a boat excursion out of Andoung Tuek.

Trail bikers and intrepid *moto* riders can bypass the newer highway and take the rugged road around the park's east coast via the scenic fishing village of Thmor Sor, which is largely built on stilts over the alluvial bay here, stretching almost a kilometre out to sea.

Chi Phat   សហគមន៍ទេសចរណ៍ជីផាត

In an effort to protect the southern Cardamom Mountains from poaching, logging and land grabbing by turning the rainforest into a source of jobs and income for local people, Wildlife Alliance (www.wildlifealliance.org) has launched a multiphase project to transform the Southern Cardamoms Protected Forest (1443 sq km), whose southern boundary is NH48 between Koh Kong and Andoung Tuek, into a world-class ecotourism destination.

Once notorious for its loggers and poachers, the river village of Chi Phat (population 630 families) is now home to Wildlife Alliance's pioneering community-based ecotourism project (CBET), offering travellers a unique opportunity to explore the Cardamoms ecosystems while contributing to their protection.

A variety of outdoor adventure activities are on offer. Visitors can take one- to five-day (four-night) treks through the jungle, go sunrise birdwatching, explore the local waterways by kayak, hire *motos* or mountain bikes to visit several nearby waterfalls and shoot (with a camera) monkeys and hornbills with a former poacher as a guide. Destinations include an area with mysterious, ancient burial jars and the Areng Valley. On overnight trips it is possible to sleep in hammocks or at one of five campsites set up by Wildlife Alliance, equipped with ecotoilets, field kitchens, and comfortable hammocks with mosquito-proof nets.

Of particular interest are the multiday mountain-bike safaris deep into the Cardamoms and the sunrise birdwatching trip. The latter involves an early wake-up call and a 1½-hour longtail boat ride before you jump in traditional stand-up rowing boats (with rower) and silently paddle along the placid Stung Proat, an unlogged tributary of the Preak Piphot River. Silver langurs, long-tailed macaques, greater hornbills and other rainforest creatures can often be seen along the banks of Stung Proat. Gibbons are hard to spot, but can often be heard calling to each other through the forest canopy.

It is also possible to visit Wildlife Alliance's million-tree nursery, where it nurtures saplings for its impressive reforestation program. This is a very educational experience and involves the chance to make a lasting mark with a plant-a-tree initiative. Adventurous travellers can spend several days roughing it in the forest on patrol with the local community rangers.

All of this is controlled through the exceptionally organised CBET Community Visitor Center (☑ 035-675 6444; www.chi-phat. com), a two-minute walk from the river pier in Chi Phat. The visitor centre has free wifi, 24-hour solar-powered electricity and a good restaurant serving both meat and vegetarian Khmer food.

Prices for all tours are extremely reasonable at less than US$35 per person per day for groups of two or more, including lunch, transport and equipment. All-inclusive multiday trips cost a bit more per day. Prices include a voluntary contribution (US$10 per person) to the community conservation fund. All tours require guides, most of whom once worked as poachers and loggers.

On arrival in Chi Phat, head to the visitor centre in the evening to join in a pre-trek orientation. You will meet the guides and other guests returning from treks. This is the time to get information about activities and the condition of the trails, and learn how the local community is now a force to protect the forests it once plundered.

🛌 Sleeping

Chi Phat's CBET project has 13 family-run guesthouses (d US$5), 10 homestays (s/d US$3/4) and two small groups of bungalows. Some of these places are in town; others are out in the countryside, surrounded by orchards. In addition there's a more upmarket place to stay at Butterfly Lodge (r US$15-25), previously known as Sothun Lodge, on a small island in the middle of a river. It has a delightful restaurant on a platform overlooking the river, and simple but sturdy bungalows with twin or double beds, balconies and en-suite bathrooms with real showers.

SOUTH COAST KOH KONG CONSERVATION CORRIDOR

CHI PHAT: AN ECOTOURISM CASE STUDY

The Chi Phat community has long supplemented their meagre agricultural income with products from the nearby forests. Gathering nontimber forest products (known in development lingo as NTFPs) and small quantities of firewood can be ecologically sustainable, but around Chi Phat the wholesale forest destruction carried out during 'the logging time' – the anarchic 1990s – left the whole ecosystem, and the villagers' livelihoods, way out of kilter. For many, poaching endangered animals became a way of life.

When Wildlife Alliance (p168) came on the scene in 2002 in a last-ditch effort to save the southern Cardamoms, local villagers and outsiders were encroaching on protected land, destroying the forest by illegal logging, and hunting endangered animals for local consumption and sale on the black market. The only way to prevent ecological catastrophe – and, among other things, to save macaques from being trapped, sold for US$60 and shipped to Vietnam to be eaten – was to send in teams of enforcement rangers to crack down on 'forestry and wildlife crimes'.

But enforcing the law impinged on local people's ability to earn income, generating a great deal of resentment. Wildlife Alliance realised that in order to save the Cardamoms, it needed the cooperation of locals, which would be forthcoming only if income-generating alternatives to poaching and logging were available.

Thus Wildlife Alliance launched what's known in NGO parlance as a community-based ecotourism (CBET) project. The first step was empowering the local community. A committee of 14 elected representatives was established to assess positive and negative impacts, set goals and manage the project. Many of those who joined as 'stakeholders' were former loggers and wildlife traders.

Today the Chi Phat CBET project is flourishing. The initially sceptical locals have warmed to the idea, and the income generated from ecotourism – income that goes into both the villagers' pockets and a community development fund – is starting to make a real difference. Chi Phat is seen as a model for other CBET projects, and delegations from around Cambodia now come here to see how it's done.

Booking in advance brings the bonus of helpful travel advice and a fact sheet about tours. Otherwise, just call in at the visitor centre when you arrive, and choose your accommodation from the display board. The guesthouse owner will come to meet you.

There's not a huge difference between the guesthouses and the homestays. Rooms – inspected monthly by the CBET committee – come with fans, mosquito nets, cotton sheets, foam mattresses, towel, free filtered water and a laminated sheet on local customs. All guesthouses and one homestay are connected to the village's electricity grid, which operates mornings and evenings only. Homestays without electricity have 12V fans powered overnight by rechargeable car battery. While Butterfly Lodge and some guesthouses have en-suite bathrooms, many homestays and bungalows have outside toilets (Western or squat) and showers (a rainwater cistern with a plastic bucket) that are clean and commodious.

✖ Eating & Drinking

There are several food stalls on the main strip between the river pier and the visitor centre. These sell simple local food for about US$2 a dish. The only full-on restaurant in town is at the visitor centre. Breakfast is US$2.50 and lunch and dinner is US$3.50. Everybody enjoys the same selection of three dishes for lunch and three different dishes for dinner, and the menu changes daily. Vegetarians are catered for and packed lunches are available. All the food is sourced locally, and much is locally grown or reared. Soft drinks and beers are available in local stores. The visitor centre boasts the only real bar in town and offers some of the best cocktails this side of Phnom Penh.

ℹ Information

At the boat dock in Andoung Tuek and in nearby coffee shops, scammers sometimes accost travellers, purveying misinformation, offering bogus tourist services and demanding spurious payments. For reliable information, contact the CBET office or check out its website. Decent imported mountain bikes are available for hire for US$10 per day.

ℹ Getting There & Away

Chi Phat is on the scenic Preak Piphot River, 21km upriver from Andoung Tuek. Andoung Tuek is on NH48, 98km from Koh Kong. All buses

travelling between Koh Kong and Phnom Penh or Sihanoukville pass through here.

A four- or six-passenger longtail boat makes the two-hour trip every day (US$10 to US$12 depending on the type of boat). Boats leave Andoung Teuk at 12 noon (or whenever the Virak Buntham bus from Phnom Penh arrives if running late). The CBET community works only with local boatmen who have been trained in safety standards and whose boats have been remodelled to offer tourists a degree of comfort. All CBET-sanctioned boats have life-vests and carry a spare engine. It is best to book the boat or *moto* in advance, as you will get pick-up information from the visitor centre. If you arrive after the CBET boat has departed (or is full), or want to make your own way to Chi Phat, you can hire a private boat (US$30 for the whole boat). These tend to be loaded with produce and locals, so are a more colourful means of transport, but you'll have to haggle on a price. Boats return to Andoung Teuk every morning in time to catch an onward bus.

It is also possible to arrange a *moto* ($US7, 45 minutes) to travel the 17km unsealed road, but the boats are far more atmospheric and relaxing. The road to Chi Phat is unsealed but in pretty good shape. Follow the telephone lines and use the car ferry to cross the river. Motorbikers can use a smaller ferry, located 100m to the left of the main ferry, if requiring a charter.

KOMPONG SOM PROVINCE

Sandwiched between Kampot and Koh Kong Provinces, this diminutive province is dominated by its main city, the dynamic port of Sihanoukville. Besides the surrounding islands, natural sites include Ream National Park, 18km east of Sihanoukville, and the Kbal Chhay Cascades.

Sihanoukville ក្រុងព្រះសីហានុ

✅ 034 / POP 221,000

Surrounded by white-sand beaches and undeveloped tropical islands, Sihanoukville (Krong Preah Sihanouk), also known as Kompong Som, is Cambodia's most happening beach destination. Visitor numbers have risen steadily in recent years and look set to skyrocket now that flights from Siem Reap are operating daily, with more routes planned.

For the time being, despite the boomtown rents, the city and its sandy bits remain pretty laidback. While backpackers continue to flock to the party zone of Serendipity Beach, the gorgeous Otres Beach, south of

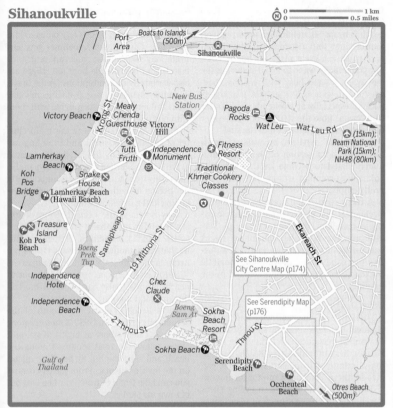

N 0 ——— 1 km
0 ——— 0.5 miles

town, has made an incredible comeback and is now equally popular for a more relaxed stay. That and the emergence of the southern islands as cradles of castaway cool give non-backpackers a reason to visit.

None of Sihanoukville's beaches would qualify as Southeast Asia's finest, but it's easy to have stretches of sand shaded by casuarina and coconut palms to yourself, especially if you venture outside the centre.

Named in honour of the then head-of-state, Sihanoukville was hacked out of the jungle in the late 1950s to create Cambodia's first and only deep-water port, strategically vital because it meant that the country's international trade no longer had to pass through Vietnam's Mekong Delta.

⊙ Sights

Wat Leu BUDDHIST TEMPLE
(វត្តលើ, Wat Chhnothean; Map p171) Spectacular views of almost the entire city and gor-

geous sunset panoramas await at Wat Leu, situated on a peaceful, forested hilltop 1.5km northwest of the city centre.

From the city centre, a *moto* ride due north up the hill costs 6000r, but drivers will likely want US$2. *Remorks* have to take the long way around and ask US$5.

Monkeys WILDLIFE
On most days in the late afternoon, three troupes of tame monkeys gather on 2 Thnou St (behind and on the chain-link fence enclosing the grounds of the Independence Hotel), hoping to score peanuts and bananas from passing humans. Locals often stop by with their kids, generating a great deal of mirth and mutual interprimate admiration.

🏖 Beaches

Sihanoukville's beaches all have wildly different characters. The most isolated are a short ride away in Ream National Park (p186).

Occheuteal Beach
BEACH

(ឆ្នេរអូរឈើទាល; Map p176) This 4km-long beach is by far Sihanoukville's most popular. Sunset views and a string of mellow beach bars make it a great place for happy hour, but you'll likely want to avoid it during the day, when it's too busy with vendors, beggars and nuisances like jet skis. It also gets packed, especially at weekends, and it's far from clean: note the rivulets of wastewater that flow from the shacks into the surf.

Escape the mayhem by walking down to the southern section of the beach, ultimately slated to become another exclusive Sokhamega-complex resort but for now pretty empty.

A rocky strip at the northwestern end of Occheuteal has emerged as a happy, easygoing travellers' hang-out known as **Serendipity Beach**. At the atmospheric resort bar-restaurants, waves lap just a few metres from the tables, providing a romantic backdrop, especially at sundown and in the evening.

Otres Beach
BEACH

(ឆ្នេរអូរត្រះ) At the southern end of Occheuteal Beach, beyond the small headland, **Phnom Som Nak Sdach** (Hill of the King's Palace), lies stunning Otres Beach, a seemingly infinite strip of casuarinas that can give southern Thailand a run for its money.

Developers have long been eyeing Otres Beach, and in 2010 a stretch of resorts was forcibly removed. However, Otres has made yet another recovery and is currently in rude health with more than 30 bungalow resorts in the area, including a couple of more upmarket boutique hotels. It's fair to say that Otres is no longer the empty beach it once was. Even so, Otres has cleaner water and is more relaxed than anything in Sihanoukville proper, and is lengthy enough that finding your own patch of private sand is not a challenge...just walk south.

Otres is split into three distinct sections: Otres 1 is the first and busiest stretch and about 2km south is Otres 2, separated by a slated resort development and currently known as 'Long Beach'. Inland lies laidback Otres Village, an up-and-coming estuary area.

Otres also has an expanding range of activities on offer. At the northern end of the beach (near where you arrive from Sihanoukville) you'll find **Hurricane Windsurfing** (☑017 471604; windsurf-cambodia.com), which rents out paddle boards (per hour US$8), windsurfers (basic/high-performance boards US$10/20 per hour), sea kayaks (single/tandem US$4/6 per hour) and skim boards (try bungee skim boarding). Otres Beach sometimes gets surf from May to October; you can rent surfboards and bodyboards here too. There are also various flying contraptions for the brave, including flyboards (see flyboardcambodia.com) and amphibious microlights with room with one passenger.

About 700m south, near the main cluster of guesthouses, you'll find **Blue Lagoon Kitesurf Centre** (☑085 511145). It's located at Sunlord Seagarden resort. The owner also runs daily **boat tours** to four islands (US$15 per person including breakfast, lunch, snorkelling and a drink or two).

Way down at the beach's sleepy southern terminus on Otres 2 is **Otres Nautica** (☑092 230065), a laidback, French-run outfit that rents tandem sea kayaks (US$4 per hour) and Hobie Cat sailing catamarans (US$10 per hour) that you can take out to nearby islands. It also has a boat for snorkelling or island-hopping excursions.

Otres Beach is about 5km south of the Serendipity area. It's a US$2/5 *moto/remork* ride to get here (more at night). If going it alone, follow the road southeast along the beach and skirt the hill by headling inland on the inviting tarmac. From the city centre, you can take Omui St from Psar Leu east out of town for 5km.

Sokha Beach
BEACH

(ឆ្នេរសុខា; Map p171) Midway between Independence and Serendipity lies Sihanoukville's prettiest beach, 1.5km-long Sokha Beach. Its fine, silicon-like sand squeaks loudly underfoot. The tiny eastern end of Sokha Beach is open to the public and rarely crowded. The rest is part of the exclusive Sokha Beach Resort. Tourists are welcome to enjoy the sand near Sokha but are expected to buy something to drink or eat. You might even duck into the resort to use the pool (US$5).

Victory Beach
BEACH

(ឆ្នេរជ័យជនះ; Map p171) This is not the best beach in town due to the looming backdrop of Sihanoukville Port. That said, it is clean, hassle-free and family-friendly, with plenty of midrange beach eateries.

Lamherkay Beach
BEACH

(ឆ្នេរឡាំម៉ែកាយ; Map p171) About 1.5km southwest of Victory Beach, next to a shady grove, is Lamherkay Beach, also known as Hawaii

Seaview Beach. It's hugely popular with car-owning Khmers on weekends and holidays but quiet on weekdays. **Koh Pos** (Snake Island), the island 800m offshore, has been leased by Russians with big resort plans, which explains the flashy new bridge linking it with the mainland. It's currently a bridge to nowhere, as work on the actual resort appears to have stalled.

Independence Beach   BEACH

(ឆ្នេរឯករាជ្យ; Map p171) Northwest of Sokha Beach, Independence Beach (7-Chann Beach) has mostly been taken over by a gargantuan new property development. The only open section is beneath the classic hotel for which the beach is named.

🏃 Activities

The diving near Sihanoukville isn't the best in Southeast Asia, but there are reefs and fish to be ogled and it gets better further afield. Just don't expect anything on a par with the best of Thailand or Indonesia.

Most serious trips will hit Koh Rong Samloem, while overnight trips target the distant islands of Koh Tang and Koh Prins. Overnight trips cost about US$100 per day including two daily dives, food, accommodation on an island and equipment. Two-tank dives out of Sihanoukville average US$80 including equipment. PADI open-water courses average about US$400 to US$450 – pretty competitive by world standards.

Marine Conservation Cambodia (MCC; www.marineconservationcambodia.org) is working to protect the area's reefs and coastal breeding grounds and occasionally has volunteer positions available at its base near M'Pay Bay Bungalows on Koh Rong Samloem.

Most dive operators have some sort of presence on Koh Rong or Koh Rong Samloem, in the shape of bungalows or an office-restaurant where you can make a pit stop. Dive shops tend to keep irregular hours, so drop in if they are open or call ahead for an appointment.

Dive Shop   DIVING

(Map p176; ☑034-933664; www.diveshopcambodia.com; road to Serendipity) PADI five-star dive centre offering National Geographic Diver certification. It has a dive shop on Koh Rong and works closely with Paradise Bungalows.

EcoSea Dive   DIVING

(Map p176; ☑034-934631; www.ecoseadive.com; road to Serendipity) PADI and SSI courses.

Frogman Diving   DIVING

(Map p176; ☑097 858 7550; www.frogman.asia; Serendipity St) This operation is popular with a French clientele.

Scuba Nation   DIVING

(Map p176; ☑012 604680; www.divecambodia.com; Serendipity St) The longest-running operator in town has a comfortable boat for liveaboard trips, and runs Cambodia's first five-star instructor-development centre. Real professionals.

Relax   SPA

(Map p176; ☑085 352213; road to Serendipity; per hr from US$10; ☺10am-9.30pm) English-owned and managed, this place's Khmer, lavender, jasmine-oil and foot massages get great reviews. Also offering facials, pedicures and waxing.

Seeing Hands Massage 3   MASSAGE

(Map p174; 95 Ekareach St; per hr US$6; ☺8am-9pm) 🕭 Some of the blind masseurs that work their magic here are English-speaking.

Starfish Bakery & Café   MASSAGE

(Map p174; 62 7 Makara St; per hr US$6-10; ☺7am-6pm) Masseuses (who are visually or physically disabled and have been trained by Western massage therapists) perform Khmer, Thai, oil, foot and Indian head massages. Profits go towards social projects.

Fitness Resort   GYM

(Map p171; ☑015 620534; www.fitness-sihanoukville.com; road to Serendipity; per day US$4, incl a class US$5; ☺6am-8pm Mon-Sat, to noon Sun) A funky French-run complex in a villa 2km northwest of the bus station with a huge open-air gym, free weights, aerobics, and Khmer and Thai boxing classes (US$8). It's between the city centre and the bus station, about 600m southeast of Mittapheap Kampuchea Soviet St.

🍳 Courses

Traditional Khmer
Cookery Classes   COOKING COURSE

(Map p171; ☑092 738615; www.cambodiancookeryclasses.com; 335 Ekareach St; per person US$23; ☺10am-2pm Mon-Sat) Teaches traditional culinary techniques in classes with no more than eight participants. Specialities include squid with Kampot pepper, whole steamed fish with sweet-and-sour sauce, and pomelo salad with prawns. Reserve classes a day ahead.

Sihanoukville City Centre

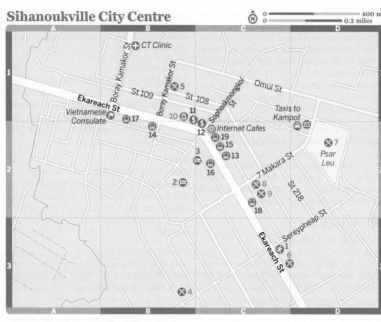

Sihanoukville City Centre

Tours

Popular day tours (US$20 per person) go to some of the closer islands and to Ream National Park. You can also hire a boat and make your own way to the islands: most travel agencies and guesthouses can arrange a boat. Figure on US$50 for a boat to Koh Ta Kiev from Occheuteal; a bit less for Koh Russei. You'll save money going from Otres Beach.

Booze cruises have been increasing in popularity. JJ's Playground is one of the main outfits offering backpackers the chance to board a boat every Saturday and spend the afternoon getting sloshed under the sun. Reports are that many a drunk has ended up in the water; don't drown or you might ruin it for everybody else.

Eco-Trek Tours   TOUR
(Map p176; ☎ 012 987073; ecotrektourscambodia@yahoo.com; road to Serendipity; ◷ 8am-10pm) Associated with the knowledgeable folks at Mick and Craig's guesthouse, this travel agency has information on just about any-

thing. It also hires out mountain bikes (per day US$4) and can direct you to good rides.

Party Boat BOAT TRIPS
(Map p176; www.thepartyboat.asia; US$25 per person) The Party Boat heads out daily to Koh Rong Samloem, departing at 9.30am and the trip includes snacks, lunch, snorkelling and a free drink. Once a month on full moon, backpackers head out to the Koh Rong Samloem full moon party (US$20) at 5pm and the boat returns to Sihanoukville around 7am.

Ravuth Travel BOAT TOUR
(Map p176; 012 439292; www.ravuthtravel.blog spot.com; Serendipity Beach) Located at Otres Beach Resort, Ravuth is one of several operations running daily trips to Koh Ta Kiev/ Koh Russei (per person US$12/15), with stops at smaller islands, departing at 9am. Tours include breakfast, a seafood barbecue lunch and snorkelling equipment.

Suntours BOAT TOUR
(016 396201; www.suntours-cambodia.com) The slightly more upscale day and overnight island cruises around Koh Rong Samloem offered by Suntours, with departures from Victory Beach, get rave reviews.

Stray Dogs of Asia MOTORCYCLE TRIP
(Map p176; 017 810125; www.straydogsasia.com; Occheuteal St; tours US$100) Runs all-day dirt-bike countryside tours that take in some of the natural attractions around Sihanoukville.

🛏 Sleeping

It's all about location in Sihanoukville, as each region has its own very distinct character and attracts a different type of clientele. Prices quoted are for the high season (approximately November to March). Rates drop during the rainy season, especially on Serendipity and Otres Beaches, but skyrocket on Khmer holidays at some establishments. Beachfront places come at a premium price on Otres Beach (or the islands), so some prefer to seek better value accommodation around the Serendipity area and commute to the beach. Ask your resort about free bus transfers.

🏖 Serendipity & Occheuteal

Small Serendipity Beach offers a string of mellow resorts spread over the hillside above the sea. Unfortunately, the buzz is partly killed by late-night noise from the nearby clubs. The din isn't too bad, especially the further east you go, but light sleepers may want to bunk elsewhere.

From Serendipity Beach, Serendipity St runs up the hill to the Road to Serendipity, which connects to Ekareach St at the Golden Lions Roundabout. The Road to Serendipity is the main backpacker hang-out. There are some excellent midrange hotels on the streets running southeast from the Road to Serendipity.

Monkey Republic HOSTEL $
(Map p176; 012 490290; monkeyrepublic.info; road to Serendipity; r US$10-12; @🛜) This self-proclaimed 'backpacker central', est. 2005, rose from the ashes in 2013 following a dramatic fire (no casualities). It offers smart new dorm beds and affordable rooms set in a striking building finished in French-colonial style. The bar-restaurant is a big draw with a happy hour from 6pm to 9pm.

Big Easy HOSTEL $
(Map p176; 081 943930; www.thebigeasy.asia; road to Serendipity; dm US$3, r US$6-10; 🛜) The Big Easy is a classic backpacker pad with accommodation, comfort food and a lively bar all rolled into one. The accommodation will have undergone a makeover by the time you read this, plus the bar has a great vibe, with occasional live music and live EPL games.

Utopia HOSTEL $
(Map p176; 034-934319; www.utopia-cambodia.com; road to Serendipity; dm US$1-2.50, r US$6-7; @🛜) Dorm beds don't come cheaper than at this backpacker escape, including 'luxury' air-con options. Most people aren't here for their beauty sleep, but to party on at the bar. Includes a superb range of bargain food outlets such as Fish & Chips and Slumdog Curry.

New Sea View Villa HOTEL $
(Map p176; 092 759753; www.sihanoukville-hotel.com; Serendipity St; r US$10-35; ❄🛜) Known more for its food, New Sea View also has popular rooms in a central (almost beachfront) location in the heart of Serendipity. Friendly, helpful staff and management make it a homely place to stay.

Sakal Guesthouse 2 GUESTHOUSE $
(Map p176; 012 806155; sakalguesthouse@ yahoo.com; road to Serendipity; dm US$3, r US$8-22) The new branch of an old Victory Beach crashpad, Sakal 2 has cheap and somewhat cheerful dorms. The rooms include large screen TVs, plus a spacious family option at US$22.

Serendipity

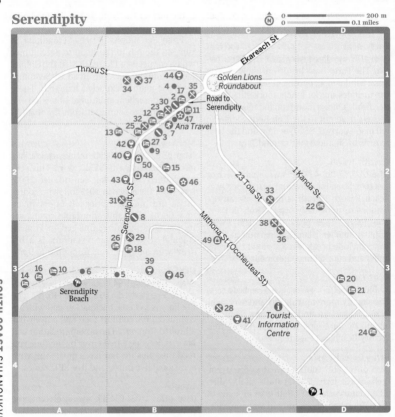

Papagayo Guesthouse   GUESTHOUSE **$**
(Map p176; ☑089 325104; 1 Kanda St; r US$9-15)
A friendly little guesthouse at the back of
the Occheuteal strip, the rooms are simple
yet spacious, including hot water bathrooms
and free wi-fi. Out front is a popular bar that
draws a regular crew of drinkers.

★**Ropanha**
Boutique Hotel   BOUTIQUE HOTEL **$$**
(Map p176; ☑012 556654; www.ropanha-boutique
hotel.com; 23 Tola St; r US$30-45) New in late
2013, this place is currently the pick of the
pack when it comes to affordable atmosphere.
Set around a lush courtyard garden and pool,
the rooms include flat-screen TVs and accom-
panying DVD players, plus rain showers in
the bathroom. It's exceptional value, although
prices may rise a little as the word spreads.

Serendipity Beach Resort   HOTEL **$$**
(Map p176; ☑034-938888; www.serendipity
beachresort.com; Serendipity St; r US$35-100;

❀@🛜🌊) Ignore the ugly ducking exterior,
for inside a Serendipity swan awaits. Prices
here remain steadfastly cheap given the impressive size and style of the rooms. There is
a huge pool, often partially in the shade of
the building, and a lift.

Cove   RESORT **$$**
(Map p176; ☑034-638 0296; www.thecovebeach.
com; Serendipity Beach; r US$21-129; ❀🛜) One
of the smarter bungalow resorts on Seren-
dipity Beach, with a variety of hillside bun-
galows and a bar lapped by waves. Most
bungalows face the sea and all have bal-
conies and hammocks. The pricier air-con
rooms are way up top in a concrete row.

Reef Resort   HOTEL **$$**
(Map p176; ☑034-934281; www.reefresort.com.
kh; road to Serendipity; d incl breakfast US$40-85;
❀🛜🌊) The apex of comfort and style in the
Serendipity area, this was the first upscale
property to open here. A smart choice if you

Serendipity

can't live without your mod-cons; the generously proportioned rooms afford views of a 12.5m pool, surrounded by a patio and lots of luscious orchids.

Nice Beach Hotel HOTEL $$
(Map p176; ☎034-659 4999; www.nicebeach-hotel.com; 14 Mithona St; r US$25-35) Just a block from the beach between Occheuteal and Serendipity, this Cambodian villa-style hotel offers enticing value for money, the rooms decked out with flat-screen TVs and swish bathrooms.

Blue Sea Boutique Hotel HOTEL $$
(Map p176; ☎034-933999; www.bluesea-boutique.com; road to Serendipity; r US$50-115) One of the smarter hotels in the Serendipity area, tucked away behind a shopping arcade at the top of the hill. Rooms are set in bungalows around a mid-size swimming pool and include more than the average decorative flourish.

Above Us Only Sky RESORT $$
(Map p176; ☎089 822318; www.aboveusonlysky-cambodia.com; Serendipity Beach; r incl breakfast with fan/air-con from US$50/55; ❄🕸) The bungalows are attractively minimalist inside, but chances are you'll be hangin' on the cosy balcony, where satellite chairs stare seaward. The bar perched over the rocks by the seashore is a gem.

Cloud 9 RESORT $$
(Map p176; ☎098 215166; www.cloud9bungalows.com; Serendipity Beach; r US$25-100; 🕸) The last place on Serendipity Beach is a fine choice, and not just because it's furthest removed from the club noise. It has a cosy tropical bar and a range of rustic, Khmer-style bungalows with fans and ocean-view balconies.

Orchidée Guesthouse HOTEL $$
(Map p176; ☎034-933639; www.orchidee-guesthouse.com; 23 Tola St; r incl breakfast US$22-50; ❄@🕸🏊) A delightful 10m pool surrounded by chairs and palms is the centre-piece of this restful place. The well-kept rooms – some poolside, others bungalow-style – have contemporary flair, in addition to more

extras than you would expect. A real find if you're happy one block back from the beach.

OC Boutique Hotel
HOTEL $$

(Map p176; ☑ 034-933658; www.ochotel.asia; 23 Tola St; r US$49-86) There are two OC hotels in one location, but we recommend the 'Boutique' option thanks to clean, contemporary lines and good views over the pool. Check out their slick OC Beach Club down on Otres, one of the smartest places on the sand.

Beach Road Hotel
HOTEL $$

(Map p176; ☑ 017 827677; www.beachroad-hotel. com; road to Serendipity; r US$18-50; ❄️ 🖥️ 🌐) Well located and efficiently run, Beach Road Hotel has 76 modern rooms, some set around the central swimming pool. It's great value for the location and has a lively little bar-restaurant out front.

Coolabah Resort
HOTEL $$

(Map p176; ☑ 017 678218; www.coolabah-hotel. com; 14 Mithona St; r US$41-80; ❄️ @ 🌐) A popular Aussie-run hotel near the Serendipity strip, this attractive place includes a small swimming pool and a good range of rooms including family options. Smart art and contemporary bathrooms complete the picture.

🖻 Around Sihanoukville

The shabby city centre, spread out along and north of Ekareach St, is preferred by some long-termers because it's cheap and it's removed from the traveller scene. Most banks and businesses are here too, as is Sihanoukville's main market.

Victory Hill (Weather Station Hill, also known as 'The Hill'), once a backpacker haven, is up the hill from Victory Beach. The main drag is now pretty sleazy and far removed from its former hippy trippy vibe, but one of the longest running guesthouses here remains a good locally owned option.

Independence Beach and Sokha Beach both have high-end resorts occupying the prime beach real estate.

Mealy Chenda Guesthouse
GUESTHOUSE $

(Map p171; ☑ 034-933472; Victory Hill; r with fan US$7-9, with air-con US$15-25; ❄️ 🖥️) The clean and spacious air-con rooms in this old classic are a fine deal. The original Sihanoukville guesthouse has survived through several Victory Hill transformations over two decades: we first stayed here in 1995 and the same friendly family still runs the show.

Check out the popular barbecue nights on Wednesday and Saturday.

Small Hotel
HOTEL $

(Map p174; ☑ 034-630 6161; www.thesmallhotel. info; r US$17-23; ❄️ @ 🌐) 🖉 Run by a cheerful, clued-up Swedish-Khmer couple, this guesthouse is as cosy as sitting in front of a fireplace on a snowy Scandinavian night. The 11 rooms lack the immense character of the lobby but are spotless and have hot water, fridge and TV.

Geckozy Guesthouse
GUESTHOUSE $

(Map p174; ☑ 012 495825; www.geckozy-guest house.com; r US$6-10; 🌐) For a slice of old-fashioned Sihanoukville hospitality, check out these basic rooms in an old wooden house on a quiet side street. Decorated with colourful flowers, the owners refuse to pay *motodop* commissions, so navigate your way here despite protestations that it's closed.

Don Bosco Hotel School
TRAINING HOTEL $$

(☑ 034-934478; www.donboscohotelschool.com; Ou Phram St; r US$25-50) Sleep easy with a good conscience at this excellent training hotel to offer disadvantaged youngsters a helping hand into hospitality. Rooms are excellent value with a three-star trim throughout. Facilities include a large swimming pool, a gym and an authentic Italian restaurant. The location is not great, but the experience more than compensates. It's clearly signposted from Omui St when travelling out of the city centre on the road to Otres Beach.

Pagoda Rocks
BOUTIQUE HOTEL $$

(Map p171; ☑ 077 524275; www.pagodarocks.com; Wat Leu Area; r US$60-105; ❄️ 🖥️ 🌐) If you're going to stay far away from the beach you might as well stay at somewhere memorable. Pagoda Rocks has a swanky restaurant, a blissful infinity pool with prime views of the port area, and smart cottages. Unfortunately, getting here is a huge hassle if you don't have your own wheels; *remork* drivers demand US$5 one way. Ask for 'Wat Leu'.

Independence Hotel
HOTEL $$$

(Map p171; ☑ 034-934300; www.independence hotel.net; 2 Thnou St; r from US$160; ❄️ @ 🖥️ 🌐) Opened in 1963, this striking seven-storey hotel still has the jet-set feel of Sihanouk's movie-star heyday. After years of neglect, it was reopened in 2007. It features classic rooms with sea views, some more modern rooms in separate wings around the landscaped gardens, and a few brand-new bungalows overlooking the water, one with a private plunge pool. Ride the elevator to the private beach.

Sokha Beach Resort RESORT $$$
(Map p171; ☑034-935999; www.sokhahotels.com; Thnou St; r/ste from US$171/210; ❋@✿⊠) This opulent Khmer-style complex has a 1.5km private beach, a huge pool with its own tiny tropical island, and a children's playground. It has almost 400 rooms and recently tacked on a prominent casino near the entrance, turning off some families. There are also some over-water bungalows on a small lagoon at the rear of the resort, but you can't help thinking they should have been built on the beach.

🛏 Otres Beach

Otres is a place to get away from the bling of Sihanoukville. Most guesthouses are in a cluster about 1km south of Queen Hill Resort, an area known as Otres 1. About 2.5km of empty beach (land slated for eventual development) separates this cluster from a smaller, more isolated colony of resorts at the far southern end of the beach, known as Otres 2. Or head inland to up and coming Otres Village where there is a cluster of cool places nestled on a river estuary. Beachside places come at a premium compared with accommodation in the Serendipity Beach area.

★ Done Right HOSTEL $
(☑034-630 1100; Otres 1; dm US$4, s/d/tr without bathroom $6/8/12, bungalows US$18) Space-age, eco-friendly bungalows known as 'geodomes' are done right here: they are a bit like concrete yurts, with skylights in lieu of windows. Above the restaurant are some simple rooms with clapboard walls and lino floors. There's an open-air gym here, plus a handy tour desk.

Otres Orchid GUESTHOUSE $
(☑034-633 8484; otres.orchid@yahoo.com; Otres 1; r US$15-20) Cracking value for this popular Otres strip, the Orchid offers a mix of 20 rooms and bungalows at sensible prices. Rooms include hot water and air-con is planned for some. Amazingly, prices don't spike at peak holiday periods.

Wish You Were Here HOSTEL $
(☑097 241 5884; wishotres.com; Otres 1; r US$10-12, bungalows US$15) The rooms are pretty standard Otres fare, but the bar-restaurant

is one of the hippest hang-outs in the Otres area. Lounge around listening to top tunes or order one of their popular wish burgers or barra burgers.

Mushroom Point HOSTEL $
(☑078 509079; mushroompoint.otres@gmail.com; Otres 1; dm US$7-10, r US$20-30; ✿) The open-air dorm over the restaurant in the shape of a mushroom wins the award for most creative dorm in Cambodia. Even those averse to communal living will be content in their mosquito-net-draped pods, good for two. The 'shroom-shaped private bungalows and food get high marks too. There is also now a small annex on the beach.

Hacienda HOSTEL $
(☑070 814643; haciendaotres@outlook.com; Otres Village; dm US$3, r US$8-15) Hacienda is a great place to escape from it all. Choose from bargain dorms (some are even free after the first night) or cheap rooms, including a large communal room with four beds. The restaurant-bar is a relaxing place to while away an afternoon or five.

Don't Tell Mama GUESTHOUSE $
(☑097 943 7201; www.donttellmama2011.jimdo. com; Otres 1; bungalows US$20) Continuing the theme of quirky names around the Otres area, this place offers some great value bungalows that are more spacious than most. The friendly owners arrived here in an overland truck and are still living in it, parked next to reception.

Sunset Lounge GUESTHOUSE $
(☑097 734 0486; www.sunsetlounge-guesthouse. com; Otres 1; r with fan/air-con US$15/25; ❋) Alright, so strictly speaking this is the far south of Occheuteal, but it is so far removed from the mainstream that it feels part of Otres. This place is quiet and secluded on an undeveloped stretch of sand and offers great value for money.

Cinderella RESORT $
(☑092 612035; www.cinderella-cambodia.com; Otres 2; bungalows US$15-25; ✿) Way down in the southernmost resort colony, this is your spot if you just want some alone time. The beach is a bit dishevelled here and the A-frame cottages basic, but you can't argue with the beachfront setting.

Footprints HOSTEL $
(☑097 262 1598; footprints.otres@gmail.com; Otres 2; dm US$8, r US$15-25) The dorms are a little ambitiously priced compared with the

competition, but the rooms represent good value. There is a lively little bar-restaurant with live sport and a boxing gym, with classes available on demand.

Tamu BOUTIQUE HOTEL $$$

(☑088 901 7451; www.tamucambodia.com; Otres 2; r US$110-170; ❄️🛜⛱) A significant statement of confidence in the Otres Beach area, Tamu is an ultra-contemporary boutique hotel offering a range of simple yet stylish rooms set around a courtyard pool. The garden bungalows include a Balinese-style al-fresco bathroom and there is a hip beachside restaurant, open to all comers.

The Secret Garden BOUTIQUE HOTEL $$$

(☑097 649 5131; www.secretgardenotres.com; Otres 2; r US$99; ❄️🛜⛱) The first upscale boutique hotel to open on Otres has started a trend. The cute bungalows here are priced at a beach premium compared with town, but the garden includes a small swimming pool. Book ahead as it's pretty popular.

Eating

Sihanoukville's centre of culinary gravity has shifted to the Serendipity area, with dozens of restaurants packed into a couple of roads. Old-timer Victory Hill still has a couple of decent restaurants amid the chaos. The gritty commercial centre also holds a few pleasant surprises. Otres has some inviting beachside places for a leisurely lunch or romantic dinner if staying in the area.

✗ Serendipity & Occheuteal

For romance, nothing beats dining on the water, either at one of the resorts at Serendipity Beach or – more cheaply – in one of the shacks along adjacent Occheuteal Beach. Two blocks inland, 12 Tola St is developing into a restaurant zone, with a plethora of barbecue places in the evening.

Nyam CAMBODIAN $

(Map p176; www.nyamsihanoukville.com; 23 Tola St; US$2-4.25; ⊙5-10pm; 🛜) The name translates as 'Eat' in Khmer, and this is a great spot for a contemporary Cambodian dinner experience. All the favourites are here such as *amok* (baked fish curry), but there are also some healthy seafood offerings reflecting its coastal location.

Beachys BARBECUE $

(Map p176; Occheuteal Beach; mains US$2.50-5; ⊙7am-10pm; 🛜) Beachys' generous mixed seafood grill, fantastic value at US$4, separates it from the pack of barbecue shacks lining Occheuteul Beach. If you aren't up for surf, order turf, a heaped platter of various grilled meats.

Cafe Mango ITALIAN $

(Map p176; Serendipity Rd; US$3-6; ⊙7am-10pm; 🛜) A cracking little Italian cafe turning out wood-fired pizza, homemade pasta and delicate gnocchi. Dine at lunchtime or before 6.30pm for a main course accompanied by garlic bread or bruschetta and a drink for just US$5.

Leisure Cafe CAFE $

(Map p176; 23 Tola St; US$1.50-3.50; ⊙7am-9pm; ❄️🛜) This contemporary cafe is located in the grounds of the Golden Sands Hotel. Take advantage of the air-con and free wi-fi to sample some of the creative coffee creations, delicious fruit shakes and New Zealand Natural ice-cream.

★Sandan CAMBODIAN $$

(Map p176; 2 Thnou St; mains US$4-10; ⊙7am-9pm Mon-Sat; 🛜) 🍃 This superb eatery is loosely modelled on the beloved Phnom Penh restaurant Romdeng (p59). It's an extension of the vocational-training programs for at-risk Cambodians run by local NGO M'lop Tapang. The menu features creative Cambodian cuisine targeted at a slightly upscale clientele. There's a kids' play area and occasional cultural shows.

★So INTERNATIONAL $$

(Map p176; New Seaview Villa, Serendipity St; mains US$4-10; ⊙8am-4pm & 6-10pm; 🛜) So is renowned for serving up some of city's tastiest cuisine at any time of day, but target dinner when the candles come out, the menu changes and the top chef is in action. Specialities include wasabi prawns, baked scallops in wine sauce, *magret* of duck in raspberry sauce and, for dessert, tiramisu and crème brûlée. Early diners benefit from two courses for two people for just US$10 before 6.30pm.

Mick & Craig's INTERNATIONAL $$

(Map p176; www.mickandcraigs.com; road to Serendipity; mains US$4-7; ⊙7am-10pm; 🛜) This long-running guesthouse and restaurant has classic comfort food from around the globe. Thursday and Friday barbecue nights include a rack of ribs, Wednesday night includes steak and Guinness pie, and two-course Indian meals are just US$6.

Marco Polo
ITALIAN $$

(Map p176; Thnou St; mains US$3-8; ⊙11am-10pm; ☎) Some of the best Italian food for miles around is created by the Italian owner and chef here. The pasta dishes are perfectly *al dente* and the thin-crust pizzas emerging from the wood-fired oven are divine.

Happa
JAPANESE $$

(Map p176; road to Serendipity; mains US$4-7; ⊙5-10pm; ☎) Authentic teppanyaki with a variety of sauce options is tastefully served amid tropical decor with Japanese touches. Fresh sushi and sashimi is also available depending on the catch of the day.

Black Grouper
SEAFOOD $$

(Map p176; Serendipity Rd; ⊙7am-10pm; ☎) For seafood with some style, check out the elevated surrounds here. The extensive, French-accented menu includes scallops, prawns, crab and various whole fish, fresh off the boats from Sihanoukville's fishing port.

Blue Ocean
JAPANESE $$

(Map p176; road to Serendipity; dishes US$2-10; ⊙11.30am-2pm & 6-10pm; ☎) One of a cluster of Japanese restaurants that has recently opened in the Serendipity area; perhaps they know something about Japanese cruise ships coming this way? Blue Ocean is stylish and affordable, with a good range of sushi and sashimi, including generous set menus.

Taj Mahal
INDIAN $$

(Map p176; 23 Tola St; curries US$3-10; ⊙7am-9pm; ☎) The new Sihanoukville outpost of the long-running Maharajah Restaurant in Siem Reap, curry-craving British expats rave about the food here. As usual, selecting bespoke dishes can add up to an expensive spread, making the *thalis* (set meals; US$4 to US$7) a particularly good deal.

✗ Around Sihanoukville

For Sihanoukville's cheapest dining, head to the food stalls in and around **Psar Leu** (Map p174; 7 Makara St; ⊙7am-9pm): the vendors across the street, next to the Kampot taxis, are open 24 hours. Options include barbecue chicken, rice porridge or noodles with chicken. Even if you're staying elsewhere in town, it might be worth checking out Victory Hill for its quirks and good-value cuisine.

★Holy Cow
ORGANIC $

(Map p174; 83 Ekareach St; mains US$2.50-5; ⊙8.30am-11pm; ☎✐) Options at this chic funky cafe-restaurant include bagels with cream cheese, pasta, sandwiches on home-made bread and a good selection of veggie options, including two vegan desserts, both involving chocolate.

Starfish Bakery & Café
ORGANIC $

(Map p174; www.starfishcambodia.org; behind 62 7 Makara St; sandwiches US$2.50-4.50; ⊙7am-6pm; ☎✐) ✐ This relaxing, NGO-run garden cafe specialises in filling Western breakfasts and healthy, innovative sandwiches heavy on Mexican and Middle Eastern flavours. Add a cookie and drink to your sandwich for $1. Income goes to sustainable-development projects.

Gelato Italiano
ICE CREAM $

(Map p174; St 108; gelato per scoop US$1; ⊙8am-9pm; ✻☎) Run by students from Sihanoukville's Don Bosco Hotel School, this Italian-style cafe specialises in gelatos (Italian ice creams) in a dizzying array of flavours, and also serves various coffee drinks and light meals in a bright, airy space.

Tutti Frutti
FRENCH $

(Map p171; Victory Hill; mains US$3-6; ☎) On Victory Hill's main drag, this is a seriously good deal, with tasty Khmer mains to supplement rich French offerings like beef burgundy, steak tartare and *steak haché oeuf au cheval* (egg on beefsteak). The continental breakfast costs US$2.75 and includes a fruit shake.

Cabbage Farm Restaurant
CAMBODIAN $

(Map p174; small/large mains 8000r/15,000r; ⊙11am-10pm) Known to locals as Chom Ka Spey, this restaurant gets rave reviews for its seafood and spicy seasonings. An authentic Khmer dining experience. A sign in English on Sereypheap St points the way.

★Chez Claude
FRENCH $$

(Map p171; www.claudecambodge.com; above 2 Thnou St; mains US$5-15; ☎) Dou Dou and Claude are your hosts at this all-wood lookout – perched high above Sokha Beach with panoramic views – with outstanding French, Vietnamese and Cambodian cuisine, especially the seafood. Order paella 48 hours in advance. Access is via an innovative tractor-pulled cable car.

Treasure Island
CHINESE $$

(Map p171; Koh Pos Beach; mains US$3.50-10; ⊙9am-10pm) This 'Hong Kong–style' seafood joint serves the freshest fish in town. Housed in tanks, just point to what you want and the staff will pluck it out. It looks shambolic, but the isolated location on windy Koh Pos Beach is wonderful, especially for kids.

Snake House
RUSSIAN $$

(Map p171; mains US$3.50-10; ⊙8am-11pm; 🐾) Snake House serves authentic Russian dishes, sushi and seafood to diners seated at glass-topped tables with live serpents inside. It also has a bar, a guesthouse, various other caged and leashed critters, and a crocodile farm (US$3; free for diners). The absolute epitome of bizarre, only a Russian could dream this up.

Samudera Supermarket
SUPERMARKET $

(Map p174; 64 7 Makara St; ⊙6am-10pm) Has a good selection of fruit, veggies and Western favourites, including cheese and wine.

✖ Otres Beach

Queenco Palm Beach
INTERNATIONAL $

(Otres 1; mains US$3-7; ⊙7am-10pm) A full-on beach club at the northern end of Otres, the prices are much more reasonable than appearances might suggest. A seafood barbecue is just US$4, which would give any of the Occheuteal beach shacks a run for their money. Activities on offer include minigolf (US$3) and sea kayaks. Chilled.

Papa Pippo
ITALIAN $

(www.papapippo.com; Otres 1; US$3-6.50; ⊙7am-10pm; 🐾) Beachfront in the main resort cluster, it brings a bit of Italian flair to Otres Beach. The homemade pasta is among the best on the coast and there are plenty of Tuscan classics on the menu. It's a popular drinking spot with a quiz night every Tuesday.

Elephant Garden
INTERNATIONAL $

(Otres 2; mains US$3-7; ⊙7am-10pm) One of the most atmospheric beach bar-restaurants on Otres, the setting is awash with Angkorian statues and tasteful furnishings. The food is predominantly international with something for everyone, no matter their taste.

The Barn
INTERNATIONAL $

(Otres Village; US$3-6; ⊙11am-11pm) Located in up-and-coming Otres Village, this large wooden restaurant-bar has a huge deck located over the estuary here. The international food includes regular barbies, plus it plays host to the famous Otres Market every Saturday night through high season (November to February), with stalls, live music and DJs.

★ Chez Paou
FRENCH $$

(Otres 1; US$4-13; ⊙7am-10pm; 🐾) This is fine dining, Otres-style where chef specials in-

---

THE LAST BATTLE OF THE VIETNAM WAR

The final bloody confrontation of the Vietnam or Indochina War took place off the coast of Sihanoukville.

On 12 May 1975, two weeks after the fall of Saigon, Khmer Rouge forces used captured US-made Swift boats to seize an American merchant ship, the SS *Mayagüez* (named after a city in Puerto Rico), while it was on a routine voyage from Hong Kong to Thailand. The vessel was anchored 50km southwest of Sihanoukville off Koh Tang – now a popular scuba-diving destination – while the 39 crew members were taken to Sihanoukville.

Determined to show resolve in the face of this 'act of piracy', President Gerald Ford ordered that the ship and its crew be freed. Naval planes from the US aircraft carrier *Coral Sea* bombed Sihanoukville's oil refinery and the Ream airbase, and Marines prepared for their first hostile boarding of a ship at sea since 1826.

On 15 May, Marines stormed aboard the *Mayagüez* like swashbuckling pirates but found it deserted. In parallel, airborne Marine units landed on Koh Tang. Thought to be lightly defended, the island turned out to have been fortified in anticipation of a Vietnamese attack (Vietnam also claimed the island). In the course of the assault, most of the US helicopters were destroyed or damaged and 15 Americans were killed.

Unbeknownst to the Americans, early on 15 May the Khmer Rouge had placed the crew of the *Mayagüez* aboard a Thai fishing boat and set it adrift – but the men weren't discovered by US ships until after the assault on Koh Tang had begun. In the chaotic withdrawal from the island, three Marines were accidentally left behind and, it is believed, later executed by the Khmer Rouge.

The Vietnam War Memorial in Washington DC lists American war dead chronologically, which is why the names of the Marines who perished in the '*Mayagüez* Incident' appear at the bottom of the very last panel.

clude sting ray cooked on embers with fresh Kampot pepper, prawns flambéed in pastis, and crabs in two different ways. Doubles as a bar by night and the owner has occasionally been known to crank out tunes on the keyboard.

 Drinking

There's no shortage of venues to quaff locally brewed Angkor Beer, available on draught for as little as US$0.50. Some of the aforementioned guesthouses have lively bars, including Monkey Republic (happy hour 6pm to 9pm), The Big Easy (sport and live music) and hedonistic Utopia, with regular US$0.25 beer promotions: yes, that does equal 20 beers for US$5.

Occheuteal Beach is lined with beach bars that are perfect for sundowners, although the beggars on Occheuteal are particularly active at sunset. Hit Serendipity Beach for a more laid-back scene, although the resorts here just miss the sunset. The late-night action is seaside around the pier dividing Occheuteal and Serendipity beaches.

The alternative Occheuteal for single gentlemen and those wanting an unplanned bar crawl are the bar courts of Golden Lions Plaza and Sihanoukville Square, but most places are heavy on hostesses and light on atmosphere.

A few longstanding regular bars remain amid the hostess bars of Victory Hill, but the overall impression is Sinville rather than the more relaxed beach vibe of Sihanoukville.

Otres Beach has a good selection of beach bar-restaurants, some of which rumble into the night.

Led Zephyr   LIVE MUSIC, BAR
(Map p176; road to Serendipity; ⏱ 7am-midnight) Sihanoukville's premier live-music venue; the house band (and friends from time to time) are rockin' here most nights. Covers include many of the big anthems from the '60s to '80s and a bit of Chili Peppers thrown in for good measure.

Maybe Later   BAR
(Map p176; Serendipity St; ⏱ 5pm-2am) A popular little Mexican taqueria that doubles as a late-night bar in the Serendipity area, it has top margaritas and some refined tequilas for those who prefer sips to shots. It's a civilised escape from the beachside party scene.

Sessions   BEACH BAR
(Map p176; Occheuteal Beach; ⏱ 5pm-1am) A sorted music selection makes Sessions the top sundowner bar on Occheuteal Beach. The crowd of expats and backpackers assembled usually lingers well into the evening before the hard-core partiers move on to Dolphin Shack or JJ's.

JJ's Playground   BEACH BAR
(Map p176; Serendipity Beach; ⏱ 5pm-late) For a while now JJ's has been the go-to spot for those seeking pure late-night debauchery. Have an absinthe shot to get you in the spirit of things, including homegrown Abyss, brewed on nearby Koh Ta Khiev.

Dolphin Shack   BEACH BAR
(Map p176; Occheuteal Beach; ⏱ 5pm-late) Long-running beach shack with a host of specials designed to get you drunk fast, and bevies of beautiful backpackers pouring drinks and passing out flyers.

Reggae Bar   BAR
(Map p176; Thnou St; ⏱ 5pm-1am) It has more Marley on the walls than we've seen in quite some time (owner Dell is an avid collector) and a clientele diligently paying homage in the most appropriate way available.

Elephant   BAR
(Map p176; Serendipity St; ⏱ 5pm-late) Blink and you'll miss it, this quirky little bar is Cambodia's leading drum 'n' bass venue. It also doubles as a bit of a head shop with regular homemade treats to put you in the mood for the music.

☆ **Entertainment**

Top Cat Cinema   CINEMA
(Map p176; ☎ 012 790630; road to Serendipity; tickets US$3.50; ⏱ 11am-3am) This minicinema shows films on an 8m high-definition screen (for groups of at least six) or on large flat-screen TVs (for smaller groups). Has cosy satellite chairs and powerful air-con.

Galaxy Cinema   CINEMA
(Map p176; ☎ 017 721677; Occheuteal St; tickets US$3; ⏱ 11am-1pm) Regular screenings starting at 7pm or you can rent it out for private viewings.

🔒 **Shopping**

Funky restaurant Holy Cow sells some fashionable clothing upstairs.

SOUTH COAST SIHANOUKVILLE

Tapang TEXTILES
(Map p176; www.mloptapang.org; Serendipity St; ⊙10am-8pm) 🥾 Run by a local NGO that works with at-risk children, this shop sells good-quality bags, scarves and T-shirts made by street kids (and their families) so that they can attend school instead of peddling on the beach. Several other handicrafts shops are right nearby.

Starfish HANDICRAFTS
(Map p174; www.starfishcambodia.org; behind 62 7 Makara St; ⊙7am-6pm) 🥾 On the premises of the bakery of the same name, the silks and other gifts sold here support a sustainable livelihood for poor local families.

Let Us Create ART
(Map p176; www.letuscreate.org; Serendipity St; ⊙10am-6pm) Another NGO that works with underprivileged kids; you can buy small paintings and postcards here. The volunteer backpackers are happy to tell you more about the project.

Q&A BOOKS
(Map p176; Mithona St; ⊙7.30am-7.30pm) An inviting secondhand bookshop behind Occheuteal Beach, with 8000 titles in over 20 languages, plus a small cafe-restaurant on site.

Mr Heinz BOOKS
(Map p174; 219 Ekareach St; ⊙9am-6pm) Stocks thousands of books in 57 varieties...well not quite, but at least 10 languages.

🛈 Information

DANGERS & ANNOYANCES
Theft is a problem on several of the beaches, especially Occheuteal Beach, so leave any valuables in your room. It's often children who do the deed, sometimes in conjunction with adults. Arriving in a team, one or more will distract you while another lifts whatever valuables are lying on your towel. Or they'll strike when you're swimming.

Even if you aren't robbed you'll probably tire of the steady stream of beggars, many of them children or amputees, on Occheuteal Beach. NGO M'lop Tapang, which exists to improve the welfare of street kids, advises to never give money or food to children begging on the beach.

As in Phnom Penh, drive-by bag snatchings occasionally happen and are especially dangerous when you're riding a *moto*. Hold your shoulder bags tightly in front of you, especially at night. The road between Otres and Sihanoukville is considered especially risky after dark, so arrange a *remork* or *moto* via your guesthouse if staying in this area, and not just a random stranger in town.

At night, men and especially women should avoid walking alone along dark, isolated beaches and roads.

The currents off Occheuteal can be deceptively strong, especially during the wet season.

One annoyance for locals is underdressed foreigners wandering about town. Cambodia is not Thailand; Khmers are generally more conservative than their neighbours. Just look at the Cambodians frolicking in the sea – most are fully dressed. Wearing bikinis on the beach is OK, but cover up elsewhere. Topless or nude bathing is a definite no-no.

INTERNET ACCESS
Most guesthouses and hotels offer free wi-fi, as do the majority of cafes, restaurants and bars. The city centre's many internet shops are on Ekareach St near the corner of Sopheakmongkol St. Many guesthouses and shops along the road to Serendipity have a few public internet terminals. Internet outfits are sprinkled along the road to Serendipity.

MEDICAL SERVICES
CT Clinic (Map p174; 📞081 886666, 936666; 47 Boray Kamakor St; ⊙24hr for emergencies) The best medical clinic in town. Can administer rabies shots and anti-venin in the event of a snake bite.

MONEY
Sihanoukville's banks – all with ATMs – are in the city centre along Ekareach St. ATMs can also be found around Serendipity and at Victory Hill. At the time of writing there were no ATMs around Otres Beach or on any of the islands, so plan ahead.

ANZ Royal Bank (Map p174; 215 Ekareach St; ⊙8am-3.30pm Mon-Fri, to 11.30am Sat) Has a 24-hour ATM. Also offers ATMs at Victory Hill and Serendipity Beach.

Canadia Bank (Map p174; 197 Ekareach St; ⊙8am-3.30pm Mon-Fri, to 11.30am Sat) No fees on ATM withdrawals.

POST
Post Office (Map p174; 19 7 Makara St; ⊙7am-5pm) Across the road from Psar Leu.

TOURIST INFORMATION
Tourist Information Centre (Map p176; 14 Mithona St; ⊙9am-11.30pm & 2-5pm Mon-Sat) Don't expect much out of Sihanoukville's tourist information centres. The best is this one just off Occheuteal Beach. It has brochures and can help you with hotel reservations.

TRAVEL AGENCIES
Ana Travel (Map p176; 📞016 499915; www.anatravelandtours.com; road to Serendipity; ⊙8am-10pm) Handles Cambodia visa extensions and arranges Vietnam visas the same day.

❶ Getting There & Away

National Highway 4 (NH4), which links Siha-noukville to Phnom Penh (230km), is in excellent condition, but because of heavy truck traffic and the prevalence of high-speed overtaking on blind corners, this is one of Cambodia's most danger-ous highways; it's doubly dicey around dusk and at night.

NH3 to Kampot (105km) and NH48 to Koh Kong (220km) and the Thailand border (230km) are also in good shape, although the road to Koh Kong took a battering in the 2013 wet season.

AIR

Temple-beach combo holidays are now possible thanks to daily direct flights between Siem Reap and Sihanoukville (US$105 one way) with **Cambodia Angkor Airlines** (www.cambodiaang-korair.com). New routes are under discussion, including direct links with Thailand and Vietnam.

The airport is 15km east of town, just off the NH4. Figure on US$5/10 for a one-way *moto/ remork*.

BOAT

Sihanoukville is the gateway to Cambodia's booming offshore islands. For more details on boat services to the various islands, see p187.

BUS

All of the major bus companies have frequent connections with Phnom Penh (US$3.75 to US$6, four hours) from early morning until at least 2pm, after which trips are sporadic. The cheapest is Capitol Tour. Virak Buntham runs the last trip at 8.30pm. **Giant Ibis** (www.giantibis. com; US$10) runs a 'luxury' service, complete with hostess and wi-fi.

Bookings made through hotels and travel agencies incur a commission. Most travel agents only work with two or three bus companies, so ask around if you need to leave at a different time from what's being offered.

Virak Buntham and Kampot Tours & Travel run minibuses to Kampot (US$6, 1½ hours), that continue to Kep (US$10, 2½ hours) the Prek Chak border crossing with Vietnam (US$16, five hours). Travel agents can arrange hotel pick-ups.

Virak Buntham and Rith Mony have morning buses to Bangkok (US$25; change buses on the Thai side) via Koh Kong (US$7, four hours). Para-mount Angkor has daily services to Koh Kong, Siem Reap, Battambang and Saigon. GST has a night bus to Siem Reap and day buses to Bat-tambang and Saigon. Virak Buntham also has a night bus to Siem Reap (US$17, nine hours) with departures at 7pm and 8pm.

Most bus departures originate at the company terminals on Ekareach St and stop at the **new bus station** (Map p171; Mittapheap Kampuchea Soviet St) on the way out of town.

Capitol Tour (Map p174; ☑034 934042; Ekareach St)

GST (Map p174; ☑034 6339666; Ekareach St)

Kampot Tours & Travel (☑in Kampot 092 125556)

Mekong Express (Map p174; ☑034 934189; Ekareach St)

Paramount Angkor (Map p174; ☑017 525366; Ekareach St)

Phnom Penh Sorya (Map p174; ☑034 933888; Ekareach St)

Rith Mony (Map p174; ☑012 644585; Ekar-each St)

Virak Buntham (Map p174; ☑016 754358; Ekareach St)

SHARE TAXI

Cramped share taxis (US$6/45 per person/ car) and minibuses (15,000r) to Phnom Penh depart from the new bus station until about

---

SINS OF COMMISSION, SINS OF OMISSION

At Sihanoukville's main bus station, only members of the official 'motodup association' (read: cartel) are allowed to pick up arriving passengers (independent drivers sent to fetch someone must show their charge's name). As a result, you may be quoted inflated prices for onward local transport. Bargaining is likely to be futile – if you don't agree to the set price (usually 8000r to the beaches) no one else will take you. You can try walk-ing out to the street, but there's not a whole lot of traffic in this part of town. You may also have trouble shaking the possibly persistent driver the cartel has assigned you according to a rotation system. Confrontations between independents and cartel driv-ers sometimes develop. The situation with *remorks* – ideal for travel with a big pack – is similar. The set price for *remorks* to the Serendipity area is US$6.

Many guesthouses pay US$2 to *moto* drivers who bring them customers, but some places pay drivers far higher sums – US$4 or even US$5 – to send custom their way, so if you've just arrived, getting your *moto* guy to take you where *you* want may turn into a battle of wills. If your chosen hostelry is one that won't pay up, don't be surprised to hear that it's closed, has contaminated water or is 'full of prostitutes'.

8pm. Avoid the minibuses if you value things like comfort and your life. Hotels can arrange taxis to Phnom Penh for US$50 to US$60 (about four hours).

Share taxis to Kampot (US$5, 1½ hours) leave mornings only from an open lot on 7 Makara St, across from Psar Leu. This lot and the new bus station are good places to look for rides to Koh Kong or the Thai border. If nobody's sharing, expect to pay US$45 to US$60 to the Thai border.

ⓘ Getting Around

TO/FROM THE BUS STATION

Arriving in Sihanoukville, buses stop at the bus terminal, then most (but not all) continue to their central terminals. Prices to the Serendipity Beach area from the new bus station are fixed at a pricey US$2/6 for a *moto/remork*, so continue to the centre if possible and get a cheaper, shorter *remork* ride from there.

BICYCLE

Bicycles can be hired from many guesthouses for about US$2 a day, or try Eco-Trek Tours at Mick & Craig's for mountain bikes.

MOTO & REMORK

Sihanoukville's *moto* drivers are notorious for aggressively hassling passers-by and, more than anywhere else in Cambodia, shamelessly trying to overcharge, so haggle hard (with a smile) over the price before setting out.

A *moto/remork* should cost about US$1/2 from the centre to Serendipity, Occheuteal and Victory Beaches and Victory Hill. *Remorks* from Serendipity to Victory Hill/Beach should cost US$3, but drivers ask US$5 for this trip.

Motorbikes can be rented from many guesthouses for US$5 to US$7 a day. For fund-raising purposes, the police sometimes 'crack down' on foreign drivers. Common violations: no driver's licence, no helmet, no wing mirrors and, everybody's favourite, driving with the lights on during the day.

Hiring a *moto* (including the driver) for the day costs US$10 plus petrol; a *remork* is about US$20 a day.

Around Sihanoukville

Ream National Park   ស្វនឧទ្យានរាម

Just 15km east of Sihanoukville, this large park offers potential trekking in primary forest, invigorating boat trips through coastal mangroves and long stretches of unspoilt beach. This is an easy escape for those looking to flee the crowds of Sihanoukville.

The park is home to breeding populations of several regionally and globally endangered birds of prey, including the Brahminy kite, grey-headed fish eagle and white-bellied sea eagle: look for them soaring over **Prek Toeuk Sap Estuary**. Endangered birds that feed on the mudflats include the lesser adjutant, milky stork and painted stork.

Despite its protected status, Ream is gravely endangered by planned tourist development, especially along its coastline. By visiting, you can demonstrate that the park, in its natural state, is not only priceless to humanity but also a valuable economic resource for Sihanoukville. Major roads have been bulldozed through the heart of the park to access the beaches and a main road will eventually connect NH4 with Otres Beach directly via this route.

◎ Sights & Activities

Jungle walks led by rangers are easy to arrange (hiking unaccompanied is not allowed) at the **park headquarters** (☏ 012 875096, 016 767686; ◷ 7am-5pm), opposite the airport entrance. Two-hour walks in the forest behind the headquarters cost US$6 per person. Four- to six-hour treks going further into the park's mountainous interior cost US$10 per person. It's best (but not obligatory) to phone ahead. The income generated goes to help protect the park.

More popular are ranger-led **boat trips** through the mangrove channels of the Prek Toeuk Sap Estuary. These leave from the Prek Toeuk Sap ranger station, which is located about 3km east of the park HQ next to a major bridge on NH4 – the rangers at HQ will help you get there and arrange for a boat to be waiting for you. From the Prek Toeuk Sap station it's a one-hour boat ride (US$35 return for one to three persons) to the fishing village of **Ta Ben**. Full-day trips (US$50 per group) continue another hour east to the village of Andoung Toeuk, where a path leads 25 minutes through the jungle to **Koh Sampoach Beach**, the park's finest, which is also nicknamed the Chinese beach as Chinese developers have the concession for this area.

To get to some **deserted beaches** on your own, drive south from the park HQ and the airport for about 9km along a sealed road until you get to Ream Naval Base. Jog left around the base and follow the dirt roads to a series of long white beaches lined with casuarina trees. Road access to Koh Sampoach Beach is possible by taking an immediate left-hand turn off the Ream National Park road when leaving NH4. If you pass the airport entrance, you've gone too far. Follow this major road for about 12km and you will eventually arrive at a small beachside restaurant on Koh Sampoach.

Ream National Park's territory includes two islands with some fine snorkelling, **Koh Thmei** and – just off Vietnam's Phu Quoc Island – **Koh Seh**, which is best accessed from Koh Thmei.

ⓘ Getting There & Around

Sihanoukville travel agencies offer day trips to the park for about US$20, including a boat ride, a jungle walk and lunch.

Ream National Park is a breeze to get to – just follow NH4 east to the airport turn-off, which is 15km from the Cambrew brewery at the junction of NH4 and Wat Leu Rd. Go right and drive 500m to the park HQ.

A return trip from Sihanoukville by *moto* should cost US$7 to US$15, a *remork* US$15 to US$20. The price depends on how well the driver speaks English and how long you stay.

Kbal Chhay Cascades ទឹកធ្លាក់ក្បាលឆាយ

Thanks to their appearance in *Pos Keng Kong* (The Giant Snake; 2000), one of the most successful Cambodian films of the post-civil war era, these **cascades** (admission US$1, picnicking platforms per day 5000r) on the Prek Toeuk Sap River draw huge numbers of domestic tourists. That's why there are so many **picnicking platforms**.

From the parking area, a rough log **toll bridge** (per local/tourist 300/500r) leads to several miniature sandy coves, more lounging areas and some perilous rapids. The best spot for a safe, refreshing dip, for children as well as adults, is across another bridge, on the far bank of a cool, crystal-clear tributary of the brown-tinted main river. Not much water flows here in the dry season.

To get here, head east along NH4 for 5.5km from the Cambrew junction and then, at the sign, head north along a wide dirt road for 8km. By *moto/remork* a return trip should cost US$7/15.

THE SOUTHERN ISLANDS

They may lack the cachet of Southern Thailand, but the two dozen or so islands that dot the Cambodian coast offer the chance to see what places like Koh Samui and Koh Pha-Ngan were like back in the early days of Southeast Asia overlanding. Until recently all signs pointed to the whole lot of them being pawned off to well-connected foreign investors for unchecked development. Instead, pretty much the opposite has happened. The global recession scared away the big boys, paving the way for DIY development to move in with rustic resorts targeting backpackers.

This is paradise the way you dreamt it: endless crescents of powdered, sugary-soft sand, hammocks swaying in the breeze, photogenic fishing villages on stilts, technicolour sunsets and the patter of raindrops on thatch as you slumber. It seems too good to last, so enjoy it while it does.

ⓘ Getting There & Away

The logical jumping-off point for any of the main habitable islands between the Koh Kong Conservation Corridor and Ream National Park is Sihanoukville. Scheduled boat services link Sihanoukville with Koh Rong, Koh Rong Samloem and Koh Sdach. Other islands are reached by private boats, usually owned by the resort you're visiting. Cambodia's largest island, Koh Kong Island (p165), is best visited from Koh Kong.

The Koh Sdach Archipelago is accessible overland from Koh Kong or even Phnom Penh, via the new four-lane highway that cuts through Botum Sakor National Park.

Koh Ta Kiev កោះតាកៀវ

Koh Ta Kiev, a delightful little island just off Ream National Park, is something of a black hole for backpacker bungalows. New resorts open and then close with alarming regularity. Ask around Sihanoukville to see if anything is operating on Koh Ta Kiev. You'd do well to stay out here, as there's a wide white beach on the northwest side along with some pretty forest walks. This may prove irrelevant anyway, as the entire island has been leased to the same French property company that is driving development on Koh Russei.

Koh Ta Kiev, along with Koh Russei and some smaller uninhabited islands in the area, appears on most island-hopping itineraries out of Sihanoukville, with day trips running from US$12 to US$15 depending whether you launch from Otres Beach or Serendipity Beach.

Koh Russei   កោះរុស្ស៊ី

Less than an hour by boat from Sihanoukville, tiny Koh Russei (Bamboo Island) was cleared of most resorts in preparation for a high-end development that is still in the construction phase, planned as a five-star Alila Hotels (www.alilahotels.com) resort. Just one resort remained at the time of research, on a pretty beach at the back of the island – the backpacker-friendly Koh Ru (☑012 388860; koh_ru@yahoo.com; dm/bungalow US$3/15). The bungalows are rudimentary and share bathrooms with scoop showers. You get a few hours of electricity after sunset. The daily boat out here costs US$10 return.

Koh Thmei   កោះថ្មី

Moving east toward the Vietnamese island of Phu Quoc, the large island of Koh Thmei is part of Ream National Park. There's only one resort on the island, German-managed Koh Thmei Resort (☑097 737 0400; www.koh-thmei-resort.com; bungalows US$25-50). It's a real gem and fantastic value, with super-simple bungalows that are just right for the setting. The resort sits on a great beach, and you can easily walk to several more, plus go sea kayaking or snorkelling (visibility varies). Khmer meals are tasty and cost US$6.

Getting here is difficult and requires private transport overland to the mainland fishing village of Koh Kchhang; turn off the NH4 in the town of Bat Kokir, about 12km east of Sihanoukville airport. From Koh Kchhang the resort is a 1¼-hour boat ride (six-passenger boat US$15).

Koh Rong & Koh Rong Samloem   កោះរុង និងកោះរុងសន្លឹម

Moving south from the Koh Sdach Archipelago, you'll eventually run into these large neighbouring islands. They share more than confusingly similar names. Both are deceptively large islands with heavily forested interiors populated by an incredible variety of bird and other wildlife, some of it endemic. And both have several head-turning beaches that in terms of sheer brilliance would give anything in Thailand a run for its money.

The larger island, Koh Rong, is the only island in Southern Cambodia that shows any hint of becoming more than a place to escape civilization entirely. Koh Tui, the village on Koh Rong's southeast foot, has a growing range of accommodation options, plus some bars where you might find a crew of drinkers until midnight or so.

In the late 2000s developers laid out plans to turn Koh Rong into a Cambodian version of Thailand's Koh Samui, complete with a paved ring road, scores of resorts and an airport. Those plans have been slow to materialise, and for now Koh Rong remains a quintessential backpacker paradise.

Koh Rong Samloem is also slowly taking off. A horseshoe-shaped, 10km-long island embracing Saracen Bay to the east, many of the most popular resorts are spread out and require separate transport to reach. The old French road network is overgrown, but you can fish, snorkel and take short treks. The island's amazing wildlife ranges from macaques, black squirrels and sea eagles to oversized salamanders, lizards and iguanas. Saracen Bay is also the venue for monthly full moon parties at The Beach Resort, accessible via the Party Boat (p175) from Sihanoukville.

🏊 Beaches

You're spoilt for choice on Koh Rong. Koh Tui Beach, also called Pinetree Beach, extends for about 1km northeast from the pier in Koh Tui and gets lonelier and lovelier the further out you go. Rounding the headland (near Treehouse Bungalows) and continuing northeast, you can walk at least another hour along the sand and encounter little more than hermit crabs.

On the back (west) side of the island is a 7km stretch of the finest white sand, dubbed Sok San Beach after the fishing village at its northern end. There are simple resorts at the extreme north and south ends of this beach, with virtually nothing in between.

Koh Rong Samloem's best beach, Lazy Beach, is unfortunately off-limits to non-guests, but circumnavigate the island by boat and you'll find no shortage of similarly idyllic expanses of white sand. Saracen Bay is the most developed area with about half a dozen small 'resorts' and counting.

🤿 Activities

Talk to Corner Bar, (p191) near the pier in Koh Tui, about deep-sea fishing opportunities and island-hopping trips that include lunch plus optional snorkelling and sea kayaking. The owners have a sturdy slow boat for big groups and a zippy little 15-horsepower outboard, plus a Zodiac with twin 60-horsepower engines.

On Koh Rong it's possible to walk 1½ hours from the main beach to Sok San Beach via a somewhat rigorous jungle track; bring insect spray and consider footwear other than flip-flops. However, it may be best not to undertake this walk alone, as an American tourist was mysteriously killed along this route in 2013. Talk to Gil at Paradise Bungalows about organised hiking options in the jungle of Koh Rong.

On Koh Rong Samloem, it's a relatively easy walk between Lazy Beach and Saracen Bay via the island's narrow waist, or you can take a guide at Lazy Beach and walk two hours to a lighthouse on a hill overlooking the ocean at the island's extreme southern tip, which is also a prime nesting spot for sea eagles.

There's good snorkelling around on both islands and resorts rent out gear for about US$5 per day. The islands also have some of Cambodia's best diving. Most dive trips are organised out of Sihanoukville. Koh Rong Dive Center (☎ 034-934744; kohrong-divecenter com; Koh Rong Pier) has an office at the main pier in Koh Rong.

Several resorts hire out sea kayaks for about US$5/8 per hour for a single/tandem kayak. From Koh Tui Beach on Koh Rong, it's a 30-minute paddle out to an idyllic island topped by a wat just offshore. With your own sea kayak you could have a go at circling either of the islands, sleeping on deserted beaches along the way.

🛏 Sleeping & Eating

As a rule resorts run their electricity only at night until about 10.30pm or so, which means no air-con and no fan, but most of the year you should be OK without it. All resorts provide mosquito nets, but only a handful provide hot water showers.

Most isolated resorts and more upscale places have booking offices on the mainland and all are located on the road to Serendipity.

Budget travellers who prefer not to book ahead should head to Koh Tui village on Koh Rong, where on either side of the pier locals run homestays and basic guesthouses with dorms for as little as US$5 and rooms from US$10 and up. These places should have vacancies for walk-in guests outside of major holiday periods, when prices also spike. Be aware that you might have to sleep in a hammock or in a tent if you turn up without a booking in the December to January period.

🛏 Koh Rong

Bunna's Place   GUESTHOUSE $
(☎ 086 446515; Koh Tui; dm US$4-5, r US$10) A classic backpacker crashpad with the cheapest dorms in Koh Tui and some cheap rooms for those who want a modicum of privacy. Downstairs is the popular beach bar famous for its shotgun beer challenge (if you dare) and nightly fire shows.

Dreamcatch Inn   GUESTHOUSE $
(kohrongdreamcatch@gmail.com; Koh Tui; r US$10-12) 🌱 Under the same ownership as party central places Island Boys and Vagabonds, this is the quieter alternative in the middle of the village. Upstairs rooms are worth the couple of extra bucks for the occasional breeze. Eco-cred includes solar power, plus a good selection of organic teas are available.

Ponleu Pich Guesthouse   GUESTHOUSE $
(Koh Tui; r US$10) One of a handful of local guesthouses in the village, this friendly, family-run place has affordable rooms, a bustling general store and a local restaurant serving cheap meals and fresh fruit shakes.

Island Boys/Vagabonds   HOSTEL $
(Koh Tui; dm US$6, r from US$10) These are two different places under the same ownership, offering a similar vibe. Island Boys has a central bar and offers free beer to inhouse guests between 6pm and 7pm. Vagabonds has more of a chilled cafe vibe, plus some upscale offerings such as cheese plates with wine.

Mango Lounge   GUESTHOUSE $
(☎ 016 405010; Koh Tui; d with shared bathroom US$10) This backpacker guesthouse near Koh Rong's pier doubles as a popular late-night bar. It has a handful of simple rooms upstairs and a new 'sky dorm' on the rooftop.

Angkor Chom   GUESTHOUSE $
(☎ 078 559959; Sok San Beach; bungalows/r US$15/20) Angkor Chum consists of six solid bungalows raised over the high-tide mark at the extreme northern end of Sok San Beach. It 's best to arrive directly here by boat.

Broken Heart Guesthouse   GUESTHOUSE $
(☎ 097 764 9424; www.bhgh.info; Sok San Beach; dm US$10, bungalows US$25-30) For full castaway effect, look no further than this quirky, electricity-free retreat at the far southern end of Sok San Beach. The rickety bungalows are

hidden in the maze-like canopy above the beach and most have sumptuous sea views. Bathrooms are rudimentary with scoop showers.

Treehouse Bungalows BUNGALOWS $$

(☑ 034-934744; www.treehouse-bungalows.com; Koh Tui; bungalows US$25-35) Treehouse is on a secluded cove around a small headland just northeast of Koh Tui, about a 15-minute beach walk from the pier. There are five pricier 'treehouses' – raised bungalows with prime sea views – and seven stand-alone bungalows nestled in the canopy at the back. They are delightfully rustic, with sturdy beds, clean private bathrooms and sea-facing balconies with hammocks. Non-guests should drop by to sample the delicious wood-fired pizza.

Monkey Island RESORT $$

(☑ 081 830992; www.monkeyisland-kohrong.com; Koh Tui; bungalow without/with bathroom US$25/35) Linked to the popular Monkey Republic on the mainland, Monkey Island is a good choice if you are looking for a semblance of action. While far from raucous, the bar does at least show a pulse on most evenings, with hip tunes, friendly bartenders and at least a few folks showing up to socialise. Bungalows have two double beds and can sleep four. The cheaper ones are down by the beach, while the pricier ones are at the back.

Paradise Bungalows BUNGALOWS $$

(☑ 092 548883; www.paradise-bungalows.com; Koh Tui; bungalows US$35-100) This is the most upscale of the options on Koh Rong's main beach, with its restaurant set up on a hill under a soaring canopy. The 16 bungalows leave little to be desired, although the cheaper ones, curiously, don't face the ocean. The US$35 rooms are set way up on the hill with sweeping sea views, while the US$55 and US$65 rooms are on the beachfront and practically lapped by waves at high tide. The food is scrumptious.

Coco Bungalow BUNGALOWS $$

(☑ 081 466880; cocos-kohrong.com; Koh Tui ; bungalows US$15-50) This place is close to the village and the pier, so it does not offer quite as much privacy as others on this stretch, but you are nonetheless just a stumble away from your own private patch of sand. The solid-wood bungalows have two beds and sleep three to four people. Cheaper bungalows share bathrooms, while pricier digs are up on the hill with prime views.

Song Saa RESORT $$$

(☑ in Phnom Penh 023-686 0360; http://songsaa. com; villas from US$1350; ❄ @ ☎ ☒) The South Coast's first ultra-luxury property occupies a pair of private islands just off the east coast of Koh Rong: Koh Bong and Koh Oeun (his and hers in Khmer), hence the sobriquet 'sweetheart' (song saa). The over-water and jungle villas are honeymoon-ready and there is a striking restaurant-bar set over the sea. Opulence pure and simple, if you can afford it.

Koh Lanta INTERNATIONAL $

(Koh Tui; US$3-6; ⊙ 7am-10pm) Named after the famous French Survivor show, which unfortunately didn't survive its second series in Cambodia, this place offers the best wood-fired pizza on the island, plus has a small bakery for fresh bread and even a newly imported ice-cream machine.

Koh Rong Samloem

M'Pay Bay RESORT $

(☑ 016 596111; mpaybay.com; s/d tents US$ 5/7, bungalows US$20) ✐ A cluster of simple bungalows nestled amid mangroves in a fishing village on the north side of Koh Rong Samloem, M'Pay Bay is all about living in harmony with nature. Efforts are made to limit waste, and management takes pains to ensure that the local fishing village benefits from tourism. From the resort it's a short walk south through the mangroves to a long crescent beach sweeping around a bay.

The Beach Resort RESORT $

(☑ 034-666 6106; www.thebeachresort.asia; Saracen Bay; dm US$5; r US$15-85) Koh Rong Samloem's funkiest place to stay, The Beach Resort offers breezy open-air dorms with mozzie nets, plus a great range of beachfront bungalows. Cheapies with share bathroom start at US$15, while the 'VIP' rondavels rise to US$50 and up at certain times. Chill-out areas abound, as this is also the venue for the monthly full moon party on Koh Rong Samloem, accessible via the Party Boat (p175).

Lazy Beach RESORT $$

(☑ 017 456536; www.lazybeachcambodia.com; bungalows US$50) Alone on the southwest coast of Koh Rong Samloem, the 16 bungalows at this idyllic getaway front one of the must stunning beaches you'll find anywhere. They have balconies and hammocks outside, and spiffy stone-floor bathrooms and duelling queen-size beds inside. The restaurant-common area is stocked with books and board games, making it a good fit for families.

Saracen Bay Resort RESORT $$
(☑016 997047; www.saracenbay-resort-cambodia.com; Saracen Bay; bungalows US$45) Impeccably well run compared with many of the island crashpads, Saracen Bay offers solid bungalows with attractive trim, including the best bathrooms on Koh Rong Samloem and great veranda views of the sea. Definitely book ahead, as this place regularly fills up.

Koh Rong Samloem Villas RESORT $$
(☑034-934631; www.kohrongsamloemvillas.com; bungalows US$25-60) New in 2013, this secluded resort is managed by long-running dive operator Ecosea. Located on the north side of the island, family bungalows will be open in 2014. A good base for those interested in a dedicated dive experience around the island.

Freedom Island Bungalows RESORT $$
(☑034-633 3830; freedom_cambodia@yahoo.com; Saracen Bay; r US$35) This resort is all by itself at the north end of Koh Rong Samloem's Saracen Bay. It has a pleasant hang-out area and is so little known that you might have the entire place to yourself. The set-up includes an attractive freshwater pool carved into the natural rocks here. Diving trips are available around the island, as they operate their own boats.

🛈 Getting There & Away

If you are going anywhere besides the Koh Tui area on Koh Rong, make arrangements through the relevant resort, most of which run daily supply trips to Sihanoukville and take passengers for about US$20 return.

For Koh Tui, **Koh Rong Island Travel** (☑034-934744; kohrong-islandtravel.com) runs two daily boats to/from the port area in Sihanoukville. Boats leave daily at 8am and 2pm, taking almost three hours, longer in choppy waters. Tickets are US$10/20 one way/return. Return trips from Koh Tui to Sihanoukville depart at 10am and 4pm. As we went to press, this company launched a fast catamaran called the *Princess*, departing Sihanoukville at 8am and 2pm daily and returning at 10am and 4pm, calling at Koh Rong Samloem in each direction. Tickets cost just US$25 return and it takes 45 minutes.

Another new catamaran option is **SEA Cambodia Fastcat** (www.seacambodia.com), which departs four times a day from the Serendipity Beach jetty, arriving at Koh Tui in less than one hour. Seating about 35 people, tickets were available for just US$13/26 one way/return during our visit, but prices may rise.

Corner Bar (☑015 703805; kohrongactivities@gmail.com) on Koh Rong offers speedboat pick-ups for about US$100 to US$150 depending on which boat you use. The six-passenger Zodiac can make the trip to Sihanoukville in less than an hour.

Koh Sdach Archipelago កោះស្តេច

Just off Botum Sakor National Park's southwest tip, this is a modest archipelago of 12 small islands, most of them uninhabited. Basing yourself at one of the two islands with accommodation – **Koh Sdach** (King Island) and **Koh Totang** – you can spend a day or two exploring the other islands, some of which have utterly isolated beaches and good snorkelling. Most island-hopping tours target **Koh Ampil**, a cluster of three tiny islands surrounding a spit of sand, and long white beaches on either side of **Koh Smach**.

The only village of any size is on Koh Sdach, which is just 10 minutes by outboard (speedboat) from the point where the new four-lane highway terminates on the mainland. This highway makes the archipelago infinitely easier to access, but as it's part of a huge tourism development, it may permanently change the southwest coast of Botum Sakor, once known for virgin beaches backed by virgin forest.

Fortunately, the islands appear to be largely excluded from the development agenda, and existing resorts are far enough from the mainland that the commotion is out of earshot, if not completely out of eyeshot. Koh Sdach has 24-hour electricity.

🛏 Sleeping

Mean Chey Guesthouse GUESTHOUSE $
(☑011 983806; Koh Sdach; r US$7.50) Budget travellers will have to settle for this simple guesthouse close to the main fishing village on the northwest side of Koh Sdach. Accommodation is in 15 powder-blue concrete cottages with basic beds, TVs and attached bathrooms. The Yvonne restaurant, on the premises, has lovely views of the neighbouring islands and serves French and Khmer food.

Nomad's Land RESORT $$
(☑011 916171; nomadslandcambodia.com; Koh Totang; bungalows US$40-135) 🚭 It's hard to imagine a more chilled-out place than Nomad's.

Owner Karim has serious Zen cred, hosting periodic yoga retreats and making this the greenest resort in the islands. The five bungalows have solar panels, and the toilets are waterless. The sturdy bungalows are funky for these parts and rates include all meals and transfers. The resort sits on a lovely stretch of white beach on Koh Totang, a speck of an island about 20 minutes from Koh Sdach by outboard. The resort is closed from the start of June to the end of October.

Belinda Beach Lovely Resort RESORT **$$$**
(☑ 017 517517; www.belindabeach.com; Koh Sdach; r incl breakfast US$130; ✱ ☀ ☎) Belinda's lacks the brilliant beach that would normally be de rigueur for a resort of this price tag, yet it somehow makes up for it in other ways. The four rooms are in a pair of duplex concrete cottages that are the most stylish of the affordable accommodation around the islands. Belgian owner Benny cooks ridiculously good food (three-course dinner US$18) and leads post-dinner trivia sessions.

❶ Getting There & Away

There are two ways to get to the archipelago. The easier and cheaper way, for now, is on a boat from Sihanoukville to Koh Sdach. The main 'passenger' ferry (it's more like small cargo boat with a few local passengers) leaves Sihanoukville's port area daily between noon and 2pm (US$10, 4½ hours with a stop or two along the way). The return leg departs at 8pm. There's also a much bigger cargo boat that stops at Koh Sdach roughly every other day on its run from Sihanoukville to Thailand. It's slower, costs only US$5 and departs Sihanoukville around 8pm. The return trip from Koh Sdach departs around 3am.

The other method is to travel overland via the new Chinese highway to the village of Poi Yopon on the mainland opposite Koh Sdach. This takes an investment in private transport. A car from Phnom Penh will cost around US$100 or so until the new highway is paved. A cheaper option is to get off the bus where the highway starts, 6km west of Andoung Tuek on the NH48. From here *moto* drivers will take you to Poi Yopon for US$15 to US$20, depending on your negotiating skills. It's a fast two-hour *moto* ride over a dirt road.

Hiring an outboard from Poi Yopon to Koh Sdach/Koh Totang costs US$10/15.

❶ Getting Around

For island hopping, all of the resorts have boats of their own or can arrange for boats to take you throughout the archipelago and to the beaches of Botum Sakor National Park.

KAMPOT PROVINCE

Kampot Province (ខេត្តកំពត) has emerged as one of Cambodia's most alluring destinations thanks to a hard-to-beat combination of old colonial architecture, abundant natural attractions and easy intraregional transport. Enchanted visitors often end up staying in the sleepy, atmospheric provincial capital of Kampot rather longer than planned. Nearby Kep is but a hop away and the province is riddled with honeycombed limestone caves, some providing shelter to centuries-old brick temples from the pre-Angkorian period.

The province is renowned for producing some of the world's finest pepper. Durian haters be warned: Kampot is also Cambodia's main producer of this odoriferous fruit.

Kampot   កំពត
☑ 033 / POP 35,000

Ever more visitors are being seduced, gently, by the charming riverside town of Kampot, with its relaxed atmosphere and one of Cambodia's finest, if dilapidated, ensembles of French colonial architecture. Eclipsed as a port when Sihanoukville was founded in 1959, Kampot makes an excellent base for exploring Bokor National Park and the verdant coast east towards Vietnam, including Kep and several superb cave-temples. Not on offer here: a beach.

◉ Sights

The most enjoyable activity is strolling along the riverside promenade and along streets lined with decrepit French-era shophouses. Some of the best colonial architecture can be found in the triangle delineated by the central **Durian Roundabout**, the post office and the **old French bridge**, which is quite a sight: as it has been repaired in a mishmash of styles. The **old cinema** (7 Makara St), **Kampot Prison** and the **old governor's mansion** – the latter two are very French – are worth a look (from the outside). Plans are afoot to develop a **museum** in the old governor's mansion, drawing on the knowledge and experience of Jean-Michel Filippi, a cultural anthropologist and some-time resident of the area.

Kampot Traditional Music School MUSIC
(☉ 6-9pm Mon-Fri) Visitors are welcome to observe training sessions and/or performances every evening at this school that trains children who are orphaned or have disabilities

in traditional music and dance. The organisation has recently experienced some funding issues, so donations are very welcome.

✗ Activities

Kampot now has several guesthouses that actively promote a range of mostly water-based activities. Most places along the river offer kayaks in some shape or form, including Champa Lodge, Greenhouse and Les Manguieres. Villa Vedici is a jack of all trades, with kitesurfing and wakeboarding (and foosball) among many pursuits.

Seeing Hands Massage 5   MASSAGE
(☎034-503012; per hr US$5; ☉7am-11pm) Blind masseurs and masseuses offer soothing bliss.

☞ Tours

Some of the riverside places send boats out on evening **firefly watching tours**. Many a sceptic has returned from these trips in awe. They're best on a starry night when the phosphorescence peaks.

The big tour is Bokor Hill Station, which everybody and their grandmother offers. Excursions also hit the pepper farms and other sights in the countryside around Kampot and nearby Kep.

Bart the Boatman   BOAT TOUR
(☎092 174280) Known simply as Bart the Boatman, this Belgian expat runs original boat tours along the small tributaries of the Kampong Bay River.

Captain Chim's   BOAT TOUR
(☎012 321043) Sunset cruises on a traditional boat cost US$5 per head and include a cold beer – a real bargain. Also offers half-day kayaking trips for US$9.

Kampot Dreamtime Tours   BOAT TOUR
(☎089 908417) Runs upmarket countryside trips in air-con vans and wine-and-cheese sunset river cruises in a boat formerly owned by King Norodom Sihanouk.

Kampot Tours & Travel   SIGHTSEEING TOUR
(☎092 125556) Leading transport supplier, they offer minibuses or taxis to just about anywhere along the south coast and beyond. They also do the standard area excursions.

Offroad Cambodia   CYCLING TOUR
(☎077 555123; offroad-cambodia.com; half-day tour US$25, rental from US$7) Offroad Cambodia offers a half-day loop through the Kam-

pot countryside taking in pretty backroads and cave pagodas.

Sok Lim Tours   SIGHTSEEING TOUR
(☎012 796919; www.soklimtours.com) Kampot's longest-running outfit, well-regarded all-round. Has trained pepper-plantation guides.

🛏 Sleeping

When it comes to accommodation, Kampot is a tale of two cities – the centre of the old town clustered near the riverside and a series of out-of-town places strung out along the riverbank. The atmospheres are quite different, so if you fall for Kampot's charms, it might be worth sampling both areas.

🏚 Old Town

★Hour Kheang Guesthouse   GUESTHOUSE **$**
(☎033-210351; hourkheang_gh@yahoo.com; Old Market; dm US$3, r with fan US$8, r with air-con US$15-20; ❄🛜) Located in a renovated block of colonial buildings opposite the Old Market, this is an inviting place in which to stay. The host family is very helpful and the rooms are very well looked after, including flat-screen TVs and hot-water bathrooms. Downstairs is a handy minimart and everything from bicycles to motorbikes are available for rent.

Little Garden   GUESTHOUSE **$**
(☎033-932396; River Rd; d with fan/air-con from US$8/15; 🛜) This high-rise punches above its weight, with clean, well-tended rooms on a prime, near-riverfront location. The rooms are very spacious for this kind of money and free wi-fi is included.

The River Lodge   GUESTHOUSE **$**
(☎033-633 3569; theriverlodgekampot@gmail.com; r US$15; ❄🛜) See Kampot from the other side with a stay at this riverside place on the east bank. Smart and shiny new bungalows feature a lilac paint scheme, flat-screen TVs, fridge and piping hot showers. There is also a small bar-restaurant on the edge of the water. The only drawback might be noise from the neighbouring Dragon Club.

The Magic Sponge   GUESTHOUSE **$**
(☎017 946428; www.magicspongekampot.com; dm US$3, r US$9-15; 🛜) This popular backpacker place has a rooftop dorm with impressive through breezes and personalised fans and reading lights. The rooms are good value with hot water bathrooms attached. Downstairs is a lively bar-restaurant with

happy hours from midday to 8pm. There's well-regarded Indian food and even mini-golf in the garden.

Blissful Guesthouse GUESTHOUSE $
(☑092 494331; www.blissfulguesthouse.com; dm US$2-3, r US$4-8; ☎) An old-time backpacker vibe lives on at this atmospheric wooden house. Cheap rooms share a bathroom. A busy bar-restaurant plays host to everything from weekly quiz nights (Tuesday) to Texas Hold'em tournaments (Wednesday). Happy hour is 4pm to 8pm.

Titch's Place GUESTHOUSE $
(☑033-650 1631; titchs.place@yahoo.com; River Rd; dm/r US$3/10; ☎) The only budget crash-pad on the riverfront, there are dorm beds aplenty here, including single sex dorms. There are also a few rooms, including a spacious family room with a double and a bunk bed – great value at just US$10. The rooftop bar is a great spot for sunset.

Pepper Guesthouse GUESTHOUSE $
(☑017 822626; guesthousepepper@yahoo.com; r US$5-30; ❀☎) Set in the heart of the back-packer backstreets, Pepper has cheap fan rooms in the original house, as well as two impressive new garden bungalows complete with rain showers and tasteful decoration.

★ The Columns BOUTIQUE HOTEL $$
(☑092 932070; www.the-columns.com; 37 Phoum 1 Ouksophear; r US$45-59; ❀☎) Set in a row of thoughtfully restored shophouses near the riverfront, this is the leading boutique hotel in Kampot, with 17 rooms. Blending the classic and the modern, rooms include flat-screen TV, i-docks, minibar and a safety deposit box. Downstairs is Green's, an inviting cafe with healthy salads and shakes, where the included breakfast is enjoyed.

Rikitikitavi BOUTIQUE HOTEL $$
(☑012 235102; www.rikitikitavi-kampot.com; River Rd; r incl breakfast US$43-59; ❀☎) Rikitikitavi has seven of the classiest and cleanest rooms in town. They have stunning wood floors and beams, four-poster beds and elegant mirrors, plus flat-screen TVs and DVD players. Breakfast is included.

La Java Bleue BOUTIQUE HOTEL $$
(☑033-667 6679; www.lajavableue-kampot.fr; Old Quarter; r incl breakfast US$45-60; ❀☎) This colonial gem in the centre of the old town now offers five spacious rooms decorated in regional themes with exquisite furniture. The Chinese room is set in the eaves of the old building

Kampot

as a secluded hideaway and there are traditional Khmer or colonial French options too. The restaurant here is well regarded, offering a daily barbecue grill and tender meats.

Mea Culpa GUESTHOUSE $$
(☑012 504769; www.meaculpakampot.com; r US$20-30; ❀☎) Behind the governor's mansion in a palatial villa, the 11 spacious rooms come with big windows, attractive decor, a DVD library and free tea and coffee. The garden restaurant here spins the best pizza in town, straight from a wood-fired oven.

Natural Bungalows HOTEL $$
(☑033-641 1888; www.natural-bungalows.com; Riverside; r US$30-50; ❀☎) Just north of the old town, Natural Bungalows has a pretty riverside setting, including a small sandy beach. Rooms are finished in wood and laterite and feature local handicrafts and textiles. The riverside restaurant is a draw, particularly for a sundowner.

Kampot

Bokor Mountain Lodge   HISTORIC HOTEL **$$**
(☏ 033-932314; www.bokorlodge.com; River Rd; r US$20-50; 🕸@🛜) This imposing century-old colonial building facing the river is a bit worn these days, but undeniably charismatic. Pricier rooms come with a river view and rates include breakfast. The riverfront bar-restaurant has live music on Sunday.

🛏 On the River

Most of the out-of-town places aren't *that* far out of town – usually just a 10-minute *remork* ride from the centre. All of them are on the river and have over-water pavilions or docks to facilitate swimming.

Bodhi Villa   HOSTEL **$**
(☏ 012 728884; www.bodhivilla.com; Tuk Chhou Rd; dm US$2.50-3, r US$5-12; 🛜) Bodhi is popular with Phnom Penh expats on weekends, when huge parties often erupt. At other times it's a peaceful hideaway on the river with a good waterfront chill-out bar and a variety of rooms, including one floating bungalow. It has a fully equipped digital recording studio and live music every Friday from 7.30pm, plus a speedboat for hire.

Arcadia Backpackers   HOSTEL **$**
(☏ 077 219756; www.arcadiabackpackers.com; Tuk Chhou Rd; dm US$3-4, r US$9-10, bungalow US$15-30; 🛜) Formerly Utopia, Arcadia Backpackers was just opening when we were in town. In a secluded riverside setting, there is a large bar-restaurant jutting out into the water, plentiful dorms and some thatched bungalows for a tad more privacy. Antics include volleyball, a rope swing and tubing. DJs crank things up some weekends.

Bungalow Kampot River   GUESTHOUSE **$**
(☏ 033-666 6418; bungalowkampotriver@yahoo.com; Tuk Chhou Rd; r US$6-10; 🛜) A Cambodian-owned family place on a bustling stretch of riverfront. It has the best-value bungalows thanks to attached bathrooms included in the price. Think basic, with a mattress on the floor, a mosquito net and a fan.

Naga House   GUESTHOUSE **$**
(☏ 012 289916; nagahousekampot@gmail.com; Tuk Chhou Rd; r US$7-10; 🛜) Another classic backpacker place by the river, Naga House offers ground level and elevated thatched bungalows with a shared bathroom. The bar-restaurant mainlines directly to the river

and there are decent imported mountain bikes available for US$4 per day.

Champa Lodge
RIVER RESORT **$$**

(☑ 092 525835; www.champalodge.com; Kompong Kreang; r US$35-50; 🐕) Blissfully set on a bend in the river amid traditional Cambodian countryside scenes, Champa Lodge is a rural hideaway. Rooms are set in traditional Khmer wooden houses. Paddy House has ricefield views and two doubles downstairs. Boat Lodge has a superb location overlooking the river. Activities include kayaking and boat trips, but relaxation is the main pursuit. The restaurant-bar includes the best selection of Belgian beers in Cambodia.

Les Manguiers
RIVER RESORT **$$**

(☑ 092 330050; www.mangokampot.com; r US$10-60; @🐕) This rambling, family-friendly garden complex, located right on the river's edge 2km north of the new bridge, is rich with activities, including kayaking (single/tandem US$4/6 for two hours), swimming, firefly-watching boat trips, badminton and pétanque. You can jump into the water from one of four over-water gazebos. The rooms and tasteful wooden bungalows all come with fan and cold water. Meals are served *table d'hôte* style.

Villa Vedici
RIVER RESORT **$$**

(☑089 290714; www.villavedici.com; r US$30-100; ✹@🐕) Villa Vedici is a playground for kids and adults alike, offering kitesurfing and a speedboat for water-skiing and wakeboarding, plus a Playstation on a gargantuan flat-screen in the main building's airy living room. In addition to functional rooms in the main building, there's a guesthouse that sleeps eight, plus one bungalow on the river.

Ganesha Riverside Eco Resort
RIVER RESORT **$$**

(☑ 092 724612; www.ganesharesort.com; r US$10-60) Offering the atmosphere of a hippy commune, this is a chilled-out place by the river. Rooms come in a variety of shapes and sizes, including riverside bungalows and the 'tower' room, almost like a windmill without its sails. There is also a bar and restaurant here, which is handy given it's quite a distance from Kampot and civilisation.

KAMPOT PEPPER

Before Cambodia's civil war, no Paris restaurant worth its salt would be without pepper from Kampot Province, but the country's pepper farms were all but destroyed by the Khmer Rouge, who believed in growing rice, not spice.

Today, thanks to a group of eco-entrepreneurs and foodies who are passionate about pepper, Kampot-grown peppercorns, delicate and aromatic but packing a powerful punch, are making a comeback.

Kampot pepper is grown on family farms that dot Phnom Voar and nearby valleys, northwest of Kompong Trach, where the unique climate and farmers' fidelity to labour-intensive growing techniques produce particularly pungent peppercorns. In fact, Kampot pepper is so extraordinary that it's Cambodia's first-ever product to receive a 'geographical indication' (GI), just like French cheeses. Increased sales have made a huge difference for Kampot's pepper families, and especially for the girls who are able to marry now their parents can afford their dowries.

Peppercorns are picked from February to May. Black pepper is plucked from the trees when the corns are starting to turn yellow and turns black during sun-drying; red pepper is picked when the fruit is completely mature; and mild white pepper is soaked in water to remove the husks. September to February is the season for green pepper, whose sprigs have to be eaten almost immediately after harvesting – the Crab Market restaurants of Kep are one of the best places to experience its gentle freshness.

A packet of pepper makes an excellent souvenir or gift: the corns are lightweight and unbreakable, and if stored properly – that is, *not* ground! – will stay fresh for years. In Kampot, you can purchase pouches of peerless pepper, and see pepper being dried and sorted, at FarmLink (☑ 033 6902354; www.farmlink-cambodia.com; ☺ 8-11am & 2-5pm Mon-Fri), one of the pioneers of GI pepper production. It's just over the New Bridge; take the first right and look for it on the left. Most countryside tours around Kampot and Kep include a visit to a working pepper farm. Starling Farm (www.starlingfarm.com) is one of the most friendly and accessible, and includes an on-site shop and restaurant.

✕ Eating & Drinking

Quite a few restaurants line River Rd south of the old French bridge. There are fruit stalls and little eateries (⊙7am-10pm) next to the Canadia Bank and, nearby, a night market (7 Makara St; ⊙4pm-midnight) where options include chicken rice soup. Both places have Khmer desserts such as sticky rice with coconut sauce.

Many of the guesthouses are worthy of a meal or two. Blissful Guesthouse and Bokor Mountain Lodge have Sunday roasts, Mea Culpa has wood-fired pizza, or enjoy a meal on the water at one of the out-of-town riverside places.

★Epic Arts Café   CAFE $
(www.epicarts.org.uk; mains US$2-4; ⊙7am-4pm; 🕾) 🍴 A great place for breakfast, homemade cakes, infused tea and light lunches, this mellow eatery is staffed by young people who are deaf or have a disability. Profits fund arts workshops for Cambodians with a disability and it's possible to learn some sign language at 3pm every Friday.

Espresso   CAFE $
(near Old Market; mains US$3-6; ⊙7am-9pm) A blink-and-you'll-miss-it cafe; we advise you not to blink. The Aussie owners are real foodies and offer a selection of specials like fresh snapper or breakfast burritos, plus the menu includes superfood salads and zesty shakes. But it is caffeine cravers that will be buzzing thanks to some fresh beans and original blends.

Captain Chim's   CAFE $
(mains US$1-3; ⊙7am-10pm; 🕾) Kampot's best budget bites are found here. Best known for breakfast, Khmer faves like *loc lak* will fill you up at any time of day. Ask about Cambodian cooking classes or join their bargain booze cruise for sunset every day.

Indo Bar   INTERNATIONAL, ASIAN $
(St 726; meals US$2-6; ⊙11am-11pm) A fun and friendly place just up from the river, Indo Bar offers an eclectic mix of regional cuisine from Thailand to China, plus home comfort favourites. It also doubles as a popular bar with the strongest Long Island iced tea in Kampot.

★Rikitikitavi   INTERNATIONAL, ASIAN $$
(www.rikitikitavi-kampot.com; River Rd; mains US$5-8; ⊙7am-10pm; 🕾🍴) Named after the mongoose in Rudyard Kipling's *The Jungle Book*, this riverfront terrace has style and ambience. It's known for its Kampot pepper chicken, burritos, slow-cooked curry and salads. Happy hour from 5pm to 7pm brings 2-for-1 cheer on all cocktails, the perfect sundowner.

Rusty Keyhole   INTERNATIONAL, KHMER $$
(River Rd; small/large/extra-large ribs US$5/7.50/10; ⊙8am-11pm Nov-May, 11am-11pm Jun-Oct; 🕾) This popular riverfront bar-restaurant turns out an impressive global menu of comfort food and Khmer home cooking. Order the famous ribs in advance, but beware the enormous extra-large portions.

Green House   INTERNATIONAL $$
(www.greenhousekampot.com; Kampot River West Bank; mains US$3-5; ⊙7am-10pm; 🕾) This chilled-out spot occupies the former house of Snowy's (aka Maxine's), a legendary bar that closed in 2011. It's in a secluded spot on the river, about 5km north of town. Dining includes some international and Khmer fare, and it's a great spot for some lazy drinks. Accommodation is also available in bungalows.

Oh Neils   BAR
(River Rd; ⊙5pm-late) The liveliest of the little bars that dot the riverfront in Kampot, Oh Neils is so much more than the standard exiled Irish bar. The walls are plastered with rock 'n' roll memorabilia and the soundtrack is a who's who of classic tunes from down the decades.

Ecran   BAR
(Old Market; 10,000r per movie; ⊙11am-10pm Wed-Mon) Ecran, the French for screen, is a little movie bar offering big-screen films and a private room for movie-watching. Cambodian classics such as *The Killing Fields* screen daily, plus cult classics and more. Handmade noodles and dumplings available, plus cold drinks.

🛍 Shopping

Kepler's Kampot Books   BOOKS
(Old Market; ⊙8am-8pm) This is the place for secondhand books in Kampot, plus pepper, *kramas* (scarves) and fine T-shirts.

Tiny Kampot Pillows   SILK
(www.tinykampotpillows.com; 2000 Roundabout; ⊙10am-6pm) Textile shop selling, well, lots of tiny pillows in handwoven silk, plus plenty of other accessories from clothing to bags.

ℹ Information

The free and often hilarious *Kampot Survival Guide* takes a tongue-in-cheek look at local expat life, and there's also the free *Coastal* guide (www.coastal-cambodia.com) to Kampot and Kep, with heaps of info on local businesses.

INTERNET ACCESS

There's a strip of copy shops with internet access southwest of the Durian roundabout on 7 Makara St.

MEDICAL SERVICES

Bokor Clinic & Maternity (☑ 033-932289; consultation US$10; ☺ emergency 24hr, consultation 7am-noon & 2-6pm) The best medical clinic in town, with four English-speaking doctors and ultrasound, X-ray and ECG machines.

MONEY

Canadia Bank (☺ 8am-3.30pm Mon-Fri, to 11.30am Sat) Has an ATM with no transaction fees and turbo air-con.

TOURIST INFORMATION

Tourist Information Centre (☑ 033-655 5541; lonelyguide@gmail.com; River Rd; ☺ 7am-7pm) Led by the knowledgeable Mr Pov, Kampot's tourist office is the main point of contact for assembling groups for Bokor National Park trips. Also doles out free advice and can arrange transport to area attractions like caves, falls and Kompong Trach.

ⓘ Getting There & Away

Kampot, on NH3, is 148km southwest of Phnom Penh, 105km east of Sihanoukville and 25km northwest of Kep.

Paramount Angkor, **Phnom Penh Sorya** and **Hua Lian** sell tickets from offices opposite the Total petrol station near the Four Nagas Roundabout. All have two or three daily trips to Phnom Penh (US$4 to US$5, four hours), the last of which depart at 1pm; some go via Kep (US$2, 45 minutes). Across the street you can catch share taxis (US$6), packed-to-the-gills minibuses (16,000r) and private taxis (US$40) to Phnom Penh. Sorya also has daily trips to Siem Reap and Battambang.

There are a couple of smarter bus services for those wanting a faster, more comfortable journey. **Giant Ibis** (www.giantibis.com) has services to Phnom Penh (US$8) departing at 8.30am and 2.45pm daily in a modern Korean bus. **Kampot Express** (www.kampotexpress.com) has express Ford Transit minibuses connecting with Phnom Penh (US$10) at 8am and 1pm daily, plus 4.30pm at weekends.

Share taxis to Sihanoukville cost US$5 and a private taxi from the taxi lot is US$30. Daily Kampot Tours & Travel and Virak Buntham minibuses go west to Sihanoukville (US$6, 1½ hours) and Koh Kong (US$13, four to five hours with a bus transfer); and east to Ha Tien, Vietnam

(US$10, 2½ hours). Guesthouses can arrange tickets and pick-ups.

A *moto/remork/*taxi to Kep should run about US$8/12/20.

ⓘ Getting Around

A *moto* ride in town costs 2000r (4000r in the evening); *remorks* cost about US$1 to US$2. To get to the nearest riverside guesthouses on the edge of town it should cost about 10,000/6000r for a *moto/remork*, more to those located further afield.

Bicycles are offered to guests for free by many guesthouses, which can also arrange motorbike hire. Try the following for motorbike or car hire:

Kampot Car Rental (☑ 088 510 2702; www.kampotcarrental.com; per day from US$20) Self-drive budget car hire available through this new company. Tiny cars for big foreigners but the freedom to explore at a bargain price. Check the small print.

Sean Ly (☑ 012 944687; ☺ 7am-9pm) Rents 125cc bikes for US$4 a day and 250cc trail bikes for US$12.

Around Kampot

The limestone hills east towards Kep are honeycombed with caves. Phnom Chhnork, surrounded by blazingly green countryside, is a real gem and can easily be visited in an afternoon along with Phnom Sorsia.

⊙ Sights

Phnom Chhnork   CAVE

(ភ្នំឆ្នក; admission US$1; ☺ 7am-6pm) The base of Phnom Chhnork is a short walk through the rice fields from Wat Ang Sdok, where a monk will collect the entry fee and a gaggle of friendly local kids, some with precociously fluent English, will offer their services as guides.

A well-tended staircase with 203 steps leads up the hillside and down into a cavern as graceful as a Gothic cathedral. There you'll be greeted by a stalactite elephant, with a second elephant outlined on the flat cliff face to the right. Tiny chirping bats live up near two natural chimneys that soar towards the blue sky, partly blocked by foliage of an impossibly green hue.

Inside the cave's main chamber stands a remarkable 7th-century (Funan-era) brick temple, dedicated to Shiva. The temple's brickwork is in superb condition thanks to the protection afforded by the cave. Poke your head inside and check out the ancient stalactite that serves as a linga. A slippery passage, flooded in the rainy season, leads through the hill.

Phnom Chhnork occupies a bucolic site surrounded by a quilt of rice paddies and meticulously tended vegetable plots (tomato, cucumber, lettuce, cabbage, mint). The view from up top, and the walk to and from the wat, is especially magical in the late afternoon.

To get to Phnom Chhnork turn left off the NH33 about 5.5km east of Kampot. Look for a sign reading 'Phnom Chhngok Resort' across the road from a Cham mosque. From the turn-off it's 6km to the cave on a bumpy road. A return *moto/remork* ride from Kampot costs about US$6/10.

Phnom Sorsia   CAVE
(ភ្នំសរសៀរ, Phnom Sia; admission free; ⊘ 7am-6pm) **FREE** Not quite as magical as Phnom Chhnork, Phnom Sorsia has a gaudily painted modern temple and several natural caves.

From the parking area in front of the school, a stairway leads up the hillside to a colourful temple. From there, steps lead left up to **Rung Damrey Saa** (White Elephant Cave). A slippery, sloping staircase – where one false step will send you into the abyss– leads down and then up and then out through a hole in the other side. Exit the cave and follow the path to the right, which leads back to the temple.

From the colourful temple, steps angle up to the right to the **Bat Cave**. Inside, countless bats flutter and chirp overhead, flying out to the forest and back through a narrow natural chimney. Locals use bamboo poles to hunt the creatures by swatting them out of the air. The circuit ends near a hilltop **stupa** with impressive views.

The turn-off to Phnom Sorsia is on NH33 13.5km southeast of Kampot and 1.3km northwest of the White Horse Roundabout near Kep. Look for a sign reading 'Phnom Sorsia Resort' – from there a dirt road leads about 1km northeast through the rice fields.

Tek Chhouu Rapids   RAPIDS
(ទឹកឈូ) Hugely popular with locals, these modest rapids are surrounded by local eateries and – a prerequisite for any proper Khmer day out – picnicking platforms.

About 5km upriver, Cambodia's largest dam, the Chinese-built **Kamchay hydroelectric dam**, was opened in late 2011. Vital stats: 115m high, 568m wide, 193.2MW. The US$280-million project flooded small parts of Bokor National Park.

Bokor National Park

This 1581-sq-km **national park** (ឧទ្យានជាតិបូរេគោ; Preah Monivong National Park; admission US$5) is famed for its once abandoned French hill station, refreshingly cool climate and lush primary rainforest. Threatened animals that live in the park include leopard, Indian elephant, Asiatic black bear, Malayan sun bear, pileated gibbon, pig-tailed macaque, slow loris and pangolin. Unfortunately it is now becoming more famous for the ugly casino that blights the summit, the Thansur Bokor Highland Resort.

An impressive new road up to the old hill station has been completed and is open to the public, fast-tracking visitors to the aforementioned casino. The huge development project includes a golf course (or a spot the ball competition in the mist?) and numerous holiday villas on sale at speculative prices, but it has sadly destroyed the atmosphere of bygone Bokor.

History

In the early 1920s the French, ever eager to escape the lowland heat, established a hill station atop Phnom Bokor (1080m), known for its dramatic vistas of the coastal plain one vertical kilometre below.

The hill station was twice abandoned to the howling winds: first when Vietnamese and Khmer Issarak (Free Khmer) forces overran it in the late 1940s while fighting for independence from France, and again in 1972, when the Lon Nol regime left it to the Khmer Rouge forces that were steadily taking over the countryside. Because of its commanding position, the site was strategically important to all sides during the civil war and was one location the Vietnamese really had to fight for during their 1979 invasion. For several months, the Khmer Rouge held out in the Catholic church while the Vietnamese shot at them from the Bokor Palace, 500m away.

The hill station became a ghost town, its once-grand buildings turned into eerie, windowless shells. Over time they became carpeted with a bright-orange lichen that gives them an other-worldly appearance. On cold, foggy days it can get pretty creepy up here as mists drop visibility to nothing and the wind keens through abandoned buildings. It's appropriate, then, that the foggy showdown that ends the Matt Dillon crime thriller *City of Ghosts* (2002) was filmed here.

◉ Sights

Bokor Hill Station
HILL STATION

The key sights of the hill station (ស្ថានីយ ភ្នំបូរ៉ែកោ), such as the Bokor Palace, a grand hotel that opened in 1925, were undergoing renovations when we visited and will become part of the new resort city.

The squat belfry of the Romanesque-style Catholic church still holds aloft its cross, and fragments of glass brick cling to the corners of the nave windows; one side window holds the barest outline of a rusty crucifix. It's easy to imagine a small crowd of French colonials in formal dress assembled here for Sunday Mass. The subdividing walls inside were built by the Khmer Rouge. A bit up the hill, a sheer drop overlooks virgin rainforest.

Other Phnom Bokor sights include lichen-caked Wat Sampeau Moi Roi (Five Boats Wat), which offers tremendous views over the jungle to the coastline below, including Vietnam's Phu Quoc Island. Wild monkeys like to hang out around the wat.

From the wat an 11km trail (four or five hours) leads to two-tiered Popokvil Falls.

⬛ Sleeping

Thansur Bokor Highland Resort
HOTEL $$

(☑ 033-683 8888; www.thansurbokor.com; Bokor Hill Station; r from US$49; ✳ @ 🛰 🛰) It's a travesty that such a beautiful location has been allowed to be blighted by such an ugly hotel.

Boasting a ludicrously ambitious 564 rooms, it was built at breakneck speed to recoup some of the huge road investment and it shows. But if you want to stay in Bokor, be their guest. We recommend Kampot or Kep.

❶ Getting There & Away

To visit the park you can take private transport up the new road, or you can join an organised tour. Trekking trips used to be very popular, but treks were recently banned due to all the development underway, a rather surreal scenario, as we have not heard of banning trekking in national parks before. Standard day trips still operate for around US$10 to US$15 per person depending on numbers. Many travellers prefer to rent a motorbike and travel under their own steam.

Kep
កែប

☑ 036 / POP 35,000

The seaside resort of Kep-sur-Mer (Krong Kep, also spelled Kaeb) is a province-level municipality that consists of little more than a small peninsula facing Bokor National Park and Vietnam's Phu Quoc Island. Famed for its spectacular sunsets and splendid seafood, it was founded as a colonial retreat for the French elite in 1908.

In the 1960s, Cambodian high rollers continued the tradition, but Khmer Rouge rule brought evacuation, which was followed, in the 1980s, by systematic looting. Today,

---

ACCOMMODATION BEYOND KAMPOT & KEP

As well as Kampot riverside accommodation and Kep's characterful offerings, there are several places to stay beyond the fringes of Kampot and Kep. Here are a few of our favourites:

Vine Retreat (☑ 036-633 3383; www.thevineretreat.com; r US$25-50; @ 🛰 🛰) This socially responsible ecolodge is near Chamcar Bei village, 13km northeast of Kep. The eight comfortable rooms, with solar hot water and decent mattresses, look out on an organic farm and a naturally filtered swimming pond; the top floor has a quiet chill-out area. Divine set meals average US$10. To get here from the White Horse Roundabout, head east for 3.5km to a well-marked turn-off on the left. The resort is 2.8km from the turn-off.

Nataya Roundhouse Coral Bay Resort (☑ 033-690201; www.natayaresort.com; Prek Ampil; r US$110-300) Located on a private beach about 16km from Kampot, it's a stylish little resort with accommodation set in well-designed rondavels. There is an inviting infinity pool fronting the beach, handy given the muddy estuary sand underfoot. There is also the Water Lily Spa. The service is not quite up to the standard of the accommodation, but there's plenty of character.

Starling Farm (☑ 017 900977; www.starlingfarm.com; r from US$60) A working pepper farm nestled in the hills on the Kampot-Kep border. It offers a luxurious two-bedroom villa for families and six traditional Khmer-style bungalows on a hillside with contemporary furnishings. There is a split-level swimming pool and a cafe-restaurant here, serving plenty of zesty pepper dishes.

scores of Kep's luxurious prewar villas remain blackened shells, relics of a once-successful (or at least rich and flashy) civilisation that met a sudden and violent end.

Some find Kep a bit soulless because it lacks a centre and accommodation options are spread out all over the place. Others revel in its sleepy vibe, content to relax at their resort, nibble on crab at the famed Crab Market and poke around the mildewed shells of modernist villas, which still give the town a sort of post-apocalyptic feel.

◉ Sights

Koh Tonsay (Rabbit Island)   ISLAND

(កោះទន្សាយ) Just off Kep, Koh Tonsay has the nicest beaches of any Kep-area island, with the exception of Phu Quoc (known as Koh Tral to Khmers), whose loss to Vietnam is still bitterly resented. Koh Tonsay is so named because locals say it resembles a rabbit, an example of what too much local brew can do to your imagination. If you like the rustic beachcomber lifestyle, come now before the island is changed forever by development.

At the 250m-long, tree-lined main beach, which faces west towards the setting sun, you can dine on seafood, lounge around on raised bamboo platforms and overnight in family-run clusters of rudimentary bungalows for around US$8 per day.

Many people call Rabbit Island a 'tropical paradise', but don't expect the sanitised resort version; this one has shorefront flotsam, flies, chickens, packs of dogs and wandering cows.

Other Kep-area islands include **Koh Pos** (Snake Island; about 30 minutes beyond Rabbit Island), which has a deserted beach and fine snorkelling but no overnight accommodation (getting out there costs about US$50 for an all-day trip by 10-person boat); and small, beachless **Koh Svay** (Mango Island), whose summit offers nice views.

Boats to Rabbit Island (30 minutes) leave from a pier 2.7km east of the Kep Beach roundabout. Your guesthouse can arrange to get you on a boat for around US$7 one way or US$10 per person return: make it clear which day you want to be picked up. A scheduled trip departs daily at 9am for the same price. A private boat arranged at the pier costs US$30 one way for up to seven passengers.

Kep National Park   NATIONAL PARK

(ឧទ្យានជាតិកែប; admission 4000r) The interior of Kep peninsula is occupied by Kep National Park, degraded in recent years by illegal logging but finally guarded by a complement of rangers. An 8km circuit around the park, navigable by foot or mountain bike, starts at the park entrance behind Veranda Natural Resort. Fuel up and grab a map of the park at the **Led Zep Cafe** (◔9.30am-6pm), which is on the trail 300m into the walk. The map is also reprinted in the *Coastal* guide to Kep and Kampot.

Led Zep Cafe has also created quirky yellow signs that point the way from the main trail to walking paths leading into the interior of the park. One such path, dubbed Stairway to Heaven, starts directly behind the Beach House guesthouse overlooking Kep Beach. It leads 800m up the hill to a pagoda, a nunnery and – 400m further on – Sunset Rock, with superb views.

Villas   HISTORIC BUILDINGS

From the Northern Roundabout, NH33A heads north past the mildewed shells of handsome mid-20th-century villas that speak of happier, carefree times, and of the terrible years of Khmer Rouge rule and civil war. Built according to the precepts of the modernist style, with clean lines, lots of horizontals and little adornment, they once played host to glittering jet-set parties and may do so again someday, though for the time being many shelter squatters (and, some say, ghosts). Don't get your hopes up about buying one, as they were all snapped up for a song in the mid-1990s by well-connected speculators.

🏃 Beaches

Most of Kep's beaches are too shallow and rocky for good swimming. It's possible to swim off the beach or the jetty at the Sailing Club, but the water is particularly shallow.

Kep Beach   BEACH

Centrally located, this is the best beach in town, but it's still somewhat pebbly and tends to fill up with locals on weekends. Back in the pre-war period, powder-white sand was trucked in from other beaches and this practice began again in 2013, ensuring the beach is in better shape than it has been for many years. The eastern end of the shaded promenade along the beach is marked by **Sela Cham P'dey**, a statue that depicts a nude fisher's wife waiting expectantly for her husband to return.

Coconut Beach   BEACH

(Chhne Derm Dont) This 'beach' has dining platforms and eateries, but not really any

Kep

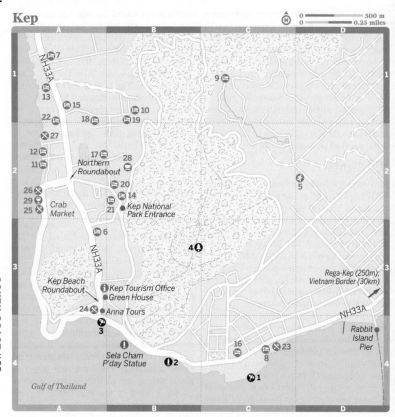

sand as such. It begins a few hundred metres southeast of Kep Beach, just past the **giant crab statue**.

🏃 Activities

For swimming, you might be better off at one of the resort pools. Veranda Natural Resort has the best in town, but those at Kep Lodge and Vanna Bungalows are also good and swimming is free if you order some food.

Sailing Club   WATER SPORTS
(⊙7am-10pm) Open to all, the club hires out sea kayaks (US$5 per hour), Hobie Cats (from US$15 per hour) and windsurfers (US$12 per hour). Decent mountain bikes are also available at US$10 per day.

Magic Tree   TREE CLIMBING
(☑099 896859; maxdiscoverycambodia.wordpress. com; US$8) 'Action' Max Discovery Cambodia organises a range of events and team building around Kep, and the Magic Tree is an al-

ternative experience for families. Explore the interior of a huge old figus tree in Kep National Park with safety ropes and instruction.

Ranch de la Plantation   HORSE RIDING
(☑097 847 4960; www.kep-plantation.com; per 1/2hr US$15/25; ⊙8am-6pm) Horse rides are available through the lower reaches of Kep National Park. Horses can be cantankerous so are more suited to experienced adult riders.

☞ Tours

Kep makes a good base for visiting several delightful cave-temples, including Wat Kiri Sela near Kompong Trach, and Phnom Chhnork and Phnom Sorsia on the road to Kampot. Guesthouses and travel agencies offer half- and full-day tours that take in a few of these sights and usually a pepper plantation, or you could hire an English-speaking *remork* driver and tailor your own countryside tour for about US$20 per day.

Kep

🛏 Sleeping

Kep meanders along the shoreline for a good 5km, with the resorts situated at intervals along its length. The ostensible centre is around the Kep Beach Roundabout and Kep Beach, but there isn't much happening there. Some of the best options are not on the water but on the other side of the highway in the hills leading up to Kep National Park. Rooms at all midrange and top-end places listed include breakfast.

★**Botanica Guesthouse** GUESTHOUSE $
(☑ 097 801 9071; www.kep-botanica.com; NH33A; r with fan US$15-19, with air-con US$23-29; ❄🤖🏊) A little way from the action (if Kep can be said to have any action), Botanica offers exceptional value for money with attractive bungalows boasting contemporary bathrooms. There is a small swimming pool and guests can use free bicycles to hit the beach.

Bacoma GUESTHOUSE $
(☑ 088 411 2424; bacoma@live.com; US$10-36; 🤖) Cheap and cheerful rondavels are available in the lush garden and include high ceilings, mosquito nets and a fan, with a generous helping of shared bathrooms. There are also larger rooms with bathroom, plus a couple of traditional wooden Khmer houses for families at US$36.

Tree Top Bungalows GUESTHOUSE $
(☑ 012 515191; khmertreetop@hotmail.com; r US$5-45; @🤖) The highlights here are the towering stilted bamboo 'treehouse' bungalows with sea views, where each pair shares a bathroom. Kep's cheapest rooms are the US$5 shacks separated by flimsy partitions. Cool off at neighbouring Kep Lodge's pool with a purchase of food and drink.

Kukuluku Beach Club GUESTHOUSE $
(☑ 036-6300150; www.kukuluku-beachclub.com; NH33A; dm US$5-7, r US$15-35; 🤖) The pool is small and the rooms are nothing to write home about, but it remains a great place for meeting fellow travellers and partying on weekends, when it sometimes imports live music (and expat crowds) from Phnom Penh.

Rega-Kep GUESTHOUSE $
(☑ 097 383 9064; keprega@hotmail.com; off NH33A; r with fan/air-con US$12/18; ❄🤖) Hidden on a side street near the Rabbit Island pier, Rega-Kep has 10 tasteful and well-appointed rooms set around a tropical courtyard. Excellent value considering Kep prices.

Kep Seaside Guesthouse HOTEL $
(☑ 036-666 4241; www.kepseaside.com; r with fan US$10, with air-con US$15-40; ❄🤖) This three-storey place is a bit decrepit, but you can't argue with the location, right on the water (although beachless). A huge new annex has recently opened with smarter rooms from US$30, but no obvious seaview.

★**Kep Lodge** RESORT $$
(☑ 092 435330; www.keplodge.com; r US$28-70; ❄🤖🏊) An uber-friendly place where the bungalows have thatched roofs, tile floors and verandas. The grounds are lush, the common area relaxing, and the restaurant

overlooking the pool serves great food and has superb sunset views. We particularly recommend the Rambutan room thanks to its breezy balcony and the views of Bokor framing the horizon.

Jasmine Valley Eco-Resort ECORESORT $$
(☑ 097 791 7635; www.jasminevalley.com; r US$24-64; 🕸 ☒) 🖋 The funky bungalows here are set dramatically amid dense jungle foliage just below Kep National Park, plus there are a couple of memorable treehouses with views over the canopy. There are good hikes around, and green credits include solar power and a natural swimming pool complete with pond critters. It's about 2.5km in from the Rabbit Island pier (follow the signs).

Brise de Kep Boutique GUESTHOUSE $$
(☑ 036-633 6339; brisedekep@yahoo.com; NH33A; r US$25) One of the very few seafront places on the western side of Kep, the neat aircon bungalows here are spacious and spotless with attractive furnishings. Only seven rooms so book ahead.

Le Bout du Monde BOUTIQUE HOTEL $$
(☑ 097 526 1761; http://leboutdumondekep.com; r US$40-130; 🕸) The French-owned 'end of the earth', the highest of all the hillside resorts, has a dozen rustic bungalows with wraparound verandas, Angkorian sculptures, beautiful wood furniture and stone-walled bathrooms. The view from the restaurant is Kep's best.

Vanna Hill Resort RESORT $$
(☑ 012 755038; www.vannahillresort.com; r US$30-80) An affordable option at the foothillls of Kep National Park, Vanna offers a range of rooms and bungalows, including some fan cheapies and smarter air-con options. The swimming pool is a real feature here, dominating the centre of the resort.

Theara Lodge HOTEL $$
(☑ 097 731 5150; theara.lodge@gmail.com; r US$23-35) A new hilltop hotel offering some great value rooms, including silk runners, flat-screen TVs and an inviting bathroom that punches above the price range. More expensive upstairs rooms include a spacious veranda.

Sea View Bungalows RESORT $$
(☑ 097 695 8582; www.seaviewbungalows.com; Off NH33A; r US$45-100) A new family-friendly guesthouse set back from the main road, the smart US$55 bungalows are a good investment with two double beds and extras

like flat-screen TV and minibar. There is also a family apartment in the main building. A swimming pool has been added and a French chef is developing a new menu.

Rock Royal Hotel HOTEL $$
(☑ 036-210168; www.rockroyalresort.com; NH33A; r US$30-100) While it won't win any beauty contests for its looks, this hotel has a dependable personality on the inside with great-value rooms including all the trims. A huge seafront swimming pool and some beachside cabanas were under construction when we visited.

★ **Veranda Natural Resort** RESORT $$
(☑ 012 888619; www.veranda-resort.com; d/tr from US$60/68; 🕸 🛜 ☒) The hillside bungalows here are built of wood, bamboo and stone and connected by a maze of stilted walkway, making for a memorable spot for a romantic getaway. Check out a few rooms because the size and shape (and price) vary wildly. It's constantly expanding and has added some striking family villas that are simply superb. The food is excellent and sunset views from the restaurant pavilion are stunning.

Knai Bang Chatt RESORT $$$
(☑ 078 888556; www.knaibangchatt.com; r US$165-325; 🕸 @ 🛜 ☒) This ultrachic boutique hotel, occupying a cluster of waterfront villas from the 1960s, has a waterfront infinity pool and its own sailing club, which is open to the public. Very classy, although there isn't actually a beach here.

Villa Romonea BOUTIQUE HOTEL $$$
(☑ 012 879486; villaromonea.com; r US$100-125; 🕸 @ 🛜 ☒) This modernist 1960s villa has been beautifully restored and converted into an evocative guesthouse with six rooms. Right on the water, it's often booked out by groups on weekends, but it's a real gem – private and with a great pool.

Le Flamboyant Resort BOUTIQUE HOTEL $$$
(☑ 017 491010; www.flamboyant-hotel.com; NH33A; r from US$75) Less flamboyant than the name would suggest, this is an attractive garden property that has doubled in size in recent years. The older bungalows are to the left and newer chalets to the right, and there are two swimming pools.

🍴 Eating & Drinking

Eating at the Crab Market – a row of wooden waterfront shacks by a wet fish market – is a quintessential Kep experience. Fresh crabs fried with Kampot pepper are a taste sensation. Crabs are kept alive in pens tethered a few metres off the pebbly beach. You can dine at one of the shacks or buy crab for around 35,000r a kilo and have your guesthouse prepare it. There are lots of great places to choose from at the crab market, so keep an eye on where the Khmer crowd are eating. **Kimly** (☑904077; Crab Market; mains US$2.50-7; ⊗9am-10pm) has a good reputation with crab prepared in 27 different ways. Or try the memorably named **Holy Crab**. The crab shacks also serve prawns, squid, fish and terrestrial offerings.

For finer dining, the best restaurants are found at the resorts: Kep Lodge, Le Bout du Monde and, especially, Veranda Natural Resort are a few of the top tables, and have great views to boot.

★**Sailing Club**   FUSION $$
(mains US$5-12; ⊗10am-10pm; 🛜) With a small beach, a breezy wooden bar and a wooden jetty poking out into the sea, this is one of Cambodia's top sundowner spots. The Asian fusion food is excellent and you can get your crab fix here too. The prices are pretty reasonable by comparison with parent and neighbour Knai Bang Chatt, especially at happy hour.

Breezes   FUSION $$
(NH33A; mains US$5-10; ⊗9am-10pm; 🛜) Sitting right on the shoreline, this inviting al-fresco restaurant out toward the Rabbit Island pier boasts sleek furnishings, excellent food and fine views of Rabbit Island. Dishes are Asian (not necessarily Khmer), Western and fusion.

Brise de Kep   FRENCH, ASIAN $$
(☑036-633 6339; Kep Beach; US$3-9; ⊗7am-10pm) Mixing up a good selection of French and Asian dishes, this seaview restaurant has a serious selection of seafood specials, including tuna, barracuda and other shellfish. Fine wines and aperitifs complete the picture.

Pasta e Basta   ITALIAN $$
(☑036-676 6667; Kep Beach; mains US$4-14.50; ⊗7am-10pm) This popular Italian eatery set back from Kep Beach offers pizza at a reasonable US$5 to US$8. Beyond the pasta are some expressive dishes of the day, including

SOUTH COAST KEP

GETTING TO VIETNAM: KEP TO HA TIEN

Getting to the border The Prek Chak/Xa Xia border crossing has become a popular option for linking Kampot and Kep with Ha Tien and the popular Vietnamese island of Phu Quoc. It is easy enough to travel between these destinations in one day with some smooth transport connections.

The easiest way to get to Prek Chak (open 6am to 5.30pm) and on to Ha Tien, Vietnam, is on a minibus from Phnom Penh (US$16, five hours), Sihanoukville (US$16, five hours), Kampot (US$10, two hours) or Kep (US$8, 1½ hours) to the border. Buses are no longer allowed to make the crossing through to Ha Tien itself. Virak Buntham has a bus from Phnom Penh; Virak Buntham and two other companies ply the Sihanoukville–Kampot–Kep–Ha Tien route.

A more flexible alternative from Phnom Penh or Kampot is to take any bus to Kompong Trach, then a *moto* (about US$3) for 15km, on a good road, to the border.

In Kep, tour agencies and guesthouses can arrange a direct *moto* (US$8, 40 minutes), *remork* (US$13, one hour) or taxi (US$20, 30 minutes). Rates and times are almost double those from Kampot. Private vehicles take a new road that cuts south to the border 10km west of Kompong Trach. It is also possible to buy through tickets to Phu Quoc, including the boat, and these cost US$18 from Kep.

At the border As always, it's necessary to have a Vietnamese visa for travel to Phu Quoc, the Mekong Delta and on to Ho Chi Minh City.

At Prek Chak, *motos* ask US$5 to take you to the Vietnamese border post 300m past the Cambodian one, and then all the way to Ha Tien (7km). You'll save money walking across no-man's land and picking up a *moto* on the other side for US$2 to US$3.

Moving on Travellers bound for Phu Quoc should arrive in Ha Tien no later than 12.30pm to secure a ticket on the 1pm ferry (230,000d or about US$11, 1½ hours). Extreme early risers may be able to make it to Ha Tien in time to catch the (slower) 8.20am car ferry to Phu Quoc. The scheduled buses from Cambodia to Ha Tien arrive before the 1pm boat departs.

fresh fish, cameralised shrimps in hot pot and salmon. Takeway available.

La Baraka
ITALIAN $$

(Crab Market; mains US$4-7; ⊙11am-10pm) A French-run pizzeria with an upstairs chill-out area and a sophisticated little seaside terrace. Try the crab with pepper pizza for an Italian-Khmer fusion experience.

Toucan
BAR

(Crab Market; snacks US$3-5; ⊙11am-10pm; 🛜) The best spot for a drink (or five) once the sun goes down. It has a pool table and usually a few punters propping up the bar until midnight or so, which is a late night for Kep.

ℹ️ Information

As in Kampot, the best source of information and maps is the *Coastal* guide to Kampot and Kep (www.coastal-cambodia.com). There is also a useful online resource in the shape of www.visitkep.com. At the time of writing, Kep did not have any banks or ATMs.

Anna Tours (📋036-652 3999; ⊙9am-6pm) Long-running Sihanoukville travel company has spread its wings and organises transport all over Cambodia and on to Vietnam.

Green House (📋089 440161; per hr US$1; ⊙9am-6pm) Travel agency with internet access.

ℹ️ Getting There & Around

Kep is 25km from Kampot and 41km from the Prek Chak/Xa Xia border crossing to Vietnam. Phnom Penh Sorya Transport and Hua Lian buses link the town with Kampot (US$2, 45 minutes) and Phnom Penh (US$4, four hours, last trips at 2pm). Stops are on request but usually include the northern roundabout and Kep Beach; guesthouses have details. A private taxi to Phnom Penh (2½ hours) costs US$40 to US$45, to Kampot US$20.

Virak Buntham's Ha Tien–Sihanoukville bus rumbles through Kep, and Kampot Tours & Travel can also get you to Sihanoukville (US$10, 2½ hours). A *moto/remork* to Kampot costs about US$8/12; private taxis are US$15 to US$20. Drivers hang out at the northern and Kep Beach roundabouts.

Motorbike rental is US$5 to US$7 per day; ask your guesthouse or any travel agency.

Around Kep

◎ Sights

Wat Kiri Sela
BUDDHIST TEMPLE

(វត្តគិរីសិលា; ⊙7am-6pm) This Buddhist temple is located at the foot of Phnom Kom-pong Trach, a dramatic karst formation riddled with more than 100 caverns and passageways. From the wat, an underground passage leads to the centre of a fishbowl-like karst formation, surrounded by vine-draped cliffs and open to the sky. Various stalactite-laden caves shelter reclining Buddhas and miniature Buddhist shrines. There's major rock-climbing opportunities around here, but no established operator to date.

Friendly local kids with torches (flashlights), keen to put their evening-school English to use, are eager (overeager?) to serve as guides. Make sure you tip them if you use them.

The closest town to Wat Kiri Sela is Kompong Trach, 28km northeast of Kep, on NH33, 18km north of the Prek Chak-Xa Xia border crossing to Vietnam. Kompong Trach makes an easy day trip from Kep or Kampot.

To get to Wat Kiri Sela, take the dirt road opposite the Acleda Bank, on NH33 in the centre of town, for 2km in the direction of the looming limestone karsts.

TAKEO PROVINCE

Often referred to as 'the cradle of Cambodian civilisation', Takeo Province was part of what Chinese annals called 'water Chenla', no doubt a reference to the extensive annual floods that still blanket much of the area. Today, this impoverished rural province is a backwater that gets few tourists. Those who do make it here get some of Cambodia's most ancient and fascinating temples virtually to themselves.

The temples of Tonlé Bati and Phnom Chisor lie in Takeo but are usually visited as day trips from Phnom Penh.

Takeo
តាកែវ

📋 032 / POP 40,000

There's not much happening at all in the quiet, lakeside provincial capital, but it makes a good base from which to take an adrenaline-fulled speedboat ride to the pre-Angkorian temples of Angkor Borei and Phnom Da. The main attraction in town is eating freshwater lobster on the waterfront (rainy season only).

◎ Sights & Activities

Some attractive French-era shophouses line the streets around Psar Nat, a concrete monstrosity built after the overthrow of the

Takeo

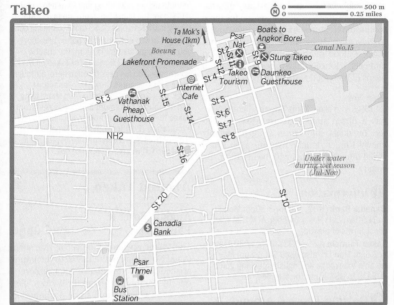

0 — 500 m
0 — 0.25 miles

Ta Mok's House (1km)

Psar Nat

Boats to Angkor Borei

Canal No.15

Boeung

Lakefront Promenade

Stung Takeo

St 2

Takeo Tourism

Daunkeo Guesthouse

St 4

St 3

Internet Cafe

Vathanak Pheap Guesthouse

St 15

St 14

St 5

St 6

St 7

St 8

NH2

St 16

Under water during wet season (Jul-Nov)

St 20

St 10

Canadia Bank

Psar Thmei

Bus Station

Khmer Rouge, but it's nothing compared with Kampot.

Ta Mok's House HISTORIC BUILDING
(ផ្ទះតាម៉ុក; ⊘7am-5pm) **FREE** A pleasant stroll via a 150m-long railings-free bridge north of the centre takes you to the house of Takeo Province's most notorious native son, Ta Mok – aka 'The Butcher' – the Khmer Rouge commander of the Southwestern Zone, where he presided over horrific atrocities. Ta Mok's House is now occupied by a police training facility, but you can wander around the grounds. Ta Mok also had a residence near Anlong Veng.

🛏 Sleeping

Few people actually overnight in Takeo, as it is daytripping distance from Phnom Penh or a brief detour on a road trip south to Kep or Kampot.

Meas Family Homestay HOMESTAY **$**
(☑011 925428; www.cambodianhomestay.com; Ang Tasaom District; per person incl all meals US$17; @🛜) This popular and friendly family homestay has 11 rooms in a spacious compound located just off the road between Ang Tasaom and Takeo. The rates include some delicious homecooked Khmer food and cooking classes are available on demand.

Popular with adventure groups like Intrepid, it's possible to volunteer to teach English at the local school.

Daunkeo Guesthouse GUESTHOUSE **$**
(☑032-210303; www.daunkeo.com; St 9; s/d with fan US$5/6, with air-con from US$11/12; ❄🛜) The smartest guesthouse in Takeo, Daunkeo is spread over three modern villas. Spotlessly clean and efficiently run, air-con rooms include satellite TV and hot water showers. Anoint yourself a VIP with a suite-like room for just US$25.

Vathanak Pheap Guesthouse GUESTHOUSE **$**
(☑032-675 5777; St 3; r US$12-15) Run by a friendly family, this place overlooks the main lake in town, one that doesn't dry up when all the other water recedes. Rooms are bright and airy and include all mod cons from TV to hot water.

🍴 Eating & Drinking

There are **food stalls** around Independence Monument. In the evening, this is the place to snack on Cambodian desserts or enjoy a *tukalok* (fruit shake).

★Stung Takeo CAMBODIAN **$$**
(St 9; mains US$2-15; ⊘7am-9pm) Perched over the seasonal lake, this is the place to come for

remarkably good – and remarkably affordable – freshwater lobster. The season for these toothsome creatures is approximately August to November. It has an English menu with other seafood offerings, as well as chicken and beef. It's easily Takeo's best restaurant in terms of both food and ambience.

Psar Nat   MARKET $

(St 10; ☺6am-about 8pm) The food court here has a dozen stalls that are great for coffee, breakfast soup, *num kong* (delectably chewy Khmer doughnuts) and *num kroch* (fried dumplings filled with beans and palm sugar).

ℹ Information

Canadia Bank (NH2; ☺8am-3.30pm Mon-Fri, to 11.30am Sat) Has a 24-hour ATM that takes most forms of plastic.

Takeo Tourism (☏032-931323; ☺7.30-11am & 2-5pm Mon-Fri, also open Sat & Sun) May be able to arrange an English-speaking guide (US$15 to US$20) to the temples.

ℹ Getting There & Around

Takeo is on NH2, 77km south of Phnom Penh, 40km north of Kirivong and 48km north of the Phnom Den/Tinh Bien border crossing to Vietnam.

Phnom Penh Sorya Transport is the only company serving Phnom Penh (10,000r, 2¼ hours), with four small buses daily to/from a lot in front of **Psar Thmei** (Central Market, NH2). If you miss those you'll have to take a shared taxi (US$25 for the whole taxi, 15,000r for a seat). These leave from the same lot throughout the day, but you may have to wait longer or hire your own taxi in the afternoon.

Occasional share taxis (10,000r) and minivans (5000r) make the 45-minute trip down to Kirivong, or you can hire a *moto* for US$10. To get to the Phnom Den/Tinh Bien border crossing to Vietnam, go to Kirivong and switch to a *moto* (US$2) for the final 8km. A private taxi to Kirivong is US$20, plus US$5 more to the border.

To get to Kep or Kampot by public transport, you need to go to Angk Tasaom, the chaotic transport junction 13km west of Takeo on NH3. Southbound buses pass through here, although there's no guarantee they'll have space. At Angk Tasaom you can also pick up share taxis and minibuses to Kampot and Kep. To get from Takeo to Angk Tasaom, hop on a trailer pulled by a motorbike (2000r) from Psar Thmei, a *remork* (US$6) from Psar Thmei or the hospital, or a *moto* (US$3) wherever you spot one.

Around Takeo

Angkor Borei & Phnom Da   អង្គរបុរី និងភ្នំដា

The 20km open-air motorboat ride along Canal No 15, dug in the 1880s, to the impoverished riverine townlet of Angkor Borei is one of Cambodia's great thrill rides. Angkor Borei is home to a small archaeological museum (☏012 201638; admission US$1; ☺8am-4.30pm) featuring locally discovered Funan- and Chenla-era artefacts. The boat then continues for 15 minutes to Phnom Da (admission US$2), which is spectacularly isolated Mont-St-Michel-style by annual floods, topped by a temple with foundations dating from the 6th century (the temple itself was rebuilt in the 11th century).

Angkor Borei, which can also be reached year-round via a circuitous land route from the north, was known as Vyadhapura when it served as the capital of 'water Chenla' in the 8th century. Angkor Borei was also an important centre during the earlier Funan period (1st to 6th centuries), when Indian religion and culture were carried to the Me-

---

GETTING TO VIETNAM: TAKEO TO CHAU DOC

Getting to the border The remote and seldom-used Phnom Den/Tinh Bien border crossing (☺7am-5pm) between Cambodia and Vietnam lies about 60km southeast of Takeo town in Cambodia and offers connections to Chau Doc. Most travellers prefer the Mekong crossing at Kaam Samnor or the newer Prek Chak crossing near Ha Tien to the south. Take a share taxi (10,000r), a chartered taxi (US$25) or a *moto* (US$10) from Takeo to the border (48km).

At the border Vietnam visas are not available at the border, so arrange one in advance through a travel company in Kampot or Kep or via the embassy in Phnom Penh.

Moving on Travellers are at the mercy of Vietnamese *xe om* (*moto*) drivers and taxis for the 30km journey from the border to Chau Doc. Prepare for some tough negotiations. Expect to pay somewhere between US$5 and US$10 by bike, more like US$20 for a taxi.

kong Delta by traders, artisans and priests from India, as the great maritime trade route between India and China passed by the Mekong Delta. The earliest datable Khmer inscription (AD 611) was discovered at Angkor Borei, which is surrounded by a 5.7km moated wall that hints at its past greatness.

The twin hills of Phnom Da shelter five artificial caves, used for centuries as Hindu and Buddhist shrines and, during the Vietnam War, as hideouts by the Viet Cong. Exceptionally, the temple entrance faces due north; the other three sides have blind doors decorated with bas-relief *nagas*. The finest carvings have been taken to museums in Angkor Borei, Phnom Penh and Paris.

Nearby, on a second hillock, is 8m-high Wat Asram Moha Russei, a restored Hindu sanctuary that probably dates from around AD 700.

❶ Getting There & Away

Hiring a boat for the trip from Takeo's dock costs around US$35 return for up to four people. The canal leading out to Angkor Borei is clearly delineated in the dry season but surrounded by flooded rice fields the rest of the year. In the rainy season the water can get rough in the afternoon, so it's a good idea to head out early.

You can travel by *moto* from Takeo to Phnom Da in the dry season only for about US$5 return.

Phnom Bayong & Environs ភ្នំបាយ័ង្គ

Affording breathtaking views of Vietnam's pancake-flat Mekong Delta, the cliff-ringed summit of Phnom Bayong (313m) is graced by a 7th-century Chenla temple built to celebrate a victory over Funan. The *linga* originally in the inner chamber is now in Paris' Musée Guimet, but a number of flora- and fauna-themed bas-relief panels can still be seen; for example, on the lintels of the three false doorways and carved into the brickwork.

The sweltering climb up to the temple takes about 1½ hours (bring plenty of water), or you can hire a *moto* in Kirivong to take you up in less than 20 minutes (US$10). It's a treacherous path, which explains the high price.

Gentle Kirivong Waterfall (Chruos Phaok Waterfall) is reached by a 1.5km access road that begins about 1km south of Kirivong. Market stalls here sell the area's most famous products: topaz and quartz, either cut like gems or carved into tiny Buddhas and *nagas*. This area is popular with locals.

❶ Getting There & Away

Phnom Bayong is about 3km west of the northern edge of Kirivong town; the turn-off is marked by a painted panel depicting the temple.

Kirivong town is on NH2, 40km south of Takeo and 8km north of the Phnom Den/Tinh Bien border crossing. From Takeo, a *moto* to Kirivong costs about US$10 (US$15 return).

Infrequent minibuses and share taxis to Phnom Penh (via Takeo) leave from Kirivong's Ton Lop Market on NH2 in the centre of town.

To get to the Vietnam border, a *moto* (US$2) from Kirivong is the best bet. Coming *from* the border, you may have to ask the Cambodian border officials to call a *moto* or taxi to pick you up.

Northwestern Cambodia

POP 3.75 MILLION / AREA 71,157 SQ KM

Best Places to Eat & Drink

➡ Cafe Eden (p224)
➡ Lonely Tree Cafe (p224)
➡ Jaan Bai (p224)
➡ Limy Restaurant (p243)
➡ Phnom Tbaeng Restaurant (p241)

Best Places to Stay

➡ La Villa (p223)
➡ Here Be Dragons (p223)
➡ Sambor Village Hotel (p248)
➡ Banteay Chhmar Homestay (p237)
➡ Preah Vihear Boutique Hotel (p243)

Why Go?

Intrepid travellers take note: northwestern Cambodia is an explorer's delight. The region is first and foremost about remote temples, many of them pillars of the Angkorian empire. The most famous is Prasat Preah Vihear, now more accessible than ever thanks to rapidly improving roads. Put Sambor Prei Kuk, in Kompong Thom province, and Banteay Chhmar, in Banteay Meanchey, on your radar as well. Preah Khan, Koh Ker, Prasat Banan...the list goes on.

The other big draw in the region is effortlessly cool Battambang, with its classic colonial architecture, burgeoning arts scene and a host of worthy day trips out of town.

At the centre of the region lies the unique Tonlé Sap lake, one of the most fish-rich lakes in the world and home to several rare bird species. Explore floating villages out of Pursat or Kompong Chhnang, or take the classic boat trip from Battambang to Siem Reap.

When to Go
Battambang

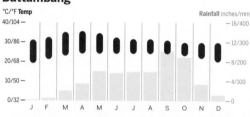

Dec–Jan Best for remote temple-hopping; dry and relatively cool climes prevail.

Nov Best time for back-country exploration; roads are neither too muddy nor too dusty.

Aug–Sep Height of rainy season; ideal for boat rides on Tonlé Sap.

KOMPONG CHHNANG PROVINCE

Kompong Chhnang Province (ខេត្ត កំពង់ឆ្នាំង) is a relatively wealthy province thanks to its proximity to the capital and its fishing and agricultural industries, supported by abundant water resources.

Kompong Chhnang កំពង់ឆ្នាំង

♪026 / POP 45,000

Kompong Chhnang (Clay Pot Port) is a tale of two cities: the sleepy centre dating back to the colonial area, arrayed around a huge park, and the bustling dockside on the Tonlé Sap River. Nearby sights include two floating villages, a hamlet famous for its distinctive pottery and drop-dead gorgeous countryside, typically Cambodian in its union of verdant rice fields and towering sugar palms.

◉ Sights & Activities

Floating Villages   BOAT TOUR

A short sail from Kompong Chhnang's river port, 2km northeast of the centre on the Tonlé Sap River, leads to a couple of colourful floating villages: **Phoum Kandal**, an ethnic Vietnamese village directly southeast of the boat dock; and the Khmer village of **Chong Kos** a bit further north. Much less

commercial than Kompong Luong, they have all the amenities of a mainland village – houses, machine-tool shops, vegetable vendors, a mosque, a petrol station – except that almost everything floats.

To get into the heart of these villages you will have to hire a motorless wooden paddle boat at the river port. These cost US$10 per hour and are good for three people. Bigger motorized tourist boats are available for river tours for US$15 per hour, but these only circle the perimeter of the villages.

Ondong Rossey & Phnom Santuk   CULTURAL TOUR

(អណ្ដូងប្រុស្សី និងភ្នំសន្ទុក) The quiet village of Ondong Rossey, where the area's famous red pottery is made under every house, is a delightful 7km ride west of town through serene rice fields dotted with sugar palms, many with bamboo ladders running up the trunk. The unpainted pots, decorated with etched or appliqué designs, are either turned on a foot-spun wheel (for small pieces) or banged into shape with a heavy wooden spatula (for large ones).

The golden-hued mud piled up in the yards is quarried at nearby **Phnom Krang Dai Meas** and pounded into fine clay before being shaped and fired; only at the last stage does it acquire a pinkish hue. Pieces can be

---

THE KHMER ROUGE AIRPORT

The Khmer Rouge were not known as great builders, but in 1977 and 1978, slave labourers built an airfield using cement of such high quality that even today the 2440m runway and access roads look like they were paved just last week.

No one knows for sure, but it seems that Kompong Chhnang airport (IATA code KZC), never operational under the Khmer Rouge, was intended to serve as a base for launching air attacks against Vietnam. Chinese engineers oversaw the work of tens of thousands of Cambodians suspected of disloyalty to the Khmer Rouge. Anyone unable to work was killed, often with a blow to the head delivered with a bamboo rod. In early 1979, as Vietnamese forces approached, almost the entire workforce was executed. Estimates of the number of victims, buried nearby in mass graves, range from 10,000 to 50,000.

In the late 1990s, a plan to turn the airport into a cargo hub for air-courier companies came to nought. These days, local teenagers come out here to tool around on their motorbikes, do doughnuts and drag race, while cows graze between the taxiway and the runway. On sunny days the sun creates convincing mirages.

On an anonymous slope a few kilometres away, the Khmer Rouge dug a **cave** – said to be 3km deep – apparently for the purpose of storing weapons flown in from China. Now home to swirling bats, it can be explored with a torch (flashlight) but, lacking ventilation, gets very hot and humid.

On a hillside near a cluster of bullet-pocked cement barracks, stripped of anything of value, is a massive cement water tank. Inside it's a remarkable echo chamber.

The airport is about 12km west of town. Take NH5 towards Battambang for 7km and then turn left onto a concrete road.

North-western Cambodia Highlights

1 Soak up the colonial-tinged charms of the riverside town of **Battambang** (p218), surrounded by lush countryside and hilltop temples

2 Make an overland pilgrimage to the majestic mountain-top temple of **Prasat Preah Vihear** (p242)

3 Explore the backwaters of the colourful floating village of **Kompong Luong** (p216), the largest floating community on Tonlé Sap lake

4 Explore Southeast Asia's first temple city, the impressive pre-Angkorian ruins of **Sambor Prei Kuk** (p248)

5 Put something back into the community with an overnight homestay at **Banteay Chhmar** (p236), a massive 12th-century complex with the signature faces of Avalokiteshvara

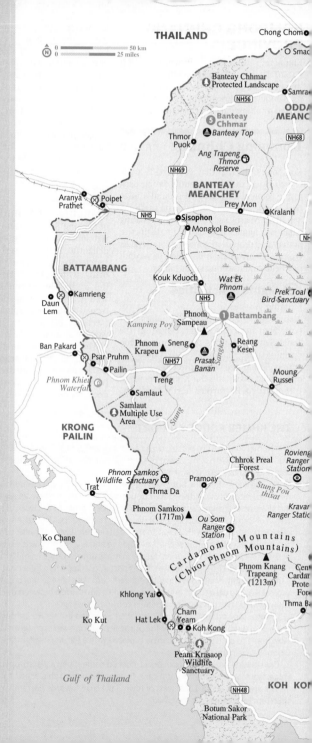

purchased at the **Pottery Development Centre**, although you'll get better deals buying directly from the pottery makers at their houses.

A visit to Ondong Rossey can be combined with Phnom Santuk, a rocky hillock behind Wat Santuk, which is a few kilometres southwest of Kompong Chhnang. The boulder-strewn summit affords fine views of the countryside, including the Tonlé Sap lake, 20km to the north.

By bicycle or *moto*, combining Ondong Rossey and Phnom Santuk makes for a rewarding circuit, especially early in the morning or late in the afternoon. There are no road signs, so it's a good idea to go with a local.

🛏 Sleeping & Eating

There are plenty of food stalls at the two markets, Psar Leu and Psar Krom.

Kompong Chhnang

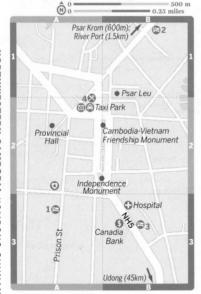

Sovann Phum Hotel   HOTEL $
(☏026-989333; sovannphumkpchotel@yahoo.com; NH5; r with fan/air-con from US$8/15; ❄@🛜) A step up from most options in town in terms of both cleanliness and style, this is a popular spot for the NGO crowd. It has 30 good-sized rooms with modern bathrooms and plenty of light, plus a decent restaurant.

Chanthea Borint Hotel   GUESTHOUSE $
(☏026-988622; cbrint@yahoo.com; Prison St; r with fan/air-con US$8/15; ❄🛜) Set in a shady garden, this 30-room family pad offers the most charming accommodation in town. The rooms are a bit small but they have fresh paint on the walls. The restaurant serves breakfast only.

Samrongsen Hotel   HOTEL $
(☏026-989011; r US$10-15) In a quiet compound 500m northeast of the centre on the road to the river port, the US$10 air-con rooms are about as good a value as you'll find anywhere. Request a room with a window.

Soksan Restaurant   CAMBODIAN $
(NH5; mains US$2-2.50; ⏱6am-8pm) It lacks English signage but there's an English menu at this restaurant next to the taxi park at Psar Leu. It specialises in fried everything and soups. Or go crazy and order the porcupine fish with omelette.

ℹ Information

Remork-moto (tuk-tuk) driver **Channy** (☏077 357361; srinchanny@yahoo.com) is the one-stop shop for all things informative about Kompong Chhnang. He hangs out near the taxi park when he's not with customers.

Canadia Bank (NH5; ⏱8am-3.30pm Mon-Fri, to 11.30am Sat, ATM 24hr) Has an ATM with no charge for withdrawals.

ℹ Getting There & Away

Kompong Chhnang is 91km north of Phnom Penh, 93km southeast of Pursat and 198km southeast of Battambang.

BUS

On NH5 it's usually pretty easy to flag down any bus heading south to Phnom Penh (12,000r, two hours) or north to Pursat (8000r, one hour) and Battambang (20,000r, 3½ hours). Phnom Penh Sorya has hourly buses during the day to Phnom Penh from near the taxi park.

TAXI

The easiest and fastest way to get to Phnom Penh is by share taxi (15,000r, 1½ hours), which wait at the taxi park west of Psar Leu. Share taxis do not generally serve destinations to the northwest, such as Battambang.

ⓘ Getting Around

A few-hour *remork* tour taking in the pottery villages and Phnom Santuk costs US$8. A *moto* should be about US$5. A *remork/moto* to the port is US$2/1 one way.

Chanthea Borint Hotel rents bicycles (US$2/1 return/one way).

PURSAT PROVINCE

Pursat Province (ខេត្តពោធិ៍សាត់), Cambodia's fourth-largest, stretches from the remote forests of Phnom Samkos, on the Thai border, eastwards to the fishing villages and marshes of Tonlé Sap lake. Famed for its oranges, it encompasses the northern reaches of the Cardamom Mountains, linked with the town of Pursat by disreputable roads.

Pursat   ពោធិ៍សាត់

ⓘ 052 / POP 38,000

The provincial capital, known for its marble carvers, is no beauty, but makes a good base for a day trip to the floating village of Kompong Luong or an expedition into the wilds of the Central Cardamoms Protected Forest.

⊙ Sights & Activities

Koh Sampovmeas   PARK
(Golden Ship Island) Koh Sampovmeas, the town's answer to Singapore's Sentosa (though there's no cable car just yet), is an island park with manicured lawns and Khmer-style pavilions. It's the place to see and be seen towards sunset as young locals drop by for aerobics (classes from 5pm), a snack, or a game of badminton.

**Bun Rany Hun Sen
Development Centre**   ARTS CENTRE
(St 109; ⊙7-11am & 2-5pm Mon-Fri, 7-11am Sat) Teaches cloth and mat weaving, sewing, marble carving and other artisanal skills to young people and sells the items they make from a large shop on premises. There are some real bargains here on beautiful *kramas* (checked scarfs) and baskets. Travellers are welcome to visit classes.

🛏 Sleeping & Eating

Pursat Century Hotel   HOTEL $
(ⓘ052-951446; pursatcenturyhotel@yahoo.com; NH5; r with fan/air-con from US$7/15; ❄@�widehat{𝕣})

The imported linens (cue contented sleep) are the highlight at this central place. Otherwise, an ordinary Cambodia high-rise: clean and good value, but with at least a few broken things.

Phnom Pech Hotel   HOTEL $
(ⓘ052-951515; St 101; r US$6-18; ❄�widehat{𝕣}) A long-running local hotel, rooms here are spacious and clean. It's the only hotel in town that dispenses any useful form of tourism advice.

Thansour Thmey Hotel   HOTEL $
(ⓘ012 962395; thansourthmey@gmail.com; St 102; r with fan/air-con US$7/15; ❄❄) This hotel, popular with the NGO crowd, has 41 rooms done up in classic Khmer shiny wood. The restaurant is one of the best in town, serving Khmer and Chinese food (mains 10,000r to 16,000r).

Village Villa   CAMBODIAN $
(www.knkscambodia.org; NH5; mains 4000-8000r; ⊙7am-9pm) 🍴 Run by a Cambodian NGO that gives job skills to at-risk young people, this place serves Khmer dishes, including ginger fish, various soups and orange juice made from fresh-squeezed Pursat oranges.

Magic Fish Restaurant   CAMBODIAN $
(St 101; mains 8000-15,000r; ⊙10am-9pm) Just north of the Khmer Rouge–era dam, this riverside place has tasty Khmer dishes and great river views.

ⓘ Information

Cheata at the Phnom Pech Hotel is relatively switched on if you need information on getting around the province, including to more remote bits such as the Cardamoms.

Canadia Bank (NH5; ⊙8am-3.30pm Mon-Fri, to 11.30am Sat) ATM with free withdrawals.

Department of Tourism (ⓘ012 838854; ⊙7-11am & 2-5pm Mon-Fri) Has a booklet on Pursat sightseeing (also available at Magic Fish Restaurant) and a map of the province and city.

Pheng Ky Computer (St 101; per hr 2000r; ⊙6am-7pm) Internet access.

ⓘ Getting There & Around

Pursat is 105km southeast of Battambang and 185km northwest of Phnom Penh along NH5.

Buses pass through Pursat virtually all day long, shuttling north to Battambang (15,000r, 1½ hours) and southeast to Kompong Chhnang and Phnom Penh (20,000r, four hours). **Phnom Penh Sorya** (NH5) has direct trips to Kompong Cham (US$9, six hours, 11.30am) and Siem Reap (US$6, five hours, 7.30am) via Battambang.

Pursat

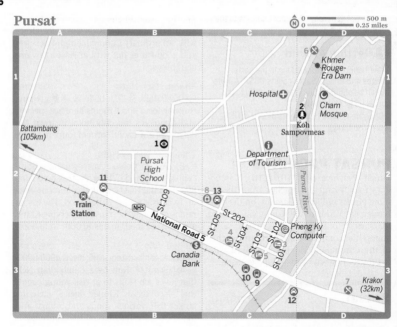

Pursat

⊚ Sights
1 Bun Rany Hun Sen Development Centre	B2
2 Koh Sampovmeas	D1

⊜ Sleeping
3 Phnom Pech Hotel	C3
4 Pursat Century Hotel	C3
5 Thansour Thmey Hotel	C3

⊗ Eating
6 Magic Fish Restaurant	D1
7 Village Villa	D3

⊜ Shopping
8 Psar Chaa	C2

⊕ Transport
9 Phnom Penh Sorya	C3
10 Rith Mony	C3
11 Taxis to Battambang	A2
12 Taxis to Phnom Penh	C3
13 Taxis to Pramoay	C2

Share taxis serve Phnom Penh (24,000r, three hours) from NH5 just east of the bridge. Share taxis to Battambang (16,000r, two hours) depart from NH5 on the west edge of town.

Pick-ups and share taxis to the remote Cardamoms town of Pramoay (Veal Veng; 30,000r,

three hours) via Kravanh (one hour) and Rovieng (two hours) leave from next to the old market, Psar Chaa.

Phnom Pech Hotel rents out bicycles (US$3 a day) and motorbikes (US$10) and can arrange a round-trip *remork* to Kompong Luong for US$15 for hotel guests or US$20 for outsiders. A *moto* round trip to Kompong Luong is about US$10.

Kompong Luong   កំពង់លួង
POP 10,000

Kompong Luong has all the amenities you'd expect to find in an oversized fishing village – except that here everything floats on water. The result is a partly ethnic-Vietnamese Venice without the dry land. The cafes, shops, chicken coops, fish ponds, ice-making factory and karaoke bars are kept from sinking by boat hulls, barrels or bunches of bamboo, as are the Vietnamese pagoda, the blue-roofed church and the colourful houses. In the dry season, when water levels drop and Tonlé Sap shrinks, the entire aquapolis is towed, boat by boat, a few kilometres north.

The population of this fascinating and picturesque village is partly Vietnamese, so – reflecting their ambiguous status in Cambodian society – you may find the welcome here slightly more subdued than in most rural Cambodian towns, at least from adults. Khmer Rouge massacres of Vietnamese villagers living around Tonlé Sap lake were commonplace during the first half of the 1990s, and even as late as 1998 more than 20 Vietnamese were killed in a pogrom near Kompong Chhnang.

The way to explore Kompong Luong, naturally, is by boat. The official tourist rate to charter a four-passenger wooden motorboat (complete with lifejackets) is US$9 per hour for one to three passengers (US$13 for four to five, US$21 for eight to 10).

Homestays (per night US$6, not incl boat ride) are available with local families and meals are available for US$1 to US$2 per person. This is an interesting way to discover what everyday life is really like on the water.

ⓘ Getting There & Around

The jumping-off point to Kompong Luong is the town of Krakor, 32km east of Pursat. From Krakor to the boat landing where tours begin is 1.5km to 6km, depending on the time of year.

Northern Cardamom Mountains ភ្នំក្រវាញ

As the Central Cardamoms Protected Forest (CCPF) and adjacent wildlife sanctuaries slowly open up to ecotourism, Pursat is emerging as the Cardamoms' northern gateway.

ⓘ Getting There & Away

Roads and bridges in the area have been upgraded to service a new hydrodam in Ou Som, and you can now get into the park at any time of the year. Areas in and near the CCPF are still being demined, so stay on roads and well-trodden trails.

From Psar Chaa in Pursat, share taxis and pick-ups serve Kravanh (one hour), Rovieng (two hours) and Pramoay (three hours) year-round. From Pramoay, the track south to Ou Som is in rougher shape. It's passable by *moto* year-round, but taxis can handle it only in the dry season. The road south from Ou Som to Koh Kong is much better and can accommodate taxis year-round. In the dry season you can go from Pursat all the way to Koh Kong by share taxi.

You can also get to Pramoay via a dirt road (no public transport) from Samlaut in Pailin Province.

Phnom Aural Wildlife Sanctuary is best accessed from Kompong Speu, 45km west of Phnom Penh.

Central Cardamoms Protected Forest (CCPF) ព្រៃអភិរក្សនៅភាគកណ្ដាលភ្នំក្រវាញ

The CCPF's enforcement ranger teams get technical and financial support from Conservation International (CI; www.conservation.org) and operate out of three stations in the north.

Rangers and military police based at Kravanh ranger station, deep in the Cardamoms jungle in the Tang Rang area south of Pursat, play an unending game of cat and mouse with loggers, poachers and encroachers.

The most valuable contraband at the front-line Rovieng ranger station is aromatic *mreah prew* (sassafras, or safrole) oil, extracted from the roots of the endangered *Cinnamomum parthenoxylon* tree. One tonne of wood produces just 30L of the oil, which has a delightful, sandalwood-like scent. Local people use it in traditional medicine, but it can also be used to make ecstasy.

A few kilometres from Rovieng (and 53km southwest of Pursat) are the L'Bak Kamronh Rapids, which attract Khmers on holidays. About 25km west of Rovieng, in Pramoay Commune, the old-growth Chhrok Preal Forest can be visited with a guide.

To pre-arrange a guide, homestay or guesthouse near the Kravanh or Rovieng ranger stations, try contacting forestry official Peau Somanak (☑ 017 464663; smpeov@gmail.com) for advice.

Phnom Samkos Wildlife Sanctuary ដែនជម្រកសត្វព្រៃភ្នំសំកុស

Sandwiched between the CCPF and the Thai frontier, the Phnom Samkos Wildlife Sanctuary (3338 sq km) is well and truly out in the sticks. It is threatened by timber laundering, agricultural concessions and, in Ou Som, the Chinese-built Atai hydroelectric dam, which will flood 52 sq km.

Boasting Cambodia's second-highest peak, Phnom Samkos (1717m), the sanctuary's main town is Pramoay (Veal Veng), 125km west of Pursat. This remote little outpost has three guesthouses (r US$5). Local *moto* drivers can take visitors to nearby ethnic minority villages.

From Pramoay it takes a couple of hours to tackle the track south to Ou Som, where there's a CCPF ranger station and a few local guesthouses next to the Atai dam.

Phnom Aural Wildlife Sanctuary ដែនជម្រកសត្វព្រៃភ្នំឱរ៉ាល់

Sadly, Phnom Aural Wildlife Sanctuary (2538 sq km), just east of the CCPF, is rapidly being destroyed from the south and the east by corrupt land speculation and rampant illegal logging.

Hiking up **Phnom Aural** (1813m), Cambodia's highest peak, can be done in a day but most do it in two or three days, including transport to and from Phnom Penh. Guides who know the way, and where to find water, can be hired through the village chief in Sra Ken at the base of the mountain (US$25 to US$30 per day). Travel from Phnom Penh to the town of Kompong Speu (45km), where early-afternoon minibuses depart for Spean Dach (12,000r, 2½ hours), then hire a *moto* to Sra Ken (US$10, one hour). Overnight in Sra Ken, which has homestay accommodation, and head up the mountain the next morning. On day two you can sleep on the mountain or return to Sra Ken.

BATTAMBANG PROVINCE

Battambang Province (ខេត្តបាត់ដំបង; Bat Dambang), said by proud locals to produce Cambodia's finest rice, sweetest coconuts and tastiest oranges (don't bring this up in Pursat), has a long border with Thailand and a short stretch of the Tonlé Sap shoreline.

Battambang has passed from Cambodia to Thailand and back again several times over the past few centuries. Thailand ruled the area from 1794 to 1907 and again during WWII (1941 to 1946), when the Thais cut a deal with the Japanese and the Vichy French.

Battambang បាត់ដំបង

📞 053 / POP 140,000

There's something about Battambang that visitors love. Forget the fact that there's really not all that much to do in the city proper. The colonial architecture, the riverside setting, the laid-back cafes – they all make up for it. It's the perfect blend of relatively urban modernity and small-town friendliness.

Outside the city's confines, meanwhile, timeless hilltop temples and bucolic villages await. The most scenic river trip in the country links Battambang with Siem Reap.

That Cambodia's best-known circus (the magnificent Phare Ponleu Selpak) is here is no coincidence: the city has an enduring tradition of producing many of Cambodia's best-loved singers, actors and artists.

⊙ Sights

Colonial-Era Architecture   NOTABLE BUILDING
Much of Battambang's special charm lies in its early-20th-century French architecture. Some of the finest **colonial buildings** are along the waterfront (St 1), especially just south of **Psar Nath**, itself an architectural monument, albeit a modernist one. The two-storey **Governor's Residence**, with its balconies and wooden shutters, is another handsome legacy of the early 1900s. Designed by an Italian architect for the last Thai governor, who departed in 1907, it has imposing balconies and a grand reception room with 5m ceilings.

The interior is closed, but you can stroll the grounds. Phnom Penh–based **Khmer Architecture Tours** (www.ka-tours.org) has collaborated with Battambang Municipality to create two heritage walks in the historic centre of Battambang, available for free download on its website. The walks concentrate both on the French period and on the modernist architecture of the '60s. This is a great way to spend half a day exploring the city.

Battambang Museum   MUSEUM
(សារមន្ទីរបាត់ដំបង; St 1; admission US$1; ⊙8-11am & 2-5.30pm) This small museum displays fine Angkorian lintels and statuary from all over Battambang Province, including Phnom Banan and Sneng. Signs are in Khmer, English and French.

Wat Kor Village   NEIGHBOURHOOD
About 2km south of the Riverside Balcony Bar, the village of Wat Kor is centred around the **temple** of the same name. It's a great place to wander, especially late in the afternoon when the opposite (east) bank of the Sangker River is back-lit in amber tones by the sinking sun. Picturesque bridges span the river, the spires of Wat Kor glow bright platinum and Khmer village life is on full display.

About 1.5km beyond Wat Kor, you'll encounter a cluster of Khmer **heritage houses** that the village is known for. Built of now-rare hardwoods almost a century ago and surrounded by orchard gardens, they have wide verandahs and exude the ambience of another era.

Two of the approximately 20 heritage houses in the Wat Kor area are open to visitors: **Bun Roerng House** (suggested donation

US$1) and neighbouring **Khor Sang House** (suggested donation US$1). The owner of each will give you a short tour in French or broken English. They have floors worn lustrous by a century of bare feet and are decorated with old furniture, family photos and old school certificates. Khor Sang House was built in 1907 by the French-speaking owner's grandfather, who served as a secretary to the province's last Thai governor. The back section dates from 1890.

Arts Quarter   NEIGHBOURHOOD
(St 2½) The name is not official yet, but all things point to the block of St 2½ that runs south of Psar Nath becoming Battambang's first concentrated arts district. A gaggle of galleries, shops and funky bars have set up, including Lotus Bar and Make Maek, with more expected to follow. Make a point to have a stroll here and check out the latest happenings.

Lotus Bar owner Darren Swallow, who helped found the respected Sammaki Gallery a bit further south on St 2½, expects to inaugurate a 'First Friday' art market, which will see the street closed to vehicular traffic.

Wats   BUDDHIST TEMPLE
Battambang's Buddhist temples survived the Khmer Rouge period relatively unscathed thanks to a local commander who ignored orders from on high. Some of the best are **Wat Phiphétaram**, **Wat Damrey Sar** and **Wat Kandal**.

Train Station   HISTORIC SITE
Here the time is always 8.02. Just along the tracks to the south, you can explore a treasure trove of derelict **French-era repair sheds**, warehouses and rolling stock.

🏃 Activities

Green Orange Kayaks   KAYAKING
(☑017 736166; feda@online.com.kh; half-day US$12) 🚩 One- to three-person kayaks can be rented from Green Orange Kayaks, run by an **NGO** (www.fedacambodia.org) that offers free English classes. The half-day trip begins at the Green Orange Cafe in Ksach Poy, 8km south of Battambang on the road to Phnom Banan. From there you paddle back to the city along the Sangker River. A guide (US$3) is optional.

There's a new homestay in Ksach Poy – **Green Orange Village Stay Bungalows** (☑012 207957; sothsarin@gmail.com; tr per person US$5). Ask for Ngarm.

Aerobics   HEALTH & FITNESS
(1000r) Head to Battambang's East Bank to see the locals burning off the rice carbs doing aerobics, from about 6am to 7am and 5pm to 7pm daily. Just five minutes of working out should be enough to teach you some numbers in Khmer.

Victory Club   SWIMMING, FITNESS
(St 1; gym/pool US$1/2; ⊙6am-8pm) Has a 25m pool and fitness machines.

Seeing Hands Massage   MASSAGE
(☑078 337499; St 121; per hr US$6; ⊙7am-10pm) 🚩 Trained blind masseurs and masseuses offer soothing work-overs.

Volunteer English Teachers   VOLUNTEERING
Teachers are welcomed by Children's Action for Development in Pheam Ek and the **Khmer New Generation Organization** (☑092-790597; www.kngo-home.org).

👉 Tours

Soksabike   CYCLING
(☑012 542019; www.soksabike.com; depending on group size half-day US$19-$27, full day US$29-40; ⊙departures 7.30am) 🚩 Based at Kinyei cafe (p224), Soksabike is a social enterprise aiming to connect visitors with the Cambodian countryside and its people. The daily half-day trip covers about 30km. It includes a fresh coconut, seasonal fruits and a shot of rice wine.

Battambang Bike   CYCLING
(☑017 905276; www.thebattambangbike.com; St 2½; tours US$25) Leads a variety of bike tours (the late-afternoon city tour is recommended) plus free weekend 'fun rides'.

Butterfly Bicycle Tours   CYCLING
(☑089 297070; www.butterflytour.asia; depending on group size half-day US$13-17; ⊙departures 7.30am & 1.30pm) The newest bike-tour operator at the time of research, this one was started by local students. The traditional livelihoods tour draws rave reviews.

🍜 Courses

Australian Centres for Development   LANGUAGE COURSE
(☑053-677 7772; acdbtb@gmail.com; St 123) 🚩 Offers well-regarded Khmer language classes.

Smokin' Pot   COOKING COURSE
(☑012 821400; vannaksmokingpot@yahoo.com; St 1½; US$10) Always wanted to learn how to prepare authentic family-style Khmer

Battambang

Vishnu Roundabout

St 501

St 501

Sanctuary Villa (200m)

19
54
57
58

65

St 101

64 42

60

Phare Ponleu
Selpak turnoff (400m);
Sisophon (68km)

62 63

59

8

St 102

St 4

12

St 115

27

61

52

NH57

St 31/2

16

Psar
Nat 5

39

CITY
CENTRE

44

20

11

51

35

50

25

55

33

36

EAST
BANK

St 119

47

1

40

Colonial
Buildings

21

34

22

28

St 121

32

31

Colonial
Buildings

St 102

St 3

13

37

43

Battambang 6

38

14

3

St 1 ½

49

24

10

St 123

Wat
Kandal

St 125

St 2 ½

St 2

Riverside Rd

Sangker River

St 127

7

2

9

St 209

41

23

Wat
Sangker

St 1

Old NH5

56

45

17

4

15

St 139

Wat
Kampheng

46

St 149

St 153

66

Psar Leu

NH57

Yi Quoc Clinic (100m);
Green Orange Kayaks (8km);
Phnom Banan (23km)

Pailin (83km)

Wat Kor (1.5km)

dishes? Smokin' Pot offers cooking classes daily from 9.30am to 12.30pm; they start with a trip to Psar Nath and culminate in a three-course lunch.

Nary Kitchen
COOKING COURSE

(☑012 763950; US$10) Another popular cooking class in town. It includes a visit to the local market, a three-course menu and a keepsake recipe book. Courses start at 9am and 4pm, lasting about three hours, plus time to eat your creations.

Woodhouse
COOKING COURSE

(☑070 496402; St 115; US$10; ⊙courses by appt) The latest restaurant to hop on the cooking-school bandwagon, run by friendly Sakorn.

🛏 Sleeping

The best budget guesthouses are in the centre close to Psar Nath, while most of the nicer boutiques are out of the centre and require a short *remork* or *moto* ride to get to the tourist belt in the old quarter.

🛏 City Centre

★Ganesha
Family Guesthouse
GUESTHOUSE $

(☑092 135570; www.ganeshaguesthouse.com; St 1½; dm US$4, r US$10-16; ☎) This is sort of an upscale backpacker (but not quite flashpacker) place. It's worth spending the premium on the double-wide dorm beds hung with privacy-protecting linens. The en-suite private rooms have attractively tiled bathrooms and plump beds draped in featherlight mozzie nets. Downstairs is a warm and inviting cafe.

Banan Hotel
HOTEL $

(☑012 739572; www.bananhotel.doodlekit.com; NH5; r without/with breakfast from US$15/20; ❄@☎☀) A modern hi-rise hotel with Khmer-style wooden decor, immaculate rooms and extremely friendly service. The 30 rooms come with all the mod cons, plus there is a new annexe with a rooftop pool.

Tomato Guesthouse
GUESTHOUSE $

(☑012 853639; www.luxguesthouse.com; St 119; dm/d US$1.50/3; ☎) Spectacular backpacker value here. The four en-suite private rooms are generally OK – no funky smells, no layers of mold, no tattered sheets – considering the ludicrous price. One fuss is that the dorm bathroom lacks a sink – use the shower to brush your teeth. The cafe downstairs is pleasant.

NORTHWESTERN CAMBODIA BATTAMBANG

Battambang

Royal Hotel   HOTEL **$**
(☏016 912034; www.royalhotelbattambang.com;
St 115; r with fan US$6-15, with air-con US$10-20;
❊@⊛) Deservedly popular with independent travellers, the 45-room Royal doesn't
have any bells and whistles, just clean and
spacious if somewhat faded lodgings with
fridge and television.

Chhaya Hotel   HOTEL **$**
(☏053-952170; www.chhayahotel.com; 118 St 3;
dm US$1.50, r US$3-12; ❊@⊛) One of the
longest-running budget hotels in Battambang, it has some of the cheapest beds in
town – just don't expect many style points.

★**Sanctuary Villa**   BOUTIQUE HOTEL **$$**
(☏097 216 7168; www.sanctuarycambodia.com; d/
tw incl breakfast US$70/80; ❊@⊛⊠) This inti-
mate poolside boutique in a lush garden has
seven attractive villas furnished with tradi-
tional woods, tasteful silks and throw rugs.
Each bungalow has a private garden out
back and marvellous bathrooms equipped

with Jacuzzi tubs. The out-of-the-way location won't be for everybody.

From the White Horse roundabout on NH5 go 500m north and take a right.

Delux Villa HOTEL $$
(☑ 077 336373; www.deluxvilla.com; St 4; r incl breakfast US$45-55; ❀ 🛜 🖵) Whereas most Battambang poolside hotels are outside the centre, Delux Villa is just a five-minute walk away. It's worth upgrading to a balcony-equipped room around the pool. The style is more Khmer than boutique, but rooms are big and clean (if a bit dark) and the grounds nice and leafy.

Its sister **Lux Guesthouse** (☑ 092 335767; www.luxguesthouse.com; 79 St 3½; s/d from US$12/15; ❀ @ 🛜), a standard Khmer highrise with clean rooms, is around the corner.

Au Cabaret Vert BOUTIQUE HOTEL $$
(☑053-656 2000; www.aucabaretvert.com; NH57; r incl breakfast US$75; ❀🛜🖵) Contemporary meets colonial at this pretty resort on the western edge of town. Rooms are stylish and include flat-screen TV and rain shower. The swimming pool is a natural self-cleaning pond.

🛏 East Bank

⭐**Here Be Dragons** HOSTEL $
(☑ 089 264895; www.herebedragonsbattambang.com; Riverside East; dm US$2, r US$8-10; 🛜) Here bedraggled backpackers find comfy dorm beds and, if they're looking to get their drink on, like-minded souls to swap yarns with at the popular bar. The clean private rooms are a dandy deal, with bamboo shelving and beds decked out in brightly colored sheets. Quiet location next to the riverside park on the East Bank is a bonus.

⭐**La Villa** BOUTIQUE HOTEL $$
(☑053-730151; www.lavilla-battambang.net; Riverside Rd; d incl breakfast US$65-92; ❀@🛜🖵) One of the most romantic boutique hotels in Cambodia, this attractive hostelry occupies a French-era villa renovated in vintage 1930s style. It has particularly ugly and tall neighbours, but the ambience and the riverside location offset that.

Bambu Hotel HOTEL $$
(☑053-953900; www.bambuhotel.com; St 203; r incl breakfast US$70-110; ❀@🛜🖵) Bambu is in the upper category of Battambang poolside boutiques in both style and price. The spacious rooms are designed in a Franco-

Khmer style. They have gorgeous tiling, stone-inlaid bathrooms, exquisite furniture and private balconies. The fusion restaurant is one of the best in town and the bar near the pool invites lingering.

Phka Villa Hotel BOUTIQUE HOTEL $$
(☑ 053-953255; www.phkavilla.com; St 203; r incl breakfast US$55; ❀@🛜🖵) Ten tastefully decorated bungalows with four-poster beds and cosy patios sit snug up against the pool here. Pink monstrosity Lotus Hotel lurks next door – position your chaise longue pointing away from it.

Sangker Villa Hotel HOTEL $$
(☑ 097 764 0017; www.sangervilla.com; off St 203; s/d incl breakfast from US$28/38; ❀🛜🖵) Sangker Villa lacks the style of Battambang's fancier poolside boutiques, but beats them on price – especially if you're travelling solo. Both the rooms and pool are best described as 'cosy'. The poolside bar, on the other hand, is big and bold. Fondue on the menu reflects Swiss ownership.

🍴 Eating

Battambang's food scene is improving rapidly and may soon become a third bona-fide culinary mecca after Phnom Penh and Siem Reap. In addition to what's listed below, the three cooking-school restaurants serve excellent Cambodian cuisine, especially Nary's (warning: it's slow).

For street food, the best place is the **night market** (🕑4-9pm) at the northeast corner of Psar Nath, facing Canadia Bank, where barbecued chicken, fish and beef can be found alongside steaming pots of curries. The neonlit **riverside night market** (St 1; 🕑3pm-midnight), across from the Battambang Museum, is more of a sit-down affair. For cheap daytime eats try the area between the two buildings at Psar Nath.

🍴 City Centre

⭐**Lonely Tree Cafe** CAFE $
(www.thelonelytreecafe.com; St 121; mains US$2-4; 🕑10am-10pm; 🛜) 🗹 Upstairs from the shop of the same name, this uber-cosy cafe has a soaring bamboo-inlaid ceiling, brick walls and white tablecloths. It serves Khmer food and a few Spanish dishes like *huevos rotos*. Its mascot is an actual tree on the road to Siem Reap. Proceeds support cultural preservation and the disabled, among other causes.

Kinyei
CAFE **$**

(www.kinyei.org; 1 St 1½; mains US$3-4; ⏰7am-7pm; 🛜) 🍴 The home base of Soksabike, this tiny cafe hidden at the end of St 1½ offers light bites and what many believe is the best coffee in town. National barista champs have been crowned here.

Flavours of India
INDIAN **$**

(85 St 2½; mains US$3-6; ⏰11am-10pm; 🛜) The new Battambang outpost of a popular Phnom Penh Indian restaurant. The inspiration for the opening came about when some curry-craving expats ordered takeaway from the capital, 293km to the southeast. Good-value veggie thalis and the usual favourites.

Chef's Corner
CAFE **$**

(St 2½; mains 10,000-16,000r) Chicago Steve is gone but his legacy lives on in the form of fat all-day breakfasts, starting early in the morning (rare for the centre). The rest of big menu is mainly Khmer, including 'happy' soup.

Vegetarian Foods Restaurant
VEGETARIAN **$**

(St 102; mains 1500-3000r; ⏰6.30am-5pm; 🍴) This hole-in-the-wall eatery serves some of the most delicious vegetarian dishes in Cambodia, including rice soup, homemade soy milk and 1000r dumplings. Tremendous value.

Fresh Eats Café
CAMBODIAN **$**

(www.mpkhomeland.org; St 2½; mains US$2.50-4; ⏰9am-9pm Mon-Sat; 🛜) 🍴 Run by an NGO that helps children whose families have been affected by HIV/AIDS, this little place complements its Khmer specialities with build-your-own baguettes (including a Philly cheesesteak) and pasta.

Lan Chov Khorko Miteanh
NOODLES **$**

(145 St 2; mains 4000-6000r; ⏰9am-9pm) More conveniently known as Chinese Noodle by resident foreigners, the Chinese chef here does bargain dumplings and serves fresh noodles a dozen or more ways, including with pork or duck soup.

★Cafe Eden
CAFE **$$**

(www.cafeedencambodia.com; 85 St 1; mains US$4-7; ⏰7.30am-9pm, closed Tue, happy hour 3-7pm; 🛜) 🍴 Tucked away in a gorgeous colonial shophouse and hung with paintings by local artists, this American-run social enterprise offers a relaxed space for a healthy breakfast or an afternoon drink. The compact menu is half-American, half-Asian. Head upstairs for air-con.

★Jaan Bai
FUSION **$$**

(📱078 263144; jaanbaibtb@gmail.com; cnr St 1½ & St 2; tapas US$3-4; ⏰5-11pm) Battambang deserves a contemporary eating space like Jaan Bai ('rice bowl' in Khmer). The design turns heads with a bright mural outside and some beautiful French-Khmer tile-work inside. The tapas likewise are successfully bold. Good cocktails too – try the lychee martini. It doubles as an art gallery and trains and employs vulnerable youth through the Cambodia Childrens Trust (www.cambodianchildrenstrust.org).

Gecko Café
INTERNATIONAL **$$**

(St 3; mains US$5-8; ⏰9.30am-10pm; 🛜) This is Battambang's answer to the Foreign Correspondents Club in Phnom Penh thanks to the glorious upstairs setting in an old French shophouse. Mellow and atmospheric and staffed by perky waitstaff, the menu runs the gamut from Mexican to burgers to Asian fusion.

Pomme d'Amour
FRENCH **$$**

(63 St 2½; mains US$6.50-10.50; ⏰8.30am-10.30pm; 🛜) 🍴 The French-run 'Apple of Love' serves fine French cuisine at elegantly set tables. Specialities include steak tartare and shrimp flambé with rice alcohol.

🍴 East Bank

A lively restaurant scene is developing on the East Bank, especially along Old NH5.

Bamboo Train Cafe
INTERNATIONAL **$**

(Old NH5; mains 8000-16,000r; ⏰7am-10pm) The affable owner ensures this place is always popular. The eclectic menu contains pizzas, pastas, curries and a delicious tofu *amok*.

Battambang BBQ & Buffet
BARBECUE **$**

(Old NH5; mains 10,000-16,000r; ⏰4-10pm) Offering an all-inclusive tabletop barbecue and serve-yourself buffet, this place is unbelievably popular with local Khmers and domestic tourists. Exceptional value.

★La Villa
INTERNATIONAL **$$**

(📱053-730151; Riverside Rd; mains US$5-15; ⏰11am-3pm & 6-9pm; 🛜) This is Battambang's finest restaurant. It dishes up delectable Khmer, Vietnamese, French and Italian dishes, plus wines from around the world. Specialities include a tender fish fillet in lemon sauce. Sit inside under the glass atrium or bask in the colonial glow of the courtyard outside.

LE CIRQUE

Battambang's signature attraction is the internationally acclaimed circus (*cirque nouveau*) of **Phare Ponleu Selpak** (☏ 053-952424; www.phareps.org; adult/student US$10/5), a multi-arts centre for disadvantaged children. Even though they are now running shows in Siem Reap, it's worth timing your visit to Battambang to watch this amazing spectacle where it all began. Performances are at 6.15pm on Monday, Thursday and Saturday, with a Friday show added during the high season.

Phare, as it's known to locals, does a ton of stuff – contrary to popular belief it is not just a circus. It trains musicians, visual artists and performing artists as well. Many of the artists you'll bump into around town, such as Ke of Choco l'art Cafe fame, lived and studied at Phare. Guests are welcome to walk in during the day to **tour** (US$5; ⊗ 8am-11am & 2-5pm) the Phare complex and observe circus, dance, music, drawing and graphic-arts classes. This is definitely five dollars well spent.

To get here from the Vishnu Roundabout on NH5, head west for 900m and then turn right (north) and continue another 600m.

🍷 Drinking

★ **Lotus Bar & Gallery**　　　　CAFE
(St 2½; ⊗ 11am-late) In a beautifully renovated shophouse, the street-level bar here is a fine place to mingle with all sorts of characters. Upstairs is a gallery while downstairs you might get film, musical performances or a themed party on any given night. The cuisine is Mediterranean meets Texas (where the chef is from).

Choco l'art Café　　　　CAFE
(www.chocolartcafe.com; St 117; ⊗ 9am-midnight; 🛜) Run with gusto by local painter Ke and his French partner, Seline, this inviting gallery cafe sees foreigners and locals alike gather to drink and eat Seline's wonderful bread, pastries and (for breakfast) crêpes. Live music gets going occasionally.

Riverside Balcony Bar　　　　BAR
(cnr St 1 & St 149; mains US$3.50-7.50; ⊗ 4-11pm Tue-Sun) Set in a gorgeous wooden house high above the riverfront, the Australian-run Riverside is Battambang's original bar and a mellow place for a sundowner. The small menu mixes pub grub and Khmer classics.

Here Be Dragons　　　　BAR
(Riverside Rd) Before there was the popular hostel Dragons, there was the popular bar Dragons. It hasn't forgotten its roots. The bar frequently rumbles 'til late with a mix of backpackers and expats, and there's a Wednesday pub quiz.

River　　　　BAR
(St 1; ⊗ 6am-11pm) The River has an enviable position on one of the prettiest stretches of the Sangker River. Late afternoon is prime time. Come nightfall it shows football and movies on giant outdoor screens. Bonus: 99¢ beers.

🛍 Shopping

Sammaki Gallery　　　　ARTS & CRAFTS
(www.sammaki.kinyei.org; St 2½; ⊗ 9am-9pm) 🖉 Battambang's original contemporary-art gallery, showcasing the work of Battambang's diverse and eclectic artistic community. It's supported by the Cambodian Children's Trust.

Jewel in the Lotus　　　　VINTAGE
(St 2½; ⊗ 11am-10pm) A wonderful little trinkets shop selling all kinds of antiques, ephemera and kitsch, plus old photos and prints by local artists. Worth stopping by even if you're not buying.

Lonely Tree Shop　　　　TEXTILES
(St 121; ⊗ 10am-10pm) 🖉 Fine silk bags, chunky jewellery, fashionable shirts and skirts. Definitely *not* your run-of-the-mill charity gift shop.

Rachana Handicrafts　　　　TEXTILES
(⊗ 7.30am-5.30pm) 🖉 A tiny NGO-run sewing workshop on the outskirts of town that trains disadvantaged women and sells purses, stuffed toys, *kramas,* and cotton and silk accessories. It's difficult to find, so it's best to go with a local *moto* driver.

Fresh Eats Café　　　　HANDICRAFTS
(St 2½; ⊗ 9am-9pm) 🖉 Small selection of colourful bags and *kramas* made by disadvantaged children.

ⓘ Information

The rival Chhaya and Royal Hotels have long been key players in the backpacker market and can help arrange guides, transport and just about anything else. Newcomer Ganesha also does this well.

The city map that the tourist office hands out details scenic routes to the bamboo train and other attractions outside of town.

ANZ Royal Bank (St 1; ☺8.30am-4pm Mon-Fri) Full international ATM, plus usual currency services.

B2B (St 2½; ☺24hr) Fast, air-conditioned internet on Battambang's arty strip.

Canadia Bank (Psar Thom; ☺7.30am-3.30pm Mon-Fri, to 11.30am Sat) Free cash withdrawals and cash advances on plastic.

Handa Emergency Centre & Medical Clinic (☑070 810812, 012 674001; NH5; ☺clinic 9am-3.30pm, emergency 24hr) Has two ambulances and usually a Western doctor or two in residence.

Institut Français (French Institute; www.institutfrancais-cambodge.com; St 501; ☺8am-noon & 2-6pm Mon-Fri) Valiantly trying to keep French culture alive in the age of the Anglophones, the French Institute has an upstairs *médiathèque* with books and DVDs available for free browsing.

Lucky Net (St 3; per hr 2000r; ☺7am-7pm) Air-conditioned internet space with modern computers.

Tourist Information Office (☑012 534177; www.battambang-town.gov.kh; St 1; ☺8-11am & 2-5pm Mon-Fri) Moderately useful office has a great map of Battambang.

Vietnamese Consulate (☑053-6888867; St 3; ☺8-11.30am & 2-4.30pm Mon-Fri) Issues 15-day visas (US$70) in 15 minutes.

Yi Quoc Clinic (☑012 530171, 053-953163; off NH57; ☺24hr) The best clinic in town.

ⓘ Getting There & Away

Battambang is 290km northwest of Phnom Penh along NH5 and 80km northeast of Pailin along NH57 (formerly NH10).

BOAT

The riverboat to Siem Reap (US$20, 7am) squeezes through narrow waterways and passes by protected wetlands, taking from five hours in the wet season to nine or more hours in the height of the dry season. Cambodia's most memorable boat trip, it's operated on alternate days by Angkor Express and **Chann Na** (☑012 354344). In the dry season, passengers are driven to a navigable section of the river. The best seats are away from the noisy motor. It may be possible to alight at the Prek Toal Bird Sanctuary and then be picked up there the next day for US$5 extra. Be aware that these fast boats, while very scenic, are not always popular with local communities along the way, as the wake has caused small boats to capsize and fishing nets are regularly snagged. They can also be overcrowded and there are rarely enough life jackets to go around.

BUS

Like Phnom Penh, Battambang does not have a central bus station. However, most companies are clustered in the centre just south of the intersection of NH5 and St 4.

Sleeper buses are popular to Phnom Penh but keep in mind it's not a very long trip so arrival at an ungodly hour is a virtual certainty. Kampuchea Angkor Express does only night trips, including fully reclining sleepers. For quicker day travel to the capital, consider an express minivan.

Buses to Bangkok involve a change at the border – usually to a minibus on the Thai side.

If you're pinching pennies, Capitol Tour generally has the lowest prices, followed by Phnom Penh Sorya, while Rith Mony's buses are priciest (odd considering its poor safety record).

BUSES FROM BATTAMBANG

DESTINATION	DURATION	PRICE	COMPANIES	FREQUENCY
Bangkok	9hr	US$13-14	Capitol/Sorya	7.45am & noon/1pm
Kompong Cham	7½hr	US$7.50-10	Sorya, Rith Mony	both at 9.30am
Pailin	1½hr	US$3	Punleu Angkor/Rith Mony	1.30pm/3pm
Phnom Penh	6hr	regular/sleeper US$5/10	all companies	frequent
Pursat	2hr	US$2.50-3	all companies	frequent
Poipet	2¼hr	US$3.25	Capitol/Kampuchea Angkor/Sorya/Rith Mony	7.45am & noon/6.30am/1pm/noon
Siem Reap	4hr	US$4-5	most companies	frequent until 2pm

CAMBODIA'S WINE COUNTRY

Midway between Battambang and Phnom Banan, in an area best known for its production of red-hot chilli peppers (harvested from October to January), one of the world's most exclusive wines is grown on 4 hectares of vines and aged for a short time.

Prasat Phnom Banon Winery (Bot Sala Village; admission free, tasting US$2; ⊘6am–6pm) `FREE`, Cambodia's only winemaking enterprise, grows Shiraz and Cabernet Sauvignon grapes to make reds, and tropics-resistant Black Queen and Black Opal grapes to make rosés – liquids it's hard to describe without resorting to superlatives. Let's just say that both have a bouquet unlike anything you've ever encountered in a bottle with the word 'wine' on the label, and a taste as surprising as the aftertaste. Officially recognised by Cambodia's Ministry of Industry, Mines & Energy, Banon wines belong to that exclusive club of wineries whose vintages improve significantly with the addition of ice cubes. Also made here is Banon brandy, which has a heavenly bouquet and a taste that has been compared favourably to turpentine. Sampling takes place in an attractive garden pavilion, and you can visit the vineyards and production facilities.

The winery is 10km south of Battambang and 8km north of Phnom Banan.

Express minivan services to Phnom Penh are run by Golden Bayon (US$10, 4½ hours, 8.30am and 2.30pm), Mekong Express (US$12, 4½ hours, 7.30am, 11am, 3pm, 4pm and 10pm) and Rith Mony (US$8, 4½ hours, 7am, 9am, 1.30pm and 4.30pm).

Angkor Express (⍾012 601287; St 4)

Capitol Tour (⍾053-953040; St 102)

Golden Bayon Express (⍾070 968905; St 101)

Mekong Express (⍾088 576 7668; St 3)

Phnom Penh Sorya (⍾053-953904; St 4)

Ponleu Angkor Khmer (⍾053-952366; St 4)

Rith Mony (⍾011 575572; St 102)

TAXI

At the **taxi station** (NH5), share taxis to Phnom Penh (40,000r, 4½ hours) and Pursat (16,000, two hours) leave from the southeast corner, while taxis to Poipet (20,000r, 1¾ hours), Sisophon (15,000r, 1¼ hours) and Siem Reap (26,000r, three hours) leave from north of the market out on NH5.

Share taxis to Pailin (US$6, 1¼ hours) and the Psar Pruhm–Ban-Pakard border (US$7) leave from the east edge of Psar Leu. Hiring a private taxi here for US$35 to US$40 will give you the option of stopping off at Phnom Sampeau and Sneng on the way.

ⓘ Getting Around

English- and French-speaking *remork* drivers are commonplace in Battambang, and all of them are eager to whisk you around on day trips. A half-day trip out of town to a single sight like Phnom Sampeau might cost US$12, while a full day trip taking in three sights – Phnom Sampeau, Phnom Banan and the Bamboo train, for instance – costs US$16 to US$20, depending on your haggling skills. A *moto* costs about half that.

A *moto* ride in town costs around 2000r, while a *remork* ride starts from US$1.

Gecko Moto (⍾089 924260; www.geckocafe-cambodia.com; St 3; ⊘8am-7pm), Chhaya Hotel and Royal Hotel rent out motorbikes for US$7 to US$8 per day. Bicycles are a great way to get around and can be ridden along both banks of the river in either direction. They can be rented at the Royal Hotel, Soksabike, Battambang Bike and several other guesthouses for about US$2 per day.

Around Battambang

The countryside around Battambang is littered with old temples, bamboo trains (p228) and other worthwhile sights. Admission to Phnom Sampeau, Phnom Banan and Wat Ek Phnom costs US$3. If you purchase a ticket at one site, it's valid all day long at the other two. For details on sites not mentioned below, check out the guidebook *Around Battambang* (US$10) by Ray Zepp, which has details on temples, wats and excursions in the Battambang and Pailin areas. Proceeds go to monks and nuns working to raise HIV/AIDS awareness and to help AIDS orphans.

Phnom Sampeau   ភ្នំសំពៅ

At the summit of this fabled limestone outcrop, 12km southwest of Battambang along NH57 (towards Pailin), a complex of **temples** (admission US$3) affords gorgeous views. Beware of the macaques that live around the summit, dining on bananas left as offerings, as some can be bad-tempered and aggressive. Access is via a steep staircase or, past the eateries, a cement road.

ALL ABOARD THE BAMBOO TRAIN

Battambang's **bamboo train** (1hr ride for 2-plus passengers US$5, for 1 passenger US$10; ⊙ 7am-dusk; 🚃 private US$8) is one of the world's all-time classic rail journeys. From O Dambong, on the East Bank 3.7km south of Battambang's old French bridge (Wat Kor Bridge), the train bumps 7km southeast to O Sra Lav along warped, misaligned rails and vertiginous bridges left by the French.

Each bamboo train – known in Khmer as a *norry (nori)* or *lorry* – consists of a 3m-long wooden frame, covered lengthwise with slats made of ultralight bamboo, that rest on two barbell-like bogies, the aft one connected by fan belts to a 6HP gasoline engine. Pile on 10 or 15 people or up to three tonnes of rice, crank it up and you can cruise along at about 15km/h.

The genius of the system is that it offers a brilliant solution to the most ineluctable problem faced on any single-track line: what to do when two trains going in opposite directions meet. In the case of bamboo trains, the answer is simple: one car is quickly disassembled and set on the ground beside the tracks so that the other can pass. The rule is that the car with the fewest passengers has to cede priority.

As you descend from the golden stupa at the summit, which dates from 1964, turn left under the gate decorated with a bas-relief of Eiy Sei (an elderly Buddha). A **deep canyon**, its vertical sides cloaked in greenery, descends 144 steps through a natural arch to a 'lost world' of stalactites, creeping vines and bats; two Angkorian warriors stand guard.

Near the westernmost of the two antennaes at the summit, two government **artillery pieces**, one with markings in Russian, the other in German, are still deployed. Near the base of the western antennae, jockey for position with other tourists on the **sunset lookout pavilion**. Looking west you'll spy **Phnom Krapeu** (Crocodile Mountain), a one-time Khmer Rouge stronghold.

About halfway up the hill, a road leads under a gate and 250m up to the **Killing Caves of Phnom Sampeau**, now a place of pilgrimage. An enchanted staircase, flanked by greenery, leads into a cavern where a golden reclining Buddha lies peacefully next to a glass-walled memorial filled with the bones and skulls of some of the people bludgeoned to death by Khmer Rouge cadres and then thrown through the skylight above. Next to the base of the stairway is the **old memorial**, a rusty cage made of chicken wire and cyclone fencing and partly filled with human bones.

Every evening at dusk, a thick column of **bats** pours out of a massive cave high up on the north side of the cliff face. The mesmerising display lasts a good 30 minutes as millions of bats turn the skies around Phnom Sampeau black. Near the bat cave, a 30m-high **Buddha** is being carved out of the cliff face. Due to a lack of funds, only the top of the Buddha's head has been liberated from the natural rock outcrop.

The road up to the summit is too steep for *remork-motos*. English-speaking *moto* drivers can whisk you up for US$3 return, or take the stairs if you're in need of a workout.

Phnom Banan   ភ្នំបាណន់

Exactly 358 stone steps lead up shaded Phnom Banan, 23km south of Battambang, to **Prasat Banan** (admission US$2); its five towers are reminiscent of the layout of Angkor Wat. Indeed, locals claim it was the inspiration for Angkor Wat, but this seems an optimistic claim.

Udayadityavarman II, son of Suryavarman I, built Prasat Banan in the 11th century, and its hillside location offers incredible views across the surrounding countryside. There are impressive carved lintels above the doorways to each tower and bas-reliefs on the upper parts of the central tower. Many of this temple's best carvings are now in the Battambang Museum (p218).

From the temple, a narrow stone staircase leads south down the hill to three **caves**, which can be visited with a local guide.

Wat Ek Phnom   វត្តឯកភ្នំ

Atmospheric, partly collapsed 11th-century temple **Wat Ek Phnom** (admission US$2) is surrounded by the remains of a laterite wall and an ancient *baray* (reservoir). A lintel showing the **Churning of the Ocean of Milk** can be seen above the eastern portal to the central temple. This is a very popular picnic and pilgrimage destination for Khmers, especially at festival times, and for women hoping to conceive.

On the way from Battambang by bicycle or *moto,* it's possible to make a number of interesting stops. About 1.2km north of Battambang's ferry landing is a 1960s **Pepsi bottling plant**, its logo faded but otherwise virtually unchanged since production ceased abruptly in 1975. You can still see the remains of the old production line (down an alley behind the cement water tanks) and, at the far end of the warehouse out back, thousands of dusty empties bearing Pepsi's old logo.

Drive 700m further, and at the sign for the Islamic Local Development Organisation, turn left (west). After 250m you'll get to a signless house, behind which is the **Slaket crocodile farm**. It's open all day, including mealtimes: the crocs are always happy to have tourists for lunch.

Return to the main road and drive another 3.5km, past several wats, to the village of **Pheam Ek**, whose speciality is making rice paper for spring rolls. All along the road, in family workshops, you'll see rice paste being steamed and then placed on a bamboo frame for drying in the sun. The coconuts grown in this area are said to be especially sweet. Wat Ek Phnom is 5.5km further on.

The nonprofit **Children's Action for Development** (www.cadcambodia.org) in Pheam Ek, 13km from Battambang, provides free English instruction to local kids and is always looking for volunteer teachers (the Khmer staff are all volunteers too). For details contact **Racky Thy** ([phone] 092 301697; rith_gentleman@yahoo.com).

Wat Ek Phnom is 11km from Battambang's ferry landing by the shortest route and 21km if you go via the Pepsi plant and Pheam Ek. Combining both routes makes for a nice 32km circuit.

Kamping Poy   កំពីងពួយ

Also known as the Killing Dam, Kamping Poy, 27km west of Battambang (go via NH5 and follow the irrigation canal), was one of the many grandiose Khmer Rouge projects intended to re-create sophisticated irrigation networks that helped Cambodia wax mighty under the kings of Angkor. As many as 10,000 Cambodians are thought to have died during its construction, worked to death under the shadow of executions, malnutrition and disease. These days, thanks to the dam, the

Kamping Poy area is one of the few parts of Cambodia to produce two rice crops a year – although at least one crop was ruined in 2013 when severe floods breached the dam's walls.

Despite the lake's grim history, and the fact that there's little to see except the dam and its sluice gates, the area's eateries, dining platforms and row boats (10,000r for two or three hours) are a popular destination for Battambangers on weekends and holidays. It's easy to combine a visit here with a stop at Phnom Sampeau.

Sneng   ស្នឹង

This town, located on NH57 20km southwest of Battambang towards Pailin, is home to two small yet interesting temples. **Prasat Yeay Ten**, dedicated to Shiva, dates from the end of the 10th century and, although in a ruinous state, has above its doorways three delicately carved lintels that somehow survived the ravages of time and war; the eastern one depicts the Churning of the Ocean of Milk. The temple is situated on the east side of the highway, so close to the road that it resembles an ancient Angkorian tollbooth.

Behind Prasat Yeay Ten is a contemporary wat; tucked away at the back of the wat compound are three **brick sanctuaries** that have some beautifully preserved carvings around the entrances.

PAILIN PROVINCE

Pailin (ខេត្តប៉ៃលិន) is best known for its gem mines, now pretty much exhausted, a surfeit of landmines and being a refuge for Khmer Rouge pensioners.

During the civil war, the Pailin area's gem and timber resources – sold on international

---

LANDMINE ALERT!

Pailin and nearby parts of Battambang Province (especially the districts of Samlot and Rotanak Mondol) are some of the most heavily mined places in the world. Demining sites are commonplace, sometimes quite close to the highway, and numerous amputees bear sad tribute to the horror of landmines. Stay well *on* the beaten track in these parts. Public roads are OK, but farm roads are risky, and venturing into Pailin's beautiful forests on foot is definitely not a good idea.

markets with help from Thai army generals – served as the economic crutch that kept the Khmer Rouge war machine hobbling along. In the mid-1990s, it was a staging area for regular dry-season offensives that overran government positions as far east as Phnom Sampeau.

In 1996, the Khmer Rouge supremo in these parts, Ieng Sary or Brother Number Three during the Democratic Kampuchea regime, defected to the government side with 3000 heavily armed troops. His reward was amnesty and free reign in Krong Pailin, a mini-province carved out of Battambang Province to serve as a Khmer Rouge fiefdom. Only in 2007 were Ieng and his wife arrested for war crimes and crimes against humanity. He died in March 2013, well before the completion of the trial. Ieng's son, Ieng Vuth, currently serves as deputy governor of Pailin.

Pailin ប៉ៃលិន

☑ 055 / POP 24,000

The remote Wild West town of Pailin has little to recommend it except a particularly colourful hilltop temple. That said, the forested Cardamom foothills surrounding the city are beautiful, just don't wander into them or you may literally be walking into a minefield.

⊙ Sights & Activities

Wat Phnom Yat   BUDDHIST TEMPLE
(វត្តភ្នំយ៉ាត) From NH57, stairs lead through a garish gate up to Wat Phnom Yat, a psychedelic temple centred on an ancient *po* tree. A life-sized cement tableau shows naked sinners being heaved into a cauldron (for the impious), de-tongued (for liars) and forced to climb a spiny tree (for adulterers). Medieval European triptychs don't portray a hell that is nearly so scary. Nearby, the repentant pray for forgiveness, a highly pertinent message given who lives around here. The sunrises and sunsets up here are usually nice enough to take your mind off the fire and brimstone. A brand-new 27m Buddha looms over it all.

At the base of the hill, an impressive gate from 1968 leads to Wat Khaong Kang, an important centre for Buddhist teaching before the Khmer Rouge madness. The exterior wall is decorated with an especially long bas-relief of the Churning of the Ocean of Milk.

Waterfalls   WATERFALL
There are numerous wateralls dropping out of the Cardamoms south of Pailin. The problem is that they're at their most impressive during the rainy season, when the roads are often impassable. Getting to the more remote falls is risky because of the lingering presence of landmines. One that's accessible and has water year-round is Phnom Keu (Blue Mountain; motorbike/car 3000/10,000r). To get there turn right off NH57 1.5km east of Wat Phnom Yat, then proceed 5km on a rough road that gets dodgy in the rainy season. From the entrance, cross the small river on foot (they were rebuilding a collapsed bridge here when we visited) and walk about 3km to the falls along the dirt road.

⊨ Sleeping & Eating

Bamboo Guesthouse   GUESTHOUSE $
(☑012 405818; r US$12-35; ❄☎) Bamboo is an oasis of calm on the northwestern outskirts,

GETTING TO THAILAND: PAILIN TO CHANTHABURI

Getting to the border This laid-back Psar Pruhm/Ban Pakard border crossing (☉7am-8pm) is 102km southwest of Battambang and 18km northwest of Pailin via rapidly improving roads. Scams are fewer here than in other remote borders.

First get to Pailin from Battambang (see p226). In Pailin, patient travellers might get a share taxi (6000r) to the border. If nothing is going, take a *moto* (US$5), private taxi (US$10) or catch the buses coming through at about 1.30pm.

At the border You actually pay the true price (US$20) for a Cambodian visa here – rare for a remote crossing. Formalities are extremely straightfoward and quick on both sides.

Moving on On the Thai side, you can avoid being overcharged for transport to Chanthaburi (150B by minibus, one hour) by hopping on a *moto* (50B) to the nearby *sŏrngtǎaou* (pick-up truck) station. From Chanthaburi's bus station there are buses to Bangkok.

On the Cambodian side, *motos* and taxis whisk you to Pailin from a stop about 150m east of the border post, near the Victoria Casino entrance. If you cross early enough, the 7.30am public buses from the border straight to Phnom Penh via Battambang are an option. A private taxi from the border to Battambang costs US$40.

with 27 comfortable bungalows. Smarter options have a forest-lodge feel. The restaurant serves excellent Khmer and Thai food (mains US$4 to US$8) in shaded outdoor pavilions. From the market head west on NH57 for 2km, turn right, and proceed 800m.

Pailin Ruby Guesthouse   GUESTHOUSE $
(☑055-636 3603; NH57; s/d with fan from US$5/7, r with air-con from US$10; ❄) A good-value city-centre place with 48 clean, spacious rooms all kitted out with spring mattresses. It's worth paying US$2 extra for some natural light.

Memoria Palace   HOTEL $$
(☑055-636 3090; www.memoriapalace.com; r US$35-90; ❄ 🛜 ☲) Located 5km west of Pailin, this well-maintained lodge-style resort has humongous bungalows with flat-screen TVs and DVD players, and a 20m hilltop swimming pool. Even the cheapest rooms have ample space and boutique touches. The fusion restaurant (mains US$5 to US$10) is Pailin's best. To get here go straight where the highway bends sharply to the right 500m beyond the Bamboo turn-off.

Diamond Crown Hotel & Casino   HOTEL $$
(☑012 400657; www.dchotelcasino.com; r 500-1500B; ❄ @ 🛜) Located in Psar Pruhm on the Thai border, this is one of several casino-hotels set up to milk cash from Thai gamblers. Choose from cheap charmless digs in the old wing or standard casino fare (plush carpets, poly bedspreads, extra-large flat-screen TVs) in the new wing.

Piphonpenh Chet 70   CAMBODIAN $
(NH 57; mains 6000-12,000r; ⏰6am-11pm; 🛜) Well-located and popular, this restaurant has a little of everything: speedy wi-fi, breakfast staples like *bei sach chrouk* (pork and rice) and *kuy teav* (noodle soup) and even a car wash. It lacks an English menu but there are a few photos.

ℹ Information

English-speaking manager Theara of the Memoria Palace hotel is about the only useful source of information in Pailin. He can put together tours taking in gem mines, farms and waterfalls, among others. The Diamond Casino has public internet access at the border (per hour US$1.50).

Canadia Bank (NH57; ⏰8am-3.30pm Mon-Fri, to 11.30am Sat) Has an ATM offering free cash withdrawals.

M@ster Internet (NH57; per hr 2000r; ⏰7am-8pm)

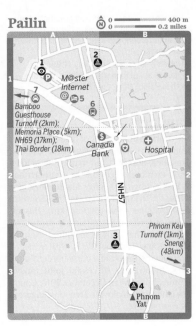

Pailin

◉ Sights

ℹ Getting There & Away

For information on getting to the Thai border at Psar Pruhm–Ban Pakard, see p230.

NH57 (sometimes still called Hwy 10) from Battambang to Pailin is now in excellent shape, making for a very straightforward journey by bus, car or motorbike.

Rith Mony (☑092-290 909) and Punleu Angkor Khmer have morning buses that originate in Psar Pruhm at the Thai border around 7.30am, pick up passengers in Pailin around 8am, and continue to Phnom Penh (38,000r, eight hours) via Battambang (15,000r, 1½ hours).

The other option to Battambang is a share taxi (20,000r, one hour) or private taxi (US$35). The taxi stand is opposite Psar Samaki on NH57.

A rough track goes from Treng District, about 25km east of Pailin, southward through the Cardamom Mountains to Koh Kong via Samlaut and Pramoay.

There's a new sealed highway, NH59, that originates about 6km west of Pailin and runs north to Poipet along the Thai border.

Samlaut សំឡូត

The northernmost tip of the Cardamom Mountains – home to elephants, gibbons, pangolins, hornbills and many other endangered creatures – covers the southern half of Pailin Province (pretty much everything south of NH57). Known as the **Samlaut Multiple Use Area** (600 sq km), this expanse of forested mountains is contiguous with two Thai parks, including Namtok Klong Kaew National Park, with which it may soon be joined in a cross-border **Peace Park**, following a successful joint ranger-training initiative in December 2010. Countless landmines make the area too dangerous for ecotrekking.

Samlaut is administered and patrolled with help from the **Maddox Jolie-Pitt Foundation** (MJP; www.mjpasia.org), named after the adopted Cambodian-born son of its founder and president, the American actress Angelina Jolie.

BANTEAY MEANCHEY PROVINCE

Sandwiched between the casinos of Poipet, Cambodia's most important border crossing with Thailand, and the glories of Angkor, agricultural Banteay Meanchey Province (ខេត្ត បន្ទាយមានជ័យ) often gets overlooked by travellers rushing to Siem Reap or Battambang. Highlights include the Angkorian temple of Banteay Chhmar and the rare birds of Ang Trapeng Thmor Reserve.

Poipet ប៉ោយប៉ែត

☑ 054 / POP 50,000

Long the armpit of Cambodia, notorious for its squalor, scams and sleaze, Poipet (poi-*peh*) has recently splurged on a facelift and no longer looks like the postapocalyptic place it once was. Thanks mainly to the patronage of neighbouring Thais, whose own country bans gambling, its casino resorts – with names like Tropicana and Grand Diamond City – are helping turn the town into the Las Vegas of Cambodia. However, beyond the border zone it's still a chaotic, trash-strewn strip mall sprinkled with dodgy massage parlours. The Khmers' gentle side is little in evidence, but don't worry, the rest of the country does not carry on like this.

The faster you get used to making quick conversions between Cambodian riel, US dollars and Thai baht, all of which are in use here, the easier: a good rule of thumb is 4000r = US$1 = 30B.

Poipet extends southeast from the border (the filthy O Chrou stream) for a few kilometres along NH5. Useful landmarks are Acleda Bank, 500m east of the border, and Canadia Bank another 500m further on.

🛏 Sleeping & Eating

Hotels in the baht-only casino zone advertise rooms for 1000B to 2000B – good value given the facilities. Cheap hotels and guesthouses, some of them brothels, are strung out along NH5 and around the bus station. However, as a general rule, unless you are an inveterate gambler, don't plan on sticking around.

The cheapest eats are around the market and along NH5 near Acleda Bank. The casino zone's night market, a block north of NH5, has clean, well-lit restaurants and pubs. The 250B all-you-can-eat Thai buffets offered by most hotels in the casino zone are a great deal.

City Poipet Hotel HOTEL $
(☑054-967576; citypoipethotel@gmail.com; d with fan/air-con from US$8/15; ❋ 🛜) By far the Poipet's nicest crash pad, it has a whiff of style, amenities like toothpaste and shampoo, plus about the only wi-fi in town. It's behind Acleda Bank.

Poipet Guesthouse GUESTHOUSE $
(☑012 565922; NH5; d US$12; ❋) Just 100m east of the border zone, the 34 functional rooms here have king-sized beds, soap, TVs and hot water.

Destiny Cafe & Spa CAFE $
(NH5; dishes US$2-3.50; ⊘7am-7pm; 🛜) 🍴 A fine place to hang out if you have some time to kill, with tasty eats, a spa and a boutique on premises. Supports an array of community projects. It's a five-minute walk beyond Canadia Bank.

LANDMINES: CAMBODIA'S UNDERGROUND WAR

Cambodia is a country scarred by years of conflict, and some of the deepest scars lie just inches beneath the surface. The legacy of landmines in Cambodia is one of the worst anywhere in the world, with an estimated four to six million dotted about the countryside. Although the conflict ended more than a decade ago, Cambodia's civil war is still claiming new victims: civilians who have stepped on a mine or been injured by unexploded ordnance (UXO), also known as explosive remnants of war (ERW).

The first massive use of mines came in the mid-1980s, when Vietnamese forces (using forced local labour) constructed a 700km-long minefield along the entire Cambodian–Thai border. After the Vietnamese withdrawal, more mines were laid by the Cambodian government to prevent towns, villages, military positions, bridges, border crossings and supply routes from being overrun, and by Khmer Rouge forces to protect areas they still held. Lots more government mines were laid in the mid-1990s in offensives against Khmer Rouge positions around Anlong Veng and Pailin.

Today, Cambodia has one of the world's worst landmine problems and the highest number of amputees per capita of any country, more than 40,000 Cambodians have lost limbs due to mines and other military explosives. Despite extensive mine-risk education (MRE) campaigns, an average of about 15 Cambodians are injured or killed every month. This is a vast improvement on the mid-1990s, when the monthly figure was more like 300, but it's still wartime carnage in a country officially at peace.

To make matters more complicated, areas that seem safe in the dry season can become dangerous in the wet season as the earth softens. It's not uncommon for Cambodian farmers to settle on land during the dry season, only to have their dreams of a new life shattered a few months later when a family member has a leg blown off.

Several groups are working furiously to clear the country of mines – one reason the mine-casualty rate has dropped (other reasons include increased awareness and improved roads). When travelling in more remote parts of the northwest you're likely to see demining teams run by the **Cambodian Mine Action Authority** (CMAA; www.cmaa. gov.kh), the **HALO Trust** (www.halotrust.org) and the **Mines Advisory Group** (MAG; www.maginternational.org) in action.

Some sage advice about mines:

➡ In remote areas, never leave well-trodden paths.

➡ Never touch anything that looks remotely like a mine or munitions.

➡ If you find yourself accidentally in a mined area, retrace your steps only if you can clearly see your footprints. If not, stay where you are and call for help – as advisory groups put it, 'better to spend a day stuck in a minefield than a lifetime as an amputee'.

➡ If someone is injured in a minefield, do *not* rush in to assist even if they are crying out for help – find someone who knows how to safely enter a mined area.

➡ Do not leave the roadside in remote areas, even for the call of nature. Your limbs are more important than your modesty.

In 1997 more than 100 countries signed a treaty banning the production, stockpiling, sale and use of landmines under any circumstances. However, the world's major producers refused to sign, including China, Russia and the USA. Cambodia was a signatory to the treaty, but mine clearance in Cambodia is, tragically, too often a step-by-step process. For the majority of Cambodians, the underground war goes on.

For more on landmines, visit the Cambodian Landmine Museum near Siem Reap.

ⓘ Information

Don't change money at the places suggested by touts, no matter how official they look. In fact, there's no need to change money at all, as baht work just fine here. The City Poipet Hotel has the only internet terminal we found.

ANZ Bank (NH5) Located a couple of hundred metres east of Canadia Bank.

Canadia Bank (NH5; ⊙8am-3.30pm Mon-Fri, to 11.30am Sat, ATM 24hr) About 1km east of the border roundabout. ATM with free withdrawals.

❶ Getting There & Away

See the boxed text below for help on crossing into Thailand. It's worth mastering the transport tricks of this scam-ridden border to save both hassle and money.

Poipet has two bus stations: the Poipet Tourist Passenger International Terminal, situated 9km east of town in the middle of nowhere, and the main bus station, which is at the main market, one block north of Canadia Bank off NH5. Unless you don't mind overpaying, avoid the international tourist terminal. Unfortunately this is easier said than done, as upon exiting immigration you'll be herded toward a 'free' tourist shuttle to this terminal, where onward buses depart to Phnom Penh (US$15, eight hours), Siem Reap (US$9, 2½ hours, 153km) and Battambang (US$10, 2½ hours, 116km). Share/private taxis to Siem Reap from the international terminal cost an inflated US$12/48.

Rather than give these scammers your business, stay solo and walk or take a *moto* (2000r) 1km along NH5 to the bus-company offices near Canadia Bank, or the main bus station nearby. You'll get bus fares here that are about half of what you pay at the international tourist terminal.

The vast majority of buses depart in the morning (before 10.30am). If you can't get a bus, just take a share taxi – these also depart from the NH5 around Canadia Bank – onward to Siem Reap (seat/whole taxi US$5/35), Battambang (seat/whole taxi US$4.25/30) or Phnom Penh (seat/whole taxi US$8/42). Don't take the taxis that hang out near the roundabout by the border – these charge tourists at least double.

The many bus companies here include Capitol Tour, Phnom Penh Sorya, Kampuchea Angkor Express and Rith Mony. Several companies offer trips to Bangkok (US$10) until about 1pm.

All roads leading out of Poipet are sealed and in fine condition.

❶ Getting Around

Moto drivers wait at the big roundabout to whisk you around the town proper – pay 2000r for a short ride.

GETTING TO THAILAND: POIPET TO ARANYA PRATHET

Getting to the border The original land **Poipet/Aranya Prathet border crossing** (⊙7am-8pm) between Cambodia and Thailand is by far the busiest and the one most people take when travelling between Bangkok and Siem Reap. It has earned itself a bad reputation over the years, with scams galore to help tourists part with their money, especially coming in from Thailand.

Frequent buses and share taxis run from Siem Reap and Battambang to Poipet. Don't get off the bus until you reach the big roundabout adjacent to the border post. Buying a ticket all the way to Bangkok (usually involving a change of buses at the border) can expedite things and save you the hassle of finding onward transport on the Thai side. The most convenient option is to take the 8am through bus to Mo Chit bus station in Bangkok run by Nattakan in Siem Reap. This costs an inflated US$28, but it's the only bus service that allows you to continue to Bangkok on the same bus you board in Siem Reap.

At the border Be prepared to wait in sweltering immigration lines on both sides – waits of two or more hours are not uncommon, especially in the high season. Show up early in the morning to avoid the crowds. You can pay a special 'VIP fee' (aka a bribe) of 200B on either side to skip the lines. There is no departure tax to leave Cambodia despite what Cambodian border officials might tell you. Entering Thailand, most nationalities are issued 15-day visa waivers free of charge.

Coming in from Thailand, under no circumstances should you deal with any 'Cambodian' immigration officials who might approach you on the Thai side – this a pure scam. Entering Cambodia you should not have to pay more than the US$20 visa fee, but again they will likely try to charge you at least 100B extra as a 'stamp' or 'overtime' fee. You should refuse to pay this, although if you do they make you wait awhile before they stamp your passport.

Moving on Minibuses wait just over the border on the Thai side to whisk you to Bangkok (300B, four hours, every 30 minutes). Or make your way 7km to Aranya Prathet by *tuk-tuk* (80B) or *sŏrngtǎaou* (15B), from where there are regular buses to Bangkok's Mo Chit station between 4am and 6pm (223B, five to six hours). Make sure your *tuk-tuk* driver takes you to the main bus station in Aranya Prathet for your 80B, not to the smaller station about 1km from the border (a common scam). The 1.55pm train is another option to Bangkok.

Sisophon

ស៊ីសុផន

♪ 054 / POP 40,000

Sisophon (also confusingly known as Svay, Svay Sisophon, Srei Sophon and Banteay Meanchey) is strategically situated at north-west Cambodia's great crossroads, the intersection of NH5 and NH6. The town is mainly a base for exploring the Angkorian temples of Banteay Chhmar. However, rather than stay in town, it's arguably more rewarding to support the community homestay project operating in the village of Banteay Chhmar.

◉ Sights & Activities

École d'Art et de Culture Khmers ARTS CENTRE

(School of Khmer Art & Culture; www.krousar-thmey.org; ⊘ 7-11am & 2-5pm Mon-Fri, 7-11am Sat) Housed in a traditional Khmer-style building, this school teaches underprivileged children traditional music, *apsara* dancing, painting, sculpture and shadow puppetry. You can observe classes but read the clearly posted ground rules first (note: no photos).

⊨ Sleeping & Eating

Golden Crown Guesthouse HOTEL $

(☑ 054-958444; r US$6-12; ❋ 🛜) One of the most central hotels in town, the rooms are pretty good value, including hot-water showers and satellite TV. Request a room with a window. It rents out motorbikes for US$10 per day and can set you up with one of the few *remorks* in town (US$30 per day).

Botoum Hotel HOTEL $

(☑ 012 687858; botoumhotel@gmail.com; r US$8-15; ❋ @ 🛜) The rooms at this middle-of-the-road place are reliably clean – if you can tolerate the pink curtains.

Red Chili CAMBODIAN $

(NH6; mains 8000-16,000r; ⊘ 6am-8.30pm) The most central and best restaurant in town. There's no menu but the English-speaking wait staff can elaborate on the offerings: *tom yam* (spicy and sour soup), fried rice/noodles, *loc lak* (peppery stir-fried beef cubes) and other Khmer faves.

❶ Information

Canadia Bank (⊘ 8am-3.30pm Mon-Fri, to 11.30am Sat) Full international ATM with free withdrawals.

Mkotmeas Internet (per hr 2000r; ⊘ 7am-8pm) Internet access facing the Golden Crown Guesthouse.

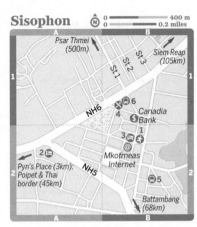

Sisophon

Psar Thmei (500m)
Siem Reap (105km)
NH6
Canadia Bank
@
Mkotmeas Internet
Pyn's Place (3km); Poipet & Thai border (45km)
NH5
Battambang (68km)

Sisophon

❹ Activities, Courses & Tours

1 École d'Art et de Culture Khmers B2

⊨ Sleeping

2 Botoum Hotel A2
3 Golden Crown Guesthouse B2

❌ Eating

4 Red Chili B1

❶ Transport

5 Bus Station B2
6 Mean Chey Express B1

❶ Getting There & Away

Sisophon is 45km east of Poipet, 105km west of Siem Reap and 68km northwest of Battambang.

Most long-haul buses call in at the bus station in the centre of town. Companies including Capitol Tour, Rith Mony and Phnom Penh Sorya each have four or five buses per day south to Battambang (7000r, 1½ hours) and Phnom Penh (US$7, eight hours). The quickest way to Phnom Penh is with comfortable minivans (US$9, 6½ hours) run by **Mean Chey Express** (☑ 054-665 1999; dara_muong@yahoo.com; NH6).

Capital Tour and Sorya have a couple of buses to Poipet. A few morning buses from Poipet come through en route to Siem Reap (two hours).

From the nearby taxi park, share taxis serve Poipet (15,000r, 40 minutes), Siem Reap (14,000r, two hours), Battambang (10,000r, 1¼ hours) and Phnom Penh (US$10, six hours); a private taxi to Siem Reap costs about US$30. Share taxis also go to Samraong via Kralanh for the O Smach border crossing (p236; 25,000r).

To get to Banteay Chhmar, see p237.

GETTING TO THAILAND: SISOPHON TO SURIN

....

Getting to the border The O Smach/Chong Chom border crossing connects Cambodia's Oddar Meanchey Province and Thailand's Surin Province, but it is very remote. Share taxis link Sisophon and Siem Reap with Samraong. From Samraong, take a *moto* (US$5) or a charter taxi (US$15) for the smooth drive to O Smach (40km, 30 minutes) and its frontier casino zone. Crossing into Thailand is a snap.

Moving on On the Thai side, walk to the nearby bus stop, where regular buses depart to Surin throughout the day (60B, 70km, 1½ hours)..

Banteay Chhmar បន្ទាយឆ្មារ

The temple complex of Banteay Chhmar was constructed by Cambodia's most prolific builder, Jayavarman VII (r 1181–1219), on the site of a 9th-century temple and is one of the most impressive remote temple complexes beyond the Angkor area. The **Global Heritage Fund** (www.globalheritagefund.org) is assisting with conservation efforts and it is now a top candidate for Unesco World Heritage Site status. The nearby village is part of a worthwhile community-based tourism (CBT) scheme to offer homestays to assist with community development. Guides for a temple tour or nature walk can be procured through the CBT office.

◎ Sights

Banteay Chhmar   BUDDHIST TEMPLE
(បន្ទាយឆ្មារ; admission US$5) Banteay Chhmar housed one of the largest and most impressive Buddhist monasteries of the Angkorian period and was originally enclosed by a 9km-long wall. Today it is one of the few temples to feature the enigmatic, Bayon-style, four-faced **Avalokiteshvaras**, with their mysterious and iconic smiles.

Banteay Chhmar is renowned for its 2000 sq metres of intricate carvings, including scenes of daily life. On the temple's east side, a huge **bas-relief** on a partly toppled wall dramatically depicts naval warfare between the Khmers (on the left) and the Chams (on the right), with the dead (some being devoured by crocodiles) at the bottom. Further south (to the left) are scenes of land warfare with infantry and elephants. There are more martial bas-reliefs along the exterior of the temple's south walls.

The once-grand entry gallery is now a jumble of fallen sandstone blocks, though elsewhere a few intersecting galleries have withstood the ravages of time, as have some almost-hidden 12th-century inscriptions. Sadly, all the *apsaras* (nymphs) have been decapitated by looters.

Unique to Banteay Chhmar was a sequence of eight **multiarmed Avalokiteshvaras** on the exterior of the southern section of the temple's western ramparts, but several of these were dismantled and trucked into Thailand in a brazen act of looting in 1998. The segments intercepted by the Thais are now on display in Phnom Penh's National Museum; the two figures that remain in situ – one with 22 arms, the other with 32 – are truly spectacular.

Banteay Top   BUDDHIST TEMPLE
(បន្ទាយទ័ព) Set among rice paddies southeast of Banteay Chhmar, Banteay Top (Fortress of the Army) may only be a small temple, but there's something special about the atmosphere here. Constructed around the same time as Banteay Chhmar, it may be a tribute to the army of Jayavarman VII, which confirmed Khmer dominance over the region by comprehensively defeating the Chams. One of the damaged towers looks decidedly precarious, like a bony finger pointing skyward. To get here from Banteay Chhmar, go south (towards Sisophon) along NH56 for 7km and then head east for 5km.

Satellite Temples   BUDDHIST TEMPLE
There are nine fascinating satellite temples in the vicinity of Banteay Chhmar, all in a ruinous state and some accessible only if you chop through the jungle. These include Prasat Mebon, Prasat Ta Prohm, Prasat Prom Muk Buon, Prasat Yeay Choun, Prasat Pranang Ta Sok and Prasat Chiem Trey.

⚡ Activities

It's possible to see silk being woven, and purchase top-quality silk products destined for the French market, at **Soieries du Mékong** (Mekong Silk Mill; www.soieriesdumekong.com; ☺7.30am-noon & 1.30-5pm Mon-Fri), 150m south of where NH56 from Sisophon meets the *baray*. It's affiliated with the French NGO **Enfants du Mékong** (www.enfantsdumekong.com).

🛏 Sleeping & Eating

⭐ **Homestay Program** HOMESTAY $

(☎ 012 237605; info@visitbanteaychhmar.org; r US$7) 🍴 Thanks to a pioneering homestay project run by the CBT office, it's possible to stay in Banteay Chhmar and three nearby hamlets. Rooms are inside private homes and come with mosquito nets, fans that run when there's electricity (6pm to 10pm) and downstairs bathrooms. Part of the income goes into a community development fund.

Banteay Chhmar Restaurant CAMBODIAN $

(mains US$1.50-4) Near the temple's eastern entrance, this rustic restaurant is the only place to dine without pre-ordering. It serves really tasty Khmer food.

ℹ Orientation

The main road through town runs west to east south of the *baray* and then takes a 90-degree turn north just after the *baray*. The market and the taxi park are at the turn; a few hundred metres north is the temple's main (eastern) entrance.

ℹ Information

Community-Based Tourism Office (CBT; ☎ 012 237605; www.visitbanteaychhmar.org) Besides arranging homestays and guides, this pioneering office also rents bicycles (US$2 per day). It's opposite and a bit south of the Banteay Chhmar main entrance.

ℹ Getting There & Away

Banteay Chhmar is 61km north of Sisophon and about 50km southwest of Samraong along NH56. This road was a mess when we visited as it was being upgraded, but should be better by the time you read this. The temple can also be visited on a long day trip from Siem Reap.

From Sisophon's Psar Thmei (1km north of NH6), most northbound share taxis go only as far as Thmor Puok, although a few continue on to Banteay Chhmar (15,000r, one hour) and Samraong. A *moto* from Sisophon to Banteay Chhmar will cost US$15 to US$20 return, a taxi US$40 to US$50.

ODDAR MEANCHEY PROVINCE

The remote, dirt-poor province of Oddar Meanchey (ខេត្តឧត្តរមានជ័យ) produces very little apart from opportunities for aid organisations. Khmer Rouge sites around Anlong Veng attract the morbidly curious, while two remote international border crossings with Thailand – Choam–Chong Sa Ngam and O Smach–Chong Chom – are becoming more popular as roads improve.

Anlong Veng   អន្លង់វែង

For almost a decade this was the ultimate Khmer Rouge stronghold, home to Pol Pot, Nuon Chea, Khieu Samphan and Ta Mok, among the most notorious leaders of Democratic Kampuchea. Anlong Veng fell to government forces in April 1998 and about the same time Pol Pot died mysteriously nearby. Soon after, Prime Minister Hun Sen ordered that NH67 be bulldozed through the jungle to ensure that the population didn't have second thoughts about ending the war.

Today Anlong Veng is a poor, dusty town with little going for it except the nearby Choam–Chong Sa Ngam border crossing, which connects with a pretty isolated part of Thailand. For those with an interest in contemporary Cambodian history, the area's Khmer Rouge sites are an important part of the picture. In this area, most of the residents, and virtually the entire political leadership and upper class, are ex-Khmer Rouge or their descendents.

The town's focal point is the Dove of Peace Roundabout at the junction of NH67 and the new highway east to Preah Vihear. The monument is a gift from Hun Sen. About 600m north of the monument, the NH67 crosses a bridge and continues to the Thai border.

⦿ Sights & Activities

To his former supporters, many of whom still live in Anlong Veng, Ta Mok (Uncle Mok, aka Brother Number Five) was harsh but fair, a benevolent builder of orphanages and schools, and a leader who kept order, in stark contrast to the anarchic atmosphere that prevailed once government forces took over. But to most Cambodians, Pol Pot's military enforcer, responsible for thousands of

NORTHWESTERN CAMBODIA ANLONG VENG

LANDMINE ALERT!

Banteay Meanchey and Oddar Meanchey are among the most heavily mined provinces in Cambodia. Do not, under any circumstances, stray from previously trodden paths. If you've got your own wheels, travel only on roads or trails regularly used by locals.

deaths in successive purges during the terrible years of Democratic Kampuchea, was best known as 'the Butcher'. Arrested in 1999, he died in July 2006 in a Phnom Penh hospital, awaiting trial for genocide and crimes against humanity.

Ta Mok's House   MUSEUM

(ផ្ទះតាម៉ុក; admission US$2) On a peaceful lakeside site is a spartan structure with a bunker in the basement, five childish wall murals downstairs (one of Angkor Wat, four of Prasat Preah Vihear) and three more murals upstairs, including an idyllic wildlife scene. About the only furnishings that weren't looted are the floor tiles.

Swampy Ta Mok's Lake was created on Brother Number Five's orders, but the water killed all the trees, their skeletons a fitting monument to the devastation he and his movement left behind. In the middle of the lake, due east from the house, is a small brick structure, an outhouse and all that remains of Pol Pot's residence in Anlong Veng.

To get to Ta Mok's house, head north from the bridge on NH67 for 600m, turn right and continue 200m past the so-called Tourism Information hut.

GETTING TO THAILAND: ANLONG VENG TO PHUSING

Getting to the border The remote **Choam/Chong Sa-Ngam border crossing** connects Anlong Veng in Oddar Meanchey Province with Thailand's Si Saket Province. A *moto* from Anlong Veng 16km to the border crossing costs US$3 or US$4 (more like US$5 in the reverse direction). This road is sealed and in good condition. The crossing is right next to the smugglers market.

At the border Formalities here are straightforward, but if you are coming in from Thailand note that they charge a premium for Cambodian visas on arrival – US$25 instead of the normal US$20. Try to talk them down to the normal rate.

Moving On Once in Thailand, it should be possible to find a *sŏrngtǎaou* (pickup truck) to Phusing and from there a bus to Khu Khan or Si Saket. Another option are the casino buses that leave hourly to/from Khu Khan (30 minutes) and Phusing.

Ta Mok's Grave   MONUMENT

From the turn-off to Ta Mok's house, driving a further 7km north takes you to Tumnup Leu village, where a signposted right turn brings you 200m to a fork. Take the left fork and proceed another 200m to Ta Mok's Angkorian-style **mausoleum**, built by a rich grandson in 2009. The cement tomb bears no name or inscription. Locals come here to light incense and, in a bizarre local tradition, hope his spirit grants them a winning lottery number.

The mausoleum is on the grounds of a modest pagoda; take a hard right (south) as you enter the grounds to find the grave.

🛏 Sleeping

Monorom Guesthouse   HOTEL $

(☏ 065-6900468; r with fan/air-con from US$6/15; ✳@⊛) An adequate hotel with big if non-descript en-suite rooms. The new wing includes VIP rooms but they are often full with visiting, well, VIPs. It's 200m north of the main roundabout. No English spoken.

Bot Uddom Guesthouse   GUESTHOUSE $

(☏ 011 500507; r with fan/air-con from US$7.50/15; ✳⊛) This establishment has 40 spacious, spotless rooms, some with massive hardwood beds. The annexe looks out on Ta Mok's Lake or swamp. It's a few hundred metres east of the dove roundabout on the road to Preah Vihear.

Sangam Resort & Casino   HOTEL $$

(☏ 087 2619886; NH67; r from 700B; ☯✳⊛) This new casino looms over the border area 16km north of Anlong Veng. You get a big room with a flat-screen TV for your baht – far from luxurious but nicer than anything else in the area. The Thai buffet is good value at 150B.

🍴 Eating

North of the roundabout are a few all-day eateries, while south of the roundabout blazing braziers barbecue chicken, fish and eggs on skewers at the lively night market.

Sheang Hai Restaurant   CHINESE $

(NH67; mains US$2-6; ⊘5am-9pm) This unsigned eatery has the best food in the town centre, not to mention about the only English menu. It's 50m north of the roundabout on the east side of NH67.

Mab Phkay Pich   CAMBODIAN $

(NH67; mains 16,000-20,000r; ⊘6am-10pm) This popular eatery serves tasty Khmer and Thai food in private pavilions and is a good place to sup on a cold Angkor Beer. Situated 500m north of town and a few buildings south of the turn-off to Ta Mok's house.

ℹ Information

Acleda Bank (◷7.30am-2pm Mon-Fri, to noon Sat) The only bank in town; has a Visa-only ATM.

Votha Internet Service (NH67; per hr 3000r; ◷7am-9pm) It doubles as the Rith Mony bus terminal.

ℹ Getting There & Around

Anlong Veng is 124km north of Siem Reap along nicely sealed NH67, and about 90km west of Sra Em, the turn-off for Prasat Preah Vihear.

The bus depots are on NH67 north of the roundabout, while share taxis gather on NH67 just southwest of the roundabout.

Share taxis to Siem Reap (20,000r, 1½ hours) and Sra Em (20,000r, two hours) are most frequent in the morning.

Rith Mony (NH67) and **Liang US Express** (☑092-905026; NH67) have a few early-morning buses buses to Phnom Penh (US$10, seven hours) and Liang adds a night service.

A *moto* circuit to the Thai border and back, via Ta Mok's house and grave, costs about US$8.

Dangrek Mountains ភ្នំដងរែក

Further north, atop the Dangkrek Mountains near the Thai border, are a number of other key Khmer Rouge sites. For years the world wondered where Pol Pot and his cronies were hiding out: the answer was right here, close enough to Thailand that they could flee across the border if government forces drew nigh.

About 2km before the frontier, where the road splits to avoid a house-sized boulder, look out for a group of **statues** – hewn entirely from the surrounding rock below by the Khmer Rouge – depicting a woman carrying bundles of bamboo sticks on her head and two uniformed Khmer Rouge soldiers (the latter were decapitated by government forces).

Just after you arrive in the bustling border village, look for a sign for the **cremation site of Pol Pot** (admission US$2) on the east side of NH67 (it's 50m south of and opposite the Sangam Casino entrance). Pol Pot's well-tended ashes lie under a rusted corrugated iron roof surrounded by rows of partly buried glass bottles. The Khmer Rouge leader was hastily burned here in 1998 on a pile of rubbish and old tyres, a fittingly inglori-

ous end, some say, given the suffering he inflicted on millions of Cambodians. Bizarre as it may sound, Pol Pot is remembered with affection by some locals, and people sometimes stop by to light incense. According to neighbours, every last bone fragment has been snatched from the ashes by visitors in search of good-luck charms. Pol Pot, like his deputy Ta Mok, is said to give out winning lottery numbers.

The **Choam–Chong Sa Ngam border crossing** is a few hundred metres north of here near a ramshackle **smugglers' market**. From behind the smugglers' market, a dirt road with potholes the size of parachutes, navigable only in the dry season by 4WD vehicles and motorbikes, heads east, parallel to the Dangrek escarpment. Domestic tourists head along this road to get to **Peuy Ta Mok** (Ta Mok's Cliff) to enjoy spectacular views of Cambodia's northern plains.

About 4km east of the smugglers' market you'll arrive at **Pol Pot's house**. Surrounded by a cinderblock wall, the jungle hideout was comprehensively looted, though you can still see a low brick building with a courtyard that hides an underground bunker.

Much more difficult to get to is **Khieu Samphan's house**, buried in the jungle on the bank of a stream about 5km east of Pol Pot's house. The Choam border crossing is a good place to find a *moto* driver who knows the snaking route to both houses.

PREAH VIHEAR PROVINCE

Bordering Thailand and Laos to the north, vast Preah Vihear Province (ខេត្តព្រះវិហារ), much of it heavily forested and extremely remote, is home to three of Cambodia's most impressive Angkorian legacies. Prasat Preah Vihear, stunningly perched on a promontory high in the Dangkrek Mountains, became Cambodia's second Unesco World Heritage Site in 2008, sparking an armed stand-off with Thailand. Further south is the mighty Preah Khan, while the 10th-century capital of Koh Ker is more accessible and lies a straightforward toll-road drive from Siem Reap, via Beng Mealea.

Preah Vihear Province, genuine 'outback' Cambodia, remains desperately poor, in part because many areas were under Khmer Rouge control until 1998, and in part because, until recently, its transport infrastructure was in a catastrophic state. The needs of the Cambodian army in its confrontation with Thailand have expedited dramatic road upgrades in the province, making travel a bit more straightforward, although public transport is still in short supply on some routes.

Preah Vihear City

☑ 064 / POP 25,000

Preah Vihear City, not to be confused with Preah Vihear Temple (Prasat Preah Vihear), is a sleepy provincial capital where dogs lounge in the middle of the streets and are only occasionally jolted awake by passing vehicles. There's very little to see or do here, but the city is a good staging point for journeys to Preah Khan and Koh Ker. For Prasat Preah Vihear, Sra Em, 27km south of the temple, makes a better base.

Preah Vihear City, which was until recently known as Tbeng Meanchey (ត្បែង មានជ័យ), may soon gain new relevance for travellers. A smooth highway running 130km east to Thala Boravit, just a short ferry hop across the Mekong to Stung Treng, has already been built; a new bridge to Stung Treng should be ready by 2015. When the bridge is up, public buses will be able to seamlessly shuttle travellers from the temples of Angkor and Preah Vihear Province to Stung Treng, Ratanakiri and Champasak Province in southern Laos.

◉ Sights

Weaves of Cambodia   SILK WEAVING
(☑092 346415; www.weavescambodia.com) 🖉
Originally established by the **Vietnam Veterans of America Foundation** (www.veteransforamerica.org), Weaves of Cambodia, known locally as Chum Ka Mo, is a silk-weaving centre that provides work and rehabilitation for landmine and polio victims, widows and orphans. Its artisans work at their hand looms from 7am to 11am and 1pm to 5pm Monday to Friday and Saturday morning, and produce silk scarves for US$30 to US$40 and sarongs for US$70 – about half of what you'll pay for its products in Phnom Penh and Siem Reap. It is now part of Vientiane-based American textile designer Carol Cassidy's silk empire.

⌂ Sleeping

Lyhout Guesthouse   HOTEL $
(☑012 737116; www.lyhoutguesthouse.blogspot.com; Koh Ker St; r US$16-20; ❋🛜) The smart

Preah Vihear City

rooms here have big wood desks, clean bathrooms with hot water, and soft white bedspreads adorned with handsome runners. Recently opened by English-speaking, switched-on Maline, the former colour master of Weaves of Cambodia.

Heng Heng Guesthouse HOTEL $

(☑ 012 900992; Mlou Prey St; r with fan/air-con from US$7/12; ❄ ☎) A bit time-worn but nonetheless a good deal. All rooms are up on the top floor, with soaring ceilings and satellite TV and a sweeping public balcony (alas, with no furniture).

Morhasambat Guesthouse GUESTHOUSE $

(☑ 012 901844; St A10; d US$5) Preah Vihear's budget lodgings are opposite the taxi station. They attract an itinerant crowd, including those in the mood for short-time love. Morhasambat is not fancy – not by a long shot – but has cheap beds on which to lay your head (and complementary H2O!).

Home Vattanak Guesthouse HOTEL $$

(☑ 064-636 3000; St A14; r US$17-35; ❄ @ ☎) It's a bit out of the way but as luxurious as it gets in Preah Vihear. The 27 well-maintained rooms include wonderful beds and such luxuries as flat-screen TVs and slick bathrooms.

✖ Eating

Food stalls can be found along the northern side of **Psar Kompong Pranak** (Koh Ker St). There are several eateries facing the taxi park and around the corner on Koh Ker St.

Phnom Tbaeng Restaurant CAMBODIAN $

(Mlou Prey St; mains US$2-3; ☺ 5am-9pm) This open-air eatery is one of the few places in town with an English menu, not to mention an English sign, an English-speaking manager and CNN. The menu includes some Western fare amid Cambodian mains like prawn soup, *tom yam,* noodle soups and steamed fish.

❶ Information

Canadia Bank (☺ 8am-3.30pm Mon-Fri, to 11.30am Sat) Fee-free ATM withdrawals and a range of banking services

Tourist office (☑ 097 997 9698, 088 885 9366; Mlou Prey St; ☺ 7.30-11am & 2-5pm Mon-Fri) With-it, English speaking Mr Thin is the man in charge here. He and temple-expert colleague Heng can guide you to Preah Khan and a few lesser-known temples in the province.

❶ Getting There & Around

Preah Vihear City is 157km north of Kompong Thom, 82km south of Sra Em, 72km east of Koh Ker and 185km northeast of Siem Reap. These roads are now all in good shape and, with the exception of parts of NH64 east of Koh Ker, surfaced.

Liang US Express (Koh Ker St), **Phnom Penh Sorya** (☑ 092 273713; Koh Ker St), Rith Mony and **Thong Ly** (bus & taxi station) have 7am buses to Phnom Penh (US$5 to US$7, seven hours) via Kompong Thom (15,000r, two hours). For Siem Reap, transfer in Kompong Thom.

Share taxis, which leave from the **bus and taxi station** (St A10), go to Kompong Thom (25,000r, 1½ hours), Siem Reap (40,000r, three hours, morning only), Sra Em (20,000r, one hour, morning only) and Choam Ksant (15,000r, one hour). Private taxis can be hired at the taxi station to Siem Reap (US$70) and Prasat Preah Vihear (one way/return US$45/70).

There is no public transport along the beautiful new road to Thala Boravit, although you might get lucky and find a morning share taxi (40,000r, two hours). Your other options are private taxi (US$70) and *moto* ($US40). Expect more public transport options once the bridge from Thala Boravit to Stung Treng is completed.

Prasat Preah Vihear ប្រាសាទព្រះវិហារ

The most dramatically situated of all the Angkorian monuments, 800m-long **Prasat Preah Vihear** (suggested donation US$2-5) is perched high atop an escarpment in the Dangkrek Mountains (elevation 625m). The views are breathtaking: lowland Cambodia, 550m below, stretches as far as the eye can see, with the holy mountain of Phnom Kulen looming in the distance.

Prasat Preah Vihear, an important place of pilgrimage during the Angkorian period, was built by a succession of seven Khmer monarchs, beginning with Yasovarman I (r 889–910) and ending with Suryavarman II (r 1112–1152), builder of Angkor Wat. Like other temple-mountains from this period, it was designed to represent Mt Meru and was dedicated to the Hindu deity Shiva, though, unlike Angkor Wat, it's laid out along a north–south processional axis. Along this axis are five cruciform *gopura* (pavilions), decorated with exquisite carvings and separated by esplanades up to 275m long.

From the parking area, walk up the hill to crumbling **Gopura V** at the north end of the temple complex. From here, the sandstone

Monumental Stairway leads down to the Thai border. Back when the temple was open from the Thai side, this stairway was how most tourists entered the temple complex. Thailand claims that this part of the temple is theirs. That Gopura V appears on both the 50,000r and 2000r banknotes is an emphatic statement that Cambodia disagrees.

East of Gopura V, you'll see a set of stairs dropping off into the abyss. This is the 1800m **Eastern Stairway.** Used for centuries by pilgrims climbing up from Cambodia's northern plains, it was recently de-mined, rebuilt as a 2242-step wooden staircase and reopened.

Prasat Preah Vihear

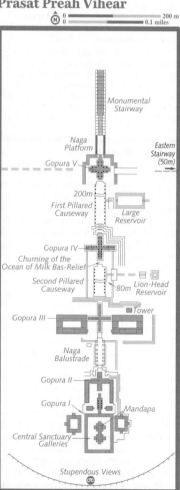

N 0 ——— 200 m
0 ——— 0.1 miles

Monumental Stairway

Naga Platform

Eastern Stairway (50m)

Gopura V

200m
First Pillared Causeway

Large Reservoir

Gopura IV
Churning of the Ocean of Milk Bas-Relief

Second Pillared Causeway

80m *Lion-Head Reservoir*

Gopura III

Tower

Naga Balustrade

Gopura II

Gopura I

Mandapa

Central Sanctuary Galleries

Stupendous Views

Walking south up the slope from Gopura V, the next pavillion you get to is **Gopura IV.** On the pediment above the southern door, look for an early rendition of the Churning of the Ocean of Milk, a theme later depicted awesomely at Angkor Wat. The galleries around **Gopura I,** with their inward-looking windows, are in a remarkably good state of repair, but the Central Sanctuary is just a pile of rubble. Nearby, the cliff affords **stupendous views** of Cambodia's northern plains and is a fantastic spot for a picnic.

The best guidebook to the architecture and carvings is *Preah Vihear,* by Vittorio Roveda. These days it may be hard to find in Cambodia, as it was published in Thailand and the text is in English and Thai.

During our most recent visit, there was still a large military presence in and around the temple. Ostensibly for security, it might make some visitors uncomfortable, and money or cigarettes are occasionally requested by soldiers. Always check the latest security situation when in Siem Reap or Phnom Penh before making the long overland journey here.

🛏 Sleeping

All accommodation in the area is in Sra Em, the bustling junction town 30km south of the temple.

Sok San Guesthouse   GUESTHOUSE $
(☑ 097 715 3839; s/d with fan US$10/11, with air-con from US$14/15; ✴ @ 🛜) In the main guesthouse cluster 1km west of Sra Em centre, Sok San has a variety of rooms and decent Thai and Cambodian food. The cheaper rooms are small and windowless, the fancier rooms have clean white bedding and spruced-up bathrooms.

Raksmey Sokon Guesthouse & Restaurant   GUESTHOUSE $
(☑ 077 516255; r with fan/air-con from US$12/16; ✴🛜) Out on the road to Anlong Veng, this place has big, clean spartan rooms that you can pile up to four people in.

★Preah Vihear Boutique Hotel   BOUTIQUE HOTEL $$$
(☑ 088 3460501; www.preahvihearhotel.com; Oknha Franna St; r from US$100; ✴🛜⊠) A slick new boutique in the unlikeliest of places, the PVBH is looking to coax higher-end temple goers from Siem Reap to stay a night or two. With lush bedding, flat-screen TVs, extravagant common areas and a shimmering 20m pool, it has a pretty good case. We'd like to see better food to justify these prices, however.

VISITING THE TEMPLE

Driving in from Sra Em, your first stop should be the **information centre** (⏲7am-5.30pm) in the village of Kor Muy. This is where you pay your donation, secure an English-speaking guide if you want one (US$15), and arrange transport via *moto* (US$5 return) or 4WD (US$25 return, maximum six passengers) up the 6.5km temple access road.

The first 5km of the access road are smooth and gradual enough, but the final 1.5km is extremely steep; nervous passengers might consider walking this last bit, especially if it's wet. Private vehicles are allowed up this road, but you'll need a motorbike or a 4WD for the steep parts at the end. Parking at the top costs 2000/5000r for a motorbike/car.

Another option is to walk up the Eastern Staircase – look for signs to the 'Ancient Staircase' on the road from Sra Em before you get to the information centre in Kor Muy.

It used to be possible to get to Prasat Preah Vihear from Thailand, where paved roads from Kantharalak led almost up to the Monumental Stairway. However, due to the long stand-off between Thailand and Cambodia, access from the Thai side has been forbidden since mid-2008. That could, of course, change so check the situation on the ground.

✕ Eating

There are simple BBQ shacks around the parking area up at the temple proper. The following are in Sra Em.

★**Limy Restaurant**   CAMBODIAN $
(mains US$3-4.50; ⏲6am-10pm) A veteran of the Siem Reap hospitality scene has moved home to open this modest eatery, where an English picture menu depicts tasty creations like fried calamari, noodle soups and curry beef with baguette. It's the last in a row of restaurants on the right just north of the roundabout (toward Prasat Preah Vihear).

Pkay Broek Restaurant   CAMBODIAN $
(mains US$2.50-6; ⏲6am-10pm) Located 3km west of the centre on the road to Anlong Veng, Pkay Prek Restaurant is famous for its grill-it-yourself *phnom pleung* (hill of fire, translated as 'Korean Fire Beef' on its menu).

❶ Getting There & Away

The roads up in this northernmost part of Cambodia have improved dramatically in recent years.

With a private car you can get to Prasat Preah Vihear in about 2½ hours from Siem Reap. The day trip usually takes in Koh Ker and/or Beng Mealea and/or Banteay Srei en route and costs US$100 to US$150.

It makes much more sense to break up the long trip with a night in Sra Em, which is 23km from Kor Muy, where the temple information office is, and 30km from the temple proper. From Sra Em's central roundabout, take a *moto* to Kor Muy (US$10 return), where another *moto* will take you up to the temple ($US5 return). There is no public transport to Kor Muy.

Sra Em is 80km from Anlong Veng and 200km from Siem Reap. From the roundabout, share taxis go to Siem Reap (US$10, 2½ hours), Phnom Penh (US$15, eight hours), Preah Vihear City (US$5, one hour) and Anlong Veng (US$5, one hour). Trips to all destinations besides Siem Reap are morning only.

Liang US Express has as morning bus from Sra Em to Phnom Penh (US10, 10 hours) via Preah Vihear City and Kompong Thom. **Rith Mony** (☑ 097 865 6018) has a morning bus to Phnom Penh (US$10, 10 hours) via Siem Reap (20,000r, 3½ hours).

Veal Krous Vulture Feeding Station

ស្ថានីយឲ្យចំណីសត្វក្ងាតនៅផែប

In order to save three critically endangered species, the white-rumped, slender-billed and red-headed vultures, the Wildlife Conservation Society (WCS) set up a 'vulture restaurant' in the village of Dongphlet, northeast of Chhep on the edge of the Preah Vihear Protected Forest. A cow carcass is put out in a field, and visitors waiting in a nearby bird hide watch as these incredibly rare vultures move in to devour the carrion.

Visits to the site are offered by Siem Reap-based Sam Veasna Centre (p246) and involve an overnight at a WCS forest camp. Access to the site is year-round now, but try to give SVC at least a week's notice to assure your spot.

Preah Khan   ប្រះខ័ន

Covering almost 5 sq km, **Preah Khan** (admission US$5) – not to be confused with a temple of the same name at Angkor – is the largest temple enclosure constructed during the Angkorian period, quite a feat when you consider the competition. Thanks to its back-of-beyond location, the site is astonishingly quiet and peaceful.

Preah Khan's history is shrouded in mystery, but it was long an important religious site, and some of the structures here date back to the 9th century. Both Suryavarman II, builder of Angkor Wat, and Jayavarman VII lived here at various times during their lives, suggesting that Preah Khan was something of a second city in the Angkorian empire. Originally dedicated to Hindu deities, it was reconsecrated to Mahayana Buddhist worship during a monumental reconstruction undertaken by Jayavarman VII in the late 12th and early 13th centuries.

At the eastern end of the 3km-long *baray* is a small pyramid temple called **Prasat Damrei** (Elephant Temple). At the summit of the hill, two of the original exquisitely carved elephants can still be seen; two others are at Phnom Penh's National Museum and Paris' Musée Guimet.

In the centre of the *baray* is **Prasat Preah Thkol** (known by locals as Mebon), an island temple similar in style to the Western Mebon at Angkor. At the western end of the *baray* stands **Prasat Preah Stung** (known to locals as Prasat Muk Buon or Temple of the Four Faces), perhaps the most memorable structure here because its central tower is adorned with four enigmatic Bayon-style faces of **Avalokiteshvara**.

It's a further 400m southwest to the walls of Preah Khan itself, which are surrounded by a moat similar to the one around Angkor Thom. Near the eastern *gopura* there's a **dharmasala** (pilgrims' rest house). Much

THE FIGHT FOR PRASAT PREAH VIHEAR

For generations, Prasat Preah Vihear (Khao Phra Wiharn to the Thais) has been a source of tension between Cambodia and Thailand. This area was ruled by Thailand for several centuries, but was returned to Cambodia during the French protectorate, under the treaty of 1907. In 1959 the Thai military seized the temple from Cambodia and then-Prime Minister Sihanouk took the dispute to the International Court of Justice in the Hague, gaining worldwide recognition of Cambodian sovereignty in a 1962 ruling.

The next time Prasat Preah Vihear made international news was in 1979, when the Thai military pushed more than 40,000 Cambodian refugees across the border in one of the worst cases of forced repatriation in UN history. The area was mined and many – perhaps several hundred – refugees died from injuries, starvation and disease before the occupying Vietnamese army could cut a safe passage and escort them on the long walk south to Kompong Thom.

Prasat Preah Vihear hit the headlines again in May 1998 because the Khmer Rouge regrouped here after the fall of Anlong Veng and staged a last stand that soon turned into a final surrender. The temple was heavily mined during these final battles and de-mining was ongoing up until the outbreak of the conflict with Thailand. Remining seems to be the greater threat right now, with both sides accusing the other of using landmines.

In July 2008, Prasat Preah Vihear was declared Cambodia's second Unesco World Heritage site. The Thai government, which claims 4.6 sq km of territory right around the temple (some Thai nationalists even claim the temple itself), initially supported the bid, but the temple soon became a pawn in Thailand's chaotic domestic politics. Within a week, Thai troops crossed into Cambodian territory, sparking an armed confrontation that has taken the lives of several dozen soldiers and some civilians on both sides. The Cambodian market at the bottom of the Monumental Stairway, which used to be home to some guesthouses, burned down during an exchange of fire in April 2009. In 2011 exchanges heated up once more and long-range shells were fired into civilian territory by both sides.

In July 2011 the International Court of Justice (ICJ) ruled that both sides should withdraw troops from the area to establish a demilitarised zone. Then in November 2013, the ICJ confirmed its 1962 ruling that the temple belongs to Cambodia, although it declined to define the official borderline, leaving sovereignty of some lands around the temple open to dispute. With a pro-Thaksin (therefore Hun Sen–friendly) government tenuously hanging on to power in Bangkok since August 2011, the border dispute has died down in recent years, but tensions can reignite any time, especially if the Yellow Shirts regain control in Thailand.

of this central area is overgrown by the forest.

As recently as the mid-1990s, the central structure was thought to be in reasonable shape, but some time in the second half of the decade looters arrived seeking buried statues under each *prang* (temple tower). Assaulted with pneumatic drills and mechanical diggers, the ancient temple never stood a chance and many of the towers simply collapsed in on themselves, leaving the depressing mess we see today. Once again, a temple that had survived so much couldn't stand the onslaught of the 20th century and its all-consuming appetite.

Among the carvings found at Preah Khan was the bust of Jayavarman now in Phnom Penh's National Museum (p35) and widely copied as a souvenir for tourists. The body of the statue was discovered in the 1990s by locals who alerted authorities, making it possible for a joyous reunion of head and body in 2000.

Most locals refer to this temple as Prasat Bakan; scholars officially refer to it as Bakan Svay Rolay, combining the local name for the temple and the district name. Khmers in Siem Reap often refer to it as Preah Khan-Kompong Svay.

Locals say there are no landmines in the vicinity of Preah Khan, but stick to marked paths just to be on the safe side.

❶ Getting There & Away

Traditionally, Preah Khan has been the toughest of Preah Vihear Province's remote temples to reach, but upgraded provincial highways and a new dirt road to the temple itself have improved things dramatically. You can now visit Preah Khan year-round, although it's still easiest in the dry season.

There's no public transport to Preah Khan, so you'll need to drive yourself or hire a *moto* or a taxi in Preah Vihear City or Kompong Thom, or in Siem Reap for an extra-long day trip (possibly combined with Sambor Prei Kuk).

To get there turn west off smooth NH62 in Svay Pak, about 64km south of Tbeng Meachey and 93km north of Kompong Thom. From here an all-season dirt road via Sangkum Thmei commune takes you to Ta Seng, about 56km from the highway and just 4km from the temple. These last 4km used to be impassable in the wet season, but are now in good shape.

Coming from Siem Reap there are other options for hard-core trail bikers. The most straight-forward route is to take NH6 to Stoeng and then head north. You can also take NH6 to Kompong

LANDMINE ALERT!

Until as recently as 1998, landmines were used by the Khmer Rouge to defend Prasat Preah Vihear against government forces. During the past decade, demining organisations made real headway in clearing the site of these enemies within. However, the advent of a border conflict with Thailand led to this area being heavily militarised once again. Both sides denied laying new landmines during the armed stand-off between Cambodia and Thailand from 2008 to 2011, but rumours persist, as several Thai and Cambodian soldiers were killed by mines in the vicinity of the temple. So do not, under any circumstances, stray from marked paths around Prasat Preah Vihear.

The rest of the province is heavily mined too, especially around Choam Ksant. Those with their own transport should travel only on roads or trails regularly used by locals.

Kdei, head north to Khvau and then ride east on a difficult stretch of NH66 (see below).

An amazing alternative is to approach from Beng Mealea along the ancient Angkor road (Cambodia's own Route 66 – NH66). You'll cross about 10 splendid Angkorian *naga* bridges, including the remarkable 77m-long **Spean Ta Ong**, 7km west of Khvau. The road from Beng Mealea to Khvau is now in fine condition. However, it deteriorates rapidly after Khvau. The 23km from Khvau to Ta Seng are impassable in the rainy season.

Only experienced bikers should attempt these alternative routes on rental motorcycles, as conditions range from difficult to extremely tough from every side and you could end up lost in the middle of nowhere.

KOMPONG THOM PROVINCE

An easy stopover when travelling overland between Phnom Penh and Siem Reap, Kompong Thom Province (ខេត្តកំពង់ធំ) is drawing more visitors thanks to several unique sites near the provincial capital, Kompong Thom, including the pre-Angkorian temples of Sambor Prei Kuk and the extraordinary hilltop shrines of Phnom Santuk. The most noteworthy geographical feature in the

NORTHWESTERN CAMBODIA PREAH KHAN

province is Stung Sen, Cambodia's second-longest river, which eventually flows into Tonlé Sap River.

Kompong Thom កំពង់ធំ

☎ 062 / POP 68,000

A bustling commercial centre, Kompong Thom is on NH6, two hours south of Siem Reap. It's a relaxed if uninspiring base from which to explore dazzling Sambor Prei Kuk. The town's focal point is the main market, Psar Kompong Thom.

◉ Sights & Activities

On the river's south bank about 500m west of the bridge, next to the old **French governor's residence**, is the most extraordinary sight: hundreds of large **bats** (in Khmer, *chreoun*), with 40cm wingspans, live in three old mahogany trees. They spend their days suspended upside down like winged fruit, fanning themselves with their wings to keep cool. Around dusk (from about 5.30pm or 6pm) they fly off in search of food.

Sambor Village Hotel offers a variety of **river cruises**, including a sunset cruise and a longer journey to the boat pagodas of Trey Leak village.

Im Sokhom Travel Agency TOUR
(☎ 012 691527; St 3) Runs guided tours, including cycling trips to Sambor Prei Kuk, and can arrange transport by *moto* to Sambor Prei Kuk (US$10) or Phnom Santuk taking in Santuk Silk Farm (US$8).

🛏 Sleeping

There are bargain-basement guesthouses on Dekchau Meas St, but some do most of their business as brothels by the hour.

TMATBOEY: ON THE TRAIL OF THE GIANT IBIS

Cambodia's remote northern plains, the largest remaining block of deciduous dipterocarp forest, seasonal wetlands and grasslands in Southeast Asia, have been described as Southeast Asia's answer to Africa's savannahs. Covering much of northwestern Preah Vihear Province, they are one of the last places on earth where you can see Cambodia's national bird, the critically endangered **giant ibis**. Other rare species that can be spotted here include the woolly-necked stork, white-rumped falcon, green peafowl, Alexandrine parakeet, grey-headed fish eagle and no less than 16 species of woodpecker, as well as owls and raptors. Birds are easiest to see from December to April.

In a last-ditch effort to ensure the survival of the giant ibis, protect the only confirmed breeding sites of the **white-shouldered ibis** and save the habitat of other globally endangered species, including the sarus crane and greater adjutant, the **Wildlife Conservation Society** (WCS; www.wcs.org) set up a pioneering community ecotourism project. Situated in the isolated village of **Tmatboey** inside the **Kulen Promtep Wildlife Sanctuary**, the initiative provides local villagers with education, income and a concrete incentive to do everything possible to protect the ibis. Visitors agree in advance to make a donation to a village conservation fund, but only if they actually *see* one or more of the birds.

Tmatboey village lies about 5km off the smooth new highway that links Preah Vihear City and Sra Em. The turn-off is 46km southeast of Sra Em and 39km northwest of Preah Vihear. The village is accessible year-round. To arrange a three-day, two-night visit (US$550 per person for a group of four, including accommodation, guides and food), contact the Siem Reap–based **Sam Veasna Center** (SVC; ☎ 063-963710; www.sam veasna.org). Visitors sleep in wooden bungalows with bathrooms and solar hot water.

For those wanting to explore the most remote corners of Cambodia, the Kulen Promtep Wildlife Sanctuary has a new birding site, about 60km from Tmatboey as the giant ibis flies, in the remote forest village of **Prey Veng**. The WCS and SVC aim to replicate the success of Tmatboey to ensure conservation of this habitat. Many of the same bird species from Tmatboey can be seen at Prey Veng, including the white-winged duck for serious enthusiasts.

A new community guesthouse in Prey Veng should be open by the time you read this. Prey Veng offers great opportunities for hiking through the open dry forest to a distant hilltop temple from the Angkor period. Trips here can include a visit to Beng Mealea and Koh Ker en route. Contact SVC for pricing details.

Kompong Thom

Arunras Hotel HOTEL $
(📞 062-961294; NH6; s/d with fan US$5/8, d with air-con US$15; ❋🖥) Dominating the accommodation scene in Kompong Thom, this seven-storey corner establishment has 58 smart, good-value rooms, as well as Kompong Thom's only lift. Operates the slightly cheaper, 53-room **Arunras Guesthouse** (📞 012 865935; NH6; s/d with fan US$6/8, with air-con US$10/13; ❋🖥) next door.

Ponleu Thmey Guesthouse HOTEL $
(📞 012 910896; NH6; s/d with fan US$3/6, d with air-con US$14-15; ❋🖥) A versatile hotel popular with NGO workers, Ponleu Thmey has tiny fan rooms for the budget-conscious along with some of the smartest midrange air-con rooms in town.

★**Sambor Village Hotel** BOUTIQUE HOTEL $$
(📞 062-961391; www.samborvillage.com; Prachea Thepatay St; r/ste US$50/85; ❋@🖥) This French-owned place brings boutique to Kompong Thom. Rooms are set in spacious bungalows and the verdant gardens include an inviting pool under the shade of a mango tree. The upstairs restaurant in the attractive main house has international cuisine and impressive hardwood flooring. Free mountain-bike use. It's located about 700m east of NH6.

✗ Eating

Prum Bayon Restaurant CAMBODIAN $
(Prachea Thepatay St; mains incl rice 6000-10,000r; ☺5am-9pm) Lacking English signs but with an English menu, this immensely popular feeding station is where locals come for flavourful Khmer cooking.

Kompong Thom

Kompong Thom

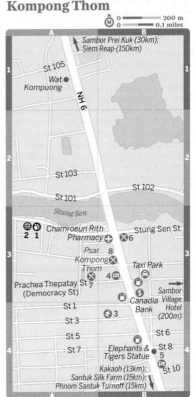

**Psar Kompong Thom
Night Market** CAMBODIAN $
(NH6; mains 2000-4000r; ☺4pm-2am) Sit on a plastic chair at a neon-lit table outside Kompong Thom's main market and dig into chicken rice soup, chicken curry noodles, Khmer-style baguettes or a *tukalok* (fruit shake).

Kompong Thom Restaurant CAMBODIAN $$
(NH6; mains US$3-5.50; ☺6.30am-9pm) The main drawcard here is the riverside setting with great views of the bridge. Easily the fanciest restaurant in town, with white tablecloths, a gorgeously designed menu and unique concoctions like water buffalo and stir-fried eel on the menu, plus a few Western offerings like pasta and burgers.

ⓘ Information

Canadia Bank (NH6; ☺8am-11.30am Mon-Fri, to 11.30am Sat) Free ATM cash withdrawals.

Chamroeun Rith Pharmacy (NH6; ☺6.30am-8pm) Internet access as well as medications.

ℹ Getting There & Around

Kompong Thom is 165km north of Phnom Penh, 147km southeast of Siem Reap and 157km south of Preah Vihear City.

Dozens of buses travelling between Phnom Penh (US$5, four hours) and Siem Reap (US$5, two hours) pass through Kompong Thom and can easily be flagged down outside the Arunras Hotel.

Share taxis are the fastest way to Phnom Penh (US$5) and Siem Reap (US$5); overcrowded local minibuses to Phnom Penh and Siem Reap save you a dollar or two. Heading north to Preah Vihear City, share taxis (US$5) depart in the morning only.

Most services depart from the taxi park, one block east of the Tela Station on NH6; Phnom Penh taxis depart from the Tela Station.

Im Sokhom Travel Agency (p247) rents bicycles (US$1 a day) and motorbikes (US$5 a day).

Around Kompong Thom

Sambor Prei Kuk   សំបូរព្រៃគុក

Cambodia's most impressive group of pre-Angkorian monuments, Sambor Prei Kuk (www.samborpreikuk.com; admission US$3) encompasses more than 100 mainly brick temples scattered through the forest, among them some of the oldest structures in the country. Originally called Isanapura, it was the capital of Upper Chenla during the reign of the early-7th-century King Isanavarman and continued to serve as an important learning centre during the Angkorian era.

The main temple area consists of three complexes, each enclosed by the remains of two concentric walls. Their basic layout – a central tower surrounded by shrines, ponds and gates – may have served as an inspiration for the architects of Angkor five centuries later. Many of the original statues are now in the National Museum (p35) in Phnom Penh.

In the early 1970s, Sambor Prei Kuk was bombed by US aircraft in support of the Lon Nol government's doomed fight against the Khmer Rouge. Some of the craters, ominously close to the temples, can still be seen. The area's last mines were cleared in 2008.

Forested and shady, Sambor Prei Kuk today has a serene and soothing atmosphere, and the sandy paths make for a pleasant stroll. It's well worth hiring a guide from the local community through Isanborei to show you around (half/full day US$6/10).

The facilities here are in line for a massive upgrade as the temple shoots for Unesco World Heritage status. At the new entrance, near the bridge about a 500m walk from the main ruins, is a giant **handicrafts market** with *kramas*, baskets and other products made by local villagers.

◉ Sights

Prasat Sambor   TEMPLE
The principle temple group, Prasat Sambor (7th and 10th centuries) is dedicated to Gambhireshvara, one of Shiva's many incarnations (the other groups are dedicated to Shiva himself). Several of Prasat Sambor's towers retain brick carvings in fairly good condition, and there is a series of large *yoni* (female fertility symbols) around the central tower.

Prasat Yeai Poeun   TEMPLE
(Prasat Yeay Peau) Prasat Yeai Poeun is arguably the most atmospheric ensemble, as it feels lost in the forest. The eastern gateway is being both held up and torn asunder by an ancient tree, the bricks interwoven with the tree's extensive, probing roots. A truly massive tree shades the western gate.

THE IRON KUY OF CAMBODIA

The Kuy are an ethnic minority found in northern Cambodia, southern Laos and northeastern Thailand. In Cambodia, the Kuy have long been renowned as smelters and smiths. It is thought that the Kuy may have produced iron – used for weaponry, tools and construction supports – since the Angkorian period.

The Kuy stopped smelting iron around 1950, but high-quality smithing continues to be practised in some communities. When travelling along NH64 between Kompong Thom and Preah Vihear City, it is possible to stop at Rumchek, about 2km south of the iron mines of Phnom Dek. Kuy smith Mr Ma Thean lives in Rumchek and can produce a traditional Kuy jungle knife in just one hour. The experience includes a chance to work the bellows and is a good way to support a dying art.

Prasat Tao   TEMPLE

(Lion Temple) The largest of the Sambor Prei Kuk complexes, Prasat Tao boasts excellent examples of Chenla carving in the form of two large, elaborately coiffed stone lions. It also has a fine rectangular pond, Srah Ne-ang Pov.

🛏 Sleeping & Eating

You'll find plenty of restaurants (mains US$2-4) that serve local fare around the new handicrafts market near the temple entrance.

Isanborei   HOMESTAY $

(☑017 936112; www.samborpreikuk.com; dm/d US$4/6) This organisation works hard to encourage visitors to Sambor Prei Kuk to stay another day. Besides running a community-based homestay program, Isanborei offers cooking courses, rents bicycles (US$2 per day) and organises ox-cart rides. It also operates a stable of *remorks* to whisk you safely to/from Kompong Thom (US$15 one way).

❶ Getting There & Away

To get here from Kompong Thom, follow NH6 north for 5km before continuing straight on NH64 towards Preah Vihear (the paved road to Siem Reap veers left). After 11km turn right at the laterite sign and continue for 14km on a brand-new sealed road to the temple entrance.

From Kompong Thom, a round-trip *moto* ride out here (under an hour) should cost US$10, a *remork* about US$20.

Phnom Santuk   ភ្នំសន្ទុក

Its forested slopes adorned with Buddha images and a series of pagodas, Phnom San-tuk (admission US$2) is the most important holy mountain (207m) in this region and a hugely popular site of Buddhist pilgrimage.

Santuk's extraordinary ensemble of wats and stupas is set high above the surrounding countryside, which means there are lots of stairs to climb – 809, in fact. You can wimp out and take the paved 2.5km road, but if you do, you'll miss the troupes of monkeys that await visitors along the stairway and the experience of winding up through the forest and emerging at a grouping of *prasat*-style wats with more *nagas* (mythical serpents) and dragons than you can possibly imagine. Just beneath the southern summit, there are a number of reclining Buddhas; several are modern incarnations cast in cement, others were carved into the living rock in centuries past. A multitiered

---

IN SEARCH OF THE BENGAL FLORICAN

The northeastern shores of Tonlé Sap lake are home to scores of bird species, including the critically endangered Bengal florican. Vaguely resembling a pheasant, the Bengal florican is one of the 'big six' critically endangered birds (along with two ibis species and three vulture species) that twitchers flock to Cambodia to see.

Straddling the borders of Siem Reap and Kompong Thom provinces, the Stung Chikreng Bengal Florican Conservation Area (BFCA) is the best place in the world to spot this rare bird. The Siem Reap–based Sam Veasna Center (p246) runs birding trips to the BFCA out of Siem Reap.

Chinese pagoda is decorated with porcelain figurines.

Phnom Santuk has an active wat and the local monks are always interested in receiving foreign tourists. Boulders located just below the summit afford panoramic views south towards Tonlé Sap.

For travellers spending the night in Kompong Thom, Phnom Santuk is a good place from which to catch a magnificent sunset over the rice fields, although this means descending in the dark – bring a torch (flashlight).

❶ Getting There & Away

The turn-off to Phnom Santuk is about 15km south of Kompong Thom. The entrance is well marked on the east side of the NH6 at about the 149km marker. From the highway it's about 2km to the base of the temple stairs. From Kompong Thom, a round trip by *moto* costs about US$8.

Kakaoh   កកោះ

The village of Kakaoh straddles the NH6 about 13km south of Kompong Thom and 2km north of the Phnom Santuk entrance. It is famous for its stonemasons, who fashion giant Buddha statues, decorative lions and other traditional Khmer figures with hand tools and a practised eye. It's fascinating to watch the figures, which range in height from 15cm to over 5m, slowly emerge from slabs of stone. Statues range wildly in price from US$20 for a statuette to US$3500 (not including excess-baggage charges) for a 2.5m-high Buddha carved from a single block of the highest-quality stone. They are often donated by wealthy Khmers to wats.

Santuk Silk Farm កសិដ្ឋានធ្វើសូត្រនៅសន្ទុក

The **Santuk Silk Farm** (☏ 012 906604; bud gibb@yahoo.com; ☺ during daylight) **FREE** is one of the few places in Cambodia where you can see the entire process of silk production, starting with the seven-week lifecycle of the silkworm, a delicate creature that feeds only on mulberry leaves and has to be protected from predators such as geckos, ants and mosquitoes. Although most of the raw silk used here comes from China and Vietnam, the local worms produce 'Khmer golden silk', so-called because of its lush golden hue.

The farm employs 18 locals, mostly women weavers. You can watch these artisans weave scarves (US$20 to US$45) and other items from 7am to 11am and 1pm to 5pm Monday to Friday and from 7am to 11am Saturday. The peaceful garden site has clean, top-quality Western toilets; complimentary coffee, tea and cold water are on offer.

The farm is run by Budd Gibbons, an American Vietnam War veteran who's lived in Cambodia since 1996, and his Cambodian wife. If possible, call ahead before your visit so they can put the scarves out. Groups of five or more can pre-order an excellent home-cooked meal.

The entrance to the farm is 200m north of the Phnom Santuk entrance, on the opposite (west) side of NH6.

Prasat Kuha Nokor ប្រាសាទគុហានគរ

This 11th-century temple, constructed during the reign of Suryavarman I, is in extremely good condition thanks to a lengthy renovation before the civil war. It is on the grounds of a modern wat and is an easy enough stop for those with their own transport. The temple is signposted from NH6 about 70km southeast of Kompong Thom and 22km north of Skuon and is 2km from the main road. From NH6, you can get a *moto* to the temple.

Eastern Cambodia

POP 6 MILLION / AREA 68,472 SQ KM

Includes ➡

Best Wildlife Experiences

➡ Gibbons in Ratanakiri (p266)

➡ Doucs in Mondulkiri (p281)

➡ Kayaking with dolphins in Stung Treng (p265)

➡ Birdwatching in Seima Protected Forest (p281)

➡ Elephant Valley Project (p280)

Best Places to Stay

➡ Tree Top Ecolodge (p269)

➡ Terres Rouges Lodge (p270)

➡ Elephant Valley Project (p280)

➡ Le Tonlé Tourism Training Centre (p263)

➡ Koh Trong Community Homestay I (p260)

Why Go?

Home to diverse landscapes and peoples, the 'Wild East' shatters the illusion that the country is all paddy fields and sugar palms. There are plenty of those in the lowland provinces, but in the northeast they yield to the mountains of Mondulkiri and Ratanakiri Provinces, where ecotourism is playing a huge role in the effort to save dwindling forests from the twin ravages of illegal logging and government-issued land concessions.

Rare forest elephants and vocal primates are found in the northeast, and endangered freshwater Irrawaddy dolphins can be seen year-round near Kratie and Stung Treng. Thundering waterfalls, crater lakes and meandering rivers characterise the landscape, and trekking, biking, kayaking and elephant experiences are all taking off. The rolling hills and lush forests also provide a home to many ethnic minority groups, known collectively as Khmer Leu (Upper Khmer) or *chunchiet* (ethnic minorities).

When to Go
Kompong Cham

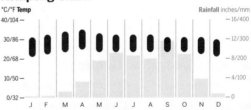

Sep–Oct Mondulkiri is particularly beautiful as blooming wildflowers colour the landscape.

Mar–Apr Low water levels, great dolphin-watching and kayaking in flooded forests of Mekong River.

May–Jun Highlands of Ratanakiri, Mondulkiri offer escape from the stifling heat of the lowlands.

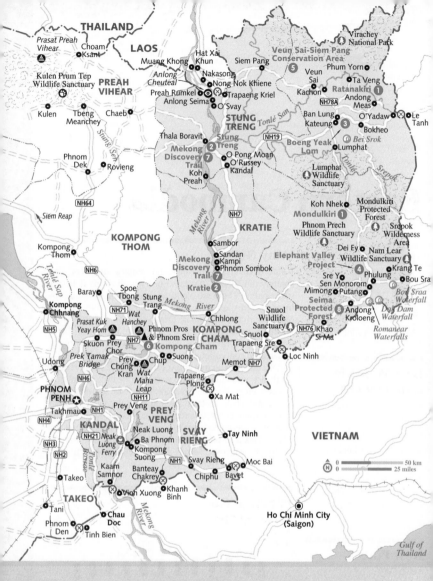

Eastern Cambodia Highlights

① Disappear for a day – or a week – in the forests of **Ratanakiri** (p266) or **Mondulkiri** (p275)

② Kayak with rare **Mekong Irrawaddy dolphins** (p258) near Kratie or Stung Treng

③ Dive into the crystal-clear waters of the crater lake of **Boeng Yeak Lom** (p267)

④ Go on an elephant safari in Mondulkiri, or observe elephants at the **Elephant Valley Project** (p280)

⑤ Observe rare **gibbons** (p266) in their element within Ratanakiri's Veun Sai-Siem Pang Conservation Area

⑥ Soak up the charms of **Kompong Cham** (p253),

gateway to temples, lush countryside and friendly locals

⑦ Experience a community-based homestay program on the **Mekong Discovery Trail** (p262)

⑧ Spot birds, black-shanked doucs and gibbons in **Seima Protected Forest** (p281)

KOMPONG CHAM PROVINCE

Kompong Cham Province (ខេត្តកំពង់ចាម) draws a growing number of visitors thanks to its role as a gateway to the northeast. Attractions include several pre-Angkorian and Angkorian temples, as well as some atmospheric riverbank rides for cyclists and motorbikers. The provincial capital offers an accessible slice of the real Cambodia, a land of picturesque villages, pretty wats and fishing communities.

Kompong Cham is the most heavily populated province in Cambodia but it sure won't feel like it. Most residents enjoy quieter lives, living off the land or fishing along the Mekong River. Rubber was the major pre-war industry here and there are huge plantations stretching eastwards from the Mekong. Some of Cambodia's finest silk is also produced in this province and many of the country's *kramas* (scarves) originate here.

Kompong Cham   កំពង់ចាម

☑ 042 / POP 70,000

More a quiet town than a bustling city, Kompong Cham is a peaceful provincial capital spread along the banks of the Mekong. It was an important trading post during the French period, the legacy of which is evident as you wander through the streets of chastened yet classic buildings.

Long considered Cambodia's third city after Phnom Penh and Battambang, Kompong Cham has lately been somewhat left in the dust by the fast-growing tourist towns of Siem Reap and Sihanoukville. However, Kompong Cham remains an important travel hub and acts as the gateway to eastern Cambodia. The big bridge south of the centre was the first to span the Mekong's width in Cambodia.

◉ Sights & Activities

There's still a fair-sized population of Cham Muslims around (hence the name 'Kompong Cham'). One Cham village is on the left (east) bank of the Mekong north of the French lighthouse. Its big, silver-domed mosque is clearly visible from the right bank. Another one is south of the bridge just beyond **Wat Day Doh**, which is worth a wander en route.

Aerobics takes place on the riverfront near the bridge at dusk if you want to get down with the locals.

Wat Nokor   BUDDHIST TEMPLE

(វត្តនគរ; admission US$2) The original fusion temple, Wat Nokor is a modern Theravada Buddhist pagoda squeezed into the walls of an 11th-century Mahayana Buddhist shrine of sandstone and laterite. It is a kitsch kind of place and many of the older building's archways have been incorporated into the new building as shrines for worship. On weekdays there are only a few monks in the complex and it's peaceful to wander among the alcoves and their hidden shrines. The entry price includes admission to Phnom Pros and Phnom Srei (p256), just outside of town.

To get here, head out of town on the NH7 to Phnom Penh, and take the left fork at the large roundabout, 2.5km west of the bridge in Kompong Cham. The temple is a couple of hundred metres down a pretty dirt road.

Koh Paen   NEIGHBOURHOOD

For a supremely relaxing bicycle ride, it's hard to beat Koh Paen (កោះប៉ែន), a rural island in the Mekong River, connected to the southern reaches of Kompong Cham town by an elaborate bamboo bridge (500r to 1000r) in the dry season or a local ferry (with/without bicycle 1500/1000r) in the wet season. The bamboo bridge is an attraction in itself, totally built by hand each year and looking like it is made of matchsticks from afar. During the dry season, several sandbars, the closest thing to a beach in this part of Cambodia, appear around the island.

Old French Lighthouse   HISTORIC BUILDING

Looming over the Mekong River opposite town is an old French lighthouse (ប៉មបារាំង ចាស់). For years it was an abandoned shell, but it's recently been renovated, including an incredibly steep metal staircase, more like a series of ladders. Don't attempt the climb if you are scared of heights. There are great views across the Mekong from the summit, especially at sunset.

🛏 Sleeping

Many visitors prefer to stay on the riverfront, with a view over the Mekong, but keep in mind that there is a lot of noise as soon as the sun comes up, including boat horns and the muezzin's call from the Cham mosque across the river.

★ Daly Hotel   HOTEL $

(☑ 042-666 6631; daly.hotel99@gmail.com; d/tw/ VIP US$18/20/40; ❋ 🛜) A newish hotel one

Kompong Cham

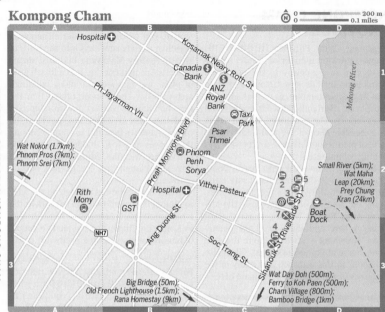

Kompong Cham

Sleeping

1	Chaplin's Guesthouse	D2
2	Daly Hotel	C2
3	Mekong Hotel	C2
4	Mekong Sunrise	C3
5	Monorom 2 VIP Hotel	D2

Eating

	Chaplin's Bar & Restaurant	(see 1)
	Destiny Coffee House	(see 7)
6	Lazy Mekong Daze	C3
7	Mekong Crossing	C2
	Smile Restaurant	(see 5)

block off the river, the Daly is easily the best of the many Khmer-style high-rise hotels in town. Rooms are huge and bright with wall-mounted flat-screen TVs, spick-and-span bathrooms, luscious linens, desks and tea tables.

Mekong Sunrise   GUESTHOUSE $
(☎011 449720; bong_tho@yahoo.com; Sihanouk St; r with fan US$5-8, with air-con US$12; ❋ ❋) A backpacker crashpad over a popular riverfront bar-restaurant, Mekong Sunrise has spacious upper-floor rooms with access to a sprawling rooftop. Furnishings are sparse, but it's cheap enough.

Monorom 2 VIP Hotel   HOTEL $
(☎092 777102; www.monoromviphotel.com; Sihanouk St; r US$15-30; ❋@❋) The smartest option on the riverfront, the rooms include heavy wood furnishings and inviting bathtubs. The lavish top-whack rooms have private balconies peering at the Mekong and large bathrooms loaded with toiletries. The US$15 rooms are windowless, however.

OBT Homestay   HOMESTAY $
(☎017 319194; p_sophal@yahoo.com; volunteer/tourist incl 2 meals US$5/10) The Organization for Basic Training accepts volunteers to teach English to local kids, but ordinary travellers looking to spend a few days going local in a Khmer village are welcome too. Tours by ox-cart, horse or boat along the Mekong are available. It's in Chiro village on the east bank of the Mekong, about 5km north of the French lighthouse.

Mekong Hotel   HOTEL $
(☎042-941536; Sihanouk St; r with fan/air-con US$8/16; ❋❋) This old timer is still popular thanks to a prime riverfront locale and its big, bright, relatively well-maintained rooms. The Shining-esque corridors here are wide enough for an ultimate Frisbee tournament.

Rana Homestay
HOMESTAY **$$**

(📞 012 686240; rana-ruralhomestay-cambodia. webs.com; per person US$25) Located in the countryside beyond Kompong Cham, this homestay offers an insight into electricity-free life in rural Cambodia. The price includes all meals and tours of the local area. There's a two-night minimum stay.

Chaplin's Guesthouse
HOTEL **$$**

(📞 078 688996; reservations@chaplinsguesthouse. com; Sihanouk St; r US$25; ❄️ 🛜) Chaplin's has six rooms with river-facing balconies above its snazzy riverfront bar-restaurant. Rooms have four-poster beds, the best bathrooms in town and flat-screen TVs.

✖️ Eating

Stalls line the waterfront, selling snacks and cold beers until late in the evening.

★ Smile Restaurant
CAMBODIAN **$**

(www.bdsa-cambodia.org; Sihanouk St; mains US$3-5; ⏰ 6.30am-9pm; 🛜) 🍴 Run by the Buddhism and Society Development Association (SDA), this handsome nonprofit restaurant is a huge hit with the NGO crowd for its big breakfasts and authentic Khmer cuisine such as *chaar k'daa* (stir-fry with lemongrass, hot basil and peanuts) and its black-pepper squid. Western and Thai dishes show up on the menu as well, and it sells BSDA-made *kramas* and trinkets.

Lazy Mekong Daze
INTERNATIONAL **$**

(Sihanouk St; mains US$3-5.50; ⏰ 7.30am-last customer; 🛜) Run by Frank, a Frenchman, this is the go-to place to assemble after dark thanks to a mellow atmosphere, a pool table and a big screen for sports and movies. The menu parades a range of Khmer, Thai and Western food, including chilli con carne, pizza baguettes and delicious Karem ice cream.

Mekong Crossing
INTERNATIONAL **$**

(Sihanouk St; mains US$2-5; ⏰ 6am-10pm; 🛜) Occupying a prime corner on the riverfront, this old favourite serves an enticing mix of Khmer curries and Western favourites, such as big burgers and tasty sandwiches.

Destiny Coffee House
CAFE **$$**

(12 Vithei Pasteur; mains US$3-5; ⏰ 7am-5.30pm Mon-Sat; ❄️ 🛜 🍴) This stylish cafe has relaxing sofas and a contemporary look. The international menu includes delicious hummus with dips, lip-smacking homemade cakes, breakfast burritos, salads and wraps.

Chaplin's Bar & Restaurant
INTERNATIONAL **$$**

(Sihanouk St; mains US$3-18; ⏰ 7am-10pm) Providing a dash of urban flair in somnolent Kompong Cham, this Scottish-owned, Charlie Chaplin–themed bistro serves excellent Cambodian food, pizzas and imported steaks in an arty space with funky lamps dangling from a towering ceiling.

ⓘ Information

Lazy Mekong Daze hands out a decent map that highlights the major sights in and around Kompong Cham.

ANZ Royal Bank (Preah Monivong Blvd; ⏰ 8.30am-4pm Mon-Fri) ATM charges US$4 for withdrawals.

Canadia Bank (Preah Monivong Blvd; ⏰ 8am-3.30pm Mon-Fri, to 11.30am Sat) Free ATM withdrawals, free cash advances on credit card.

Mekong Internet (Vithei Pasteur; per hr 1500r; ⏰ 6.30am-10pm) Among a gaggle of internet cafes on Vithei Pasteur St.

ⓘ Getting There & Away

Phnom Penh is 120km southwest. If you are heading north to Kratie or beyond, secure transport via the sealed road to Chhlong rather than taking a huge detour east to Snuol on NH7.

Phnom Penh Sorya (Preah Monivong Blvd) is the most reliable bus company operating out of Kompong Cham.

GST/Liang US Express (Preah Monivong Blvd) has morning buses to Battambang, Kratie

---

GETTING TO VIETNAM: KOMPONG CHAM TO TAY NINH

Getting to the border The Trapeang Phlong/Xa Mat border crossing (⏰ 7am-5pm) has become increasingly popular for those traveling between Northeast Cambodia and Ho Chi Minh City. From Kompong Cham take anything heading east on NH7 towards Snuol, and get off at the roundabout in Krek (Kraek), on NH7 55km east-south-east of Kompong Cham. From there, it's 13km south by *moto* (US$3) along NH72 to snoozy Trapeang Phlong, marked by a candy-striped road barrier and a few tin shacks.

At the border This border is a breeze, just have your Vietnamese visa ready.

Moving on On the Vietnamese side, motorbikes and taxis go to Tay Ninh, 45km to the south.

PHNOM PENH SORYA BUSES FROM KOMPONG CHAM

DESTINATION	PRICE	DURATION	FREQUENCY
Ban Lung	36,000r	7hr	10am
Battambang	35,000r	7hr	7.30am
Kratie via Chhlong	20,000r	2hr	9.30am
Kratie via Snuol	21,000r	4hr	10.30am, 2pm
Pakse (Laos)	US$22	12hr	10am
Phnom Penh	19,000	3hr	hourly until 3.45pm
Sen Monorom	31,000r	5hr	noon
Siem Reap	24,000r	5hr	7.30am, noon
Stung Treng via Chhlong	30,000r	5½hr	10am

and Siem Reap. **Rith Mony** (NH7) adds buses to Ban Lung (10am), Battambang and Siem Reap.

Share taxis (US$3.50) dash to Phnom Penh from the taxi park near the New Market (Psar Thmei). The trip takes two to 2½ hours. Overcrowded local minibuses also do the run (10,000r).

Morning share taxis and minibuses to Kratie (US$5, 1½ hours) depart when full from the **Caltex station** (NH7) at the main roundabout, and there are morning minibuses from the taxi park as well.

There are no longer any passenger boats running on the Mekong.

❶ Getting Around

Kompong Cham has a surplus of *moto* and *remork-moto (tuk-tuk)* drivers who speak great English and can guide you around the sites. If you sip a drink overlooking the Mekong, one of them will find you before too long. **Mr Vannat** (☑012 995890; vannat_kompongcham@yahoo.com) is the veteran of the group and has a 4WD for hire (he also speaks French), but all of these guys are pretty good. Figure on US$10/15 or less per day for a *moto/remork* (slightly more if including Wat Maha Leap in your plans). Round-trip *remork* journeys to Wat Hanchey or Phnom Pros and Phnom Srei are a negotiable US$10.

Most guesthouses and restaurants on the riverfront rent motorbikes (US$5 to US$7 per day) and bicycles (US$1 per day).

Around Kompong Cham

Consider hiring an outboard at the boat dock opposite the Mekong Hotel and heading upstream for about 30 minutes to a clutch of idyllic Mekong islands where you'll encounter smiling children and other slices of rural life. It costs about US$40. Turn it into a sunset cruise.

Phnom Pros & Phnom Srei ភ្នំប្រុសភ្នំស្រី

'Man Hill' and 'Woman Hill' are the subjects of local legends with many variations, one of which describes a child taken away at infancy only to return a powerful man who falls in love with his own mother. Disbelieving her protestations, he demanded her hand in marriage. Desperate to avoid this disaster, the mother cunningly devised a deal: a competition between her team of women and his team of men to build the highest hill by dawn. If the women won, she would not give her hand. As they toiled into the night, the women built a fire with the flames reaching high into the sky. The men, mistaking this for sunrise, lay down their tools and the impending marriage was foiled. Locals love to relay this tale, each adding their own herbs and spices as the story unfolds. Admission is US$2 and includes entry to Wat Nokor (p253).

Phnom Srei has fine views of the countryside during the wet season and a very stroke-able statue of Nandin (the sacred bull that was Shiva's mount). Phnom Pros is a good place for a cold drink, among the inquisitive monkeys that populate the trees. The area between the two hills was once a killing field. A small, gilded brick stupa on the right as you walk from Man Hill to Woman Hill houses a pile of skulls.

The hills are about 7km out of town on the road to Phnom Penh. Opposite the entrance to Phnom Pros lies **Cheung Kok** village, home to a local ecotourism initiative, run by the NGO **Amica** (www.amica-cambodge.org), aimed at introducing visitors to rural life in Kompong Cham. Villagers can teach visitors about harvesting rice, sugar palm and other crops. There is also a small shop in the village selling local handicraft products.

Wat Maha Leap វត្តមហាលាភ

Sacred Wat Maha Leap is one of the last remaining wooden pagodas left in the country. More than a century old, it was only spared devastation by the Khmer Rouge because they converted it into a hospital. Many of the Khmers who were put to work in the surrounding fields perished here; 500 bodies were thrown into graves on-site, now camouflaged by a tranquil garden.

The pagoda itself is beautiful. The wide black columns supporting the structure are complete tree trunks, resplendent in gilded patterns. The Khmer Rouge painted over the designs to match their austere philosophies, but monks later stripped it back to its original glory. Sadly, the roof collapsed in 2012; a temporary roof had been put in place at the time of our last visit.

The journey to Wat Maha Leap is best done by boat from Kompong Cham. You follow the Mekong downstream for a short distance before peeling off on a sublime tributary known as Small River, which affords awesome glimpses of rural Cambodian life. A 40HP outboard (US$50 round trip including stops in nearby weaving villages) gets there in less than an hour each way. Slower long boats once made this trip too for about US$35 but we could not find any on our last visit. Outboards can be found at the boat dock.

Small River is only navigable from about July to late December. At other times you'll have to go overland. It's pretty difficult to find on your own without some knowledge of Khmer, as there are lots of small turns along the way, so hire a *moto* (US$10 per round trip including a stop in Prey Chung Kran, one hour each way). It's 20km by river and almost twice that by road.

Prey Chung Kran ព្រែកចង្រ្កាន

Kompong Cham is famous for high-quality silk. The tiny village of Prey Chung Kran is set on the banks of the river and nearly every household has a weaving loom. Under the cool shade provided by their stilted homes, weavers work deftly to produce *kramas* that are fashionable and traditional. The most interesting thing to watch is the dyeing process, as the typical diamond and dot tessellations are formed at this stage. Prey Chung Kran is about 4km from Wat Maha Leap. There are additional weavers all along the road between Wat Maha Leap and Prey Chung Kran.

Wat Hanchey វត្តហាន់ជ័យ

Wat Hanchey is a hilltop pagoda that was an important centre of worship during the Chenla period when, as today, it offered some of the best Mekong views in Cambodia. During the time of the Chenla empire, this may have been an important transit stop on journeys between the ancient cities of Thala Boravit (near Stung Treng to the north) and Angkor Borei (near Takeo to the south), and Sambor Prei Kuk (near Kompong Thom to the west) and Banteay Prei Nokor (near Memot to the east).

Sitting in front of a large, contemporary wat is a remarkable brick sanctuary dating from the 8th century. The well-preserved inscriptions on the doorway are in ancient Sanskrit. A hole in the roof lets in a lone shaft of light. The foundations of several

KRAMA CHAMELEON

The colourful checked scarf known as the *krama* is almost universally worn by rural Khmers and is still quite popular in the cities. The scarves are made from cotton or silk and the most famous silk *kramas* come from Kompong Cham and Takeo Provinces.

Kramas have a multitude of uses. They are primarily used to protect Cambodians from the sun, the dust and the wind, and it is for this reason many tourists end up investing in one during a visit. However, they are also slung around the waist as mini-sarongs, used as towels for drying the body, knotted at the neck as decorations, tied across the shoulders as baby carriers, placed upon chairs or beds as pillow covers, used to tow broken-down motorbikes and stuffed inside motorbike tyres in the advent of remote punctures – the list is endless.

Kramas are sold in markets throughout Cambodia and are an essential purchase for travellers using pick-up trucks or taking boat services. They have become very much a symbol of Cambodia and, for many Khmers, wearing one is an affirmation of their identity.

other 8th-century structures, some of them destroyed by American bombs, are scattered around the compound, along with a clutch of bizarre fruit and animal statues.

The smooth trip out here takes about 40 minutes from Kompong Cham on a motorbike. Cycling out here through the pretty riverbank villages is a good way to pass a day.

Rubber Plantations

Kompong Cham was the heartland of the Cambodian rubber industry and rubber plantations still stretch across the province. Many of them are back in business and some of the largest plantations can be visited. Using an extended scraping instrument, workers graze the trunks until the sap appears, dripping into the open coconut shells on the ground. At **Chup Rubber Plantation**, about 15km east of Kompong Cham, you can observe harvesting in action and wander at will around the **factory** (admission US$1) where workers process the rubber.

KRATIE PROVINCE

Pretty Kratie Province (ខេត្តក្រចេះ) spans the Mekong, from which much of Kratie's population makes its living. Beyond the river, it's a remote and wild land that sees few outsiders. Many visitors are drawn to the rare freshwater Irrawaddy dolphins found in Kampi, about 15km north of the provincial capital. The town of Kratie is a little charmer and makes a good base from which to explore the surrounding countryside.

The provincial capital was one of the first towns to be 'liberated' by the Khmer Rouge (actually it was the North Vietnamese, but the Khmer Rouge later took the credit) in the summer of 1970. It was also one of the first provincial capitals to fall to the liberating Vietnamese forces in the overthrow of the Khmer Rouge on 30 December 1978.

Kratie   ក្រចេះ
♪ 072 / POP 42,000

A supremely mellow riverside town, Kratie (kra-*cheh*) has an expansive riverfront and some of the best Mekong sunsets in Cambodia. It is the most popular place in the country to see Irrawaddy dolphins, which live in the Mekong River in ever-diminishing numbers. There is a rich legacy of French-era architecture, as it was spared the wartime bombing that destroyed so many other provincial centres.

Kratie is the natural place to break the journey when travelling overland between Phnom Penh and Champasak in southern Laos.

◑ Sights & Activities

The main draw is the chance to spot the elusive Irrawaddy dolphin. Riding a bike around

---

DOLPHIN-WATCHING AROUND KRATIE

The freshwater Irrawaddy dolphin *(trey pisaut)* is an endangered species throughout Asia, with shrinking numbers inhabiting stretches of the Mekong in Cambodia and Laos, and isolated pockets in Bangladesh and Myanmar. The dark blue to grey cetaceans grow to 2.75m long and are recognisable by their bulging foreheads and small dorsal fins. They can live in fresh or salt water, although they are seldom seen in the sea. For more on this rare creature, see www.panda.org/greatermekong.

Before the civil war, locals say, Cambodia was home to as many as 1000 dolphins. However, during the Pol Pot regime, many were hunted for their oils, and their numbers continue to plummet even as drastic protection measures have been put in place, including a ban on fishing and commercial motorised boat traffic on much of the Mekong between Kratie and Stung Treng. The dolphins continue to die off at an alarming rate, and experts now estimate that there are fewer than 85 Irrawaddy dolphins left in the Mekong between Kratie and the Lao border.

The place to see them is at Kampi, about 15km north of Kratie, on the road to Sambor. A *moto/remork* should be around US$7/10 return depending on how long the driver has to wait. Motorboats shuttle visitors out to the middle of the river to view the dolphins at close quarters. It costs US$9 per person for one to two persons and US$7 per person for groups of three to four. Encourage the boat driver to use the engine as little as possible once near the dolphins, as the noise is sure to disturb them. It is also possible to see them near the Lao border in Stung Treng Province.

nearby Koh Trong (p260) or along either bank of the Mekong River is always enjoyable.

Wat Roka Kandal
BUDDHIST TEMPLE

(វត្តរកាកណ្តាល; admission 2000r) About 2km south of Kratie on the road to Chhlong is this beautiful little temple dating from the 19th century, one of the oldest in the region. To see the beautifully restored interior, ask around for someone with the key. Even if you can't get in, the shaded grounds, adjacent to some lovely traditional wooden houses, are worth a wander.

Sorya Kayaking Adventures
KAYAKING

(☑090 241148; www.soryakayaking.com; Rue Preah Suramarit) Run by a socially conscious American woman, Sorya has a fleet of eight kayaks and runs half-day trips and multiday trips (with homestay accommodation) on the Mekong north of Kratie or on the Te River to the south. This is a great way to get close to the dolphins. Other highlights include a small flooded forest north of Kampi, Vietnamese floating villages, and a sunset trip around Koh Trong. There's a small cafe on premises and it sells handicrafts woven by disadvantaged widows.

🚶 Tours

CRD Tours
TOUR

(☑099 834353; www.crdtours.org; Tonlé Traning Centre, St 3; ⊙8am-noon & 2-5.30pm) 🏍 Run by the Cambodian Rural Development Team (CRDT), this company focuses on sustainable tours along the Mekong Discovery Trail. Homestays, volunteer opportunities and various excursions are available on the Mekong island of Koh Pdao, 20km north of Kampi. The typical price is US$40 to US$60 per day, including all meals and tours. Tours and homestays on Koh Preah (near Stung Treng) and Koh Trong are also possible. CRDT can also organise boat trips from Stung Treng to Kratie sleeping in remote river villages along the way (US$130 to US$300 depending on amount of people). Bike tours from Kratie to Koh Pdao are another option.

Cambodian Pride Tours
TOUR

(☑088 836 4758; www.cambodianpridetours.com) Local tours website operated by two enthusiastic young guides from the Kratie area keen to promote real life experiences.

🛏 Sleeping

For something even more relaxed than Kratie, consider staying directly on the island

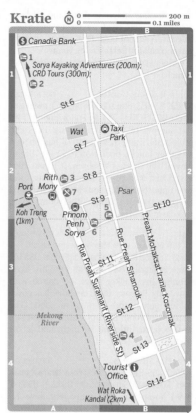

Kratie Ⓝ

🛏 Sleeping
1 Balcony Guesthouse	A1
2 Le Bungalow	A1
3 Santepheap Hotel	A2
4 Silver Dolphin Guesthouse	B4
5 Star Backpackers	B2
6 U-Hong II Guesthouse	A3

✪ Eating
7 Red Sun Falling	A2
Tokae Restaurant	(see 5)

of Koh Trong (p260), where homestays and two midrange guesthouses await.

Silver Dolphin Guesthouse
HOSTEL $

(☑012 999810; silver.dolphinbooking@yahoo.com; 48 Rue Preah Suramarit; dm/s/tr US$2/4/12, d US$6-14; ▣🎧) Kratie's newest hostel is a superb deal. Even the cheapest doubles have a TV, bathroom and some furniture, and the dorm is plenty big, with a soaring ceiling.

There are fine spaces to drink and eat both downstairs and upstairs on the riverfront balcony. A school next door means an early wakeup call for north-facing rooms.

Owner Pech speaks great English and French.

Tonlé Training Center
GUESTHOUSE $

(☑ 099 834353; http://letonle.org; St 3; r with fan/air-con US$15/30; ✹ 🅰) 🖉 Following on from the success of its long-running Le Tonlé project in Stung Treng, CRDT has opened a slightly fancier operation in Kratie. Brand new at the time of research, it boasts four rustic but attractive rooms in a beautiful wood house and delicious food prepared by at-risk program trainees. The rooms share two clean bathrooms.

Balcony Guesthouse
GUESTHOUSE $

(☑ 016 604036; www.balconyguesthouse.net; Rue Preah Suramarit; s/d without bathroom US$3/6, r with bathroom US$7-20; ✹ @ 🅰) This long-running backpacker place, partnered with Ban Lung Balcony in Ratanakiri, has good-value rooms and impressive food. The shared bathroom has hot water. Doubles up as a popular little bar by night and is gay friendly.

Star Backpackers
GUESTHOUSE $

(☑ 097 455 3106; starbackpackerskratie@gmail.com; Rue Preah Sihanouk; dm US$2, d US$5-6; ✹ 🅰) Young Spanish managers have revived this once-faded backpacker stalwart, installing a rooftop bar and hammock lounge, slapping colourful paint and murals on the walls, and installing a roomy 10-bed dorm room. It's above the Tokae Restaurant.

Santepheap Hotel
HOTEL $

(☑ 072 210210; santepheaphotel@yahoo.com; Rue Preah Suramarit; r with fan US$7, with air-con US$15-20; ✹ 🅰) The elder statesman of hotels in Kratie, this expansive riverfront place has large fan rooms at the back with TV and bathroom. Air-con rooms come in various shapes and sizes and are clean and well appointed, including desks.

U-Hong II Guesthouse
GUESTHOUSE $

(☑ 085 885168; 119 St 10; r US$5-13; ✹ @ 🅰) A lively little shoes-off guesthouse with a buzzing little bar-restaurant between the market and the riverfront. The six rooms are pretty basic but there are 11 more in a nearby annex.

Le Bungalow
BOUTIQUE HOTEL $$

(☑ 012 660902; www.rajabori-kratie.com; Rue Preah Suramarit; incl breakfast s/d without bathroom US$25/31, r with bathroom US$65; ✹ @ 🅰) Akin to a boutique homestay, here you'll find three rooms in a traditional wooden house decorated with Sino-Khmer furnishings from the colonial period. Two rooms are spacious with modern bathrooms, while the third is more suited to children travelling with their parents and has an outside bathroom. If you don't appreciate the traditional style it will seem overpriced.

KOH TRONG, AN ISLAND IN THE MEKONG

Lying just across the water from Kratie is the island of Koh Trong, an almighty 6km-long sandbar in the middle of the river. Cross here by boat and enjoy a slice of rural island life. Attractions include an **old stupa** and a small **floating village**, as well as the chance to encounter one of the rare **Mekong mud turtles** who inhabit the western shore.

There are two homestays on the island. Best is **Koh Trong Community Homestay I** (per person US$4), set in an old wooden house, offering two proper bedrooms and fancy-pants bathrooms, meaning thrones not squats. It is located about 2km north of the ferry dock near Rajabori Villas. Ride your bike, take a *moto* (US$1) or ride an ox-cart.

Rajabori Villas (☑ 012 770150; www.rajabori-kratie.com; r incl breakfast US$52-95; ✹) is a boutique lodge with a swimming pool and attractive bungalows that provide the best accommodation in the Kratie region. It's located at the northern tip of the island; a private boat from Kratie costs US$4/5 day/night.

Practically next door is the slightly more rustic **Arun Mekong** (www.arunmekong.wordpress.com; r US$22-27, bungalow US$33), with a nice mix of tastefully furnished rooms and bungalows. Electricity runs only from 6pm to 11pm here.

Catch the little ferry from the port (with/without bicycle 2000r/1000r) in Kratie. Bicycle rental is available on the island near the ferry landing for US$1, or do the loop around the island on a *moto* (US$2.50) steered by a female *motodup* (driver) – a rarity for Cambodia.

✖ Eating

When in Kratie keep an eye out for two famous specialities, sold on the riverfront and elsewhere: *krolan* (sticky rice, beans and coconut milk steamed inside a bamboo tube) and *nehm* (tangy, raw, spiced river fish wrapped in banana leaves). The south end of the *psar* (market) turns into a carnival of barbecue stands hawking meat-on-a-stick by night. Among aforementioned guesthouses, Balcony Guesthouse and more upscale Le Bungalow have noteworthy restaurants.

Red Sun Falling INTERNATIONAL **$**
(Rue Preah Suramarit; mains 7000-14,000r; ⊙7am-9pm; 🛜) One of the liveliest spots in town, with a relaxed cafe ambience, supreme riverfront location, used books for sale and a good selection of Asian and Western meals.

Tokae Restaurant CAMBODIAN **$**
(St 10; mains US$2-3; ⊙6am-11pm; 🛜) Although French-run, the focus at this lively restaurant underneath Star Guesthouse is very much on cheap Cambodian food like curries and *amok* (a baked fish dish), plus equally affordable Western breakfasts.

ℹ Information

All of the recommended guesthouses are pretty switched on to travellers' needs. You Hong II (per hour US$1) and Silver Dolphin (per hour 3000r) guesthouses have public internet access.
Canadia Bank (Rue Preah Suramarit) ATM offering free cash withdrawals, plus currency exchange.

ℹ Getting There & Away

Kratie is 250km northeast of Phnom Penh via the Chhlong road and 141km south of Stung Treng.
  Phnom Penh Sorya (☑ 081 908005) operates three buses per day to Phnom Penh (US$8, eight hours) along the slow route (via Snuol); Sorya's bus from Laos comes through at roughly 3.30pm and goes to Phnom Penh via the much-shorter Chhlong route (six hours). Sorya buses to Siem Reap involve a change in Suong.
  Going the other way, Sorya's bus from Phnom Penh to Pakse, Laos (US$20, eight hours) via Stung Treng collects passengers in Kratie at about 11.30am. Sorya also has a 1pm bus to Ban Lung (US$8, five hours), and a 3pm bus to Stung Treng (US$5, three hours). Rith Mony also has a bus to Ban Lung (11.30am).
  Express vans, which pick you up from your guesthouse, are a faster way to Phnom Penh (US$7, 4½ hours, about six per day), and usually offer transfers onward to Sihanoukville. There's an express van to Siem Reap as well (US$13, six

> ### GETTING TO VIETNAM: KRATIE TO BINH LONG
>
> **Getting to the border** The **Trapeang Sre/Loc Ninh border crossing** (⊙7am-5pm) is useful for those trying to get straight to Vietnam from Kratie or points north. First get to the much-maligned junction town of Snuol by bus, share taxi or minibus from Sen Monorom, Kratie or Kompong Cham. In Snuol catch a *moto* (US$5) for the 18km trip southeastward along the smooth NH74.
>
> **At the border** As always you'll need a prearranged visa to enter Vietnam, and US$20 for a visa-on-arrival to enter Cambodia.
>
> **Moving on** On the Vietnamese side, the nearest town is Binh Long, 40km to the south. Motorbikes wait at the border.

hours, 7.30am). Share taxis (US$10) head to Phnom Penh between 6am and 8am, with possible additional departures after lunch.
  For Sen Monorom, take a local minibus (30,000r, four hours, two or three early morning departures) from the taxi park or backtrack to Soung. Local minibuses also serve Ban Lung, with most departures between 11am and 2pm.

ℹ Getting Around

Most guesthouses can arrange bicycle (from US$1) and motorbike hire (from US$5). An English-speaking *motodup* will set you back US$10 to US$15 per day, a *remork* about US$25.

Around Kratie

Phnom Sombok ភ្នំ សំបុក

Phnom Sombok is a small hill with an active wat, located on the road from Kratie to Kampi. The hill offers the best views across the Mekong on this stretch of the river and a visit here can easily be combined with a trip to see the dolphins for an extra couple of dollars.

Sambor សំបូរ

Sambor was the site of a thriving pre-Angkorian city during the time of Sambor Prei Kuk and the Chenla empire. Not a stone remains in the modern town of Sambor, which

THE MEKONG DISCOVERY TRAIL

It's well worth spending a couple of days exploring the various bike rides and activities on offer along the **Mekong Discovery Trail** (www.mekongdiscoverytrail.com), an initiative to open up stretches of the Mekong River around Stung Treng and Kratie to community-based tourism. Once managed by the government with foreign development assistance, the project is now being kept alive by private tour companies – mainly Xplore-Asia in Stung Treng and CRD Tours in Kratie. It deserves support, as it intends to provide fishing communities an alternative income in order to protect the Irrawaddy dolphin and other rare species on this stretch of river.

There's a great booklet with routes and maps outlining excursions around Kratie and Stung Treng, but you'll be hard-pressed to secure your own copy. Ask tour operators if you can photograph theirs. The routes can be tackled by bicycle or motorbike. They range in length from a few hours to several days, with optional overnights in village homestays. Routes criss-cross the Mekong frequently by ferry and traverse several Mekong islands, including Koh Trong.

is locally famous for having the largest wat in Cambodia, complete with 108 columns. Known locally as **Wat Sorsor Moi Roi** (100 Columns Temple), it was constructed on the site of a 19th-century wooden temple, a few pillars of which are still located at the back of the compound.

Within the temple grounds is the **Mekong Turtle Conservation Centre** (☑012 712071; www.mekongturtle.com; adult/child US$4/2; ◷8.30am-4.30pm). Established by **Conservation International** (www.conservation.org), it is home to several species of turtle, including the rare Cantor's giant softshell, which was only rediscovered along this stretch of the Mekong in 2007. One of the largest freshwater turtles, it can grow to nearly 2m in length. Hatchlings are nurtured here for 10 months before being released in the wild. Tourists can participate in the release on select weeks, usually in September and May/ June. Check the website for the exact dates.

To get to Sambor, follow the Kampi road north to Sandan, before veering left along a reasonable 10km stretch of road – it's about 35km in total.

Chhlong   ឆ្លង

Chhlong is a somnolent riverside town 31km south of Kratie. The main attraction is the **old governor's residence**, a gorgeous, yellow-and-white French-colonial mansion near the river. Once a top-end boutique hotel, it is now shuttered up and falling into disrepair. Architecture buffs might also drop in at the **house of a hundred pillars** (1884), about 500m north of Le Relais. According to the owner, the Khmer Rouge removed many of the pillars and today only 56 remain. A few more decrepit French-colonial buildings line the river.

Chhlong is worth a wander if you are driving through with your own transport, but is probably not worth a special trip from Kratie. Keen cyclists might like to follow the old river road between Kratie and Chhlong, as it passes through some traditional Cham minority villages along the way.

STUNG TRENG PROVINCE

For a long while, poor Stung Treng Province (ខេត្តស្ទឹងត្រែង) was the neglected middle child, sandwiched between the luminary siblings of Ratanakiri Province and Kratie Province, not to mention the languid charms of Champasak in southern Laos. But a new bridge over the Mekong in Stung Treng town may soon change that. The bridge, scheduled for completion in 2015, will feed into the new highway running west to Preah Vihear City, cutting about four hours off the journey from Champasak to Siem Reap – a key route on the Southeast Asia backpacker trail.

Loaded with largely untapped tourist potential, Stung Treng could benefit hugely from the increased traffic. The main attractions are up near the Lao border, where you can kayak out to a pod of Irrawaddy dolphins then continue downstream along a heavenly stretch of the Mekong known as the flooded forest. Further north, thundering rapids cascade over the border from Laos – a spectacular sight. Further east, hard-core travellers can access Virachey National Park from remote Siem Pang.

Stung Treng ស្ទឹងត្រែង

074 / POP 34,000

Located on the Tonlé San near its confluence with the Mekong, Stung Treng is a dusty city with not much to offer, but this may change when the new bridge is completed. Some locals call the Tonlé San the 'Tonlé Kong', as it merges with the Tonlé Kong (well known as the Sekong in Laos) 10km east of town. Just north of the town centre, a major bridge across the San leads north to the Lao border.

◉ Sights & Activities

Dolphin-watching and **kayaking** trips near the Lao border can be done as day trips out of Stung Treng. Get the blood pumping with sunset **aerobics** sessions just off the river opposite the boat dock.

Thala Boravit　　　　　　　　　TEMPLE

This crumbling temple is across the Mekong from Stung Treng in the town of the same name. It is hardly worth the effort for the casual visitor, but temple fiends may feel the urge to tick it off. Thala Boravit (ថាឡាបុរៈវិត) was an important Chenla-period trading town on the river route connecting the ancient city of Champasak and the sacred temple of Wat Phu with the southern reaches of the Chenla empire, including the ancient cities of Sambor Prei Kuk (Isanapura) and Angkor Borei. For all its past glories, there is very little to see today. Thala Boravit is on the west bank of the Mekong River and boats cross from the boat dock in Stung Treng roughly every 30 minutes throughout the day (5000/1500r with/without a motorbike). The new bridge, when completed, will terminate in Thala Boravit.

Mekong Blue　　　　　SILK-WEAVING CENTRE

(មេតងប្លូ; ☎ 012 622096; www.mekongblue.com; ⊙ 7.30-11.30am & 2-5pm Mon-Sat) ✎ Part of the Stung Treng Women's Development Centre, Mekong Blue is a silk-weaving centre on the outskirts of Stung Treng. Mekong Blue specialises in exquisite silk products for sale and export. At this centre it is possible to observe the dyers and weavers, most of whom come from vulnerable or impoverished backgrounds. There is a small showroom on-site with a selection of silk on sale, plus a cafe. However, it only serves cold drinks unless you book a meal in advance. The centre is located about 4km east of the centre on the riverside road that continues under the bridge.

🛌 Sleeping

★**Le Tonlé Tourism Training Centre**　　　　　GUESTHOUSE $

(☎ 074-973638; http://letonle.org; s/d with shared bathroom from US$6/8; 🛜) Located in a shady spot on the riverfront about 500m west of the ferry dock, this small guesthouse doubles as a training centre to help underprivileged locals get a start in the tourism industry. Rooms are simple but tastefully furnished. The bathroom is immaculate bathroom and the four rooms share a comfy balcony, where delicious meals can be ordered in advance.

Golden River Hotel　　　　　　HOTEL $$

(☎ 074-690 0029; www.goldenriverhotel.com; r US$15-35; ❄ @ 🛜) Still the smartest hotel in town, although that's not saying much. It has the province's only lift and 50 well-appointed rooms with a few quirks (odd wall-socket placement, faulty remote controls, crowing roosters out back). The riverview rooms in front cost a bit more.

Riverside Guesthouse　　　　GUESTHOUSE $

(☎ 012 257207; timtysou@gmail.com; r US$5-8; @) Overlooking the riverfront area, the Riverside

Stung Treng

has long been a popular travellers' crossroads. Rooms are basic, but so are the prices. Good for travel information and there is a popular bar-restaurant downstairs.

Mekong Bird Lodge BUNGALOW $
(012 796699; www.mekongbirdeco-lodge.com; s/d/tw US$13/15/18) This self-styled ecolodge sits on a bluff overlooking a peaceful Mekong eddy north of town. It has recently been upgraded but remains exceedingly rustic. The sturdy wood bungalows are spacious and fragrant, and have balconies with sunset views, but lack furniture. Request a mozzie net. To get here turn left off NH7 4km north of the bridge and continue 1.5km.

Ly Hang Guesthouse HOTEL $
(074-636 3868; dm US$3-4, r with fan/air-con from US$7/12) A pretty solid deal off the river. Air-con rooms are gargantuan, with dueling king-sized beds, flat screens, fridges and private balconies with no furniture. Dorms were not yet a reality when we dropped by but they planned to convert one of the rooms.

Eating

On the riverside promenade west of the ferry dock, a handful of streetside vendors peddle cold beer and noodle soup until late in the evening. The southwest corner of the market has cheap-and-quick eateries with pots for your perusal.

Ponika's Palace INTERNATIONAL $
(mains US$2-5; 6am-10pm) Need a break from *laab* after Laos? Burgers, pizza and English breakfast grace the menu, along with Indian food and wonderful Khmer curries. The affable owner Ponika speaks English.

Dara Canteen INTERNATIONAL $
(7am-9pm) This is a good refuge for French travellers, with baguettes, US$5 filet mignon and a French-speaking owner.

Information

Canadia Bank (near market) Has a full international ATM with free withdrawals.

Rany Neh Internet (per hr 2500r; 7am-8pm) Internet access.

Riverside Guesthouse (012 257207; timtysou@gmail.com) Specialises in getting people to/from Laos, Siem Reap or just about anywhere else. Also runs boat tours to the Lao border via the resident dolphin pod (US$100/120 for two/four people). English-speaking guides

GETTING TO LAOS: STUNG TRENG TO DON DET

Getting to the border The remote Trapeang Kriel/Dong Kalaw border (6am-6pm), 60km north of Stung Treng, is a popular crossing point on the Indochina overland circuit. For many years, there was a separate river crossing here, but that's gone now. Sorya Phnom Penh Transport, in partnership with Pakse-based Lao operator Sengchalean, has buses from Phnom Penh straight through to Pakse's 2km Bus Station (US$27, 12 to 14 hours). This bus leaves Phnom Penh at 6.45am, with pick-ups possible in Kompong Cham (around 9.30am), Kratie (around 11.30am) or Stung Treng (around 3pm). Trips in the other direction depart Pakse at 7.30am. Services to Laos from Siem Reap are also possible, with a bus change in Soung. The only other option to the border is a private taxi (US$35 to US$45) or *moto* (US$15 to US$20) from Stung Treng.

At the border Both Lao and Cambodian visas are available on arrival. Entering Laos, you'll pay US$35 to US$42 for a visa, depending on nationality, plus a US$2 fee (dubbed either an 'overtime' or a 'processing' fee, depending on when you cross) upon both entry and exit.

Entering Cambodia, they jack up the price of a visa to US$25 from the normal US$20. The extra US$5 is called 'tea money', as the poor border guards have been stationed at such a remote crossing. In addition, the Cambodians charge US$2 for a cursory medical inspection upon arrival in the country, and levy a US$2 processing fee upon exit. These fees might be waived if you protest, but don't protest for too long or your bus may leave without you. The bus companies want their cut too, so they charge an extra US$1 to US$2 to handle your paperwork with the border guards. To avoid this fee, insist on doing your own paperwork and go through immigration alone.

Moving on Aside from the Sorya bus, there's virtually zero traffic on either side of the border. If you're dropped at the border, expect to pay 150,000/50,000 kip (US$12/4) for a taxi/*săhm-lór* heading north to Ban Nakasang (for Don Det).

can take you places on motorbikes, including to Preah Vihear City.

Tourist Information Centre (☑074-210001; ⊙8-11am & 2-7pm; ☎) Inconveniently located near the new bridge, it's run by the ever-helpful Theany.

Xplore-Asia (☑011 433836, 074-973456; www.xplore-cambodia.com) Doles out brochures, booklets and advice, and tailors one- to several-day cycling-and-kayak combo tours along the Mekong Discovery Trail, including kayaking with the dolphins. Rents out kayaks (US$10 per day), motorbikes (US$10 per day) and sturdy Trek mountain bikes (US$5 per day).

❶ Getting There & Around

NH7 north to the Lao border is in great shape these days. The same cannot be said for NH7 south to Kratie.

Express minibuses with guesthouse pickups as early as 4am are the quickest way to Phnom Penh (US$10 to US$13, eight hours). Book through Riverside Guesthouse.

Phnom Penh Sorya (☑092 181805) has a 6.30am bus to Phnom Penh (40,000r, nine hours) via Kratie (20,000r, three hours) and Kompong Cham (30,000r, six hours). Sorya's bus from Laos to Phnom Penh comes through Stung Treng around 11.30am. Additionally, local minibuses to Kratie depart regularly until 2pm from the market area.

There is a comfortable tourist van to Ban Lung (US$6, two hours, 8am), with additional morning trips in cramped local minibuses from the market (15,000, three hours). If you want to leave later in the day make your way to O Pong Moan and hail a more frequent bus or minibus en route from Kratie.

From the riverfront taxi park, minibuses go to Phnom Penh (50,000r, eight hours) and Ban Lung (30,000r, four hours).

The new highway west from Thala Boravit to Preah Vihear via Chhep is in great shape. There's no public transport, but that will no doubt start once the bridge is finished. For now you'll need to hire a car (US$110) or motorbike (US$40 to US$50) to Preah Vihear. Riverside Guesthouse does minivan trips when there is demand (US$25 per person).

Riverside Guesthouse rents out motorbikes (from US$8) while Riverside and Ponika's Place have bicycles for hire (US$1 to US$2).

Around Stung Treng

In addition to the homestay program at Preah Rumkel, there are some worthwhile community-based tourism initiatives, including homestays, in **O'Russey Kandal**,

about 28km south of Stung Treng, and in **Koh Preah**, about 15km south of Stung Treng. Both programs have a slew of tours and activities on offer and there are volunteer opportunities as well. Contact **Mlup Baitong** (☑012 899471; www.mlup-baitong.org) in Stung Treng for information on O'Russey Kandal, and CRDT (p259) in Kratie for information on Koh Preah. Xplore-Asia can also help fit you into these programs.

Preah Rumkel   អ្នកស្វាយ និងព្រះរំកិល

This small village is emerging as hotbed of ecotourism thanks to its proximity to the **Anlong Cheuteal** Irrawaddy dolphin pool near the Lao border. With its Ramsar-recognised wetlands, dozens of islands, a rich array of bird life and various rapids and waterfalls cascading down from Laos, this is one of the Mekong River's wildest and most beautiful stretches.

The half-dozen frolicking dolphins in the Anlong Chuteal pool (known as Boong Pa Gooang in Laos) can easily be sighted from shore in Preah Rumkel, where there is an excellent community-based **homestay** (per person US$3, plus per meal US$3) program if you want to stay another day. There's a US$2 per person charge to see the dolphins.

Excursions out of Preah Rumkel include a hike up a nearby mountain and a boat/hiking trip to view the rampaging **Mekong rapids** cascading down from Laos. The rapids are an awesome display of nature's force, especially in the wet season.

Hire a longtailed boat in O'Svay or, closer to the Laos border, Anglong Morakot, to explore the area and view the dolphins at Anlong Cheuteal. Boats cost a negotiable US$25 round trip to Preah Rumkel and the dolphin pool. Add US$10 if you want to continue upstream to the rapids. Anlong Morakot is only 4km from the border so travellers coming in from Laos could get there in about 10 minutes on the back of a *moto* (about US$2). Be sure to arrange onward transport to Stung Treng – either at the border or in advance through Xplore-Asia or Riverside Guesthouse in Stung Treng. These companies can also prearrange your *moto* and boat ride from the border to Preah Rumkel. A taxi to Stung Treng from this area costs about US$45.

Better yet, through Xplore-Asia you can **kayak** with the dolphins and then paddle downstream to O'Svay – or through bird-infested flooded forests all the way to Stung

Treng. A full-day kayak excursion south of O'Svay costs US$65 per person; add US$20 per person to include the boat trip upstream to the dolphin pool and the Mekong rapids.

Siem Pang ស្យៀមប៉ាង

POP 5000

A relatively prosperous town that stretches for about 6km along the Tonlé Kong, Siem Pang is a good place to observe rural life or just relax by the riverside in a remote outpost.

Siem Pang acts as the western gateway to Virachey National Park and is renowned for its rich wildlife. Rare giant ibises and white-shouldered ibises roost around here. You can arrange a park permit (preferably well in advance) and find a guide through Theany Guesthouse.

BirdLife International (✆ 097 974 5966, in Phnom Penh 023-993631; www.birdlife.org) runs a 'vulture restaurant' (feeding station) that attracts all three species of critically endangered vultures found in Cambodia. It's set up for research rather than tourism, but if you time your visit for the twice-monthly 'feed', which involves killing a water buffalo or cow and leaving it in a field near an observation hideout, you may get a chance to spot the vultures. Or you can up the ante with US$300 to organise a private feed.

A ferry takes passengers (1000r) and motorbikes (2500r) across the river, where the scenic trail to Veun Sai in Ratanakiri starts. Theany Guesthouse (✆ 097 810 2888; r 25,000r) offers one-way motorbike rentals for this ride (US$70, including the cost of returning the motorbike to Siem Pang), along with simple rooms in a traditional wooden house.

Regular morning and occasional afternoon vans do the trip from Stung Treng to Siem Pang (US$5, 2½ hours). From Stung Treng, drive 50km north on NH7, turn right, and proceed another 52km on a rather sandy unsealed road. There are no longer any public boats along the Tonlé Kong to/from Stung Treng.

RATANAKIRI PROVINCE

Popular Ratanakiri Province (ខេត្តរតនគិរី) is a diverse region of outstanding natural beauty that provides a remote home for a mosaic of minority peoples. The Jarai, Tompuon, Brau and Kreung are the Khmer Leu (Upper Khmer) people, with their own languages, traditions and customs. There is also a large Lao population throughout the province and

---

THE REAL GIBBON EXPERIENCE

The Mekong region is awash in tours that have 'gibbon' in their name but don't involve seeing gibbons. Now Cambodia offers a gibbon experience where you actually observe gibbons in their natural habitat.

Set up as a community-based ecotourism project (CBET; veunsaicbet@gmail.com) by Conservation International (CI; www.conservation.org), the new project takes place within the Veun Sai-Siem Pang Conservation Area (VSSPCA), just outside the border of Virachey National Park north of Veun Sai. You stay at least one night in the jungle sleeping in hammocks or in a community-based homestay, rising well before dawn to spend time with semihabituated northern buff-cheeked gibbons.

This species was only discovered in 2010 and the population in Veun Sai is believed to be one of the largest at about 500 groups. Hearing their haunting dawn call echo through the jungle and seeing them swing through the canopy is memorable. These tours also offer the opportunity to experience dense jungle, open savannah, rivers and waterfalls, and to visit Kavet and Lao villages.

CI has an exclusive arrangement with the village near the gibbon site to run these tours. The gibbon-viewing season runs from November to mid-June – it's too wet at other times – and the visits are limited to six people at a time. The tours cost US$100 to US$200 per person for a one-night/two-day tour, depending on group size and which tour company you choose. The fee includes entrance to the VSSPCA, guide, homestays and camps, and all meals. Most companies in Ban Lung can arrange these trips on behalf of CI. For details contact the CBET.

CBET payments are used as a substitute for destructive forest use so this is a very worthwhile way to contribute something positive to wildlife conservation and community development.

multiple languages will be heard in villages such as Veun Sai.

Adrenalin activities are abundant. Swim in clear volcanic lakes, shower under waterfalls, or trek in the vast Virachey National Park – it's all here. Tourism is taking off even as lowland politicians and generals plunder the place. Ratanakiri is the frontline in the battle for land, and the slash-and-burn minorities are losing out thanks to their tradition of collective ownership. The forest is disappearing at an alarming rate, being replaced by rubber plantations and cashewnut farms. Hopefully someone wakes up and smells the coffee – there's plenty of that as well – before it's too late.

Gem mining is big business in Ratanakiri, hardly surprising given the name means 'hill of the precious stones'. There is good-quality zircon mined in several parts of the province, as well as other semiprecious stones. Just don't get suckered into a dream deal, as gem scams are as old as the hills themselves.

Roads in Ratanakiri are not as impressive as the sights. In the dry season, prepare to do battle with the dust of 'red-earth Ratanakiri', which will leave you with orange skin and ginger hair. The roads look like a papaya shake during the wet season. The ideal time to explore is November, after the rains have stopped and before the dust begins to swirl.

Ban Lung បានលុង

♫ 075 / POP 30,000

Affectionately known as '*dey krahorm*' (red earth) after its rust-coloured affliction, Ban Lung provides a popular base for a range of Ratanakiri romps.

The town itself is busy and lacks the backwater charm of Sen Monorom in Mondulkiri, but with attractions such as Boeng Yeak Lom just a short hop away, there is little room for complaint. Many of the minorities from the surrounding villages come to Ban Lung to buy and sell at the market.

◉ Sights & Activities

There are no real sights in the centre of town. The big draw is Boeng Yeak Lom, while multiday treks around Ban Lung are picking up steam.

Boeng Yeak Lom   LAKE
(បឹងយក្សឡោម; admission US$1, inner tubes per hr 4000r) At the heart of the protected area of **Yeak Lom** is a beautiful emerald crater

lake set amid the vivid greens of the towering jungle. The lake is believed to have been formed 700,000 years ago and some people swear it must have been formed by a meteor strike as the circle is so perfect. The indigenous minority people in the area have long considered Yeak Lom a sacred place and their legends talk of mysterious creatures that inhabit the waters. It is one of the most peaceful, beautiful locations Cambodia has to offer and the water is extremely clear. Several wooden piers are dotted around the perimeter, making it perfect for swimming (don't worry, we're pretty sure those creature legends are just that).

A small Cultural & Environmental Centre has a modest display on ethnic minorities in the province and hires out life jackets for the young 'uns. The local Tompuon minority has a 25-year lease to manage the lake through to 2021, and proceeds from the entry fee go towards improving life in the nearby villages. However, developers, backed by local politicians, have long been clamoring for the sacred lands around the lake. One can only hope they are kept at bay and that Boeng Yeak Lom is preserved in all of its pristine glory – an all too rare occurrence in Cambodia.

To get to Boeng Yeak Lom from Ban Lung's central roundabout, head east towards Vietnam for 3km, turn right at the prominent minorities statue and proceed 2km or so. *Motos* charge US$3 return (more if you make them wait), while *remorks* have been known to charge up to US$10 return. It takes almost an hour to reach the lake on foot from Ban Lung.

Waterfalls   WATERFALL
Tucked amid the sprawling cashew and rubber plantations just west of Ban Lung are three waterfalls worth visiting: **Chaa Ong** (admission 2000r), **Ka Tieng** (admission 2000r) and **Kinchaan** (Kachang; admission 2000r). All are within a 20-minute *moto* ride of town, and visits to all three are usually included in half- and full-day excursions offered by tour companies.

The most spectacular and tallest of the three is 25m Chaa Ong, as it is set in a jungle gorge and you can clamber behind the waterfall or venture underneath for a power shower. However, it dries up from about January to May. Ka Tieng is the most enjoyable, as it drops over a rock shelf allowing you to clamber all the way behind. There are some vines on the far side that are strong enough to swing on for some Tarzan action.

Ban Lung

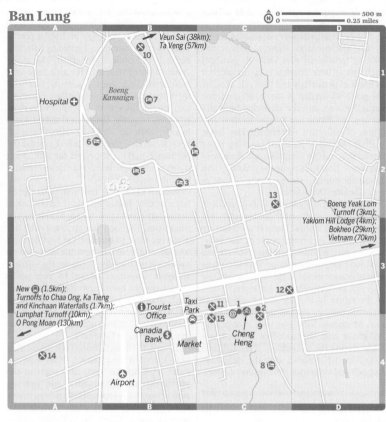

Veun Sai (38km);
Ta Veng (57km)

Boeng
Kansaign

Hospital

Boeng Yeak Lom
Turnoff (3km);
Yaklom Hill Lodge (4km);
Bokheo (29km);
Vietnam (70km)

New (1.5km);
Turnoffs to Chaa Ong, Ka Tieng
and Kinchaan Waterfalls (1.7km);
Lumphat Turnoff (10km);
O Pong Moan (130km)

Tourist
Office

Taxi
Park

Canadia
Bank

Market

Cheng
Heng

Airport

Ban Lung

The turn-offs to all three waterfalls are 200m west of the new bus station, just beyond a Lina petrol station. There's signage but it's barely visible. The Chaa Ong turn-off is on the right (north) side of NH19; the waterfall is 5.5km from the highway along a dirt road. The turn-off to Ka Tieng and Kinchaan is on the left side of NH19; proceed 5.5km to a fork in the road. Go left 200m to Kinchaan, or right 2.5km to Ka Tieng.

You can access all three falls year-round, but think twice about driving yourself on a motorbike in the rainy season as the red-clay access roads are extremely slippery when wet and you're almost guaranteed to wipe out. *Motos* (return US$6 for one waterfall, or US$10 for all three) and *remorks* (US$10/20 for one/three waterfalls) can get you here safely.

Elephant Rides
ELEPHANTS
(☎ 097 303 3680) Ban Lung's two resident elephants tote tourists for rides in the vil-

lage of Kateung near the Ka Tieng Waterfall. The one-hour loop, which starts and ends near the waterfall entrance, takes place in a small patch of jungle improbably preserved amid fields of cashew and rubber trees. The usual charge is US$15/20 per elephant for one/two riders if you arrange it through the owner, Mr Bunma, and get there on your own. Guesthouses will obviously charge a bit more to set this up.

👉 Tours

Overnight treks with nights spent camping or staying in minority villages north of Veun Sai or Ta Veng are popular. Day tours usually take in some combination of waterfalls, Boeng Yeak Lom, elephant rides, minority villages, gem mines and jungle walks. Figure on US$45 or $50 per day per person for a couple (less for bigger groups).

Keep in mind that trekking in Virachey National Park is the exclusive domain of Virachey National Park Eco-Tourism Information Center (p271). Private tour operators also offer multiday treks, but these only go as far as the park's buffer zone. There's little forest left standing outside the park boundary, so be careful that you're not being taken for a loop – literally – around and around in the same small patch of forest. Despite being shut out from the park, private operators can still design creative treks that take in minority villages and scenic spots around the province.

Backpacker Pad, Tree Top Ecolodge, Terres Rouges (which can provide French-speaking guides) and Yaklom Hill Lodge are good at arranging tours, but we recommend using one of the following dedicated tour companies:

Highland Tours   TOUR
(☑097 658 3841, 088 870 3080; highland.tour@yahoo.com) Kimi and Horng are husband-and-wife graduates of the Le Tonlé Tourism Training Centre (p263) in Stung Treng who have moved to the highlands to run a range of tours, including fun day trips and a multiday tour from Itub (northwest of Veun Sai) to Siem Pang by bike, then on to Stung Treng by boat. Horng is the only female guide in Ratanakiri.

Khieng   TOUR
(☑097 923 0923; khamphaykhieng@yahoo.com) Bespectacled Khieng is an indigenous Tompuon guide who runs unique one- to two-night trips in some fairly well-preserved jungle around Lumphat with overnights in minority villages. His tours are cheap – he seems genuinely interested in seeing money go to Tampuon communities and guides – so tip him well. He also has a truly stunning hand-drawn map of Ratanakiri province. Khieng can often be found around Boeng Yeak Lom.

DutchCo Trekking Cambodia   TOUR
(☑097 679 2714; www.trekkingcambodia.com) One of the most experienced trekking operators in the province, run by – wait for it – a friendly Dutchman. Runs four- to five-day treks north of Veon Sai through Kavet villages and community forests, and one- to two-day trips around Kalai (south of Veun Sai), among many other tours.

Parrot Tours   TOUR
(☑012 764714; www.jungletrek.blogspot.com) Sitha Nan is a national-park-trained guide with expert local knowledge. Runs a range of overnight treks in the gibbon-infested forests north of Itub.

🛏 Sleeping

In addition to the following there are a host of bog-standard high-rise hotels near the market, none worth writing home about.

★ Tree Top Ecolodge   BUNGALOW $
(☑012 490333; www.treetop-ecolodge.com; d US$7, cottage with cold/hot water US$12/15; 🛜) How do you improve the northeast's best deal? Start by expanding to 17 rooms so it's actually possible to get a room. 'Mr T's' place boasts rough-hewn walkways leading to huge, boutique-quality bungalows with mosquito nets, thatch roofs and hammock-strewn verandahs with verdant valley vistas. Like the bungalows, the restaurant is fashioned from hardwood and dangles over a lush ravine.

Up-to-date travel advice is plentiful, especially for those Laos bound.

Banlung Balcony   GUESTHOUSE $
(www.balconyguesthouse.net; d US$4-7; @🛜) This has survived the recent passing of its expat owner and remains Ban Lung's best deal at the bargain-basement end. The rooms are basic but have high ceilings and odour-combating wood floors, and there's a huge public balcony. The pub-restaurant has decent food and a pool table.

Backpacker Pad   HOSTEL $
(☑092 785259; banlungbackpackerpad@yahoo.com; dm $US2, d without/with bathroom US$4/5;

☎) Penny pinchers rejoice, it doesn't get cheaper than this. The rooms are small and dark and the dorm grubby, but a cosy common area out front makes up for it. A good place to meet other travellers. Owner Sophat is a great source of info and runs a tour company.

Lakeside Chheng Lok Hotel HOTEL $

(☏ 012 957422; lakeside.chhenglokhotel@gmail.com; r with fan/air-con from US$5/15; ❋ @ 🛜 🛉) The ever-expanding Lakeside has tacked on a swimming pool, a vast new wing and a sister hotel (the Lakeside Hotel, next door) in recent years. A lot to choose from here, from large but generic air-con rooms to bare-bones fan-cooled rooms. The original wing is an afterthought these days, as the newer buildings have the lake views.

Colonial Lake Palace HOTEL $

(r with fan/air-con from US$10/15; ☏ 088 993 0384; ❋🛜) Grandiose name for a fairly modest place down by the lake. The rooms have a touch of class with flat screens and indigenous runners on white bedspreads, but are on the small side. It's the sister hotel of Backpacker Pad, which means tours and other handy things offered by owner Sophat.

Yaklom Hill Lodge LODGE $

(☏ 011 725881; www.yaklom.com; s/d/tr US$10/15/20) 🏝 Ratanakiri's only true ecolodge, staffed by Tompuon, is set amid lush forest near Boeung Yeak Lom, 5km east of Ban Lung's central roundabout. It will appeal to those who like camping. The all-wood bungalows are atmospheric but starting to show their age, and can get damp. A generator enables hot showers and light from 6pm to 9pm.

Hiking trails lead to the lake and beyond. Breakfast is included in the low season only.

★ Terres Rouges Lodge BOUTIQUE HOTEL $$

(☏ 075-974051; www.ratanakiri-lodge.com; incl breakfast s/d US$46/52, ste US$86-92; ❋ @ 🛜 🛉) Undoubtedly one of the most atmospheric places to stay in provincial Cambodia. The fan-cooled standard rooms are done up in classy colonial style, with beautiful Cambodian furniture, tribal artefacts and a long common verandah. The suites consist of spacious Balinese-style bungalows set in the gorgeous garden near the 14m pool.

If you're travelling with kids and/or looking for a little more comfort in Ban Lung, staying here is a no-brainer.

🍴 Eating & Drinking

Among the guesthouses, Terres Rouge has the most sophisticated menu, while Treetop and Banlung Balcony are also reliable. To get down with the locals, head to the lakefront near Coconut Shake Restaurant around sunset, plop down on a mat, and order cheap beer and snacks from waterfront shacks. Or try the market, where you'll find delicious noodles for 4000r.

Night owls don't have much to choose from – see if Cafe Alee or Gecko House have action. Otherwise Banlung Balcony has a great bar occasionally brimming with backpackers; ditto Backpacker Pad.

★ Sal's Restaurant & Bar INTERNATIONAL $

(mains US$1.75-5) This welcoming restaurant-bar, popular with Ban Lung's small expat community, is the place to come for comfort food from home, including Indian curries, spicy Mexican and great burgers. All dishes are freshly prepared, so order ahead if you don't want to wait around.

Cafe Alee INTERNATIONAL $

(7am-last customer) In a new space out in front of DutchCo Trekking, American-run Cafe Alee has a classic Ban Lung menu: the full gamut of Khmer food plus a few token Western dishes – veggie burgers, lasagne, pizza, baguettes and hearty breakfasts and breads for trekkers. Do try the homemade potato crisps.

Gecko House INTERNATIONAL $

(mains 10,000-20,000r; ⊙8am-10pm; ☎) A charming little restaurant-bar with soft lighting and famously frosty beer mugs, this is a great place by day or night. The menu features mainly Thai tastes and Khmer classics, plus burgers, pasta and pizza. The bathrooms have squatters, but clean squatters.

A'Dam Restaurant CAMBODIAN $

(mains US$2-4; ⊙11am-10pm) Long a popular bar, A'Dam has reinvented itself as one of Ban Lung's more refined eateries (for what that's worth). A bright picture menu does justice to the tasty, freshly made Khmer-Chinese food. Our green mango salad was particularly successful.

Taman CAMBODIAN $

(dishes 6000-12,000r; ⊙6am-8pm) Locals flock to this place a block east of the market to tuck into steaming bowls of noodle soup. It's especially popular for breakfast.

Everest INDIAN $

(mains US$3-4; ☉7am-11pm) OK so it's not the greatest Indian food in the world but it's a welcome relief from ye-old familiar Ban Lung menu of Khmer faves, burgers and pasta.

Coconut Shake Restaurant CAMBODIAN $

(northeast cnr of Boeng Kansaign; mains 6000-16,000r; ☉7am-9pm) The best coconut shakes in the northeast cost just 4000r – we drink at least one a day when in Ban Lung. It has fried noodles and other Khmer fare if you care to sit down and stay.

Rith Any Banh Chav CAMBODIAN $

(dishes US$1; ☉2-7pm) The proprietess here specialises in *banh chav* - meat, baby shrimps, sprouts, veggies and spices wrapped inside a thin egg pancake wrapped inside a piece of cabbage, and dipped in a tangy orange sauce.

❶ Information

Visitors will find their guesthouse or the recommended tour companies to be most useful in the quest for local knowledge.

Canadia Bank Full-service bank with fee-free ATM.

Srey Mom Internet (097 295 9111; per hr 4000r; ☉6.30am-10pm) Fan-cooled internet access.

Virachey National Park Eco-Tourism Information Centre (☏075-974013, 097 896 4995; virachey@camintel.com; ☉8am-noon & 2-5pm)

❶ Getting There & Away

Ban Lung is 588km northeast of Phnom Penh and 129km west of O Poang Moan, the junction town 19km south of Stung Treng. Hwy NH19 between Ban Lung and O Pong Moan is flat, empty and fully sealed, but leave early as very little public transport departs Ban Lung in the afternoon.

The new **bus station** (NH19) is on the western outskirts of town, 2.5km east of Ban Lung's main roundabout. All bus departures and most long-distance minibus services depart from here. Tour companies in town usually offer free rides out here with the purchase of a ticket.

Phnom Penh Sorya, Rith Mony and Thong Ly operate early-morning buses to Phnom Penh (US$9 to US$10, 11 hours) via Kratie and Kompong Cham. Long-distance bus services to Siem Reap or Pakse are also promoted, but in reality this is a scam and you will be forced to change buses, often with significant wait times, in Kompong Cham or Stung Treng respectively.

Speedy express-van services pick you up at your guesthouse and head to Phnom Penh (US$15, eight hours, 6am and 4pm) and Stung Treng (US$6, two hours, around 7.30am). Organise these through your guesthouse, or alternatively through **Sok Kun** (☏011 433939). Call Tree Top Ecolodge to arrange an express van pick-up if coming from Phnom Penh.

From the bus station, various local minibuses depart in the morning to Phnom Penh (50,000r), Stung Treng (20,000r) and O'Yadaw (12,000r), and throughout the day to Lumphat (10,000r, one hour) and Kratie (25,000r, four hours). See

---

RESPONSIBLE TREKKING AROUND RATANAKIRI

Overnight treks in the forests of Ratanakiri are very popular these days. Die-hard trampers spend up to eight days sleeping in replica US Army hammocks and checking out some of the country's last virgin forest in and around Virachey National Park.

Where possible, we recommend using indigenous guides for organised treks and other excursions around Ban Lung. They speak the local dialects and can secure permission to visit cemeteries that are off limits to Khmer guides.

Unfortunately, with a few notable exceptions (namely Khieng; p269), the level of English among indigenous guides tends to be only fair. If you need a more fluent English guide, we suggest hiring both an English-speaking Khmer guide and a minority guide, if it's within your budget.

A loose association of Tompuon guides is based at Boeng Yeak Lom. They have neither a phone number nor an email so you'll just have to rock up. They can take you on an exclusive tour of several Tompuon villages around Boeng Yeak Lom. You can observe weavers and basket makers in action, learn about animist traditions and eat a traditional indigenous meal of bamboo-steamed fish, fresh vegetables, 'minority' rice and, of course, rice wine.

Among private tour companies, only Yaklom Hill Lodge employs a full-time indigenous (Tompuon) guide, but you'll need to request him. Virachey National Park also employs some indigenous guides and uses minority porters, while tour companies listed in this section can all hire indigenous guides on request.

GETTING TO VIETNAM: BAN LUNG TO PLEIKU

....

Getting to the border Opened to tourists only in 2008, the **O'Yadaw/Le Thanh border crossing** (⊘ 7am to 5pm) is 70km east of Ban Lung along smooth NH19. From Ban Lung, guesthouses advertise a 6.30am van to Pleiku (US$12, three hours) involving a change of vehicles at the border. These pick you up at your guesthouse. Alternatively, take a local minibus to O'Yadaw from Ban Lung's new bus station, and continue 25km to the border by *moto*. A *moto* from Ban Lung to the border will set you back US$20 (one hour).

At the border Formalities are straightforward and lines nonexistent, just make sure you have a Vietnamese visa.

Moving on Once on the Vietnamese side of the frontier, the road is nicely paved and *motos* await to take you to Duc Co (20km), where there are buses (15,000d) to Pleiku, Quy Nhon and Hoi An.

---

the boxed text above for more information on getting to Vietnam via O'Yadaw.

Pick-up trucks head to more remote Ratanakiri villages from the taxi park next to the market. Share taxis out of Ban Lung are rare.

Ratanakiri's airport has been closed to commercial flights for years.

ⓘ Getting Around

Bicycles (US$1 to US$3), motorbikes (US$5 to US$7), cars (from US$30) and 4WDs (from US$45) are available for hire from most guesthouses in town.

Cheng Heng (☑ 088 851 6104; ⊘ 6am-8pm) has some 250cc trail bikes for rent (US$25) in addition to a stable of well-maintained smaller motorbikes (US$6 to US$8). Next door, Srey Mom Internet (p271) hires out motorbikes (from US$5) and 4WD Pajeros (per day US$45).

Motodops hang out around the market, and some double as guides. Figure on US$15 to US$20 per day for a good English-speaking driver-guide (less for a Khmer speaker). A *moto* to Yeak Lom costs US$3 to US$4 return; to Veun Sai is US$15 return; to any waterfall is about US$6 return.

Remorks have finally made it to Ban Lung, but there are only about eight of them in town and they are expensive by Cambodia standards – about double what a *moto* costs.

Around Ban Lung

Veun Sai   វើនសៃ

Located on the banks of Tonlé San, Veun Sai is a cluster of Chinese, Lao and *chunchiet* villages. Originally, the town was located on the north bank of the river and known as Virachey, but these days the main settlement is on the south bank.

From the south side, cross the river on a small ferry (500r; 3000r with a motorbike) and walk west for a couple of kilometres, passing through the Khmer village, a Lao community and a small *chunchiet* area, before finally emerging in a wealthy Chinese village complete with large wooden houses and inhabitants who still speak Chinese. Note how neat and tidy it is compared with the surrounding communities.

The Veun Sai area is known for Tompuan cemeteries, but most of them are closed to outsiders these days. The bans are at least partially the result of tourists flaunting behavioral protocols.

At the time of writing, the closest cemetery to Veun Sai open to visitors was an ethnic Kachah cemetery in Kaoh Paek, a 45-minute boat ride upriver from Veun Sai. Expect to pay around US$40 for the boat trip from Veun Sai, or about half that from Kachon, 10km upriver (east) of Veun Sai. Tour companies in Ban Lung charge US$50 for an excursion here.

Veun Sai is 39km northwest of Ban Lung on an unsealed but smooth all-weather road. It is easy enough to get here under your own steam on a motorbike or with a vehicle. English-speaking guides ask US$15 or so to return to take you out here on a *moto*.

Skilled motorbike and mountain-bike riders can ride from Veun Sai to Siem Pang in Stung Treng via Itub (a few hours' walk south of the gibbon zone) along a scenic trail that begins on the north side of the river.

Ta Veng   តាវែង

Ta Veng is an insignificant village on the southern bank of Tonlé San, but it acts as the main gateway to Virachey National Park and the base for many treks run by private operators in the park's buffer zone. It was in the Ta Veng district that Pol Pot, Ieng Sary and other leaders of the Khmer Rouge established their guerrilla base in the 1960s. Locals say nothing today remains of the remote base, although, in a dismal sign of decline, they point out that Ta Veng had electricity before the war.

Ta Veng is about 57km north of Ban Lung on a roller-coaster road through the mountains that affords some of the province's better views. The road passes through several minority villages, where it is possible to break the journey. There are some very steep climbs in sections, and for this reason, it wouldn't be much fun in the rain. Travel by motorbike or charter a vehicle.

It is possible to hire small boats in Ta Veng for river jaunts (US$15 to US$20 in the local area or US$80 to US$90 for the five-hour trip to Veun Sai).

Lumkut Lake (បឹងលំកុត) & Bokheo

Lumkut is a large crater lake hemmed in by dense forest on all sides, similar to the more illustrious and accessible Boeng Yeak Lom (p267). To get to the lake turn south off the highway to O'Yadaw about 33km east of Ban Lung. The lake is 15km south along a rough road. Access is difficult in the rainy season.

On the way to the lake you can stop off in Bokheo, the current hot spot for gem mining, 29km east of Ban Lung. Locals dig a large pit in the ground and then tunnel horizontally in their search for amethyst and zircon. The mines tend to move around so ask around where to find them.

Virachey National Park ឧទ្យានជាតិវីរៈជ័យ

This park (admission US$5) is one of the largest protected areas in Cambodia, stretching for 3325 sq km east to Vietnam, north to Laos and west to Stung Treng Province. The park has never been fully explored and is home to a number of rare mammals, including elephants, clouded leopards, tigers and sun bears, although your chances of seeing any of these beasts are extremely slim. However, you'll probably hear endangered gibbons and might spot great hornbills, giant ibises, Germain's peacock-pheasants and other rare birds. So important is the park to the Mekong region that it was designated an Asean Heritage Park in 2003. However, the bad news is that it is seriously under threat from developers, and Cambodian authorities have already sold more remote regions of the park to Vietnamese rubber-plantation developers.

Virachey has one of the most organised ecotourism programs in Cambodia, focusing on small-scale culture, nature and adventure trekking. The program aims to involve and benefit local minority communities. All treks into the park must be arranged through the Virachey National Park Eco-Tourism Information Centre (p271) in Ban Lung. The park offers two- to eight-day treks led by English-speaking, park-employed rangers. Private operators offer tours in the park buffer zone

RESPECT THE DEAD

The chunchiet (minorities) of Ratanakiri bury their dead amid the jungle, carving effigies of the deceased to stand guard over the graves.

When a lengthy period of mourning is complete, villagers hold a big celebration and add two carved wooden likenesses of elephant tusks to the structures. Some of these tombs date back many years and have been abandoned to the jungle. Newer tombs of wealthy individuals have been cast in concrete and show some modern touches like shades and mobile phones.

There are many cemeteries scattered throughout the forests of Ratanakiri, but most of them are strictly off limits to visitors. Cemeteries are sacred sights for the chunchiet; enter them only with permission from the village chief and preferably in the company of a local. If you are lucky enough to be allowed into a cemetery, touch nothing, act respectfully and ask permission before taking photos.

Unfortunately, there have been many reports of tourists ignoring clearly marked signs (in English) urging outsiders to abstain from entering chunchiet cemeteries. Worse, unscrupulous art collectors and amateur anthropologists from Europe have reportedly been buying up the old effigies from poor villagers.

TREAD LIGHTLY IN THE HILLS

Tourism can bring many benefits to highland communities: cross-cultural understanding, improved infrastructure, cheaper market goods, employment opportunities and tourist dollars supporting handicraft industries. However, there are also negatives, such as increased litter and pollutants, domination of the tourism business by lowland Khmers at the expense of highland minorities, and the tendency of tourists to disregard local customs and taboos.

One way to offset the negatives in a big way is to hire indigenous guides. Not only does this ensure that your tourist dollars go directly to indigenous communities, it will also enrich your own visit. Indigenous guides can greatly improve your access to the residents of highland communities, who are animists and rarely speak Khmer. They also understand taboos and traditions that might be lost on Khmer guides. Their intimate knowledge of the forests is another major asset.

More tips on visiting indigenous communities responsibly:

Interaction

➡ Be polite and respectful – doubly so with elderly people.

➡ Dress modestly.

➡ Taste traditional wine if you are offered it, especially during a ceremony. Refusal will cause offence.

➡ Honour signs discouraging outsiders from entering a village, for instance during a spiritual ceremony. A good local guide will be able to detect these signs.

➡ Learn something about the community's culture and language and demonstrate something good about yours.

Gifts

➡ Individual gifts create jealousy and expectations. Instead, consider making donations to the local school, medical centre or community fund.

---

but are forbidden from taking tourists into the park proper. However, private tour companies can be useful in setting things up in advance with park staff, who are not always responsive.

The signature trek is an eight-day, seven-night **Phnom Veal Thom Wilderness Trek** (per person 1/2 people US$400/350). It starts from Ta Veng with an overnight homestay in a Brau village. The trek then goes deep into the heart of the Phnom Veal Thom grasslands, an area rich in wildlife such as sambar deer, gibbons, langurs, wild pigs, bears and hornbills. Trekkers return via a different route and pass through areas of evergreen forest. The price includes transport by *moto* to the trail head, park admission, food, guides, porters, hammocks and boat transport. Prices drop the larger the group. There are also one- and two-night treks available in the park.

Lumphat   លំផាត់

The former provincial capital of Lumphat, on the banks of Tonlé Srepok, is something

of a ghost town these days thanks to sustained US bombing raids in the early 1970s. The Tonlé Srepok is believed to be the river depicted in the seminal antiwar film *Apocalypse Now,* in which Martin Sheen's Captain Benjamin Willard goes upriver into Cambodia in search of renegade Colonel Kurtz, played by Marlon Brando.

Bei Srok (Tuk Chrouu Bram-pul; admission 2000r) is a popular waterfall with seven gentle tiers. It's about 20km east of Lumphat. You can also get here on a rough road that leads south/southwest from Boeng Yeak Lom. Many Ban Lung tour companies offer Bei Srok as a day tour combined with some abandoned gem mines nearby and bomb-crater spotting around Lumphat. Access is difficult to impossible in the rainy season.

To get to Lumphat from Ban Lung, take the road to Stung Treng for 10km before heading south. The 35km journey takes about 45 minutes. Pick-ups to the taxi park in Ban Lung leave early in the morning from Lumphat and return in the afternoon on most days.

* If you do give individual gifts, keep them modest (such as matches).
* Do not give children sweets or money.
* Do not give clothes – communities are self-sufficient.

Shopping

* Haggle politely and always pay the agreed (and fair) price.
* Do not ask to buy a villager's personal household items, tools or the jewellery or clothes they are wearing.
* Don't buy village treasures, such as altar pieces or totems.

Photographs

* Do not photograph without asking permission first – this includes children. Some hill tribes believe the camera will capture their spirit.
* Don't photograph altars.
* Don't use a flash.
* Don't show up for 15 minutes and expect to be granted permission to take photos. Invest some time in getting to know the villagers first.

Travel

* Make a point of travelling in small, less disruptive groups.
* Try to spend some real time in minority villages – at least several hours if not an overnight. If you don't have a few hours to invest, don't go.

MONDULKIRI PROVINCE

A world apart from lowland Cambodia, Mondulkiri Province (ខេត្តមណ្ឌលគិរី) is the original Wild East of the country. Climatically and culturally, it's also another world, which comes as a relief after the heat of the plains. Home to the hardy Bunong (Pnong) people and their noble elephants, it is possible to visit traditional villages and learn about elephants in their element at the Elephant Valley Project. The landscape is a seductive mix of pine clumps, grassy hills and windswept valleys that fade beguilingly into forests of jade green and hidden waterfalls. Wild animals, such as bears, leopards and especially elephants, are more numerous here than elsewhere, although sightings are usually limited to birds, monkeys and the occasional wild pig.

Mondulkiri means 'Meeting of the Hills', an apt sobriquet for a land of rolling hills. In the dry season it is a little like Wales with sunshine; in the wet season, like Tasmania with more rain. At an average elevation of 800m, it can get quite chilly at night, so carry something warm.

Mondulkiri is the most sparsely populated province in the country, with just four people per square kilometre. Almost half the inhabitants come from the Bunong minority group, with other minorities making up much of the rest of the population. Hunting remains the profession of choice for many minorities.

Conservationists have grand plans for the province, creating wildlife sanctuaries and initiating sustainable tourism activities, but are facing off against speculators and industrialists queuing up for natural resources.

Sen Monorom សែនមនោរម្យ

♪ 073 / POP 10,000

The provincial capital of Mondulkiri, Sen Monorom is really an overgrown village; a charming community set in the spot where the famous hills meet. In the centre of town are two lakes, leading some dreamers to call it 'the Switzerland of Cambodia'. The area around Sen Monorom is peppered with minority villages and picturesque water-falls, making it the ideal place to spend some time. Many of the Bunong people from nearby villages come here to trade, the distinctive baskets they carry on their backs making them easy to distinguish from the immigrant lowlanders. Set at more than 800m, when the winds blow it's notably cooler than the rest of Cambodia, so bring warm clothing.

◉ Sights & Activities

Not much happens in Sen Monorom itself, but there are a few worthwhile sights within a short motorbike ride or a long walk from town.

Monorom Falls   WATERFALL
FREE A 10m drop into a popular swimming hole, Monorom Falls is lovely if you can beat the crowds. From the west side of the air strip, head northwest for 2.3km, turn left and proceed 1.5km. There's no legible sign at the turnoff; if you hit the Forrest Guest-house turnoff you've gone too far.

Wat Phnom Doh Kromom   BUDDHIST TEMPLE
Looming over the northeast corner of the air strip, Wat Phnom Doh Kromom has Mondulkiri's best sunset vista. Continue another 5km north beyond to the wat for **Samot Cheur** (Ocean of Trees), another viewpoint overlooking an emerald forest to the east.

⚐ Tours

As in Ratanakiri, multiday forest treks are immensely popular. We recommend secur-ing indigenous Bunong guides for these trips. They know the forests intimately and can break the ice with the locals in any Bu-nong villages you visit.

The Bunong Place employs a female Bu-nong guide, **Vanny** (☎097 826 9741; tounvanny@gmail.com), who can take you into Bunong villages and/or lead any of the popular day excursions. Other tour operators, such as Nature Lodge and Green House, usually employ Bunong people as porters on long-er excursions, but you should request this service.

All of the guesthouses listed run the full gamut of treks and tours around Sen Mono-rom. Figure on about US$50 per person, per day for overnight trips, including all meals, transfer to the trail head by *moto,* and an English-speaking guide. Per-person prices drop for larger groups.

Elephant Rides   ELEPHANTS
The Elephant Valley Project grabs all the headlines, but you can actually ride an ele-phant in the villages of Phulung, 7km north-east of Sen Monorom, and Putang, 9km southwest of town. Treks arranged in Sen Monorom cost US$25 to US$30 per person, including lunch and transport to and from the village. It can get pretty uncomfortable up on top of an elephant after a couple of hours; carry a pillow to ease the strain.

It is also possible to negotiate a longer trek with an overnight stay in a Bunong vil-lage, costing US$50 to US$80 per person. For a much shorter trek, mahouts hang-ing out at Monorom Falls offer 10-minute rides for US$5. Lastly, Nature Lodge does bareback elephant riding (US$38 including lesson).

COMMUNITY HOMESTAYS IN MONDULKIRI

WWF has recently helped two villages in Mondulkiri's **Phnom Prich Wildlife Sanctu-ary** launch projects geared towards giving tourists a glimpse into traditional Bunong lifestyles.

About 55km north of Sen Monorom on the road to Koh Nhek, the village of **Dei Ey** offers homestays, traditional meals, walking with elephants owned by the local Bunong, and trekking. Cultural activies such as resin collecting and honey making are also on the docket. Prices for a two-day trip start at US$135 for one person and go down substan-tially with each added person. Included are transport, meals cooked by Bunong, guides and accommodation in the Dei Ey Community Lodge.

WWF has launched a similar program in **Sre Y**, about 30km northwest of Sen Mono-rom. Day trips here involve walking with elephants, followed by a trek to a waterfall, then returning to Sen Monorom on mountain bikes.

Contact Nimith at WWF for details on both projects, which can also be booked through tour operators in Sen Monorom. Portions of the proceeds from these initiatives go into a community fund designed to improve local livelihoods and protect the forest.

Sen Monorom

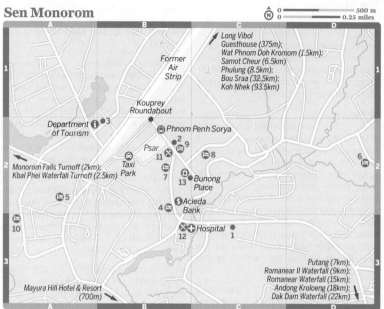

Long Vibol
Guesthouse (375m);
Wat Phnom Doh Kromom (1.5km);
Samot Cheur (6.5km);
Phulung (8.5km);
Bou Sraa (32.5km);
Koh Nhek (93.5km);

Former
Air
Strip

Kouprey
Roundabout

Department 🛈 3
of Tourism

Phnom Penh Sorya

Psar
2 9
11 8

Taxi
Park
7
13 Bunong
Place

Monorom Falls Turnoff (2km);
Kbal Phei Waterfall Turnoff (2.5km)

5

10

Acleda
Bank
4

Hospital
12 1

Putang (7km);
Romanear II Waterfall (9km);
Romanear Waterfall (15km);
Andong Kroloeng (18km);
Dak Dam Waterfall (22km)

Mayura Hill Hotel & Resort
(700m)

Adventure Rider Asia TOUR

(☏078 250350; www.adventureriderasia.com; NH76; tours from US$65 per day) Reini tailors trail-bike tours on the rugged back roads of Mondulkiri, and well beyond for multiday trips. Tours include a high-quality bike and full riding gear.

Green House TOUR

(☏017 905659; www.greenhouse-tour.blogspot. com) Sam Nang works closely with conservation groups on designing ecofriendly tours and is a good source of information about just about everything. Green House helped pilot the Wildlife Conservation Society's black-shank douc project. Besides the normal trekking it also runs full-day mountain-bike tours (about US$20). Trek and Giant mountain bikes (per day US$8) and motorbikes (US$7) are available for hire. He also arranges transport by *moto* to Ban Lung (US$60). Internet access is available.

Veha Jungle Tours TREKKING

(☏097 544 8832; vehatour2012@yahoo.com) A local tour guide offering trips around Mondulkiri Province.

WWF TOUR

(☏073-6900096; www.panda.org) Involved in a host of ecotourism initiatives around Mon-

Sen Monorom

dulkiri and runs its own set of tours north of Sen Monorom in the Phnom Prich Wildlife Sanctuary and Mondulkiri Protected Forest.

Wildlife Conservation Society TOUR

(WCS; ☏023-219443; www.wcscambodia.org) Runs tours to support several initiatives in the Seima Protected Forest west of town.

🛏 Sleeping

Hot water is a nice bonus in chilly Mondulki-ri, but you'll pay extra for it. Places without hot-water showers can usually provide flasks of boiling water for bathing. There is rarely need for air-conditioning in this neck of the woods. The Elephant Valley Project offers an alternative lodging experience.

★ **Nature Lodge** GUESTHOUSE $
(☎012 230272; www.naturelodgecambodia.com; r US$10-30; 🛜) Sprawling across a windswept hilltop near town are 30 solid wood bungalows with private porches, hot showers and mozzie nets. Among them are incredible Swiss Family Robinson–style chalets with sunken beds and hidden rooms. The magnificent restaurant/common area has comfy nooks, a pool table and an enviable bar where guests belly up and swap traveller tales.

Trek-fuelling burgers and pasta are the speciality; an array of tours are neatly outlined on the menu.

Phanyro Guesthouse GUESTHOUSE $
(☎017 770867; r US$8-12; 🛜) This is a favourite with visiting volunteers and NGOs, offering a clutch of tasteful cottages perched on a ridge overlooking the river valley. The rooms fail to exploit the views, but are clean with a capital C and have hot water.

Tree Lodge BUNGALOW $
(☎097 723 4177; www.treelodge-senmonorom. blogspot.com; r with cold/hot water from US$3/5; 🛜) Basic (think bed, floor, mosquito net) A-frame huts made from native materials extend in perfect linear formation down a hill at the back. Hanging out happens at the restaurant, where hammocks and decent Khmer food await. The young family in charge here couldn't be nicer, and are helpful in arranging tours.

Happy Elephant GUESTHOUSE $
(☎097 616 4011; motvil@hotmail.com; d from US$5; 🛜❄) French-Khmer tandem Vivi and Mot are your capable hosts at this backpacker special, which features a half-dozen sturdy cold-water bungalows on a hill behind the pleasingly simple wooden restaurant. Tours galore available, including elephant rides in Bunong communities.

Sovankiri HOSTEL $
(☎097 474 4528; dm per bed US$3, r US$5-8) Run by a Tasmanian-Khmer couple, this centrally situated guesthouse targets backpackers with no-nonsense, clean, affordable rooms. The big dorm beds can sleep two. The popular restaurant has the best Western food in town, fine Khmer food and an attached bar.

Long Vibol Guesthouse GUESTHOUSE $
(☎012 589958; www.longvibol.com; r US$10-25; 🛜) An attractive wooden resort set amid a lush garden just outside the centre. The 20 rooms are smallish but well-appointed compared with what else is in town. Tour guide legend Vibol retired from trekking and is now mayor of Sen Monorom. His old tours are still available with new guides.

Green House Guesthouse GUESTHOUSE $
(Boran Sortha Guesthouse; ☎017 280694; r US$5-20; ❄🛜) Partnered with the tour company of the same name, here you'll find a wide range of rooms from singles with cold water right through to a two-bedroom family suite with air-con.

Pech Kiri Guesthouse GUESTHOUSE $
(☎012 932102; r US$5-30; ❄🛜) Once upon a time, this was the only guesthouse in town and it is still going strong under the lively direction of Madame Deu. Cheap rooms are near the front, while more opulent new digs are at the back.

Mayura Hill Hotel & Resort HOTEL $$$
(☎077 980980; www.mayurahillresort.com; r incl breakfast US$100-120, ste incl breakfast US$150; ❄🛜🏊) It's considerably overpriced for Cambodia (calling the 10 cottages 'villas' is a stretch), but if you are looking for a modicum of comfort and boutique-style amenities like imported linens and a modest-sized pool, Maruya is really the only game in town.

🍴 Eating & Drinking

Most of the guesthouses have restaurants, the most noteworthy of which are Nature Lodge and Sovankiri; the latter also has a good bar if you want to stay up until, oh, 11pm.

Khmer Kitchen CAMBODIAN $
(mains US$2-4; ☉6am-10pm; 🛜) This unassuming streetside eatery whips up some of the most flavoursome Khmer food in the hills. The *kari saik trey* (fish coconut curry) and other curries are particularly scrumptious.

Green House Restaurant & Bar INTERNATIONAL $
(mains US$1.50-3.50) As well as internet access and tour information, Green House is a popular place for inexpensive Khmer and

DEATH OF THE 'DEATH HIGHWAY'?

For years, Mondulkiri and Ratanakiri Provinces were connected by a spider's web of ox-cart trails known as the 'death highway'. Hard-core bikers would get hopelessly lost on this route. Intrepid and knowledgable local drivers would charge tourists US$50 to make the nine-hour trip from Sen Monorom to Ban Lung on the back of a Honda Dream. Completing the trip was a badge of courage on the backpacker trail.

Alas, the death highway is no more. A real highway has been built from Koh Nhek, Mondulkiri, to Lumphat, Ratanakiri, where a new bridge over the Srepok River is scheduled to be ready by late 2014.

If progress is not for you, the cattle tracks of the old 'death highway' do still exist (the new highway takes a different path). Look around in Ban Lung or Sen Monorom for a *moto* driver who will take you on the old route – Mony (see below) is one.

Western dishes plus cocktails against a backdrop of ambient reggae beats.

Mondulkiri Pizza PIZZA **$**
(☑ 097 522 2219; small/large pizza US$5/10; ⊙ 10am-10pm) The big electric oven here churns out a half-decent pie, and will deliver to your guesthouse.

Hefalump Cafe CAFE
(☏) ✐ A collaboration of various NGOs and conservation groups in town, this cafe doubles as a training centre for Bunong people in hospitality. Coffee, tea, cake and sandwiches.

🛍 Shopping

Bunong Place HANDICRAFTS
(☑ 012 474879; www.bunongcenter.org; ⊙ 6am-6pm) Sells authentic Bunong textiles, and local coffee, sodas and beers are available.

ℹ Information

The leading guesthouses in town are also good sources of information.
Acleda Bank (NH76) Changes major currencies and has a Visa-only ATM.
Bunong Place (☑ 012 474879; www.bunongcenter.org; ⊙ 6am-6pm) This NGO-run 'drop-in centre' for Bunong people is a good source of information on sustainable tourism and provides trained Bunong guides for local tours, costing US$15/25 per half/full day, including motorbike. Also sells handicrafts.

ℹ Getting There & Away

The stretch of NH76 connecting Sen Monorom to Snuol and Phnom Penh (370km) is in fantastic shape and passes through large tracts of protected forest. Hardcore dirt bikers may still prefer the old French road heading east from Kao Seima, which runs roughly parallel to NH76.

Phnom Penh Sorya runs a 7.30am bus to Phnom Penh (US$8, eight hours). Express vans run by Chim Vuth Mondulkiri Express and Kim Seng Express do the trip in 5½ hours (US$10). Share taxis are another speedy option to Phnom Penh; try reserving a day ahead through your guesthouse or at the taxi park.

Vehicles to Phnom Penh go via Kompong Cham. Any advertised trip to Siem Reap usually involves a change in Soung.

Local minibuses (departing from the taxi park) are the way forward to Kratie (30,000r, four hours), with at least one early-morning departure and two or three departures around 12.30pm. It's wise to reserve the morning van in advance.

To get to Ratanakiri by public transport, you must backtrack to Snuol or Kratie and pick up transportation there. The new road to Ratanakiri via Koh Nhek (estimated completion date: 2015) will cut many kilometres off this trip and may be served by public transport.

ℹ Getting Around

English-speaking *moto* drivers cost about US$15 to US$20 per day. Sample round-trip *moto* prices for destinations around Sen Monorom are US$12 to Bou Sraa, US$10 to Dak Dam Waterfall, US$5 to Samot Cheur and US$3 for Monorom Falls. **Mony** (☑ 088 593 5588; www.mondulkiritourguide.com) is a *moto* driver who can take you deep into the bush for wildlife-spotting, either on a day trip out of Sen Monorom or on overnights en route to Mimong or Ratanakiri.

Most guesthouses rent out motorbikes for US$6 to US$8 and a few have bicycles for US$2. Adventurer Asia has well-maintained 250cc dirt bikes (US$25) for rent. Pick-up trucks and 4WDs can be chartered for the day. It costs about US$50 around Sen Monorom in the dry season, and more again in the wet season.

Around Sen Monorom

In addition to the waterfalls listed here, look out for a newly accessible **Kbal Phei** waterfall, in the jungle some 20km north-west of town. Follow the signs to Angkor Forest Guesthouse and keep going on the new road (which had not quite yet been completed at the time of writing).

Bou Sraa Waterfall ទឹកជ្រោះប៊ូស្រា

Plunging into the dense Cambodian jungle below, this is one of the country's most impressive falls (ទឹកជ្រោះប៊ូស្រា; admission 5000r). Famous throughout the country, this double-drop waterfall has an upper tier of some 10m and a spectacular lower tier with a thundering 25m drop. To get to the bottom of the lower falls, cross the bridge over the river and follow a path to a precipitous stair-case that continues to the bottom; it takes about 15 minutes to get down.

Bou Sraa is a 33km, one-hour journey east of Sen Monorom on a mostly sealed road.

THE ELEPHANT VALLEY PROJECT

For an original elephant experience, visit the Elephant Valley Project (☏099-696041; www.elephantvalleyproject.org). The project entices local mahouts to bring their over-worked or injured elephants to this sanctuary, where, in the words of project coordinator Jack Highwood, 'they can learn how to act like elephants again'.

A Briton with a contagious passion for elephants, Highwood is on a mission to im-prove the lot of Mondulkiri's working elephants. While Bunong tradition calls for giving elephants a certain amount of down time, Highwood says that economic incentives to overwork elephants prove too great for the impoverished mahouts of Mondulkiri. In addition to toting tourists around on their backs, elephants are hired to haul around anything and everything, including illegally cut timber. 'In Mondulkiri, the elephant is basically seen as a cheap tractor', he says.

Most tour companies in Mondulkiri stress that their tours employ only humanely treated elephants. Highwood commends this, but says it's the exception rather than the rule. 'Most elephants in Mondulkiri are in a highly abused state', he says. 'They are beaten on the head and made to do things they aren't meant to be doing.'

Enter the Elephant Valley Project. Mahouts who bring their elephants here are paid a competitive working wage to retire their elephants full time to ecotourism. Mahouts continue to work with their elephants, feeding and caring for them and making sure they don't escape into the wild. The elephants, for their part, can spend their days blasting through the forest in search of food, uprooting saplings to get to their yummy roots and hanging out by the river spraying mud on one another.

You are not allowed to ride the elephants here. Instead, you simply walk through the forest with them and observe them in their element. In the process you learn a lot about not only elephant behaviour but also Bunong culture and forest ecology. Other project components include health care for Bunong communities in the project area, and health and veterinary care for the mahouts of Mondulkiri. The Wildlife Conservation Society lauds the Elephant Valley Project for helping to protect the eastern reaches of the Seima Protected Forest.

There are two options for visiting the Elephant Valley Project. Option one is a day trip (half/full day US$40/70) in which half the day is spent observing the the elephants, and half the day is spent washing the elephants and doing other tasks around the project site. The other option is an overnight in exquisite bungalows tucked into the jungle on a ridge overlooking the valley. Dorm-style accommodation costs US$20, while private bungalows cost US$30 to US$50. You must still pay the day-trip fee on top of this. Prices include full board. Short- and long-term volunteers who want to help the project while learning mahout skills are welcome.

Access to the site is tightly controlled so don't show up unannounced (there are free-range elephants wandering around after all). It's popular so book well in advance. The maximum amount of day trippers allowed per day is 12. Green House (p278) can handle bookings in Sen Monorom.

The project does not take overnight visitors on Friday and Saturday nights and is not open to visitors on Saturday and Sunday; however, there are plans in place to open six days a week.

MONKEY BUSINESS IN MONDULKIRI

A recent Wildlife Conservation Society (p277) study estimated populations of 30,500 black-shanked doucs in Seima and 2600 yellow-cheeked crested gibbons – the world's largest concentration of both species. You can trek into the wild and possibly spot these primates, along with other wild beasts, thanks to an exciting new project supported by the WCS in the Bunong village of Andong Kraloeng, which lies on the highway just 20km southwest of Sen Monorom. The project site is just a few kilometres north of the highway, so access is relatively easy.

This scheme provides local villagers with an incentive to conserve the endangered primates and their habitat through providing sustainable income. Day treks and overnight trips wind their way through mixed evergreen forest and waterfalls with an excellent chance of spotting the doucs along the way (the gibbons were still being habituated at the time of research). Many other species are present in this area, including abundant bird life, with the world's largest diversity of woodpeckers, the spectacular giant hornbill and resplendent green peafowl. The area is also rich with waterfalls.

Registered guides accompany visitors together with local Bunong guides to identify the trails. A $10 conservation contribution is included in the cost of the trip, which supports community development projects. Sample prices: about $50 per person for a one-day tour, or US$100 for an overnight tour, including all guides, equipment for overnight stays in hammocks, and food. Plans call for building a community guesthouse near the project site in the style of a traditional Bunong house. For information and booking contact Green House (p277) in Sen Monorom.

Basic snacks and drinks are available at the falls, but pack a picnic if you want something more sophisticated.

Other Waterfalls

Other popular waterfalls in Mondulkiri include Romanear Waterfall, 18km southeast of Sen Monorom, and Dak Dam Waterfall, 25km southeast of Sen Monorom. Both are very difficult to find without assistance, so it's best to take a *moto* driver or local guide. Romanear is a low, wide waterfall with some convenient swimming holes. There is also a second Romanear Waterfall, known rather originally as Romanear II, which is near the main road between Sen Monorom and Snuol. Dak Dam is similar to the Monorom Falls, albeit with a greater volume of water. The waterfall is several kilometres beyond the Bunong village of Dak Dam and locals are able to lead the way if you can make yourself understood.

Bunong Villages

Several Bunong villages around Sen Monorom make for popular excursions, although the frequently visited villages that appear on tourist maps have assimilated into modern society. In general, the further out you go, the less exposed the village. Trips to Bunong villages can often be combined with waterfalls or elephant treks. Each guesthouse has a preferred village to send travellers to, which is a great way to spread the wealth.

Seima Protected Forest តំបន់ការពារព្រៃឈើកែវសីមា

The 3000-sq-km Seima Protected Forest may host the country's greatest treasure trove of mammalian wildlife. Besides unprecedented numbers of black-shanked doucs and yellow-cheeked crested gibbons, an estimated 150 wild elephants – accounting for more than half of the total population in Cambodia – roam the park, along with bears and seven species of cat. The bird life is also impressive, and the jungle, which is lusher and denser than the dry forest in eastern Mondulkiri, has been relatively well preserved.

WCS supports the government's Forestry Administration to manage the forest, and there are a range of ecotourism enterprises in development, including douc- and gibbon-spotting in Andong Kraloeng. WCS' partner and birdwatching specialist Sam Veasna Center (☎ 063-963710; www.samveasna.org) runs birdwatching trips in Seima not far from Kao Seima for around US$100 per

MONDULKIRI PROTECTED FOREST: THE AFRICAN EXPERIENCE IN CAMBODIA

Before the civil war, the vast grasslands of northern Mondulkiri were home to huge herds of gaur, banteng and wild buffalo. Visitors lucky enough to witness their annual migrations compared the experience to the Serengeti and the annual wildebeest migrations. Sadly, the long civil war took its toll and, like Uganda and other African countries, thousands of animals were killed (and are still killed) for bush meat.

WWF (☑ 012 776003, 073-690 0096; www.mondulkiritourism.org) has been working hard to return this area to its former glory through conservation initiatives in the Mondulkiri Protected Forest, one of the largest protected areas in Cambodia, which provides a home to leopards, bears, langurs, gibbons, wild cows and rare bird life (tigers have not been spotted since roughly 2007). During our most recent visit, we saw several herds of banteng, a rare type of wild cow. Ecotourism is part of the mix, but several initiatives, including a high-end jungle ecolodge on the Srepok River, have been scrapped because of the remoteness of the place. Another problem is that many of the cats, bears and other exotic prowlers that patrol the area are more elusive than banteng. Check with the WWF to find out the latest on tours into this area.

person per day, including highly trained guides, plus a flat US$30-per-person conservation fee. Guests usually opt to sleep in Sen Monorom.

For the latest developments on tours in the park contact Green House (p277), Sam Veasna Center or CRD Tours (p259) in Kratie.

The road to Sen Monorom passes right through Seima Protected Forest – look out for monkeys!

Koh Nhek   កោះញែក

POP 6000

The final frontier as far as Mondulkiri goes, this village in the far north of the province is a strategic place on the overland route be-

tween Sen Monorom and Ratanakiri Province. This is traditionally where the road from Sen Monorom ended and the cattle track to Lumphat, Ratanankiri, began. Now it is a rest stop on the new Mondulkiri–Ratanakiri highway.

As well as making it easier for travellers to get from Mondulkiri to Ban Lung, the new road should provide a little economic boost to Koh Nhek. An Acleda Bank (no ATM) is a sign of changing times.

There is a pair of unnamed guesthouses in town. The store on the northeast corner of the main intersection has food and some basic supplies, including cold beer – well earned by the time you get here.

Understand Cambodia

Cambodia Today

Cambodia is a compelling country to visit, in part due to the complex socio-political system in which the country is cocooned. The political landscape shifted decisively in the 2013 election and that promises to make for some interesting years ahead. The economy continues to grow at a dramatic pace, albeit from a low base, but many observers are beginning to question at what cost to the delicate environment.

Best on Film

The Killing Fields (1984) This definitive film on the Khmer Rouge period in Cambodia tells the story of American journalist Sydney Schanberg and his Cambodian assistant Dith Pran during and after the war.

Apocalypse Now (1979) In Francis Ford Coppola's masterpiece, a renegade colonel, played by Marlon Brando, goes AWOL in Cambodia. Martin Sheen plays a young soldier sent to bring him back, and the ensuing encounter makes for one of the most powerful indictments of war ever made.

Best in Print

Cambodia's Curse (Joel Brinkley) Pulitzer Prize–winning journalist pulls no punches in his criticism of the government and donors alike.

Cambodia Now (Karen Coates) A no-holds-barred look at contemporary Cambodia through the eyes of its diverse population.

The Gate (François Bizot) Bizot was kidnapped by the Khmer Rouge, and later held by them in the French embassy.

Voices from S-21 (David Chandler) A study of the Khmer Rouge's interrogation and torture centre.

Politics

The Cambodian People's Party (CPP) has dominated the politics of Cambodia since 1979 when it was installed in power by the Vietnamese. Party and state are intertwined and the CPP leadership has been making plans for the future with dynastic alliances between its offspring. Just look at the roll call of marriages in the past decade and it soon becomes apparent that senior leaders such as Prime Minister Hun Sen have their eyes firmly on a potential handover of power to the children of the elite.

However, this sophisticated system of control was shaken in the 2013 national election when the united opposition was able to make significant gains in the national assembly. Long-standing opposition leader Sam Rainsy united with Human Rights Party leader Kem Sokha to launch the Cambodia National Rescue Party (CNRP).

Official results from the National Election Commission (NEC) showed the CPP had won 68 seats and the CNRP 55 seats, a dramatic decline for the previously unassailable CPP. However, the opposition cried foul, as the NEC is seen by observers as a tool of the ruling party. According to official opposition counts and some independent observers, the CNRP may have even won the popular vote by a slight majority and claimed 62 seats to the CPP's 61 seats.

The CPP pushed ahead with official results and the new assembly was sworn in with only 68 MPs, as the opposition refused to take its seats. Mass demonstrations were called and petitions delivered to embassies around Phnom Penh. At the time of writing, the demonstrations remained largely peaceful, but the political impasse continued. Many Cambodians hope that both sides will reach a compromise and that in time this surprise result will put pressure on the CPP to introduce much-needed political and electoral reform. The next five years will be very interesting indeed.

Economy

Badly traumatised by decades of conflict, Cambodia's economy was long a gecko amid the neighbouring dragons. This has slowly started to change, as the economy has been liberalised and investors are circling to take advantage of the new opportunities. Asian investors are flocking to Phnom Penh, led by the Chinese and South Koreans who have inked deals for skyscrapers all over the low-rise city.

The government, long shunned by international big business, is keen to benefit from all these new-found opportunities. Contracts are being signed off like autographs and there are concerns for the long-term development of the country. China has come to the table to play for big stakes, and is now annually pledging as much as all the other donors put together, with no burdensome strings attached.

Aid was long the mainstay of the Cambodian economy, supporting half the government's budget, and NGOs have done a lot to force important socio-political issues onto the agenda. However, Cambodia remains one of Asia's poorest countries. Income remains desperately low for many Khmers, with annual salaries in the hundreds rather than thousands of dollars, and public servants, such as teachers, are unable to eke out a living on their meagre wages.

Economy Versus Environment

Cambodia's pristine environment may be a big draw for adventurous ecotourists, but much of it is currently under threat. Ancient forests are being razed to make way for plantations, rivers are being sized up for major hydroelectric power plants and the South Coast is being explored by leading oil companies. Places like the Cardamom Mountains are in the front line and it remains to be seen whether the environmentalists or the economists will win the debate. All this adds up to an ever-stronger economy, but it's unlikely to encourage the ecotourism that is just starting to take off.

Media

Cambodia's media scene looks to be in good shape on paper, with freedom of the press enshrined in the constitution, but the everyday reality is a different story. The governing CPP control all the national television stations and most of the radio stations and newspapers. Opposition demonstrations or antigovernment activities are almost never reported via official channels. However, social media is plugging the gap and a new generation of young Cambodians are avid Facebook and YouTube users. Armed with smartphones, people are now capturing police and military abuses on camera, making it harder for the government to deny responsibility for heavy-handed crackdowns on dissent. With opposition support officially hovering around the 50% mark, some of the official media may need to change its tune to remain in touch with the popular mood.

POPULATION: **15.5 MILLION**

GDP: **US$14.25 BILLION (2012)**

LIFE EXPECTANCY: **65 YEARS**

ADULT LITERACY RATE: **78%**

INFANT MORTALITY: **45 PER 1000 BIRTHS**

if Cambodia were 100 people

90 would be Khmer
5 would be Vietnamese
3 would be Cham
1 would be Chinese
1 would be ethnic minority

origin of visitors (%)

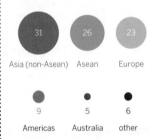

31 Asia (non-Asean)
26 Asean
23 Europe

9 Americas
5 Australia
6 other

population per sq km

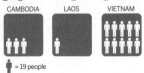

CAMBODIA LAOS VIETNAM

≈ 19 people

History

'The good, the bad and the ugly' is a simple way to sum up Cambodian history. Things were good in the early years, culminating in the vast Angkor empire, unrivalled in the region during four centuries of dominance. Then the bad set in, from the 13th century, as ascendant neighbours steadily chipped away at Cambodian territory. In the 20th century it turned downright ugly, as a brutal civil war culminated in the genocidal rule of the Khmer Rouge (1975–79), from which Cambodia is still recovering today.

Cambodia's Funan-period trading port of Oc-Eo, now located in Vietnam's Mekong Delta, was a major commercial crossroads between Asia and Europe, and archaeologists there have unearthed Roman coins and Persian pottery.

The Origin of the Khmers

Like many legends, the one about the origin of Cambodia is historically opaque, but it does say something about the cultural forces that brought Cambodia into existence, in particular its relationship with its great subcontinental neighbour, India. Cambodia's religious, royal and written traditions stemmed from India and began to coalesce as a cultural entity in their own right between the 1st and 5th centuries AD.

Very little is known about prehistoric Cambodia. Much of the southeast was a vast, shallow gulf that was progressively silted up by the mouths of the Mekong, leaving pancake-flat, mineral-rich land ideal for farming. Evidence of cave-dwellers has been found in the northwest of Cambodia, and carbon dating on ceramic pots found in the area shows that they were made around 4200 BC. Examinations of bones dating back to around 1500 BC suggest that the people living in Cambodia at that time resembled the Cambodians of today. Early Chinese records report that the Cambodians were 'ugly' and 'dark' and went about naked. A healthy dose of scepticism may be required, however, when reading the reports of imperial China concerning its 'barbarian' neighbours.

The Early Cambodian Kingdoms

Cambodian might didn't begin and end with Angkor. There were a number of powerful kingdoms present in this area before the 9th century.

From the 1st century AD, the Indianisation of Cambodia occurred through trading settlements that sprang up on the coastline of what is

TIMELINE	4200 BC	AD 100	245
	Cave-dwellers capable of making pots inhabit caves around Laang Spean; archaeological evidence suggests their vessels were similar to those still made in Cambodia today.	The religions, language and sculpture styles of India start to take root in Cambodia with the arrival of Indian traders and holy men.	The Chinese Wei emperor sends a mission to the countries of the Mekong region and is told that a barbarous but rich country called Funan exists in the Delta region.

now southern Vietnam, but was then inhabited by the Khmers. These settlements were important ports of call for boats following the trading route from the Bay of Bengal to the southern provinces of China. The largest of these nascent kingdoms was known as Funan by the Chinese, and may have existed across an area between modern Phnom Penh and the archaeological site of Oc-Eo in Kien Giang Province in southern Vietnam. Funan would have been a contemporary of Champasak in southern Laos (then known as Kuruksetra) and other lesser fiefdoms in the region.

Funan is a Chinese name and may be a transliteration of the ancient Khmer word *bnam* (mountain). Although very little is known about Funan, much has been made of its importance as an early Southeast Asian centre of power.

It is most likely that between the 1st and 8th centuries Cambodia was a collection of small states, each with its own elites who strategically intermarried and often went to war with one another. Funan was no doubt one of these states, and as a major sea port would have been pivotal in the transmission of Indian culture into the interior of Cambodia.

The little that historians do know about Funan has mostly been gleaned from Chinese sources. These report that Funan-period Cambodia (1st century to 6th century AD) embraced the worship of the Hindu deities Shiva and Vishnu and, at the same time, Buddhism. The *linga* (phallic totem) appears to have been the focus of ritual and an emblem of kingly might, a feature that was to evolve further in the Angkorian cult of the god-king. The people practised primitive irrigation, which enabled successful cultivation of rice, and traded raw commodities such as spices and precious stones with China and India.

Cambodia's turbulent past is uncovered in a series of articles, oral histories and photos in an excellent website called Beauty and Darkness: Cambodia, the Odyssey of the Khmer People. Find it at www.mekong.net/cambodia.

JAYAVARMAN VII

A devout follower of Mahayana Buddhism, Jayavarman VII (r 1181–1219) built the city of Angkor Thom and many other massive monuments. Indeed, many of the temples visited around Angkor today were constructed during Jayavarman VII's reign. However, Jayavarman VII is a figure of many contradictions. The bas-reliefs of the Bayon depict him presiding over battles of terrible ferocity, while statues of the king depict a meditative, otherworldly aspect. His program of temple construction and other public works was carried out in great haste, no doubt bringing enormous hardship to the labourers who provided the muscle, and thus accelerating the decline of the empire. He was partly driven by a desire to legitimise his rule, as there may have been other contenders closer to the royal bloodline, and partly by the need to introduce a new religion to a population predominantly Hindu in faith. However, in many ways he was also Cambodia's first progressive leader, proclaiming the population equal, abolishing castes and embarking on a program of school, hospital and road building.

600	802	889	924
The first inscriptions are committed to stone in Cambodia in ancient Khmer, offering historians the only contemporary accounts of the pre-Angkorian period other than from Chinese sources.	Jayavarman II proclaims independence from Java in a ceremony to anoint himself a *devaraja* (god-king) on the holy mountain of Phnom Kulen, marking the birth of the Khmer Empire of Angkor.	Yasovarman I moves the capital from the ancient city of Hariharalaya (Roluos today) to the Angkor area, 16km to the northwest, and marks the location with three temple mountains.	Usurper king Jayavarman IV transfers the capital to Koh Ker and begins a mammoth building spree, but the lack of water sees the capital move back to Angkor just 20 years later.

From the 6th century, Cambodia's population gradually concentrated along the Mekong and Tonlé Sap Rivers, where msot people remain today. The move may have been related to the development of wet-rice agriculture. Between the 6th and 8th centuries, Cambodia was a collection of competing kingdoms, ruled by autocratic kings who legitimised their rule through hierarchical caste concepts borrowed from India.

This era is generally referred to as the Chenla period. Like Funan, this is a Chinese term and there is little to support the idea that Chenla was a unified kingdom that held sway over all of Cambodia. Indeed, the Chinese themselves referred to 'water Chenla' and 'land Chenla'. Water Chenla was located around Angkor Borei and the temple mount of Phnom Da, near the present-day provincial capital of Takeo, and land Chenla in the upper reaches of the Mekong River and east of Tonlé Sap lake, around Sambor Prei Kuk, an essential stop on a chronological jaunt through Cambodia's history.

> The Documentation Center of Cambodia is an organisation established to document the crimes of the Khmer Rouge as a record for future generations. Its excellent website has a wealth of information about Cambodia's darkest hour. Take your time to visit www.dccam.org.

The Rise of the Angkorian Empire

Gradually the Cambodian region was becoming more cohesive. Before long the fractured kingdoms of Cambodia would merge to become a sprawling Asian empire.

A popular place of pilgrimage for Khmers today, the sacred mountain of Phnom Kulen, northeast of Angkor, is home to an inscription that tells of Jayavarman II (r 802–50) proclaiming himself a 'universal monarch', or *devaraja* (god-king) in 802. It is believed that he may have resided in the Buddhist Shailendras' court in Java as a young man and was inspired by the great Javanese temples of Borobudur and Prambanan near present-day Yogyakarta. Upon his return to Cambodia, he instigated an uprising against Javanese control over the southern lands of Cambodia. Jayavarman II then set out to bring the country under his control through alliances and conquests, becoming the first monarch to rule most of what we call Cambodia today.

Jayavarman II was the first of a long succession of kings who presided over the rise and fall of the greatest empire mainland Southeast Asia has ever seen, one that was to bequeath the stunning legacy of Angkor. The key to the meteoric rise of Angkor was a mastery of water and an elaborate hydraulic system that allowed the ancient Khmers to tame the elements. The first records of the massive irrigation works that supported the population of Angkor date to the reign of Indravarman I (r 877–89), who built the *baray* (reservoir) of Indratataka. His rule also marks the flourishing of Angkorian art, with the building of temples in the Roluos area, notably Bakong.

> India wasn't the only power to have a major cultural impact on Cambodia. The island of Java was also influential, colonising part of 'water Chenla' in the 8th century.

By the turn of the 11th century, the kingdom of Angkor was losing control of its territories. Suryavarman I (r 1002–49), a usurper, moved

1002	1112	1152	1177
Suryavarman I comes to power and expands the extent of the kingdom by annexing the Buddhist kingdom of Louvo (known as Lopburi in modern-day Thailand). He also increases trade links with the outside world.	Suryavarman II commences the construction of Angkor Wat, the mother of all temples, dedicated to Vishnu and designed as his funerary temple.	Suryavarman II is killed in a disastrous campaign against the Dai Viet (Vietnamese), provoking this rising northern neighbour and sparking centuries of conflict between the two countries.	The Chams launch a surprise attack on Angkor by sailing up the Tonlé Sap. They defeat the powerful Khmers and occupy the capital for four years.

into the power vacuum and, like Jayavarman II two centuries before, re-unified the kingdom through war and alliances, stretching the frontiers of the empire. A pattern was beginning to emerge, which was repeated throughout the Angkorian period: dislocation and turmoil, followed by reunification and further expansion under a powerful king. Architecturally, the most productive periods occurred after times of turmoil, indicating that newly incumbent monarchs felt the need to celebrate, even legitimise, their rule with massive building projects.

By 1066, Angkor was again riven by conflict, becoming the focus of rival bids for power. It was not until the accession of Suryavarman II (r 1112–52) that the kingdom was again unified. Suryavarman II embarked on another phase of expansion, waging costly wars in Vietnam and the region of central Vietnam known as Champa. Suryavarman II is immortalised as the king who, in his devotion to the Hindu deity Vishnu, commissioned the majestic temple of Angkor Wat. For an insight into events in this epoch, see the bas-reliefs on the southwest corridor of Angkor Wat, which depict the reign of Suryavarman II.

Suryavarman II had brought Champa to heel and reduced it to vassal status, but the Chams struck back in 1177 with a naval expedition up the Mekong and into Tonlé Sap lake. They took the city of Angkor by surprise and put King Dharanindravarman II to death. The following year a cousin of Suryavarman II rallied the Khmer troops and defeated the Chams in another naval battle. The new leader was crowned Jayavarman VII in 1181.

Decline & Fall of Angkor

Angkor was the epicentre of an incredible empire that held sway over much of the Mekong region, but like all empires, the sun was to eventually set.

A number of scholars have argued that decline was already on the horizon at the time Angkor Wat was built, when the Angkorian empire was at the height of its remarkable productivity. There are indications that the irrigation network was overworked and slowly starting to silt up due to the massive deforestation that had taken place in the heavily populated areas to the north and east of Angkor. This was exacerbated by prolonged periods of drought in the 14th century, which was more recently discovered through the advanced analysis of dendrochronology, or the study of tree rings, in the Angkor area.

Massive construction projects such as Angkor Wat and Angkor Thom no doubt put an enormous strain on the royal coffers and on thousands of slaves and common people who subsidised them in hard labour and taxes. Following the reign of Jayavarman VII, temple construction effectively ground to a halt, in large part because Jayavarman VII's public works had quarried local sandstone into oblivion and left the population exhausted.

During much of the 1980s, the second-largest concentration of Cambodians outside Phnom Penh was in the Khao I Dang refugee camp on the Thai border.

1181
The Chams are vanquished as Jayavarman VII, the greatest king of Angkor and builder of Angkor Thom, takes the throne, changing the state religion to Mahayana Buddhism.

1219
Jayavarman VII dies aged in his 90s, and the empire of Angkor slowly declines due to a choking irrigation network, religious conflict and the rise of powerful neighbours.

➡ Statues of serpent-carrying giants, Angkor Thom (p139)

Another challenge for the later kings was religious conflict and internecine rivalries. The state religion changed back and forth several times during the twilight years of the empire, and kings spent more time engaged in defacing the temples of their predecessors, than building monuments to their own achievements. From time to time this boiled over into civil war.

Angkor was losing control over the peripheries of its empire. At the same time, the Thais were ascendant, having migrated south from Yunnan, China, to escape Kublai Khan and his Mongol hordes. The Thais, first from Sukothai, later Ayuthaya, grew in strength and made repeated incursions into Angkor before finally sacking the city in 1431 and making off with thousands of intellectuals, artisans and dancers from the royal court. During this period, perhaps drawn by the opportunities for sea trade with China and fearful of the increasingly bellicose Thais, the Khmer elite began to migrate to the Phnom Penh area. The capital shifted several times over the centuries but eventually settled in present-day Phnom Penh.

From 1500 until the arrival of the French in 1863, Cambodia was ruled by a series of weak kings beset by dynastic rivalries. In the face of such intrigue, they sought the protection – granted, of course, at a price – of either Thailand or Vietnam. In the 17th century the Nguyen lords of southern Vietnam came to the rescue of the Cambodian king in return for settlement rights in the Mekong Delta region. The Khmers still refer to this region as Kampuchea Krom (Lower Cambodia), even though it is well and truly populated by the Vietnamese today.

In the west, the Thais controlled the provinces of Battambang and Siem Reap from 1794 and held influence over the Cambodian royal family. Indeed, one king was crowned in Bangkok and placed on the throne at Udong with the help of the Thai army. That Cambodia survived through the 18th century as a distinct entity is due to the preoccupations of its neighbours: while the Thais were expending their energy and resources fighting the Burmese, the Vietnamese were wholly absorbed by internal strife. The pattern continued for more than two centuries, the carcass of Cambodia pulled back and forth between two powerful tigers.

THE LEGEND OF KAUNDINYA & THE NAGA PRINCESS

Cambodia came into being, so the legend says, through the union of a princess and a foreigner. The foreigner was an Indian Brahman named Kaundinya and the princess was the daughter of a naga (mythical serpent-being) king who ruled over a watery land. One day, as Kaundinya sailed by, the princess paddled out in a boat to greet him. Kaundinya shot an arrow from his magic bow into her boat, causing the fearful princess to agree to marriage. In need of a dowry, her father drank up the waters of his land and presented them to Kaundinya to rule over. The new kingdom was named Kambuja.

1253	1296	1353	1431
The Mongols of Kublai Khan sack the Thai kingdom of Nanchao in Yunnan, sparking an exodus southwards, which brings Thais into direct conflict with the weakening Khmer empire.	Chinese emissary Chou Ta Kuan spends one year living at Angkor and writes *The Customs of Cambodia*, the only contemporary account of life in the great Khmer capital.	Lao prince Chao Fa Ngum ends his Angkor exile and is sponsored by his Khmer father-in-law on an expedition to conquer the new Thai kingdoms, declaring himself leader of Lan Xang (Land of a Million Elephants).	The Thais sack Angkor definitively, carting off most of the royal court to Ayuthaya, including nobles, priests, dancers and artisans.

The French in Cambodia

The era of yo-yoing between Thai and Vietnamese masters came to a close in 1863, when French gunboats intimidated King Norodom I (r 1860–1904) into signing a treaty of protectorate. Ironically, it really was a protectorate, as Cambodia was in danger of going the way of Champa and vanishing from the map. French control of Cambodia developed as a sideshow to its interests in Vietnam, uncannily similar to the American experience a century later, and initially involved little direct interference in Cambodia's affairs. The French presence also helped keep Norodom on the throne despite the ambitions of his rebellious half-brothers.

By the 1870s, French officials in Cambodia began pressing for greater control over internal affairs. In 1884 Norodom was forced into signing a treaty that turned his country into a virtual colony, sparking a two-year rebellion that constituted the only major uprising in Cambodia before WWII. The rebellion only ended when the king was persuaded to call upon the rebel fighters to lay down their weapons in exchange for a return to the status quo.

During the following decades, senior Cambodian officials opened the door to direct French control over the day-to-day administration of the country, as they saw certain advantages in acquiescing to French power. The French maintained Norodom's court in splendour unseen since the heyday of Angkor, helping to enhance the symbolic position of the monarchy. In 1907 the French were able to pressure Thailand into returning the northwest provinces of Battambang, Siem Reap and Preah Vihear in return for concessions of Lao territory to the Thais. This meant Angkor came under Cambodian control for the first time in more than a century.

King Norodom I was succeeded by King Sisowath (r 1904–27), who was succeeded by King Monivong (r 1927–41). Upon King Monivong's death, the French governor-general of Japanese-occupied Indochina, Admiral Jean Decoux, placed 19-year-old Prince Norodom Sihanouk on the Cambodian throne. The French authorities assumed young Sihanouk would prove pliable, but this proved to be a major miscalculation.

During WWII, Japanese forces occupied much of Asia, and Cambodia was no exception. However, with many in France collaborating with the occupying Germans, the Japanese were happy to let their new Vichy France allies control affairs in Cambodia. The price was conceding to Thailand (a Japanese ally of sorts) much of Battambang and Siem Reap Provinces once again, areas that weren't returned until 1947. However, after the fall of Paris in 1944 and with French policy in disarray, the Japanese were forced to take direct control of the territory by early 1945. After WWII, the French returned, making Cambodia an autonomous state

One of the definitive guides to Angkor is *A Guide to the Angkor Monuments* by Maurice Glaize, first published in the 1940s and now out of print. Download it free at www.theangkorguide.com.

The French did very little to encourage education in Cambodia, and by the end of WWII, after 70 years of colonial rule, there were no universities and only one high school in the whole country.

HISTORY THE FRENCH IN CAMBODIA

1594	**1772**	**1834**	**1863**
Temporary Cambodian capital of Lovek falls when, legend says, the Siamese fire a cannon of silver coins into its bamboo defences. Soldiers cut down the bamboo to retrieve the silver, leaving the city exposed.	Cambodia is caught between the powerful Vietnamese and Siamese, and the latter burn Phnom Penh to the ground, another chapter in the story of inflamed tensions, which persist today.	The Vietnamese take control of much of Cambodia during the reign of Emperor Minh Mang and begin a slow revolution to 'teach the barbarians their customs'.	The French force King Norodom I into signing a treaty of protectorate, which prevents Cambodia being wiped off the map and thus begins 90 years of French rule.

within the French Union, but retaining de facto control. The immediate postwar years were marked by strife among the country's various political factions, a situation made more unstable by the Franco-Vietminh War then raging in Vietnam and Laos, which spilled over into Cambodia. The Vietnamese, as they were also to do 20 years later in the war against Lon Nol and the Americans, trained and fought with bands of Khmer Issarak (Free Khmer) against the French authorities.

For more on the incredible life and times of Norodom Sihanouk, read the biography *Prince of Light, Prince of Darkness* (1994) by Milton Osborne.

The Sihanouk Years

The postindependence period was one of peace and prosperity. It was Cambodia's golden era, a time of creativity and optimism. Phnom Penh grew in size and stature, the temples of Angkor were the leading tourist destination in Southeast Asia and Sihanouk played host to a succession of influential leaders from across the globe. However, dark clouds were circling, as the American war in Vietnam became a black hole, sucking in neighbouring countries.

In late 1952 King Sihanouk dissolved the fledgling parliament, declared martial law and embarked on his 'royal crusade', a travelling campaign to drum up international support for his country's independence. Independence was proclaimed on 9 November 1953 and recognised by the Geneva Conference of May 1954, which ended French control of Indochina. In 1955, Sihanouk abdicated, afraid of being marginalised amid the pomp of royal ceremony. The 'royal crusader' became 'citizen Sihanouk'. He vowed never again to return to the throne. Meanwhile his father became king. It was a masterstroke that offered Sihanouk both royal authority and supreme political power. His newly established party, Sangkum Reastr Niyum (People's Socialist Community), won every seat in parliament in the September 1955 elections and Sihanouk was to dominate Cambodian politics for the next 15 years.

Journalist Henry Kamm spent many years filing reports from Cambodia and his book *Cambodia: Report from a Stricken Land* is a fascinating insight into recent events.

Although he feared the Vietnamese communists, Sihanouk considered South Vietnam and Thailand – both allies of the mistrusted USA – the greatest threats to Cambodia's security, even survival. In an attempt to fend off these many dangers, he declared Cambodia neutral and refused to accept further US aid, which had accounted for a substantial chunk of the country's military budget. He also nationalised many industries, including the rice trade. In 1965 Sihanouk, convinced that the USA had been plotting against him and his family, broke diplomatic relations with Washington and veered towards the North Vietnamese and China. In addition, he agreed to let the communists use Cambodian territory in their battle against South Vietnam and the USA. Sihanouk was taking sides, a dangerous position in a volatile region.

1884	1907	1942	1947
Rebellion against French rule in Cambodia erupts in response to a treaty giving French administrators wide-ranging powers. The treaty is signed under the watch of French gunboats in the Mekong River.	French authorities successfully negotiate the return of the northwest provinces of Siem Reap, Battambang and Preah Vihear, which have been under Thai control since 1794.	Japanese forces occupy Cambodia, leaving the administration in the hands of Vichy France officials, but fan the flames of independence as the war draws to a close.	The provinces of Battambang, Siem Reap and Sisophon, seized by the Thais during the Japanese occupation, are returned to Cambodia.

These moves and his socialist economic policies alienated conservative elements in Cambodian society, including the army brass and the urban elite. At the same time, left-wing Cambodians, many of them educated abroad, deeply resented his domestic policies, which stifled political debate. Compounding Sihanouk's problems was the fact that all classes were fed up with the pervasive corruption in government ranks, some of it uncomfortably close to the royal family. Although most peasants revered Sihanouk as a semidivine figure, in 1967 a rural-based rebellion broke out

SIHANOUK: THE LAST OF THE GOD-KINGS

Norodom Sihanouk was a towering presence in the topsy-turvy world of Cambodian politics. A larger-than-life character of many enthusiasms and shifting political positions, amatory exploits dominated his early life. Later he became the prince who stage-managed the close of French colonialism, led Cambodia during its golden years, was imprisoned by the Khmer Rouge and, from privileged exile, finally returned triumphant as king. He is many things to many people, but whatever else he may be, he has proven himself a survivor.

Sihanouk, born in 1922, was not an obvious contender for the throne, as he was from the Norodom branch of the royal family. He was crowned in 1941, at just 19, with his education incomplete. In 1955 Sihanouk abdicated and turned his attention to politics, his party winning every seat in parliament that year. By the mid-1960s Sihanouk had been calling the shots in Cambodia for a decade.

The conventional wisdom was that 'Sihanouk is Cambodia', his leadership the key to national success. However, as the country was inexorably drawn into the American war in Vietnam and government troops battled with a leftist insurgency in the countryside, Sihanouk was increasingly seen as a liability.

On 18 March 1970 the National Assembly voted to remove Sihanouk from office. He went into exile in Beijing and joined the communists. Following the Khmer Rouge victory on 17 April 1975, Sihanouk returned to Cambodia as head of the new state of Democratic Kampuchea. He resigned after less than a year and was confined to the Royal Palace as a prisoner of the Khmer Rouge. He remained there until early 1979 when, on the eve of the Vietnamese invasion, he was flown back to Beijing.

Sihanouk never quite gave up wanting to be everything for Cambodia: international statesman, general, president, film director and man of the people. On 24 September 1993, after 38 years in politics, he settled once more for the role of king. On 7 October 2004 he once again abdicated, and his son King Sihamoni ascended to the throne. However, Sihanouk's place in history is assured, the last in a long line of Angkor's god-kings.

Norodom Sihanouk passed away on 15 October 2012 in Beijing and his body was flown back to Cambodia a few days later. More than one million Cambodians lined the streets from the airport to the Royal Palace and his body was laid in state for 100 days before an elaborate state funeral.

1953	1955	1962	1963
Sihanouk's royal crusade for independence succeeds and Cambodia goes it alone without the French on 9 November, ushering in a new era of optimism.	King Sihanouk abdicates from the throne to enter a career in politics; he founds the Sangkum Reastr Niyum (People's Socialist Community) party and wins the election with ease.	The International Court rules in favour of Cambodia in the long-running dispute over the dramatic mountain temple of Preah Vihear, perched on the Dangkrek Mountains on the border with Thailand.	Pol Pot and Ieng Sary flee from Phnom Penh to the jungles of Ratanakiri. With training from the Vietnamese, they launch a guerrilla war against Sihanouk's government.

BOMBS

in Samlot, Battambang, leading him to conclude that the greatest threat to his regime came from the left. Bowing to pressure from the army, he implemented a policy of harsh repression against left-wingers.

By 1969 the conflict between the army and leftist rebels had become more serious, as the Vietnamese sought sanctuary deeper in Cambodia. Sihanouk's political position had also decidedly deteriorated – due in no small part to his obsession with film-making, which was leading him to neglect affairs of state. In March 1970, while Sihanouk was on a trip to France, General Lon Nol and Prince Sisowath Sirik Matak, Sihanouk's cousin, deposed him as chief of state, apparently with tacit US consent. Sihanouk took up residence in Beijing, where he set up a government-in-exile in alliance with an indigenous Cambodian revolutionary movement that Sihanouk had nicknamed the Khmer Rouge. This was a definitive moment in contemporary Cambodian history, as the Khmer Rouge exploited its partnership with Sihanouk to draw new recruits into their small organisation. Talk to many former Khmer Rouge fighters and they'll say that they 'went to the hills' (a euphemism for joining the Khmer Rouge) to fight for their king and knew nothing of Mao or Marxism.

During the US bombing campaign, more bombs were dropped on Cambodia than were used by all sides during WWII.

Descent into Civil War

The lines were drawn for a bloody era of civil war. Sihanouk was condemned to death in absentia, a harsh move on the part of the new government that effectively ruled out any hint of compromise for the next five years. Lon Nol gave communist Vietnamese forces an ultimatum to withdraw their units within one week, which amounted to a declaration of war, as the Vietnamese did not want to return to the homeland to face the Americans.

To the End of Hell: One Woman's Struggle to Survive Cambodia's Khmer Rouge is the incredible memoir of Denise Affonço, one of the only foreigners to live through the Khmer Rouge revolution, due to her marriage to a senior intellectual in the movement.

On 30 April 1970, US and South Vietnamese forces invaded Cambodia in an effort to flush out thousands of Viet Cong and North Vietnamese troops who were using Cambodian bases in their war to overthrow the South Vietnamese government. As a result of the invasion, the Vietnamese communists withdrew deeper into Cambodia, further destabilising the Lon Nol government. Cambodia's tiny army never stood a chance and within the space of a few months, Vietnamese forces and their Khmer Rouge allies overran almost half the country. The ultimate humiliation came in July 1970 when the Vietnamese occupied the temples of Angkor.

In 1969 the USA launched Operation Menu, the secret bombing of suspected communist base camps in Cambodia. For the next four years, until bombing was halted by the US Congress in August 1973, huge areas of the eastern half of the country were carpet bombed by US B-52s, killing what is believed to be many thousands of civilians and turning hundreds of thousands more into refugees. Undoubtedly, the bombing

1964	1969	1970	1971
After the US-sponsored coup against President Diem in South Vietnam, Sihanouk veers left, breaking diplomatic ties with the USA and nationalising the rice trade, antagonising the ethnic Chinese business community.	US President Nixon authorises the secret bombing of Cambodia, which starts with the carpet bombing of border zones, but spreads to the whole country, continuing until 1973 and killing up to 250,000 Cambodians.	Sihanouk throws in his lot with the Khmer Rouge after being overthrown by his cousin Prince Sirik Matak and military commander Lon Nol, and sentenced to death in absentia, marking the start of a five-year civil war.	Lon Nol, leader of the Khmer Republic, launches the disastrous Chenla offensive against Vietnamese communists and their Khmer Rouge allies in Cambodia. He suffers a stroke, but struggles on as leader until 1975.

campaign helped the Khmer Rouge in their recruitment drive, as more and more peasants were losing family members to the aerial assaults. While the final, heaviest bombing in the first half of 1973 may have saved Phnom Penh from a premature fall, its ferocity also helped to harden the attitude of many Khmer Rouge cadres and may have contributed to the later brutality that characterised their rule.

Savage fighting engulfed the country, bringing misery to millions of Cambodians; many fled rural areas for the relative safety of Phnom Penh and provincial capitals. Between 1970 and 1975, several hundred thousand people died in the fighting. During these years, the Khmer Rouge came to play a dominant role in trying to overthrow the Lon Nol regime, strengthened by the support of the Vietnamese, although the Khmer Rouge leadership would vehemently deny this from 1975 onwards.

The leadership of the Khmer Rouge, including Paris-educated Pol Pot and Ieng Sary, had fled into the countryside in the 1960s to escape the summary justice then being meted out to suspected leftists by Sihanouk's security forces. They consolidated control over the movement and began to move against opponents before they took Phnom Penh. Many of the Vietnamese-trained Cambodian communists who had been based in Hanoi since the 1954 Geneva Accords returned down the Ho Chi Minh Trail to join their 'allies' in the Khmer Rouge in 1973. Many were dead by 1975, executed on the orders of the anti-Vietnamese Pol Pot faction. Likewise, many moderate Sihanouk supporters who had joined the Khmer Rouge as a show of loyalty to their fallen leader rather than a show of ideology to the radicals were victims of purges before the regime took power. This set a precedent for internal purges and mass executions that were to eventually bring the downfall of the Khmer Rouge.

It didn't take long for the Lon Nol government to become very unpopular as a result of unprecedented greed and corruption in its ranks. As the USA bankrolled the war, government and military personnel found lucrative means to make a fortune, such as inventing 'phantom soldiers' and pocketing their pay, or selling weapons to the enemy. Lon Nol was widely perceived as an ineffectual leader, obsessed by superstition, fortune tellers and mystical crusades. This perception increased with his stroke in March 1971 and for the next four years his grip on reality seemed to weaken as his brother Lon Non's power grew.

Despite massive US military and economic aid, Lon Nol never succeeded in gaining the initiative against the Khmer Rouge. Large parts of the countryside fell to the rebels and many provincial capitals were cut off from Phnom Penh. Lon Nol fled the country in early April 1975, leaving Sirik Matak, who refused evacuation to the end, in charge. 'I cannot alas leave in such a cowardly fashion... I have committed only one mistake, that of believing in you, the Americans' were the words Sirik

AM RONG

Lon Nol's military press attaché was known for his colourful, even imaginative media briefings that painted a rosy picture of the increasingly desperate situation on the ground. With a name like Major Am Rong, few could take him seriously.

1973	1975	1977	1979
Sihanouk and his wife, Monique, travel down the Ho Chi Minh Trail to visit Khmer Rouge allies at the holy mountain of Phnom Kulen near Angkor, a propaganda victory for Pol Pot.	The Khmer Rouge march into Phnom Penh on 17 April and turn the clocks back to Year Zero, evacuating the capital and turning the whole nation into a prison without walls.	The Pol Pot faction of the Khmer Rouge launch their bloodiest purge against the Eastern Zone of the country, sparking a civil war along the banks of the Mekong and drawing the Vietnamese into the battle.	Vietnamese forces liberate Cambodia from Khmer Rouge rule on 7 January 1979, just two weeks after launching the invasion, and install a friendly regime in Phnom Penh.

Matak poignantly penned to US ambassador John Gunther Dean. On 17 April 1975 – two weeks before the fall of Saigon (now Ho Chi Minh City) – Phnom Penh surrendered to the Khmer Rouge.

The Khmer Rouge Revolution

Upon taking Phnom Penh, the Khmer Rouge implemented one of the most radical and brutal restructurings of a society ever attempted; its goal was a pure revolution, untainted by those that had gone before, to transform Cambodia into a peasant-dominated agrarian cooperative. Within days of the Khmer Rouge coming to power, the entire population of Phnom Penh and provincial towns, including the sick, elderly and infirm, was forced to march into the countryside and work as slaves for 12 to 15 hours a day. Disobedience of any sort often brought immediate execution. The advent of Khmer Rouge rule was proclaimed Year Zero. Currency was abolished and postal services ground to a halt. The country cut itself off from the outside world.

In the eyes of Pol Pot, the Khmer Rouge was not a unified movement, but a series of factions that needed to be cleansed. This process had already begun with attacks on Vietnamese-trained Khmer Rouge and Sihanouk's supporters, but Pol Pot's initial fury upon seizing power was directed against the former regime. All of the senior government and military figures who had been associated with Lon Nol were executed within days of the takeover. Then the centre shifted its attention to the outer regions, which had been separated into geographic zones. The loyalist Southwestern Zone forces, under the control of one-legged general Ta Mok, were sent into region after region to 'purify' the population, a process that saw thousands perish.

The cleansing reached grotesque heights in the final and bloodiest purge against the powerful and independent Eastern Zone. Generally considered more moderate than other Khmer Rouge factions, the Eastern Zone was ideologically, as well as geographically, closer to Vietnam. The Pol Pot faction consolidated the rest of the country before moving against the east from 1977 onwards. Hundreds of leaders were executed before open rebellion broke out, sparking a civil war in the east. Many Eastern Zone leaders fled to Vietnam, forming the nucleus of the government installed by the Vietnamese in January 1979. The people were defenceless and distrusted – 'Cambodian bodies with Vietnamese minds' or 'duck's arses with chicken's heads' – and were deported to the northwest with new, blue *kramas* (scarves). Had it not been for the Vietnamese invasion, all would have perished, as the blue *krama* was a secret party sign indicating an eastern enemy of the revolution.

It is still not known exactly how many Cambodians died at the hands of the Khmer Rouge during the three years, eight months and 20 days

For the full flavour of Cambodian history, from humble beginnings in the prehistoric period through the glories of Angkor and right up to the present day, grab a copy of *The History of Cambodia* (1994), by David Chandler.

1980	1982		1984
Cambodia is gripped by a terrible famine, as the dislocation of the previous few years means that no rice has been planted or harvested, and worldwide 'Save Kampuchea' appeals are launched.	Sihanouk is pressured to join the Khmer Rouge as head of the Coalition Government of Democratic Kampuchea (CGDK), a new military front against the Vietnamese-backed government in Phnom Penh.		The Vietnamese embark on a major offensive in the west of Cambodia and the Khmer Rouge and its allies are forced to retreat to refugee camps and bases inside Thailand.

ANDREW BURKE / GETTY IMAGES ©

➡ Phnom Penh (p30)

of its rule. The Vietnamese claimed three million deaths, while foreign experts long considered the number closer to one million. Yale University researchers undertaking ongoing investigations estimated that the figure was close to two million.

Hundreds of thousands of people were executed by the Khmer Rouge leadership, while hundreds of thousands more died of famine and disease. Meals consisted of little more than watery rice porridge twice a day, but were meant to sustain men, women and children through a back-breaking day in the fields. Disease stalked the work camps, malaria and dysentery striking down whole families; death was a relief for many from the horrors of life. Some zones were better than others, some leaders fairer than others, but life for the majority was one of unending misery and suffering in this 'prison without walls'.

As the centre eliminated more and more moderates, Angkar (the organisation) became the only family people needed and those who did not agree were sought out and crushed. The Khmer Rouge detached the Cambodian people from all they held dear: their families, their food, their fields and their faith. Even the peasants who had supported the revolution could no longer blindly follow such insanity. Nobody cared for the Khmer Rouge by 1978, but nobody had an ounce of strength to do anything about it...except the Vietnamese.

Only a handful of foreigners were allowed to visit Cambodia during the Khmer Rouge period of Democratic Kampuchea. US journalist Elizabeth Becker was one who travelled there in late 1978; her book *When the War Was Over* (1986) tells her story.

Enter the Vietnamese

Relations between Cambodia and Vietnam have historically been tense, as the Vietnamese have slowly but steadily expanded southwards, encroaching on Cambodian territory. Despite the fact the two communist parties had fought together as brothers in arms, old tensions soon came to the fore.

From 1976 to 1978, the Khmer Rouge instigated a series of border clashes with Vietnam, and claimed the Mekong Delta, once part of the Khmer empire. Incursions into Vietnamese border provinces left hundreds of Vietnamese civilians dead. On 25 December 1978, Vietnam launched a full-scale invasion of Cambodia, toppling the Pol Pot government two weeks later. As Vietnamese tanks neared Phnom Penh, the Khmer Rouge fled westward with as many civilians as it could seize, taking refuge in the jungles and mountains along the Thai border. The Vietnamese installed a new government led by several former Khmer Rouge officers, including current Prime Minister Hun Sen, who had defected to Vietnam in 1977. The Khmer Rouge's patrons, the Chinese communists, launched a massive reprisal raid across Vietnam's northernmost border in early 1979 in an attempt to buy their allies time. It failed and after 17 days the Chinese withdrew, their fingers badly burnt by their Vietnamese enemies. The Vietnamese then staged a show trial in Cambodia in which

1985	1989	1991	1993
There is a changing of the guard at the top and Hun Sen becomes prime minister of Cambodia, a title he still holds today with the Cambodian People's Party (CPP).	As the effects of President Gorbachev's perestroika (restructuring) begin to impact on communist allies, Vietnam feels the pinch and announces the withdrawal of its forces from Cambodia.	The Paris Peace Accords are signed, in which all parties, including the Khmer Rouge, agree to participate in free and fair elections supervised by the UN.	The pro-Sihanouk royalist party Funcinpec, under the leadership of Prince Ranariddh, wins the popular vote, but the communist CPP threatens secession in the east to muscle its way into government.

Pol Pot and Ieng Sary were condemned to death in absentia for their genocidal acts.

A traumatised population took to the road in search of surviving family members. Millions had been uprooted and had to walk hundreds of kilometres across the country. Rice stocks were decimated, the harvest left to wither and little rice planted, sowing the seeds for a widespread famine in 1979 and 1980.

As the conflict in Cambodia raged, Sihanouk agreed in 1982, under pressure from China, to head a military and political front opposed to the Phnom Penh government. The Sihanouk-led resistance coalition brought together – on paper, at least – Funcinpec (the French acronym for the National United Front for an Independent, Neutral, Peaceful and Cooperative Cambodia), which comprised a royalist group loyal to Sihanouk; the Khmer People's National Liberation Front, a noncommunist grouping under former prime minister Son Sann; and the Khmer Rouge, officially known as the Party of Democratic Kampuchea and by far the most powerful of the three. The crimes of the Khmer Rouge were swept aside to ensure a compromise that suited the realpolitik of the day.

For much of the 1980s Cambodia remained closed to the Western world, save for the presence of some humanitarian aid groups. Govern-

THE POLITICS OF DISASTER RELIEF

The Cambodian famine became a new front in the Cold War, as Washington and Moscow jostled for influence from afar. As hundreds of thousands of Cambodians fled to Thailand, a massive international famine relief effort, sponsored by the UN, was launched. The international community wanted to deliver aid across a land bridge at Poipet, while the new Vietnamese-backed Phnom Penh government wanted all supplies to come through the capital via Kompong Som (Sihanoukville) or the Mekong River. Both sides had their reasons – the new government did not want aid to fall into the hands of its Khmer Rouge enemies, while the international community didn't believe the new government had the infrastructure to distribute the aid – and both fears were right.

Some agencies distributed aid the slow way through Phnom Penh, and others set up camps in Thailand. The camps became a magnet for half of Cambodia, as many Khmers still feared the return of the Khmer Rouge or were seeking a new life overseas. The Thai military convinced the international community to distribute all aid through their channels and used this as a cloak to rebuild the shattered Khmer Rouge forces as an effective resistance against the Vietnamese. Thailand demanded that, as a condition for allowing international food aid for Cambodia to pass through its territory, food had to be supplied to the Khmer Rouge forces encamped in the Thai border region as well. Along with weaponry supplied by China, this international assistance was essential in enabling the Khmer Rouge to rebuild its military strength and fight on for another two decades.

1994	1995	1996	1997
The Khmer Rouge target foreign tourists in Cambodia, kidnapping and killing groups travelling by taxi and train to the South Coast, reinforcing Cambodia's overseas image as a dangerous country.	Prince Norodom Sirivudh is arrested and exiled for allegedly plotting to kill Prime Minister Hun Sen, removing another potential rival from the scene.	British deminer Christopher Howes, working in Cambodia with the Mines Advisory Group (MAG), is kidnapped by the Khmer Rouge and later killed, together with his interpreter Houn Hourth.	Second Prime Minister Hun Sen overthrows First Prime Minister Norodom Ranariddh in a military coup, referred to as 'the events of 1997' in Cambodia.

ment policy was effectively under the control of the Vietnamese, so Cambodia found itself very much in the Eastern-bloc camp. The economy was in tatters for most of this period, as Cambodia, like Vietnam, suffered from the effects of a US-sponsored embargo.

In 1984 the Vietnamese overran all the major rebel camps inside Cambodia, forcing the Khmer Rouge and its allies to retreat into Thailand. From this time the Khmer Rouge and its allies engaged in guerrilla warfare aimed at demoralising its opponents. Tactics used by the Khmer Rouge included shelling government-controlled garrison towns, planting thousands of mines in rural areas, attacking road transport, blowing up bridges, kidnapping village chiefs and targeting civilians. The Khmer Rouge also forced thousands of men, women and children living in the refugee camps it controlled to work as porters, ferrying ammunition and other supplies into Cambodia across heavily mined sections of the border.

The Vietnamese, for their part, laid the world's longest minefield, known as K-5 and stretching from the Gulf of Thailand to the Lao border, in an attempt to seal out the guerrillas. They also sent Cambodians into the forests to cut down trees on remote sections of road to prevent ambushes. Thousands died of disease and from injuries sustained from landmines. The Khmer Rouge was no longer in power, but for many the 1980s were almost as tough as the 1970s – it was one long struggle to survive.

The UN Comes to Town

The arrival of Mikhail Gorbachev in the Kremlin saw the Cold War draw to a close. It was the furthest-flung Soviet allies who were cut adrift first, leaving Vietnam internationally isolated and economically crippled. In September 1989, Vietnam announced the withdrawal of all of its troops from Cambodia. With the Vietnamese gone, the opposition coalition, still dominated by the Khmer Rouge, launched a series of offensives, forcing the now-vulnerable government to the negotiating table.

Diplomatic efforts to end the civil war began to bear fruit in September 1990, when a peace plan was accepted by both the Phnom Penh government and the three factions of the resistance coalition. According to the plan, the Supreme National Council (SNC), a coalition of all factions, would be formed under the presidency of Sihanouk. Meanwhile, the UN Transitional Authority in Cambodia (Untac) would supervise the administration of the country for two years, with the goal of free and fair elections.

Untac undoubtedly achieved some successes, but for all of these, it is the failures that were to cost Cambodia dearly in the 'democratic' era. Untac was successful in pushing through many international human-rights covenants; it opened the door to a significant number of NGOs; and, most importantly, on 25 May 1993, elections were held with an

Western powers, including the USA and UK, ensured the Khmer Rouge retained its seat at the UN General Assembly in New York until 1991, a scenario that saw those responsible for the genocide representing their victims on the international stage.

1998	1999	2000	2002
Pol Pot passes away on 15 April 1998 as Anlong Veng falls to government forces, and many observers ponder whether the timing is coincidental.	Cambodia finally joins Asean after a two-year delay, taking its place among the family of Southeast Asian nations, who welcome the country back onto the world stage.	The Cambodian Freedom Fighters (CFF) launch an 'assault' on Phnom Penh. Backed by Cambodian-American dissidents, the attackers are lightly armed, poorly trained and politically inexperienced.	Cambodia holds its first ever local elections at commune level, a tentative step towards dismantling the old communist system of control and bringing grass-roots democracy to the country.

89.6% turnout. However, the results were far from decisive. Funcinpec, led by Prince Norodom Ranariddh, took 58 seats in the National Assembly, while the Cambodian People's Party (CPP), which represented the previous communist government, took 51 seats. The CPP had lost the election, but senior leaders threatened a secession of the eastern provinces of the country. As a result, Cambodia ended up with two prime ministers: Norodom Ranariddh as first prime minister, and Hun Sen as second prime minister.

Even today, Untac is heralded as one of the UN's success stories. Another perspective is that it was an ill-conceived and poorly executed peace because so many of the powers involved in brokering the deal had their own agendas to advance. To many Cambodians who had survived the 1970s, it was unthinkable that the Khmer Rouge would be allowed to play a part in the electoral process after presiding over a genocide.

The UN's disarmament program took weapons away from the rural militias who for so long provided the backbone of the government's provincial defence network against the Khmer Rouge and this left communities throughout the country vulnerable to attack. Meanwhile the Khmer Rouge used the veil of legitimacy conferred upon it by the peace process to re-establish a guerrilla network throughout Cambodia. By 1994, when it was finally outlawed by the government, the Khmer Rouge was arguably a greater threat to the stability of Cambodia than at any time since 1979.

Untac's main goals had been to 'restore and maintain peace' and 'promote national reconciliation', and in the short term it achieved neither. It did oversee free and fair elections, but these were later annulled by the actions of Cambodia's politicians. Little was done during the UN period to try to dismantle the communist apparatus of state set up by the CPP,

> The commercial metropolis that is now Ho Chi Minh City (Saigon) in Vietnam was, in 1600, a small Cambodian village called Prey Nokor.

THE NAME GAME

Cambodia has changed its name so many times over the last few decades that there are understandable grounds for confusion. To the Cambodians, their country is Kampuchea. The name is derived from the word Kambuja, meaning 'those born of Kambu', the mythical founder of the country. It dates back as far as the 10th century. The Portuguese 'Camboxa' and the French 'Cambodge', from which the English name 'Cambodia' is derived, are adaptations of 'Kambuja'.

It was the Khmer Rouge that insisted the outside world use the name Kampuchea. Changing the country's official English name back to Cambodia was intended as a symbolic move to distance the present government in Phnom Penh from the bitter connotations of the name Kampuchea, which Westerners associate with the Khmer Rouge regime.

2003	2004	2005	2006
The CPP wins the election, but political infighting prevents the formation of the new government for almost a year until the old coalition with Funcinpec is revived.	In a move that catches observers by surprise, King Sihanouk abdicates from the throne and is succeeded by his son King Sihamoni, a popular choice as Sihamoni has steered clear of politics.	Cambodia joins the WTO, opening its markets to free trade, but many commentators feel it could be counterproductive, as the economy is so small and there is no more protection for domestic producers.	Lawsuits and counter-lawsuits see political leaders moving from conflict to courtroom in the new Cambodia. The revolving doors stop with opposition leader Sam Rainsy back in the country and Prince Ranariddh out.

a well-oiled machine that continues to ensure that former communists control the civil service, judiciary, army and police today.

The Slow Birth of Peace

When the Vietnamese toppled the Pol Pot government in 1979, the Khmer Rouge disappeared into the jungle. The guerrillas eventually boycotted the 1993 elections and later rejected peace talks aimed at establishing a ceasefire. In 1994, the Khmer Rouge resorted to a new tactic of targeting tourists, with horrendous results for a number of foreigners in Cambodia. During 1994, three people were taken from a taxi on the road to Sihanoukville and subsequently shot. A few months later another three foreigners were seized from a train bound for Sihanoukville and in the ransom drama that followed they were executed as the army closed in.

The government changed course during the mid-1990s, opting for more carrot and less stick in a bid to end the war. The breakthrough came in 1996 when Ieng Sary, Brother No 3 in the Khmer Rouge hierarchy and foreign minister during its rule, was denounced by Pol Pot for corruption. He subsequently led a mass defection of fighters and their dependants from the Pailin area, and this effectively sealed the fate of the remaining Khmer Rouge. Pailin, rich in gems and timber, had long been the economic crutch that kept the Khmer Rouge hobbling along. The severing of this income, coupled with the fact that government forces now had only one front on which to concentrate their resources, suggested the days of civil war were numbered.

By 1997, cracks were appearing in the coalition and the fledgling democracy once again found itself under siege. But it was the Khmer Rouge that again grabbed the headlines. Pol Pot ordered the execution of Son Sen, defence minister during the Khmer Rouge regime, and many of his family members. This provoked a putsch within the Khmer Rouge leadership, and the one-legged hardliner general Ta Mok seized control, putting Pol Pot on 'trial'. Rumours flew about Phnom Penh that Pol Pot would be brought there to face international justice, but events dramatically shifted back to the capital.

A lengthy courting period ensued in which both Funcinpec and the CPP attempted to win the trust of the remaining Khmer Rouge hardliners in northern Cambodia. Ranariddh was close to forging a deal with the jungle fighters and was keen to get it sewn up before Cambodia's accession to the Association of South-East Asian Nations (Asean), as nothing would provide a better entry fanfare than the ending of Cambodia's long civil war. He was outflanked and subsequently outgunned by Second Prime Minister Hun Sen. On 5 July 1997, fighting again erupted on the streets of Phnom Penh as troops loyal to the CPP clashed with those loyal to Funcinpec. The heaviest exchanges were around the airport

When Jemaah Islamiyah (affiliated with Al Qaeda) bomber Hambali was arrested in Thailand in August 2003, it later surfaced that he had been living in a backpacker hostel on Boeng Kak lake for about six months.

2007	2008	2009
Royalist party Funcinpec continues to implode in the face of conflict, intrigue and defections, with democrats joining Sam Rainsy, loyalists joining the new Norodom Ranariddh Party and others joining the CPP.	Elections are held and the CPP increases its share of the vote to 58%, while the opposition vote is split across several parties.	Comrade Duch, aka Kaing Guek Eav, commandant of the notorious S-21 prison, goes on trial for crimes committed during the Khmer Rouge regime.

MATTHEW MICAH WRIGHT/GETTY IMAGES ©

➡ S-21 prison, now Tuol Sleng Museum (p35)

and key government buildings, but before long the dust had settled and the CPP once again controlled Cambodia. Euphemistically known as the 'events of 1997' in Cambodia, much of the international community condemned the violence as a coup.

As 1998 began, the CPP announced an all-out offensive against its enemies in the north. By April it was closing in on the Khmer Rouge strongholds of Anlong Veng and Preah Vihear, and amid this heavy fighting Pol Pot evaded justice by dying a natural death on 15 April in the captivity of his former Khmer Rouge comrades. The fall of Anlong Veng in April was followed by the fall of Preah Vihear in May, and the surviving big three, Ta Mok, Khieu Samphan and Nuon Chea, were forced to flee into the jungle near the Thai border with their remaining troops.

The 1998 election result reinforced the reality that the CPP was now the dominant force in the Cambodian political system and on 25 December Hun Sen received the Christmas present he had been waiting for: Khieu Samphan and Nuon Chea were defecting to the government side. The international community began to pile on the pressure for the establishment of some sort of war-crimes tribunal to try the remaining Khmer Rouge leadership. After lengthy negotiations, agreement was finally reached on the composition of a court to try the surviving leaders of the Khmer Rouge. The CPP was suspicious of a UN-administered trial as the UN had sided with the Khmer Rouge–dominated coalition against the government in Phnom Penh, and the ruling party wanted a major say in who was to be tried and for what. The UN for its part doubted that the judiciary in Cambodia was sophisticated or impartial enough to fairly oversee such a major trial. A compromise solution – a mixed tribunal of three international and four Cambodian judges requiring a super majority of two plus three for a verdict – was eventually agreed upon.

Early 2002 saw Cambodia's first-ever local elections to select village- and commune-level representatives, an important step in bringing grassroots democracy to the country. Despite national elections since 1993, the CPP continued to monopolise political power at local and regional levels and only with commune elections would this grip be loosened. The national elections of July 2003 saw a shift in the balance of power, as the CPP consolidated its grip on Cambodia and the Sam Rainsy Party overhauled Funcinpec as the second party. This trend continued into the 2008 election when the CPP's majority grew. However, the 2013 election saw a massive reversal in the trend as the opposition managed to stay united through the election campaign. The return of Cambodian National Rescue Party (CNRP) leader Sam Rainsy from self-imposed exile saw his party come close to victory over the CPP. For more on the election and recent events in Cambodia, see the Cambodia Today chapter (p284).

During the 1960s, Cambodia was an oasis of peace while wars raged in neighbouring Vietnam and Laos. By 1970 that had all changed. For the full story, read *Sideshow: Kissinger, Nixon and the Destruction of Cambodia*, by William Shawcross (1979).

2010	2011	2012	2013
As the annual Bon Om Tuk (Water Festival) draws to a close on 22 November, more than 350 people die as revellers swarm across a narrow bridge in huge numbers.	The simmering border conflict over the ancient temple of Preah Vihear spills over into actual fighting between Cambodia and Thailand. A ceasefire is negotiated by Asean chair Indonesia.	Cambodia assumes the chair of Asean.	In Cambodia's fifth post-war election the united opposition Cambodia National Rescue Party (CNRP) win 55 seats in the National Assembly to CPP's 68. CNRP cites voting irregularities but the CPP ignores calls for an investigation.

Pol Pot & the Legacy of the Khmer Rouge

The Khmer Rouge controlled Cambodia for three years, eight months and 20 days, a period etched into the consciousness of the Khmer people. The Vietnamese ousted the Khmer Rouge on 7 January 1979, but Cambodia's civil war rumbled on for another two decades before drawing to a close in 1999. Finally, more than 20 years after the collapse of the Khmer Rouge regime, serious discussions began about a trial to bring those responsible for the deaths of about two million Cambodians to justice.

The Khmer Rouge Tribunal

Case 001

Case 001, the trial of Kaing Guek Eav, aka Comrade Duch, began in 2009. Duch was seen as a key figure as he provided the link between the regime and its crimes in his role as head of S-21 prison. Duch was sentenced to 35 years in 2010, but this was reduced to just 19 years in lieu of time already served and his cooperation with the investigating team. For many Cambodians this was a slap in the face, as Duch had already admitted overall responsibility for the deaths of about 17,000 people. Convert this into simple numbers and it equates to about 10 hours of prison time per victim. However, an appeal verdict announced on 3 February 2012 extended the sentence to life imprisonment.

Case 002

Case 002 began in November 2011, involving the most senior surviving leaders of the Democratic Kampuchea (DK) era: Brother Number 2 Nuon Chea (age 84), Brother Number 3 and former foreign minister of Democratic Kampuchea Ieng Sary (age 83), and former DK head of state Khieu Samphan (age 79). Justice may prove elusive, however, due to the slow progress of court proceedings and the advancing age of the defendants. Ieng Sary died on 14 March 2013 and his wife and former DK Minister of Social Affairs Ieng Thirith (age 78) was ruled unfit to stand trial due to the onset of dementia. To keep abreast of developments in Case 002, visit the official Extraordinary Chambers in the Courts of CAmbodia (ECCC) website at www.eccc.gov.kh or the Cambodian Tribunal Monitor at www.cambodiatribunal.org.

Case 003

Case 003 against head of the DK navy, Meas Muth, and head of the DK air force, Sou Met, is politically charged; it threatened to derail the entire tribunal during 2011. Investigations into this case stalled back in 2009 under intense pressure from the Cambodian government, which wanted to draw a line under proceedings with the completion of Case 002. Prime Minister Hun Sen made several public statements objecting to the continuation of Case 003 and the subsequent impasse has led to criticism from many quarters including Human Rights Watch. Many independ-

Pol Pot travelled up the Ho Chi Minh trail to visit Beijing in 1966, at the height of the Cultural Revolution there. He was obviously inspired by what he saw, as the Khmer Rouge went even further than the Red Guards in severing links with the past.

To learn more about the origins of the Khmer Rouge and the Democratic Kampuchea regime, read How Pol Pot Came to Power (1985) and The Pol Pot Regime (1996), both written by Yale University academic Ben Kiernan.

ent observers have called for the replacement of at least two Cambodian judges for their lack of political impartiality, and German judge Siegfried Blunk resigned under pressure for failing to conduct full investigations into Case 003. It remains to be seen who will prevail in this battle of wills, but to many observers the entire credibility of the trial continues to remain under threat.

Brother Number One (2011) is a feature-length documentary that follows New Zealand rower Rob Hamill on a personal journey to discover who was responsible for the murder of his brother Kerry Hamill in S-21 prison in 1978.

Cost

In the meantime, the budget for the trial just keeps on rising. A total of US$100 million was spent in the first five years, against a backdrop of allegations of corruption and mismanagement on the Cambodian side. Some Cambodians feel the trial will send a message about accountability that may resonate with some of the Cambodian leadership today. However, others argue that the trial is a major waste of money given the overwhelming evidence against surviving senior leaders and that a truth and reconciliation commission may have provided more compelling answers for Cambodians who want to understand what motivated the average Khmer Rouge cadre.

Pol Pot & His Comrades

Pol Pot: Brother Number One

Pol Pot is a name that sends shivers down the spines of Cambodians and foreigners alike. It is Pol Pot who is most associated with the bloody madness of the regime he led between 1975 and 1979, and his policies heaped misery, suffering and death on millions of Cambodians.

Pol Pot was born Saloth Sar in a small village near Kompong Thom in 1925. As a young man he won a scholarship to study in Paris, where he came into contact with the Cercle Marxiste and communist thought, which he later transformed into politics of extreme Maoism.

In 1963, Sihanouk's repressive policies sent Saloth Sar and his comrades fleeing to the jungles of Ratanakiri. It was from this moment that Saloth Sar began to call himself Pol Pot. Once the Khmer Rouge was allied with Sihanouk, following his overthrow by Lon Nol in 1970 and subsequent exile in Beijing, its support soared and the faces of the leadership became familiar. However, Pol Pot remained a shadowy figure, leaving public duties to Khieu Samphan and Ieng Sary.

Enemies of the People (2010) follows Cambodian journalist and genocide survivor Thet Sambath as he wins the confidence of Brother Number Two in the Khmer Rouge, Nuon Chea, eventually coaxing him to give new testimony on his role in the genocidal regime.

When the Khmer Rouge marched into Phnom Penh on 17 April 1975, few people could have anticipated the hell that was to follow. Pol Pot and his clique were the architects of one of the most radical and brutal revolutions in the history of mankind. It was Year Zero and Cambodia was on a self-destructive course to sever all ties with the past.

After being ousted by the Vietnamese, Pol Pot was not to emerge as the public face of the revolution until the end of 1976, after he returned from a trip to see his mentors in Beijing. He granted almost no interviews to foreign media and was seen only on propaganda movies produced by government TV. Such was his aura and reputation that, by the last year of the regime, a cult of personality was developing around him.

Pol Pot spent much of the 1980s living in Thailand and was able to rebuild his shattered forces and once again threaten Cambodia. His enigma increased as the international media speculated on his real fate. His demise was reported so often that when he finally passed away on 15 April 1998, many Cambodians refused to believe it until they had seen his body on TV or in newspapers. Even then, many were sceptical and rumours continue to circulate about exactly how he met his end. Officially, he was said to have died from a heart attack, but a full autopsy was not carried out before his body was cremated on a pyre of burning tyres.

For more on the life and times of Pol Pot, pick up one of the excellent biographies written about him: *Brother Number One* by David Chandler or *Pol Pot: The History of a Nightmare* by Phillip Short.

Nuon Chea: Brother Number Two

Long considered one of the main ideologues and architects of the Khmer Rouge revolution, Nuon Chea studied law at Bangkok's Thammasut University before joining the Thai Communist Party. He was appointed Deputy Secretary of the Communist Party of Kampuchea upon its secretive founding in 1960 and remained Pol Pot's second in command throughout the regime's rule, with overall responsibility for internal security. He is currently on trial at the ECCC as part of Case 002.

Ieng Sary: Brother Number Three

One of Pol Pot's closest confidants, Ieng Sary fled to the jungles of Ratanakiri in 1963, where he and Pol Pot both underwent intensive guerrilla training in the company of North Vietnamese communist forces. Ieng Sary was one of the public faces of the Khmer Rouge and became foreign minister of Democratic Kampuchea. Until his death, he maintained that he was not involved in the planning or execution of the genocide. However, he did invite many intellectuals, diplomats and exiles to return to Cambodia from 1975, the majority of whom were subsequently tortured and executed in S-21 prison. He helped hasten the demise of the Khmer Rouge as a guerrilla force with his defection to the government side in 1996 and was given an amnesty for his earlier crimes.

Khieu Samphan: Brother Number Nine

Khieu Samphan studied economics in Paris and some of his theories on self-reliance were credited with inspiring Khmer Rouge economic policies. During the Sihanouk years of the 1960s, Khieu Samphan spent several years working with the Sangkum government and putting his more moderate theories to the test. During a crackdown on leftists in 1967, he fled to the jungle to join Pol Pot and Ieng Sary. During the DK period, he was made head of state from 1976 to 1979. He is currently on trial as one of the accused in Case 002.

Comrade Duch: Commandant of S-21

Born Kaing Guek Eav in Kompong Thom in 1942, Duch initially worked as a teacher before joining the Khmer Rouge in 1967. Based in the Cardamom Mountains during the civil war of 1970–75, he was given responsibility for security and political prisons in his region, where he refined his interrogation techniques. Following the Khmer Rouge takeover, he was moved to S-21 prison and was responsible for the interrogation and execution of thousands of prisoners. He fled Phnom Penh as Vietnamese forces surrounded the city, and his whereabouts was unknown until he was discovered living in Battambang Province by British photojournalist Nic Dunlop. The first to stand trial and be sentenced in Case 001, Comrade Duch cooperated through the judicial process. He was sentenced to life in early 2012.

The Future

It remains to be seen whether the wheels of justice will turn fast enough to deliver a verdict on the remaining Khmer Rouge leaders on trial. However, that justice has already been served in the case of Comrade Duch has provided a measure of closure for some victims and sends an important political message to the current Cambodian leadership regarding accountability for their actions.

Khieu Samphan tries to exonerate himself in his 2004 publication, *Cambodia's Recent History and the Reasons Behind the Decisions I Made.*

The Khmer Rouge period is politically sensitive in Cambodia, due in part to the connections the current leadership have with the communist movement – so much so that the history of the genocide was not taught in high schools until 2009.

POL POT & THE LEGACY OF THE KHMER ROUGE THE FUTURE

People & Culture

Since the glory days of the Angkorian empire, the Cambodian people have been on the losing side of many a historical battle, their country all too often a minnow amid the circling sharks. Popular attitudes have been shaped by this history, and the relationship between Cambodia and its neighbours Thailand and Vietnam is marked by a cocktail of fear, admiration and animosity.

The National Psyche

Lowland Khmers are being encouraged to migrate to Cambodia's northeast where there is plenty of available land. But this is home to the country's minority peoples, who have no indigenous concepts of property rights or land ownership, so this may see their culture marginalised in coming years.

Cambodian attitudes towards the Thais and Vietnamese are complex. The Thais aren't always popular, as some Cambodians feel they fail to acknowledge their cultural debt to Cambodia and generally look down on their less affluent neighbour. Cambodian attitudes towards the Vietnamese are more ambivalent. There is a certain level of mistrust, as many feel the Vietnamese aspire to colonise their country. (Many Khmers still call the lost Mekong Delta 'Kampuchea Krom', meaning 'Lower Cambodia'.) However, this mistrust is balanced with a grudging respect for the Vietnamese role in Cambodia's 'liberation' from the Khmer Rouge in 1979. But when liberation became occupation in the 1980s, the relationship soured once more.

At first glance, Cambodia appears to be a nation of shiny, happy people, but look deeper and it is a country of evident contradictions. Light and dark, rich and poor, love and hate, life and death – all are visible on a journey through the kingdom. Most telling of all is the evidence of the nation's glorious past set against the more recent tragedy of its present.

Angkor is everywhere: on the flag, the national beer, cigarettes, hotels and guesthouses – anything and everything. It's a symbol of nationhood and fierce pride – no matter how ugly things got in the bad old days, the Cambodians built Angkor Wat and it doesn't come better than that.

Contrast this with the abyss into which the nation was sucked during the years of the Khmer Rouge. Pol Pot is a dirty word in Cambodia due to the death and suffering he inflicted on the country.

CAMBODIAN GREETINGS

Cambodians traditionally greet each other with the *sompiah,* which involves pressing the hands together in prayer and bowing, similar to the *wai* in Thailand. The higher the hands and the lower the bow, the more respect is conveyed – important to remember when meeting officials or the elderly. In recent times this custom has been partly replaced by the handshake but, although men tend to shake hands with each other, women usually use the traditional greeting with both men and women. It is considered acceptable (or perhaps excusable) for foreigners to shake hands with Cambodians of both sexes.

The Cambodian Way of Life

For many older Cambodians, life is centred on family, faith and food, an existence that has stayed the same for centuries. Family is more than the nuclear family we now know in the West, it's the extended family of third cousins and obscure aunts – as long as there is a bloodline, there is a bond. Families stick together, solve problems collectively, listen to the wisdom of the elders and pool resources. The extended family comes together during times of trouble and times of joy, celebrating festivals and successes, mourning deaths and disappointments. Whether the Cambodian house is big or small, there will be a lot of people living inside.

For the majority of the population still living in the countryside, these constants carry on as they always have: several generations sharing the same roof, the same rice and the same religion. But during the dark decades of the 1970s and 1980s, this routine was ripped apart by war and ideology, as the peasants were dragged into a bloody civil war and later forced into slavery. The Khmer Rouge organisation Angkar took over as the moral and social beacon in the lives of the people, and families were forced apart – children turned against parents, brother against sister. The bond of trust was broken, and it is only slowly being rebuilt today.

For the younger generation, brought up in a postconflict and post-communist period of relative freedom, it's a different story – arguably thanks to their steady diet of MTV and steamy soaps. Cambodia is experiencing its very own '60s-style swing, as the younger generation stands ready for a different lifestyle to the one their parents had to swallow. This creates plenty of friction in the cities, as rebellious teens dress as they like, date whoever they wish and hit the town until all hours. More recently this generational conflict spilled over into politics as the Facebook generation helped deliver a shock result that saw the Cambodian Peoples' Party majority slashed in half.

Cambodia is set for major demographic shifts in the next couple of decades. Currently, just 20% of the population lives in urban areas, which contrasts starkly with the country's more developed neighbours, such as Malaysia and Thailand. Increasing numbers of young people are likely to migrate to the cities in search of opportunity, forever changing the face of contemporary Cambodian society. However, for now at least, Cambodian society remains much more traditional than that of Thailand and Vietnam, and visitors need to keep this in mind.

Multiculturalism

According to official statistics, more than 90% of the people who live in Cambodia are ethnic Khmers, making the country the most ethnically homogeneous in Southeast Asia. However, unofficially, the figure is probably smaller due to a large influx of Chinese and Vietnamese in the past century. Other ethnic minorities include Cham, Lao and the indigenous peoples of the rural highlands.

Ethnic Khmers

The Khmers have inhabited Cambodia since the beginning of recorded regional history (around the 2nd century), many centuries before Thais and Vietnamese migrated to the region. Over the centuries, the Khmers have mixed with other groups residing in Cambodia, including Javanese and Malays (8th century), Thais (10th to 15th centuries), Vietnamese (from the early 17th century) and Chinese (since the 18th century).

The Cambodian and Lao people share a close bond, as Fa Ngum, the founder of the original Lao kingdom of Lan Xang (Land of a Million Elephants), was sponsored by his Khmer father-in-law.

PEOPLE & CULTURE MULTICULTURALISM

THE POPULATION OF CAMBODIA

Cambodia's second postwar population census was carried out in 2008 and put the country's population at about 13.5 million. The current population is estimated at nearly 15 million and, with a rapid growth rate of about 2% per year, it's predicted to reach 20 million by 2025.

Phnom Penh is the largest city, with a population of 1.5 million. Other major population centres include the boom towns of Siem Reap, Sihanoukville, Battambang and Poipet. The most populous province is Kompong Cham, where more than 10% of Cambodians live.

The much-discussed imbalance of men to women due to years of conflict is not as serious as it was in 1980, but it's still significant: there are about 95 males to every 100 females, up from 86.1 to 100 in 1980. There is, however, a marked imbalance in age groups: more than 40% of the population is under the age of 16.

Ethnic Vietnamese

The Vietnamese are one of the largest non-Khmer ethnic groups in Cambodia. According to government figures, Cambodia is host to around 100,000 Vietnamese, though unofficial observers claim the real figure may be somewhere between half a million and two million. The Vietnamese play a big part in the fishing and construction industries in Cambodia. There is still some distrust between the Cambodians and the Vietnamese, though, even of those who have been living in Cambodia for generations.

Friends of Khmer Culture (www.khmerculture.net) is dedicated to supporting Khmer arts and cultural organisations, and Meta House (p69), an exhibition space in Phnom Penh, promotes Khmer arts and culture.

Ethnic Chinese

The government claims there are around 50,000 ethnic Chinese in Cambodia; however, informed observers estimate half a million to one million in urban areas. Many Chinese Cambodians have lived in Cambodia for generations and have adopted the Khmer culture, language and identity. Until 1975, the ethnic Chinese controlled the economic life of Cambodia and in recent years they have re-emerged as a powerful economic force, mainly due to increased investment by overseas Chinese.

Ethnic Cham

Cambodia's Cham Muslims (known locally as the Khmer Islam) officially number around 200,000. Unofficial counts put the figure higher at around 500,000. The Cham live in villages on the banks of the Mekong and Tonlé Sap Rivers, mostly in the provinces of Kompong Cham, Kompong Speu and Kompong Chhnang. They suffered vicious persecution between 1975 and 1979, when a large part of their community was targeted. Many Cham mosques that were destroyed under the Khmer Rouge have since been rebuilt.

Ethno-Linguistic Minorities

Cambodia's diverse Khmer Leu (Upper Khmer) or *chunchiet* (ethnic minorities), who live in the country's mountainous regions, probably number around 100,000.

There are just 20 female parliamentarians out of 123 seated in the National Assembly in Cambodia, making up just over 15% of MPs.

The majority of these groups live in northeast Cambodia, in the provinces of Ratanakiri, Mondulkiri, Stung Treng and Kratie. The largest group is the Tompuon (many other spellings are also used), who number nearly 20,000. Other groups include the Bunong, Kreung, Kavet, Brau and Jarai.

The hill tribes of Cambodia have long been isolated from mainstream Khmer society, and there is little in the way of mutual understanding. They practise shifting cultivation, rarely staying in one place for long.

Finding a new location for a village requires a village elder to mediate with the spirit world. Very few of the minorities retain the sort of colourful traditional costumes found in Thailand, Laos and Vietnam.

Religion

Buddhism

Buddhism arrived in Cambodia with Hinduism but only became the official religion from the 13th and 14th centuries. Most Cambodians today practise Theravada Buddhism. Between 1975 and 1979 many of Cambodia's Buddhist monks were murdered by the Khmer Rouge and nearly all of the country's wats (more than 3000) were damaged or destroyed. In the late 1980s, Buddhism once again became the state religion and today young monks are a common sight throughout the country. Many wats have been rebuilt or rehabilitated and money-raising drives for this work can be seen on roadsides across the country.

The ultimate goal of Theravada Buddhism is nirvana – 'extinction' of all desire and suffering to reach the final stage of reincarnation. By feeding monks, giving donations to temples and performing regular worship at the local wat, Buddhists hope to improve their lot, acquiring enough merit to reduce their number of rebirths.

Every Buddhist male is expected to become a monk for a short period in his life, optimally between the time he finishes school and starts a career or marries. Men or boys under 20 years of age may enter the *sangha* (monastic order) as novices. Nowadays men may spend as little as 15 days to accrue merit as monks.

Hinduism

Hinduism flourished alongside Buddhism from the 1st century AD until the 14th century. During the pre-Angkorian period, Hinduism was represented by the worship of Harihara (Shiva and Vishnu embodied

Look out for Chinese and Vietnamese cemeteries dotting the rice fields of provinces to the south and east of Phnom Penh. Khmers do not bury their dead, but practise cremation, and the ashes may be interred in a stupa in the grounds of a wat.

PEOPLE & CULTURE RELIGION

KHMER KROM

The Khmer Krom people of southern Vietnam are ethnic Khmers separated from Cambodia by historical deals and Vietnamese encroachment on what was once Cambodian territory. Nobody is sure just how many of them there are and estimates vary from one million to seven million, depending on who is doing the counting.

The history of Vietnamese expansion into Khmer territory has long been a staple of Khmer textbooks. King Chey Chetha II of Cambodia, in keeping with the wishes of his Vietnamese queen, first allowed Vietnamese to settle in the Cambodian town of Prey Nokor in 1623. It was obviously the thin end of the wedge, as Prey Nokor is now better known as Ho Chi Minh City (Saigon).

The Vietnamese government has pursued a policy of forced assimilation since independence, which has involved ethnic Khmers taking Vietnamese names and studying in Vietnamese. According to the Khmer Kampuchea Federation (KKF), the Khmer Krom continue to suffer persecution, including lack of access to health services, religious discrimination and outright racism. Several monks have been defrocked for nonviolent protests in recent years and the Cambodian government has even assisted in deporting some agitators, according to Human Rights Watch.

Many Khmer Krom would like to see Cambodia act as a mediator in the quest for greater autonomy and ethnic representation in Vietnam. The Cambodian government, for its part, turns a blind eye to the vast numbers of illegal Vietnamese inside its borders, as well as reports of Vietnamese encroachments on the eastern borders of Cambodia. The Cambodian government takes a softly, softly approach towards its more powerful neighbour, perhaps borne of the historic ties between the two political dynasties.

For more about the ongoing struggles of the Khmer Krom, visit www.khmerkrom.org.

in a single deity). During the time of Angkor, Shiva was the deity most in favour with the royal family, although in the 12th century he was superseded by Vishnu. Today some elements of Hinduism are still incorporated into important ceremonies involving birth, marriage and death.

Animism

The purest form of animism is practised among the minority people known as Khmer Leu. Some have converted to Buddhism, but the majority continue to worship spirits of the earth and skies and their forefathers.

Both Hinduism and Buddhism were gradually absorbed from beyond the borders of Cambodia, fusing with the animist beliefs already present among the Khmers before Indianisation (p286). Local beliefs didn't disappear but were incorporated into the new religions to form something uniquely Cambodian. The concept of Neak Ta has its foundations in animist beliefs regarding sacred soil and the sacred spirit around us. Neak Ta can be viewed as a mother-earth concept, an energy force uniting a community with its earth and water. It can be represented in many forms, from stone or wood to termite hills – anything that symbolises both a link between the people and the fertility of their land. The sometimes phallic representation of Neak Ta helps explain the popularity of Hinduism and the worship of the *lingam* (phallic symbol).

Islam

Cambodia's Muslims are descendants of Chams, who migrated from what is now central Vietnam after the final defeat of the kingdom of Champa by the Vietnamese in 1471. Like Buddhists in Cambodia, the Cham Muslims call the faithful to prayer by banging a drum, rather than with the call of the muezzin.

Christianity

Christianity has made limited headway into Cambodia compared with neighbouring Vietnam. There were a number of churches in Cambodia before the war, but many of these were systematically destroyed by the Khmer Rouge, including Notre Dame Cathedral in Phnom Penh. Christianity made a comeback of sorts throughout the refugee camps on the Thai border in the 1980s, as a number of 'food for faith'-type charities set up shop dispensing religion with every meal. Many Cambodians changed their public faith for survival, before converting back to Buddhism on their departure from the camps, earning the moniker 'rice Christians'.

The Arts

Rithy Panh's 1996 film *Bophana* tells the true story of Hout Bophana, a beautiful young woman, and Ly Sitha, a regional Khmer Rouge leader, who fall in love and are executed for their 'crime'.

The Khmer Rouge's assault on the arts was a terrible blow to Cambodian culture. Indeed, for a number of years the consensus among Khmers was that their culture had been irrevocably lost. The Khmer Rouge not only did away with living bearers of Khmer culture but also destroyed cultural artefacts, statues, musical instruments, books and anything else that served as a reminder of a past it was trying to efface. The temples of Angkor were spared as a symbol of Khmer glory and empire, but little else survived. Despite this, Cambodia is witnessing a resurgence of traditional arts and a growing interest in experimentation in modern arts and cross-cultural fusion.

Architecture

Khmer architecture reached its peak during the Angkorian era (9th to 14th centuries). Some of the finest examples of architecture from this period are Angkor Wat and the structures of Angkor Thom.

Today, most rural Cambodian houses are built on high wood pilings (if the family can afford it) and have thatched roofs, walls made of palm mats and floors of woven bamboo strips resting on bamboo joists. The shady space underneath is used for storage and for people to relax at midday. Wealthier families have houses with wooden walls and tiled roofs, but the basic design remains the same.

The French left their mark in Cambodia in the form of some handsome villas and government buildings built in neoclassical style, Romanesque pillars and all. Some of the best architectural examples are in Phnom Penh, but most of the provincial capitals have at least one or two examples of architecture from the colonial period. Battambang and Kampot are two of the best-preserved colonial-era towns, with handsome rows of shophouses and the classic governor's residences.

During the 1950s and 1960s, Cambodia's so-called golden era, a group of young Khmer architects shaped the capital of Cambodia in their own image, experimenting with what is now called New Khmer Architecture. Vann Molyvann was the most famous proponent of this school of architecture, designing a number of prominent Phnom Penh landmarks such as the Olympic Stadium, the Chatomuk Theatre and Independence Monument. The beach resort of Kep was remodelled at this time, as the emergent Cambodian middle class flocked to the beach, and there are some fantastic if dilapidated examples of New Khmer Architecture around the

The famous Hindu epic the *Ramayana* is known as the *Reamker* in Cambodia. Reyum Publishing has issued a beautifully illustrated book, *The Reamker* (1999), telling the story.

PEOPLE & CULTURE THE ARTS

TOP 10 TIPS TO EARN THE RESPECT OF THE LOCALS

Take your time to learn a little about the local culture in Cambodia. Not only will you avoid inadvertently causing offence, it will also ingratiate you with your hosts. Here are a few top tips:

Dress code Respect local dress standards, particularly at religious sites. Covering the upper arms and upper legs is appropriate, although some monks will be too polite to enforce this. Always remove shoes before entering a temple, as well as hats. Nude sunbathing is considered totally inappropriate, even on beaches.

Make a contribution Since most temples are maintained through donations, remember to make a contribution when visiting a temple. When visiting a Khmer home, a small token of gratitude in the form of a gift is always appreciated.

Meet and greet Learn the Cambodian greeting, the *sompiah*, and use it when introducing yourself to new friends. When beckoning someone over, always wave towards yourself with the palm down, as palm up with fingers raised can be suggestive, even offensive.

A woman's touch Monks are not supposed to touch or be touched by women. If a woman wishes to pass something to a monk, the object should be placed within reach of the monk or on his 'receiving cloth'.

Keep your cool No matter how high your blood pressure rises, do not raise your voice or show signs of aggression. This will lead to a 'loss of face' and cause embarrassment to the locals, ensuring the situation gets worse rather than better.

Business cards Exchanging business cards is an important part of even the smallest transaction or business contact in Cambodia. Get some printed before you arrive and hand them out like confetti. Always present them with two hands.

Deadly chopsticks Leaving a pair of chopsticks sitting vertically in a rice bowl looks very much like the incense sticks that are burned for the dead. This is a powerful sign and is not appreciated in Asia.

Mean feet Cambodians like to keep a clean house and it's usual to remove shoes when entering somebody's home. It's rude to point the bottom of your feet towards other people. Never, ever point your feet towards anything sacred, such as an image of Buddha.

Hats off As a form of respect to the elderly or other esteemed people, such as monks, take off your hat and bow your head politely when addressing them. Never pat or touch an adult on the head – in Asia, the head is considered the most sacred part of the body.

Toothpicks While digging out those stubborn morsels from between your teeth, it's polite to use one hand to perform the extraction and the other hand to cover your mouth.

small town. Boutique hotels Knai Bang Chatt and Villa Romonea in Kep are both restored examples from this period.

To discover examples of New Khmer Architecture, visit the website of **Khmer Architecture Tours** (www.ka-tours.org) or sign up for one of its walking tours of Phnom Penh or Battambang. The website includes downloadable printouts for DIY tours of each city.

Cinema

Back in the 1960s, the Cambodian film industry was booming. Between 1960 and 1975, more than 400 films were made, some of which were exported all around Asia, including numerous films by then head-of-state Norodom Sihanouk. However, the advent of Khmer Rouge rule saw the film industry disappear overnight and it didn't recover for more than a quarter of a century.

The film industry in Cambodia was given a new lease of life in 2000 with the release of *Pos Keng Kong* (The Giant Snake). A remake of a 1960s Cambodian classic, it tells the story of a powerful young girl born from a rural relationship between a woman and a snake king. It's an interesting love story, albeit with dodgy special effects, and achieved massive box-office success around the region.

The success of *Pos Keng Kong* heralded a mini revival in the Cambodian film industry and local directors now turn out several films a year. However, many of these are amateurish horror films of dubious artistic value.

At least one overseas Cambodian director has enjoyed major success in recent years: Rithy Panh's *People of the Rice Fields* was nominated for the Palme d'Or at the Cannes Film Festival in 1995. The film touches only fleetingly on the Khmer Rouge, depicting the lives of a family living an arduous existence in the rice fields. His other films include *One Night after the War* (1997), the story of a young Khmer kickboxer falling for a bar girl in Phnom Penh; and the award-winning *S-21: The Khmer Rouge Killing Machine* (2003), a powerful documentary in which survivors from Tuol Sleng are brought back to confront their guards.

The definitive film about Cambodia is *The Killing Fields* (1985), which tells the story of American journalist Sydney Schanberg and his Cambodian assistant Dith Pran. Most of the footage was actually shot in Thai-

Australian-Cambodian film *Ruin* (2013), directed by Amiel Courtin-Wilson and Michael Cody, won the special Orizzonti jury prize at the Venice Bienniale Film Festival.

RUIN

SIHANOUK & THE SILVER SCREEN

Between 1965 and 1969 Sihanouk (former king and head of state of Cambodia) wrote, directed and produced nine feature films, a figure that would put the average workaholic Hollywood director to shame. Sihanouk took the business of making films very seriously, and family and officials were called upon to play their part: the minister of foreign affairs acted as the male lead in Sihanouk's first feature, *Apsara* (1965), and his daughter Princess Bopha Devi, the female lead. When, in the same movie, a show of military hardware was required, the air force was brought into action, as was the army's fleet of helicopters.

Sihanouk often took on the leading role himself. Notable performances saw him as a spirit of the forest and as a victorious general. Perhaps it was no surprise, given the king's apparent addiction to the world of celluloid dreams, that Cambodia should challenge Cannes with its Phnom Penh International Film Festival. The festival was held twice, in 1968 and 1969. Perhaps unsurprisingly, Sihanouk won the grand prize on both occasions. He continued to make movies in later life and made around 30 films during his remarkable career. For more on the films of Sihanouk, visit the website www.norodomsihanouk.org.

land, as it was filmed in 1984 when Cambodia was effectively closed to the West.

Quite a number of international films have been shot in Cambodia in recent years, including *Tomb Raider* (2001), *City of Ghosts* (2002) and *Two Brothers* (2004), all worth seeking out for their beautiful Cambodian backdrops. Australian independent feature film *Wish You Were Here*, partly shot in Cambodia in 2011, opened the Sundance Festival in 2012.

For more on Cambodian films and cinema, pick up a copy of *Kon: The Cinema of Cambodia* (2010), published by the Department of Media and Communication at the Royal University of Cambodia.

Dance

More than any of the other traditional arts, Cambodia's royal ballet is a tangible link with the glory of Angkor. Its traditions stretch long into the past, when the art of the *apsara* (nymph) resounded to the glory of the divine king. Early in his reign, King Sihanouk released the traditional harem of royal *apsara* that went with the crown.

Dance fared particularly badly during the Pol Pot years. Very few dancers and teachers survived. In 1981, with a handful of teachers, the University of Fine Arts was reopened and the training of dance students resumed.

Much of Cambodian royal dance resembles that of India and Thailand (the same stylised hand movements, the same sequined, lamé costumes and the same opulent stupa-like headwear), as the Thais incorporated techniques from the Khmers after sacking Angkor in the 15th century. Although royal dance was traditionally an all-female affair (with the exception of the role of the monkey), more male dancers are now featured. Known as *robam preah reachtrop* in Khmer, the most popular classical dances are the Apsara dance and the Wishing dance.

Folk dance is another popular element of dance performances that are regularly staged for visitors in Phnom Penh and Siem Reap. Folk dances draw on rural lifestyle and cultural traditions for their inspiration. One of the most popular folk dances is *robam kom arek,* involving bamboo poles and some nimble footwork. Also popular are fishing and harvest-themed dances that include plenty of flirtatious interaction between male and female performers.

Other celebrated dances are only performed at certain festivals or at certain times of year. The *trot* is very popular at Khmer New Year to ward off evil spirits from the home or business. A dancer in a deer costume runs through the property pursued by a hunter and is eventually slain.

Chinese New Year (*Tet* to the Vietnamese in Cambodia) sees elaborate lion dances performed all over Phnom Penh and other major cities in Cambodia.

Contemporary dances include the popular *rom vong* (circle dance), which is likely to have originated in neighbouring Laos. Dancers move around in a circle taking three steps forward and two steps back. Hip hop and break-dancing is fast gaining popularity among urban youngsters and is regularly performed at outdoor events.

Music

The bas-reliefs on some of the monuments in the Angkor region depict musicians and *apsara* holding instruments similar to the traditional Khmer instruments of today, demonstrating that Cambodia has a long musical tradition all of its own.

Customarily, music was an accompaniment to a ritual or performance that had religious significance. Musicologists have identified six types of Cambodian musical ensemble, each used in different settings. The

PEOPLE & CULTURE THE ARTS

Amrita Performing Arts (p71) has worked on a number of ground-breaking dance and theatre projects in Cambodia, including collaborations with French and Japanese performers.

Cambodia's great musical tradition was almost lost during the Khmer Rouge years, but the Cambodian Master Performers Program is dedicated to reviving the country's musical tradition. Visit its website at www.cambodianmasters.org.

most traditional of these is the *arek ka,* an ensemble that performs at weddings. The instruments of the *arek ka* include a *tro khmae* (three-stringed fiddle), a *khsae muoy* (single-stringed bowed instrument) and *skor areak* (drums), among others. *Ahpea pipea* is another type of wedding music that accompanies the witnessing of the marriage, and *pin peat* is the music that can be heard at ballet performances and shadow-puppet displays.

Much of Cambodia's golden-era music from the pre-war period was lost during the Pol Pot years. The Khmer Rouge targeted famous singers, and the great Sinn Sisamouth and female divas Ros Sereysothea and Pen Ron, Cambodia's most famous songwriters and performers, all disappeared in the early days of the regime.

After the war, many Khmers settled in the USA, where a lively Khmer pop industry developed. Influenced by US music and later exported back to Cambodia, it has been enormously popular.

A new generation of overseas Khmers growing up with influences from the West is producing its own sound. Cambodians are now returning to the homeland raised on a diet of rap in the US or France, and lots of artists are breaking through, such as the ClapYaHandz collective started by Sok 'Cream' Visal.

There's also a burgeoning pop industry, and many of its stars perform at outdoor concerts in Phnom Penh. It's easy to join in the fun by visiting one of the innumerable karaoke bars around the country. Preap Sovath is the Robbie Williams of Cambodia and, if you flick through the Cambodian channels for more than five minutes, chances are he will be performing. Aok Sokun Kanha is one of the more popular young female singers, with a big voice, but it's a changeling industry and new stars are waiting in the wings.

Dengue Fever is the ultimate fusion band, rapidly gaining a name for itself beyond the USA and Cambodia. Cambodian singer Chhom Nimol fronts five American prog rockers who dabble in psychedelic sounds. Another fusion band fast gaining a name for itself is the Cambodian Space Project, comprising a mix of Cambodians and expats. They regularly play in Phnom Penh and are well worth catching if you happen to be in town.

One form of music unique to Cambodia is *chapaye,* a sort of Cambodian blues sung to the accompaniment of a two-stringed wooden instrument similar in sound to a bass guitar played without an amplifier. There are few old masters, such as Kong Nay (the Ray Charles of Cambodia), left alive, but *chapaye* is still often shown on late-night Cambodian TV before transmission ends. Kong Nay has toured internationally in countries such as Australia and the US, and has even appeared with Peter Gabriel at the WOMAD music festival in the UK.

One of the greatest '70s legends to seek out is Nuon Sarath, the Jimi Hendrix of Cambodia, with his screaming vocals and wah-wah pedals. His most famous song, 'Chi Cyclo', is an absolute classic.

Check out www.tinytoones.org for more on a hip-hop cooperative seeking to inspire the youth of Cambodia to adopt a healthier lifestyle free of drugs and exposure to HIV. Keep an eye out for their performances around Phnom Penh.

SPORT IN CAMBODIA

The national sport of Cambodia is *pradal serey* (Cambodian kickboxing). It's similar to kickboxing in Thailand (don't make the mistake of calling it Thai boxing over here, though) and there are regular weekend bouts on CTN and TV5. It's also possible to go to the TV arenas and watch the fights live.

Football is another national obsession, although the Cambodian team is a real minnow, even by Asian standards. Many Cambodians follow the Premier League in England religiously and regularly bet on games.

The French game of *pétanque,* also called *boules*, is also very popular here and the Cambodian team has won several medals in regional games.

For more on Cambodian music, pick up a copy of *Dontrey: The Music of Cambodia* (2011), published by the Department of Media and Communication at the Royal University of Cambodia.

Sculpture

The Khmer empire of the Angkor period produced some of the most exquisite carved sculptures found anywhere on earth. Even in the pre-Angkorian era, the periods generally referred to as Funan and Chenla, the people of Cambodia were producing masterfully sensuous sculpture that was more than just a copy of the Indian forms on which it was modelled. Some scholars maintain that the Cambodian forms are unrivalled, even in India itself.

The earliest surviving Cambodian sculpture dates from the 6th century AD. Most of it depicts Vishnu with four or eight arms. A large eight-armed Vishnu from this period is displayed at the National Museum in Phnom Penh.

Also on display at the National Museum is a statue of Harihara from the end of the 7th century, a divinity who combines aspects of both Vishnu and Shiva but looks more than a little Egyptian with his pencil moustache and long, thin nose – a reminder that Indian sculpture drew from the Greeks, who in turn were influenced by the Pharaohs.

Innovations of the early Angkorian era include freestanding sculpture that dispenses with the stone aureole that in earlier works supported the multiple arms of Hindu deities. The faces assume an air of tranquility, and the overall effect is less animated.

The Banteay Srei style of the late 10th century is commonly regarded as a high point in the evolution of Southeast Asian art. The National Museum has a splendid piece from this period: a sandstone statue of Shiva holding Uma, his wife, on his knee. Sadly, Uma's head was stolen some time during Cambodia's turbulent years. The Baphuon style of the 11th century was inspired to a certain extent by the sculpture of Banteay Srei, producing some of the finest works to have survived today.

The statuary of the Angkor Wat period is felt to be conservative and stilted, lacking the grace of earlier work. The genius of this period manifests itself more clearly in the immense architecture and incredible bas-reliefs of Angkor Wat itself.

The final high point in Angkorian sculpture is the Bayon period from the end of the 12th century to the beginning of the 13th century. In the National Museum, look for the superb representation of Jayavarman VII, an image that projects both great power and sublime tranquility.

As the state religion swung back and forth between Mahayana Buddhism and Hinduism during the turbulent 13th and 14th centuries, Buddha images and Bodhisattvas were carved only to be hacked out by militant Hindus on their return to power. By the 15th century, stone was generally replaced by wood and polychrome as the material of choice for Buddha statues. A beautiful gallery of post-16th-century Buddhas from around Angkor is on display in the National Museum.

Cambodian sculptors are rediscovering their skills now that there is a ready market among visitors for reproduction stone carvings of famous statues and busts from the time of Angkor.

Even the destructive Khmer Rouge paid homage to the mighty Angkor Wat on its flag, with three towers of the temple in yellow, set against a blood-red background.

Jayavarman VII was a Mahayana Buddhist who directed his faith towards improving the lot of his people, with the construction of hospitals, universities, roads and shelters.

PEOPLE & CULTURE THE ARTS

Food & Drink

It's no secret that the dining tables of Thailand and Vietnam are home to some of the finest food in the world, so it should come as no surprise to discover that Cambodian cuisine is also rather special. Unlike the culinary colossi that are its neighbours, Cambodia is not that well known in international food circles, but all that looks set to change. Just as Angkor has put Cambodia on the tourist map, so too *amok* (baked fish with lemongrass-based *kreung* paste, coconut and chilli in banana leaf) could put the country on the culinary map.

As well as eating the notorious tarantulas of Skuon, Cambodians also like to eat crickets, beetles, larvae and ants. Some scientists have suggested insect farms as a way to solve food problems of the future. This time, Cambodia might be ahead of the curve.

Cambodia has a great variety of national dishes, some similar to the cuisine of neighbouring Thailand and Laos, others closer to Chinese and Vietnamese cooking, but all come with a unique Cambodian twist.

Freshwater fish forms a huge part of the Cambodian diet thanks to the natural phenomenon that is the Tonlé Sap lake. The fish come in every shape and size, from the giant Mekong catfish to teeny-tiny whitebait, which are great beer snacks when deep-fried. The French left their mark too, with baguettes becoming the national bread and Cambodian cooks showing a healthy reverence for tender meats.

Cambodia is a crossroads in Asia, the meeting point of the great civilisations of India and China, and, just as its culture has drawn on both, so too has its cuisine. You're bound to find something that takes your fancy, whether your tastes run to spring rolls or curry. Add to this a world of dips and sauces to complement the cooking and a culinary journey through Cambodia becomes as rich a feast as any in Asia.

Staples & Specialities

No matter what part of the world you come from, if you travel much in Cambodia, you are going to encounter food that is unusual, strange, maybe even immoral, or just plain weird. The fiercely omnivorous Cambodians find nothing strange in eating insects, algae, offal or fish bladders. They will dine on a duck foetus, brew up some brains or snack on some spiders. They will peel live frogs to grill on a barbecue or down wine infused with snake to increase their virility.

To the Khmers there is nothing 'strange' about anything that will sustain the body. To them a food is either wholesome or it isn't; it's nutritious or it isn't; it tastes good or it doesn't. And that's all they worry about. They'll try anything once, even a burger.

COOKING COURSES

If you are really taken with Cambodian cuisine, it's possible to learn some tricks of the trade by signing up for a cooking course. This is a great way to introduce your Cambodian experience to your friends – not everyone wants to sit through the slide show of photos, but offer them a mouth-watering meal and they will all come running.

There are courses available in Phnom Penh, Siem Reap, Battambang and Sihanoukville, and more are popping up all the time.

WE DARE YOU: TOP FIVE

Crickets Anyone for cricket?

Duck foetus Unborn duck, feathers and all.

Durian Nasally obnoxious spiky fruit, banned on flights.

Prahoc Fermented fish paste, almost a biological weapon.

Spiders Just like it sounds, deep-fried tarantulas.

Rice, Fish & Soup

Cambodia's abundant waterways provide the fish that is fermented into *prahoc* (fermented fish paste), which forms the backbone of Khmer cuisine. Built around this are the flavours that give the cuisine its kick: the secret roots, the welcome herbs and the aromatic tubers. Together they give the salads, snacks, soups and stews a special aroma and taste that smacks of Cambodia.

Rice from Cambodia's lush fields is the principal staple, enshrined in the Khmer word for 'eating' or 'to eat', *nyam bai* – literally 'eat rice'. Many a Cambodian, particularly drivers, will run out of steam if they run out of rice. It doesn't matter that the same carbohydrates are available in other foods, it is rice and rice alone that counts. Battambang Province is Cambodia's rice bowl and produces the country's finest yield.

For the taste of Cambodia in a bowl, try the local *kyteow,* a rice-noodle soup that will keep you going all day. This full, balanced meal will cost you just 5000r in markets and about US$2 in local restaurants. Don't like noodles? Then try the *bobor* (rice porridge), a national institution, for breakfast, lunch and dinner, and best sampled with some fresh fish and a splash of ginger.

A Cambodian meal almost always includes a *samlor* (traditional soup), which will appear at the same time as the other courses. *Samlor machou bunlay* (hot and sour fish soup with pineapple and spices) is popular.

Much of the fish eaten in Cambodia is freshwater, from the Tonlé Sap lake or the Mekong River. *Trey ahng* (grilled fish) is a Cambodian speciality (*ahng* means 'grilled' and can be applied to many dishes). Traditionally, the fish is eaten as pieces wrapped in lettuce or spinach leaves and then dipped into *teuk trey,* a fish sauce that is a close relative to Vietnam's *nuoc mam,* but with the addition of ground peanuts.

Salads

Cambodian salad dishes are popular and delicious, although they're quite different from the Western idea of a cold salad. *Phlea sait kow* is a beef and vegetable salad, flavoured with coriander, mint and lemongrass. These three herbs find their way into many Cambodian dishes.

Desserts & Fruit

Desserts can be sampled cheaply at night markets around the country. One sweet snack to look out for is the ice-cream sandwich. Popular with the kids, it involves putting a slab of homemade ice cream into a piece of sponge or bread.

Cambodia is blessed with many tropical fruits and sampling these is an integral part of a visit to the country. All the common fruits can be found in abundance, including *chek* (banana)*, menoa* (pineapple) and *duong* (coconut). Among the larger fruit, *khnau* (jackfruit) is very common, often weighing more than 20kg. The *tourain* (durian) usually

Friends is one of the best-known restaurants in Phnom Penh, turning out a fine array of tapas, shakes and specials to help street children in the capital. Its cookbook *The Best of Friends* is a visual feast showcasing its best recipes.

Teuk trey (fish sauce), one of the most popular condiments in Cambodian cooking, cannot be taken on international flights, in line with regulations on carrying strong-smelling or corrosive substances.

WINE

needs no introduction, as you can smell it from a mile off; the exterior is green with sharp spines, while inside is a milky, soft interior regarded by the Chinese as an aphrodisiac. It stinks, although some maintain it is an acquired taste...best acquired with a nose peg.

The fruits most popular with visitors include the *mongkut* (mangosteen) and *sao mao* (rambutan). The small mangosteen has a purple skin that contains white segments with a divine flavour. Similarly popular is the rambutan, with an interior like a lychee and an exterior covered in soft red and green spines.

Best of all, although it's common throughout the world, is the *svay* (mango). The Cambodian mango season is from March to May. Other varieties of mango are available year-round, but it's the hot-season ones that are a taste sensation.

Drinks

Cambodia has a lively local drinking culture, and the heat and humidity will ensure that you hunt out anything on offer to quench your thirst. Coffee, tea, beer, wine, soft drinks, fresh fruit juices and some of the more exotic 'firewaters' are all widely available. Tea is the national drink, but these days it is just as likely to be beer in the glass.

The local brew for country folk is sugar-palm wine, distilled daily direct from the trees and fairly potent after it has settled. Sold in bamboo containers off the back of bicycles, it's tasty and cheap, although only suitable for those with a cast-iron stomach.

Beer

It's never a challenge to find a beer in Cambodia and even the most remote village usually has a stall selling a few cans. Angkor is the national beer, produced in vast quantities in a big brewery down in Sihanoukville. It costs around US$2 to US$3 for a 660ml bottle in most restaurants and bars. Draught Angkor is available for around US$0.50 to US$1.50 in the main tourist centres. Other popular local brands include newcomer Cambodia Beer, aiming to topple Angkor as the beer of choice, and provincial favourite Crown Lager.

A beer brand from neighbouring Laos, Beerlao, is very drinkable and is also one of the cheapest ales available. Tiger Beer is produced locally and is a popular draught in the capital. Some Khmer restaurants have a bevy of 'beer girls', each promoting a particular beer brand. They are always friendly and will leave you alone if you prefer not to drink.

A word of caution for beer seekers in Cambodia: while the country is awash with good brews, there's a shortage of refrigeration in the countryside. Go native and learn how to say, '*Som teuk koh*' (Ice, please).

Some Cambodian nightclubs allow guests to rent premium bottles of spirits, like Johnnie Walker Blue Label, to display on the table – a way of maintaining face despite the fact it's actually Johnnie Walker Red Label in the glass.

Wine & Spirits

Local wine in Cambodia generally means rice wine; it is popular with the minority peoples of the northeast. Some rice wines are fermented for months and are superstrong, while other brews are fresher and taste more like a demented cocktail. Either way, if you are invited to join a session in a minority village, it's rude to decline. Other local wines include light sugar-palm wine and ginger wine.

In Phnom Penh and Siem Reap, foreign wines and spirits are sold in supermarkets at bargain prices, given how far they have to travel. Wines

---

BOTTOMS UP

When Cambodians propose a toast, they usually stipulate what percentage must be downed. If they are feeling generous, it might be just *ha-sip pea-roi* (50%), but more often than not it is *moi roi pea-roi* (100%). This is why they love ice in their beer, as they can pace themselves over the course of the night. Many a *barang* (foreigner) has ended up face down on the table at a Cambodian wedding when trying to outdrink the Khmer boys without the aid of ice.

from Europe and Australia start at about US$5, while the famous names of the spirit world cost between US$5 and US$15.

Tea & Coffee

Chinese-style *tai* (tea) is a bit of a national institution, and in most Khmer and Chinese restaurants a pot will automatically appear for no extra charge as soon as you sit down. *Kaa fey* (coffee) is sold in most restaurants. It is either black or *café au lait,* served with dollops of condensed milk.

Water & Soft Drinks

Drinking tap water *must* be avoided, especially in the provinces, as it is rarely purified and may lead to stomach complications. Locally produced mineral water starts at 1000r per bottle at shops and stalls.

Although tap water should be avoided, it is generally OK to have ice in your drinks. Throughout Cambodia, *teuk koh* (ice) is produced with treated water at local ice factories, a legacy of the French.

All the well-known soft drinks are available in Cambodia. Bottled drinks are about 1000r, while canned drinks cost about 2000r, more again in restaurants or bars.

Teuk kalohk are popular throughout Cambodia. They are a little like fruit smoothies and are a great way to wash down a meal.

Dining Out

Whatever your tastes, some eatery in Cambodia is sure to help out, be it the humble peddler, a market stall, a local diner or a slick restaurant.

It's easy to sample inexpensive Khmer cuisine throughout the country, mostly at local markets and cheap restaurants. For more refined Khmer dining, the best restaurants are in Phnom Penh and Siem Reap, where there is also the choice of excellent Thai, Vietnamese, Chinese, Indian, French and Mediterranean cooking. Chinese and Vietnamese food is available in towns across the country due to the large urban populations of both of these ethnic groups.

There are few Western fast-food chains in Phnom Penh as yet, with the exception of KFC and Burger King, but there are a few local copycats. The most successful have been Lucky Burger and BB World, with lots of branches in the capital.

There are often no set hours for places to eat but, as a general rule of thumb, street stalls are open from very early in the morning until early evening, although some stalls specialise in the night shift. Most restaurants are open all day, while some of the fancier places are only open for lunch (usually 11am to 2.30pm) and dinner (usually 5pm to 10pm).

Dining Out with Kids

Both Phnom Penh and Siem Reap have child-friendly eateries. Check out Le Jardin (p64) in Phnom Penh, or Kanell (p106) or Tangram Garden (p106) in Siem Reap, and sit back and relax. Some of the fast-food places in the capital also have children's playgrounds.

Street Snacks

Street food is an important part of everyday Cambodian life. Like many Southeast Asians, Cambodians are inveterate snackers. They can be found at impromptu stalls at any time of the day or night, delving into a range of unidentified frying objects. Drop into the markets for an even greater range of dishes and the chance of a comfortable seat. It's a cheap, cheerful and cool way to get up close and personal with Khmer cuisine.

FOOD & DRINK DINING OUT

A popular food blog on Cambodia can be found at www.phnomenon.com, which covers Khmer food, surfing the streets and the up-and-coming dining scene. It's dated, but the archives are a treasure trove. For a more up-to-date food blog, check out Nyam Penh at nyampenh.com.

Before it become a member of the World Trade Organization, copyright protection was almost unknown in Cambodia. During that period there was a host of copycat fast-food restaurants, including Khmer Fried Chicken, Pizza Hot and Burger Queen, all now sadly defunct.

In the Cambodian Kitchen

Enter the Cambodian kitchen and you will learn that fine food comes from simplicity. Essentials consist of a strong flame, clean water, basic cutting utensils, a mortar and pestle, and a well-blackened pot or two.

Cambodians eat three meals a day. Breakfast is either *kyteow* or *bobor*. Baguettes are available at any time of day or night, and go down well with a cup of coffee.

Lunch starts early, around 11am. Traditionally, lunch is taken with the family, but in towns and cities many workers now eat at local restaurants or markets.

Dinner is the time for family bonding. Dishes are arranged around the central rice bowl and diners each have a small eating bowl. The procedure is uncomplicated: spoon some rice into your bowl, and lay 'something else' on top of it.

When you're ordering multiple courses from a restaurant menu, don't worry – don't even think – about the proper succession of courses. All dishes are placed in the centre of the table as soon as they are ready. Diners then help themselves to whatever appeals to them, regardless of who ordered what.

One of the most popular street snacks in Cambodia is the unborn duck foetus. The white duck eggs contain a little duckling, feathers and all. Don't order *kaun pong tier* if you want to avoid this.

Table Etiquette

Sit at the table with your bowl on a small plate, chopsticks or fork and spoon at the ready. Some Cambodians prefer chopsticks, some prefer fork and spoon, but both are usually available. Each place setting will include a small bowl, usually located at the top right-hand side for the dipping sauces.

When serving yourself from the central bowls, use the communal serving spoon so as not to dip your chopsticks or spoon into the food. To begin eating, just pick up your bowl with your left hand, bring it close to your mouth, and spoon in the rice and food.

Some dos and don'ts:

➡ *Do* wait for your host to sit first.

➡ *Don't* turn down food placed in your bowl by your host.

➡ *Do* learn to use chopsticks.

➡ *Don't* leave chopsticks in a V-shape in the bowl, a symbol of death.

➡ *Do* tip about 5% to 10% in restaurants, as wages are low.

➡ *Don't* tip if there is already a service charge on the bill.

➡ *Do* drink every time someone offers a toast.

➡ *Don't* pass out face down on the table if the toasting goes on all night.

For the scoop on countryside cooking in Cambodia, pick up *From Spiders to Waterlilies* (2009), a cookbook produced by Romdeng restaurant in Phnom Penh.

Vegetarians & Vegans

Few Cambodians understand the concept of strict vegetarianism and many will say something is vegetarian to please the customer when in fact it is not. If you are not a strict vegetarian and can deal with fish sauces and the like, you should have few problems ordering meals, and those who eat fish can sample Khmer cooking at its best. In the major tourist centres, many of the international restaurants feature vegetarian meals, although these are not budget options. In Khmer and Chinese restaurants, stir-fried vegetable dishes are readily available, as are vegetarian fried-rice dishes, but it is unlikely these 'vegetarian' dishes have been cooked in separate woks from other fish- and meat-based dishes. Indian restaurants in the popular tourist centres can cook up genuine vegetarian food, as they usually understand the vegetarian principle better than the *prahoc*-loving Khmers.

Environment

Cambodia's landscape ranges from the highs of the Cardamom Mountains to the lows of the Tonlé Sap basin, and includes some critically endangered species clinging on in the protected areas and national parks. However, these species and their habitat are under threat from illegal logging, agricultural plantations and hydroelectric dams for electricity. Cambodia faces a challenge to balance the economy and its need for electricity against the desire to develop sustainable ecotourism.

The Land

Cambodia's borders as we know them today are the result of a classic historical squeeze. As the Vietnamese moved south into the Mekong Delta and the Thais pushed west towards Angkor, Cambodia's territory, which in Angkorian times stretched from southern Burma to Saigon and north into Laos, began to shrink. Only the arrival of the French prevented Cambodia from going the way of the Chams, who became a people without a state. In that sense, French colonialism created a protectorate that actually protected.

Modern-day Cambodia covers 181,035 sq km, making it a little more than half the size of Vietnam or about the same size as England and Wales combined. To the west and northwest it borders Thailand, to the northeast Laos, to the east Vietnam, and to the south is the Gulf of Thailand.

Cambodia's two dominant geographical features are the mighty Mekong River and a vast lake, the Tonlé Sap. At Phnom Penh the Mekong splits into three channels: the Tonlé Sap River, which flows into, and out of, the Tonlé Sap lake; the Upper River (usually called simply the Mekong or, in Vietnamese, Tien Giang); and the Lower River (the Tonlé Bassac, or Hau Giang in Vietnamese). The rich sediment deposited during the Mekong's annual wet-season flooding has made central Cambodia incredibly fertile. This low-lying alluvial plain is where the vast majority of Cambodians live – fishing and farming in harmony with the rhythms of the monsoon.

In Cambodia's southwest quadrant, much of the land mass is covered by mountains: the Cardamom Mountains (Chuor Phnom Kravanh), covering parts of the provinces of Koh Kong, Battambang, Pursat and Krong Pailin, which are now opening up to ecotourism; and, southeast of there, the Elephant Mountains (Chuor Phnom Damrei), situated in the provinces of Kompong Speu, Koh Kong and Kampot.

Cambodia's 435km coastline is a big draw for visitors on the lookout for isolated tropical beaches. There are islands aplenty off the coast of Sihanoukville, Kep and Koh Kong.

Along Cambodia's northern border with Thailand, the plains collide with a striking sandstone escarpment more than 300km long that towers up to 550m above the lowlands: the Dangkrek Mountains (Chuor Phnom Dangkrek). One of the best places to get a sense of this area is Prasat Preah Vihear.

The Tonlé Sap lake provides a huge percentage of Cambodians' protein intake, 70% of which comes from fish. The volume of water in the Tonlé Sap can expand by up to a factor of 70 during the wet season.

For a close encounter with tigers at the temples of Angkor, watch Jean-Jacques Annaud's 2004 film *Two Brothers*, the story of two orphaned tiger cubs during the colonial period.

In the northeastern corner of the country, the plains give way to the Eastern Highlands, a remote region of densely forested mountains that extends east into Vietnam's Central Highlands and north into Laos. The wild provinces of Ratanakiri and Mondulkiri provide a home for many minority (hill-tribe) peoples and are taking off as an ecotourism hot spot.

Wildlife

Cambodia's forest ecosystems were in excellent shape until the 1990s and, compared with its neighbours, its habitats are still relatively healthy. The years of war took their toll on some species, but others thrived in the remote jungles of the southwest and northeast. Ironically, peace brought increased threats as loggers felled huge areas of primary forest and the illicit trade in wildlife targeted some endangered species. Due to years of inaccessibility, scientists have only relatively recently managed to research and catalogue the country's plant and animal life.

Researchers estimate that about 50 to 100 wild elephants live in Mondulkiri Province. A similar number live in the Cardamom Mountains.

Animals

Cambodia is home to an estimated 212 species of mammal, including tigers, elephants, bears, leopards and wild oxen. Some of the biggest characters, however, are the smaller creatures, including the binturong (nicknamed the bear cat), the pileated gibbon (the world's largest population lives in the Cardamoms) and the slow loris, which hangs out in trees all day. The country also has a great variety of butterflies.

Most of Cambodia's fauna is extremely hard to spot in the wild. The easiest way to see a healthy selection is to visit the Phnom Tamao Wild-

---

TONLÉ SAP: HEARTBEAT OF CAMBODIA

The Tonlé Sap, the largest freshwater lake in Southeast Asia, is an incredible natural phenomenon that provides fish and irrigation waters for half the population of Cambodia. It is also home to 90,000 people, many of them ethnic Vietnamese, who live in 170 floating villages.

Linking the lake with the Mekong at Phnom Penh is a 100km-long channel known as the Tonlé Sap River. From June to early October, wet-season rains rapidly raise the level of the Mekong, backing up the Tonlé Sap River and causing it to flow northwestward into the Tonlé Sap lake. During this period, the lake surface increases in size by a factor of four or five, from 2500 sq km to 3000 sq km up to 10,000 sq km to 16,000 sq km, and its depth increases from an average of about 2m to more than 10m. An unbelievable 20% of the Mekong's wet-season flow is absorbed by the Tonlé Sap. In October, as the water level of the Mekong begins to fall, the Tonlé Sap River reverses direction, draining the waters of the lake back into the Mekong.

This extraordinary process makes the Tonlé Sap an ideal habitat for birds, snakes and turtles, as well as one of the world's richest sources of freshwater fish: the flooded forests make for fertile spawning grounds, while the dry season creates ideal conditions for fishing. Experts believe that fish migrations from the lake help to restock fisheries as far north as China.

This unique ecosystem was declared a Unesco Biosphere Reserve in 2001, but this may not be enough to protect it from the twin threats of upstream dams and rampant deforestation. Dams are already in operation on the Chinese section of the Mekong, known locally as the Lancang, and the massive new Xayaboury Dam in Laos is now under construction, the first major dam on the Middle or Lower Mekong.

You can learn more about the Tonlé Sap and its unique ecosystem at the Gecko Centre (p115) near Siem Reap.

life Rescue Centre near Phnom Penh, which provides a home for rescued animals and includes all the major species.

A whopping 720 bird species find Cambodia a congenial home, thanks in large part to its year-round water resources. Relatively common birds include ducks, rails, cranes, herons, egrets, cormorants, pelicans, storks and parakeets, with migratory shorebirds, such as waders, plovers and terns, around the South Coast estuaries. Serious twitchers should consider a visit to Prek Toal Bird Sanctuary; Ang Trapeng Thmor Reserve, home to the extremely rare sarus crane, depicted on the bas-reliefs at Angkor; or the Tmatboey Ibis Project, where the critically endangered giant ibis, Cambodia's national bird, can be seen. For details on birdwatching in Cambodia, check out the Siem Reap–based Sam Veasna Center (p114).

Cambodia is home to about 240 species of reptile, including nine species of snake whose venom can be fatal, such as members of the cobra and viper families.

Endangered Species

Unfortunately, it is getting mighty close to checkout time for a number of species in Cambodia. The kouprey (wild ox), declared Cambodia's national animal by King Sihanouk back in the 1960s, and the Wroughton's free-tailed bat, previously thought to exist in only one part of India but recently discovered in Preah Vihear Province, are on the 'Globally Threatened: Critical' list, the last stop before extinction.

Other animals under serious threat in Cambodia include the Asian elephant, tiger, banteng, gaur, Asian golden cat, black gibbon, clouded leopard, fishing cat, marbled cat, sun bear, pangolin, giant ibis and Siamese crocodile.

Cambodia has some of the last remaining freshwater Irrawaddy dolphins (*trey pisaut* in Khmer), instantly identifiable thanks to their bulging forehead and short beak. Viewing them at Kampi is a popular activity.

In terms of fish biodiversity, the Mekong is second only to the Amazon, but dam projects threaten migratory species. The Mekong giant catfish, which can weigh up to 300kg, is critically endangered due to habitat loss and overfishing.

The following environmental groups are staffed in Cambodia, mainly by Khmers, and are playing leading roles in protecting Cambodia's wildlife:

Conservation International (www.conservation.org)
Fauna & Flora International (www.fauna-flora.org)
Maddox Jolie-Pitt Foundation (www.mjpasia.org)
Wildlife Alliance (WildAid; www.wildlifealliance.org)
Wildlife Conservation Society (www.wcs.org)
WWF (www.worldwildlife.org)

Plants

No one knows how many plant species are present in Cambodia because no comprehensive survey has ever been conducted, but it's estimated that the country is home to 15,000 species, at least a third of them endemic.

In the southwest, rainforests grow to heights of 50m or more on the rainy southern slopes of the mountains, with montane (pine) forests in cooler climes above 800m and mangrove forests fringing the coast. In the northern mountains there are broadleaved evergreen forests, with trees soaring 30m above a thick undergrowth of vines, bamboos, palms and assorted woody and herbaceous ground plants. The northern plains

ENVIRONMENT WILDLIFE

The *khting vor* (spiral-horned ox), so rare that no one had ever seen a live specimen, was considered critically endangered until DNA analysis of its distinctive horns showed that the creature had never existed – the 'horns' belonged to ordinary cattle and buffalo!

Snake bites are responsible for more amputations in Cambodia than landmines these days. Many villagers go to the medicine man for treatment and end up with infection, gangrene and/or a funeral.

support dry dipterocarp forests, while around the Tonlé Sap there are flooded (seasonally inundated) forests. The Eastern Highlands are covered with deciduous forests and grassland. Forested upland areas support many varieties of orchid.

The sugar palm, often seen towering over rice fields, provides fronds to make roofs and walls for houses, and fruit that's used to produce medicine, wine and vinegar. Sugar palms grow taller over the years, but their barkless trunks don't get any thicker, hence they retain shrapnel marks from every battle that has ever raged around them.

National Parks

In the late 1960s Cambodia had six national parks, together covering 22,000 sq km (around 12% of the country). The long civil war effectively destroyed this system and it wasn't reintroduced until 1993, when a royal decree designated 23 areas as national parks, wildlife sanctuaries, protected landscapes and multiple-use areas. Several more protected forests were added to the list in the last decade, bringing the area of protected land in Cambodia to over 43,000 sq km, or around 25% of the country.

This is fantastic news in principle, but in practice the authorities don't always protect these areas in any way other than drawing a line on a map. The government has enough trouble finding funds to pay the rangers who patrol the most popular parks, let alone to recruit staff for the remote sanctuaries, though in recent years a number of international NGOs have been helping to train and fund teams of enforcement rangers.

The Mondulkiri Protected Forest, at 4294 sq km, is now the largest protected area in Cambodia and is contiguous with Yok Don National Park in Vietnam. The 4013-sq-km Central Cardamoms Protected Forest borders the Phnom Samkos Wildlife Sanctuary to the west and the Phnom Aural Wildlife Sanctuary to the east, creating almost 10,000 sq km of designated protected land. The noncontiguous Southern Cardamoms Protected Forest (1443 sq km) is along the Koh Kong Conservation Corridor, the ecotourism potential of which is as vast as its jungles are impenetrable.

In 2005 three rangers working with the NGO Flora & Fauna International to prevent illegal hunting and logging in the Cardamom Mountains were murdered in two separate incidents, apparently by poachers. In 2012, popular environmental activist Chhut Vuthy, founder of the Natural Resource Protection Group, was shot dead in Koh Kong province.

TIGERS UNDER THREAT

In the mid-1990s, somewhere between 100 and 200 Cambodian tigers were being killed every year, their carcasses bringing huge sums around Asia (especially China) because of their supposed aphrodisiacal powers. By 1998 annual incidents of tiger poaching had dropped to 85 and in 2005 just two tigers were killed. Sadly, it's more likely that these estimates reflect a crash in tiger numbers rather than increased community awareness or more effective law enforcement.

Experts fear there may be only 50 of the big cats left in the wild in Cambodia. Numbers are so low that, despite repeated efforts, camera traps set by researchers in recent years have failed to photograph a single tiger, though footprints and other signs of the felines' presence have been recorded. As far as anyone can tell, the surviving tigers live in very low densities in very remote areas, making it difficult for both poachers and scientists to find them, and hard for environmentalists to protect them.

At present, tigers are known to inhabit two areas: the central part of the Cardamom Mountains and Mondulkiri Province. In addition, they are thought to be present in small numbers in Ratanakiri and Preah Vihear.

For insights, stories and links about tigers in Cambodia and what's being done to protect them, visit the website of the Cat Action Treasury at www.felidae.org.

CAMBODIA'S MOST IMPORTANT NATIONAL PARKS

PARK	SIZE	FEATURES	ACTIVITIES	BEST TIME TO VISIT
Bokor	1581 sq km	hotel-casino, ghost town, views, waterfalls	trekking, biking, wildlife-watching	Nov-May
Kirirom	350 sq km	waterfalls, vistas, pine forests	hiking, wildlife-watching	Nov-Jun
Ream	150 sq km	beaches, islands, mangroves, dolphins, monkeys	boating, swimming, hiking, wildlife-watching	Nov-May
Virachey	3325 sq km	unexplored jungle, waterfalls	trekking, adventure, wildlife-watching	Nov-Apr

Environmental Issues

Logging

The greatest threat to Cambodia's globally important ecosystems is logging for charcoal and timber and to clear land for cash-crop plantations. During the Vietnamese occupation, troops stripped away swaths of forest to prevent Khmer Rouge ambushes along highways. The devastation increased in the 1990s, when the shift to a capitalist market economy led to an asset-stripping bonanza by well-connected businessmen.

International demand for timber is huge and, as neighbouring countries such as Thailand and Vietnam began to enforce much tougher logging regulations, foreign logging companies flocked to Cambodia. At the height of the country's logging epidemic in the late 1990s, just under 70,000 sq km of the country's land area, or about 35% of its total surface area, had been allocated as concessions, amounting to almost all of Cambodia's forest land except national parks and protected areas. However, even in these supposed havens, illegal logging continued. According to environmental watchdog **Global Witness** (www.globalwitness.org), the Royal Cambodian Armed Forces (RCAF) is the driving force behind much of the recent logging in remote border regions.

In the short term, deforestation is contributing to worsening floods along the Mekong, but the long-term implications of logging are hard to assess. Without trees to cloak the hills, rains will inevitably carry away large amounts of topsoil during future monsoons and in time this will have a serious effect on Tonlé Sap.

Since 2002 things have been looking up. Under pressure from donors and international institutions, all logging contracts were effectively frozen, pending further negotiations with the government. However, small-scale illegal logging has continued, including cutting for charcoal production and slash-and-burn for settlement.

The latest threat to Cambodia's forests comes from 'economic concessions' granted to establish plantations of cash crops such as rubber, mango, cashew and jackfruit, or agro-forestry groves of acacia and eucalyptus to supply wood chips for the paper industry. The government argues these plantations are necessary for economic development and counts them as reforestation, but in reality the damage to the delicate ecosystem is irreparable.

Pollution

Phnom Penh's air isn't anywhere near as bad as Bangkok's, but as vehicles multiply it's getting worse. In provincial towns and villages, the smoke from garbage fires can ruin your dinner...or worse.

Cambodia has extremely primitive sanitation systems in its urban areas, and nonexistent sanitary facilities in rural areas, with only a tiny percentage of the population having access to proper facilities. These

Banned in Cambodia, the damning 2007 report *Cambodia's Family Trees*, by the UK-based environmental watchdog Global Witness (www.globalwitness.org), exposes Cambodia's most powerful illegal-logging syndicates.

In the mid-1960s Cambodia was reckoned to have around 90% of its original forest cover intact. Estimates today vary, but 25% is common.

DOING YOUR BIT

Every visitor to Cambodia can make at least a small contribution to the country's ecological sustainability.

➡ Lead by example and dispose of your rubbish responsibly.

➡ Drink fresh coconuts, in their natural packaging, rather than soft drinks in throwaway cans and bottles.

➡ Choose trekking guides who respect both the ecosystem and the people who live in it.

➡ Avoid eating wild meat, such as bat, deer and shark fin.

➡ Don't touch live coral when snorkelling or diving, and don't buy coral souvenirs.

➡ If you see wild animals being killed, traded or eaten, take down details of what and where, and contact the **Wildlife Alliance** (☏012 500094; wildlifealliance@online.com. kh), an NGO that helps manage the government's Wildlife Rapid Rescue Team. Rescued animals are either released or taken to the Phnom Tamao Wildlife Rescue Centre.

conditions breed and spread disease: epidemics of diarrhoea are not uncommon and it is the number-one killer of young children in Cambodia.

Detritus of all sorts, especially plastic bags and bottles, can be seen in distressing quantities on beaches, around waterfalls, along roads and carpeting towns, villages and hamlets.

Damming the Mekong

The Mekong rises in Tibet and flows for 4800km before continuing through southern Vietnam into the South China Sea. This includes almost 500km in Cambodia, where it can be up to 5km wide. With energy needs spiralling upwards throughout the region, it is very tempting for developing countries like Cambodia and its upstream neighbours to build hydroelectric dams on the Mekong and its tributaries.

Despite responsibility for nearly 20% of the Mekong River's waters, China is not a member of the Mekong River Commission (MRC) and has only recently begun to discuss its extensive dam developments with the MRC members downstream.

Environmentalists fear that damming the mainstream Mekong may be nothing short of catastrophic for the flow patterns of the river, the migratory patterns of fish, the survival of the freshwater Irrawaddy dolphin and the very life of the Tonlé Sap. Plans now under consideration include the Sambor Dam, a massive 3300MW project 35km north of Kratie, and the Don Sahong (Siphandone) Dam just north of the Cambodia–Laos border.

Also of concern is the potential impact of dams on the annual monsoon flooding of the Mekong, which deposits nutrient-rich silt across vast tracts of land used for agriculture. A drop of just 1m in wet-season water levels on the Tonlé Sap would result in around 2000 sq km less flood area, with potentially disastrous consequences for Cambodia's farmers.

Overseeing development plans for the river is the **Mekong River Commission** (MRC; www.mrcmekong.org). Formed by the United Nations Development Programme and involving Cambodia, Thailand, Laos and Vietnam, it is ostensibly committed to sustainable development.

Sand Extraction

Sand dredging in the estuaries of Koh Kong Province, including inside the protected Peam Krasaop Wildlife Sanctuary, threatens delicate mangrove ecosystems and the sea life that depends on them. Much of the sand is destined for Singapore. For details, see Global Witness' 2009 report *Country for Sale* (www.globalwitness.org/library/country-sale).

Survival Guide

Directory A–Z

BOOK YOUR STAY ONLINE

For more accommodation reviews by Lonely Planet authors, check out http://lonelyplanet.com/hotels/. You'll find independent reviews, as well as recommendations on the best places to stay. Best of all, you can book online.

Accommodation

Accommodation in Cambodia has improved immensely during the past decade and everything is available, from the classic budget crash pad to the plush palace. Most hotels quote in US dollars, but some places in the provinces quote in riel, while those near the Thai border quote in baht. We provide prices based on the currency quoted to us at the time of research.

Hotels & Guesthouses

Budget guesthouses used to be restricted to Phnom Penh, Siem Reap and Sihanoukville, but as tourism takes off in the provinces, they are turning up in most of the other provincial capitals. Costs hover around US$3 to US$10 for a bed. In many rural parts of Cambodia, the standard rate for cheap hotels is US$5, usually with bathroom and satellite TV.

In Phnom Penh, Siem Reap and the South Coast, which see a steady flow of tourist traffic, hotels improve significantly once you start spending more than US$10 a night. For US$15 it is usually possible to find an air-con room with satellite TV and attached bathroom. If you spend between US$20 and US$50 you can arrange something very comfortable with the possible lure of a swimming pool. Most smaller provincial cities also offer air-conditioned comfort in the US$10 to US$20 range.

There are now a host of international-standard hotels in Siem Reap, several in Phnom Penh and a couple on the coast in Sihanoukville and Kep. Most quote hefty walk-in rates and whack 10% tax and 10% service on as well. Book via a hotel-booking website for a lower rate including taxes and service.

There are substantial low-season (April through September) rates available at major hotels in Phnom Penh, Siem Reap and Sihanoukville. Discounts of 50% or more are common, as are specials such as 'stay three, pay two'. Check hotel websites for details on any promos or offers.

Some guesthouses in Cambodia do not have hot water, but most places have at least a few more expensive rooms where it is available.

While many of the swish new hotels have lifts, older hotels often don't and the cheapest rooms are at the top of several flights of stairs. It's a win-win-win situation: cheaper rooms, a bit of exercise and better views.

Homestays

Homestays are popping up in the provinces and offer a good way to meet the local people and learn about the Cambodian lifestyle. There are several organised homestays around the country in provinces like Kompong Cham and Kompong Thom, as well as lots of informal

SLEEPING PRICE RANGES

The following price ranges refer to a double room in high season.

$ less than US$20

$$ US$20–80

$$$ more than US$80

homestays in out-of-the-way places such as Preah Vihear. In the minority areas of Mondulkiri and Ratanakiri, it is often possible to stay with tribal villagers. The Mekong Discovery Trail includes several homestays between Kratie and the Lao border.

Activities

Tourism in Cambodia is catching up fast and there are now more activities than ever to get that adrenaline buzz. Phnom Penh and Siem Reap remain the places with most of the action, but Sihanoukville and Kep are making a name for themselves for fun in the sun with water sports.

Birdwatching

Birdwatching is a big draw, as Cambodia is home to some of the region's rarest large waterbirds including adjutants, storks and pelicans.

Boat Trips

With so much water around the country, it's hardly surprising that boat trips are popular with tourists. Some of these are functional, such as travelling up the Tonlé Sap River from Phnom Penh to Siem Reap, or along the Sangker River from Siem Reap to Battambang. Others are the traditional tourist trips, such as those available in Phnom Penh, Siem Reap and Sihanoukville, or dolphin-spotting boat trips in Kratie.

Cycling

As Cambodia's roads continue to improve, cycling tourists are an increasingly common sight. It's a real adventure and brings visitors that much closer to the uber-friendly locals. The most popular place for cycling is around the majestic temples of Angkor, where the roads are paved and the forest shade welcome. For more on cycling in Cambodia, see p343.

PRACTICALITIES

Newspapers The *Phnom Penh Post* offers the best balance of Cambodian and international news, including business and sport. The *Cambodia Daily* is another long-running English-language newspaper.

Magazines *AsiaLife* is a free monthly listings magazine (a sort of *Time Out: Phnom Penh*). A variety of international magazines and newspapers are also widely available in Phnom Penh and Siem Reap.

TV Cambodia has a dozen or so local Khmer-language channels, but most of them support the ruling CPP and churn out a mixture of karaoke videos, soap operas and ministers going about their business. Most midrange hotels have cable TV with access to between 20 and 120 channels, including some obscure regional channels, international movie channels and the big global news and sports channels such as BBC and ESPN.

Radio BBC World Service broadcasts on 100.00FM in Phnom Penh. Cambodian radio and TV stations are mainly government-controlled and specialise in phone-ins and product placements.

Video Cambodia uses the PAL and NTSC video systems.

Weights and measures Cambodians use the metric system for everything except precious metals and gems, where they prefer to use the Chinese units of measurement.

Dirt Biking

For experienced riders, Cambodia is one of the most rewarding off-road biking destinations in the world. The roads are generally considered some of the worst in Asia (or best in Asia for die-hard biking enthusiasts). There are incredible rides all over the country, particularly in the north and northeast, but it is best to stay away from the main highways as traffic and dust make them a choking experience. For more on dirt biking in Cambodia, see p344.

Diving & Snorkelling

Snorkelling and diving are available off the coast of Sihanoukville. While it may not be as spectacular as Indonesia or the Philippines, there is plenty out there in the deep blue yonder. It's best to venture to the more remote dive sites, such as Koh Tang and Koh Prins, staying overnight on a boat. There are many unexplored areas off the coast between Koh Kong and Sihanoukville that could one day put Cambodia on the dive map of Asia.

Golf

Cambodia is an up-and-coming golfing destination thanks to several world-class courses in Siem Reap, one of which now hosts an annual PGA event on the Asian tour. There are also a couple of courses in Phnom Penh.

Trekking

Trekking is not the first activity most people would associate with Cambodia, due to the rather disconcerting presence of landmines, but there are several relatively safe areas of the country, including the nascent national parks, where walking can be enjoyed. The northeastern provinces of Mondulkiri and Ratanakiri were never mined, for example, and with their wild, natural scenery, abundant waterfalls and ethnic-minority populations, they are emerging as the country's leading trekking destinations.

Cambodia is steadily establishing a network of national parks with visitor facilities; Bokor National Park, Kirirom National Park and Ream National Park all promise trekking potential, while Virachey National Park in Ratanakiri has multiday treks. Chi Phat and the Cardamom Mountains also offer the possibility of a walk on the wild side.

Angkor is emerging as a good place for gentle walks between the temples – one way to experience peace and solitude as visitor numbers skyrocket.

Water Sports

As the Cambodian coast takes off, there are more adrenalin buzzes available, including boating, windsurfing and kitesurfing off the beaches of Sihanoukville.

Children

Children can live it up in Cambodia, as they are always the centre of attention and almost everybody wants to play with them. This is great news when it comes to babes in arms and little toddlers, as everyone wants to entertain them for a time or babysit while you tuck into a plate of noodles. For the full picture on surviving and thriving on the road, check out Lonely Planet's *Travel with Children*, which contains useful advice on how to cope on the road. There is also a rundown on health precautions for kids and advice on travel during pregnancy.

Customs Regulations

If Cambodia has customs allowances, it is tight-lipped about them. You are entitled to bring into the country a 'reasonable amount' of duty-free items. Travellers arriving by air might bear in mind that alcohol and cigarettes are on sale at prices well below duty-free prices on the streets of Phnom Penh – a branded box of 200 cigarettes costs just US$10 and international spirits start as low as US$7 a litre.

Like any other country, Cambodia does not allow travellers to import any weapons, explosives or narcotics – some might say that there are more than enough in the country already.

It is also illegal to take ancient stone sculptures from the Angkor period out of the country.

Discount Cards

Senior travellers and students are not eligible for discounts in Cambodia.

Electricity

230V/50Hz

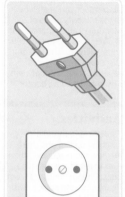

230V/50Hz

Embassies & Consulates

Quite a few countries have embassies in Phnom Penh, though some travellers will find that their nearest embassy is in Bangkok. It's important to realise what an embassy can and can't do to help if you get into trouble. Generally speaking, it won't be much help if the trouble is your own fault. Visitors are bound by the laws of the country they are in. The embassy won't be sympathetic if you end up in jail after committing a crime, even if such actions are legal in your own country.

In genuine emergencies assistance may be available, but only if all other channels have been exhausted. If you have all your money and documents stolen, the embassy can assist with getting a new passport, but a loan for onward travel is out of the question.

Australian Embassy (☑023-213413; 16 National Assembly St, Phnom Penh)

Chinese Embassy (☑023-720920; 256 Mao Tse Toung Blvd, Phnom Penh)

French Embassy (☏023-430020; 1 Monivong Blvd, Phnom Penh)

German Embassy (☏023-216381; 76-78 St 214, Phnom Penh)

Indian Embassy (☏023-210912; 5 St 466, Phnom Penh)

Indonesian Embassy (☏023-216148; 1 St 466, Phnom Penh)

Japanese Embassy (☏023-217161; 194 Norodom Blvd, Phnom Penh)

Lao Embassy (☏023-982632; 15-17 Mao Tse Toung Blvd, Phnom Penh)

Malaysian Embassy (☏023-216177; 220 Norodom Blvd, Phnom Penh)

Myanmar Embassy (☏023-223761; 181 Norodom Blvd, Phnom Penh)

Philippine Embassy (☏023-222303; 15 St 422, Phnom Penh)

Singaporean Embassy (☏023-221875; 92 Norodom Blvd, Phnom Penh)

Thai Embassy (☏023-726306; 196 Norodom Blvd, Phnom Penh)

UK Embassy (☏023-427124; 27-29 St 75, Phnom Penh)

US Embassy (☏023-728000; 1 St 96, Phnom Penh)

Vietnamese Battambang consulate (☏053-6888867; St 3; ⊙8-11.30am & 2-4.30pm Mon-Fri); Phnom Penh embassy (☏023-726274; 436 Monivong Blvd); Sihanoukville consulate (Map p174;☏034-934039; 310 Ekareach St; ⊙8am-noon & 2-4pm Mon-Sat) Fifteen-day visas cost US$60 (US$45 plus a US$15 processing fee) for one-

day processing or US$70 on the spot. Bring a passport photo.

Food

Cambodian cuisine may be less well known than that of its popular neighbours Thailand and Vietnam, but it is no less tasty. See p316 for more.

Gay & Lesbian Travellers

While Cambodian culture is tolerant of homosexuality, the gay and lesbian scene here is certainly nothing like that in Thailand. The former King Norodom Sihanouk was a keen supporter of equal rights for same-sex partners and this seems to have encouraged a more open attitude among younger Cambodians. Both Phnom Penh and Siem Reap have a few gay-friendly bars, but it's a low-key scene compared with some parts of Asia.

With the vast number of same-sex travel partners – gay or otherwise – checking into hotels across Cambodia, there is little consideration over how travelling foreigners are related. However, it is prudent not to flaunt your sexuality. As with heterosexual couples, passionate public displays of affection are considered a basic no-no.

Cambodia Out (www.cambodiaout.com) Promoting the GLBT community in Cambodia and the gay-friendly Adore Cambodia campaign.

Sticky Rice (www.stickyrice.ws) Gay travel guide covering Cambodia and Asia.

Utopia (www.utopia-asia.com) Gay travel information and contacts, including some local gay terminology.

Insurance

Health insurance is essential. Make sure that your policy covers emergency evacuation:

limited medical facilities mean that you may have to be airlifted to Bangkok in the event of serious injury or illness. For more on health insurance see p347. For car and motorcycle insurance see p344.

Worldwide travel insurance is available at www.lonely planet.com/travel_services. You can buy, extend and claim online any time, even if you're already on the road.

Internet Access

Internet access is widespread and there are internet shops in all but the most remote provincial capitals. Charges range from 1500r to US$2.50 per hour.

Many hotels, guesthouses, restaurants and cafes now offer free wi-fi, although connections are easiest to find in Phnom Penh and Siem Reap.

Language Courses

The only language courses available in Cambodia at present are in Khmer and are aimed at expat residents of Phnom Penh rather than travellers. Try the Institute of Foreign Languages at the **Royal University of Phnom**

Penh (☐012 866826; www. rupp.edu.kh; Russian Blvd). Also check out the noticeboards at popular guesthouses, restaurants and bars, where one-hour lessons are often advertised by private tutors. There are also regular listings under the Classifieds in the *Phnom Penh Post* and *Cambodia Daily*.

Legal Matters

Marijuana is not legal in Cambodia and the police are beginning to take a harder line on it. There have been several busts (and a few setups, too) of foreigner-owned bars and restaurants where ganja was smoked – the days of free bowls in guesthouses are definitely history. Marijuana is traditionally used in some Khmer food, so it will continue to be around for a long time, but if you are a smoker, be discreet. It's probably only a matter of time before the Cambodian police turn the regular busting of foreigners into a lucrative sideline.

This advice applies equally to other narcotic substances, which are also illegal. And think twice about buying from an unfamiliar *moto* driver, as

it may end with you getting robbed after passing out.

Travellers should note that they can be prosecuted under the law of their home country regarding age of consent, even when abroad.

Maps

The best all-rounder for Cambodia is the Gecko *Cambodia Road Map*. At 1:750,000 scale, it has lots of detail and accurate place names. Other popular foldout maps include Nelles *Cambodia, Laos and Vietnam Map* at 1:1,500,000, although the detail is limited, and the Periplus *Cambodia Travel Map* at 1:1,000,000, with city maps of Phnom Penh and Siem Reap.

Lots of free maps, subsidised by advertising, are available in Phnom Penh and Siem Reap at leading hotels, guesthouses, restaurants and bars.

Money

Cambodia's currency is the riel, abbreviated in our listings to a lower-case 'r' written after the sum. Cambodia's second currency (some would say its first) is the US dollar, which is accepted everywhere and by everyone, though change may arrive in riel. Dollar bills with a small tear are unlikely to be accepted by Cambodians, so it's worth scrutinising the change you are given to make sure you don't have bad bills. In the west of the country, the Thai baht (B) is also commonplace. If three currencies seems a little excessive, perhaps it's because the Cambodians are making up for lost time: during the Pol Pot era, the country had *no* currency. The Khmer Rouge abolished money and blew up the National Bank building in Phnom Penh.

The Cambodian riel comes in notes of the following denominations: 100r,

---

DANGEROUS DRUGS 101

Watch out for *yaba,* the 'crazy' drug from Thailand, known rather ominously in Cambodia as *yama* (the Hindu god of death). Known as ice or crystal meth back home, it's not just any old diet pill from the pharmacist but homemade meta-amphetamines produced in labs in Cambodia and the region beyond. The pills are often laced with toxic substances, such as mercury, lithium or whatever else the maker can find. *Yama* is a dirty drug and more addictive than users would like to admit, provoking powerful hallucinations, sleep deprivation and psychosis. Steer clear of the stuff unless you plan on an indefinite extension to your trip.

Also be very careful about buying 'cocaine'. Most of what is sold as coke, particularly in Phnom Penh, is actually pure heroin and far stronger than any smack found on the streets back home. Bang that up your hooter and you'll be doing impressions of Uma Thurman in *Pulp Fiction*.

200r, 500r, 1000r, 2000r, 5000r, 10,000r, 20,000r, 50,000r and 100,000r.

We give prices in the currency quoted to the average punter. This is usually US dollars or riel, but in the west it is sometimes baht. While this may seem inconsistent, this is the way it's done in Cambodia and the sooner you get used to thinking comparatively in riel, dollars or baht, the easier your travels will be.

ATMs

There are now credit card–compatible ATMs (Visa, MasterCard, JCB, Cirrus) in most major cities. There are also ATMs at the Cham Yeam, Poipet and Bavet borders if arriving by land from Thailand or Vietnam. Machines dispense US dollars or riel. Large withdrawals of up to US$2000 are possible, providing your account can handle it. Stay alert when using ATMs late at night. ANZ Royal Bank has the most extensive network, including ATMs at petrol stations and popular hotels, restaurants and shops, closely followed by Canadia Bank. Acleda Bank has the widest network of branches in the country, including all provincial capitals, making remote travel that much easier to plan. Most ATM withdrawals incur a charge of US$3 to US$5, but Canadia Bank offers free withdrawals.

Bargaining

It is important to haggle over purchases made in local markets in Cambodia, otherwise the stallholder may 'shave your head' (local vernacular for 'rip you off'). Bargaining is the rule in markets, when arranging share taxis and pick-ups, and in some guesthouses. The Khmers are not ruthless hagglers, so a persuasive smile and a little friendly quibbling is usually enough to get a fair price. Try to remember that the aim is not to get the lowest possible price, but a price that is acceptable to both you and

the seller. Remember that in many cases a few hundred riel is more important to a Cambodian with a family to support than to a traveller on an extended vacation.

Cash

The US dollar remains king in Cambodia. Armed with enough cash, you won't need to visit a bank at all as it is possible to change small amounts of dollars for riel at hotels, restaurants and markets. It's always handy to have about US$10 worth of riel kicking around, as it is good for *motos*, *remork-motos* and markets. Pay for something cheap in US dollars and the change comes in riel.

The only other currency that can be useful is Thai baht, mainly in the west of the country. Prices in towns such as Krong Koh Kong, Poipet and Sisophon are often quoted in baht, and even in Battambang it is common.

In the interests of making life as simple as possible when travelling overland, organise a supply of US dollars before arriving in Cambodia. Cash in other major currencies can be changed at banks or markets in Phnom Penh or Siem Reap. However, most banks tend to offer a poor rate for any non-dollar transaction so it can be better to use moneychangers, which are found in and around every major market.

Western Union and Money Gram are both represented in Cambodia for fast, if more expensive, money transfers. Western Union is represented by SBC and Acleda Bank, and MoneyGram is represented by Canadia Bank.

Credit Cards

Top-end hotels, airline offices and upmarket boutiques and restaurants generally accept most major credit cards (Visa, MasterCard, JCB and sometimes American Express), but many pass the charges straight on to the customer, meaning an extra 3% on the bill.

TIPPING TIPS

In many Cambodian restaurants, change will be returned in some sort of bill holder. If you leave the change there it will often be taken by the restaurant proprietor. If you want to make sure the tip goes to the staff who have served you, then leave the tip on the table or give it to the individuals directly.

Cash advances on credit cards are available in Phnom Penh, Siem Reap, Sihanoukville, Kampot, Battambang, Kompong Cham and other major towns. Most banks advertise a minimum charge of US$5, but Canadia Bank offers this service for free.

Several travel agents and hotels in Phnom Penh and Siem Reap can arrange cash advances for about 5% commission; this can be particularly useful if you get caught short at the weekend.

Tipping

Tipping is not traditionally expected here, but in a country as poor as Cambodia, tips can go a long way. Salaries remain extremely low and service is often impressive. Many of the upmarket hotels levy a 10% service charge, but this doesn't always make it to the staff. If you stay a couple of nights in the same hotel, try to remember to tip the staff that clean your room. Consider tipping drivers and guides, as the time they spend on the road means time away from home and family.

It is considered proper to make a small donation at the end of a visit to a wat, especially if a monk has shown you around; most wats have contribution boxes for this purpose.

Travellers Cheques

Acleda Bank now offers travellers cheque encashment at most branches, bringing financial freedom to far-flung provinces like Ratanakiri and Mondulkiri. It is best to have cheques in US dollars. Expect to pay about 2% commission to change travellers cheques.

Opening Hours

Most Cambodians get up very early and it's not unusual to see people out and about exercising at 5.30am if you are heading home – ahem, sorry, getting up – at that time. Attractions such as museums are normally open seven days a week.

Government offices Open from Monday to Friday and on Saturday mornings. They theoretically begin the working day at 7.30am, break for a siesta from 11.30am to 2pm, and end the day at 5pm.

Banks Hours vary slightly according to the bank, but most keep core hours of 8am to 3.30pm Monday to Friday, plus Saturday morning.

Restaurants Local restaurants generally open from about 6.30am until 9pm and may stay open throughout that time. International restaurants stay open until a little later and sometimes close between sittings.

Bars Many are open all day, but some open only for the night shift, especially if they don't serve food.

Local markets Operate seven days a week and usually open and close with the sun, running from 6.30am to 5.30pm. They close for a few days during the major holidays of Chaul Chnam Khmer (Khmer New Year), P'chum Ben (Festival of the Dead) and Chaul Chnam Chen (Chinese New Year).

Shops Tend to open from about 8am until 6pm, sometimes later.

Photography

Many internet cafes in Cambodia will burn CDs or DVDs from digital images using card readers or USB connections. The price is about US$2.50 if you need a DVD or US$1.50 for a CD. Digital memory sticks are widely available in Cambodia and are pretty cheap. Digital cameras are a real bargain in Cambodia thanks to low tax and duty, so consider picking up a new model in Phnom Penh rather than Bangkok or Saigon.

Make sure you have the necessary charger, plugs and transformer for Cambodia. Take care with some of the electrical wiring in guesthouses around the country, as it can be pretty amateurish.

Photographing People

The usual rules apply. Be polite about photographing people, don't push cameras into their faces, and show respect for monks and people at prayer. In general, the Khmers are remarkably courteous people and if you ask nicely, they'll agree to have their photograph taken. The same goes for filming, although in rural areas you will often find children desperate to get in front of the lens and astonished at seeing themselves played back on an LCD screen. It is the closest most of them will get to being on TV. Some people will expect money in return for their photo being snapped; be sure to establish this before clicking away.

Post

The postal service is hit and miss from Cambodia; send anything valuable by courier or from another country. Ensure postcards and letters are franked before they vanish from your sight.

Letters and parcels sent further afield than Asia can take up to two or three weeks to reach their destination. Use a courier to speed things up; **EMS** (☑023-723511; www.ems.com.kh; Main Post Office, St 13, Phnom Penh) has branches at every major post office in the country.

Public Holidays

Banks, ministries and embassies close down during public holidays and festivals, so plan ahead if visiting Cambodia during these times. Cambodians also roll over holidays if they fall on a weekend and take a day or two extra during major festivals. Add to this the fact that they take a holiday for international days here and there, and it soon becomes apparent that Cambodia has more public holidays than any other nation on earth!

International New Year's Day
1 January

Victory over the Genocide
7 January

International Women's Day
8 March

SHOPPING

High-quality handmade crafts, including silk clothing and accessories, stone and wood carvings, and silver, are widely available, especially in Siem Reap, Phnom Penh and towns with particular handicraft specialities. Hill tribes in Mondulkiri and Ratanakiri produce handwoven cotton in small quantities. In our coverage of Phnom Penh and Siem Reap, we focus on shops and organisations that contribute to reviving traditional crafts and support people who are disadvantaged or disabled.

International Workers' Day
1 May

International Children's Day
8 May

King's Birthday 13-15 May

King Mother's Birthday 18 June

Constitution Day 24 September

Commemoration Day 15 October

Independence Day 9 November

International Human Rights Day 10 December

FESTIVAL WARNING

In the run-up to major festivals such as P'chum Ben or Chaul Chnam Khmer, there is a palpable increase in the number of robberies, particularly in Phnom Penh. Cambodians need money to buy gifts for relatives or to pay off debts, and for some individuals theft is the quickest way to get this money. Be more vigilant at night at these times and don't take valuables out with you unnecessarily.

Safe Travel

Cambodia is a pretty safe country for travellers these days, but remember the golden rule: *stick to marked paths in remote areas (because of landmines)*.

The *Cambodia Daily* (www. cambodiadaily.com) and the *Phnom Penh Post* (www. phnompenhpost.com) are both good sources for breaking news. Check their websites before you hit the road.

Crime & Violence

Given the number of guns in Cambodia, there is less armed theft than one might expect. Still, hold-ups and motorcycle theft are a potential danger in Phnom Penh and Sihanoukville. There is no need to be paranoid, just cautious. Walking or riding alone late at night is not ideal, certainly not in rural areas.

There have been incidents of bag snatching in Phnom Penh in the last few years and the motorbike thieves don't let go, dragging passengers off *motos* and endangering lives.

Should anyone be unlucky enough to be robbed, it is important to note that the Cambodian police are the best that money can buy! Any help, such as a police report, is going to cost you. The going rate depends on the size of the claim, but anywhere from US$5 to US$50 is a common charge.

Violence against foreigners is extremely rare, but it pays to take care in crowded bars or nightclubs in Phnom Penh. If you get into a stand-off with rich young Khmers in a bar or club, swallow your pride and back down. Still think you can 'ave 'em? Many carry guns and have an entourage of bodyguards, 'nuff said.

Mines, Mortars & Bombs

Never touch any rockets, artillery shells, mortars, mines, bombs or other war material you may come across. The most heavily mined part of the country is along the Thai border area, but mines are a problem in much of Cambodia. In short: *do not stray from well-marked paths under any circumstances*. If you are planning any walks, even in safer areas such as the remote northeast, it is imperative you take a guide as there may still be unexploded ordnance (UXO) from the American bombing campaign of the early 1970s.

Scams

Most scams are fairly harmless, involving a bit of commission here and there for taxi or *moto* drivers, particularly in Siem Reap.

There have been one or two reports of police set-ups in Phnom Penh, involving planted drugs. This seems to be very rare, but if you fall victim to the ploy, it may be best to pay them off before more police get involved at the local station, as the price will only rise when there are more officials to pay off.

There is quite a lot of fake medication floating about the region. Safeguard yourself by only buying prescription drugs from reliable pharmacies or clinics.

The Filipino blackjack scam has made it to Cambodia in the last couple of years, so don't get involved in any gambling with seemingly friendly Filipinos unless you want to part with plenty of cash.

Beggars in places such as Phnom and Siem Reap are asking for milk powder for an infant in arms. Some foreigners succumb to the urge to help, but the beggars usually request the most expensive milk formula available and return it to the shop to split the proceeds after the handover.

Telephone

Cambodia's landline system was totally devastated by the long civil war, leaving the country with a poor communications infrastructure. The advent of mobile phones has allowed Cambodia to catch up with its regional neighbours by jumping headlong into the technology revolution. Mobile phones are everywhere in Cambodia, but landline access in major towns is also improving, connecting more of the country to the outside world than ever before.

Landline area codes appear under the name of each city, but in many areas service is spotty. Mobile phones, the numbers for which start with 01, 06, 07, 08 or 09, are hugely popular with both individuals and commercial enterprises. Foreigners need to present a valid passport to get a local SIM card.

The easiest way to make a local call in most urban areas is by heading to one of the many small private booths on the kerbside, usually plastered with numbers like 012 and 016 and with prices around 300r. Many internet shops offer cheap international calls for about 1000r per minute, though in places with broadband speeds you can Skype for the price of an internet connection (usually 2000r to 4000r *per hour*).

For listings of businesses and government offices, check out www.yellowpages -cambodia.com.

Mobile Phones

When travelling with a mobile phone on international roaming, just select a network upon arrival, dial away and await a hefty phone bill once you return home. Note to self: Cambodian roaming charges are extraordinarily high.

Those who plan on spending longer in Cambodia should purchase a SIM card for one of the local service providers. Most mobile companies now offer cheap internet-based phone calls accessed through a gateway number. Use the cheap prefix and calls will be just US 20¢ or less per minute.

Time

Cambodia (like Laos, Vietnam and Thailand) is seven hours ahead of Greenwich Mean Time or Universal Time Coordinated (GMT/UTC). When it is midday in Cambodia, it is 10pm the previous evening in San Francisco, 1am in New York, 5am in London, 6am in Paris and 3pm in Sydney.

Toilets

Cambodian toilets are mostly of the sit-down variety. The occasional squat toilet turns up here and there, particularly in the most budget of budget guesthouses in the provinces.

The issue of toilets and what to do with used toilet paper is a cause for concern. Generally, if there's a wastepaper basket next to the toilet, that is where the toilet paper goes, as many sewerage systems cannot handle toilet paper. Toilet paper is seldom provided in the toilets at bus and train stations or in other public buildings, so keep a stash with you at all times.

Many Western toilets also have a hose spray in the bathroom, aptly named the 'bum gun' by some. Think of this as a flexible bidet, used for cleaning and ablutions as well as hosing down the loo.

Public toilets are rare, the only ones in the country being along Phnom Penh's riverfront and some beautiful wooden structures dotted about the temples of Angkor. The charge is usually 500r for a public toilet, although they are free at Angkor. Most local restaurants have some sort of toilet.

Should you find nature calling in rural areas, don't let modesty drive you into the bushes: *there may be landmines not far from the road or track*. Stay on the roadside and do the deed, or grin and bear it until the next town.

Tourist Information

Cambodia has only a handful of tourist offices, and those encountered by the independent traveller in Phnom Penh and Siem Reap are generally of limited help. However, in the provinces it is a different story, as the staff are often excited to see visitors. These offices generally have little in the way of brochures or handouts though. Generally, fellow travellers, guesthouses, hotels and free local magazines are more useful than tourist offices.

Cambodia has no official tourist offices abroad and it is unlikely that Cambodian embassies will be of much assistance in planning a trip, besides issuing visas, which are available on arrival anyhow.

Travellers with Disabilities

Broken pavements, potholed roads and stairs as steep as ladders at Angkor ensure that for most people with mobility impairments, Cambodia is not going to be an easy country in which to travel. Few buildings have been designed with the disabled in mind, although new projects, such as the international airports at Phnom Penh and Siem Reap, and top-end hotels include ramps for wheelchair access. Transport in the provinces is usually very overcrowded, but taxi hire from point to point is an affordable option.

On the positive side, the Cambodian people are usually very helpful towards all foreigners, and local labour is cheap if you need someone to accompany you at all times. Most guesthouses and small hotels have ground-floor rooms that are reasonably easy to access.

The biggest headache also happens to be the main attraction – the temples of Angkor. Causeways are uneven, obstacles common and staircases daunting, even for able-bodied people. It is likely to be some years before things improve, although some ramping is now being introduced at major temples.

Wheelchair travellers will need to undertake a lot of research before visiting Cambodia. A growing network of information sources can put you in touch with others who have wheeled through Cambodia before. Try contacting the following:

Disability Rights UK (☎020-7250 3222; http://disabilityrightsuk.org)

Mobility International USA (☎54-1343 1284; www.miusa.org)

Society for Accessible Travel & Hospitality (SATH; ☎212-447 7284; www.sath.org)

Visas

Most visitors to Cambodia require a one-month tourist visa (US$20). Most nationalities receive this on arrival at Phnom Penh and Siem Reap airports, and at land borders, but do check if you are carrying an African, Asian or Middle Eastern passport, as there are some exceptions. Citizens of Asean (Association of Southeast Asian Nations) member countries do not require a visa to visit Cambodia. One passport-sized photo is required and you'll be 'fined' US$1 if you don't have one. It is also possible to arrange a visa through Cambodian embassies overseas or an online e-visa (US$20, plus a US$5 processing fee) through the **Ministry of Foreign Affairs** (www.mfaic.gov.kh).

Those seeking work in Cambodia should opt for the business visa (US$25) as it is easily extended for long periods, including multiple entries and exits. A tourist visa can be extended only once and only for one month, and does not allow for re-entry.

Travellers are sometimes overcharged when crossing at land borders with Thailand, as immigration officials demand payment in baht and round up the figure considerably. Overcharging is also an issue at the Laos border, but not usually at Vietnam borders. Arranging a visa in advance can help avoid overcharging.

Overstaying a visa currently costs US$5 a day.

For visitors continuing to Vietnam, one-month single-entry visas cost US$55 taking two days in Phnom Penh, or just one day via the Vietnamese consulate in Sihanoukville. Most visitors to Laos can obtain a visa on arrival and many visitors heading to Thailand do not need a visa.

Visa Extensions

Visa extensions are issued by the large immigration office

THE PERILS OF ORPHANAGE TOURISM

In recent years, visiting orphanages in the developing world – Cambodia in particular – has become a popular activity, but is it always good for the children and the country in the longer run? Tough question. 'Orphan tourism' and all the connotations that come with it are a disturbing development that is bringing unscrupulous elements into the world of caring for Cambodian children. There have already been reports of new orphanages opening up with a business model to bring in a certain number of visitors per month. In other cases, the children are not orphans at all, but are 'borrowed' from the local school for a fee.

In a report released in November 2009, Save the Children stated that most children living in orphanages throughout the developing world have at least one parent still alive. More than eight million children worldwide are living in institutions, with most sent there by their families because of poverty rather than the death of a parent. Many are in danger of abuse and neglect from carers, as well as exploitation and international trafficking, with children aged under three most at risk.

'One of the biggest myths is that children in orphanages are there because they have no parents. This is not the case,' the report states. 'Most are there because their parents simply can't afford to feed, clothe and educate them.' From 2005 to 2010, the number of orphanages in Cambodia almost doubled from 153 to 269. Of the 12,000 Cambodian children in institutions, only about 28% are genuine orphans without both parents.

Many orphanages in Cambodia are doing a good job in tough circumstances. Some are world class, enjoy funding and support from wealthy benefactors, and don't need visitors; others are desperate places that need all the help they can get. However, if a place is promoting orphan tourism, then proceed with caution, as the adults may not always have the best interests of the children at heart. Cambodia is a confusing and confounding place and it's not for us to play judge and jury, but we do believe travellers should be informed before they make a decision.

Friends International and Unicef joined forces in 2011 to launch the 'Think Before Visiting' campaign. Learn more at www.thinkchildsafe.org/thinkbeforevisiting/ before you inadvertently contribute to the problem.

located directly across the road from Phnom Penh International Airport.

Unofficial extensions are the easiest to arrange for visitors, taking just a couple of days to arrange. It costs US$45 for one month, US$75 for three months, US$155 for six months and US$285 for one year. It's pretty straightforward to extend the visa ad infinitum. Travel agencies and some motorbike-rental shops in Phnom Penh can help with arrangements, sometimes at a discounted price.

Volunteering

There are fewer opportunities for volunteering than one might imagine in a country as impoverished as Cambodia. This is partly due to the sheer number of professional development workers based here, and development is a pretty lucrative industry these days.

Cambodia hosts a huge number of NGOs, some of which do require volunteers from time to time. The best way to find out who is represented in the country is to drop in on the **Cooperation Committee for Cambodia** (CCC; ☏023-214152; www.ccc-cambodia.org; 9-11 St 476) in Phnom Penh. This organisation has a handy list of all NGOs, both Cambodian and international, and is extremely helpful.

There are a couple of professional Siem Reap–based organisations helping to place volunteers. **ConCERT** (Map p90; ☏063-963511; www.concertcambodia.org; 560 Phum Stoeung Thmey; ☉9am-5pm Mon-Fri) has a 'responsible volunteering' section on its website that offers some sound advice on preparing for a stint as a volunteer. **Globalteer** (☏063-761802; www.globalteer.org) coordinates the Cambodia Kids

Project and offers volunteer placements with various projects, but this does involve a weekly charge.

The other avenue is professional volunteering through an organisation back home that offers one- or two-year placements in Cambodia. One of the largest organisations is **Voluntary Service Overseas** (VSO; www.vso.org.uk) in the UK, but other countries also have their own organisations, including **Australian Volunteers International** (AVI; www.australianvolunteers.com) and New Zealand's **Volunteer Service Abroad** (VSA; www.vsa.org.nz). The UN also operates its own volunteer program; details are available at www.unv.org. Other general volunteer sites with links all over the place include www.worldvolunteerweb.com and www.volunteerabroad.com.

For general tips on voluntourism in Cambodia, visit www.voluntourism101.org.

Women Travellers

Women will generally find Cambodia a hassle-free place to travel, although some of the guys in the guesthouse industry will try their luck from time to time. Foreign women are unlikely to be targeted by local men, but at the same time it pays to be careful. As is the case anywhere in the world, walking or riding a bike alone late at night is risky, and if you're planning a trip off the beaten track it would be best to find a travel companion.

Despite the prevalence of sex workers and women's employment as 'beer girls', dancing companions and the like, foreign women will probably find Khmer men to be courteous and polite. It's best to keep things this way by being restrained in

your dress. Khmer women dress fairly conservatively, and it's best to follow suit, particularly when visiting wats. In general, long-sleeved shirts and long trousers or skirts are preferred. It is also worth having trousers for heading out at night on *motos*, as short skirts aren't too practical.

Tampons and sanitary napkins are widely available in the major cities and provincial capitals, but if you are heading into very remote areas for a few days, it is worth having your own supply.

Work

Jobs are available throughout Cambodia, but apart from teaching English or helping out in guesthouses, bars or restaurants, most are for professionals and are arranged in advance. There is a lot of teaching work available for English-language speakers; salary is directly linked to experience. Anyone with an English-language teaching certificate can earn considerably more than those with no qualifications.

For information about work opportunities with NGOs, call into the CCC, which has a noticeboard for positions vacant. If you are thinking of applying for work with NGOs, you should bring copies of your education certificates and work references. However, most of the jobs available are likely to be on a voluntary basis, as most recruiting for specialised positions is done in home countries or through international organisations.

Other places to look for work include the classifieds sections of the *Phnom Penh Post* and the *Cambodia Daily*, and on the noticeboards at guesthouses and restaurants in Phnom Penh.

Transport

GETTING THERE & AWAY

Flights and tours can be booked online at lonelyplanet.com/bookings.

Air

Airports & Airlines

Phnom Penh International Airport (☎023-890890; www.cambodia-airports.com) is the gateway to the Cambodian capital, while **Siem Reap International Airport** (Map p120; ☎063 761 261; www.cambodia-airports.com) serves visitors to the temples of Angkor. Both airports have a good range of services, including restaurants, bars, shops and ATMs. **Sihanoukville International Airport** (☎012-333524; www.cambodia-airports.com) currently only offers domestic links with Phnom Penh and Siem Reap.

Flights to Cambodia are expanding, but most connect only as far as regional capitals. However, budget airlines have taken off in recent years and are steadily driving down prices.

If you are heading to Cambodia for a short holiday and want a minimum of fuss, Thai Airways offers the easiest connections from major cities in Europe, the USA and Australia. Singapore Airlines' regional wing, Silk Air, and budget airline Jetstar offer at least one flight per day connecting Cambodia to Singapore. Other regional centres with flights to Cambodia are Ho Chi Minh City (Saigon), Hanoi, Vientiane, Luang Prabang, Pakse, Kuala Lumpur, Seoul, Taipei, Hong Kong, Guangzhou and Shanghai. Further afield, there is also a route to Doha in the Middle East.

Domestic airlines in Cambodia tend to open up and close down regularly. Given the choice, enter the country on an international carrier rather than a local outfit.

Some airlines offer open-jaw tickets into Phnom Penh and out of Siem Reap, which can save some time and money. The majority of the following telephone numbers are for Phnom Penh offices (☎023). See the Siem Reap section for airline offices there.

Air Asia (☎023-356011; www.airasia.com) Daily budget flights connecting Phnom Penh and Siem Reap to Kuala Lumpur and Bangkok.

Asiana Airlines (☎023-890440; www.asiana.co.kr) Regular connections between Phnom Penh and Seoul.

Bangkok Airways (☎023-722545; www.bangkokair.com) Daily connections from Phnom Penh and Siem Reap to Bangkok.

Cambodia Angkor Air (☎023-212564; www.cambodiaangkorair.com) Daily connections from Phnom Penh and Siem Reap to Bangkok and Ho Chi Minh City (Saigon).

CLIMATE CHANGE & TRAVEL

Every form of transport that relies on carbon-based fuel generates CO_2, the main cause of human-induced climate change. Modern travel is dependent on aeroplanes, which might use less fuel per kilometre per person than most cars but travel much greater distances. The altitude at which aircraft emit gases (including CO_2) and particles also contributes to their climate change impact. Many websites offer 'carbon calculators' that allow people to estimate the carbon emissions generated by their journey and, for those who wish to do so, to offset the impact of the greenhouse gases emitted with contributions to portfolios of climate-friendly initiatives throughout the world. Lonely Planet offsets the carbon footprint of all staff and author travel.

China Eastern Airlines (063-965229; www.ce-air.com) Regular flights from Siem Reap to Kunming.

China Southern Airlines (023-430877; www.cs-air.com) Regular flights from Phnom Penh to Guangzhou.

Dragon Air (023-424300; www.dragonair.com) Daily flights between Phnom Penh and Hong Kong.

Eva Air (023-219911; www.evaair.com) Daily flights between Phnom Penh and Taipei.

Jetstar (023-220909; www.jetstar.com) Daily budget flights from both Phnom Penh and Siem Reap to Singapore.

Korean Air (023-224047; www.koreanair.com) Regular flights connecting Phnom Penh and Siem Reap with Seoul and Incheon.

Lao Airlines (023-216563; www.laoairlines.com) Regular flights from Phnom Penh and Siem Reap to Pakse, Vientiane and Luang Prabang.

Malaysia Airlines (023-426688; www.malaysiaairlines.com) Daily connections from Phnom Penh and Siem Reap to Kuala Lumpur.

Myanmar Airways International (023-881178; www.maiair.com) Regular flights from Phnom Penh and Siem Reap to Yangon.

Qatar Airways (023-424012; www.qatarairways.com) Regular flights from Phnom Penh to Ho Chi Minh City and Doha.

Shanghai Airlines (023-723999; www.shanghai-air.com) Regular flights linking Phnom Penh with Shanghai.

Silk Air (023-426807; www.silkair.com) Regular flights linking Phnom Penh and Siem Reap with Singapore, plus some flights between Siem Reap and Danang.

Thai Airways (023-214359; www.thaiair.com) Daily flights connecting Phnom Penh and Bangkok.

Tiger Air (023-551 5888; www.tigerair.com) Daily budget flights between Phnom Penh and Singapore.

Vietnam Airlines (023-363396; www.vietnamair.com.vn) Daily flights linking both Phnom Penh and Siem Reap with both Hanoi and Ho Chi Minh City, as well as Phnom Penh with Vientiane, and Siem Reap with Luang Prabang.

Tickets

Buying direct from the airline is usually more expensive, unless the airline has a special promotion or you are flying with a budget carrier offering online deals. As a rule, it is better to book as early as possible, as prices only get higher as the seats fill up.

The time of year has a major impact on flight prices. Starting out from Europe, North America or Australia, figure on prices rising dramatically over Christmas and during July and August, and dropping significantly during lax periods of business like February, June and October.

Cheapflights (www.cheapflights.com) No-frills website with a number of destinations.

Lonely Planet (www.lonelyplanet.com) Use the Trip Planner service to book multi-stop trips.

Lowest Fare (www.lowestfare.com) They promise...'the lowest fares'.

STA Travel (www.statravel.com) Leading student-travel agency with cheap fares, plus separate websites for the UK, Australia and New Zealand.

Land

Border Crossings

During the bad old days of communism and the Cold War, pretty much none of the land borders were open to foreigners. Times have changed and there are now more than a dozen border crossings connecting Cambodia with its neighbours.

Cambodia shares one border crossing with Laos, six crossings with Thailand and eight with Vietnam. Cambodian visas are now available at all the land crossings with Laos, Thailand and Vietnam. Neighbouring visas are available on arrival in Laos and Thailand but are not available on arrival in Vietnam. Most borders are open during the core hours of 7am to 5pm. However, some of the most popular crossings are open later in the evening and other more remote crossings close for lunch.

There are few legal money-changing facilities at some of the more remote border crossings, so be sure to have some small-denomination US dollars handy.

Tourist visas are available at all crossings for US$20, but Cambodian immigration officers at the land border crossings, especially with Thailand, have a reputation for petty extortion. Travellers are occasionally asked for a small 'immigration fee' of some kind or some sort of bogus health certificate costing US$1. More serious scams include overcharging for visas by demanding payment in Thai baht (anywhere between 1000B and 1200B instead of 600B) and forcing tourists to change US dollars into riel at a poor rate. Hold your breath, stand your ground, and don't let this experience flavour your impression of Cambodians overall.

Before making a long-distance trip, be aware of border closing times, visa regulations and any transport scams. Border details change regularly, so ask around or check the Lonely Planet Thorn Tree (www.lonelyplanet.com/thorntree). For the latest on Cambodian border crossings, check out the Immigration Department website at http://cambodia-immigration.com.

LAOS

Cambodia and Laos share a remote frontier that includes some of the wildest areas of both countries. There is only one border crossing open to foreigners.

THAILAND

Cambodia and Thailand share an 805km border and there are now six legal international border crossings, and many more options for locals.

VIETNAM

Cambodia and Vietnam share a long frontier with a bevy of border crossings. Foreigners are currently permitted to cross at eight places. Cambodian visas are now available at all crossings, but Vietnamese visas should be arranged in advance, as they are not available on arrival.

Car & Motorcycle

Car drivers and motorcycle riders will need registration papers, insurance documents and an International Driving Licence (although not officially recognised) to bring vehicles into Cambodia. It is complicated to bring in a car but relatively straightforward to bring in a motorcycle, as long as you have a *carnet de passage* (vehicle passport). This acts as a temporary import-duty waiver and should save a lot of hassles when dealing with Cambodian customs.

Tours

In the early days of tourism in Cambodia, organised tours were a near necessity. Things have changed dramatically and it is now much easier to organise your own trip. Budget and midrange travellers in particular can go it alone, as arrangements are cheap and easy on the ground. If you are on a tight schedule, it can pay to book a domestic flight in advance if you're planning to link the temples of Angkor and Siem Reap with Cambodia's capital, Phnom Penh. Once at Angkor, guides and all forms of transport under the sun are plentiful.

Shop around before booking a tour, as there is lots of competition and some companies offer more interesting itineraries than others. The following are some of the best companies based in Cambodia, many of which are trying to put a little something back into the country.

About Asia (☑063-760190; www.asiatravel-cambodia.com) Small bespoke travel company specialising in Siem Reap. Profits help build schools in Cambodia.

Hanuman (☑023-218396; www.hanuman.travel) A long-running locally owned and operated company with innovative tours like Temple Safari. Big supporter of responsible tourism initiatives.

Journeys Within (☑063-964748; www.journeys-within.com) A boutique tourism company offering trips to Cambodia and the Mekong region. Operates a charitable arm (see www.journeyswithinourcommunity.org

POPULAR LAND CROSSINGS

Laos

For Laos, the Trapeang Kriel–Nong Nok Khiene crossing connects Stung Treng in Cambodia with Don Det in Laos.

Thailand

BORDER CROSSING	CAMBODIAN TOWN	CONNECTING TOWN
Poipet–Aranya Prathet	Siem Reap	Bangkok
Cham Yeam–Hat Lek	Koh Kong City	Trat
O Smach–Chong Chom	Samraong	Surin
Psar Pruhm–Ban Pakard	Pailin	Chanthaburi
Choam–Chong Sa-Ngam	Anlong Veng	Phusing

Vietnam

BORDER CROSSING	CAMBODIAN TOWN	CONNECTING TOWN
Bavet–Moc Bai	Phnom Penh	Ho Chi Minh City
Kaam Samnor–Vinh Xuong	Phnom Penh	Chau Doc
Prek Chak–Xi Xia	Kep, Kampot	Ha Tien, Phu Quoc
Phnom Den–Tinh Bien	Takeo	Chau Doc
O Yadaw–Le Thanh	Ban Lung	Pleiku, Quy Nhon, Hoi An
Trapeang Phlong–Xa Mat	Kompong Cham	Tay Ninh, Ho Chi Minh City
Trapeang Sre–Loc Ninh	Kratie, Kompong Cham	Binh Long

Border Crossings

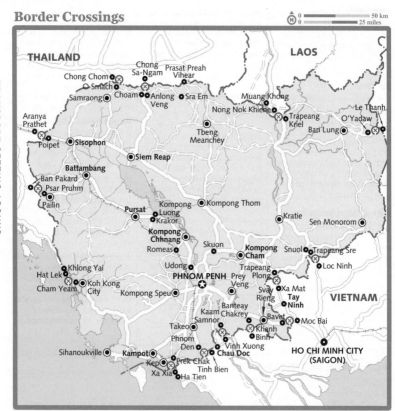

for more information) helping schools and communities.

Local Adventures (☏023-990460; www.cambodia.nl) Cambodian-based company specialising in off-the-beaten-path tours to the less-visited regions of the country. Assists Cambodian children through the Cambodian Organisation for Learning and Training (www.colt-cambodia.org).

PEPY Ride (☏023-222804; www.pepyride.org) Specialist cycling company that runs adventurous bike rides through Cambodia to raise funds to build schools and improve education. Also offers noncycling trips.

Sam Veasna Center (☏063-963710; www.samveasna.org) Day trips that combine birdwatching with visits to outlying temples.

GETTING AROUND

Air

Airlines in Cambodia

Domestic flights offer a quick way to travel around the country. The problem is that the airlines themselves seem to come and go pretty quickly as well. There is currently only one fully-operational domestic airline, **Cambodia Angkor Air** (☏023-212564; www.cambodiaangkorair.com), and this company operates almost as an offshoot of Vietnam Airlines. It serves the Phnom Penh to Siem Reap route. Flights between Siem Reap and Sihanoukville have

finally taken off after much travel-industry lobbying.

There are up to four flights a day between Phnom Penh and Siem Reap (from US$75 one way). It's usually possible to get on a flight at short notice. Book ahead in peak season. There are currently three flights per week between Siem Reap and Sihanoukville (from US$110 one way).

Helicopter

Helicopters Cambodia (Map p90; ☏012 814500; www.helicopterscambodia.com) has offices in Phnom Penh and Siem Reap and operates reliable choppers that are available for charter. **Helistar** (Map p90; ☏088 8880016; www.helistarcambodia.com) is a newer company offering similar services.

Bicycle

Cambodia is a great country for adventurous cyclists to explore. Needless to say, given the country's legendary potholes, a mountain bike is the best bet. Top bikes, safety equipment and authentic spare parts are now readily available in Phnom Penh at very reasonable prices. Many roads remain in bad condition, but there is usually a flat unpaved trail along the side. Travelling at such a gentle speed allows for much more interaction with the locals. Although bicycles are common in Cambodian villages, cycling tourists are still very much a novelty and will be wildly welcomed in most small villages. In many parts of the country there are new dirt tracks being laid down for motorcycles and bicycles, and these are a wonderful way to travel into remote areas.

Much of Cambodia is pancake flat or only moderately hilly. Safety, however, is a considerable concern on the newer surfaced roads, as local traffic travels at high speed. Bicycles can be transported around the country in the back of pick-ups or on the roof of minibuses.

Cycling around Angkor is a rewarding experience as it really helps to get a measure of the size and scale of the temple complex. Mountain biking is likely to take off in Mondulkiri and Ratanakiri Provinces over the coming years, as there are some great trails off the beaten track. It is already a reality around Chi Phat in the Cardamom Mountains. Guesthouses and hotels throughout Cambodia rent out bicycles for around US$2 per day, or US$7 to US$15 for an imported brand.

PEPY Ride (☑023-222804; www.pepyride.org) is a bicycle and volunteer tour company offering adventures throughout Cambodia. PEPY promotes 'adventurous living, responsible giving' and uses proceeds to help build schools in rural Cambodia and fund education programs.

Boat

Cambodia's 1900km of navigable waterways are not as important as they once were for the average tourist, given major road improvements. North of Phnom Penh, the Mekong is easily navigable as far as Kratie, but there are no longer regular passenger services on these routes, as buses have taken all the business. There are scenic boat services between Siem Reap and Battambang, and the Tonlé Sap lake is also navigable year-round, although only by smaller boats between March and July.

Traditionally the most popular boat services with foreigners are those that run between Phnom Penh and Siem Reap. The express services do the trip in as little as five hours, but it's not the most interesting boat journey in Cambodia, as the Tonlé Sap lake is like a vast sea, offering little scenery. It's more popular (and much cheaper) to take a bus on the paved road instead.

The small boat between Siem Reap and Battambang is more rewarding, as the river scenery is truly memorable, but it can take as long as a whole day with delays.

Bus

The range of road transport is extensive. On sealed roads, the large air-conditioned buses are the best choice. Elsewhere in the country, a shared taxi or minibus is the way to go.

Bus services have come on in leaps and bounds in the last few years and the situation is getting even better as more roads are upgraded. Bus travel is arguably the safest way to get around the country these days. The services used most regularly by foreigners are those from Phnom Penh to Siem Reap, Battambang, Sihanoukville, Kompong Cham and Kratie, and the tourist buses from Siem Reap to Poipet. 'Express minibuses' now connect Phnom Penh and major cities around the country and these can be faster than the bigger buses. These minibuses are usually modern Ford Transits or Toyota HiAces and operate a one seat/one passenger policy. Older minibuses serve most provincial routes but are not widely used by Western visitors. They are very cheap but often uncomfortably overcrowded and sometimes driven by maniacs. Only really consider them if there is no alternative.

Car & Motorcycle

Car and motorcycle rental are comparatively cheap in Cambodia and many visitors rent a car or bike for greater flexibility to visit out-of-the-way places and to stop when they choose. Almost all car rental in Cambodia includes a driver, which is good news given the abysmal state of many roads, the lack of road signs and the disregard for road rules displayed by some drivers.

Driving Licence

A standard driving licence is not much use in Cambodia. In theory, to drive a car you need an International Driving Licence, usually issued through your automobile association back home, but Cambodia is not currently a recognised country. It is very unlikely that a driving licence will be of any use to most travellers, save for those coming to live and work in Cambodia.

When it comes to renting motorcycles, it's a case of no licence required. If you can drive the bike out of the shop, you can drive it anywhere, or so the logic goes.

Fuel & Spare Parts

Fuel is relatively expensive in Cambodia compared with other staples, at around 5000r to 6000r (US$1.25 to US$1.50) a litre. Fuel is readily available throughout the country, but prices generally rise in rural areas. Even the most isolated communities usually have someone selling petrol out of Fanta or Johnnie Walker bottles. Some sellers mix this fuel with kerosene – use it sparingly, in emergencies only.

When it comes to spare parts, Cambodia is flooded with Chinese, Japanese and Korean motorcycles, so it's easy to get parts for Hondas, Yamahas or Suzukis, but finding a part for a Harley or a Ducati is another matter. The same goes for cars – spares for Japanese cars are easy to come by, but if you are driving something obscure, bring substantial spares.

Hire

CAR

Car hire is generally only available with a driver and is most useful for sightseeing around Phnom Penh and Angkor. Some tourists with a healthy budget also arrange cars or 4WDs with drivers for touring the provinces. Hiring a car with a driver is about US$30 to US$35 for a day in and around Cambodia's towns. Heading into the provinces it rises to US$50 or more, plus petrol, depending on the destination. Hiring 4WDs will cost around US$60 to US$120 a day, depending on the model and the distance travelled. Driving yourself is just about possible, but this is inadvisable due to chaotic road conditions, personal liability in the case of an accident and higher charges.

MOTORCYCLE

Motorcycles are available for hire in Phnom Penh and some other popular tourist destinations. In Siem Reap (and at times in Sihanoukville), motorcycle rental is forbidden, so anyone planning any rides around Siem Reap will need to arrange a bike elsewhere. In other provincial towns, it is usually possible to rent a small motorcycle after a bit of negotiation. Costs are US$3 to US$10 per day for a 100cc motorcycle and around US$10 to US$25 for a 250cc dirt bike.

Drive with due care and attention, as medical facilities and ambulances are less than adequate beyond Phnom Penh, Siem Reap and Battambang. If you have never ridden a motorcycle before, Cambodia is not the best place to start, but once out of the city it does get easier. If you're jumping in at the deep end, make sure you are under the supervision of someone who knows how to ride.

The advantage of motorcycle travel is that it allows for complete freedom of movement and you can stop in small villages that Westerners rarely visit. It is possible to take motorcycles upcountry for tours, but only experienced off-road bikers should take to these roads with a dirt bike. Anyone planning a longer ride should try out the bike around Phnom Penh for a day or so first to make sure it is in good health.

For those with experience, Cambodia has some of the best roads in the world for dirt biking, particularly in the provinces of Preah Vihear, Mondulkiri, Ratanakiri and the Cardamom Mountains.

There are several specialised dirt-bike touring companies.

Cambodia Expeditions (www.cambodiaexpeditions. com) This team has been running motorbike tours and rallies in Cambodia since 1998. Very professional with some great routes in the north of the country.

Dancing Roads (www.dancingroads.com) Offers motorbike tours around the capital and gentle tours further afield to the South Coast. Based in Phnom Penh, the driver-guides are fun and friendly.

Hidden Cambodia (www.hiddencambodia.com) A Siem Reap–based company specialising in motorcycle trips throughout the country, including the remote temples of northern Cambodia and beyond.

Red Raid Cambodia (www.motorcycletourscambodia.com) More expensive but experienced French-run outfit offering trips throughout Cambodia, including the Cardamoms.

Siem Reap Dirt Bikes (www.siemreapdirtbikes.com) Based in Siem Reap, as you might guess; offers everything from day trips to six-day remote temple adventures.

Insurance

If you are travelling in a tourist vehicle with a driver, then the car is usually insured.

ROAD SAFETY

Many more people are now killed and injured each month in traffic accidents than by landmines. While this is partly down to landmine awareness efforts and ongoing clearance programs, it is also due to a huge rise in the number of vehicles on the roads and drivers travelling at dangerous speeds. Be extremely vigilant when travelling under your own steam and take care crossing the roads on the high-speed national highways. It's best not to travel on the roads at night due to a higher prevalence of accidents at this time. This especially applies to bikers, as several foreigners are killed each year in motorbike accidents.

When it comes to motorcycles, many rental bikes are not insured and you will have to sign a contract agreeing to a valuation for the bike if it is stolen. Make sure you have a strong lock and always leave the bike in guarded parking where available.

Do not even consider hiring a motorcycle if you are daft enough to be travelling in Cambodia without medical insurance. The cost of treating serious injuries, especially if you require an evacuation, is bankrupting for budget travellers.

Road Conditions & Hazards

Whether travelling or living in Cambodia, it is easy to lull yourself into a false sense of security and assume that down every rural road is yet another friendly village. However, even with the demise of the Khmer Rouge, odd incidents of banditry and robbery do occur in rural areas. There have also been some nasty bike-jackings in Sihanoukville. When travelling in your own vehicle, and particularly by motorcycle in rural areas, make certain you check the latest security information in communities along the way.

Be particularly careful about children on the road – you'll sometimes find kids hanging out in the middle of a highway. Livestock on the road is also a menace; hit a cow and you'll both be pizza.

Other general security suggestions for those travelling by motorcycle:

➡ Try to get hold of a good-quality helmet for long journeys or high-speed riding.

➡ Carry a basic repair kit, including some tyre levers, a puncture-repair kit and a pump.

➡ Always carry a rope for towing on longer journeys in case you break down.

➡ In remote areas always carry several litres of water,

as you never know when you will run out.

➡ Travel in small groups, not alone.

➡ When in a group, stay close together in case of any incident or accident.

➡ Don't be cheap with the petrol – running out of fuel in a rural area could jeopardise your health, especially if water runs out too.

➡ Do not smoke marijuana or drink alcohol and drive.

➡ Keep your eyes firmly fixed on the road; Cambodian potholes eat people for fun.

Road Rules

If there are road rules in Cambodia it is doubtful that anyone is following them. Size matters and the biggest vehicle wins by default. The best advice if you drive a car or ride a motorcycle in Cambodia is to take nothing for granted.

In Cambodia traffic drives on the right. There are some traffic lights at junctions in Phnom Penh, Siem Reap and Sihanoukville, but where there are no lights, most traffic turns left into the oncoming traffic, edging along the wrong side of the road until a gap becomes apparent. For the uninitiated it looks like a disaster waiting to happen, but Cambodians are quite used to the system. Foreigners should stop at crossings and develop a habit of constant vigilance. Never assume that other drivers will stop at red lights; these are considered optional by most Cambodians, especially at night.

Phnom Penh is the one place where, amid all the chaos, traffic police take issue with Westerners breaking even the most trivial road rules. Make sure you don't turn left at a 'no left turn' sign or travel with your headlights on during the day (although, strangely, it doesn't seem to be illegal for Cambodians to travel without headlights at night). New laws requiring that bikes have mirrors, and

THE MOTO BURN

Be careful not to put your leg near the exhaust pipe of a *moto* after long journeys; many travellers have received nasty burns, which can take a long time to heal in the sticky weather, and often require antibiotics to recover.

that drivers (not passengers, even children) wear helmets, are being enforced around the country by traffic police eager to levy fines. Foreigners are popular targets.

Local Transport

Bus

There are currently no local bus networks in Cambodia, even in Phnom Penh.

Cyclo

As in Vietnam and Laos, the *cyclo* (pedicab) is a cheap way to get around urban areas. In Phnom Penh *cyclo* drivers can either be flagged down on main roads or found waiting around markets and major hotels. It is necessary to bargain the fare if taking a *cyclo* from outside an expensive hotel or popular restaurant or bar. Fares range from 2000r to US$1 (about 4000r). There are few *cyclos* in the provinces, and in Phnom Penh the *cyclo* has almost been driven to extinction by the *moto*.

Moto

Motos, also known as *motodups* (meaning *moto* driver), are small motorcycle taxis. They are a quick way of making short hops around towns and cities. Prices range from 1000r to US$1 or more, depending on the distance and the town; expect to pay more at night. In the past it was rare for prices to be agreed in advance, but with the increase in visitor numbers, a lot of drivers have got into the habit of overcharging. It's probably best to negotiate up front, particularly in the major tourist centres, outside fancy hotels or at night.

Outboards

Outboards (pronounced 'outboor') are the equivalent of Venice's *vaporetto*, a sort of local river-bus or taxi. Found all over the country, they are small fibreglass boats with 15HP or 40HP engines, and can carry up to six people for local or longer trips. They rarely run to schedules, but locals wait patiently for them to fill up. Those with time on their hands can join the wait; those in a hurry can charter the whole boat and take off. Another variation are the longtail rocket boats imported from Thailand that connect small villages on the upper stretches of the Mekong. Rocket is the definitive word and their safety is questionable.

Remork-moto

The *remork-moto* is a large trailer hitched to a motorcycle and pretty much operates as a low-tech local bus with ohso-natural air-conditioning. They are used throughout rural Cambodia to transport people and goods, and are often seen on the edge of towns ready to ferry farmers back to the countryside.

Most popular tourist destinations, including Phnom

Penh, Siem Reap and the South Coast, have their very own tourist versions of the *remork*, with a canopied trailer hitched to the back of the motorbike for two people in comfort or as many as you can pile on at night. Often referred to as *tuk-tuks* by foreigners travelling in Cambodia, they're a great way to explore temples, as you get the breeze of the bike but some protection from the elements.

Rotei Ses

Rotei means 'cart' or 'carriage' and *ses* is 'horse', but the term is used for any cart pulled by an animal. Cambodia's original 4WD, ox carts, usually pulled by water buffalo or cows, are a common form of transport in remote parts of the country, as only they can get through thick mud in the height of the wet season. Some local community-tourism initiatives include cart rides.

Taxi

Taxi hire in towns and cities is getting easier, but there are still very few metered taxis, with just a couple of operators in Phnom Penh. Guesthouses, hotels and travel agents can arrange cars for sightseeing in and around towns.

Share Taxis

In these days of improving roads, pick-up trucks are

losing ground to 'express minibuses' or pumped-up Toyota Camrys that have their suspension jacked up like monster trucks. When using share taxis or pick-ups, it is an advantage to travel in numbers, as you can buy spare seats to make the journey more comfortable. Double the price for the front seat and quadruple it for the entire back row. It is important to remember that there aren't necessarily fixed prices on every route, so you have to negotiate, and prices do fluctuate with the price of petrol.

Share taxis are widely available for hire. For major destinations they can be hired individually, or you can pay for a seat and wait for other passengers to turn up. Guesthouses are also very helpful when it comes to arranging share taxis, at a price, of course.

Train

Cambodia's rail system is, like the old road network, one of the most notorious in Asia. There are currently no passenger services, but this may change as the railway continues to be rehabilitated by a private company. Eventually, the Cambodian network will be plugged into the Trans-Asian Railway, which will eventually link Singapore and China, but connecting Phnom Penh with Ho Chi Minh City via a Mekong bridge will take a few years yet.

The rail network consists of about 645km of single-track metre-gauge lines. The 385km northwestern line, built before WWII, links Phnom Penh with Pursat and Battambang. The 254km southwestern line, which was completed in 1969, connects Phnom Penh with Takeo, Kampot and Sihanoukville. The prettiest sections of the network are between Takeo and Kampot and from there to Sihanoukville.

REMORK VERSUS TUK-TUK

So just what are those motorbikes with the cute little carriages pulled behind? *Remork-motos? Remorks? Tuk-tuks*? The debate rumbles on. Officially, Cambodians call them *remork-motos*, which is often shortened to *remork*. In Thailand, the high-octane three-wheeled taxis in Bangkok are known as *tuk-tuks*, and this moniker has hopped across the border into common usage in Cambodia. However, some Cambodians take offence at the use of the name *tuk-tuk*, so for the time being we are opting for *remork*. Remorkable.

Health

General health is more of a concern in Cambodia than most other parts of South-east Asia, due to a lack of effective medical-treatment facilities, a prevalence of tropical diseases and poor sanitation. Once you venture into rural areas you are very much on your own, although most towns have a reasonable clinic these days.

If you feel particularly unwell, try to see a doctor rather than visit a hospital; hospitals in rural areas are pretty primitive and diagnosis can be hit and miss. If you fall seriously ill in Cambodia you should head to Phnom Penh or Siem Reap, as these are the only places in the country with decent emergency treatment. Pharmacies in the larger towns are remarkably well stocked and you don't need a prescription to get your hands on anything from antibiotics to antimalarials. Prices are also very reasonable, but do check the expiry date, as some medicine may have been on the shelves for quite a long time.

While the potential dangers can seem quite frightening, in reality few travellers experience anything more than an upset stomach. Don't let these warnings make you paranoid.

BEFORE YOU GO

Insurance

Do not visit Cambodia without medical insurance. Hospitals are extremely basic in the provinces and even in Phnom Penh the facilities are generally not up to international standards. Anyone who has a serious injury or illness while in Cambodia may require emergency evacuation to Bangkok. With an insurance policy costing no more than the equivalent of a bottle of beer a day, this evacuation is free. Without an insurance policy, it will cost between US$10,000 and US$20,000 – somewhat more than a six-pack. Don't gamble with your health in Cambodia or you may end up another statistic.

Medical Checklist

Following is a list of items to consider including in your medical kit – consult your pharmacist for brands available in your country.

➡ aspirin or paracetamol – for pain or fever

➡ antihistamine – for allergies, or to ease the itch from insect bites or stings

➡ cold and flu tablets, throat lozenges and nasal decongestant

➡ multivitamins – especially for long trips, when dietary vitamin intake may be inadequate

➡ loperamide or diphenoxylate – 'blockers' for diarrhoea

➡ rehydration mixture – to prevent dehydration, which may occur during bouts of diarrhoea

➡ insect repellent, sunscreen, lip balm and eye drops

➡ calamine lotion or aloe vera – to ease irritation from sunburn

➡ antifungal cream or powder – for fungal skin infections and thrush

➡ antiseptic (such as povidone-iodine) – for cuts and grazes

➡ bandages, plasters and other wound dressings

➡ water-purification tablets or iodine

EVERYDAY HEALTH

Normal body temperature is up to 37°C (98.6°F); more than 2°C (4°F) higher indicates a high fever. The normal adult pulse rate is 60 to 100 beats per minute (children 80 to 100, babies 100 to 140). As a general rule, the pulse increases about 20 beats per minute for each 1°C (2°F) rise in fever.

➡ sterile kit (sealed medical kit containing syringes and needles) – highly recommended, as Cambodia has potential medical-hygiene issues

Vaccinations

Plan ahead for getting your vaccinations; some of them require more than one injection over a period of time, while others should not be given together.

Record all vaccinations on an International Certificate of Vaccination, available from your doctor. It is a good idea to carry this as proof of your vaccinations when travelling in Cambodia.

IN CAMBODIA

Availability & Cost of Health Care

Self-diagnosis and treatment of health problems can be risky: always seek professional medical help.

Antibiotics should ideally be administered only under medical supervision. Take only the recommended dose at the prescribed intervals and use the whole course, even if the illness seems to be cured earlier. Stop immediately if there are any serious reactions.

The best clinics and hospitals in Cambodia are found in Phnom Penh and Siem Reap. A consultation usually costs in the region of US$20 to US$50, plus medicine. Elsewhere, facilities are more basic, although a private clinic is usually preferable to a government hospital. For serious injuries or illnesses, seek treatment in Bangkok.

Infectious Diseases

Dengue

This viral disease is transmitted by mosquitoes. There is only a small risk to travellers, except during epidemics, which usually occur during and just after the wet season.

Unlike the malaria mosquito, the *Aedes aegypti*

mosquito, which transmits the dengue virus, is most active during the day and is found mainly in urban areas.

Signs and symptoms of dengue fever include a sudden onset of high fever, headache, joint and muscle pains (hence its old name, 'breakbone fever'), plus nausea and vomiting. A rash of small red spots appears three to four days after the onset of fever.

Seek medical attention if you think you may be infected. A blood test can diagnose infection, but there is no specific treatment for the disease. Aspirin should be avoided, as it increases the risk of haemorrhaging, but plenty of rest is advised.

There is no vaccine against dengue fever. The best prevention is to avoid mosquito bites at all times.

Fungal Infections

Fungal infections occur more commonly in hot weather and are usually on the scalp, between the toes (athlete's foot) or fingers, in the groin and on the body (ringworm). Ringworm, a fungal infection, not a worm, is contracted from infected animals or other people. Moisture encourages these infections.

To prevent fungal infections wear loose, comfortable clothes, avoid artificial fibres, wash frequently and dry yourself carefully.

Hepatitis

Hepatitis is a general term for inflammation of the liver. Several different viruses cause hepatitis, and they differ in the way that they are transmitted. The symptoms are similar in all forms of the illness, and include fever, chills, headache, fatigue, feelings of weakness, and aches and pains, followed by loss of appetite, nausea, vomiting, abdominal pain, dark urine, light-coloured faeces, jaundiced (yellow) skin and yellowing of the whites of the eyes.

RECOMMENDED VACCINATIONS

Recommended vaccinations for a trip to Cambodia are listed here, but it is imperative that you discuss your needs with your doctor.

Diphtheria and tetanus Vaccinations for these two diseases are usually combined.

Hepatitis A This vaccine provides long-term immunity after an initial injection and a booster at six to 12 months. The hepatitis A vaccine is also available in a combined form with the hepatitis B vaccine – three injections over a six-month period are required.

Hepatitis B Vaccination involves three injections, with a booster at 12 months.

Polio A booster every 10 years maintains immunity.

Tuberculosis Vaccination against TB (BCG vaccine) is recommended for children and young adults who will be living in Cambodia for three months or more.

Typhoid Vaccination against typhoid may be required if you are travelling for more than a couple of weeks in Cambodia.

Hepatitis A and E are both transmitted by ingesting contaminated food or water. Seek medical advice, but there is not much you can do apart from resting, drinking lots of fluids, eating lightly and avoiding fatty foods.

There are almost 300 million chronic carriers of hepatitis B in the world. It is spread through contact with infected blood, blood products or body fluids; for example, through sexual contact, unsterilized needles, blood transfusions or contact with blood via small breaks in the skin. Hepatitis C and D are spread in the same way as hepatitis B and can also lead to long-term complications.

HIV/AIDS

Infection with the human immunodeficiency virus (HIV) may lead to acquired immune deficiency syndrome (AIDS), which is a fatal disease. Any exposure to blood, blood products or body fluids may put the individual at risk.

The disease is often transmitted through sexual contact or dirty needles, so vaccinations, acupuncture, tattooing and body piercing can be potentially as dangerous as intravenous drug use.

Intestinal Worms

These parasites are most common in rural Cambodia. The various worms have different ways of infecting people. Some may be ingested in food such as undercooked meat (eg tapeworms) and some enter through your skin (eg hookworms). Consider having a stool test when you return home to check for worms and to determine the appropriate treatment.

Malaria

This serious and potentially fatal disease is spread by mosquitoes. If you are travelling in endemic areas it is extremely important to avoid mosquito bites and to take tablets to prevent the disease developing if you become infected. There is no malaria in Phnom Penh, Siem Reap and most other major urban areas in Cambodia, so visitors on short trips to the most popular places do not need to take medication. Malaria self-test kits are widely available in Cambodia, but are not that reliable.

Symptoms of malaria include fever, chills and sweating, headache, aching joints, diarrhoea and stomach pains, usually preceded by a vague feeling of ill health. Seek medical help immediately if malaria is suspected, as, without treatment, the disease can rapidly become more serious or even fatal.

Sexually Transmitted Infections (STIs)

Gonorrhoea, herpes and syphilis are among these infections. Sores, blisters or a rash around the genitals and discharges or pain when urinating are common symptoms. With some STIs, such as wart virus or chlamydia, symptoms may be less marked or not observed at all, especially in women. Reliable condoms are widely available throughout urban areas of Cambodia.

Typhoid

Typhoid fever is a dangerous gut infection caused by contaminated water and food. Medical help must be sought.

In its initial stages sufferers may feel they have a bad cold or flu on the way, as early symptoms are a headache, body aches and a fever that rises a little each day until it is around 40°C (104°F) or higher. There may also be vomiting, abdominal pain, diarrhoea or constipation.

In the second week the high fever and slow pulse continue, and a few pink spots may appear on the body; trembling, delirium, weakness, weight loss and dehydration may occur.

Traveller's Diarrhoea

Simple things like a change of water, food or climate can all cause a mild bout of diarrhoea, but a few rushed toilet trips with no other symptoms are not indicative of a major problem. Almost everyone gets a mild bout of the runs on a longer visit to Cambodia.

Dehydration is the main danger with diarrhoea, particularly in children or the elderly as it can occur quite quickly. Under all circumstances *fluid replacement* is the most important thing to remember. Stick to a bland diet as you recover. Commercially available oral rehydration salts are very useful; add them to boiled or bottled water.

Gut-paralysing drugs such as Lomotil or Imodium can be used to bring relief from the symptoms of diarrhoea, although they do not actually cure the problem. Only use these drugs if you do not have access to toilets and *must* travel.

Environmental Hazards

Food

There is an adage that says, 'If you can cook it, boil it or peel it you can eat it...otherwise forget it'. This is slightly extreme, but many travellers have found it is better to be safe than sorry. Vegetables and fruit should be washed with purified water or peeled

CONTACT LENSES

People wearing contact lenses should be aware that Cambodia is an extremely dusty country and this can cause much irritation when travelling. It is generally bearable in cars, but when travelling by motorcycle or pick-up, it is most definitely not. Pack a pair of glasses.

where possible. Beware of ice cream that is sold in the street (or anywhere), as it might have been melted and refrozen. Shellfish such as mussels, oysters and clams should be avoided, as should undercooked meat, particularly in the form of mince.

Heat Exhaustion

Dehydration and salt deficiency can cause heat exhaustion. Take time to acclimatise to high temperatures, drink sufficient liquids and do not do anything too physically demanding.

Salt deficiency is characterised by fatigue, lethargy, headaches, giddiness and muscle cramps; salt tablets may help, but adding extra salt to your food is better.

Heatstroke can occur if the body's heat-regulating mechanism breaks down, causing the body temperature to rise to dangerous levels. Long, continuous periods of exposure to high temperatures and insufficient fluids can leave you vulnerable to heatstroke.

Insect Bites & Stings

Bedbugs live in various places, but particularly in dirty mattresses and bedding, and are evidenced by spots of blood on bedclothes or on the wall. Bedbugs leave itchy bites in neat rows. Calamine lotion or Stingose spray may help.

All lice cause itching and discomfort. They make themselves at home in your hair (head lice), your clothing (body lice) or in your pubic hair (crabs). You catch lice through direct contact with infected people or by sharing combs, clothing and the like. Powder or shampoo treatment will kill the lice, and infected clothing should be washed in very hot, soapy water and left to dry in the sun.

Leeches may be present in damp rainforest conditions; they attach themselves to your skin to suck your blood. Trekkers often get them on their legs or in their boots. Salt or a lighted cigarette end will make them fall off.

Prickly Heat

Prickly heat is an itchy rash caused by excessive perspiration trapped under the skin. It usually strikes people who have just arrived in a hot climate. Keeping cool, bathing often, drying the skin, using a mild talcum or prickly heat powder, or finding air-conditioning, may help.

Snakes

To minimise the chances of being bitten by a snake, always wear boots, socks and long trousers when walking through undergrowth where snakes may be present.

Water

The number-one rule is *be careful of water and ice,* although both are usually factory produced, a legacy of the French. If you don't know for certain that the water is safe, assume the worst. Reputable brands of bottled water or soft drinks are usually fine, but you can't safely drink tap water. Only use water from containers with a serrated seal. Tea and coffee are generally fine, as they're made with boiled water.

Traditional Medicine

Traditional medicine or *thnam boran* is very popular in rural Cambodia. There are *kru Khmer* (traditional medicine men) in most districts of the country and some locals trust them more than modern doctors and hospitals. Working with tree bark, roots, herbs and plants, they boil up brews to supposedly cure all ills. However, when it comes to serious conditions like snake bites, their treatments can be counterproductive.

Language

The Khmer language is spoken by approximately nine million people in Cambodia, and is understood by many in neighbouring countries. Although Khmer as spoken in Phnom Penh is generally intelligible to Khmers nationwide, there are several distinct dialects in other parts of the country. Most notably, inhabitants of Takeo Province tend to modify or slur hard consonant/vowel combinations, especially those with 'r'. For example, *bram* (five) becomes *pe-am*, *sraa* (alcohol) becomes *se-aa*, and *baraang* (French for foreigner) becomes *be-ang*. In Siem Reap there's a Lao-sounding lilt to the local speech – some vowels are modified, eg *poan* (thousand) becomes *peuan*, and *kh'sia* (pipe) becomes *kh'seua*.

Though English is fast becoming Cambodia's second language, the Khmer population still clings to the Francophone pronunciation of the Roman alphabet and most foreign words. This is helpful to remember when spelling Western words and names aloud – 'ay-bee-see' becomes 'ah-bey-sey' and so on.

The pronunciation guides in this chapter are designed for basic communication rather than linguistic perfection. Read them as if they were English, and you shouldn't have problems being understood. Some consonant combinations are separated with an apostrophe for ease of pronunciation, eg 'j-r' in j'rook (pig) and 'ch-ng' in ch'ngain (delicious). Also note that k is pronounced as the 'g' in 'go'; kh as the 'k' in 'kind'; p as the final 'p' in 'puppy'; ph as the 'p' in 'pond'; r as in 'rum' (hard and rolling); t as the 't' in 'stand'; and th as the 't' in 'two'.

Vowels and vowel combinations with an h at the end are pronounced with a puff of air at the end. Vowels are pronounced as follows:

- a and ah shorter and harder than aa
- aa as the 'a' in 'father'
- ae as the 'a' in 'cat'
- ai as in 'aisle'
- am as the 'um' in 'glum'
- av like a nasal ao (without the 'v')
- aw as the 'aw' in 'jaw'
- awh as the 'aw' in 'jaw' (short and hard)
- ay as ai (slightly nasal)
- e as in 'they'
- eh as the 'a' in 'date' (short and hard)
- eu like 'oo' (with flat lips)
- euh as eu (short and hard)
- euv like a nasal eu (without the 'v')
- ey as in 'prey'
- i as in 'kit'
- ia as the 'ee' in 'beer' (without the 'r')
- ih as the 'ee' in 'teeth' (short and hard)
- ii as the 'ee' in 'feet'
- o as the 'ow' in 'cow'
- œ as 'er' in 'her' (more open)
- oh as the 'o' in 'hose' (short and hard)
- ohm as the 'ome' in 'home'
- ow as in 'glow'
- u as the 'u' in 'flute' (short and hard)
- ua as the 'ou' in 'tour'
- uah as ua (short and hard)
- uh as the 'u' in 'but'
- uu as the 'oo' in 'zoo'

WANT MORE?

For in-depth language information and handy phrases, check out Lonely Planet's *Southeast Asia Phrasebook*. You'll find it at **shop.lonelyplanet.com**, or you can buy Lonely Planet's iPhone phrasebooks at the Apple App Store.

BASICS

The Khmer language reflects the social standing of the speaker and the subject through personal pronouns and 'politeness words'. These range from the simple *baat* for men and *jaa* for women, placed at the end of a sentence and meaning 'yes' or 'I agree', to the very formal and archaic *Reachasahp* or 'royal language', a separate vocabulary reserved for addressing the king and very high officials. Many of the pronouns are determined on the basis of the subject's age and gender in relation to the speaker.

Foreigners are not expected to know all of these forms. The easiest and most general personal pronoun is *niak* (you), which may be used in most situations, for either gender. Men of your age or older can be called *lowk* (Mister). Women of your age or older can be called *bawng srei* (older sister) or, for more formal situations, *lowk srei* (Madam). *Bawng* is an informal, neutral pronoun for men or women who are (or appear to be) older than you. For the third person (he/she/they), male or female, singular or plural, the respectful form is *koat* and the common form is *ke*.

Hello.	ជម្រាបសួរ	johm riab sua
Goodbye.	លាសិនហើយ	lia suhn hao-y
Excuse me./ Sorry.	សូមទោស	sohm toh
Please.	សូម	sohm
Thank you.	អរគុណ	aw kohn
You're welcome.	អត់អីទេ/ សូមអញ្ជើញ	awt ei te/ sohm anjœ-in
Yes.	បាទ/ចាស	baat/jaa (m/f)
No.	ទេ	te

How are you?
អ្នកសុខសប្បាយទេ? niak sohk sabaay te

I'm fine.
ខ្ញុំសុខសប្បាយ kh'nyohm sohk sabaay

What's your name?
អ្នកឈ្មោះអ្វី? niak ch'muah ei

My name is ...
ខ្ញុំឈ្មោះ... kh'nyohm ch'muah ...

Does anyone speak English?
មានៈមានអ្នកចេះ
ភាសាអង់គ្លេសទេ? tii nih mian niak jeh
phiasaa awngle te

I don't understand.
ខ្ញុំមិនយល់ទេ/
ខ្ញុំស្ដាប់មិនបាន kh'nyohm muhn yuhl te/
kh'nyohm s'dap muhn baan te

ACCOMMODATION

Where's a hotel?
អ្នកតើលនៅឯណា? ohtail neuv ai naa

I'd like a room ...	ខ្ញុំសុំបន្ទប់...	kh'nyohm sohm bantohp ...
for one person	សម្រាប់ មួយនាក់	samruhp muy niak
for two people	សម្រាប់ ពីរនាក់	samruhp pii niak
with a bathroom	ដែលមាន បន្ទប់ទឹក	dail mian bantohp tuhk
with a fan	ដែលមាន កង្ហារ	dail mian dawnghahl
with a window	ដែលមាន បង្អួច	dail mian bawng-uit

How much is it per day?
តម្លៃមួយថ្ងៃ
ប៉ុន្មាន? damlay muy th'ngay
pohnmaan

DIRECTIONS

Where is a/the ...?
...នៅឯណា? ... neuv ai naa

How can I get to ...?
ផ្លូវណាទៅ...? phleuv naa teuv ...

Go straight ahead.
ទៅត្រង់ teuv trawng

Turn left.
បត់ឆ្វេង bawt ch'weng

Turn right.
បត់ស្ដាំ bawt s'dam

at the corner
នៅកាច់ជ្រុង neuv kait j'rohng

behind
នៅខាងក្រោយ neuv khaang krao-y

in front of
នៅខាងមុខ neuv khaang mohk

next to
នៅជាប់ neuv joab

opposite
នៅទល់មុខ neuv tohl mohk

EATING & DRINKING

Where's a ...? ...នៅឯណា? ... neuv ai naa

food stall កន្លែងលក់ម្ហូប kuhnlaing loak m'howp

market ផ្សារ psar

restaurant រ៉េស្ស៊ីរ៉ង់ resturawn

Do you have a menu in English?
មានម៊ីនុយជា mien menui jea
ភាសាអង់គ្លេសទេ? piasaa awnglay te

What's the speciality here?
ទីនេះមានម្ហូប tii nih mien m'howp
អីពិសេសទេ? ei piseh te

I'm vegetarian.
ខ្ញុំតមសាច់ kh'nyohm tawm sait

I'm allergic to (peanuts).
កុំដាក់ (សណ្ដែកដី) kohm dak (sandaik dei)

Not too spicy, please.
សូមកុំធ្វើហឹរពេក sohm kohm twœ huhl pek

This is delicious.
អានេះឆ្ងាញ់ណាស់ nih ch'ngain nah

The bill, please.
សូមគិតលុយ sohm kuht lui

Fruit & Vegetables

apple	ផ្លែប៉ោម	phla i powm
banana	ចេក	chek
coconut	ដូង	duong
custard apple	ទៀប	tiep
dragonfruit	ផ្លែស្រកានាគ	phlai srakaa neak
durian	ធូរេន	tourain
grapes	ទំពាំងបាយជូរ	tompeang baai juu
guava	ត្របែក	trawbaik
jackfruit	ខ្នុរ	khnau
lemon	ក្រូចឆ្មារ	krow-it ch'maa
longan	មៀន	mien
lychee	ផ្លែគូលេន	phlai kuulain
mandarin	ក្រូចខ្វិច	krow-it khwait
mango	ស្វាយ	svay
mangosteen	មង្ឃុត	mongkut

orange	ក្រូចពោធិ៍សាត់	krow-it pow saat
papaya	ល្ហុង	l'howng
pineapple	ម្នាស់	menoa
pomelo	ក្រូចថ្លុង	krow-it th'lohng
rambutan	សាវម៉ាវ	sao mao
starfruit	ស្ពឺ	speu
vegetables	បន្លែ	buhn lai
watermelon	ឪឡឹក	euv luhk

Meat & Fish

beef	សាច់គោ	sait kow
chicken	សាច់មាន់	sait moan
crab	ក្ដាម	k'daam
eel	អន្ទង់	ahntohng
fish	ត្រី	trey
frog	កង្កែប	kawng kaip
lobster	បង្កង	bawng kawng
pork	សាច់ជ្រូក	sait j'ruuk
shrimp	បង្គា	bawngkia
snail	ខ្យង	kh'jawng
squid	មឹក	meuk

Other

bread	នំប៉័ង	nohm paang
butter	ប៊ីរ	bœ
chilli	ម្ទេស	m'teh
curry	ការី	karii
fish sauce	ទឹកត្រី	teuk trey
fried	ចៀន/ឆា	jien/chaa
garlic	ខ្ទឹមស	kh'tuhm saw
ginger	ខ្ញី	kh'nyei
grilled	អាំង	ahng
ice	ទឹកកក	teuk koh
lemongrass	ស្លឹកគ្រៃ	sluhk kray
noodles (egg/rice)	មី/គុយទាវ	mii/kyteow
pepper	ម្រេច	m'rait

rice	បាយ	bai
salt	អំបិល	uhmbuhl
soup	ស៊ីប	sup
soy sauce	ទឹកស៊ីអ៊ីវ	teuk sii iw
spring rolls (fresh/fried)	ណែម/ឆាយ៉	naim/chaa yaw
steamed	ចំហុយ	jamhoi
sugar	ស្ករ	skaw

Drinks

beer	ប៊ីយ៉ែរ	bii-yœ
coffee	កាហ្វេ	kaa fey
lemon juice	ទឹកក្រូច ឆ្មា	teuk krow-it ch'maa
orange juice	ទឹកក្រូច ពោធិ៍សាត់	teuk krow-it pow sat
tea	តែ	tai
water	ទឹក	teuk

EMERGENCIES

Help!
ជួយខ្ញុំផង!   juay kh'nyohm phawng

Call the police!
ជួយហៅប៉ូលិសមក!   juay hav polih mao

Call a doctor!
ជួយហៅ   juay hav
គ្រូពេទ្យមក!   kruu paet mao

I've been robbed.
ខ្ញុំត្រូវចោរប្លន់   kh'nyohm treuv jao plawn

I'm ill.
ខ្ញុំឈឺ   kh'nyohm cheu

I'm allergic to (antibiotics).
ខ្ញុំមិនត្រូវជាតុ   kh'nyohm muhn treuv thiat
(អង់ទីប៊ីយ៉ូទិក)   (awntiibiowtik)

Where are the toilets?
បង្គន់នៅឯណា?   bawngkohn neuv ai naa

SHOPPING & SERVICES

I want to see the ...
ខ្ញុំចង់ទៅមើល...   kh'nyohm jawng teuv mœl ...

What time does it open?
វាបើកម៉ោងប៉ុន្មាន?   wia baok maong pohnmaan

What time does it close?
វាបិទម៉ោងប៉ុន្មាន?   wia buht maong pohnmaan

I'm looking for the ...
ខ្ញុំរក...   kh'nyohm rohk ...

bank	ធនាគារ	th'niakia
post office	«ប្រៃសណីយ៍	praisuhnii
public telephone	ទូរសព្ទ សាធារណៈ	turasahp saathiaranah
temple	វត្ត	wawt

How much is it?
នេះថ្លៃប៉ុន្មាន?   nih th'lay pohnmaan

That's too much.
ថ្លៃពេក   th'lay pek

No more than ...
មិនលើសពី...   muhn lœh pii ...

What's your best price?
អ្នកដាច់ប៉ុន្មាន?   niak dait pohnmaan

I want to change US dollars.
ខ្ញុំចង់ដូរ   kh'nyohm jawng dow
ដុល្លារអាម៉េរិក   dolaa amerik

What is the exchange rate for US dollars?
មួយដុល្លារ   muy dolaa
ដូរបានប៉ុន្មាន?   dow baan pohnmaan

TIME & DATES

What time is it?
ឥឡូវនេះម៉ោងប៉ុន្មាន?   eileuv nih maong pohnmaan

in the morning	ពេលព្រឹក	pel pruhk
in the afternoon	ពេលរសៀល	pel r'sial
in the evening	ពេលល្ងាច	pel l'ngiat
at night	ពេលយប់	pel yohp

yesterday	ម្សិលមិញ	m'suhl mein
today	ថ្ងៃនេះ	th'ngay nih
tomorrow	ថ្ងៃស្អែក	th'ngay s'aik

Monday	ថ្ងៃចន្ទ	th'ngay jahn
Tuesday	ថ្ងៃអង្គារ	th'ngay ahngkia
Wednesday	ថ្ងៃពុធ	th'ngay poht
Thursday	ថ្ងៃព្រហស្បតិ៍	th'ngay prohoah
Friday	ថ្ងៃសុក្រ	th'ngay sohk
Saturday	ថ្ងៃសៅរ៍	th'ngay sav
Sunday	ថ្ងៃអាទិត្យ	th'ngay aatuht

TRANSPORT

Where's the ...?	...នៅឯណា?	... neuv ai naa
airport	វាលយន្ត	wial yohn
	ហោះ	hawh
bus stop	ចំណត	jamnawt
	ឡានឈ្នួល	laan ch'nual
train station	ស្ថានីយ	s'thaanii
	រថភ្លើង	roht plœng

When does the ... leave?	...ចេញម៉ោង ប៉ុន្មាន?	... jein maong pohnmaan
boat	ទូក	duk
bus	ឡានឈ្នួល	laan ch'nual
train	រថភ្លើង	roht plœng
plane	យន្តហោះ	yohn hawh

What time does the last bus leave?

ឡានឈ្នួលចុងក្រោយ / laan ch'nual johng krao-y
ចេញទៅម៉ោងប៉ុន្មាន? / jein teuv maong pohnmaan

I want to get off (here).

ខ្ញុំចង់ចុះ(ទីនេះ) / kh'nyohm jawng joh (tii nih)

How much is it to ...?

ទៅ...ថ្លៃប៉ុន្មាន? / teuv ... th'lay pohnmaan

Please take me to (this address).

សូមជូនខ្ញុំទៅ / sohm juun kh'nyohm teuv
(អាសយដ្ឋាននេះ) / (aasayathaan nih)

Here is fine, thank you.

ឈប់នៅទីនេះក៏បាន / chohp neuv tii nih kaw baan

Numbers

Khmers count in increments of five – after reaching the number five *(bram)*, the cycle begins again with the addition of one, ie 'five-one' *(bram muy)*, 'five-two' *(bram pii)* and so on to 10, which begins a new cycle. For example, 18 has three parts: 10, five and three.

There's also a colloquial form of counting that reverses the word order for numbers between 10 and 20 and separates the two words with *duhn: pii duhn dawp* for 12, *bei duhn dawp* for 13 and so on. This form is often used in markets, so listen keenly.

1	មួយ	muy
2	ពីរ	pii
3	បី	bei
4	បួន	buan
5	ប្រាំ	bram
6	ប្រាំមួយ	bram muy
7	ប្រាំពីរ	bram pii
8	ប្រាំបី	bram bei
9	ប្រាំបួន	bram buan
10	ដប់	dawp
11	ដប់មួយ	dawp muy
12	ដប់ពីរ	dawp pii
16	ដប់ប្រាំមួយ	dawp bram muy
20	ម្ភៃ	m'phei
21	ម្ភៃមួយ	m'phei muy
30	សាមសិប	saamsuhp
40	សែសិប	saisuhp
100	មួយរយ	muy roy
1000	មួយពាន់	muy poan
1,000,000	មួយលាន	muy lian
1st	ទីមួយ	tii muy
2nd	ទីពីរ	tii pii
3rd	ទីបី	tii bei
4th	ទីបួន	tii buan
10th	ទីដប់	tii dawp

GLOSSARY

apsara – heavenly nymph or angelic dancer, often represented in Khmer sculpture

Asean – Association of Southeast Asian Nations

Avalokiteshvara – Bodhisattva of Compassion and the inspiration for Jayavarman VII's Angkor Thom

baray – reservoir

boeng – lake

Chenla – pre-Angkorian period, 6th to 8th centuries

chunchiet – ethnic minorities

CPP – Cambodian People's Party

cyclo – pedicab; bicycle rickshaw

devaraja – cult of the god-king, established by Jayavarman II, in which the monarch has universal power

devadas – goddesses

EFEO – École Française d'Extrême Orient

essai – wise man or traditional medicine man

Funan – pre-Angkorian period, 1st to 5th centuries

Funcinpec – National United Front for an Independent, Neutral, Peaceful and Cooperative Cambodia; royalist political party

garuda – mythical half-man, half-bird creature

gopura – entrance pavilion in traditional Hindu architecture

Hun Sen – Cambodia's prime minister (1985–present)

Jayavarman II – the king (r 802–50) who established the cult of the god-king, kicking off a period of amazing architectural productivity that resulted in the extraordinary temples of Angkor

Jayavarman VII – the king (r 1181–1219) who drove the Chams out of Cambodia before embarking on an ambitious construction program, including the walled city of Angkor Thom

Kampuchea – the name Cambodians use for their country; to non-Khmers, it is associated with the bloody rule of the Khmer Rouge, which insisted that the outside world adopt for Cambodia the name Democratic Kampuchea from 1975 to 1979

Khmer – a person of Cambodian descent; the language of Cambodia

Khmer Krom – ethnic Khmers living in Vietnam

Khmer Rouge – a revolutionary organisation that seized power in 1975 and implemented a brutal social restructuring, resulting in the suffering and death of millions of Cambodians during its four-year rule

krama – scarf

linga – phallic symbols

Mahayana – literally, 'Great Vehicle'; a school of Buddhism (also known as the Northern School) that built upon and extended the early Buddhist teachings; see also Theravada

moto – small motorcycle with driver; a common form of transport in Cambodia

Mt Meru – the mythical dwelling of the Hindu god Shiva

naga – mythical serpent, often multiheaded; a symbol used extensively in Angkorian architecture

nandi – sacred ox, vehicle of Shiva

NGO – nongovernmental organisation

NH – national highway

Norodom Ranariddh, Prince – son of King Sihanouk and former leader of Funcinpec

Norodom Sihanouk, King – former king, head of state, film director and a towering figure in modern-day Cambodia

Pali – ancient Indian language that, along with Sanskrit, is the root of modern Khmer

phnom – mountain or hill

Pol Pot – the former leader of the Khmer Rouge; responsible for the suffering and deaths of millions of Cambodians; also known as Saloth Sar

prasat – stone or brick hall with religious or royal significance

preah – sacred

psar – market

Ramayana – an epic Sanskrit poem composed around 300 BC featuring the mythical Ramachandra, the incarnation of the god Vishnu

remork-moto – trailer pulled by a motorcycle; often shortened to remork

rom vong – Cambodian circle dancing

Sangkum Reastr Niyum – People's Socialist Community; a national movement, led by King Sihanouk, that ruled the country during the 1950s and 1960s

Sanskrit – ancient Hindu language that, along with Pali, is the root of modern Khmer language

stung – river

Suryavarman II – the king (r 1112–52) responsible for building Angkor Wat and for expanding and unifying the Khmer empire

Theravada – a school of Buddhism (also known as the Southern School or Hinayana) found in Myanmar (Burma), Thailand, Laos and Cambodia; this school confined itself to the early Buddhist teachings; see also Mahayana

tonlé – large river

UNDP – UN Development Programme

Unesco – UN Educational Scientific and Cultural Organization

Untac – UN Transitional Authority in Cambodia

vihara – temple sanctuary

WHO – World Health Organization

Year Zero – 1975; the year the Khmer Rouge seized power

yoni – female fertility symbol

Behind the Scenes

SEND US YOUR FEEDBACK

We love to hear from travellers – your comments keep us on our toes and help make our books better. Our well-travelled team reads every word on what you loved or loathed about this book. Although we cannot reply individually to postal submissions, we always guarantee that your feedback goes straight to the appropriate authors, in time for the next edition. Each person who sends us information is thanked in the next edition – the most useful submissions are rewarded with a selection of digital PDF chapters.

Visit **lonelyplanet.com/contact** to submit your updates and suggestions or to ask for help. Our award-winning website also features inspirational travel stories, news and discussions.

Note: We may edit, reproduce and incorporate your comments in Lonely Planet products such as guidebooks, websites and digital products, so let us know if you don't want your comments reproduced or your name acknowledged. For a copy of our privacy policy visit lonelyplanet.com/privacy.

OUR READERS

Many thanks to the travellers who used the last edition and wrote to us with helpful hints, useful advice and interesting anecdotes:

Letizia Bordoli, Francesco Bozzi, Luigi Ciullo, Claire Donohue, Anoop Gannerkote, Raymond N Greenwell, John Hoffmann, Thomas Imcielcik, Gabrielle Innes, Danka József, Sriram Karra, Suzanne Kho, Wancy Lam, Panos Loupasis, Regina Meyer, Raegan Moynes, Jacopo Occhini, Munjin Park, Claire Peirce, Paul Putz, Nikki Rozario, Dagmar Ruehl, Miriam Schaper, Riley Simas, Burghard Thiele, Linda Torres, James Whitehead, Joanie Williams, Christian Winther, Milin Young

AUTHOR THANKS

Nick Ray

A huge and heartfelt thanks to the people of Cambodia, whose warmth and humour, stoicism and spirit make it a happy yet humbling place to be. Biggest thanks are reserved for my lovely wife Kulikar Sotho and our children Julian and Belle, as without their support and encouragement the adventures would not be possible.

Thanks to fellow travellers and residents, friends and contacts in Cambodia who have helped shaped my knowledge and experience in this country. There is no room to thank everyone, but you all know who you are, as we meet for anything from beers to ecotourism conferences regularly enough.

Thanks also to my co-author and good friend Greg Bloom for going the extra mile to ensure this is a worthy new edition. Finally, thanks to the Lonely Planet team who have worked on this title. The author may be the public face, but a huge amount of work goes into making this a better book behind the scenes and I thank everyone for their hard work.

Greg Bloom

The cumulative knowledge of my gang (both real and Twitter-based) in Phnom Penh was elemental in writing this book. Special shout-outs to Jared, colleague Nick and the likes of @HayleyFlack. Thanks to Zach and Joe for tagging along on several gruelling bar crawls. Thanks to Anna for being my 'travel with children' guinea pig in places like Anlong Veng, Preah Vihear, Stung Treng and Ratanakiri, and to Ofie for helping out with Anna. And thanks to Lucy for joining me on many a restaurant review and rolling with this crazy lifestyle.

ACKNOWLEDGMENTS

Climate map data adapted from Peel MC, Finlayson BL & McMahon TA (2007) 'Updated World Map of the Köppen-Geiger Climate Classification', Hydrology and Earth System Sciences, 11, 1633-44.

Illustration pp132-3 by Michael Weldon.

Cover photograph: Buddhist monks, Angkor, Martin Puddy/Corbis

THIS BOOK

This 9th edition of Lonely Planet's *Cambodia* guidebook was researched and written by Nick Ray and Greg Bloom, who also wrote the previous two editions. This guidebook was commissioned in Lonely Planet's Melbourne office, and produced by the following:

Commissioning Editor
Ilaria Walker

Coordinating Editors
Elin Berglund, Kate James

Senior Cartographer
Diana Von Holdt
Senior Editor
Catherine Naghten
Managing Editors Sasha Baskett, Bruce Evans
Assisting Editors Penny Cordner, Peter Cruttenden, Carly Hall, Kate Kiely, Rosie Nicholson, Charlotte Orr
Assisting Cartographers
Jeff Cameron, Julie Dodkins, Mick Garrett

Book Designer
Katherine Marsh
Cover Research
Naomi Parker
Language Content
Branislava Vladisavljevic
Thanks to Anita Banh, Seda Douglas, Ryan Evans, Larissa Frost, Genesys India, Jouve India, Indra Kilfoyle, Wayne Murphy, Lorna Parkes, Chad Parkhill, Trent Paton, Martine Power, Dianne Schallmeiner, John Taufa, Juan Winata

Index

Map Legend

Sights

- Beach
- Bird Sanctuary
- Buddhist
- Castle/Palace
- Christian
- Confucian
- Hindu
- Islamic
- Jain
- Jewish
- Monument
- Museum/Gallery/Historic Building
- Ruin
- Sento Hot Baths/Onsen
- Shinto
- Sikh
- Taoist
- Winery/Vineyard
- Zoo/Wildlife Sanctuary
- Other Sight

Activities, Courses & Tours

- Bodysurfing
- Diving
- Canoeing/Kayaking
- Course/Tour
- Skiing
- Snorkelling
- Surfing
- Swimming/Pool
- Walking
- Windsurfing
- Other Activity

Sleeping

- Sleeping
- Camping

Eating

- Eating

Drinking & Nightlife

- Drinking & Nightlife
- Cafe

Entertainment

- Entertainment

Shopping

- Shopping

Information

- Bank
- Embassy/Consulate
- Hospital/Medical
- Internet
- Police
- Post Office
- Telephone
- Toilet
- Tourist Information
- Other Information

Geographic

- Beach
- Hut/Shelter
- Lighthouse
- Lookout
- Mountain/Volcano
- Oasis
- Park
- Pass
- Picnic Area
- Waterfall

Population

- Capital (National)
- Capital (State/Province)
- City/Large Town
- Town/Village

Transport

- Airport
- Border crossing
- Bus
- Cable car/Funicular
- Cycling
- Ferry
- Metro/MRT station
- Monorail
- Parking
- Petrol station
- Skytrain/Subway station
- Taxi
- Train station/Railway
- Tram
- Underground station
- Other Transport

Routes

- Tollway
- Freeway
- Primary
- Secondary
- Tertiary
- Lane
- Unsealed road
- Road under construction
- Plaza/Mall
- Steps
- Tunnel
- Pedestrian overpass
- Walking Tour
- Walking Tour detour
- Path/Walking Trail

Boundaries

- International
- State/Province
- Disputed
- Regional/Suburb
- Marine Park
- Cliff
- Wall

Hydrography

- River, Creek
- Intermittent River
- Canal
- Water
- Dry/Salt/Intermittent Lake
- Reef

Areas

- Airport/Runway
- Beach/Desert
- Cemetery (Christian)
- Cemetery (Other)
- Glacier
- Mudflat
- Park/Forest
- Sight (Building)
- Sportsground
- Swamp/Mangrove

Note: Not all symbols displayed above appear on the maps in this book

OUR STORY

A beat-up old car, a few dollars in the pocket and a sense of adventure. In 1972 that's all Tony and Maureen Wheeler needed for the trip of a lifetime – across Europe and Asia overland to Australia. It took several months, and at the end – broke but inspired – they sat at their kitchen table writing and stapling together their first travel guide, *Across Asia on the Cheap*. Within a week they'd sold 1500 copies. Lonely Planet was born.

Today, Lonely Planet has offices in Melbourne, London and Oakland, with more than 600 staff and writers. We share Tony's belief that 'a great guidebook should do three things: inform, educate and amuse'.

OUR WRITERS

Nick Ray

Coordinating Author, Siem Reap, Temples of Angkor, South Coast A Londoner of sorts, Nick comes from Watford, the sort of town that makes you want to travel. He lives in Phnom Penh with his wife Kulikar and his young children Julian and Belle. He has written for countless guidebooks on the Mekong region, including Lonely Planet's *Cambodia, Laos, Myanmar* and *Vietnam* books, as well as *Southeast Asia on a Shoestring*. When not writing, he is often out exploring the remote parts of Cambodia as a location scout and manager for the world of television and film, including everything from *Tomb Raider* to *Top Gear*. Motorbikes are a part-time passion (riding them a passion, maintaining them part-time) and he has travelled through most of Indochina on two wheels.

Greg Bloom

Phnom Penh, Northwestern Cambodia, Eastern Cambodia After five years in Manila, Greg crossed the pond to 'small town' Phnom Penh in 2008. Since then, he has covered virtually every inch of Cambodia for Lonely Planet, from Koh Kong to Sen Monorom to Ban Lung to Anlong Veng. When not writing about Southeast Asia for Lonely Planet, Greg might be found kicking around the former Soviet Union (he was editor of the *Kyiv Post* in another life), or running around Asia's ultimate frisbee fields. Read about his trips at www.mytripjournal.com/bloomblogs.

Read more about Greg at:
lonelyplanet.com/members/gbloom4

Published by Lonely Planet Publications Pty Ltd
ABN 36 005 607 983
9th edition – August 2014
ISBN 978 1 74220 557 1
© Lonely Planet 2014   Photographs © as indicated 2014
10 9 8 7 6 5 4 3 2 1
Printed in China